: Back and Forth, **Aaliyah:** At your best you are love, **Aaliyah:** Age ain't nothin' but a number, **Aaliyah:** Down with the clique, **Aaliyah:** , **Baby Bird:** Your gorgeous, Backstreet Boys: We've got it going on, **Backstreet Boys:** I'll never break your heart, **Backstreet Be** ving games with my heart, **Backstreet Boys:** Anywhere for you, **Backstreet Boys:** Everybody Backstreets back, **Backstreet Boys:** As **i** ove me, **Backstreet Boys:** All I have to give, **Backstreet Boys:** I want it that way, **Backstreet Boys:** Larger than life, **Backstreet B** e the meaning of being lonely, Backstreet Boys: The one, **Backstreet Boys:** Shape of my heart, **Backstreet Boys:** The call, **Backst** ore than that, **Backstreet Boys:** Drowning, **Band Aid:** Do they know it's Christmas, **Bangles:** Walk like an Egyptian, **Pato Banton: B** ck, **Toni Basil:** Mickey, **Big Fun:** Blame it on the boogie, **Big F** **Biork:** Army of me, **Blow Monkeys:** Di **e,** **David Bowie:** Absolute Beginners, **Elkie Brooks:** No more

G000061523

Word up, **Mar** **s and Dave:** **ry, The Cure:** **us and Pliers:** **I'll be there, Belinda Carlisle:** Heaven is a place on earth, **David** **ng you, Chas and Dave:** Snooker loopy, **Cher:** The shoop s **Hazel Dean:** Searchin', **Hazel Dean:** Whatever I do, wherevo **, Jason Donov** obody, **Divine:** You think you're a man, **Dr and the medics:** S **for you, Jason Donovan:** Too many broken hearts, **Jason D** **, Jason Donov** come back to me, **Jason Donovan:** Hang on to your love, **Ja** n of the rain, **Ja** : I'm doing fine, **Jason Donovan:** Happy together, **Candy Du** **s:** Sisters are d aselves, **Joe Fagin:** That's livin' alright, **The Farm:** Altogether **amantha Fox: T** antha Fox: Do ya Do ya, **Samantha Fox:** Nothings gonna st **i Fox:** Naughty **a Fox:** Love house, **Frankie goes to Hollywood:** Relax, **Warren G:** Regulate, **The Gap band:** **ollow me, follow** ordon: Happening all over again, **Groove Armada:** If everybody looked the same, **Groove Armada:** At the river, **Groove Armada:** I **Groove Armada:** Superstylin', **Groove Armada:** My friend, **Groove Armada:** Purple haze, **Haircut 100:** Favourite shirts, **Haircut** one, **Haircut 100:** Fantastic day, Hall and Oates: Maneater, **Hall and Oates:** One on one, **Hall and Oates:** Out of touch, **Hall and Oa** modern love, **Paul Hardcastle:** Nineteen, **Chesney Hawkes:** The one and only, **Bruce Hornsby and The Range:** The way it is, **Ho** ump around, **Whitney Houston:** One moment in time, **Human League:** Love action, **Billy Idol:** White Wedding, **Billy Idol:** Rebel **on:** Body Talk, **Jazzy Jeff and the Fresh Prince:** Summertime, **Jazzy Jeff and the Fresh Prince:** Boom shake the room, **Elton Jo** **y, Tom Jones:** Kiss, **R. Kelly:** She's got that vibe, **R. Kelly:** Bump and Grind, **R. Kelly:** Your Body's calling, R. Kelly: I believe I can **otham City, R. Kelly:** I'm your Angel, **R. Kelly:** If I could turn back the hands of time, **R. Kelly:** The world's greatest, **R. Kelly:** Igni **Box:** Living in a Box, **Kylie Minogue:** I should be so lucky, **Kylie Minogue:** Got to be certain, **Kylie Minogue:** The Locomotion, **K** Jen ne sais pas pourquoi, **Kylie Minogue:** Especially for you, **Kylie Minogue:** Hand on your heart, **Kylie Minogue:** Wouldn't cha **e Minogue:** Never too late, **Kylie Minogue:** Tears on my pillow, **Kylie Minogue:** Better the devil, **Kylie Minogue:** Step back in t **gue:** What do I have to do, **Kylie Minogue:** Shocked, Kylie Minogue: Word is out, **Kylie Minogue:** If you were with me now, **K** **eep on pumpin' it, Kylie Minogue:** Give me just a little more time, **Kylie Minogue:** Finer feelings, **Kylie Minogue:** What kind of **gue:** Celebration, **N'Sync:** Bye bye bye, **N'Sync:** I'll never stop, **N'Sync:** It's gonna be me, **N'Sync:** This I promise you, **N'Sync:** friend, **Billy Ocean:** Carribean Queen, **Billy Ocean:** Loverboy, **Billy Ocean:** Suddenly, **Billy Ocean:** Mystery Lady, **Billy Ocean:** W **ts tough, Billy Ocean:** There'll be sad songs, **Billy Ocean:** Love is forever, **Billy Ocean:** Get Outta my dre **car, Billy Ocean:** The colour of love, **Rednex:** Cotton eyed joe, **Rose Royce:** Car wash, **Rose Royce:** I wanna get next to you, **nake me feel like dancing, Leo Sayer:** When I need you, **Leo Sayer:** How much Love, **Shanks and Bigfoot:** Sweet like choco **ington:** Dat, **Simple Minds:** Don't you forget about me, **Sinitta:** So Macho, **Sinitta:** Toy boy, **Sinitta:** Cross my broken heart, **Sin** **here we started, Small Faces:** Itchicoo Park, **Sonia:** You'll never stop me from loving you, **Spandau Ballet:** I'll fly for you, **Bri** **y One more time, Britney Spears:** Sometimes, **Britney Spears:** Crazy, **Britney Spears:** Born to be happy, **Britney Spears:** Oops **ey Spears:** Lucky, **Britney Spears:** Stronger, **Britney Spears:** Don't let me be the last to know, **Britney Spears:** I'm a slave for **ars:** Overprotected, **Britney Spears:** I'm a girl not yet a woman, Britney Spears: Boys, **Britney Spears:** I love Rock n Roll, **Bri** **, Britney Spears:** Me against the music, **Alvin Stardust:** Pretend, **Alvin Stardust:** I feel like Buddy Holly, **Steps:** Five, six, se **Last thing on my mind, Steps:** One for sorrow, **Steps:** Heatbeat/Tragedy, Steps: Better best forgotten, **Steps:** Thank Abba fo **: Love's got a hold of my heart, Steps:** After the love has gone, **Steps:** Say you'll be mine/Better the devil, **Steps:** Deeper shad **When I said goodbye/Summer of love, Steps:** Stomp, **Steps:** It's the way you make me feel/Too busy thinking about my baby, **St** **/You'll be sorry, Steps:**Chain Reaction, **Steps:** Words are not enough/I know him so well, **The Stone Roses:** She bangs the d **ses:** What the world is waiting for/Fools Gold, **The Stone Roses:** elephant Stone, **The Stone Roses:** Made of Stone, **The St** **ve, The Stone Roses:** I want to be adored, **The Stone Roses:** Waterfall, **The Stone Roses:** I am the resurrection, Sybil: Walk o **e I lost, Sybil:** When I'm good and ready, **Justin Timberlake:** Like I love you, **Justin Timberlake:** Cry me a river, **Justin Timberl **y, Justin Timberlake:** Senorita, **A tribe called Quest:** Can I kick it, **2 Unlimited:** Get ready for this, **2 Unlimited:** Twilight zo **orkaholic, 2 Unlimited:** Tribal Dance, **Wham:** Wham rap, **Jackie Wilson:** Reet petite, **Jackie Wilson:** I get the sweetest fee

and Forth, **Aaliyah:** At your best you are love, **Aaliyah:** Age ain't nothin' but a number, **Aaliyah:** Down with the clique, **Aaliyah:** **y Bird:** Your gorgeous, Backstreet Boys: We've got it going on, **Backstreet Boys:** I'll never break your heart, **Backstreet E** mes with my heart, **Backstreet Boys:** Anywhere for you, **Backstreet Boys:** Everybody Backstreets back, **Backstreet Boys:** As **e,** **Backstreet Boys:** All I have to give, **Backstreet Boys:** I want it that way, **Backstreet Boys:** Larger than life, **Backstreet E** meaning of being lonely, Backstreet Boys: The one, **Backstreet Boys:** Shape of my heart, **Backstreet Boys:** The call, **Backs** **n that, Backstreet Boys:** Drowning, **Band Aid:** Do they know it's Christmas, **Bangles:** Walk like an Egyptian, **Pato Banton:** **ni Basil:** Mickey, **Big Fun:** Blame it on the boogie, **Big Fun:** Can't shake the feeling, **Bjork:** Army of me, **Blow Monkeys:** D **vid Bowie:** Absolute Beginners, **Elkie Brooks:** No more the fool, **Buggles:** Video killed the radio star, **Cameo:** Word up, **Ma** **here, Belinda Carlisle:** Heaven is a place on earth, **David Cassidy:** The last kiss, **Chas and Dave:** Rabbit, **Chas and Dave: , Chas and Dave:** Snooker loopy, **Cher:** The shoop shoop song (its in his kiss), **The Cult:** She sells sanctuary, **The Cure **Dean:** Searchin', **Hazel Dean:** Whatever I do, wherever I go, **Hazel Dean:** Who's leaving who, Chaka Demus and Pliers **Divine:** You think you're a man, **Dr and the medics:** Spirit in the sky, **Jason Donovan:** Nothing can divide us, **Jason Dona** **, Jason Donovan:** Too many broken hearts, **Jason Donovan:** Sealed with a kiss, **Jason Donovan:** Everyday, **Jason Dona** back to me, **Jason Donovan:** Hang on to your love, Jason Donovan: Another night, **Jason Donovan:** Rhythm of the rain, **J** **ing fine, Jason Donovan:** Happy together, **Candy Dulfer:** Lily was here, **Sheena Easton:** 9 to 5, **Eurythmics:** Sisters are **Joe Fagin:** That's livin' alright, **The Farm:** Altogether now, **Fine Young Cannibals:** She drives me crazy, Samantha Fox: **Fox:** Do ya Do ya, **Samantha Fox:** Nothings gonna stop me now, **Samantha Fox:** Hold on tight, **Samantha Fox:** Naughty **Love house, Frankie goes to Hollywood:** Relax, **Warren G:** Regulate, **The Gap band:** Big fun, **Genesis:** Follow me, follow **Happening all over again. Groove Armada:** If everybody looked the same, **Groove Armada:** At the river, **Groove Armada: e Armada:** Superstylin', **Groove Armada:** My friend, **Groove Armada:** Purple haze, **Haircut 100:** Favourite shirts, Haircut **ircut 100:** Fantastic day, Hall and Oates: Maneater, **Hall and Oates:** One on one, **Hall and Oates:** Out of touch, **Hall and O**

For Susan

Special thanks to my friend Jon Tolanski, former musician
and award winning music documentary maker.

www.stevejenkinsuk.com

Nick Fleming Ltd
nick@fclpr.com
020 7636 7441
www.flemingassociatespr.com

Sue Buckler
Plug and Play Promo
Regional Radio/T.V. Promotions/ PR.
sue@plugandplaypromo.com
+(0) 7976 971540

An exclusive inside picture of the popular music industry's zenith years, related in the autobiography of one of the most influential creative producers in the history of popular music recording and promotion.

Justin Timberlake, Britney Spears, Elton John, David Bowie, George Michael, Kylie Minogue, STEPS, R. Kelly, The Stone Roses, John Lee Hooker, Tom Jones, Whitney Houston, Billy Ocean, Prince, Mariah Carey, N'Sync and The Backstreet Boys – these are some of the celebrity artists that have been signed or promoted and marketed by Steve Jenkins in an extraordinary career in which he has been awarded over 260 Platinum, Gold and Silver discs. During his tenures as founder and Chairman of Impulse Promotions and Managing Director of Jive Records, Steve Jenkins partnered with the song-writing and production team Stock Aitken Waterman (Mike Stock, Matt Aitken and Pete Waterman) and was involved in a pop music boom that is now seen as a legendary period in music history.

This autobiographical memoir, however, is greatly more than just a recollection of exceptional commercial success. Steve Jenkins is a philosophical, private and serious person with not a trace of the superficial brashness that many people associate with the moguls of the popular music industry. His life has been devoted both to nurturing and furthering the artistry of the superstars he has discovered and also to giving these artists' fans the best possible access to their idols, not only through recordings, but also in live appearances and broadcasts. His idealistic love of the artists and their audiences managed to withstand the many increasing economic, bureaucratic and plutocratic pressures imposed by a vastly changing industrial environment that has turned the world of popular music into an almost unrecognisable scene from how it was only a few years before this book was written. And so, in *The Future Is In The History*, Steve Jenkins not only takes the reader backstage to encounter the lives and souls of the legendary personalities he has been so closely involved with – he also presents a vivid and penetrating first-hand eyewitness account of massive changes taking place in the musical world over a substantial period of time: changes in values, communications, economics and the entire way performers and their audiences are connected. He places this panorama within the descriptive historical perspective of his own life from its earliest days in 1950s Walsall up to the present time when he can look back on immense social as well as artistic variants in the course of more than half a century.

The Future Is In The History is not only a unique personal entry into the human and artistic world of people who have been at the centre of some of the most influential and high powered music entertainment of recent decades – it is also a compelling and colourful journey of struggles and dramas set against a vividly painted backdrop of changing social environments and communications of the last five decades.

JON TOLANSKY

ISBN 978-1-907540-53-0

Written by Steve Jenkins

First published April 2012

Printed and Published by Anchor Print Group Ltd.

Cover design by Susan Gregory-Jenkins & Richard Linnett

Cover photograph by Paul Pickard/ Walsall Museum

Authors' acknowledgements
Personal thanks for work on the book go to, Jon Tolansky, Richard Linnett,
Simon Bradshaw, Emily Linnett, Dan Slee, Elliott Engers and Sue Buckler.
Also to all the people I've mentioned in the book, my many thanks for the memories and
allowing me to relay these stories.

The author and publisher would like to thank the following
for permission to reproduce their photographs:
Opening page plus Pages 172, 243, 450, 454, 455, 456 Paul Pickard/Walsall Museum
Pages 9, 36, 45, 50, 100, 244 , 426, 434, 460 Steve Jenkins Personal Collection
Page 10 SJ/Walsall Museum – Pages 174, 178, 210, 222 The Impulse Promotion Company
Page 264 Jive Records – Page 292 Jive Records/SJ Personal – Page 312 SJ Personal/Internal Affairs Records
Page 334 Mark Allen/Jive Records – Page 406 SJ Personal & Paul Pickard/Walsall Museum

Front Page: shows a list of Steve Jenkins career hits. Last Page: shows a list of his musical influences

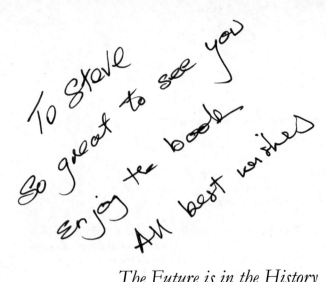

To Steve

So great to see you

enjoy the book

All best wishes

The Future is in the History

PROLOGUE
WALSALL: MY HOME TOWN

Walsall's History:

I have always been proud of my home town; it was the place where I spent my first twenty years before beginning to seek a life further afield. All of my childhood memories are around Walsall, my family had resided in this part of the world for many generations, and during the growing-up years I never pictured myself not being part of that town. When eventually I did leave I did so with regret, and throughout my life I have maintained that I never wanted to go – I was obliged to if I wanted to give my music career a chance. I would be 29 years old before I was to buy a property outside Walsall, and ever since I left I have returned constantly to visit my family.

Walsall has a long history – and a very colourful one. The most favoured interpretations of the name's origins are 'the hall of a stranger' or 'the house in the wood.' Early records state that in 1337 there were 367 taxpayers in the town. By 1811 it was recorded that 11,189 people lived in Walsall, and just 50 years later, in 1861, this had risen to 39,793. Only 30 years later, in 1891, the figure had reached 71,789 due to the influx of people drawn to the busy thriving industry of the time. Steam driven machinery had spawned factories throughout the borough, and coal mines, blast furnaces and casting shops produced iron and brass castings for all manners of uses. The town was famous for its saddlery trade, and for decades Walsall had been England's dominating producer of bridles, bits, stirrups, fancy leather goods, bags, purses and wallets. Other manufactured goods included a very wide variety of artefacts – bricks, locks, brushes, electric fittings, artificial teeth and church organs.

In 1900, Walsall became a major English town at war when the Independent Boer Republic of Transvaal and The Orange Free State challenged the British Empire. As Walsall flourished in the manufacture of saddlery and horse tackle, many local volunteers were sent to defend the Empire. Music Hall songs about war were the hits of the day: 'We don't want to lose you but we think you ought to go', 'Comrades', and 'Goodbye Dolly Grey', were melodies that filled the air of the town at this time.

Celebrities of Walsall:

One of Walsall's most famous ladies was a nurse, Dorothy Windlow Pattison, known affectionately as Sister Dora. She has also been referred to as Walsall's saint: taking charge of Walsall's first hospital in 1865, Sister Dora worked tirelessly for the sick and injured of the town until her death in 1878. She was, in fact, born in Yorkshire, but she became so loved by the people of Walsall that before her death she asked to be buried in Walsall with 'her own people.' Her wish was respected and she was buried in the Queen Street Cemetery. There are, and always will be, statues of Sister Dora in Walsall – the original, paid for by the people of Walsall, was erected in 1886, but factory smoke and the ravages of weather seriously affected the marble statue and it was replaced in 1954 by one made of bronze. The plaster cast of the statue stood in the General Hospital for many years, but through the constant human traffic it sustained much damage. In 1974, the School of Arts restored the plaster cast statue, which now stands proudly in the entrance to the Council House in Lichfield Street.

Sister Dora was also honoured by the London and North Western Railway Company. The Chief Mechanical Engineer, Francis William Webb, a celebrated figure who was known as 'The Uncrowned King of Crewe', was aware of her special work for the railwaymen of the time who had sustained many serious injuries. In 1895, Webb, a successful locomotive designer who gave names to many of his engines, designated a 2–4–0 passenger locomotive, a rebuild of a Precedent Class 'Jumbo', as No. 2158 *Sister Dora*. The management at Crewe Station, one of the country's most important railway line junctions, decided that *Sister Dora* would visit Walsall as often as possible. The locomotive was housed at Derby and pulled the morning train from Derby to Walsall via Burton, Birmingham New Street and Soho (Staffordshire). It would then go to Ryecroft Shed in Walsall for maintenance, and after a few hours, would return to Derby – so it spent plenty of time daily in Walsall.

No. 2158 *Sister Dora* had a long and demanding career, eventually being scrapped in 1924. However, the story does not end there: in 1988 a modern diesel locomotive, a class 31, became the proud bearer of the new 'Sister Dora' nameplate. These locomotives and statues illustrate the magnitude of love Walsall has expressed for Sister Dora, who gave the best part of her life to the town. In 1876, she attended 12,127 people, an exceptional workload that seriously affected her health, and indeed only one year later she was diagnosed with breast cancer. On Christmas Eve, 1878, she passed away. To the people of Walsall Sister Dora is a legend equalled only by Florence Nightingale.

Jerome Klapka Jerome is one of Walsall's most famous sons. Born in Walsall in 1859, his family lived in Bradford Place, and today their home houses the Jerome K Jerome museum. His father, Jerome Clapp Jerome, was wealthy and came to

Walsall in 1855. He helped found and design the Wednesbury Road Congregational Chapel and was part owner of Birchills Ironworks. Jerome senior invested in the coal mines in Norton Canes, which proved to be a financial disaster, prompting the family to move first to Stourbridge and then to London. There, Jerome K Jerome started work with the London and North Western Railway at Euston Station, beginning by collecting coal that fell along the railway. He remained there for four years, but he was soon smitten by show business and became an actor. While 'resting' from the acting profession he worked as a newspaper reporter and schoolmaster and began to write short stories, including satirical pieces. He published his first book, entitled *On Stage And Off*, in 1888, but it was in the following year that he achieved worldwide fame when *Three Men In A Boat* came out. In 1927, Jerome was made a Freeman of the borough of Walsall, and in 1984, the Jerome Birthplace Museum opened to celebrate his life. Now called The Jerome K Jerome Birthplace, it contains photographs, books, letters and personal items. Jerome K Jerome's desk upon which he wrote *Three Men In A Boat* now rests in the Council House inside the Mayor's chambers.

In 1859, Walsall became only the third town in England to open its own library. Outside the library today stands the memorial statue to John Henry Carless. During the First World War, Walsall sent 12,000 men into action, 2,000 of which never saw their home town again. One of them was J H Carless. Born in Walsall in 1896, he was originally refused acceptance into the Army on medical grounds. He was determined to serve his country, and so, undeterred, he enlisted in the Royal Navy. Ordinary Seamen John Henry Carless served aboard HMS Caledon, and despite being seriously wounded in the battle of Heligoland Bight, continued serving at his gun and helping his friends and the wounded. He lost his life later that day, on 17th November 1917, and he was subsequently awarded the nation's highest honour, the Victoria Cross, in recognition of his selfless bravery. His VC 'for most conspicuous bravery and devotion to duty' was awarded by King George V and received by his proud but grieving parents. Carless Street and Caledon Street within the town are reminders of this brave Walsall hero.

Joseph Leckie was a successful businessman in the leather trade. He became a councillor and Alderman and served for a total of 21 years, becoming a Member of Parliament from 1931 until his death in 1938. Joe Leckie, as he was known, was a popular man, and he stood as a National Liberal Unionist candidate, winning comfortably in 1931 and again in 1935. He also served as Mayor of Walsall in 1926. On his death, in 1938, he left money for the town to have a carillon in the Council House Tower, although, because of the Second World War, his wishes were not fulfilled until 1953. Since then the carillon has been played on a regular basis, particularly at Christmas, when carols are played as the people of Walsall go about their Christmas shopping.

The Arboretum – glorious public park:

The Arboretum is on the edge of Walsall town centre. Originally the site was used for mining limestone, but when this ceased it did not take long for the large working quarry to fill with water from the Holbrook stream. The lake became known as Hatherton Lake, and Walsall people began to swim in it and use the surroundings as an unofficial park.

This was the catalyst for a development in 1870, when the Walsall Arboretum and Lake Company was formed and leased two lakes and seven acres of land from Lord Hatherton to lay out a public park. At the time this was considered a 'healthy change' for the area and the local newspaper wrote that eventually this move would help bring to an end the old sports of cock fighting in Wednesbury, bull baiting in Darlaston and dog fighting in Walsall. The Arboretum was officially opened on 4th May 1874. In 1884, the Council purchased the freehold to the land from Lord Hatherton and Lord Mellish and the Arboretum then became, in the words of the Mayor, 'a free recreation ground for the inhabitants of Walsall forever.' More land was purchased in 1890 and 1921, enabling the opening of playing fields.

In 1923, the Prince of Wales came to Walsall to open the ring road now known as the Broadway, which passes alongside the Arboretum. The crowds were enormous, children from all schools in the area were there to wave flags, and the people living in Lichfield Street rented out their bedrooms for the day to those who wanted a special view of the procession. The evening brought a programme of entertainment at the Arboretum and one of the performers that night was a star from the silent screen – Charlie Chaplin.

Following the Second World War, the Festival of Britain was created in 1951 as an initiative to revive the country's spirits. Walsall played its part in inaugurating the Illuminations. The exhibition was mounted by borrowing the lights that had brought so much joy to the visitors at Blackpool. Such was the success of the event, that from 1952 until 2009, each autumn, for a six week period, the Walsall Arboretum Illuminations have twinkled brightly in the night air. Thousands and thousands of visitors from near and far now come to see the Illuminations, and Walsall is second only to Blackpool in the field. In the summer of 1953, a new attraction was added to the Arboretum, a playground for children, including slides, roundabouts, seesaws, swings and two paddling pools. The funding had mainly been raised from the profits of the annual horticultural show and fete. That year the event had been blessed with perfect weather, unlike each of the previous thirteen years when most people remembered the heavens opening. Over 30,000 people packed the Arboretum for the opening ceremony, which was performed by Berlita, the ice skating star of the day. For more than a century and a quarter the young and old of Walsall have visited the Arboretum, myself included, and a common conversation has to be pronounced in the local dialect: 'Wherem yow gooin'?' 'Down the Arbo!'

Walsall Football Club – "The Saddlers":

In the 1870s there were two prominent football teams in Walsall: Walsall Town and the Walsall Swifts (the Swifts had originally been called the Victoria Swifts for a short time). Walsall Town was formed on 17th September 1874 at The Dragon Inn, a year after the Swifts had been created. Amid great rivalry, both teams played on adjacent pitches in Chuckery. Whenever they played each other, crowds of two to three thousand would turn up to see these amateur footballers confront each other. The final game between Swifts and Town was held in March 1888 in the semi-final of the Walsall Cup. Swifts won the match 1–0. Soon afterwards the competing teams amalgamated to form Walsall Town Swifts, and *The Observer* newspaper wrote 'this ends the battle of the giants and henceforth let all dissension cease.' Walsall Town Swifts would soon become the team we know today, simply Walsall Football Club, their team badge being a flying swift. The new club's first game was against Aston Villa in the final of the Birmingham Cup at their ground in Perry Barr. The game drew a crowd of 12,000, who didn't see a single goal scored, and a replay was called. Walsall rightly insisted that the rematch should be played at their Chuckery ground, but the Birmingham Association said no and ordered the game to be played at Aston Villa. Walsall stuck to their guns and pressed for Chuckery. The Birmingham Association would not relent and so they awarded the trophy to Aston Villa – typical!

In 1882, Walsall FC became a founding member of the Football League Second Division. They were still playing games in Chuckery and the local residents had become unhappy about the noise and disturbance on match days. So the club was given its marching orders and sometime later settled at the Hillary Street ground. Walsall lost its league status in 1901 and would not return until 1920, when the club became a founding member of the Third Division North. Some people of the day blamed the players for the loss of our league status, noting that on Boxing Day only eight men turned up and we went down 12–0.

In 1930, the Hillary Street ground was re-named Fellows Park, after the long time director H L Fellows, who would later become Chairman, and the Hillary Street End became the home of Walsall's most passionate supporters. The following year, record goal scorer Gilbert Alsop was signed from Coventry City, and he would feature in 222 games scoring 169 goals. The club's greatest moment of glory was just around the corner. In January 1933, the third round of the FA Cup forced the mighty Arsenal to Fellows Park and a passionate full capacity Walsall crowd turned up in full voice to see the Saddlers pull off the most remarkable 2–0 victory with goals from Gilbert Alsop and a penalty from Bill Sheppard. The Arsenal team featured all the superstars of the day including David Jack, Alex James and Cliff Bastin. One of the newspapers of the time wrote: 'Arsenal, the rich, the confident, the league leaders, the £30,000 aristocrats, against a little Midland Third Division South team that cost £69. Arsenal train on ozone, brine baths, champagne, golf and electrical massage in an atmosphere of prima donna preciousness, they own £87 worth of football boots. Walsall footballers eat fish and chips, drink beer and the entire running costs of the club this year has been £75.' That game has been spoken about for generations in Walsall, and although promotions and further giant killing games were to come, the first giant killers in England came from Fellows Park, Walsall. Up the Saddlers!

Visitors to Walsall – refugees and royalty:

During the Second World War, Walsall received evacuees from London. Two thousand children along with their mothers came in 1944, and *The Observer* reported: 'Walsall hearts and homes have been opened to women and children from London to escape Hitler's flying bombs.' Many of the cockney kids that came said they liked Walsall, stating 'Walsall was alright, once you had learnt the language.'

Royalty has visited the cultural backwater of Walsall – most prominent was the visit of Her Majesty Queen Elizabeth II on 24th May 1962: it was the tenth year of her reign. The Queen made visits to The Council House to sign the register, Crabtree's, the large company in Chuckery that manufactured electrical components, and the Arboretum, where hundreds of Girl Guides lined up for her inspection. The procession brought out crowds several tiers deep standing on tiptoe, boxes or bricks to get a small glimpse as Her Majesty passed. I was in the Arboretum that day aged 9, with my sister Helen aged 5 and a half. My mother filmed the Queen passing and some scenes from the event on my father's rare movie camera. Dad was at work, so Mom filmed it for him to see later, and the footage has remained in our family. I have seen it many times over the years. We woz there gov!

Barrie Blower – a special figure:

Barrie Blower MBE, a prominent name in the Borough of Walsall over the past 30 to 40 years, deserves special mention among the people I have grown up to know in Walsall. Barrie was the Chief Executive of The Caldmore Area Housing Association, which became a large landlord in a small area of Walsall. The Association started in 1973 and soon became a national leader: by 1976 it was the largest outside London and definitely the most active in the country. The Manpower Service Commission helped train the town's young people in the building trade, carpentry and motor mechanics, and in 1979 the Afro-Caribbean hostel opened, followed in 1980 by two blocks of flats that housed over a hundred single occupants. Purpose built dwellings for the Asian community's elderly opened in 1988. Five years later, in 1993, the Association redeveloped the Sister Dora Hospital into 98 units and then began to expand at a pace. In 1994 the CHAT shop opened, selling second hand goods, 1995 saw the old White Hart pub converted to flats, in 1997 46 new houses were built at Hatherton Road and in 1999, 25 flats in Station Street.

In 2000, the Association owned 2,000 homes costing over £70 million. Barrie had presided over this entire incredible expansion and he had become well known to the residents of Walsall. It was Barrie that greeted HRH Diana Princess of Wales to the town in 1986; Diana was officiating at the opening of the Association's project for the deaf in Lichfield Street.

Barrie Blower has had an altogether extraordinary career in the history of Walsall, but in many quarters he will be remembered most of all for saving our Football Club in 1986. These were dark days for the Saddlers – there was talk of ground sharing with Birmingham City, which financially could have been a saving factor, but it would have surely killed our club: it was unthinkable to have to travel to Birmingham to see our home town team, no-one in Walsall wanted this to happen. Barrie Blower stepped in, and it is worth relating the inside story of what happened, as I know it, as an illustration of passionate belief and vision bringing about action. Barrie visited the hairdressers in Bloxwich one Saturday morning and met with Jeff Bonser, a friend and interested partner in the 'Save Walsall FC' plan. Barrie, aroused by this initiative, mentioned to Jeff that he had read in a newspaper about a London businessman, Terry Ramsden. 'We need him,' said Barrie. Now, Terry Ramsden did not know of the existence of Barrie Blower and had probably never given Walsall Football Club a thought in his lifetime, but Barrie phoned his office over and over again until he was eventually able to arrange a meeting with him in London. That day Barrie told Terry Ramsden of Walsall FC's predicament, and during his meeting he convinced him on the spot to be involved. Ramsden made an immediate decision and bought Walsall Football Club, thereby saving the Saddlers and keeping the team in the town. Today, Barrie Blower is President of Walsall Football Club and rarely misses a match. I have had the pleasure of seeing him at so many Walsall games, chatting with him and Jeff Bonser at their lunch club before home games and also at away games on the occasions when I have been invited into the directors' boxes. Barrie Blower – a true Walsall boy through and through.

Nearby villages of importance:

In this short history of my home town, some of the surrounding villages are important factors in my family background and upbringing. Bloxwich was the local village, and later town, where my family roots began. Originally known as Bloc's Village, its history extends back before the Norman Conquest. The Romans left and Britain was invaded by the Anglo-Saxons, the Midlands becoming known as the Kingdom of Mercia. The Mercians established small communities, and the family 'Bloc' settled in the area we now know as Bloxwich, where the oldest surviving building is the 'Cottage Shop' on the corner of Samuel Street: the foundations are said to go back to the 15th century. Bloxwich had started life as a small agricultural village, but it expanded in the 18th century when the coal mines were opened, growing substantially from the neighbourhood of 600 people who had first lived there. Cottage industries of nails, needles and saddle blades expanded quickly when the goods could be transported easily by the new canal waterways surrounding Bloxwich.

One of Bloxwich's most famous sons was Pat Collins, known as the 'King of Showmen.' He used to live in Lime Tree House and held the Bloxwich Wakes every year in August. It was Pat Collins who built one of Bloxwich's cinemas, The Grosvenor, in the High Street, in 1922. The cinema ceased operations in 1959 but the building still stands today. Pat Collins developed his fairground business in Bloxwich and had fairs in Walsall, Wolverhampton, Bilston and the surrounding areas. I visited these fairgrounds regularly as a child and everyone had heard of Pat Collins. I vividly remember his name painted across all the fair rides and transport, and it was always a big deal when he opened for a week or two in the Arboretum – much fun and excitement was to be had.

Rushall also plays a major part in my life. The Domesday Book of 1086 lists Rushall, and its total value to its Lord was noted as 10 shillings. Rushall means 'a place in marshy ground where rushes grow.' The main settlement of Rushall was established on the Lichfield Road at the junction of Pelsall Lane, Daw End Lane and Coalpool Lane, where in 1766 a toll bar was set up after the main road was made a Turnpike. At the start of the 20th century Rushall, was a thriving village set around the square, but with the passing of time much of the area's character was lost due to road improvements. After 1945 the population was increased considerably by new housing developments, particularly around Barnes Lane. In 1953, Barnes Lane was where I was taken after my birth and it became my first home.

Rushall Hall has a very long and interesting history. The fortified gate house and walls were built in the 13th and 14th centuries. At the start of the Civil War in 1642, it was occupied by the writer and Member of Parliament Edward Leigh, who was a staunch opponent of the King. He fortified the building when he joined the army fighting the King as a colonel, but the following year his wife, left in charge, was not able to hold the Hall against the forces of Prince Rupert. However, in 1644, the royalists were ejected after a short siege. Among the people that subsequently came and went, the Leigh, Mellish and Buchanan families all enjoyed periods of time at Rushall Hall before the estate was finally sold off in 1945.

My childhood was enhanced by hundreds of visits to Park Lime Pits. Limestone of high quality lies near the surface at Rushall and it had been exploited since the times of the Romans for building and agricultural purposes. Park Lime Pits was a thriving quarry as limestone was used as flux in the production of iron, and blocks of limestone were taken in small trucks from the quarry face to the canal, from where they were transported by barge to the iron foundries of the Black Country. When the quarrying ceased 150 years ago the Victorians started to landscape the old workings. The magnificent beech trees were planted at this time and the quarry was filled with water, creating the pools. Park Lime Pits in my childhood was a fascinating area to explore: it gave me hours of pleasure and a true sense of freedom and nature. Today, Park Lime Pits is a 25-acre nature reserve just 2.5 miles from Walsall town centre, and it is home to an extraordinary variety of wildlife. Over 100 species of birds and over 300 species of plants have been recorded there. To me, though, it will always remain an indelible part of my childhood. And Walsall will forever be my home, even though I left there for so many faraway travels so long ago.

A future Pop Mogul with sister Helen

My Mom and Dad's Wedding Day

1959 Bournemouth, Dad, Helen, Me and Mom

I knew early on, you gotta have wheels if you wanna make deals

1950's Walsall and District Co-operative Society, Bridge Street, where my Dad was Footwear Manager

CHAPTER 1

THE 1950s

1953 – and all that

During 1953, I made my debut into a vastly different world to the one we know today. That year Dwight D Eisenhower became President of the United States, the movie *Peter Pan* premiered in New York and the Academy Awards were televised live for the very first time. Ian Fleming's first James Bond novel, *Casino Royale*, appeared, and Aldous Huxley first tried the psychedelic hallucinogen mescaline that would inspire his book *The Doors of Perception*. Sir Edmund Hillary and Tenzing Norgay were the first to reach the summit of Mount Everest. A motorcar was built that would inspire many songs and become a youth icon – the still famous Chevrolet Corvette. Hugh Hefner published the first edition of *Playboy* magazine selling 54,175 copies for the princely sum of $.50 cents each, and the first colour television sets went on sale in America for roughly $1,175.

The huge event of the year occurred on 2nd June: Queen Elizabeth II was crowned at a coronation ceremony in Westminster Abbey in London. She was 25 years old. Eight thousand guests were inside the Abbey including prime ministers and heads of state from around, what was then known as, the British Commonwealth. The Queen took the Coronation Oath and was then bound to serve her people and maintain the laws of God. After being handed the four symbols of authority – the orb, the sceptre, the rod of mercy and the royal ring of sapphire and rubies, the Archbishop of Canterbury, Dr Geoffrey Fisher, placed St Edward's Crown on her head to complete the ceremony. Over three million people lined the streets of London to catch a glimpse of the new monarch as she made her way to and from Buckingham Palace in the golden state coach. The ceremony was watched by millions more around the world as the BBC set up their biggest ever outside broadcast to provide live coverage on radio and television. Street parties were held all over the UK as people crowded around TV sets to watch the event. It was estimated that over 20 million people watched the BBC coverage – some had never seen television before and only did so on neighbours' sets, while many families bought their first televisions so they could watch the historic broadcast, which was relayed in 44 languages. The weather that day was overcast, no surprise, but the RAF marked the occasion with a fly past down The Mall and that evening the skies of London were lit up by a firework display above Victoria Embankment.

The greatest ever FA Cup Final was held on 2nd May 1953 at Wembley Stadium. In front of 100,000 fans Blackpool beat Bolton Wanderers 4–3 in Wembley's highest ever scoring Cup Final. It was the first time they ever won the Cup, and it was the culmination of five great years of endeavour that had seen them at Wembley in 1948 and 1951, each time unsuccessfully. This Cup Final is still talked about and remains the pinnacle for this outstanding competition: 100,000 people were there but millions watched it on television. The day was full of spring sunshine, and even before a ball was kicked the game was dubbed the Stanley Matthews Final. One of England's greatest all time wingers, Stanley Matthews was 38 years old and the country (apart from the people of Bolton) wanted him to win a Cup Final medal after failing to do so twice before. That afternoon they saw him turn from brilliance to genius as over and over again he raced down the right touchline and provided centres and crosses to create chances for his Blackpool teammates. The country watched on TV, thrilled as Matthews continually cut deep into Bolton's defences again and again, and the excitement rose like the swell of the ocean. Finally, Blackpool were victorious 4–3 and Stanley Matthews won his FA Cup medal. The final will also be remembered for the unparalleled way the Bolton players took their defeat.

The Top 10 films in America in 1953 all found success here in the UK: *Peter Pan, The Robe, From Here to Eternity, House of Wax, Shane, The Glen Miller Story, How to Marry a Millionaire, Gentlemen Prefer Blondes, Knights of the Round Table*, and *Salome*. The Academy Award would go to *From Here to Eternity* as Best Picture, Best Actor was William Holden for *Stalag 17*, Best Actress was Audrey Hepburn for *Roman Holiday* and best supporting actor was Frank Sinatra, for *From Here to Eternity*. The short film series would see Mickey Mouse have his final outing this year; however, a 15 year run was ahead with the launch of Speedy Gonzales, a name my father would call me for several years in my childhood.

I came into this world on 16th October 1953. During that month Winston Churchill was awarded the Nobel Prize for literature and the Royal Air Force Canberra won the London to New Zealand air race. Our Prime Minister was Winston Churchill, the Leader of the Opposition was Clement Attlee and the population of Britain was 50,954,000.

An average three bedroom house cost £2,750, average income was £550 per year, a postage stamp cost 1.5p, petrol was 21p per gallon, a loaf of bread 10.5p and a bottle of milk 2.75p. In sport, the Derby was won by Gordon Richards on Pinza, the Grand National by B Marshall on Early Mist, Wimbledon Ladies by Maureen Connolly, Wimbledon Men's by Victor Seixas, and the Open by the great Ben Hogan.

Famous people I share my birthday with include Oscar Wilde in 1854, Max Bygraves in 1922, Angela Lansbury in 1925, and Terry Griffiths, the snooker player, in 1947. On TV, *The Good Old Days* was first shown in 1953, also the first edition of *Panorama*. On radio came the first broadcasts of 'Hello Playmates' with Arthur Askey and 'Hancock's Half Hour' with Tony Hancock.

Musically, the biggest hit of the year came from Frankie Laine – 'I Believe' spent 18 weeks at No. 1, to where it ascended on 16th October. Also by Frankie Laine, 'Answer Me' stayed at No. 1 for eight weeks at the end of the year. Other hit records of 1953 were 'Don't Let The Stars Get In Your Eyes', by Perry Como; 'She Wears Red Feathers', by Guy Mitchell; '(How Much Is) That Doggie In The Window?', by Lita Roza; 'Outside Of Heaven' and 'I'm Walking Behind You', by Eddie Fischer (both No 1s); Jo Stafford's No 1, 'You Belong To Me; Look At That Girl', by Guy Mitchell; and 'Song From *The Moulin Rouge*', by Mantovani and his Orchestra. This was the flavour of the records being broadcast on the radio during 1953 that brushed past my young ears and probably soothed those baby squeals.

98 Barns Lane, Rushall Aldridge

Number 286 in the Register Book of Births for the Sub-District Wednesbury in the County of Stafford is one Stephen Jenkins. It states I was born on 16th October 1953 at Portland House Maternity Home to William Alan Jenkins and Evelyn Nance Jenkins formerly Smith. The profession of father was listed as Assistant Departmental Manager (Boots and Shoes) and I was registered on 22nd October 1953 by a registrar named Whitehouse. I presume on that day I was taken to 98 Barns Lane, Rushall, to begin my life with my mother and father. Barns Lane was a long and winding road with fields on the right as you travelled from the Rushall Square end, and it was a quiet road, mainly due to few people owning their own cars in those days. On the left, houses had been built in lines at right angles to the road. There were terraced houses opposite our house, probably around twenty homes that went from the road to a small stream and then into the fields on the left of Barns Lane. 98 Barns Lane was the first house opposite the terraces, and on our side the houses were newer council houses – a little wider, hence probably ten or twelve homes stood opposite the 20 terraces. In between the two lines of houses was a grassed area which went from the stream, or brook as we knew it, to the road, and this would become my childhood playground as soon as I could walk. The houses opposite had no garages, as they had been built before the need to have one, but on our side garages had been built at the back of the homes in a cluster, approached by a small lane that ran at the side of our house.

In those days few women worked after the birth of their children and there were no nursery schools to be dropped off at for a few hours, hence the first few years were spent exclusively with my Mom and with my Dad when he was not working. One of my first real memories was when I was somewhere between two and three years old. As the lane that led to the garages was next to the house, my Mom could see the top of my father's car as he drove to put it in the garage on his return from work in the evening. That would signal my Mom's call to go and meet my Dad down the lane; I remember that this little trip brought me immense joy. There was no access to the garages via the bottom of our garden, so it meant going out of the front door, opened by Mom, and off I went down the lane and most times would arrive just as Dad was squeezing himself down the side of the car along the inner wall of the garage and locking up. I was usually greeted with 'Hello little man', or 'Speedy Gonzales', after one of my favourite TV characters. Dad would then lift me onto what seemed the highest wall in the world between our garden and the lane and hold my hand as I walked along the top. This was a moment of great excitement, being so high up and overjoyed that my Dad was home. At the end of the wall he would catch me as I jumped and carry me into the house. We would instantly play for a while and then he would eat his evening meal with Mom and soon after it was bedtime for yours truly.

My days were spent with Mom going about her daily business, shopping in Rushall Square, almost daily, as she picked up fresh food, bread and vegetables. At this time I was completely infatuated with cars. I would pester Mom and show her the required car in the toyshop window I wanted to add to the collection, but Mom always had a great reason to wait for a few days. Usually on a Friday I would get one, but not every Friday. I had to learn the lessons of being patient and respectful, and if I had changed my mind when the time came to get one, I would always be questioned why and told how wise it was to have waited. We also went on trips into Walsall that seemed like long rides on the bus. This occurred once a week to get supplies, buy clothes as I was growing, make payment of bills and carry out general jobs. For the next few years I would hear regularly: 'Come on Steve, you walk so slow, let's get a move on.' The walk around town was always punctuated with Mom meeting people she knew – having lived around Walsall all her life and been a supervisor at Woolworths, she seemed to know everyone. 'So, this is little Steve, isn't he growing?' 'Hello Mrs so and so.' Mother had taught me to be very polite and proper when meeting people and to be quiet and speak when spoken to – absolutely no childish tantrums. I never found this a hardship, I was happy to please my Mom. She took me everywhere, she was the most fantastic cook, she cared for me in every way and she loved my father. My world was warm, secure and happy.

On these trips we would always call in to my Dad's shop. He had become Manager of the Walsall and District Co-operative Society Shoe Department. The shop was on the right hand side of Bridge Street in the town centre. Dad had been the youngest Assistant Manager in the Co-op's history and had followed that up by becoming the youngest Manager. My Dad's office overlooked the street over the top of the men's shoe department and I loved going there. The staff all seemed to like my Mom and always made a fuss of Speedy Gonzales, who was passed around from shop assistant to shop assistant, squeezed, cuddled, tickled – all great stuff. Then upstairs to Dad's office. Margaret was his secretary, who would stay with him until he became ill years later. She was part of my world, always smiling, and good friends with my Mom. So, another great environment. Dad always picked me up and we would look out of the window to the street below, watching the people and the cars going by, calling out the make and model. I remember his desk, paperwork, shoe boxes, shoe horns, polish and brushes that were everywhere and all around. They were samples of everything that representatives from all sorts of companies would leave for him to look at and think about, as he was responsible for buying what would be sold in nine Co-op stores under his control.

As the weeks and months went by, I was allowed more and more freedom on the grass that separated the two lines of houses in Barnes Lane. There were plenty of kids from those homes, and the stream at the bottom of the grass, far away from the road, was a magnet to us all – probably just below the knee of a 3 year-old, but constantly moving, with mud, stones and newts – just perfect for a young boy. Small games of football, cricket in the summer, and rounders organised by one of the parents filled what seemed like an idyllic life. As we grew, we ventured across the stream and up into the fields that followed but never straying very far. I could always see my Mom coming out of the house and scanning the area to see where I was, and I was not allowed to lose sight of our house.

As my father was in the retail trade he always worked on a Saturday but had Thursdays off. It took many years before I realised that the working week was not split in that way for most people. To me it was fantastic, as midweek we would always do something: we might go into the huge city of Birmingham, or go to the Arboretum and feed the swans and ducks, or travel to Sutton Park, go up Barr Beacon or drive further afield to Drayton Manor Park. Sundays were the same too, we were always off somewhere. Mom would make the most delicious sandwiches and bake cake for the journey. I loved travelling in the back of Dad's car, and he loved to drive: it was his freedom from work and his reward, and he always cleaned the car on Sunday morning. The working week was broken by occasional Tuesday night visits to Fellows Park. I was too young to accompany him, but Dad would go to see the mighty Walsall Football Club play, usually with my Grandfather, Harry Jenkins, and my Uncle George. George Baldock was married to my Dad's sister Joan. He was a policeman in Walsall, having arrived from Grimsby many years before. George always had a soft spot for Grimsby Town football club but through a love of football and no real chance to watch Grimsby he had become a Saddlers fan. Throughout the remainder of their lives, all three would attend and live the highs and lows of the town's football team.

Joan was three years older than my Dad and they both had a younger sister Iris who married Geoff Smith. Unfortunately, he was a Wolverhampton Wanderers supporter, which did not go down too well with Harry, George or my Dad and caused many comic rivalries over the years. Walsall people grow up being taught that Wolves are to be disliked, and much joy and applause can be heard all over the borough when Wolves suffer defeat. The bad feeling had developed over the years mainly because Wolverhampton Wanderers were the big club, had great support, had won first division titles and had many international players. All of that in itself was fine, but it wasn't fine when Walsall, a small club that had carefully nurtured its own players, saw Wolves come in and buy the best ones and then go and win the league with them. Johnny Hancocks and Doug Lishman, for instance, were Walsall regulars that would go on to accomplish this feat. In today's world this movement of players is inevitable, but in those days the world was much smaller and the local pain was at a much higher level. Within the family, however, this was taken much more lightly and Geoff just had to suffer the constant flow of 'ribbing' that occurred each week.

In 1957, the final addition to our family would appear: 17th March would see the birth of my sister Helen. I have no clear recollection of having a baby in the household, but I know from the years that followed that Helen was not an easy one to handle. In years to come my mother would say that if Helen had been the first child in the family there would have been no second. Hence I am pleased and forever thankful that I was first and Helen decided to be second. Throughout my life Helen has been my friend, cohort, defender and greatest supporter – she was so all through the years I struggled to find an opportunity and direction and she continued to be so through all the glory years and on until today. My parents always said that I was a good baby, which I believe meant I didn't disrupt their sleep patterns too much and I could also be put in the sitting room with a few toy cars and left to myself, as I would play quietly and contentedly for hours. Helen on the other hand was a livewire, into everything, and up all night, and the nickname 'speedy' should have been hers and not mine. As soon as Helen became mobile she was off here, there and everywhere into anything she could get her hands on. My Dad loved me, no doubt, but Helen was his little girl and he bestowed upon her that extra protection that all fathers should give their daughters. He also instilled in me that I would always protect both my sister and my mother no matter what: in their cause no mountain was too high to climb, we were and always would be a close-knit unit.

As soon as Helen could walk, she would come with me down to the stream, which fascinated her. She loved getting messy, she loved mud, and not just the mud on the side of the stream but the softer kind found beneath the water level. She would get plastered in it, all over her clothes, splashing, kicking the water and laughing. Helen thought this was great fun. When we returned home, if I heard it once I heard it hundreds of times: 'Helen what have you been doing?' Helen always had an embarrassed smile but it made no difference, she would do it all again whenever possible. I remember those early years as a warm family unit.

Helen would join in the evening ritual of meeting Dad by the garages, she would come with me to play on the grass area in front of the house with the other kids, she would be there on Wednesday night visits to granddad's, and at Joan and George's home she would slowly join in the games with their daughter Susan.

My father was now doing well as manager of the shoe department for the Co-op, Helen was growing, and at the coming age of 5 it would soon be school time for me. My parents had enough money to put a deposit on their own home, and so we left 98 Barns Lane and moved closer to Walsall on a new development of houses on The Rushall Manor Estate. This would be my home for the next twenty years. I do recall the pride and joy of the move to 26 Regina Drive, Walsall, especially for my Mom. We had a corner house at the bottom of the cul-de-sac with its own drive and front lawn and a side gate to the yard, now known as the patio. Dad had a veranda built on the side of the house. It doubled as a playroom and greenhouse where each year Dad grew beautiful tasting tomatoes that we picked when ripe. The back garden was vast with four generous lawns and separating flower beds. Mom and Dad worked in it on Thursday and Sunday mornings, and they made the ornamental bricks that surrounded the square lawn. I remember my Dad teaching me to mix the cement and put it in metal holders that would then shape the bricks, leaving them to dry in preparation for the continued building a few days later. When Mom and Dad went in the garden, so did Helen and I, working to landscape the ground and generally helping. Happy times. Upstairs in the house, almost directly opposite the entrance to Helen's room and Mom and Dad's room, was the door to my smaller room overlooking the drive. Lots of schemes and dreams would be hatched in that room.

Young School Days – with music and football

Butts Primary School was the place where I would spend the majority of my time in the next few years, before moving into Butts Junior School, also on the same small site. Dad would drop me off at school in the morning and off into the playground I'd go, although after much protesting. I wanted to go on to work with my Dad, I hated going into school and would cry almost daily at having to get out of the car and go in. One day as Dad drove off down the road, I turned shouting "Dad!" and made a bolt for the car chasing down the hill. At this point some of the juniors were coming up the hill: 'Oh do you want your daddy, little boy? Ahhh, shame.' This pretty much stopped me in my tracks and my tears. I don't think I had encountered put downs by older boys at that time and I realised I didn't like it. I was angry but had no-one to blame other than myself. Quietly, I turned and began to walk up the street into school. The boys slightly ahead had moved on with their own thoughts and chatter, while I just walked into school where the whole affair settled in my mind. That was not going to happen again. I quit the crying game and got on with everything.

My first taste of show business came at Butts school in the Christmas nativity play. I was the lead shepherd, which had a good speaking part, sort of third or fourth on the bill. I remember being proud of my efforts as Mom and Dad came to watch. Helen came too and probably just pointed at me and giggled.

We were all in fear of the headmistress. She was very strict and would stand at the end of corridors and bellow 'Walk', if any of us got a little energetic and dared to break into a trot. Fortunately, I was still in my quiet mode at this time and didn't get told off that often. The primary years for me were peaceful, I was not out of line that much, my world was secure.

This was the latter end of the 1950s. Rock 'n' Roll was just beginning, Elvis Presley was just having his first hits, Cliff Richard and the Shadows recorded 'Move It.' The music world was beginning to change. Our house was always full of music, my Dad loved it, and from a very early age I can remember him coming home with records. He had bought a top of the range Rediffusion radiogram and radio or records would play constantly in our house. The first song I sang when I had mastered parts of the language was Love and Marriage – you know, it goes together like a horse and carriage. My pronunciation was not so good: 'Lull and mallidge, lull and mallidge, goes together like a horse and callidge.' It became my family party piece, but from that you can tell the amount of times it had been played at home. Dad always played to me the artists he liked: Frank Sinatra, Dean Martin, Sammy Davis Junior, Perry Como, Peggy Lee, they all became the soundtrack to our life at Regina Drive. He also liked Gershwin, Rodgers and Hammerstein, and *West Side Story*, which he thought was one of the best shows he had seen. He also tried me out with opera – the tenor Richard Tauber. He said Tauber was exceptional, but that went way over my head.

Dad knew all the artists, songwriters and shows of the day. In his youth he had played drums in a local band, 'The Rhythm Rascals.' They were well known locally and played many venues, especially the Gaumont in the centre of Walsall, where they had their greatest successes. Dad could also dance. He used to put on a record and get out a square piece of wood he had made three feet by three feet and treat us to his tap dancing in the kitchen. At the time I thought this was hilarious and Helen would smile and giggle too, but I knew then from the beats he tapped out that he was good at it. I would also take my turn on the wood but could not get the foot movements of my Dad. He made it look so easy when in reality it is difficult. Without doubt my love for music and the influence it was to have over me grew from this time. Mom used to do a bit on the piano too, as when she was a young girl there had been a piano at one of her relatives homes. Although no-one had bothered to teach her to play, she had mastered a little ability by ear, just sitting there until she got it right.

In junior school the highlight of the day was the morning and afternoon break, when 20-a-side football would dominate the playground. You not only had to negotiate the opposition but also the girls who lined the walls and scattered as the small sized football came their way. It was here that I would first feel that rush of scoring a goal for your team, a feeling I could not get enough of, so I was always up for a game. The holidays were filled with playing at home – football in the cul-de-sac and also cricket, another sport that I would love all my life.

Music and football were beginning to make real marks on my life. On Sundays we would have the radio on in the mornings for 'Two Way Family Favourites.' This is when requests would be played from families in the UK to the troops abroad and vice versa. On this show they played all kinds of music, but always including the current hits. This is where I heard Bill Haley's 'Rock Around The Clock' and 'See You Later Alligator'; 'Why Do Fools Fall In Love', by Frankie Lyman & the Teenagers; 'Singing The Blues', by Tommy Steele & the Steelmen; 'Cumberland Gap', by Lonnie Donegan; 'That'll Be The Day', by Buddy Holly & the Crickets; 'Diana', by Paul Anka; 'Great Balls Of Fire', by Jerry Lee Lewis; 'All I Have To Do Is Dream', by the Everly Brothers; 'Dream Lover', by Bobby Darin; and 'Only Sixteen', by Craig Douglas. I was also touched by Perry Como's 'Magic Moments'; 'Who's Sorry Now', by Connie Francis; 'It's Only Make Believe', with Conway Twitty; 'Smoke Gets In Your Eyes', by the Platters; and 'Side Saddle', by Russ Conway. The great awakening though was all down to The Tupelo Mississippi Flash – Elvis Presley's 'Heartbreak Hotel', 'All Shook Up', 'Jailhouse Rock', and 'One Night.' I was sold, and when Dad took me to see the movies, as far as I was concerned Elvis was King. The UK's equivalent in the late 1950s was Cliff Richard & the Shadows. Cliff seemed to explode from nowhere and capture the nation. He was England's Elvis complete with the sneered lip.

News of Cliff Richard's huge impact spread north to Walsall from what became a legendary coffee bar in London – The Two I's. Back in 1953 Gina Lollobrigida had opened the Moka coffee bar at 29 Frith Street which provided London with its first Gaggia espresso coffee machine. Londoners quickly took advantage of having the option of early morning espressos to kick start the day or lunchtime kicks of caffeine to speed the afternoon and before long many other coffee bars began to appear around Soho. Some of them began to provide live music: the Top 10 in Berwick Street as well as Heaven and Hell and The Two I's, both next door to each other at 57 and 59 Old Compton Street respectively, were places that young people could call their own. Almost overnight the 'teenagers', as they were referred to for the first time, were heading to Soho to listen to music, preferably live, and drink coffee. It was a force that seemed unstoppable. The Two I's was bought in 1955 by an Australian wrestler Paul Lincoln, who purchased it from two brothers in a family called Irani – hence its name Two I's. The coffee bar started slowly as a business and began losing money, but this all changed when Lincoln started putting on skiffle groups that were becoming popular, especially after Lonnie Donegan had a hit with Rock Island Line. Skiffle suited the Two I's as the bands were minimal, cheap and the unamplified instruments meant they could fit onto the tiniest, sweatiest cellar stage. The Two I's legend began to be created one night when a skiffle group The Vipers played their set and one of their friends Tommy Hicks helped out on vocals. Tommy's vocals so impressed a watching record producer from Decca that he was signed to the label. Hicks was managed by a former shopkeeper, Larry Parnes, and he persuaded him to change his name to Tommy Steele. The name stuck and a hit single 'Rock with the Caveman' turned Tommy Steele into Britain's first genuine teenage pop idol. Steele's overnight success turned the Two I's basement cellar into the country's most famous music venue and prompted teenagers with guitars to come to the Two I's to seek fame and fortune. Larry Parnes now considered himself an impresario and he started to manage and create new stage names for other singers: Reg Smith became Marty Wilde, Ronald Wycherly became Billy Fury and Clive Powell became Georgie Fame. Joe Brown it seems rejected his name Elmer Twitch but went on to have hits anyway. Most famous of all, Cliff Richard (he was Harry Webb and in fact was turned down by Parnes) and the Shadows also met in the Two I's, and other celebrity musicians there were Eden Kane, Screaming Lord Sutch, Tony Sheridan, Johnny Kidd and Paul Gadd, who years later found fame as Gary Glitter. On 18th September 2006, a green plaque was unveiled at the site of the Two I's to commemorate its existence. Today, it is known as The Boulevard Bar and Dining Room, and the basement is now just a lobby.

Back in the late 1950s, I believed the Two I's to be a palace, full of names I knew from records I had heard and the grand place to be. It would be many years before I realised that the Two I's was a small basement with a tiny eighteen inch high stage, speakers on the wall and a Gaggia expresso coffee machine. But the coffee bar was here to stay and eventually it would reach every town in the country. Walsall's was the Cosmopolitan, better known as the 'Cos.' I was still a few years away from being a regular.

CHAPTER 2
1960s, SCHOOL AND TRAGEDY

The 1960s Revolution:

Music was becoming increasingly important in my life. I listened to the radio whenever possible and searched for the programmes that might occasionally play some of the pop records of the day. In 1963 there was no Radio One, there were no commercial radio stations and no chart programmes: it was mainly only on a Saturday or Sunday morning that you might catch the current hits mixed in with the older favourites. Looking back now, this gave me a great knowledge of Frank Sinatra, Dean Martin, Sammy Davis, Perry Como, Doris Day, Ella Fitzgerald, Peggy Lee and alike, most of whom I knew from my Dad's record collection. On occasions, Dad would introduce me to more artists he loved – these came in the form of Sunday afternoon films. *The Glen Miller Story* was always one of my favourites, and Dad explained to me how Miller had found his sound. I remember how Dad said that to be successful you had to bring a new sound to the people. After the movie Dad would get out his records and we would listen again to 'Moonlight Serenade', 'Pennsylvania 65000', 'Little Brown Jug' and 'In The Mood.'

The Sunday movies that my Dad loved so much were from the great years of the Hollywood Studio System. Now, I saw for the first time Marilyn Monroe, Fred Astaire, Ginger Rogers, Rock Hudson, John Wayne, Jane Russell and Tony Curtis in those great movies with music throughout. One of my favourite songs of all time was Gene Kelly in *Singin' In The Rain*. Dad would sing along and dance in the lounge to all the songs from the movies, and his joy made the movies and songs incredibly attractive to me. The family loved to watch the *Perry Como Show* from America, but favourite of all was the *Dean Martin Show*. My Dad adored Dean and still to this day I too have a great love of him.

Then, one day in this year of 1963 my world was shaken to the core by a pop record that had just come out. When I first heard *Please Please Me* by The Beatles my whole being opened up and from that moment on I had to know all I could about John Lennon, Paul McCartney, George Harrison and Ringo Starr. Now it was my turn to introduce my Dad to a song. The Beatles caused some ructions in the older generation of the time and I was proud that my Dad stood firm and stated to all the doubters, 'You're wrong, those boys are really good.'

My first guitar appeared that year on my tenth birthday, bought by my parents along with a copy of The Beatles debut album *Please Please Me* which the band had recorded in a one day session. That Parlophone LP album, which I still own, was never off the record player. I knew all the words of the 14 songs and would sing along with my guitar around my neck playing any chord I could find, making one hell of a noise, but basking in complete paradise.

On the night of 4th November when The Beatles appeared on the Royal Command Performance and Lennon said, 'The people in the cheaper seats clap your hands, and the rest of you, if you'd just rattle your jewellery,' I was in my pyjamas, guitar around my neck, standing next to my Dad's chair as we both watched the Beatles play – absolute magic. As soon as they stopped my mother said, 'Right, bedtime.' I had only been allowed to stay up to watch if I washed, cleaned my teeth and put on my pyjamas before the show started. It was worth it, and still is today.

I gleefully took *Please Please Me* to Joan and George's to play to my cousin Susan. She was three years older than me and in my mind was super cool. It was Susan who had taught us to twist at the previous Christmas get-together and she owned copies of 'The Twist' by Chubby Checker and 'Twistin' the Night Away' by Sam Cooke. Susan was also taken by The Beatles but shortly afterwards I was distraught when she told me the Beatles were old hat and the new band that was even better was The Rolling Stones. We would disagree for many years, Susan in the Rolling Stones corner and me firmly with The Beatles. This was a country-wide debate over the coming years and both groups were fiercely supported by their own fans. For me, The Beatles were and still are the best group ever and their achievements set the bench mark for all that followed, although I have to own up that The Rolling Stones are also up there for me and some of their records are still to this day simply outstandingly brilliant.

The *New Musical Express* became a 'must have' paper at this time, and my Dad knowing I was completely obsessed with all the pop music of the day would buy a copy and bring it home for me. I became known at school as the one who knew most about the current records and this made me popular both with the boys and for the first time the girls.

School Days:

The year 1964 blew into my idyllic life, and change, as it always does, began to come with it. Butts Junior School was much the same in terms of the break time football matches and evening games in the street, but the lessons seemed to intensify. My mother also started to talk constantly about the eleven plus and that if I wanted to succeed in life this was one of the first tests. Mother explained in great detail that it was a must that I pass so as not to let my father down. Father was not so intense about it all and regularly used to say that he didn't care what I did in life as long as I was the best at it. 'If you turn out to be a dustbin man Steve, that's OK as long as you're happy doing it and you become the best at it. That will be good enough for me.' This was not good enough for my Mom but in their own ways they both got through to me. I learned that a pass in the eleven plus was either a place at Queen Mary's Grammar School or at Joseph Leckie Comprehensive School.

What seemed like all of a sudden, the summer of 1965 was approaching and the eleven plus loomed. I was constantly asked by Mom if I was working hard at school. I thought I was holding my own and was fairly sure that I would pass and not let my father down. Finally the results were issued and I had in fact passed and been awarded a place at Joseph Leckie Comprehensive School for the autumn. I was relieved. Mom, happy, sprang into action with uniforms, gym shoes and everything else I would need. In those days all boys wore short trousers, the jeans revolution was only just beginning, so along with a new school came long trousers for the first time. These took a little getting used to and seemed a bit restrictive but also made me feel a little more grown up.

As I walked through the gate at Leckie on my first day that September I had no idea that the next five years would be traumatic. My warm and wonderful family world was due to change forever and with it my outlook on life. It was a little scary going to senior school for the first time, I was not in the same class as the only two others from Butts Junior School – Stephen Fellows and Lesley Grew – and so as I entered that first form room I knew no-one. I sat myself down one row from the back of the class and almost central looking at the teacher's desk. I had tried for the back row of seats but they were all taken as everyone had the same idea. We sat there for what seemed like an age as each person in the school was released from the opening assembly and directed to their designated form room.

'Anyone sitting here, mate?'

'No, help yourself.'

The opening lines to what would be a friendship that lasted for years. John Oebel would be a daily confidant for the next eleven years and a friend for the next thirty-five. Our form teacher was Mrs Prole who in the next eighteen months would become a fantasy figure for some of us young boys. She was not only our form teacher but also our French teacher, which added to her attraction. Tall, blonde, long legs, always-high heels and at that time probably in her late 20s, in a short period of time the boys would all look forward to the French class, although not necessarily to learn the language.

1966 arrived and England was the centre of the world. The Beatles and The Rolling Stones led the way in pop music, Mary Quant and Twiggy were the fashion icons and David Bailey photographed it all. We were all Cool Britannia and Swingin' London, and it seemed that everything was possible. It was the height of the exciting new society of the sixties, breaking down generations of barriers. Gone was the stiffness of what had been before, there was a boom in young people and we were the future. No-one could stop our ideas, the pill was just around the corner and we were one year away from the Summer of Love.

Britain's rise to King of the World was cemented in the summer of 1966 when England beat West Germany 4–2 to win the World Cup. Life just couldn't get any better. The Jenkins family had taken a two and a half week summer break to Cornwall, where we travelled around staying in a different town every three or four days. I watched the World Cup Final with my Dad, Mom and Helen through a serving hatch from the dining room to the kitchen, on a farm in Cornwall.

The World Cup in our possession, the Jenkins squad moved onto a caravan site in St Ives, a pretty little village on the north coast of Cornwall, made famous a year later by the hippies, and there I met a girl also staying with her family on the site. Today, I have no recollection of her name, but what I remember is that for the first time I wanted to be around a girl and talk to her. She was pretty and attractive in a way I had never noticed in a girl before. I really had no idea why, as I knew nothing about sex at that time. During the 1950s and early '60s no-one mentioned sex and there was no such thing as sex education. So my head was in a complete spin not knowing what this emotional, sick feeling in my stomach was. When our few days in St Ives came to an end I was trying everything to get Mom and Dad to stay there for a few more days, but all to no avail. I said goodbye to a pretty girl with long brown hair and she gave me her trogg to remember her by. It stayed with me for a long time and resided in my bedroom.

Holidays over and back to school with summer stories; after the seven weeks off everyone returns with new experiences and school becomes a learning place about life as other kids share their recent knowledge. Girls were now becoming more and more interesting, their personal equipment was arriving on a daily basis and I learned a little about sex from the other lads, well at least where it was all supposed to fit. Mary Quant's miniskirt had caused many problems for the school: almost overnight a lot of the girls had cut their knee length skirts into minis. At first the schoolmasters sent the girls home, then as the wave of short skirts washed over the teachers, who began to look like stranded King Canutes, a new rule was issued. It stated that girls' skirts could be no more than three inches above the knee. Girls were called into masters' offices if the teachers thought the offending skirts were higher than three inches, and the girl would then have to kneel on the floor while a ruler was used to measure the distance from knee to skirt. If the skirt was more than three inches, initially the girl was sent home, but as time went by the punishment would change to one, two or three nights' detention, known by the pupils as 'Jug.' Later the girls at Leckie would adjust their skirts by just folding them over at the waist, and if they were caught with the blatantly obvious five to six inches above the knee, while walking behind the master to his office they would release a roll or two of the waist material and arrive at the required three inches above length. The teachers had no chance, the girls were way ahead of them all the time. The boys became more and more interested in the length of skirts at this time and with that came an acknowledgement of what a cracking pair of legs looked like. You see what a learning curve school can be.

During the first couple of years at Leckie, I was a pretty quiet lad during lessons, sport, with football and cricket, brought me some respect from the other pupils, and the odd fight here and there made all concerned know I stand up for myself if need be. My father was not too keen on my fighting but he bought me some boxing gloves and sent me to have a few lessons, believing that if it was going to happen I would then have some knowledge about what I was doing. I believe those boxing lessons encouraged me not to fight rather than the opposite. Once you go in a ring and take a few punches from someone who really knows what he is doing, it sure makes you think, and fighting eventually becomes your last option.

Sign of the Times:

1967 arrived and the Summer of Love was upon us. My Wrangler jacket and cord jeans meant I was as cool as can be, it was all San Francisco and we all wore flowers in our hair – well not us lads, but we were down with the vibe, if you know what I mean. And now my life began its change. Mom became ill with kidney trouble, suffering colossal pain and hallucinations. I am not sure whether the doctors understood this condition so well in those days. Mom went into hospital and her half sister Molly came to look after Helen and me while Dad was at work. He would pick us up and then we would go and see her at Walsall General. Most of the time Mom was in another world – sometimes she knew who we were and other times not. Just a week or so later I developed stomach trouble and was sent to Joan and George's to recover, but instead my condition worsened. I was examined for suspected appendicitis, but in fact it was a false alarm, and I believe the fear of an operation aided my complete recovery. A few days later, as I was on the mend, I found my Auntie Joan in the front room holding my Dad who was crying and in a bad way. I quickly left the room and went into the sitting room not knowing what I should do, but he came in and said all was OK – Mom really wasn't well but all would be fine. Soon after, I returned to school for the new term and some weeks later Mom came home. It was a fright but she was eventually going to be all right. Mom being seriously tough made light of it all and for a short while life returned back to normal.

As it became cool to now have girls as friends Sharon Lunt became one of mine. She lived just around the corner from where we used to catch the number 35 bus in the morning and we would catch the same bus home after school. I had a crush on her for a very long time, but Sharon was one of those girls who seemed older than her age and so attracted the boys from the years above at school. So I had no chance, but we became really good friends. I learned a lot from Sharon in those tender years and she was always someone I could talk to and ask questions to, and in return if any of the lads were playing her up I would always spring to her defence.

In the summer of 1968 the family went to Bournemouth, where we were to have our holidays in the following years. We had a beach hut that we would go to everyday and Mom had brought her travelling stove to cook hot lunches while we played on the beach. Dad pretty much sat in his chair most of the time. It seemed that he was always tired and work was taking it out of him. He began not to want to play cricket, which I found disappointing, but he was still the same, cracking jokes, having fun as long as he didn't move around too much. Helen was always at Dad's side, he was always cuddling her – and I was beginning to wander in search of something, but I didn't know what it was.

One day a couple came past with their daughter and as they went by their daughter leaned forward and looked at me. I think this was the first time a girl had ever really given me the look. I can't say I blame her as I was sitting there with my John Lennon hat on, which I believed at the time almost turned me into a Beatle. Thinking back now, she probably wanted the hat. For days I searched for that girl like a needle in a haystack until to my amazement I finally found her and gave her my look. But with her parents so close by, we couldn't speak. Finally, some days later, on what I thought was my final check out trip past her beach hut, I could tell her parents were packing up to leave, so it was now or never. The girl started to lag behind her parents as they walked the prom, enabling me to catch her up and finally say hello. We spoke for a few minutes as we walked along and I told her of a disco I had seen by the pier called The Ritz. Would she like to go? She said she would have to ask her Mom and Dad, they were going home tomorrow and she was meant to be going out for dinner. Well, she went to her parents and they had a discussion. I stood a few yards away, these were terrible moments – I didn't know what to do with myself. Then she came back and said she could possibly go with me, but I had to speak to her Mom and Dad first. We both went over and we spoke for a few moments. I had to collect her at 7.30 from their hotel and she must be back by 10.30 at the latest. They were prepared to trust me and I was not to let them down. Having pulled off the impossible, I now had to ask my Mom and Dad if it was OK for me to go out to the disco. They said that after all that effort they saw no reason why not and if the girl's parents had trusted me to take her out I would not let them or my Mom and Dad down. From that day, Silvana was to become my first girlfriend. We would spend the next three years of our lives staying at each others' parents' houses for weekends and my parents became friends with Silv's parents, Len and Carole.

Music, Music, Music:

All the time, music was more and more on my agenda. I had progressed through Radio Luxembourg, listening at night in bed to Tony Prince and Kid Jensen, to the pirate station Radio Caroline, where Johnnie Walker was my favourite, and now came the newly launched Radio One on the BBC. In those days Tony Blackburn was a must in the morning, we had it on in the house before school every day. Along with the boom of pop records came all the music magazines. I couldn't get enough. I knew about all the groups and who wrote the songs and I started to become interested in the labels themselves. George Martin's Parlophone, part of the EMI Group, was my first interest with The Beatles, Gerry and the Pacemakers, Billy J Kramer and the Dakotas, and Cilla Black. But then, this new sound from Detroit appeared in the form of Tamla Motown. I was sold: Diana Ross and the Supremes, Martha Reeves and The Vandellas, The Temptations, The Four Tops, The Isley Brothers, Marvin Gaye and Tammi Tyrell, that sound was the best I had ever heard next to The Beatles. I had to find a map and find out where Detroit was. The same happened with Stax Records: I heard Booker T and the MGs, Sam and Dave, Carla Thomas, Isaac Hayes and Joe Tex, and once again I was at the map to find out exactly where Memphis was.

An entire completely new musical world had opened up and I was infatuated. I was going to youth club where all these records were played and everyone would have a dance, and I especially watched the girls and learned how to move a little so that I wouldn't feel so self-conscious and could get involved with that sound. On Saturdays they had a disco at St Paul's Hall in Walsall and I couldn't wait to go. Inside it was completely dark except for the lights coming from the stage and the seats all around the edge, as well as a small room off the main hall where you could buy a coke. It was packed every week, with Motown blaring out and new records being played. I was mesmerised. The DJ was a god. He had all the records at his fingertips, he had everyone dancing and they were all staring at him when he back announced the previous record and announced what was coming next. I wanted to be him.

He's a Rebel:

By now my sister Helen had also passed her eleven plus and had secured a seat at Joseph Leckie, so I could look out for her as she began life at senior school. This became a mixed blessing for Helen over the coming two or three years. Yes, her brother made sure she would come to no harm but as my character began to change, Helen was constantly asked the same question as she went to different lessons and the registrar was called.

'Name?'

'Helen Jenkins.'

'Do you have a brother, Miss Jenkins?'

'Yes Sir.'

Helen became marked by my forthcoming rebellion, which was completely unfair, as she has always been a little ray of sunshine and not a problem for anyone. One day, we both turned up late to school by 20 minutes or so, as we had missed the bus and caught the next one. Leckie put monitors from the senior year on gate duty to catch the latecomers and the penalty was detention for the following evening. As we walked through the gate the prefect said, 'Names.' I said, 'Listen, put me in the book, no problem, but leave her out, it's her first year.' 'No, you are both going in the book. I know your name, what's her first name?' 'Look, I'll take double "jug", just let her go.' Helen, sensing all was not going to be well, said, 'It's OK, Steve.' Now, I felt I had made a reasonable request and was starting to think the situation unfair. 'What's her first name?' 'OK, here's the way it's going to go. I'll give you her first name and as soon as you write the first letter of it I'm going to kick your head in. Get going sis, see you later.' Helen reluctantly walked on. 'Do you still want her name?' 'Yes.' He wrote 'H' and all hell broke loose, which ended with him in a holly bush screaming. I had only been in class five minutes when the Head of Senior School, a certain Mr Smith, walked into the classroom. After a short discussion with our teacher, I was told: 'Jenkins, Mr Smith would like to see you.' The result was one night of detention for Helen, and for me, a good belt across the head and four nights in detention.

Paul West became a good pal at school around this time and it was Paul who would give me the nickname that would stick for years throughout my schooldays. I had bought a pair of hush puppy suede Chelsea boots from Dad's shop – they were top fashion back then and I wore them to school. One day Paul looked at the shoes and said, 'Hey Elvis, don't step on my brown suede shoes.' That was it, I would spend years known only as Elvis. Now, that might not seem too bad today, but at the time Elvis Presley was definitely not cool. The Beatles, The Stones and Motown had rendered Elvis 'old hat' before Elvis made his comeback some years later. I really didn't like it but there was no way out, I'd walk into classrooms and pupils had already written Elvis on the black board, which brought me even more under the suspicious eye of the teachers who thought I was being 'big' on myself. I heard hundreds of renditions of Elvis's hits as I walked through the corridors, which for a teenage boy was not cool and a complete nightmare when everything around was built on being cool. My pal John Oebel was also suffering at this time. A British boxer coming to the end of his career, Jack Bodell, was beginning to look slow and awkward, and John became known as Jack Bobel – Jack and Elvis were attached as brothers even more. Around this time John's father died and almost at the same time my family's biggest trauma began: we were thrust together even more.

Family Tragedy – The Beginning:

I arrived home one day from school and Mom told me Dad had been taken to hospital after suffering a heart attack. Mom said he was OK but would remain in hospital for at least three weeks and maybe more before coming home. After a few days Helen and I were allowed to visit him but we were told to be very calm. When we arrived, although Dad didn't look well, he said he would be fine in a while and not to worry. For the next two weeks we visited every other night and the reports said all was going to plan. Then one morning my Mom woke me from my sleep and said Dad had suffered another two heart attacks which had brought on a stroke. She was leaving for the hospital and I was to get Helen and myself up and off to school. At this point I had never heard of a stroke and didn't know what it meant. I did as I was asked and took Helen with me to school. Everything really passed me by that day, I had no idea or knew what to expect. When we returned home Mom explained what a stroke was and that Dad had been struck by the worst kind. He had lost the use of the left side of his body, his face was distorted and he could not speak. Mom explained that some of the use could return to his limbs, but when we were to go and see him we must act normally and not look shocked. A couple of days later we went to see Dad, but he was not really there. I thought I saw recognition in his eyes and I tried to be strong and keep my face impassive, but after a few minutes I had to remove myself slowly and exit the room. I went outside and wept. The greatest man I knew was so drastically reduced in his powers and I knew then that a recovery was unlikely. This was bad enough for me but Helen was three and a half years younger than I was, although at the time it seemed that she handled it all better.

The next four months were spent at Walsall General Hospital. Dad did make little improvements but they were small. A voice of sorts returned but it was not the voice I had known. The family rallied around and we saw lots of our relatives. By the time the day came for Dad to return home Mom had turned the dining room into his room as it was impossible to get him upstairs. From then on, every day my Mom dressed Dad without fail, massaged his limbs, carried him to the bathroom and worked on him every minute. She never once felt sorry for herself and never outwardly accepted that Dad would not make a full recovery. I have never seen love that big to this day.

I could no longer speak with Dad like before. He was not the same man and it seemed I had been cut off overnight. My mind went into overdrive. Religion and Church went flying out the window: no God would do that to a charming, intelligent man who did no harm to anyone. School became irrelevant, the only way I could escape was to physically exhaust myself. At football I'd career into tackles with no fear of being hurt, running as fast and as hard as I could. At cricket I'd bowl as fast as I could and when batting after getting my eye in, I would smash anything that was just a little loose. I began to suffer the most horrendous migraines. They could come along at anytime and when they came I just couldn't lift my head up. I became introverted at school and really couldn't care less. If I was well I would answer back and if I was unwell I would just get through it. The teachers had no idea of what was going on in my life and so I suppose what happened next was not completely their fault.

One day, when I couldn't lift my head up from the desk because of a migraine, our physics teacher Mr Hodges, not a pleasant man, decided I was sleeping in his class. When I told him I had a migraine, he made me stand, whacked me round the head and asked me how it felt now. The pain was unbelievable, I was holding back the tears, and when I said I was hurting really badly, he whacked me again and told me to stand in the hallway. I couldn't stand up properly, so I went to the toilets to run cold water on my hands and face. I dried off and then sat on the cold toilet seat, which helped. After a while I went back and stood in the hallway. After the class had finished Hodges called me back in and said that after missing the class I had two hundred lines to write out by next week – and where had I been when he had come out to look for me? I again told him I had a migraine and the cold of the toilets helps. He just replied: '200 lines for next week.'

I took a few more whacks from teachers over the coming weeks, some my fault, some not, and then one day I thought 'my Dad is the greatest man I have ever known and he has never raised his hand to me in his life.' Dad's philosophy was that if he could not make me understand by talking to me then it really wasn't worth the trouble, as either I would never understand or maybe life would teach me. Yet here, people who did not know me thought they were somehow going to punch understanding in to me. After that day, my world changed. I felt I was on my own and that was the way it was going to be. I would make my own decisions and face the consequences of those decisions myself. Slowly, after about a year the migraines began to subside – but my school work was slipping. Sometimes I was interested, sometimes not. Sport and music were the only escape, along with every other weekend spent with Silvana.

The coffee bar culture was in full swing in Walsall at this time, and whenever we got the chance, all the lads would assemble at The Cosmopolitan towards the top of Bridge Street. We would all drink coffee or Coke, and would normally have to make the drink last as long as possible as money was tight and you had to have a drink or be thrown out. But what else could you want? It was paradise for teenage girls and boys, including teenagers from other schools. We didn't think much of the lads from Queen Mary's, posh and always full of themselves, but we all liked the girls from Bluecoat and we made a few friends from there. In particular, Susan McClusky was a good friend. Susan was a good singer too, so with my passion for records we had lots to talk about. Susan would go on to have a couple of hit records, with Silver Convention by the time she was 20 – her stage name being Zenda Jacks.

The jukebox in the Cosmopolitan was everything and regularly restocked with new records. Tamla Motown was huge there, it was always Isley Brothers, Marvin Gaye, and The Temptations. 'Behind A Painted Smile', 'This Old Heart Of Mine' and 'I Guess I'll Always Love You' from the Isleys repeated all the time. The Temptations' 'Get Ready', 'I Think It's Gonna Rain', 'The Things You Do

For Love' and the magnificent 'Ain't Too Proud To Beg' were the soundtracks of our lives. Plenty of British bands were also mixed in with the soul records – The Who, especially, were blaring out all the time. The Cos was the teenager's home in Walsall, a lot of us had happy years there, and I was one of them.

The Cosmopolitan was my only refuge from the traumas of both home life and school – and they were about to worsen, just when I thought things had to get better. Dad would sit me down on his good days and give me the benefit of his knowledge and conclusions on a huge range of subjects and life in general. I particularly valued these conversations because they only occurred on the days when he was able to think clearly. Each subject was well worked out and put to me in simple terms. Those directives were to last my lifetime – they were to form the basis of how I would operate through the next forty years. From them I learned how to manage in a variety of situations that would occur in my life and I truly believe Dad knew he would not be there to tell me when they happened. We spoke about everything: gambling, drinking, smoking, fighting, money, mortgages, work, honesty, belief in one's ability, failure, effort, success; when to walk away, when to stand your ground, opportunities, decisions, responsibility – no stone was left unturned and all was delivered from actual experiences in his life. A calm and intelligent man doing all he could to protect me and put me on the best possible road for the future while fighting his own physical and mental frailties at the same time. A champion, no doubt.

Then one day he had another heart attack and was taken into Walsall General again. Mom, who under the most enormous stress had worked so hard to make everything as normal as possible in our lives, could take no more, and was also admitted to Walsall General. Dad had never worked again since the first heart attack, and I remember the Co-op, who had been good to him and kept his job open for a long time, had to move on. Mom then had to juggle the finances and learn all the issues in running the home that Dad had always managed. The daily physical work that Dad's illness had created, as well as many other issues that were kept from me, took their toll. Molly and Joan were again on duty with regards to Helen and myself, but the whole thing was a mess. Helen and I would go to Walsall General at night and run between wards, one with Mom and one with Dad, and then after 30 minutes we would swap. Joan, George, Iris and Geoff would also visit and take it in turns with the changeover. The consensus of opinion was that probably both our parents were not going to make it. This became a reality to me when one day Dad told everyone to leave except me. He told me it was I who now had to look after my Mom and sister, he knew it was unfair that he was asking this, but from here on in I would be the man of the house. He would rely on me to protect, look after and take care not only of Mom but also particularly Helen. He said Helen was his little princess and this should not be happening to her at such a young age. It was tragic, and no matter what might happen I should always make sure that no harm would come to her. I told him I would always do exactly what he had asked and he said he knew that already. Dad also told me that although I had not been so good at school, he knew I was smart and I should live as he had told me in our conversations during the last few months. 'Now go see your Mom.'

I don't know how many weeks both my parents were in hospital, it seemed like a lifetime. I was trying to be a man but I was filled with anger. I just couldn't believe that good honest people should be treated so badly by life itself. Some friends of my parents, who were doing the best they could, thought I might find some help in God. At that moment I hated God and all he stood for. One night at the hospital my aunts and uncles were outside my father's ward as I returned from seeing Mom. In all fairness they were doing what they thought was right – the conversation was about what was going to happen to Helen and myself, where were we going to live, who was going to look after us. I got the gist of this as I was approaching, and Helen looked up at me crying, a look I will never forget. In protection of my sister and much pain I yelled 'Don't discuss that in front of Helen.' I took her to outside Mom's ward and tried to reassure her that all would be fine and I would be the one to look after her if anything happened. Helen, little toughie that she was, did as I asked, and we managed to get through another night. I couldn't think any further than the next day or the next night at that stage. I knew nothing of weekly bills, even putting food in the pantry was something I had never thought of before. I can only believe that our mother was aware of all that and decided with her usual ruthless determination that she would now get well. Slowly she did recover, and finally, although weak, she returned home. Dad remained in hospital and would never again leave it; we visited every night and watched as he slowly declined.

Mother woke me up again one morning. Dad had died, she was going to the hospital and had to arrange a lot of things. 'Get Helen to school, be brave.' 'OK Mom.' The sheets came back over my head as I wept, then I pulled myself together and went to get Helen. I think all the family knew Dad was not going to make it and there was some relief in that he did not have to live his life that way anymore – he deserved better.

Dad had decided to be cremated. He had said to me, he did not want to have a grave that people would visit as he would not be there anyway. Dad wanted to live on only in the minds of the people that loved him; he believed that was the best way forward. I remember not knowing about cremation at that time. I thought everyone had a gravestone and I thought it would always be a place I could go to talk with Dad when I had decisions to make or problems I had to solve. It came as a shock when I understood what cremation was and I decided I would have to think about that one later in my life as I really couldn't get it then. But, it was my father's wish and so it happened. My mother seemed to agree with the whole idea and many years later she would be cremated in exactly the same place and manner. My most vivid memory of the day is everyone standing and the coffin moving towards some red curtains that parted. Everyone was still and just at that moment my mother waved, just once, a sort of 'bon voyage' half wave. In that one single movement I saw the deepest love, the most desperate loss and the greatest beauty in the knowledge that she would see Dad again. They were most definitely a pair.

Mom was tougher than anyone believed she could be and slowly she put one foot in front of the other and took charge of our small unit. Helen would suffer a couple of years later, a backlash to what had occurred. I was just plain angry at everything and everyone. I just could not come to terms with what had happened to Dad, with seeing my Mom ill and suffering and my sister just lost sometimes in all that had occurred. I just wanted to get out to work, start to earn some money, help with the home, take care of Mom and Helen, and pretty much get on with the tasks that had been set me by my Dad.

School's Out:

School was now a very serious problem. With everything that had been going on, I had no respect at all for anything to do with Joseph Leckie. The teachers, unaware of my home traumas, set about bringing me into line. I was sent to the Head of Senior school, Mr Smith, on several occasions after being dismissed from class for answering back or disrupting class. Finally, I was formally accused of being a 'ring leader', which all the other kids thought was funny, although some had followed my lead.

'What are you here for again Jenkins?'

'Dismissed from class, Sir.'

'What for?'

'I disagreed with the teacher and answered back when told to be quiet.'

'I don't know what to do with you Jenkins, what are you going to do with your pathetic life?'

'I'm going to be a footballer, Sir.'

'Very few boys make it to being a professional footballer Jenkins; let's say that's not going to happen. What will you do then?'

'I'll be a film star, Sir.'

At which point he whacked me as hard as possible around the head.

'I'm going to break you Jenkins, I'm going to make it my business to do so.'

'You can try, Sir.'

Whack.

'Get out!'

And so my life went on getting worse and worse at Leckie. In due course I was up in front of the Headmaster, Mr Williams. Unlike Smith and Hodges, who had no compassion, heart or understanding, Williams had all of that and more. He explained to me how I had become the subject of debate in the staff room. I had somehow generated genuine hatred from some of his most experienced staff and yet other teachers simply would not agree and spoke up passionately on my behalf and in my defence. But he also explained how this could not go on – either we must somehow find a solution or he would have no choice but to force me to go a separate way from Joseph Leckie School.

I knew I was now not far from being expelled. To get out of Leckie any way would be joyous for me at that time, but my Mom would see the situation as very damaging to my father's name and it would bring a whole host of problems and repercussions. I agreed with Mr Williams I would try and behave better in class, but I did make him aware that I would not put up with being whacked around the head and I would not tolerate being expected to take it without some kind of repercussion. He said that he did not want to hear my thoughts – at some point in the future he would review the situation.

Mr Williams did call me to his office some weeks later, he had decided that I should spend an afternoon with a therapist. The therapist turned out to be a good man and I was sorry the meeting had to end. He told me I was bright and he could find nothing wrong with me at all. He said my passion and belief in the future were admirable and he would recommend that I stay at the school. He thought I would do well in my life whichever avenue I would take. I have never seen him again from that day to this but I have good memories of whoever he was and I thank him.

I told my great friend John all that had happened. He said 'Well we know all that don't we, and we know you're smart – let's go.' It was over as far as he was concerned and I suppose it grew a little quieter between a few of the teachers and me after that for a time, for two reasons I believe: first, I was in the final year and sooner or later would be gone, there was no way I was staying on for 'A' levels; and second, I was a little bigger and not so easy to push around. The end was inevitably near. I had the strap again after jumping school one Friday afternoon to go to the opening of The Hideaway Café in Walsall – the beginnings of the Californian West Coast sound were reaching Walsall, the riots were starting against Vietnam in the

States, the 1970s were approaching with great expectation and Friday afternoons were not meant to be spent in school. A disappointed Mr Williams handed over the punishment to Mr Smith who pulled the ultimate foul: against all regulations he delivered the third blow across my back rather than backside, which can cause permanent injury. There were more beatings before the final event that sealed my expulsion: I had an altercation with a teacher from Bluecoat's school who tried to stop me taking a friend and some of her pals to the Hideaway. Altercation is a mild word, actually – I told him to ….. off. For Mr Williams, I had now reached the end of the road; the guy at Bluecoat was a headteacher there and a personal friend. Although the O-level exams were due to start in about one month's time, Williams said, 'You are no longer required to attend school. You will arrive at the gate at the times I allocate to you, sit your exams, and then be escorted back to the gate. I will write to your parents. Goodbye Jenkins.'

That was it. I left school. In those days boys rarely confessed to parents about traumas they may have experienced at school, it was too embarrassing and schools had limited personal contact with parents. My mother knew nothing of the beatings over the years, nothing of the battles that had gone on and nothing of the therapist. When she was invited to the school to be told god knows what about me, it was a complete bolt out of the blue. She returned home to give me the best right body punch I had ever taken. Such was the surprise and the power of that punch, it sent me flying and the sofa saved my embarrassment.

After being excused from school, I don't think I was registered as being officially expelled, because they let me back in for the final exams. The worst to come from it all was that my Mom thought I had scarred my father's name. It would take 20 years for me to prove that I had not, and that I was not, in fact, one of life's great losers.

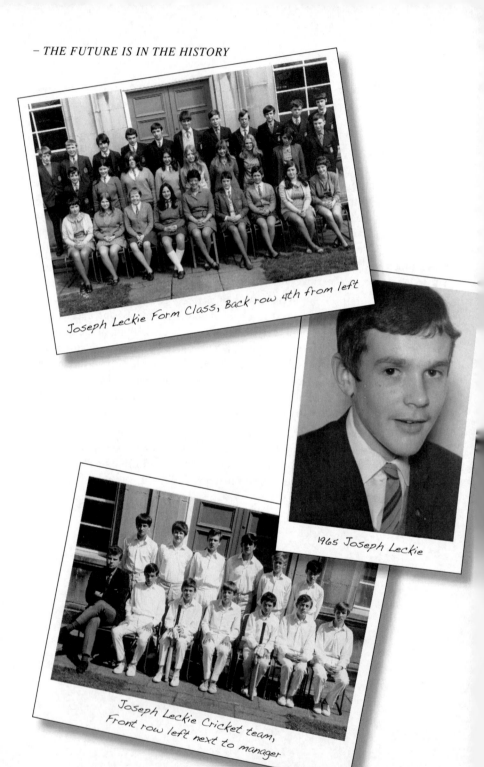

Joseph Leckie Form Class, Back row 4th from left

1965 Joseph Leckie

Joseph Leckie Cricket team,
Front row left next to manager

36

CHAPTER 3

WORK, DISCOVERY, DJING, AND THE EARLY SONGS OF THE 1970s

Wishing and Hoping

During my last year at Leckie, I had written a book on China. I don't know why I had become so interested either in writing a book or in China, however, I spent many evenings of my own time at Walsall Library researching everything I could find out about China. When I handed in the work I remember the look of amazement on the teacher's face. He read it all and when he returned it he said that the book was outstanding. I received a pass of 40 out of 40. I told Mom about it, but by now, at the end of my time at school, I think she had pretty much given up on me and there was no way back into her good books.

The only O-level pass I had obtained in the summer examinations was in English, so I now had the dreaded prospect of having to attend Walsall Technical College in the autumn to prepare for a re-sit of the exams. What a contrast to the ever growing thrill I was feeling about music. Ever since I had attended my first gig, when Desmond Dekker had come to Walsall Town Hall a couple of years earlier, live music had really hit home to me in a new way, and for the rest of my life I will never forget the experience of the Stax Records Volt Tour at the Birmingham Odeon, which was the first time I had ever seen a gig in the City. The opening of the show was fantastic: sirens, horns and American motorbike police walking in front of the stage – then lights, dancers and 'Green Onions' by Booker T and the MG's. The crowd went wild and I'd never seen anything like it. Knowing all these years later what a special label Stax Records would be in the history of popular music, it was an honour to be there. During the previous twelve months, music had taken on an even greater significance as certain songs had been introduced into my life through all sorts of different means and people. Others obviously realised my passion. Everyone seemed to come to me and ask what I thought of this record or that group and then tell me their own particular favourite record or group, and I always had time to listen and chat about songs and records.

It was during this summer of impasse that an experience came along that was to be a seminal influence on my future: the Radio 1 Roadshow visited Walsall. This annual summer roadshow hosted and broadcast by BBC Radio 1 would broadcast from a different town each day for two hours at lunchtime – midday until two in the afternoon. All the DJs were household names and on this occasion it was Emperor Rosko. Johnnie Walker was my favourite DJ, but for pure show business Rosko was the man. There was a colossal queue to get into the George Hotel, large numbers were going to be turned away, but through some nifty work I managed to make it inside. As I listened to Rosko warming up, I was mesmerised. This was really it, the crew running around, Rosko playing records to a packed hall. I never moved for two and a half hours, I just milked up the atmosphere, the records, Rosko talking on air and then off air to the crowd while the records were playing, the lights – I was transfixed. The record that set the place on fire that day was Rescue Me by Fontella Bass. The single had not been a hit the first time around, but it had been re-released and this time it had started to explode in the clubs and on radio. By the time the show was over I was exhausted. My eyes, ears and very soul had been wide open to all that was going on. I was beginning to believe that I had to be a DJ, I had to play records and get that kind of reaction from a crowd. Of course, at that point it was all a daydream: I had no money, not enough records, no equipment, no microphone, no gigs and no hope – but it had registered in my mind.

The year of the Tech

The day came to go to Walsall Technical College. It was a completely different matter to school – you were there of your own accord to re sit O-level exams and if you played up in class or weren't bothering to learn you were invited to leave the class or the College: the teachers did not care, it was your problem not theirs.

My Mom constantly asked if I was trying hard and working. I was, I liked it at Walsall Tech, the teachers and pupils were fine, we were all getting on with our lives. I rarely played hooky, there was no point: no one told you off and no one cared if you didn't show up, it was your loss. I think, had I been able to leave school a year earlier and spend two years at the college doing my O-levels the outcome would have been much different. It was a much more adult environment and in my opinion the teachers were better and not so petty minded. After a year, I passed the Maths O-level my Mom had insisted on. I obtained a grade three pass, which was a good level, and my worried mother breathed a sigh of relief.

Many evenings this year were spent in the Dirty Duck pub – even though I was under age. The Dirty Duck was in the centre of Walsall and is still there today. Back then it had six bars all with a different theme and a couple of restaurants, and it became a focal social point of Walsall. In the cellar the DJ played discs. This was not a dancing place, in fact, there was no facility for dancing at all. The DJ played album tracks and a lot of Eric Clapton: 'After Midnight' was a big record from this era. There was a lot of Cream, The Bryds and some of the chart hits. Allan England was the DJ. He had been contracted from an agency in London and told to move to Walsall and play five nights a week at The Dirty Duck. All his equipment was set up for him by the pub and his records were sent up free of charge from London. He drove a white Ford Consul with a black bonnet and Allan England painted on it. I most definitely wanted to be Allan England. I could see myself working there five nights a week and it was more like a radio show than a dancehall. I wanted the free records, the wages and the Ford Consul. I hadn't learned to drive at that time, I was still underage, but it wouldn't be long. I got to know Allan and occasionally in the week he would teach me the record decks and show me how to switch over, queue the next record, operate the microphone, play the discs and so on. I think Allan thought I may be able to fill in for him if he was ill or something happened. I hoped so too, and I did do half an hour here and there when it was quiet, but being underage it was asking for trouble and the landlord eventually said no.

Just down the road from The Duck, on the opposite side of the road, was another place we would all go to occasionally. You never knew if it would be open, it was always dark and sometimes there would be plenty of people there and sometimes very few, probably because no one knew when it was going to be open. It was sort of a 'Happening' only sometimes it never happened at all. They called it The 'Commodore' or something like that, and it was there that I first heard the sound of Northern Soul: soul records with a pacy dance beat and boys and girls flinging themselves across the dance floor in a heavenly trance of movement and sound. To see this way back then was just pure excitement, it was very underground and you had never heard these records on the radio. It would cost a fortune to buy a copy, it was very elitist. Again, I was sold and I kept checking to see if this strange place was open whenever I passed. It is where I heard records like 'Sliced Tomatoes' by The Just Brothers, 'Long After Tonight Is All Over' by Jimmy Radcliffe, 'Skiing In The Snow' by The Invitations, and 'Afternoon Of The Rhino' by Mike Post.

1970 was here, I was longing to be seventeen so I could drive and spread my wings a little further than Walsall. I was still seeing Silvana but that was all about to change. One day she told me it was all over, she had a new boyfriend who lived in Kettering and that was most likely where her future lay. I couldn't quite get my head around that and was lost on the issue of girls for some time after. Nevertheless, we all learn to take those things on the chin, fortunately our friendship has passed the test of time, and we still remember each others' birthdays.

Work – and closing in on a dream

Mom had told me there would no hanging around when College was over, no more long summer holidays. It was straight out for work. My mantra at this time was 'No nuts and bolts': basically this meant no factory work, even though

Walsall and The Midlands at that time were all about industry of all kinds. There were two main choices: factory work of some description or the motor trade, the other industry that dominated the area. After two attempts I passed my driving test and before long I bought an old car with money I had saved doing odd jobs over the years.

They say, 'Gotta have wheels if you wanna make deals.' I'm sure that's from a song somewhere or other, but at least I was in business, I had the wheels. After a couple of weeks the dawning comes of how expensive it is to run a car, and the mantra of 'No nuts and bolts' went clean out of the window. I needed to earn money, I had to pay off my debts, and I was responsible for paying rent to my Mom both for living at home and to help the family. I also needed a few new clothes to look the part.

Charles Richards Fasteners Ltd, manufacturers of bolts, nuts, rivets and washers, appeared in my life and I was taken on as an office apprentice in the sales department. In due course, every Monday I would go on day release to Wednesbury Technical College to learn theory in manufacturing. Being a factory, even though you work in the office, first off you have to clock on and off. 8.30 was the morning start point and as you put your card in at 8.30 it stamped the time in black. If you clocked in at 8.31 it was still black. At 8.32, it went red. Two or three 'reds' in a week and you were up in front of the boss with nowhere to hide. Everyone, including me, was always on time. I was to be paid seven pounds, ten shillings a week. Mother, on hearing from me about the wage, said that rent at home would be three pounds a week and that would always come out of the wages first. I had no problem with this, I was happy to contribute and help Mom, and although I would have liked three more quid a week, our family was not in a position for an alternative. To celebrate my first week's wages I did go out and buy two new shirts as a statement to myself that I could afford this and that I was on my way – but such luxuries did not happen too often in the next couple of years.

In due course, I moved from sales to the progress department, but after five months everything was dragging so much, and I hated the Monday attendances at the Wednesbury Technical College, so I started looking for another job. I managed to obtain work at Ductile Sections in Wednesbury – which was hardly any better except that I was no longer going to the Technical College each week. It was a lonely place, I really had little in common with anybody there and I was beginning to withdraw into my own world of records, music, clubs, DJs, music magazines, record shops, record labels, producers, songwriters, artists, record label owners – anything I could read or learn about the music world was worth its weight in gold and my only escape.

About this time I heard a record that would stay with me for the rest of my life and I still love it to this day. I was at a party and someone brought me the Carole King single 'It's Too Late', from the A & M album Tapestry. Carole King had been a writer in the famous Brill Building, working on great pop songs for many artists, such as 'Up On The Roof' by The Drifters. Neil Sedaka had fallen in love with her and written the hit 'Oh Carol.' After years in New York, Carole King had moved to Laurel Canyon, California, which would become the home of hundreds of hit songs, and there she recorded an album called Tapestry. It would become one of the biggest selling albums of all time and sell vast quantities every year from its release in 1970 until today. James Taylor, a friend of Carole King, played on the album and would re-record a track from Tapestry for his own album, having a huge hit with 'You've Got A Friend.' I was hooked on both King and Taylor who would both remain in my top ten favourite artists all my life.

One day, I was listening to Radio 1's Johnnie Walker in my car as I was eating sandwiches in my lunch break, the only way I could get through the day, and he was telling the story of how he was selling cars for Patrick Motors in Birmingham, but he was so obsessed with records that one day he decided someway, somehow, he would make his living out of the record industry. Regardless of how successful he would be, at least he would be around it all. This was the final spur, it just hit me like a siren going off in my head. Suddenly, I didn't care if I was successful or not, I just had to be around records. Ductile Sections was killing me on a daily basis, I was trying to make a go of it for my Mom and trying to be a good son to both Mom and the memory of my Dad, but I was not cut out for this kind of life, it was a slow painful death.

That afternoon I couldn't get Walker off my mind, I needed to be a DJ and play records for a living. This meant buying some equipment, increasing the record collection and then getting some gigs. There was also the matter of transport, it was all a huge expense, but no matter what, I was going to do it and do it as quickly as I could. I think Mom was at least pleased that I had some determination about something that wasn't football and cricket, and although she didn't understand where it was going, at least to see me working all hours for something and not getting into trouble gave her some relief.

Carolyn Darnley came into my life at this time and would help me greatly during our relationship in the next eighteen months. Carol loved Northern Soul music, which was never heard on the radio. The records were exclusively played by name Northern Soul DJs, who became heroes to a vast part of the teenage population north of London. Carol had perfected the somewhat complicated movements that go with the music and when we met we both had a love of this genre, which Carol was particularly knowledgeable about. I was still working most days and nights but we would go out at the weekends and slowly our relationship developed. Carol knew of my ambitions, as I probably never talked about much else, and it was through her father Les, who was the Managing Director of a large car sales firm, that I obtained an interview with J W Stocks, which was part of Patrick Motors. Les must have paved the way for a job for me, because two weeks later I was a car salesman with the opportunity of earning some really decent money on commissions. As Bruce Hipwell, the General Manager of Patrick Motors, had been a junior salesman to Johnnie Walker many years before, I felt I was now in exactly the right place.

I was almost nineteen when I started as a car salesman at J W Stocks and I would stay there for the next eighteen months of my life, driving into Birmingham daily, staying in the showroom all day, getting sandwiches from the shop three doors down, hanging out with the mechanics, and sometimes driving new cars from Leyland to Patrick Motors main depot, something all junior salesmen had to do. Opposite Stocks was a small music exchange shop that sold guitars, drums, bass, in fact anything they could get hold off, and most of the musicians in Birmingham went in there at some time or another. I was in the shop one lunchtime when a delivery of turntables, speakers, amplifiers and microphone turned up; a DJ had quit the mobile circuit and traded in his equipment. The lads in the store said they were going to get it set up and going in the next day or so to see how good it was, what needed doing to it and what it was worth. I told them I was interested and would be back tomorrow to have a look at it. My mind was racing: this could possibly be the chance I had been waiting for, and I wondered how much it might cost and if I could afford to get on the bottom rung of my ambitions.

That night I counted up all the money I had saved and hoped I may be able to buy the equipment. Next day at lunchtime there the equipment was, up and running for me – the boys in the shop had learned how it all worked and showed me the basics. Within minutes I was cueing up, switching over, cueing up again, switching back, absolute heaven. The equipment came almost ready to go, except that it needed a new microphone and new headphones. I could afford the price and took my first DJ equipment home, setting it up in the garage with the speakers facing into the wall. I began to rehearse and get used to it all. I showed my Mom, who really was not keen on having the equipment in the garage and wondered what on earth was going to happen next – which was that I put an advertisement in the *Walsall Observer*, which closed its doors in 2010 (I didn't dare advertise in a Birmingham paper, confidence was not that high just yet). All it said was: 'DJ requires work, available most nights, call Walsall 27061.' The paper came out on a Friday and on the following Monday I received a call from Pelsall Community Centre. Would I like to play the Community Centre a week on Saturday, 7.00pm to 10.30pm, six pounds was the fee? I accepted.

My excitement and fear were at an all time high. This was my very first paying gig for real, would the Vauxhall Victor (my latest car) start? Would the equipment work? Did I know what I was doing? Could I pull it off? This could be over before I'd even got going and yet I did have confidence that I could really be a good DJ.

The day came. I remember standing on the stage, equipment positioned, with the records at the back of me in racks, looking out into an empty hall apart from the girls getting the drinks and crisps stalls loaded. Here it is, sunshine, I hope this stuff 'fires up.' I need not have worried. The equipment worked brilliantly and was far more powerful than Pelsall Community Centre had experienced before. Slowly the place filled up and with each record my confidence grew. The dance floor was packed, I experimented with different records at different times and kept up the chat and banter with the crowd. The evening flew by, I just didn't want it to end. I was totally at home, all nerves had disappeared. The noise, the movement, the dancing, the sounds of the records, everything was so good it gave me one of the best feelings of my young life. At the end so many people came up to talk to me, asking about records and where was I playing next. The lady who was in charge of the Community Centre came up on stage and said that usually she did not re-book the same DJ, but would I like to come back in four weeks time? 'I'd love to.' The lady gave me a brown envelope, which I still have to this day. On it is written, 'Six Pounds, Two Pounds extra,' which she said they were paying me for being excellent.

The gigs did not come in fast and furious, but slowly Saturdays became full. Then David Virr opened Graduate Records at the top of Park Street in Walsall, and for the next few years that would be my home, listening to all the new singles, imports, soul, northern soul, rock, etc. I was now 20, and in Graduate Records I met Susan Parsons, who would play a major part in my life and career. I am delighted to say after all these years of working together we are still great friends.

Playing more and more gigs, I was getting to know more like-minded people. I was reading more music papers and beginning to know where the record companies were in London. Susan knew representatives from companies who would call on Graduate Records to sell or promote their new singles or artists – there was a small community and an information flow and I was beginning to know a few people in it.

Dinner dances were still going on all the time, complete with big bands, so I would have the opportunity to play some really big halls where the guests would have dinner and dance to a big band playing all sorts of songs by Frank Sinatra, Dean Martin and Ella Fitzgerald. When the band took a break I would go on for maybe an hour or maybe I would do an hour at the end. My mother was still very wary of this occupation of playing records in clubs. It all became very confusing for her and she constantly carried that look of 'Why does this have to happen to Steve? Why can't he be like everyone else? Where is all this leading to?' But some respite was fortunately just around the corner. I had been booked to play Bloxwich Baths at a dinner and dance with a 15-piece big band, and unknown to me my aunt Joan and uncle George had bought three tickets – two for themselves and one for Mom. I had plenty of time to study my mother from the stage, her head was doing the full 360 like an owl: she just couldn't take it all in. But when the band came back on to finish the evening and the bandleader finished with his closing speech before the last number, he called me back to the stage and said he thought everyone had witnessed something special that night. He added that he neither knew nor liked what DJs did, but after this night everyone must give credit to Steve Jenkins. There was an ovation and there was my mother joining in the clapping while still doing a 360 with her head.

Bloxwich Baths bought me time in my mother's mind. It would still be a rough ride to try and forge a career in records and music, but she realised she just could not stop it now.

Professional DJ – and Ken Dodd

It was my friend John who would be responsible for me turning professional as a DJ, and it happened in the most bizarre set of circumstances. One evening he came to have dinner with Mom, Helen and me and he said he had been on a crossed line phone call. Back in 1972, crossed lines were frequent occurrences. Sometimes you would pick up your phone and find that two unknown people would be talking or you would dial the number you wanted and jump straight into some stranger's private conversation. John had crossed lines with a woman who was starting a new club in Lichfield and he told us she had invited us to the opening, which would be three months ahead. We both thought 'great, another night out in our tour of nightclubs' and thought no more of it. Three weeks later, by a really remarkable coincidence he crossed lines with her again. She told him they were looking for DJs for the new club and John, as always, said, 'My mate Steve is the best DJ I have ever heard, you should hire him.' This time he obtained the lady's number and about a month later I was on my way to Barnaby's in Lichfield to audition for a brand new nightclub.

In due course Barnaby's Nightclub offered me a full-time job. The disco downstairs was four nights a week, the cabaret room was six nights a week and there was an opportunity to be a Compere. My mother didn't really like the idea, but I negotiated thirty five pounds a week at Barnaby's for six nights and I was a professional, playing records and introducing well known acts.

Barnaby's opened in a blaze of glory. The place was packed, the people of Lichfield were very supportive, we made the local news and Ken Dodd was the first in a long line of stars that graced our stage. The resident band was the Brian Ford Trio and Brian inducted me into all that happened on stage and how to handle situations. I would play records in a radio show kind of way to begin the evening – calm, easy pop records, with gentle banter, and information as to who was appearing in the coming weeks and what the running order of the evening was. As the dinner came to an end we would do 30 minutes of dancing to records, then Brian Ford and the boys would play for 15 minutes. After that I would introduce a support act, which could be an up-and-coming vocalist or comedian. I would get them off, back for a bow, Brian and the boys would play a number to allow me to get into the DJ booth, then thirty minutes dancing, bring back Brian and the boys, get the main attraction, introduce them, they do their show and I'm back to do the encores. Brian plays a number and I am back in the booth until closing time. That's me – I'm a professional.

1973 *Professional DJ and Compere*

I worked with a lot of artists during that period at Barnaby's and I learned a lot about show business just being around them – also about the hazards of the profession. A new act called Airborne came to us not long after success on the influential TV show *Opportunity Knocks*. They were a four piece harmony group that did versions of old songs and their fame was built on their former lives as ex pilots in the British Air Force who had formed the group, done gigs in the mess and then had a go at *Opportunity Knocks* and come out trumps with the public. They had stopped being pilots and were now on their way to being superstar vocalists, and they felt rather special. Normally. artists tell you roughly what they want you to say and you put it together in your own style and bring them onto the stage. The introduction they wanted me to give went on forever, it was like the second coming of the Beatles. I took their notes and rearranged the way I was going to present them, but the day after the first night the leader of Airborne took it upon himself to tear me to pieces. It was one of those military drubbings that I really had never experienced. When I went on that evening to introduce Airborne, having tried hard to memorise this long and extensive introduction, I got lost about half way through and had to busk the rest. The same happened each night. The boys in Airborne, wherever they are now, will remember me as one of the worst comperes they encountered. Fortunately, that was not the same for the majority of the artists I worked with – in particular, Ken Dodd and I got on especially well. I would introduce him onto the stage and then after ten or fifteen minutes, on a certain cue, I would go back on as his butler. Ken would proceed to rip me to pieces for a few minutes, then put his diddy hat on my head, which would fall down to my shoulders so I couldn't see a thing. With my arms outstretched, he would place this massive coat across my arms, all the time sending me up, and almost every night with a different patter. I loved working with him. He is a great ventriloquist and I would be on and off stage all night, bringing on Dickie Mint, my favourite, and Nigel Poncenby-Smallpiece, both great diddymen.

After Ken's show had finished and I had done my final hour I used to meet up with him in the dressing room and stay for an hour or two. He never seemed to want to leave and go back to his hotel, it took him ages to wind down. After my time at Barnaby's I went to work with him for a few weeks in Stoke, Manchester and Blackpool, just doing the butler bit, he was a real pleasure to be with.

It would be 35 years before I met up with Ken again at the annual Gold Badge awards in central London. I had been invited with my partner of today Susan (you'll find out all about her later on) and didn't know that Ken was one of the recipients. Ken got up to take his award and as usual did a few gags, and then afterwards at the photo session Susan and I went to say 'Hello.' I told Ken I had been involved in the sales of over one hundred million records, but that I started as his onstage butler. He looked at me, smiled, and said: 'Good lord, was that you?' It most definitely was.

One of my most taxing early compere stories involved Max G Beasley, another *Opportunity Knocks* winner, and a well-known mimic at the time. I really enjoyed working with him. His main character, and the one people came to see, was his impression of Marlon Brando in *The Godfather*. Max was exceptional in that role, it always came at the end of his show and it took him about two and half minutes to put on all the make-up and wig, which he did just off stage. My job was to go on and set the scene for his entrance as the Godfather. The lights would slowly go down and I would relay the story and bring the audience to the point of the particular scene that Max was going to do. When you are on stage with just a microphone and relaying a story, you cannot look at your watch to see how you are doing, you just have to feel it. On occasion I was a little quicker than I should have been, but Max always made his entrance perfectly and only after the show would sometimes joke 'you cut it fine tonight Steve.'

The biggest hits and most played discs at Barnaby's were George McCrae's 'Rock Your Baby', Hues Corporations's 'Rock The Boat', and 'Get Down Tonight' by KC and The Sunshine Band. Barnaby's was where I met Sue Chapman, a secretary, who had taken a job there to earn some extra money as a barmaid and do something different. We didn't know it then, but she would be my girlfriend for the next eleven years and she would work in many of the clubs where I was a DJ. We weren't prepared for the sudden change in the club's fortunes. Despite its auspicious beginning, it began to lose its audiences, and before long it closed. My professional DJ career was in tatters. I had gambled, sold all my equipment, given up my day job and lost. Mom was sad that Barnaby's had closed, but a part of her wanted this strange life of going to work at 7.00pm and returning at 4.00am to end and I knew I would come under immense pressure to get a normal job and settle down. So there was no time to rest on my laurels, feel sorry for myself or even think. I had to move quickly.

Starting over

As predicted, mother was at me right away. I told her that I would not be giving up on being a DJ. However, until I got going again I would take any job that came along, as I would soon return to working at night.

Barrett's Office Furniture was my next port of call; I would arrive at 7.30 in the morning, get my delivery sheet for the day, load up the van with the warehouse boys and be on my way. Just ten days after being a professional DJ, I was a van driving delivery boy, who assembled the desks on arrival at small offices around Birmingham. Tough to take, but at least I was out on the road on my own and I could daydream the hours away. Also, I could nip into as many record stores as I liked as long as the desks had been delivered. My record collection at this time was vast and I knew that it would only be a matter of time before I would get a gig at a club. I didn't want to be a mobile DJ again, I wanted to work in the Birmingham clubs and then I might be able to be on the radio and have my own show. Nothing was going to stop me.

The following weeks were tough, carrying desks and assembling them on the floor, and after suffering a knee injury kneeling was difficult. After four weeks of Barretts I walked into Barbarella's nightclub in Birmingham and asked for the manager. Chris Fewtrell came to meet me. Chris was one of the famous Fewtrell Brothers that ran many of Birmingham's nightclubs back in the day. They also owned most of the second hand car sales pitches around town and were not to be messed with. The story goes that the Kray Twins' gang from London came north to take over Birmingham in the protection racket game and encountered the Fewtrells. They were beaten black and blue and returned to London never to touch the Birmingham area again.

Barbarella's was a purpose built club and had three rooms, of which the largest had a big stage and held probably 800 people. All the groups of the day played that stage. The Take Two, as it was known, was a disco styled pop and soul nightclub, also with a stage, which could be used as a cabaret room or a disco with a local band, which normally happened at weekends. The third room was extremely dark, still large, could probably hold two hundred people, but was mainly used as a reggae or heavy soul room and pretty much taken over by the black community of Birmingham at the weekends.

An audition was fixed for me and after I had given it Chris said he needed a compere for the main room to bring the bands on and off and also a 'fill in' DJ for the other rooms in case the regular boys didn't turn up or were late. Thirty pounds a week, six nights, and if the club needs you to do other things it will let you know. 'Are you interested?' 'Yes – when can I start?' 'This very minute, right now.' And so it was that I became a member of the Barbarella's staff that very evening and got home around 3.00am. Three and a half hours later, at 6.30am, I was up again and off to deliver desks for Barretts – but not for long. My friend John came to the rescue again, and as he was now General Manager of the Leon Berners steel company and ran the show, he wanted me on the road talking to steel buyers. I told him I was going to be a DJ and he knew more than anyone that I was going to do it. He knew as well as I did that I would ultimately have to let him down as the evenings were more important than the day jobs, but although I refused he persisted and would never let go. I am sure he was doing this for Mom as well as me. So it came to pass that I quit Barrett's Office Equipment and started as a representative for Leon Berner, with a brand new Ford Escort car, a proper salary, and my insurance stamps paid. At last Steve Jenkins was respectable in the eyes of his mother – he just kept disappearing every night to Barbarella's, doing god knows what and returning at three in the morning.

What Mom didn't realise was that Barbarella's was absolute heaven for me: music six hours every night and meeting all the bands of the day. My first night as a compere was a riot. Several weeks earlier, the bookers at Barbarella's had taken a gamble on an unknown act, some kid who sang and dressed up like a clown. In the intervening weeks before his appearance, 'The Show Must Go On' had become a Top 10 record and everyone wanted to see Leo Sayer. Eddie Fewtrell was delighted, he had booked Leo as an unknown and was paying him tuppence, while the queue was right the way back to Broad Street – Eddie was making a fortune. Wayne, the principal DJ, handed over to me and I just about got out 'The Show Must Go On – please welcome Leo Sayer', before I was drowned out by cheers. I had never been on stage before and seen that happen so close, it was mesmerising, electric, red hot. Then the band started up and there was another wave as Leo passed me, I was off, he was on, and I watched from the side of the stage, just brilliant. I would work with Leo Sayer again in later years.

Ken Boothe and the Cimarons also came to town and played Barbarella's. Ken Boothe had the No 1 single with 'Everything I Own', and again he was booked for one night at the club. The Real Thing, who I would also work with in later years, worked Barbarella's regularly, and the band's members Chris, Eddie and Dave became good mates of mine as we spent so much time together in the band room. Chris always said, 'One day I'm going to be a fuckin' star,' and I guess he was right, they did have their moment and I was truly delighted when 'You To Me Are Everything' and 'Can't Get By Without You' became No 1 records.

As I proved myself to Chris and Eddie Fewtrell, I began to DJ in both the Take Two and the reggae and deep Soul room on Fridays and Saturdays. The six or seven months I spent at Barbarella's were a fun time in my life, it was always exciting, there were always up-and-coming and established acts performing at the club and the Fewtrell Brothers were nothing but fantastic to me. They paid me, gave me a chance, protected me and I thank them.

Now that I was established at Barbarella's, I was very tired from working at Leon Berner in the day and the club at night. John and Leon Berner had been great for me and I had managed to be reasonably successful for John, which was all that mattered, but I had decided it was now time to go. A couple of weeks later I had left Leon Berner, I had a few quid stashed away to see me through the bad times should they come, I had a great record collection, I still had my latest Austin 1100 car, I was at Barbarella's six nights a week and Mom had given up all hope that her son would just be normal.

Backstage after DJing with Radio 1's David Hamilton

Ken Dodd with his onstage Butler, 35 years on...

CHAPTER 4

1974 THE YEAR IT HAPPENED

Records, Records, Records

Barbarella's made me feel good. It was not what I wanted, but at least I was in the right area and I could be around music, show business and night people. I felt I belonged there.

I keenly waited for the arrival of KC and the Sunshine Band – they were appearing at Barb's for just one night and touring on the back of the single 'That's The Way I Like It', which had been a huge hit follow-up to 'Get Down Tonight', a big club record in the UK that set up 'That's The Way I Like It' to become a major hit. I was well aware of the band and knew that they had signed with the Miami label Jay Boy Records and were kings of that white boy funk sound. Howard Casey was lead singer, hence KC, and his song-writing partner of all those Sunshine Band hits was Richard Finch, who played bass in the band. I spent a couple of hours in the band room with the group and an hour or so with Richard Finch, who seemed to be in complete control of the band on and off stage. He was an articulate, quiet but great lad to be around for a while. I introduced KC and the Sunshine Band that night to a packed Barbarella's and they ripped it, a great band. I stood just off stage but almost on it with them – another great night at Barb's for me.

Working at Barb's you got to meet all the Birmingham musicians that came into the club on nights off or played with various bands during the week. The Steve Gibbons Band played many times at Barb's and I compered them a lot – they would, years later, have a big record with 'Tulane.' Roy Wood, a great player and songwriter with the Move in the 1960s, was always around. He also had those big records with his other group Wizzard and was the founder member of The Electric Light Orchestra with Jeff Lynne, who also spent time in Barb's. So did Carl Wayne, lead singer with The Move: you may remember 'Flowers in the Rain', their big hit that was the first ever record played on Radio One in 1967. Bev Bevan, drummer with both The Move and the Electric Light Orchestra was also always in Barb's. Ozzie Osbourne and a whole host of rock artists were always welcome and would just pop in to see the new bands that were having hit records and playing the big room. I did lots of gigs with the Raymond Froggatt Band and The Cissy Stone

Band, both of which would go on to have a couple of minor hits. They were much loved in the Midlands and Froggart would sell a lot of albums locally.

Finishing at Leon Berner meant my days were free, and although for the first couple of weeks I spent them in bed just recovering from that day and night working schedule, I was already planning the next moves. At this time I had no intention of working for any record companies, as my mind was set on a broadcasting career for the day and DJ gigs at night, but London and the UK record companies were on my mind because I wanted to try to get free promotional copies of their new releases so that I could be at the cutting edge at Barbarella's. So I started to make regular visits to see record companies – fully expecting to be rejected, so when I was, I felt no pain at all and used to say to the receptionists, 'Tell them I'll be back in two or three weeks and I'll keep coming until they see me.' Slowly but surely each of the record companies began to see me and send the free copies through the post to my Mom's house.

DJing as a barometer – a gauge for the Record Companies

At this time CBS Records opened an office in Birmingham that was run by John Aston. He controlled the sales operations for the Midlands and he employed Bob Hermon to take all the records to the local radio stations in the area. The BRMB radio station had just started and was getting a large audience, the Chris Tarrant Saturday morning kids show *Tiswas* was not far away, and BBC Birmingham broadcast plenty of big listenership radio shows. The Birmingham area was beginning to become important in the exposure of new records and their sales base, from that exposure, would affect national chart positions. John Aston and Bob Hermon were leaders in this area at the time and they were soon followed by Brian Hancock when EMI opened their office in Birmingham. This was great for me. My Fridays were now spent at CBS and EMI getting the new records as they came in, having a listen, telling the lads what I thought and then playing them in the clubs.

The main objective of the record companies was of course to expose their records to the widest audience possible. The most resourceful of the local club DJs were of great value in creating an early demand for a record by playing them in the clubs. If the record went down well with the audience then the public would start to ask for the record in record stores and request the record on radio shows. This would help the promotion people and sales people at the record companies in their daily occupation of getting records played and eventually sold. Hence, local DJs were important and at the cutting edge of all that was new and interesting musically and the best ones were also the most dedicated lovers of records. They worked firstly because they loved what they did and secondly to make money. I loved what I did, but without my knowing it at the time, the seeds of my future career-to-be were being unconsciously planted. I would gauge the reaction to the discs in the clubs and then the following week I would let John and Brian know which records were starting to work with the audience and which ones weren't. Looking back now, the excitement I felt being involved with the launch and growth of a record's appeal was the first intimation of what was to drive me so passionately in the record industry.

John Aston would go on to have a 35 year career with CBS and live through Sony's buyout of the company. He would work for some of the most flamboyant, difficult, but brilliant chairmen on both sides of the Atlantic, all of whom rated him highly, and he would become Sales Director of the entire company for many years. In those days, he took great delight in giving me a lot of stick when I arrived in the office on Fridays. Some weeks he would be fantastic, play me records and ask my opinion, and then the next week it would be 'what do you want?' – all of which kept me on my toes never knowing what to expect. In future years, we were to work together with tremendous results and a fantastic strong and loyal friendship exists to this day.

On my many trips to London by train during these days, when I eventually got to see the record companies, they all asked 'What is your total audience?' If you played six nights a week to 300 people on average, your audience was 1,800. Depending on the size of your audience, that determined what level of free promotional records you received as a local DJ. I knew I needed to increase the size of my audience and so I made a visit to one of my old haunts to bump up the numbers.

Walsall Football Club broadcasts, Hospital Radio – and a man called Waterman

The name Barbarella's helped me get onto the mailing lists of a lot of the record companies for promotional singles. Friday mornings were spent at CBS and EMI in their Birmingham offices, on Thursdays I was at the Diskery Record shop in Birmingham and on Friday afternoons I went to Graduate Records in Walsall. On Mondays and Tuesdays I would write reports to the record companies on the discs they had sent me and the reactions I had seen from playing them at Barbarella's at the weekends. I would also add my own personal response as to whether I thought the singles had chances of being a hit or otherwise. At the end of each week I would have plenty of new records to play along with the regular favourites and the current hits.

I knew that record companies graded their promotion lists to the size of the audience the DJ played to and although Barbarella's name put me up there on the lists there were higher levels to achieve. I knew I needed to be playing to a wider audience and I wanted to get onto the radio: I could then do 'one off' gigs for a lot more money, play to a wide audience during the day via the radio and be more in control of what I was doing.

First up was to increase my audience, so back I went to Walsall Football Club. Being at many matches over the years, I had heard the big loudspeaker announcements and chat before and at half time during the games. They were like mini broadcasts, and it seemed to me that I should be the one doing them and thereby increase my audience by at least 6,000 people a week. If Walsall had two home games in a week that put my audience up to 12,000. I knew that would be irresistible to the record companies and it also meant that I would be part of Walsall Football Club and have a free opportunity to see all the games from a ringside seat on the half way line – perfect, just perfect. I went to see the Club Secretary John Westmancoat, a very charming man and a perfect gentleman. I told him about my career, ambitions and how I felt I would make a very good match day broadcaster. John told me that Cyril (I can't recall his other name now) had been his match day broadcaster for many years, but he would think about the situation and consider me should Cyril ever want to stop broadcasting at the games. He was true to his word as in due course, in that summer of 1974, I was invited to 'sit in' with Cyril while he did the broadcasts at the games. I was in charge of the records and the one record player in a small booth under the main stand at Fellows Park. Cyril and I got on well, he just let me get on with playing the records, which I did on his cue when he was coming to the end of the notices and advertisements he had been asked to read, along with the team changes and attendance totals and up-and-coming fixtures. We did a whole season together and eventually I was to take over from him, after which, I missed him and our regular banter very much. Cyril was a good man.

The Walsall Football Club audience boost worked a treat. Record companies were now begging me to play certain records at the games, however, I chose the singles I would play and I did so on the basis of what I thought was best for the audience there. I would be at Fellows Park for four seasons in all and I enjoyed every minute of it. The staff at the club treated me well and a lot of the players from those days were to become lifelong friends.

Meanwhile, I had been searching for opportunities to broadcast on radio and was singularly unsuccessful in getting anywhere at the BBC's Pebble Mill studios, but I did receive a useful tip from Peter York, who had worked for the BBC in Birmingham and had even filled in for a couple of weeks on Radio One when one of the DJs had gone on holiday. He said a lot of radio DJs learnt their trade in Hospital Radio and that would be the place to start. I researched and found out that Hospital Radio Stafford broadcast to seven or eight hospitals in the area reaching up to Stoke-on-Trent. Some radio enthusiasts had put the station together and the Station Manager was Dick Fisher, so I set about making contact. After a few meetings, I had been invited to learn how to operate the equipment at HRS and then began filling in for DJs who were on holiday or absent for a week or so. Eventually, I was given my own and very first radio show for one hour on a Sunday afternoon between 3.00pm and 4.00pm every week. It goes to show – always chase your dream and give it a go!

It was around this time, although neither of us can remember exactly where or when, that I had my first encounter with a DJ from Coventry, who like me was making trips to London to try to get records from the companies. Today, it seems we have always been in each others' lives as inseparable friends, and so we just can't pinpoint precisely when we first met – it may even have been in Barbarella's, although I doubt it, or it might have been at Mr George's in Coventry where he was the DJ, as I did just one gig there on a single night. Or it might have been on a Thursday or Friday at the Diskery in Birmingham searching for new import records from America. But, if I had to put money on where our first meeting place was, I would bet on the Birmingham to London train that made only one stop, at Coventry, the hometown of Peter Alan Waterman. Pete and I were both experiencing those trips that started with so much hope on the journey south and normally ended on the return journey north with exhaustion, dejection and bruises from having had every door slammed shut in our faces or backsides – and still having to get to a club that night and work until two in the morning. However, no matter how tough it got I would be on the train from Birmingham and every now and again getting on at Coventry was Pete Waterman. One of my earliest memories of Pete is of him telling me about some bridge that we were passing under and how it had been important in the building of the railway network. I would learn a lot about the British railway system from him over the next 35 years, some of which I could have done without.

The Moulin Rouge – Strippers aren't what you might expect

I was still at Barbarella's six nights a week but I was beginning to feel frustrated. I had done well in the Take Two room which was full on Wednesday, Thursday, Friday and Saturday and I was still compering the artists in the main room and occasionally playing the Soul Room, but it all seemed like bits and pieces. Wayne was still the main DJ and there was no dislodging him from that spot. I would be first pick to fill in for him, but there was never a chance to take over from him permanently. Dave Possall was Barbarella's General Manager at the time and really ran everything to do with the club. If he had special evenings planned in the Take Two, I was his preferred DJ, but he knew I was frustrated at Barb's and felt I was not having the recognition I deserved. One warm night in that summer of '74 Dave called me over in the main room and said a friend of his had bought a club at the top of Broad Street and was going to change it into a dinner club. Dave thought I would be ideal as the DJ and had mentioned me to the owner. At the time the place was a strip club named Moulin Rouge, and I said I was not sure about going there, but Dave had said I should just go and listen to what the owner Ron had to say (another surname that has faded from memory with time).

A few days later I was at the Moulin Rouge. It was a small club with a bar area and the club opened from the bar into a restaurant seating about thirty people. There was a stage next to the restaurant surrounded by small alcoves in semi circular shapes, each with a table seating maybe six people, who were all facing the stage, and there was a bar at the end of the club with a standing area. The DJ area was in between the restaurant and the stage and was accessed from the side of the stage. It faced the entire club so you could see both bars and the entire restaurant and seating areas from that position. Ron and his General Manager Gerry Foley took me into the top bar to talk about their vision for the new club. Although, at the moment, the place was a strip club, they had good investment and were going to refurbish it so that from Monday to Thursday it would be a dinner club with cabaret and on Friday and Saturday it would be a nightclub for older people, and definitely not kids. They wanted a DJ who could handle both operations and do some publicity for the new club, which was to be called Chaplin's, with its restaurant 'The Moonlight Restaurant', named after one of Charlie Chaplin's hits. There would be a huge advertising campaign, promotions at the Motor Show and any big events that came to Birmingham. I would compere the cabaret acts and play records before and after, but to more of an adult crowd, and then at the weekend we would turn it into a club for a 'cool' crowd. I agreed to come to the club and play for a try-out night.

Even though I knew it was only an audition, I was a little unsure about playing records in a strip club. I didn't tell Mom anything about it as she would definitely have not approved, but I did tell Sue Chapman to see what she thought and she said I should give it a go and see what happens. Well, certainly playing records at the Moulin Rouge for one night was not going to be a problem, Hospital Radio Stafford had taught me how to programme a radio show and I thought the Moulin Rouge would be no different: a little bit of calm chat and a few hits and oldies mixed in with one or two album tracks. I can remember playing George Benson's 'This Masquerade' and 'Breezin'' from the same album that night, records that normally I couldn't have played, but which sat right into the atmosphere of the club. People were eating and drinking, the atmosphere was very calm and then on came the stripper. They had three strippers a night and a vocalist who came on and did a few numbers. The vocalist introduced the stripper and I started a cassette on cue as the curtain parted for the young lady to make her entrance. This was all new to me and I had a seat right next to the stage. During the first strip I didn't know quite where to look, but by the time the third stripper came on later in the evening, it had become the norm and I just got on with it.

The evening had gone well, I had enjoyed being in more of a radio environment in terms of playing records than just banging out dance tunes and the hits, everyone was very complimentary about the records I had played, and there was no doubt that Ron and Gerry thought I was the DJ they needed. It was a difficult decision to consider, but finally I went for it –

I wanted to be a radio DJ and a sit down restaurant with an older generation environment could be advantageous to my future. The owners wanted me to start as soon as possible, which meant I would be working in a strip club for a month before the Moulin Rouge was replaced by Chaplin's. I did feel nervous about that, but I was nearly doubling my wages, all the people seemed pleasant and as long as mother didn't find out all would be well. Sue was also OK with it all and she had been promised a bar job on Friday and Saturday nights when the new club opened, so all seemed to be working out well.

Finally, one Monday in the summer of 1974 I started work at the Moulin Rouge with 'Good evening and welcome along, Steve Jenkins here at the Moulin Rouge with the music through until 2.00.' Into the first record and off we go. There were always three strippers and they would perform two strips a night, starting in different costumes. Each strip would last about five minutes. Somewhere during the evening a male or female vocalist would come on and perform two or three numbers and then come back on again later in the evening, so there was always something going on. I would be at the console while the strippers were on and my time off came when the vocalists performed. I was in charge of cueing the music for the girls, which was normally on cassette, and all the 'on stage' lighting was controlled from my area. The music I played went down well and changed the whole environment of the club. I have no idea what was played prior to my arrival there, but everyone was complimentary about my choice of music and the way my collection of records enabled me to vary the music night after night.

The stripper girls were great and soon became friends of mine over the next few weeks. It was not long before I came in early to make new cassettes for them with dubs of different records. Constantly they would come to me during the evenings and say 'keep that one for me' and 'I like that one.' I would just make a note and then we would piece the music together before the club opened.

I always found it remarkable how the girls arrived at the club and transformed themselves from almost 'the everyday housewife' into a 'nightlife sex bomb.' They would arrive at the club dressed very plainly, hair pulled back or tied up, wearing glasses and with very little make-up, you really would not look twice. Then they would disappear into the dressing room and re-appear an hour later, completely different women: high heels, dresses, make-up, just unbelievable. The main Madam, Michele, who worked at the club and brought in the strippers on a weekly basis, was a housewife, with a young daughter and a husband that had run a large company. They lived in a well-to-do area of Birmingham and when the husband had lost his job and had not been able to find another job that was as well paid, Michele began supplementing the family income by organising strippers around town. She had already worked at the Moulin Rouge for quite some time and would occasionally strip there when I believe the mood took her. One night Michele came in after she had been to the parent/teacher association at her daughter's school. She looked as though butter wouldn't melt in her mouth and said, laughing, 'If only they knew.' I swear you would not recognise her 45 minutes later.

Some of the girls were single mothers, some had husbands or boyfriends and some were single and just making their way in life. Overall, I found them down-to-earth and fun to be with.

Chaplin's, Graduate Records – and the moment it happened

After about five or six weeks of watching strippers perform, the Moulin Rouge closed its doors for the last time and Chaplin's opened with plenty of publicity. It sure was a transformation. The new Chef was up and running, there were new kitchens and I had to learn how to handle new sound equipment. There were new waitresses and Tony Rome was the resident vocalist four nights a week. 'Good evening and welcome along to Chaplin's, Steve Jenkins here with the music through until 2.00.' Another new phase in my life had begun, and I had made it to opening night without my mother knowing I had been working in a strip club, a great result.

The moment that would change my life was just around the corner, but for now, I loved working at Chaplin's. I was being employed for six nights a week doing something I loved. On Saturdays, I broadcast at Walsall Football Club, killing two birds with one stone, as I was also watching the match from a ringside seat. On Sundays, I had my own radio show for one hour a week on Hospital Radio Stafford between 3.00pm and 4.00pm, and I worked hard at making that show entertaining for the patients just lying there, waiting for or recovering from treatment.

It was my Mom who made me aware that sooner or later I would have to pay an income tax bill after all the time I had been earning in self-employment. I had known nothing about this procedure as no-one had ever contacted me, nor that I was supposed to pay self-employed insurance stamps, which was also going to mean a bill for arrears. So, I put some money aside and I decided that if I could work in a record store for maybe two or three days a week, I could then declare the tax that I would earn on this income, hopefully through the record shop accounts, and keep all the money I was earning in the evening at Chaplin's. I figured that the tax people were more likely to leave me alone if I was contributing in some way rather than dropping off the radar completely. In today's world it seems the most naive idea, but back then I thought it was a way of keeping going almost legitimately and staying out of any serious trouble. It would also keep Mom quiet and allow me to continue to push my career forward without the constant, 'you'll have to get a proper job' routine that came my way weekly.

So, one Friday, in September of 1974, I went to Graduate Records in Walsall to see Susan Parsons. I had spent many hours with her on previous Fridays listening to and playing the new releases and American imports that had arrived in the store. I would then purchase the records I thought would become hits, or just the ones

I liked or had read about so that I could play them at the club that weekend and the following week. I knew which record companies would send me free products and the ones that I needed to buy – the best buys were always the United States' imports. If you played the hits from America long before they were issued in England, you were seriously cool and well ahead of the game. Susan had been working at Graduate Records for quite some time and she knew a large number of the local DJs and regular customers that bought records for their own personal collections. We all liked Sue, she was one of us, she worked in a record store because it kept her close to records and music and she had great knowledge of the artists and records of the past and the current day, as well as the imports that would be the hits of tomorrow. She was also fun to hang out with for a couple of hours each week and had no problem playing record after record, expressing her opinion with me and responding with a yes or a no. If Sue thought I was wrong she would say so and the debate on certain records would go on for weeks until eventually it would fail or I would have to buy it as the single was getting so many requests at the club. All this over a long period of time developed a good friendship, one that lasts to this day, 35 years later.

That Friday, I went carrying the idea of working in Graduate Records to pay a little tax – Sue would know if there was any chance or not of a job for a couple of days a week. The moment that would change my life appeared that day. Susan said that they didn't have any opportunities at the shop and she didn't think anything would come along for quite some time. Susan stated: *'You should work for a record company, you know all about the records, you should work for them.'* I had never considered working for a record company, I had never had any desire to do so and I can honestly say no thought of this had ever entered my head. I was most definitely going to be a broadcaster, a DJ on the radio, helping people enjoy their day, playing the best records with some topical chat in between. That was me and that was my future, it was everything I had dreamed of for the past six or seven years. The record companies I had visited in London were full of poseurs who seemed to know little about the records they were paid to work on and if it meant working with them or being in London, it was not for me. All of this was instantly going around my head and yet out of my mouth came, 'Doing what?'

'I think you should be a promotion man,' replied Sue.

'What does a promotion person do?'

'They promote the records to radio and get them played – I'd love to do that!'

'Yeh, but that means going to London and I'm not doing that. I've got Chaplin's, Walsall Football Club and Radio Stafford and it's taken me ages

to get all of that together. I'm not giving that up to go to London, I don't like it there and they are all poseurs.'

'All I'm saying is, I think you would be good at it. Look, here's Music Week, the jobs are all in the back. Look, there's one here: "Promotion Man Wanted".'

I had never looked at the *Music Week* journal before in any great detail. I would look at the chart, but I knew the positions from Radio 1 so I only skimmed it. The front page and the articles inside were about people I had never heard of and were really of no interest to me at all, in fact, I remember thinking what a boring publication it was. And yet, as Sue was off serving and talking to other customers, I found myself trying to come to terms with the words 'Promotion Man', 'Record Company', 'You would be good at it.' For the rest of the afternoon I went back to the usual procedure of listening to records and talking to Sue about them, and then at the end of the day as I was paying for the singles I wanted, I said to Sue, 'I'll take the advert and have a think about it.' Sue said, 'Fine, but if you get the job, then when you get in, you have to get me a job too.'

'Sue, if I apply, then if I get the job, then, I promise I'll get you in as well.'

'Promise?'

'Yeh, promise.'

I left Graduate Records that day with not much real intention of answering that record company's small advertisement for a promotion man. I was more disappointed that Graduate Records could not provide me with a couple of days work each week to keep both the taxman and my Mom at bay. But during the next few days the thought of working for a record company kept coming back into my mind. I was thinking that if promotion men had to call on radio stations and get records played it meant that the promotion man was welcome and at last I may be able to make some contacts at radio stations and land a job on air. And so, for all the wrong reasons, the idea began to grow.

The advertisement had no information other than 'Promotion Man wanted for top record company, apply to P.O.Box so and so.' When I began to focus on it I remember being concerned that I did not know which record company I was applying to. It may have been one that I didn't like the music of. However, I decided to get on with it and start writing my application. I spent the week writing and rewriting it – I had never done this before in my life. All the jobs I had obtained before were from face-to-face interviews or recommendations. Finally, my application was ready, in my mind, after a week. I mentioned my career in music, the clubs I had worked at, the size of my record collection, my passion for certain styles of music and my feelings about which records would be big sellers in the coming months. I stayed away from qualifications and school days, not having left school with a great reputation, and only having O-levels in Maths and English. My main objective was solely to get an interview: from that I could judge what this was all about.

Seven or eight days after first seeing the advertisement in *Music Week* I posted my application. I did not hang around waiting for a response or looking for the post in the morning – after my experiences with trying to get on mailing lists and the many fruitless journeys I had made to London visiting record companies, I expected nothing. A response saying 'No thank you' was the most I thought may happen. I just got right on with life – Chaplin's was going well and I was enjoying it.

Two weeks later, a letter did arrive at 26 Regina Drive, Walsall. It was from The Nems and Immediate Record Company requesting me to go to London for an interview with the General Manager, Rod Duncombe. Would I like to call and make a date and time?

The First Hits

CHAPTER 5

NEMS AND IMMEDIATE RECORDS

1974–1976

The Beatles Boardroom:

September 1974. I was wearing a suit, the only one I owned, and I caught the 9.00am train from Walsall to Birmingham and then was leaving on the 10.05 from Birmingham to London. When I arrived in London I used the tube, which I had got used to during my mailing list hustling days. I intended to continue a series of record company mailing visits during this trip, but first up was Rod Duncombe, Nems and Immediate Records, 3 Hill Street, London W1.

All these years later, I remember it being one of those sunny late mornings in London. I had never been in Hill Street before. Back then it was a great London street, the buildings had class, the road was not a busy hustling street and there was more of a calm air about it. Looking pristine, there in front of me, was 3 Hill Street. There was nothing from the outside to suggest this was a record company. A small plaque by the door just said 'NEMS.'

I would learn soon that these were once the offices of Brian Epstein, famed manager of The Beatles, Gerry and the Pacemakers, Billy J Kramer and the Dakotas and Cilla Black. NEMS stood for North End Music Stores and had been the name of Epstein's music shops in and around Liverpool in the early sixties. It had been the import sales of 'My Bonnie', recorded by Tony Sheridan and backed, by a then unknown, Beatles, that had drawn Brian Epstein's attention to the group and it was from the NEMS music shop that he had, one lunchtime, walked over to the Cavern to see The Beatles perform.

The office that I would be interviewed in was once known as the Beatles Boardroom and it was there that the Fab Four would make decisions on albums, singles, tours, movies and the day-to-day running of the band with Epstein. The history that had occurred in that building was immense and it would be there that my life course would change. I really could not have requested a finer place for that to happen and 3 Hill Street will always be a favourite and fond building in my life.

I walked into reception that day not knowing what to expect. NEMS to me was not a record company but a management company and Immediate Records had been a label famous in the sixties for The Small Faces, P P Arnold, Chris Farlow, Amen Corner, The Nice, Humble Pie, John Mayall and The Herd, all of which were no longer having hit records. I waited in reception for a few minutes and then was shown into Rod Duncombe's office. Rod was tall, bearded, had a ready smile and pretty soon would show a great sense of humour, I think we got on well straight from the off.

My interview lasted about 45 minutes. I learned that Nems and Immediate Records were on the up. They had signed a couple of artists to Nems, were about to work the back catalogue from Immediate Records, owned the first four Black Sabbath albums and had a tie up with Opel Records in Jamaica to release new reggae artists from the Islands. They wanted a Regional Promotions man who would call on radio stations in the Midlands and get their records played, fix interviews for the artists, promote to the largest record stores to increase orders and get to know the Birmingham press and clubs to increase exposure for the artists and ultimately the records.

At this time, in late 1974, regional commercial radio stations were springing up fast, far and wide following the opening of the first ever UK independent radio station in October 1973 (LBC). Radio Clyde in Glasgow was on air, so was Radio Forth in Edinburgh, Radio City in Liverpool, Piccadilly Radio in Manchester, Metro Radio in Newcastle, Radio Tees in Stockton, Pennine Radio in Bradford, Radio Trent in Nottingham, BRMB in Birmingham, Beacon Radio in Wolverhampton, Swansea Sound in Swansea, Radio Orwell in Ipswich and Capital Radio and LBC in London. These stations were an alternative to the national radio stations, the BBC's Radio One, Two, Three and Four networks. They played pop music in a local environment and were beginning to take listeners from Radio One. In those days, DJs on radio were real DJs and not radio presenters DJing. They had a love of music rather than their own voice and they wanted to pick new records and champion them, building a reputation in that way. The DJ also had an amount of freedom to play a couple of records an hour that were not on the playlist, something that is taboo today – which is why we now have to turn off the radio station we listen to every three weeks or so, as we are tired of the rigid playlist during that time. In '74, different DJs played slightly different styles of music and increased their listeners by doing so: seventy-five percent of their show was playlist material, but they were allowed to be inventive. The combination of a growing commercial radio audience and the availability of some free choice in the records that were played made record companies look to have their own promotion men in the regions for the first time ever. Hence CBS had opened an office in Birmingham with John Aston as had EMI with Brian Hancock. These early moves by the large record companies were seen to be positive, successful and rewarding and it was this background that created the opportunity for me to enter the Beatles Boardroom for an interview at NEMS.

Rod Duncombe explained what he was looking for and I became more and more interested as I realised I would be based in the Midlands. If I were to be offered the job, they would want me to stay in Walsall, as it was so central, and from there I would visit radio stations in Birmingham, Wolverhampton, Nottingham, Swansea and Ipswich. As well as the commercial stations, local BBC stations were also on the list – BBC Derby, Birmingham, Nottingham, Cardiff and Ipswich. Initially, I was to look out for any pop shows on these local BBC's, call on a weekly basis and get our records played. For my work expanding the label's contacts in the Midlands, I would be paid a monthly salary and given a company car and an expense account.

I left Nems that day thinking this might be a very good idea. If I could manage working at night, as well as in the day, again, I could probably make a lot of contacts at radio stations and after a while maybe get a job in broadcasting. Rod had also told me that he had received a great response to the advert and there were a lot of people to interview, so I probably would not hear from him for two to three weeks. I would learn several weeks later that there had been nearly eighty applicants for the job. My feeling was that the interview had gone well, I liked Rod and thought I had made a favourable impression on him. He knew I was working in a nightclub and had asked what I would do if I was offered the job, and I was honest and said I couldn't think about that until I received an offer, but, if he were to want me, we would work it out together. I felt I had done my best. Afterwards, I went to Phonogram Records to try once again to get on their mailing list. Once again I failed and headed for Euston and the train back to Birmingham, then to Walsall. At home I told Mom I thought it went OK, got changed and was at Chaplin's at 9.00pm to play until 2.00 the following morning.

Three weeks later a letter dropped through the door at Regina Drive. I opened it slowly, expecting, after my mailing list experiences, a polite 'thanks – but no thanks.' To my surprise, I was invited again to 3 Hill Street to attend a second interview – phone in and the date and time would be agreed. I phoned and the date and time were set: 2.30pm, 16th October 1974.

The day came. Around 3.00pm, Rod came through the door at speed: 'Sorry I'm late, come on in. We would like to offer you the job covering the radio stations around the Midlands along with Swansea and Ipswich. The wages will be £2,750.00, plus a company car and expenses. We would like you to start on 1st November, come to London to pick up the car and start work the following day.' I agreed to the deal straight away and then told Rod it was my birthday, in fact, my 21st birthday. We must have a drink to celebrate! I settled on vodka and orange juice, which appeared from somewhere in the building together with Rod's favourite tipple. We celebrated my 21st birthday and my joining the record industry that day, right there in the Beatles Boardroom. The first record I ever owned, which my Dad bought for me on my tenth birthday, was *Please Please Me*, The Beatles' first album – now, some eleven years later, on my 21st birthday, I was in the record business in the boardroom bearing their name: I couldn't quite believe it.

Rod was also looking for another promotion man who would cover the north of England, Liverpool, Manchester, Glasgow, Edinburgh, Newcastle, Stockton and Bradford. Whoever that would be would arrive at the company on 1st November, when we would be introduced to everyone and pick up the cars.

Mom was delighted. It seemed a more legitimate job and involved working during the daylight hours, so from her point of view it was just fantastic. Sue was pleased for me, but never pressured me to give up DJing in clubs. Sue Parsons was happy for me and constantly reminded me of my promise to somehow get her into the record business as well. My old mate John was equally delighted – and I have never forgotten how he had helped my confidence to chase my dreams and give them a go.

1st November came and down to London I went. I met a few members of staff: two girls worked in the office as assistants, Neil Ferris was an office junior who was going to assist on radio promotion in London and Steve Beaver from Liverpool would be the Northern promotion man. With myself in the Midlands, that completed the promotion team at that time, although expected in two or three weeks, was a top London radio promotion man. I was then introduced to Peter Parkinson. He controlled the finances for the label and was what would now be known as Financial Director. I got on well with Peter for the most part of my time at Nems, he was someone who rarely lost his temper and held the company together when the water got choppy a little later.

That day I also met the owners of NEMS and Immediate Records, Patrick Meehan and Tony Calder. In 1974, these guys were industry veterans, although still in their early to mid thirties. They had grown up as the industry exploded into worldwide sales and had worked with and managed some of the biggest grossing bands of the sixties and seventies. They had strong reputations, were clever in their manipulation of radio, press, television and artists and had travelled the world first class generating millions of pounds.

Patrick Meehan was a big man, bearded and imposing. He had managed Black Sabbath, and legend had it that he had stolen them from Don Arden, leading to a war between Arden and Meehan that had raged ever since, with the two constantly injuring each other in whatever way possible as the years went by. If there was a UK record business mafia, then Arden and Meehan were the heads of the families and they controlled their territories with great passion, strength and force.

Tony Calder had learned the record business with Andrew Loog Oldham. They had found The Rolling Stones and masterminded their rise to fame when they were both very young. Throughout the sixties Oldham and Calder had reigned supreme making hit records with The Stones and Marianne Faithfull, then starting Immediate Records and having a great run of hits with exceptional and inspirational marketing and flair.

The flavour of radio – mid 1970s:

On that first day, Steve Beaver and I collected our company cars and a few boxes of records and headed back up the motorway to Liverpool and the Midlands. On Monday we would start work as promotion men. We had received no real instruction from Rod Duncombe or anyone at Nems as to how to promote records to radio. All I was told was 'get the records played on the radio and go and see the librarian.' So, armed just with transport, a box of records and a card bearing my name with the company logo I set off that Monday morning to BBC Radio Derby.

I arrived at around 10.30 and asked for the librarian, a woman by the name of Liz. Here I was in a radio station where, first and foremost, I had been welcomed – this was a first for me. Liz was a wonderful, friendly woman who had worked at Radio Derby for many years and was just getting used to promotion men turning up and leaving records for the library. She told me what programmes played pop records and who the presenters/DJs were that might play them. I gave her all the information on the singles and artists I was carrying and hoped that the records would be played. Liz was so friendly and pleasant that I took it for granted that the singles would get a play or two. And now, as I was reaching the end of my first radio promotion meeting, the door opened and in walked Dave 'The Rave' Cave, as I would get to know him, the promotion man for ABC/Anchor Records. He instantly went into his routine with suggestive jibes at Liz who laughed. 'Got to get this one played Liz, big record, have a listen.' Dave had been doing the job for about a year and was on top of his game – a ladies' man, but fun, always up, and every record he was carrying was a massive hit, no matter how bad it was. Dave worked on the philosophy of 'promote everything and the ones that are good will stick, the others will fall by the wayside.' Over the next couple of years he would refine his act and be selective about the records he put all his effort into: he had to, as more and more promotion men arrived on the scene, and the radio programmers, librarians and playlist guys did not want their time wasted.

For now though, Dave the Rave was King, and ABC/Anchor had Steely Dan, Ace and a host of great artists that were making great music. I watched intensely as Dave did his work: this was the first promotion man I had seen in action. After a while I thought I should leave and I started to excuse myself.

'Where are you going next?' asked Dave.

'BBC Radio Nottingham,' I said, 'and then Radio Trent.'

'I'll be five minutes, wait for me, we can go in together.'

I went out into the car park at BBC Radio Derby for a much needed cigarette after my first try at being a promo man. Dave was soon out and lit-up too.

'What the hell are you wearing?' Dave's opening line.

I was wearing my one suit with a waistcoat and tie, dressed up to be a promotion man. Dave was wearing jeans, trainers, a tee shirt and a sort of cardigan that was five sizes too big or had been seriously messed up in the wash.

'You'll get us all shot. Get rid of the tie and waistcoat, I'll put up with the shirt and suit today, but don't ever wear it again. Follow me to BBC Radio Nottingham, I'll introduce you to a few people, plug your records after me, just do what I do, let's go.'

Off we went. Dave had a sporty little car and I thrashed the NEMS Escort Estate to keep up with him. Everything with Dave was done at pace, we screamed into BBC Nottingham, the girls on reception all smiled at Dave like they all wanted him and he breezed through without stopping on his way to see John Holmes, who did the playlist for years at BBC Nottingham. Dave plugged his records to John, introduced me, took the mickey out of the suit and told him it was my first day and he would soon have me in shape. I presented my records and John said he would take a listen and let me know if he would put any of them up for plays.

Dave and I then went for a sandwich and during that lunch Dave, bless him, gave me his knowledge about being a Plugger, a Radio Plugger. It was the first time I had heard that phrase.

The real trick was to get your records on the playlist at the commercial radio stations. Normally there were A, B and C lists and some stations even had a D list. If there was a D list and you could get your record on it, it could mean three or four plays a week and the playlist operator could then judge the reaction both from the public in the form of repeat requests and from the DJs that played the records. If the reaction was positive the record might move to the C list or B list next week or hold its D list position for another week. The C list records would receive seven or eight plays per week, one a day usually, and again would be reviewed and possibly moved up. The B list records got maybe 12 to 15 plays per week and the A list 20 to 25 plays per week. Most weeks maybe between eight and 12 records would be added or dropped. Some weeks there were only four or five adds and drops, on other weeks more, it just depended on the records released and the pluggers' drive and influence in those early days of commercial radio. The good part, though, was that those radio stations wanted to create their own sound and be different to all that had gone before, therefore, there was a chance to have new records played. Playlist operators would take a chance on what their ears told them, which sadly is not the case today, when most operators' first question is, 'What's the plot?' That means, 'will the artist do an interview and free appearance for us if we back the record?' Playlist operators today do not listen to the record, they just judge the financial outlay of the record company or the size of a musical following, the fan base of an artist, what the artist's last record achieved – in fact, anything rather than allowing their ears to judge the record.

Dave 'the Rave' Cave was a mine of information for me that day and we went off to Radio Trent in Nottingham in the afternoon. Radio Trent would soon be the home of Kid Jensen who was joining from Radio Luxembourg. Kid had been a well-known and popular DJ in Luxembourg and was arriving to do the morning show. No-one at the time could understand why Kid would leave a national radio station for a commercial one, but he had been promised a job on Radio One if he worked on a UK radio station for a year or so. Kid Jensen going to the regional, Radio Trent, did give the impression that commercial radio was much more important than it actually was and this helped all us regional promo guys to influence the airwaves of the UK by pushing new records that might otherwise not have been heard. Dale Winton, who became nationally famous later on *The National Lottery, Supermarket Sweep* and a few other TV shows, started on Radio Trent as the Breakfast DJ. He also had a spell as playlist controller, so, for a few years, we all had meetings to play records to him. I always found him knowledgeable about music and especially soul records – his favourite music was Northern Soul records, of which, at that time, he had a great collection.

After Radio Trent, I drove back to Walsall and called the office from home. Rod asked if I had got any records playlisted, which came as a bit of a shock as I had not expected to have to get anything on the playlist so soon. In fact, it had only been a few hours earlier when I had realised what a playlist was. I managed to wriggle out by saying the playlists were released on Thursday, which was another piece of information I had learned that day. I had no time to ponder, as after a quick sleep and something to eat, I was off into Birmingham to play at Chaplin's from 9.00 until 2.00 in the morning. I had decided to do both jobs for as long as I could, just in case being a promotion man was not a good move.

The next few weeks were all about making contacts and understanding how radio stations worked, how to get the records played, meeting people in the local press that may write about the records and working to get to know people at ATV (Associated Television), the high powered Midlands commercial television station. One of the major ATV shows, important to the record business, came from Birmingham: it was *Tiswas* on Saturday mornings, and it was seen nationwide on the ITV (Independent Television) network.

I also made trips to the NEMS London headquarters once every two or three weeks, usually on Fridays. I would listen to the new records that were to be released, hear where the company was going and learn what the expectations of certain records were. On one of these trips I was introduced to Lyndon Holloway, who was to become the new Head of Promotion for Nems and Immediate. Although Rod was General Manager and we all reported to him, Steve Beaver and I now also reported to Lyndon, who tried to co-ordinate the promotion in a tighter fashion with the hope of making our efforts have more impact.

Lyndon took me to Radio One for my first time, where he introduced me to Alan Freeman, who had been presenting the rock shows and the chart run down on a Sunday. Freeman's many catchphrases such as 'Greetings Pop Pickers' and 'Not Half' were nationally known and he was a respected figure. He and Lyndon had got to know each other over the years and they had become firm friends. They took me out to a few places on a couple of visits to London and were always very keen for me to stay over at either Lyndon's or Alan's place, which was impossible as I always had to get back to Birmingham to play at Chaplin's. I could never mention to anyone at NEMS that I was still DJing, as I had told them I was only doing weekends now. I had in fact arranged with Gerry at Chaplin's, who knew I was working for a record company, that if I couldn't make it for some reason we would agree on a 'fill in' DJ and as long as it didn't happen too often all was fine. I think both Lyndon and Alan secretly wanted to introduce me into 'batting for the other side', but being so naive at the time it all went over my head and even Alan's famous nickname of 'Fluff' didn't register. Walsall was indeed a place far, far away, where the gay revolution had yet to reach.

After what seemed like a very short time, probably about four months, Steve Beaver resigned and as NEMS decided that they were not going to replace him, I was now given the responsibility of covering the whole of the UK outside London. This would mean travelling on a three week rota to Glasgow, Edinburgh, Newcastle, Bradford, Sheffield, Liverpool and Manchester along with the Midlands, Swansea and Ipswich. It felt good – although we were not really having hit records, we seemed more and more like a record company and we had great ideas for the future. Our back catalogue sales of Black Sabbath albums were basically taking care of all company bills and expenses.

I had been working day and night for about four months at this time and although I had a good surplus of cash, I was exhausted. I spoke with Gerry and Ron at Chaplin's and although I didn't want to leave, we all knew it was impossible for me to continue. The three of us had a good chat and decided that I would work Friday and Saturday at the club, but if I was free and they needed me for a special function in the week then I would do it.

My first hit record

In my new position as UK NEMS promotion man I devised a system for visiting Liverpool's Radio City and BBC Radio Merseyside, Manchester's Piccadilly Radio, BBC Manchester and Granada Television, Glasgow's Radio Clyde and BBC Glasgow, Edinburgh's Radio Forth, Newcastle's Metro Radio and Radio Tees, Bradford's Pennine Radio, Sheffield's Radio Hallam and BBC Sheffield, Birmingham's BRMB, BBC Birmingham and ATV, Wolverhampton's Beacon Radio, Nottingham's Radio Trent and BBC Nottingham, BBC Derby, Swansea Sound, Radio Orwell in Ipswich – the list just kept growing. It meant driving all day, every day, all week, but in all honesty, I loved it.

My first hit record was now only weeks away. We had all assembled one Friday in London and the Company had decided to rework the Immediate Records back catalogue. Immediate owned a lot of hits from the Sixties and was considered a fashionable label. It had originally been known as the Sound of Swinging London, mainly due to The Small Faces. The jewel in the crown was the The Small Faces album *Ogden's Nut Gone Flake*, which included the hit 'Lazy Sunday Afternoon.' The album was most famous for its round sleeve, the first ever one of its kind in the history of the record business, when it was issued. It was a parody of a tobacco tin, the tobacco being Ogden's Nut Brown Flake. Originally released in 1968, the album went to No 1 on 26th June and stayed there for six weeks. To manufacture the sleeve back then would have been immensely difficult, so the people involved – Andrew Oldham, Tony Calder and the group – must take full marks for persistence, passion and inventiveness. In 1975, these records had been unavailable for some time and so we felt that if we promoted a single and then the album as 'new releases' rather than back catalogue, we may stand a chance of having a hit record with the single, which would then help us sell some albums. We felt that 'Itchycoo Park' would be a stronger release than 'Lazy Sunday Afternoon' and would have the most impact, but if we were successful then 'Lazy Sunday' would lead us straight into the album.

The key was most definitely the style in which we promoted. We attacked from day one and believed 'Itchycoo Park' was a brand new record, not a reissue that had been a hit in 1967. The single had originally reached No 3 in the charts. Written by Steve Marriott and Ronnie Lane, it had been known as the first psychedelic pop song. Now it was to be released on the original label imprint and so it looked both historical and a collector's timepiece. Lyndon Holloway used his friendship with Alan Freeman to get a few weekend plays on Radio One. The record sounded fresh on the radio in 1975 even though it had been made some eight years earlier and other Radio One shows picked up on how good it sounded and programmed it for their shows. I set about promoting it to regional radio stations across the country and now for the first time when I visited the stations I had DJs coming to find me looking for a copy of 'Itchycoo Park.'

When a record is destined to become a hit a wave of positivity begins to build around it. As a promotion man you receive phone calls from people at radio stations and TV companies whom you have never spoken to or met but have probably heard of, and members of the press, who have never returned your calls but have obviously kept your number, are now ringing you for a copy. Information you previously have had to force feed is now being requested: 'When is the single out? When is the album out? Can I get a copy of the album? What do the Faces think of the reissue? Are the Faces doing any interviews to support the record?' A hit record begins to gather its own momentum and in the recording industry this phase in a disc's life was known as 'Growing its own legs': the record gathers and gathers momentum until it grows legs and begins to run and then there is no stopping it. That is what happened to 'Itchycoo Park' in 1975 and it was the first time I had ever seen or experienced a hit record at close quarters. Radio and TV had initially not believed it could be a hit record again and now shortly after making that decision they could not get enough of it. The Small Faces were a hit group all over again and the press hunt was on for Steve Marriott.

In December 1975, the single was Top 10 in the UK and finally peaked at No 8, we as a company were delighted and I was feeling on top of the world. I had been involved in a hit record, Christmas was here and I was doing a few extra gigs for a lot of money, as well as Chaplin's. 1976 was just around the corner and all that effort of the previous five years since leaving school seemed to be paying off.

New blood – Opel Records – and another hit:

The record business is in some ways like football – sometimes, even when you are winning, everything can change. Suddenly, and without any previous warning, Rod Duncombe was gone and it was announced that Peter Knight Jnr would be Managing Director of NEMS and Immediate Records. I was to report to him in London one Friday morning that January of 1976. I had never heard of Peter Knight, but soon found out he had a good and indeed interesting reputation within the record business and publishing world. He had been the co-producer of the original cast recording of the musical *Hair* and his father Peter Knight had been a celebrated conductor and arranger for radio and television. I was nervous as I drove south, it could mean the end of my involvement with a record company, as my relationship had always been with Rod Duncombe and Peter may have his own ideas. I need not have worried. Pretty much instantly when I met Peter Knight we became friends and remain so to this day. Back then, mind you, to me, Peter was definitely London: average height, big glasses and smoking cigarettes with those plastic filters that had been invented to catch the tar and nicotine and stop it going into your lungs; they were sort of orange in colour and were supposed to eventually help you to stop smoking by weaning you off the nicotine. I'm not sure that method worked for Peter, but he did eventually give up the ciggies.

Peter told me he had heard good things about me and hoped we could work well together. There were to be changes at the record company, but I would not be one of them, and he felt we were hitting a good streak and would have more hits. I was to continue promoting the records to the whole of the regions but the London promotion team would change. That happened within a week and I was back in London to meet Oliver Smallman, the new Head of Promotion. Out had gone Lyndon Holloway and the Company was on the up with a new team and 'Itchycoo Park' still selling well. Peter Knight told us that 'Lazy Sunday' would be the follow-up to 'Itchycoo' and we would be issuing the album *Ogden's Nut Gone Flake* with big budget advertising spends. The reissues on Immediate would continue with the single 'You Were On My Mind' by Chris Farlow, followed by a *Best of Chris Farlow*, a new single and album by Marianne Faithful and two singles from our newly acquired Jamaican label, Opel Records.

The two singles we played that day were a big learning curve for me in the business of records and one I would always remember. We played 'The Power And The Glory' by Ernie Smith and 'DAT' by Pluto Shervington. Ernie Smith was a well known Jamaican artist, although not in the UK. He had won many awards and was historically the first artist to be recognised by the Jamaican government. Knight considered Smith had potential for hit singles and also had the depth of ability in songwriting terms to sell albums. Pluto was considered a singles artist with a novelty record, the song being delivered in a patios reggae style that had not yet become popular outside of the Caribbean. The instruction was: 'service Pluto to radio, but "go after" Ernie Smith – if you have a choice of plays get Smith played not Pluto.'

We set about launching Opel Records with Ernie Smith and Pluto. Regardless of what we had been instructed, within a week both Oliver and I were back at the office saying the same thing: 'can't get arrested with Ernie, but Pluto is a flyer.' Quickly we turned our attentions to Pluto and DAT. Oliver got a couple of daytime plays for it on Radio One and soon the public and the regional stations were after it. By the middle of February, Pluto Shervington was No 6 on the UK chart and on a plane from Jamaica to a cold London to perform on *Top Of The Pops*. Within three months we had hit the Top 10 twice and NEMS and Immediate were a proper label.

Marianne Faithfull:

During February and March of 1976 we were working hard on rebuilding the career of Marianne Faithfull. I had been called to London to meet Marianne with Peter Knight and then to set up an interview tour of the UK for radio, which would eventually last three weeks. Marianne was not well during this time, she had been living in Ireland, but had visited London on and off to record an album. The wild living and drug taking of the sixties had ravaged what had been a beautiful young girl and Peter had warned me beforehand that she was in a particularly delicate condition. Her confidence was severely shaken and she was trying desperately to leave behind the drugs that had been so readily available through the sixties. She was falling on and off the wagon and you never knew which Marianne would turn up on any given day.

At our first meeting I realised this was not going to be an easy job. Marianne was quiet all the way through. I tried my best to be upbeat and reassure her that all would be well, but looking back now I can see that she knew more about everything than I did – more about life, the record business and radio interviews. She was an experienced professional and I was still learning the game. Still, I set up the interviews for her and we were to start in Liverpool on a Tuesday morning. I had picked up Marianne in Manchester the previous day and booked us into the Albany Hotel in Liverpool, where we would have dinner together at 8.00 in the restaurant. I waited and waited but no sign. At around 8.45 I called up to her room. A sleepy Marianne answered the phone. 'Marianne, it's Steve – dinner?' In that trademark husky voice, Marianne declined and said she would see me in the morning. That pretty much set the tone for the next three weeks. In the evenings, Marianne would disappear and in the mornings you just could not get her up and out.

Our first day and our first interview was with Billy Butler at BBC Merseyside. Billy had a very successful morning show in Liverpool at the time and it beat Radio City's morning show by a large number of listeners. He had been particularly interested in having Marianne on his show and had promised great support for her album and single if I would get her on the show for him. At our initial meeting in London there had been a list of dos and don'ts – first on the list was: 'No questions about Mick Jagger and no references to Mars Bars.' I had particularly told Billy to stay away from the Mars Bars, warm her into the interview and not talk about Mick Jagger. Billy agreed.

> *'Here, on BBC Merseyside,' started Billy, 'today we are delighted to have Marianne Faithfull on the show. Hello Marianne.'*

> *'Hello Billy.'*

> *'Let's get right to it, what is all the fuss about Mars Bars?'*

I was outside the studio listening and hoped for a hole to swallow me up. Billy then laughed and quickly changed the subject and before long he had Marianne talking about the sixties, where she had been, the new album and her hopes for the future. By the time the interview was over Marianne was relieved – the first one was done and she had quite enjoyed the experience.

Every other interviewer on the tour steered clear of Mars Bars as I had stipulated – that Billy Butler was a real lad but a good radio host and interviewer.

During that first week on the road, we travelled from Liverpool to Manchester, Carlisle, Glasgow and Edinburgh. The following week we did Newcastle, Sheffield and Nottingham, and during the third week we were in Swansea, Wolverhampton and Birmingham, where we finished. As the tour progressed, the more I saw of Marianne in the evenings. Eventually, she would go for dinner, but only at the hotel – never to a restaurant. The drug taking had destroyed her taste buds and she would put salt and pepper regularly on her food throughout the meal until it was covered in it, but she didn't seem to notice. I became more protective of her as we travelled, she really did not want to be doing these interviews and I could see the stress and strain they put on her as each day went by. Nevertheless, Marianne did all the interviews and stuck to the schedule throughout the tour.

The best interview was her last. Adrian Juste was doing the late night show on BRMB in Birmingham and we were due to arrive at 11.00pm, which was the time of day when Marianne truly was at her best. Adrian is light and funny and by the end of the show when Marianne must have done a two hour interview, we were all sitting on the floor. The mikes were down there too and Adrian got up every now and then to play a record. Marianne told stories of parties, life in the sixties, Mick Jagger, The Beatles, hit records and was totally at ease. I took her back to the hotel after the interview and then put her on a train to London the following morning. The single and album didn't work and I would never see her again in all these years, but I have fond memories of Marianne.

One door closes – and another one opens:

Ogden's Nut Gone Flake came out and started doing great business, the sleeve was a collector's item, and there was a rush on the early sale copies. We issued 'Lazy Sunday Afternoon' in early March and that too started to sell. Because of the success of 'Itchycoo Park' we got more play on 'Lazy' and it really helped the sales of *Ogden's*. All through these first few months of 1976, NEMS and Immediate Records were having their most successful time: hits were coming, our catalogue was selling and all of us in sales and promotion felt we were building a future record company that could last. Patrick Meehan and Tony Calder, the owners, had different ideas. That, I guessed, was their right. They had been through a lot of change in the record industry and were highly sensitive to the extreme highs and lows that the business can subject you to – as well as the sudden changes of fortune. It wasn't long before the hits dried up at NEMS and although the catalogue was doing well, soon there was no real signing of new artists. At that time I was not really aware of what a record company should or should not be doing, but as the months went on I was aware of clouds starting to form above this one. My wages were being paid but the expenses that I had incurred driving all over the country and staying in hotels were not being paid. I let this ride for a couple of months then started to worry about the money I had already laid out. I decided I could no longer afford to pay for NEMS promotion in the regions and so I didn't promote any more records to radio or TV.

Meanwhile, that summer, my sister got married at the age of 19. Too young, my mother thought and to be honest so did I, but Helen is my sister and I would support her in anything she wanted to do as long as there was no personal danger to her, just as my Dad had instructed me. I was the one who had to give her away, standing in for my Dad – next to him a real poor second choice and I always remember being upset that he couldn't give away Helen, just one of the many things a great man missed out on.

During August, the money for the expenses finally arrived and I was back out on the road for NEMS – but it would only be for a short time. As the autumn came I was called to London. It was a normal call, nothing out of the ordinary. 'We are having a meeting, be here for midday, see you then.' I drove to London on the day required. On arrival I was told that Peter Knight wanted to see me and he would be ready in 20 minutes. I hung around the promo office and chatted to the girls and Neil Ferris. All seemed well. Twenty minutes later I was in to see Peter, and I was welcomed as usual. Peter is and always has been a gentleman, and he was still using the orange tar-catching filters, as he had not yet given up the cigarettes almost a year later.

> *'Steve, we are closing the Company in the next couple of weeks, so unfortunately, we are not going to be working together anymore.'*

This was a blow. I had never really thought about not working at Nems, even though the warning signs were all around and had been for some time. I was calm and said:

> *'Oh well, Peter, I shall miss working here, you know I've really enjoyed it.'*

> *'We think you are a very good promotion man and have proved yourself to us, so I'm pleased to say I've got you another job with Chrysalis Records. Go to the company at 2.30 and ask for Chris Stone, he is a friend of mine. He's the General Manager of the Company, he knows all about you and is expecting you.'*

> *'Peter, you mean I've already got another job?'*

> *'Yes, it's all agreed, they are expecting you.'*

CHAPTER 6

CHRYSALIS RECORDS
AND STARS OF 1976 AND 1977

The Art and Craft of Promotion

I walked out of Peter Knight's office in a bit of a daze. The only record company I had ever worked for was closing and I would soon be on my way to Chrysalis Records to meet Chris Stone, who would evidently be hiring me to be a regional promotion man. Peter had said that I was to return to Nems next Friday and that would be the day that I would bring back the company car and receive my pay and outstanding expenses.

At my Chrysalis meeting Chris Stone said I was highly recommended and he wanted me to join immediately. They were expanding their regional promotions, and as well as having a representative in the North covering Glasgow, Edinburgh and the North East, someone in the South, and Chris Griffin in the Midlands, they wanted me to work in Liverpool, Manchester, Bradford, Sheffield and Nottingham. Chris knew that I had relationships with radio stations in these cities and he wanted me to start as soon as I could. There was the usual company car and expenses, plus an increase in wages over Nems and Immediate.

I accepted the offer and was ready to begin in ten days time. Suddenly, I realised my life had changed, I was about to work for a front-running organisation. Chrysalis Records had been founded in 1969 by Chris Wright and Terry Ellis and started as a licensed label through Chris Blackwell's Island company. The initial success was based on two groups – Procul Harum and Jethro Tull. Both owners had been social secretaries at University and were used to booking bands to entertain the students. By the time I was arriving at the label it had grown and had a roster of artists that were mainly rock based and album sellers – the company had not been a hit singles driven company, more a rock gigging company that developed record sales through their bands being out on tour most of the time. Chrysalis were beginning to develop into the 'pop' field, but when I started our mainstay artists were Procul Harum, Jethro Tull, Rory Gallagher, Gentle Giant, Steeleye

Span, Ten Years After, Robin Trower, UFO, Uriah Heep and Pat Benatar. The company was also developing Leo Sayer, The Babys and an Australian group, Split Enz. These artists brought a constant flow of album sales, which would build a good financial footing for Chrysalis and enable the move into the pop world with, eventually, massive worldwide sales of Blondie, Spandau Ballett, Billy Idol, Go West, Ultravox, Huey Lewis and the News and latterly Robbie Williams.

In the week before I went down to Nems for the final time I went over to see Chris Griffin. He had been working for Chrysalis for some time and I already knew him, although not really well. He explained that he was due to be promoted but would be hanging on to BRMB, Beacon Radio, BBC Birmingham and ATV Television as well as being in charge of the other regional promotion men. Hence a vacancy had occurred for Liverpool, Manchester and across the Pennines to Bradford and Sheffield. It was suggested that it would make sense that I live in Manchester to service the area properly, also Chrysalis was a gigging company so it meant plenty of nights out on the road with artists: if I lived in Manchester it would cut down the hotel bills and it would be easier to get home from Liverpool, Bradford and Sheffield late at night. This all did make perfect sense, except I was not keen on living in Manchester, in fact, at that time, I couldn't think of anything worse. I also had a well paid two nights a week at Chaplin's, which I had no intention of giving up, some fill in evenings DJing at clubs that came along every now and again, Walsall Football Club broadcasting and a Sunday show on Radio Stafford that I loved. My belief, at that time, was that I was still destined for a career in broadcasting, but working for record companies could only help to propel me closer to that aim. Chris was great, though, and we remain friends to this day even though we rarely see each other. He went through the reporting systems, what was expected, how many nights we were out on the road with the artists, how often we were meant to call on the radio stations, interview set ups for artists, newspaper interviews, gig guides, in fact, any type of exposure we could get for the acts. It was a much more professional set-up than Nems: they knew exactly what they were doing and how they wanted it done and it was a step up from what I had been used to.

I was sad to leave Nems and Immediate. In the office during my final weeks we had all fallen in love with an album Abandoned Luncheonette by an unknown group, Daryl Hall and John Oates. The single was 'She's Gone' (it was written about Hall's divorce) and the girls bought me a copy of the album as a leaving present. Little did I know that some years later I would work with Daryl Hall and John Oates and have some influence over their career in the UK; back then, it was just a great record with which to remember my times at Nems and Immediate Records.

There was no doubt I wanted to give it a go with Chrysalis. I was impressed with the way they set out how they wanted everything done and I felt I was part of a team and not just 'busking it' on my own, deciding what was best and where

I would be going each day. Chrysalis was to bring some discipline to my weekly routine and educate me properly in the true art of promoting records and artists. I left Chris's house just outside Birmingham with a lot of paperwork: expenses sheets, report forms for each radio station, files to send to the office on what records had been playlisted each week and from which record companies, ideas sheets in which we would write about what the other record companies were doing and if certain promotions were working, in fact, just about anything and everything that may give us an edge in making a record or artist successful.

Chrysalis's London headquarters was together and ready for me. I met with the accountants, signed the relevant paperwork, went into the promotion office and met Geoff Goy our Radio One Promo Manager. I shook hands with Chris Wright, the owner, and Chris Stone took me out to the Blue Ford Cortina Estate that would be my car for the time I spent at Chrysalis. I loaded up with all the current records we were working with and headed back up the motorway. Chaplin's again filled my Friday and Saturday night, I was at Fellows Park to broadcast for Walsall Football Club on Saturday afternoon, Sunday I was at Radio Stafford and soon enough it was Monday morning. Off I went: Steve Jenkins, Chrysalis Records, to see Dave Lincoln, head of playlist at Radio City Liverpool. I soon established myself at Radio City with Dave and Phil Easton was a great supporter as he did the evening rock show in those days and I had a lot of albums that were featured on his show. I also became good mates with Johnny Jason who did the late night show and Billy Butler was, as ever, great fun at BBC Merseyside. Roger Day was head of playlist at Piccadilly Radio and I always got on well with him. At Piccadilly you never really had relationships with the other DJs, Roger organised everything and it was his call alone with regard to what was played on air, but he always had time to listen to your records and what was happening with your artists. Pennine Radio and Radio Trent chopped and changed their head of playlist and DJs, while Beverley Chubb controlled Radio Hallam in Sheffield. Now, Beverley did not suffer fools gladly: if you made an appointment to see Bev, you were on time or suffered. If Bev asked for certain copies of records or interviews with certain artists and you didn't deliver, you suffered. But, if you did your job to the best of your ability, then occasionally she would allow you to mess up. Personally, I had a great relationship with Bev, she played lots of my records over the years and always treated me well, rewarding me with interviews too. So, fitting in to my new area was very easy.

Touring with UFO – around the clock:

At Chrysalis, you worked nights as well as the days. We always had someone on tour and when they hit a town in your area you were responsible for exposure before and leading up to the gig. If they were in your area the next night the same would occur until they moved onto someone else's area, when the other promo man took over. One of the first tours I was involved in with Chrysalis was with UFO. At the time the band were selling good amounts of albums, probably a hundred and fifty thousand to two hundred thousand in the UK and probably the same amount again around the world. They were a good band and were on the verge of maybe going to the next stage and selling a million.

In the routing of a tour I would be with UFO on Wednesday in Nottingham, Thursday at City Hall, Sheffield, then they would go on to Newcastle, Edinburgh and Glasgow on the Northern promo man's area and then probably the next Tuesday I would be back with them in Liverpool or Manchester. The tours in those days were normally thirty to thirty-five dates in maybe forty days, so the band would criss-cross the country; there were no big arena dates back then. The week before the band hit my area I would be onto the local radio station, say Radio Trent in Nottingham and BBC Nottingham, topping up the stations with the band's previous albums and their new album and single. Also providing all the new information, where they had been recording, how the tour was going, what was next after the tour, anything that the DJs could use in introducing tracks from the album. I would also get interviews for members of the band, either live on air the day of the gig or pre-recorded at the sound check. The local papers would also be serviced for reviews and the main one would be offered an interview. The local six o'clock news TV show would normally have a gig guide as to who was appearing that week in the area, so again, I would offer an interview and also give out a few tickets for DJs or important media people to come and watch the show. The day of the gig would start with a visit to the radio station to make sure the plays and interviews were happening, then onto the sound check either to organise interviews at the gig or hotel or to take a band member for a live radio or TV interview. Then back to the gig. Normally, I ate with the band backstage and then I would look after the guests we had invited, watch the show and do what we all called a 'grip and grin' after the show, where the band shook hands with people we wanted support from in the media. At around midnight all would be over, and if it was an early start the following morning you would stay in a hotel with the band and then move onto the next town and radio station first thing and start doing the same all over again.

These were Rock 'n' Roll days when bands were out on the road on tour for many years building up their fan bases. The stories go that these bands were out of control and wild – well, at times that was the case, but usually it was a case of letting off steam after a show when the adrenalin rush usually meant that they could not sleep for a few hours after a gig. Drinking and a few drugs normally occurred at this time to relieve the sudden boredom and assist with the 'come down' from the adrenalin. Today, we are all aware of the pitfalls of self-abuse in drugs and alcohol, but back then that was all new and only a few had paid the price.

The tours in those days were well organised, although the routing sometimes left a lot to be desired and to cope with that, and indeed everything else, the movement of the band, equipment, lights and crew was a military exercise. The band had a tour manager, who dealt with all the flights, hotels, checking in and out, passports and crossing boundaries, and the promotion people had to be in constant communication with him or her. You had to be on good terms with these people, without them you could not get it all together – they always had some control over the band and pretty much knew where they were at all times. The road crew were normally good hard-working lads who set up the gig, and while we were all in bed at the hotel they had already broken down the equipment and were on their way to the next town, where they would sleep late and then be in at the next gig at midday setting up for that day's soundcheck. On tour it was perpetual motion and until you learned the rhythm of the days it could make you feel sick. There were times when I just had to stop the car in a lay-by late at night and sleep, only to wake up freezing cold at four in the morning not knowing then whether to continue home or just drive to the next town. It was a life out of the norm; a constant circus on the move.

Rock 'n' Roll bands attract Rock 'n' Roll girls. Maybe it's all that posturing, thrashing of guitars, sweat and hair that gets them going, but after every gig in those towns there were always girls after the band. The press and films portray how every member of the band and the crew are getting their share every night and I can tell you that is not realistic. Even so, certainly, every tour has its moments. My first eyewitness experience of the legend of Rock 'n' Roll occurred at City Hall Sheffield in those early days at Chrysalis with UFO. The gig had gone well and I had a couple of people from the Sheffield local papers and the BBC with me. Immediately after the gig we headed backstage to do the 'grip and grin' with the band and were moving at speed. I knew my way around the backstage area of City Hall as I had been there quite a few times – through one door into a corridor, through the next, and right there in full view were two guys we knew, one doing a girl doggy style and the other having sex up against the wall. It seemed more shocking to my guests as it could only have been five minutes since the curtain had gone down. Obviously, the boys were not asked 'if they had enjoyed the gig or went to City Hall often' – my guests declined the 'grip and grin' and after show drinks, but at least they had a story to tell.

Jethro Tull: Who wants promotion?

Not long after the UFO tour Jethro Tull were out promoting their new album. Tull's record sales had been responsible for the building of Chrysalis Records and Ian Anderson, Tull's lead vocalist, writer and chief operator, was a close friend of the owners Chris Wright and Terry Ellis. All the staff knew this and we were all on our toes around him. I was to meet Ian for the first time at the opening gig of the tour in Manchester, where we had not pre-arranged any interviews as he evidently only did what he wanted to do and it depended on his mood. Our maiden meeting did not go well. I knocked on his dressing room door a couple of hours before the gig to find out if he wanted to do any interviews in my area with press, radio or TV and if so what kind of interview and where: at the gig, in the hotel, at the studios, live or recorded.

> *'Come' was all I heard. I went in. Ian was standing looking in the mirror wearing a pair of red riding trousers and black riding boots and tying a yellow cravat in front of his neck.*

> *'Yes.'*

> *'I'm Steve Jenkins, Chrysalis Promotions for this area.'*

> *'Well fucking hooray, what do you want?'*

> *'I was wanting to talk to you about what promotion you might like to do for the album.'*

> *'I don't want to do any!'*

> *'Would you like me to bugger off?'*

> *'Perfect.'*

And so ended my first meeting with Ian Anderson. I told Chris Griffin about it and he said yes, Ian could be like that, don't bother about the promotion, just turn up at the gigs, see the tour manager to let him know you are there and leave it at that.

Two nights later, at Liverpool Empire, backstage and passing Ian's dressing room the door was open and there was Ian. I stopped: 'No need to tell me Ian, I'm already buggering off.' He looked at me as if he didn't know what I was talking about but said nothing. In the months that followed I did talk to Ian a couple of times, once at a party in Glasgow, where I told him of our first meeting. He put it down to first night of the tour nerves and a general hatred of promotion. I found Ian Anderson to be an intelligent and thoughtful man, he owned huge lakes and had salmon fisheries, and he knew a lot about nature and the environment all those years ago before that became national news. I met him again a few months later in London, and again, he was charming and interesting, but we never did any promotion together.

Mick Jagger – by chance:

As I got to know more and more people in the record business I was able to go out to more venues and working for a label gave me the confidence to talk to the artists and celebrities as I was in the same industry. On the rare occasions when we were called to London by Chrysalis for meetings it was usually for two days and this meant an overnight stay. On one of the overnight stays I had been given a ticket to see an up-and-coming band at the Electric Ballroom in Victoria. With nothing else to do and time to kill, off I went and pitched up about eight thirty on the night. I approached the door with a few people milling about and probably three or four people in front of me in the queue. Someone appeared on my left, I looked, and to my surprise it was Mick Jagger. Without thinking I said 'Alright Mick?' Mick replied, 'Yeh, alright mate.' I enquired if he was going to see the band and if he had the private passes, which he did. So, Mick Jagger and I walked into the private area together and ordered some drinks. We spoke for maybe seven or eight minutes in total, and from that chance meeting, and the way Mick handled himself with a complete stranger, I have always thought he was an alright lad. He was out on the town on his own. There was no entourage, he was pleasant, good to talk to, easy going and not big on himself at all. I noticed how he watched the band set and then just disappeared into the night. The boy from Walsall had met a hero and an icon of the music industry in a moment I will always remember.

On the other hand – Johnnie Walker:

Sometimes it is best not to meet your heroes. You put them on a pedestal from where they can fall too easily and destroy years of faith and hope without knowing what they have done. Johnnie Walker was my all time broadcasting DJ hero and it was his radio style that propelled me to believe I could be a DJ and a broadcaster. After I had joined Patrick Motors and learned that Walker too had been a car salesman for the company, the parallels were too great and he became a driving force in my life, something he of course was completely unaware of. I discovered that Walker was doing a gig at The Lafayette in Wolverhampton. This was Wolverhampton's premier nightclub where I had been to on many occasions and I had to go and meet Walker, it was to be a crowning glory moment. I waited with anticipation all week until the night came and went along with John Oebel, who I had asked to accompany me. I used the Chrysalis business card to propel us backstage and into Walker's dressing room. I think I was all of a blabber when the doorman took me in:

'Steve Jenkins, Chrysalis, I brought some records for you.'

'Yeh, got all of them.'

'I used to work at Patrick Motors, I know you worked there too.'

'Don't talk about those days.'

'Well, just wanted to say Hello and see the show.'

'Got any gear?'

'Er, no.'

'OK, say see you later.'

Johnnie left. John had witnessed the conversation and we left too. I have to say it took me a long time to get over that night. Walker had been a driving force for me for years, and that he really didn't have the time to speak civilly for such a short period of time was a huge disappointment. Then, as the years went by, I thought about it and realised of course, how really he had no idea how important those few minutes were for me. So, if you have a similar experience when a hero lets you down the best advice I can give is to forgive and move on. As for Walker and me, it would be almost thirty years before I would meet him again.

And the bands played on:

The gigs kept rolling at Chrysalis, and next up were Steeleye Span. We opened the tour for the new album in Chester, where I met Maddy Prior and the band. I would get to know Maddy best of all as she did the bulk of the interviews and TV appearances that I always accompanied her to. The band was in its most successful period, having had their biggest hit 'All Around My Hat.' The album we were now promoting was 'Rocket Cottage', which would not be as successful, but the tour was a sell out as 'All Around My Hat' had brought in a huge level of support. Bob Johnson, the band's guitarist, also became a friend during this period and did an interview for me on my Sunday Radio Stafford show. Bob knew it was the first time I had interviewed anyone on the radio and he was the perfect guest.

Steeleye Span was the most famous electric folk band in Britain and along with Fairport Convention remains so to this day. For me, it was great to work with so many different styles of music and see the different types of people that turned up at the gigs. In those days music was very diverse: Steeleye Span were successful with traditional folk songs, Jethro Tull were an individualistic band entirely unlike any other, UFO were a hard driving rock band and these bands had very different audiences. It was a fantastic music education.

The regular promotion at radio and TV continued daily. Chrysalis had signed a band called The Babys, a youthful rock group that really looked their title's part, although they were not a metal band. Their first single was 'Isn't It Time?' and we set about promoting it with organised gusto. There were no videos in those days, but Chrysalis was an inventive and forward thinking company and it had shot film footage of the band performing 'Isn't It Time?' We were given fold-away TVs that could show the footage for promotion to radio so that the playlist people could actually see what the band looked like. The TV folded into a briefcase and was pretty easy to erect and play and every radio station I went into with this contraption pulled a crowd. Each station had a DJ room where all the DJs had a desk and I must have played this early film of the band ten times at each station.

The promotion worked to a degree, we got plenty of playlists and airplay, but the song itself was never quite embraced by the public and only became a minor hit. Some years later, the lead singer would have a worldwide massive No 1 single with 'Missing You' – I was delighted when John Waite's moment finally came having originally known him as a lad with The Babys.

Leo Sayer – My first No 1 hit:

Leo Sayer was the most successful artist of my time with Chrysalis. I had compered Leo that night a few years earlier at Barbarella's, which I reminded him of when we met again at BBC Manchester to record a radio segment for Tony Hale and pre-record a slot for *Top Of The Pops*. The album we were working was 'Endless Flight', which had been produced by Richard Perry, who had made a lot of hit records in America. His production made Leo sound a little smoother, and the album would establish him in America and sell a million copies. The first single from the album 'You Make Me Feel Like Dancing' had already been a hit before I joined the company, but I was well established as a Chrysalis promotion man when we released 'When I Need You.' I did all the promotion in my area on this single, the record was all over the radio and although Leo was not on tour, we did a lot of radio interviews and TV appearances. We generally had a fun time as everything was going so well: the album went to No 1 and just kept selling. The greatest moment of all for me was when 'When I Need You' finally, was the UK's No 1 single on 19th February 1977. I'd done it, I had worked and been involved in a No 1 single. Even if it never happened again, I had been to No 1 once in my life – and the single would stay on top of the charts for three weeks. It was a big day for Chrysalis: No 1 records in those days were few and far between and meant so much, both to the artist in terms of credibility with a massively increasing fan base, and to the label in terms of sales. We were invited to London for a party and were all presented with bottles of champagne labelled No 1, 'When I Need You', Leo Sayer. I took the champagne home and presented it to my Mom, it was a small statement that after all those years of pain and worry she had to suffer from her wayward son, something had come out of it, a No 1 record. Mom kept the bottle of champagne for years and it stood proudly in the house – we never drank it. Chrysalis would release a further two singles from the album during my time with them and they would have another two hits, but neither went to No 1. And yet the album just went on selling. I saw a lot of Leo during this time and then he was off to promote and enjoy his success in America.

More artists, more hits:

Touring and promoting continued, and next up was Rory Gallagher, a truly great guitar player and an even greater lad. It was a real pleasure to work with Rory, he gigged endlessly and played his heart out every night, and although his audiences were smaller, his fans adored him. In 1976, Rory had enjoyed his most successful album to date, 'Against The Grain', which had increased his audiences at live gigs, and so when Chrysalis released 'Calling Card' in 1977, he was on top form. We played gig after gig and Rory did every interview I could get for him with the same passion and commitment he gave when playing guitar. I can tell you it was an honour and a privilege to work with and know Rory Gallagher. His brother Don was his manager and taught me how to play backgammon backstage at many venues. Unfortunately, I was never as good as those two.

I managed to score big in the eyes of Chrysalis executives with a single from Split Enz entitled 'Another Great Divide.' The band hailed from New Zealand and would gain a massive audience in later years as Crowded House with Tim Finn. Back then, they had a small following, but enough to come to England and tour. They had some of the most impressive haircuts I had ever seen! Chrysalis were always giving targets and incentives for getting records on the regional playlists and Split Enz was a major priority, so it was very good news when I managed to achieve a playlisting of 'Another Great Divide' on Piccadilly Radio in Manchester through my friend Roger Day. Piccadilly was one of the biggest stations outside London in terms of listeners and the airing of the single made the up-and-coming gigs in the area sell out. For a short time I was a hero at Chrysalis and Promotion Man of the Month, it seemed I could do no wrong – oops here we go again.

Chrysalis had been working steadily on me to move north and live in Manchester. At the start of my time there it had been 'we would like you to move', but as time went on the matter became more of a pressure issue. My success rate with playlists, interviews, gigs and artist support could not be questioned, I had no problem driving through the night, and as a matter of fact, I enjoyed being on my own listening to the radio and driving. My expenses were quite normal as I drove rather than stayed in hotels and I felt that would stop the questioning of the move to Manchester. I suppose accountants could see by the petrol receipts that I was doing more driving than I should, even though I maintained that it did not affect my work and I was obtaining the results. Chris Stone once called me into his office and asked how the move was coming along and when would it occur. I told him I hadn't had a lot of time to go flat hunting but would step up my search. I did toy with the idea, but could not bring myself to move to Manchester. I decided if I had to move it would be Liverpool and so I started to look for a flat there whenever I had the chance. I must admit it was a half-hearted attempt and the two or three flats I saw and the areas they were in, really, were not for me. Another couple of months went by and then Chris Griffin came out on the road with me and said the time was now, time to move. I told him of my attempts in Liverpool and Chris, bless him, said Liverpool was just about acceptable, Manchester was still preferable, but I would have to do something in the next month.

'Another Great Divide' was a double edged sword: the single got everyone to back off about the move as Chrysalis thought they could build plays on other radio stations off the back of Piccadilly's success, but this unfortunately didn't happen. Meanwhile, Splitz Enz arrived in Manchester to play the biggest gig of the tour. I had met the boys before at previous gigs in my area and had already completed the radio interviews for that gig. I went to the soundcheck in Manchester and hung out with the guys until about 5pm, when they went to eat and prepare for the show. The next day we were to be in Liverpool and I had a problem. On the same night that we were in Manchester, Walsall Football Club were at home to Crystal Palace and I was due to broadcast at the ground. I had no guests at the Split Enz show that needed taking care of and there was no 'grip and grin' scheduled. Hence, I said to the boys, 'see you later', slipped out by the backstage exit and headed for the motorway. Down the M6 and straight off into the Fellows Park players car park and Jenkins is at the turntables announcing team changes, spinning records, reading the adverts and up-and-coming fixtures, job done, no problem.

The following morning, bright and early, I was up and off to Liverpool and into Radio City and BBC Merseyside preparing for the afternoon interviews with Split Enz, and then onto soundcheck. All went well, the boys had not missed my 'no show' after last night's gig, we did the interviews and the show and Phil Easton went backstage after a very good night. Then back down the motorway at midnight to Walsall. By Friday I was at home collecting the playlists by phone and that week's plays, ready to relay them to Chris Griffin for the weekend's report. The phone rings. It's Chris. We chat for a few minutes and then he asks, 'How were the Split Enz gigs in Manchester and Liverpool?'

'All good, went well.'

'Manchester?'

'Yeh, good.'

'Steve, I'm a Crystal Palace supporter.'

'Oh... well I was there until 5.00pm and back in Liverpool by 10.30 Wednesday, but I can't deny I was at the match.'

'I know and that was you broadcasting.'

'True.'

'This is the problem with not living in your area.'

'Well, I'm caught cold Chris.'

In the years that have followed Chris and I have had good laughs about that night. I would have loved to have seen his face when he arrived at Fellows Park to see his beloved Crystal Palace and my dulcet tones welcomed him to the ground. Chris did not go running to the bosses at Chrysalis telling them that I was not where I should have been, but I guess we both knew something had to change: the move to Manchester had to happen or I had to leave.

That weekend I seriously began to weigh up the options: working for Chrysalis, a proper record company, meant moving to Manchester; that would mean giving up Walsall Football Club broadcasting, probably Chaplin's on Fridays and Saturdays and probably my Sunday Radio Show as well – unhappy decisions no matter which way I went. The Sunday Radio Show had been going from strength to strength and I had recovered from my greatest faux pas, one that I will never forget. Before I managed to get the two hour 4pm to 6pm slot my first show had been 3pm to 4pm: I played hit singles, a few oldies and some new tracks from the week's new album releases, and that was all interspersed with general chatter about what I had been doing in the week, a look back at the week's news and a few inside stories from the music industry. The show had brought me notice and I had a good listenership. I had all the new releases sent to me, which I would let the other broadcasters use for their shows, as long as I had them back for my Friday night gig at Chaplin's. The key is to remember this is Hospital Radio: broadcasting to people who are ill, people who are recovering, doctors and nurses. When you reach the end of the show you must finish precisely on time as the feed comes from the BBC for the News exactly on the hour – you absolutely cannot be one second late. In your headphones you cue the last record, listen to the feed from the BBC and finish with, 'Goodbye and see you next week.' One Sunday I am due to play 'Writing' from Elton John's 'Captain Fantastic and The Brown Dirt Cowboy' album. Seeing that 'Writing' is about four minutes long and I only have two and a half minutes left, I pick up the album while chatting and look for the shortest track, which was a simple task to see as in those days the albums were vinyl. Track 2 looked the shortest, so while continuing to chat, I queued it and said 'Thanks for listening, see you next week, today I leave you with a track from 'Captain Fantastic and the Brown Dirt Cowboy', here's Elton John (I quickly look at the album for the title) with 'Better Off Dead.' The technicians in the other room are shocked and in horror I'm paralysed. I cannot stop the record or get it off, the News is coming and Elton is chanting at speed Better off dead, Better off dead, Better off dead. That day I died on the radio.

I told Chris Griffin I would look in earnest to find a flat in the North. I couldn't face Manchester, as I had an immovable mental block on that idea, but I decided I would start to look on the edge of Liverpool for a bedsit, thinking it would appease Chrysalis. I could use it as a stopover a couple of nights a week.

I never got to look at any bedsits; life was about to change again.

CHAPTER 7

MCA RECORDS AND STARS OF COUNTRY, STAGE AND SCREEN – 1977 AND 1978

In at the start:

A week after the crisis had arisen at Chrysalis about where I should live the phone rang at 26 Regina Drive around six in the evening. Mom answered and passed on the message when I arrived home. 'Martin Sattherswaite called from MCA Records and wants you to call him, the number's by the phone.' I thought nothing of it, as I'd had no real contact with the company over the years, apart from unsuccessfully trying to get promotional records for DJing from them, but the following day I called the number and asked for Martin. He explained that he was the new Head of Promotion for MCA Records which was setting up a new operation in the UK. At that moment they were a licensed label through EMI, but in the next month they would be obtaining new offices in Soho and were recruiting staff for the new autonomous company. Martin had spoken to a lot of people at radio stations and other record companies and my name had kept coming up in conversations. In short: would I be interested in joining MCA as Regional Promotions Manager for the Midlands? In short, yes I would. Martin asked if I could arrange a day off from Chrysalis, come to London and meet everyone, and they would explain their vision for the company. We agreed I would try and come to London in the next week or so.

This was really exciting news. Here was a company that was setting up with full enthusiasm and I would be in at the start. Instead of having to live in Manchester or Liverpool I could stay in Walsall and hopefully keep my other jobs at Chaplin's, Walsall Football Club and Radio Stafford. I liked working for Chrysalis and was thankful they had given me a chance, but the move north was really causing both parties serious problems. I thought I would listen to everything that MCA had to say, and if it looked solid and I thought I could work with their people, then this could be just the right move at the right time. I arranged a day off at Chrysalis with no problem, as I never took the holidays I was entitled to.

The day came and I was off to London. I had to meet everyone at the EMI offices as the new MCA offices would not be available for another three weeks. I had been to EMI before but had never made it past the reception. I had always been forced to sit there waiting for someone to see me, as I was trying to get on their mailing lists for records, with no success. It felt finally good to get into the building.

MCA Records' headquarters in London at that time was just a couple of rooms within EMI. A licensed label has a skeleton staff and just acts as a product source for the major label, that being EMI. MCA had few UK acts and the staff really just dealt with the records and artists that were signed in the USA – a little outpost for America in simple terms. However, Julie Covington's No 1 hit 'Don't Cry For Me Argentina' in February 1977 and an association with Andrew Lloyd Webber had begun to change the standing of MCA in the UK, and I must say, I had been particularly delighted at Chrysalis just a few months earlier when Leo Sayer's 'When I need You' had knocked Julie Covington off the No 1 spot after only one week.

MCA Records stands for the Music Corporation of America. It had started as a label in 1962 with the purchase of the American branch of Decca Records. MCA also acquired Universal Pictures as part of that deal and would transform Universal into the top film studio in Hollywood producing hit after hit in the film business. Through further acquisitions and expansion, the company would become the biggest label in Nashville for Country music and, in due course, MCA was to grow into what today is the world's largest conglomerate of record labels, the Universal Music Group. Back in 1977, it was already a huge company in the USA with the combination of its film soundtracks and the signing of major artists. The success of the movie company and the vast income from several hit films meant that the expansion of the sister record label around the world was now at the forefront of the US agenda. The UK was to be the first part of that expansion.

Martin told me of the plans: a new A & R Department (Artist and Repertoire Departments are responsible for the signing of new artists and the recording of the albums and singles), a new Sales and Marketing Department and a new Promotion Department, headed by Martin and two Regional Promotion Managers. Steve McCaughley would be working Leeds, Stockton on Tees, Newcastle, Glasgow and Edinburgh, and my area would be Birmingham, Wolverhampton, Manchester, Liverpool, Nottingham and Swansea. The offer was an improvement on my terms at Chrysalis Records and there would be a brand new car and expenses. The start date would be anytime in the next month.

All this seemed perfect. I informed Martin that I still operated as a DJ at the weekends and wanted to know if that was a problem. 'No', was the firm answer. I felt Radio Stafford being a Sunday job was my business and Walsall Football Club being Saturday with only a few Tuesday evenings should not be a problem and not worth putting on the table. I accepted Martin's offer and said that when I received a letter confirming everything we had discussed I would inform Chrysalis of my decision. The start date would have to be left open, as I wanted to give them enough time to find a replacement and be honourable.

Martin then took me in to meet Roy Featherstone, the Managing Director, and Stewart Watson, the General Manager. Roy had been in the record and music publishing industry for years and Stewart had previously worked for Harvest Records, a UK EMI label, and been successful there.

Finally, before I left that day, I asked Martin if he knew on which floor in those Manchester Square offices The Beatles had posed for the photo that became the cover for the *Please Please Me* album. He said he did – would I like to go? 'You bet I would!'

Should you ever see the cover of The Beatles' first album, it is shot on a stairwell in the EMI Manchester Square building. The Beatles are facing the Square and leaning over the banister. The photo was taken at the time of the recording and it remains the cover to this day. Ringo had not at that stage changed his hairstyle into 'the Beatle cut.' Pop history, and I had finally made it into the EMI offices, got a job and stood in the exact spot that the Beatles had that photo taken. 'How about that Dad?'

A few days later the paperwork arrived from MCA confirming all that we had discussed and the start date was to be determined by me after conversations with Chrysalis. They were not pleased that I was going to leave, but they respected that the Manchester situation was something that we could not get around and so they decided to end it all quickly. It was all over within ten days, Chris Griffin took over my area and everything was executed with great ease.

In the early years of working for these record companies I think I was lucky to work on all styles of music. At Nems and Immediate, I had worked on the flower power, psychedelic records of the sixties, Marianne Faithfull's return, Reggae with Opal Records and the hit DAT, and the initial Black Sabbath albums. At Chrysalis, I had been inducted into the world of touring with Jethro Tull, UFO, Rory Gallagher, all varying styles of rock music, the traditional folk music of Steeleye Span and the 'pop' explosion of Leo Sayer. I had also worked in nightclubs for years playing soul, dance and pop records for people to dance to, and altogether I had been involved in a very wide range of musical styles. Especially as I had been earning my living from all this, it had been essential to be professional and learn about the various audiences that preferred different styles.

I signed on for MCA Records and waiting was a brand new red Ford Cortina car. We spent some time sorting out the paperwork, picking up records, biographies and the general tools of the trade of promotion. I met Steve McCauphley for the first time. He would become a lifelong friend and a good promotion man to have on your team. Steve was bright, intelligent and switched on to life in 1977: he had already adopted the tight drainpipe jeans that were blowing into fashion with the advent of 'Punk Rock Music.' I was still wearing the slightly flared ones of the dying disco phase and he told me I immediately had to move on and change the jeans, which I did a short time later. I remember not liking it initially as the flares had more room in them, while the punk ones didn't leave much room for 'The Crown Jewels', and it felt really uncomfortable to start with, especially after several hours in a car. The things we do for fashion.

We did not have any immediate hit records coming down the track, so we started work at the radio stations presenting our catalogue, filling the libraries with our music and looking for playtime on past albums to get the catalogue selling. The catalogue was enormous and generated a lot of sales as it had not been worked for some time, and this gave the company breathing space to get new albums ready from UK artists. It also enabled our relationships with the radio stations to grow without the constant pressure to playlist singles and get hits. We knew that the touring of our UK acts was in the pipeline and in a few short months we would be up to full speed. This was a good time to be a promotion man for MCA, it was all about setting up the future.

Evita:

We were buoyant in the album chart with the Andrew Lloyd Webber and Tim Rice album from the show *Evita*: the soundtrack had been recorded way in advance of the West End show and had come hard on the heels of Julie Covington's hit single 'Don't Cry For Me Argentina.' I had the pleasure of picking up Tim Rice from Birmingham New Street Station and taking him to ATV for an interview on the six o'clock news programme. A charming man and a great lyricist, we spoke for the journey to and from ATV mainly about cricket, a great passion for him and for me. Tim made no demands, he just needed transport to the interview and taking back to the train station. There was no entourage, he was just an ordinary man doing a job quickly and smoothly.

We issued the second single, 'Another Suitcase in Another Hall', by Barbara Dickson a tremendous song from *Evita*, and this time I met Barbara in Manchester at the railway station, from where we went to do interviews with BBC Manchester and then moved over to Granada for the six o'clock show. Barbara again was a joy to be with. She came in, just did the job, and then went back to the train station. I remember her in knee-length black boots, black jeans, white shirt, jacket and jewellery, she looked fantastic. I told her the record was going to be a hit, but it had been some time since she had been on the UK chart and didn't believe it: 'I don't know, let's wait and see.' I knew from the sales patterns that it would chart the following week and I enjoyed phoning her seven days later with a 'told you so.' Barbara was delighted and enjoyed the popularity of the hit – lovely lady.

Celebrity Stars of Country Music:

MCA introduced me to Country Music – another completely different style and world.

Back in 1977, Wembley Arena hosted the Country Music Show of America each year. It would last three days over the summer bank holiday weekend and large numbers of Americans would fly in for the nonstop concert when a whole host of American artists would perform. The concerts also encouraged a community of English people who wanted to be cowboys. The first year I attended the concert I could not believe that people from Rochdale, Southport, Bolton, Manchester and Liverpool would dress that way, but they did, and had a great time doing so. McCauphley and I were drafted in to look after the artists during their four day stay and get interview time for some of our radio stations that specially made the journey south. The big stars would only do limited interviews, but that enabled us to bounce the newer artists into the interview arena. During 1977 and 1978, I spent time with and watched the performances of Tammy Wynette, most famous in England for her hits 'Stand By Your Man' and 'D.I.V.O.R.C.E.', but a huge selling albums artist in America for many years. Tammy had her time as The First Lady of Country Music and was good to work with, always on time, ready to do the interviews and always professional.

Meeting Conway Twitty was a special moment for me. All those years before when I was at school and heard 'It's Only Make Believe', I really couldn't believe that anyone would be so unfortunate as to be called Twitty – but the song and the vocal was fantastic. I would learn now that the name Conway Twitty, was in fact, not real; his name was Harold Lloyd Jenkins, the same as my Grandfather without the Lloyd. Harold Lloyd Jenkins believed that his name was not show business, and it was while he was one day looking at a map of America and saw Conway Arkansas and Twitty Texas that he had his revelation, and history was made. Conway Twitty had a career in the States that lasted all his life and he would total fifty-five No 1 records on all charts. The day I met him he was wearing a bright red suit, red trousers and red jacket – you could see him coming miles away. I introduced myself as Steve Jenkins MCA Records. He said in an American drawl 'Good name son, you'll do alright.' He did his interviews, winked at me and left. That night I watched his show, great performer.

Don Williams was just beginning to become a world star back in 1977. Six years earlier he had gone solo when the folk group he played in, Pozo-Seco Singers, disbanded, and now he had just come off three consecutive No 1 country records in America: 'Turn Out The Lights And Love Me Tonight', 'Some Broken Hearts Never Mend', and 'I'm Just A Country Boy.' Everyone wanted to see him play. I was in the room with Don Williams during his interviews, but I never spoke with him: on his way out after he had finished he just looked at me and touched his cowboy hat. I watched and loved his show: class act.

The second year that I worked at The Country Festival at Wembley, I was put in charge of promotion for Loretta Lynn. Loretta had been the biggest selling female country singer in America throughout the sixties and seventies, accumulating over seventy hits. Her autobiography had been made into an Oscar winning movie *The Coal Miner's Daughter,* starring Sissy Spacek and Tommy Lee Jones. Sue and I had gone to see the movie in Walsall at the ABC Cinema at the top of Park Street; I thought I should watch the film as research before meeting with such a huge Country star. Loretta had been married before her fourteenth birthday and had four children by the time she was eighteen. Her husband, whom she was to stay with until his death in 1996, was Doolittle Lynn, played by Tommy Lee Jones in the movie. He had discovered Loretta's talent and managed her career, and in her autobiography she recalled that he 'thought I was something special, more special than anyone in the world, and never let me forget it.'

Well, Doolittle was not a man to be messed with. I spent three days in the company of Loretta and her husband. Loretta was fantastic and treated me as if she had known me for years. She did every interview with great charm and ease. Doolittle, who was a man mountain, hardly spoke to me but constantly looked at me and seemed as though if I said one word out of place he was going to shoot me and then go and have a steak and beer to celebrate. It was Doolittle who decided when each interview was over: he just looked at me and said 'End.' I would then signal to the interviewer that it was time to wind up. Doolittle didn't look at the interviewer, he just kept looking at me. I remember ushering Loretta into another room – we had two rooms, with an interview taking place in one while the other was being used to set up the next interview, and I would work from one room to the other. I was under pressure, moving Loretta from one room to the other, and Doolittle followed one step behind. I was blowing a bit at one point and Loretta said, 'Don't worry I'll handle Doo.' I was thankful she tried to calm me, but Doolittle was menacing. I watched Loretta perform, she had complete control of the band, the show and the audience – a true Country Legend.

The new artists we were working in those years were Joe Ely and Tanya Tucker. Joe, who is still performing today with many albums behind him, was just releasing his first solo album. He notably worked with Bruce Springsteen and The Clash, in fact, when Joe was in the UK in 1977 he formed a friendship with The Clash and sang backing vocals on 'Should I Stay Or Should I Go' – a good artist right at the start of his career back then. Tanya was a 16 year-old country singer with a big future. She came to the UK back then to play and promote her records. In the time I had with Tanya she was quiet and simply trying to get through everything in a foreign country. Two years later she would become the wild child of Country Music and embark on a notorious relationship with Glen Campbell. During their years together Tanya would be blamed for Glen's decline and drug addiction, Glen would be charged with knocking out her front teeth and the newspapers would have a field day. Over many years Tanya would eventually become one of Nashville's biggest female artists. Back then she was just a young girl.

After each Country Festival one of our artists would go on tour around the UK and off I would go with them, as usual, arranging all the interviews and TV appearances around the shows in different towns. In 1977, it was the turn of Merle Haggard. He is known as 'The Okie From Muskogee' and was a tough individual who was loved by Country Music folk for his down to earth manner and songs. He had been inspired by Johnny Cash's performances while he was serving time for robbery at San Quentin. Haggard had then turned his life around and would score thirty-eight No 1 country records. He is acclaimed as one of the most important country artists in history. Merle had little to say, didn't really like doing interviews and didn't really have much time for yours truly; he did what he had to do and left as fast as possible.

In lighter moments he was OK, though, and undoubtedly he was a great performer. He had a small but strong following in England and we did about ten gigs in twelve days. Merle has been divorced four times and said 'Willie Nelson told me the reason divorce is so expensive is because it's worth it.'

The following year I was on tour with Bill Anderson. In the States, Bill Anderson has fame as a performer whose whispering style of vocal brought him many hits, a TV presenter of some big TV shows and most of all, a songwriter. As I began the tour I didn't know who he was and the eight gigs we were booked to do were two thousand seaters. It was unusual for me not to know something about the artist, so I read about Bill and learned that he had written 'Happiness' for Ken Dodd and scored a lot of No 1s in the Country charts. But, I couldn't see how the gigs would sell. Well, they did not sell out, but they were pretty full and Bill delivered a good show, with a good band, to a responsive audience who were obviously fans. I did my job in obtaining interviews, and after playing Manchester we had a couple of sold out gigs in Southport, a Country stronghold for some reason, before heading off to Liverpool the following day. I sat with Bill before the last Southport show to go through the following day's interviews at Radio City, BBC Merseyside and with the press. In trying to keep the conversation light while finalising the upcoming times and approvals I said 'Liverpool tomorrow Bill, home of the Beatles.' Bill was a quite mild mannered man and his response took my breath away. 'Beatles, fucking Beatles, don't mention them to me, they came to America and fucked it up for all of us.' He got up and left. We did the interviews the following day and I never mentioned the Beatles for the rest of the tour.

New genres:

On the UK artist front, we were beginning to work new products, and one of the surprise chart hit selling albums was Julian Lloyd Webber's *Variations*. Julian, a cellist, was pure classical in terms of music, whereas Andrew, composer of hit musicals, was far more commercially minded. The two brothers had not worked together, but after Andrew lost a bet one day while watching a game at Leyton Orient Football club with Julian, he had to come up with a project. Variations was that project and it would eventually become a No 2 album on the UK chart. A piece from the album has been heard for years as the introduction music for the ITV cultural magazine programme *The South Bank Show*. Our job again, was to get plays and interviews for Julian, which at first was tough, but *The South Bank Show* dedicated an entire programme to the album and we started to pick up some momentum. The interviews then started to come in and increased as the record began to climb the charts. The musicians we used on the album were mainly from one of our bands, Colosseum II: Don Airey, Keyboards, Gary Moore, Guitar, John Hiseman, Drums, and John Mole, Bass. Also playing on the album were Rod Argent, Piano, Barbara Thompson, Flute and Saxophone, Phil Collins and Herbie Flowers.

Colossium II were a band I would be on constant tour with for a year or more. We tried hard to get their two albums of Jazz Fusion selling and ultimately we would fail, but we put a great deal of effort in for the albums *Electric Savage* and *War Dance* at radio rock shows and with touring. On these tours, I became Gary Moore's personal guitar tuner. Gary would sit with one guitar and I was with another for what seemed like an hour every night plucking string after string time and time again until he was happy. I really didn't mind, Gary and I were good friends during that time and I used to look forward to our nightly meeting and guitar session. Airey, Hiseman and 'the Mole' were also good lads to be around, and we all worked well together. I placed them on all the rock shows and they appreciated the effort I put into the albums.

My work with Colosseum helped me in my progress within MCA Records. In the Seventies, the business of music was growing and the gulf between the record company and the artist was beginning to widen. Record companies tried to narrow the divide by creating a position titled Artist Liaison Manager. It was a go between for both the artist and the company and it worked at its best when both sides were in opposite corners, most usually, over single selection, timing of tours, album artwork and promotion (financial issues were handled directly by the artists' managements). The Artist Liaison Manager spent more and more time with the artist on tour and in the studio recording. Martin Sattherswaite told me one day when I was in London that Colosseum II, Wishbone Ash and a new punk band I had been on tour with named London, had all spoken highly of me, and he asked if I would be interested in adding these duties to the promotion duties and combining both jobs. It seemed to me it was more or less what I was already doing except that it might mean a few more visits to the office. I agreed and was given a small pay rise, so I was now Artist Liaison Manager & Promotions. It sounded a little grander and I took it that I was making my way up the ladder inside MCA.

I did two tours with Wishbone Ash, thirty dates in thirty-six days. The group were always professional, they had been on the road a long time and they had a great following. Almost every move was rehearsed: if you were watching for the first time it was a fantastic rock show, but watching for the twentieth time you knew exactly when the guitarists would throw their 'picks' into the crowd, every night it was just like clockwork. It made me realise, that although everything is supposed to be wild and 'Rock 'n' Roll', the shows were, in fact, precisely worked out and religiously routined to give maximum enjoyment to the fans. I suppose we all know that these days, but back then, to me, it was a revelation.

One of my worst experiences was coming off the relative calm of a thirty date Wishbone Ash tour straight onto a huge punk band tour with London. Wherever the band stayed so did you and I had become accustomed to Holiday Inns or similar with Wishbone, Merle, Bill Anderson, Jethro Tull, Steeleye Span and alike. The punk tours were known by the older bands as 'The Toilet Tours', not because of the places you played, but more because of where you stayed. I joined the band for the first show of the tour at The Porterhouse in Retford, a place I will never forget. I had never done a punk gig before, but I was up to date on all the groups and records and knew that 'spitting' at the band was a sign of respect. I thought it was completely out of order, but that was what came with punk. The bands would 'spit' back at the audience, unbelievable, I also thought that the 'spitting' was while the band played and was some kind of interaction. When you are touring with a band, if you are the Tour Manager, Artist Liaison Manager or head of the crew, the band normally follow you in a line from the dressing room to the stage, and sometimes you have to pass through the side of the audience to get to the stage. I had been out front to organise the way to the stage, and having done more touring than the band, I led them out. Big mistake. As I walked through the side door and went to pass the audience, with the band close behind me, the Retford audience knew the routine and all had mouthfuls of saliva ready. It was World War Three of spit, it thudded against your head and hit and ran down your coat, and by the time we made the stage, we were covered. How the bands then went on to play a set, I really do not understand. I was covered and wanted to fight, but who are you going to start with? The whole lot are doing it and in their world it is not a foul. Then, that night, we all checked into a Bed & Breakfast guest house that was just a hell hole. It was one of those places where as you open the door the bed moves to greet you. I couldn't sleep a wink. Two lessons learned: never lead out a punk group and wherever the band is playing try and drive home, don't stay in the 'Toilet.' But there was one consolation prize: the drummer of London would become a good mate during that year, and a few years later, he would be a world star – Jon Moss would leave London and join Culture Club, touring the world with Boy George.

Big Movie Band:

Being the company that owned Universal Pictures, MCA Records often had soundtracks from movies to promote. Most had one single plus film incidental music on the album, but on one occasion the movie launched a band and the band launched the movie. I had to promote the film around the country and get press, radio and TV to the special showings we had arranged at either 11.00 in the morning or 3.00 in the afternoon, and then we would give everyone the album and the single to play on radio, or a film clip for TV with the single as the soundtrack. *Car Wash*, directed by Michael Schultz, remains to this day the movie I have seen most in my life.

In October 1977 the promotion for *Car Wash* began and it was my first involvement with a movie. We worked with the film company Universal Pictures – they booked the cinemas, dates and times of showings and we 'promotion people' went about spreading the word to radio and TV. The whole promotion took about three weeks and, for between three and four days of those weeks, I was positioned at cinemas welcoming DJs, radio staff, TV staff and press to the showings. The film had started to be a success in America and both the movie and the record 'Car Wash' were moving up the respective charts of popularity. The film's band Rose Royce, with Gwen Dickey as lead singer, was starting to become famous.

Promoting a film may appear to be an exciting job and to begin with I thought it was. In reality, you can watch the movie maybe three times before you get used to the dialogue and all the surprises are gone, you know the jokes and, pretty soon you just can't watch it anymore. After the first week of two showings a day I'd had it with the movie, but you have to be professional and be 'up' for the new media people on their first showing in each town. I would settle everyone in and then go out for coffee, returning half way through the movie when I would watch five minutes. Then I would leave again and come back towards the end. Needless to say, over twenty years later and without having seen the film again since, I still know it well.

Rose Royce had originally been signed to Tamla Motown, but left in 1975 along with the well known producer Norman Whitfield. Norman was probably best known for his work with The Temptations, it was he who changed their sound and produced records like 'Cloud Nine' and 'I Can't Get Next To You.' He was commissioned to do the soundtrack to *Car Wash* after at first not wanting to be involved – it was only when the film company embarrassed him with money that he felt he had to accept and he also thought this might be a way to give a break to the then unknown Rose Royce. After trying for weeks to come up with a song for the film's main theme, inspiration finally came while Norman was playing basketball: rumour has it that he wrote the style and lyric on the back of a fried chicken bag. Wherever he wrote it, 'Car Wash' would become an American No 1 in January 1977 and would peak in England, on Christmas day 1977, at No 9. The next single, 'Put Your Money Where Your Mouth Is', was a minor success but the third single catapulted the double album into great sales: 'I Wanna Get Next To You' was a great record and peaked at No 14 in the UK.

That was it for MCA Records and Rose Royce. The band were only contracted to do the soundtrack album and although the company tried to sign them long-term, they went to Warner Brothers and over the years produced another couple of classic tracks, 'Wishing On A Star' and 'Love Don't Live Here Anymore.' I never toured with Rose Royce, but when they did come to England in late 1977, I was invited to see them play at Birmingham Odeon by Warner Brothers in recognition of my work and I went back stage to meet the band and Gwen, who I would meet again years later. The band were fantastic on that tour. At one point during the show and in mid song they would completely stop and stand motionless. The lighting made them look like statues and the longer they stayed still the more the crowd went mad. Then, on cue, the band hit a groove and all hell broke loose. To this day it was one the best stage stunts I have seen.

During my first few months at MCA I gained a reputation, not only as an accomplished promotion man, but also as someone not to mess with. For a long time I had no idea about this, although I was occasionally aware that people were gentle in certain circumstances. In my time in the clubs of Birmingham and on the tours with many bands I had seen a lot of aggression and fighting, it was part of the night life scene. I always tried to stay away from most of it, but I had become conditioned to it all the same. On Fridays, for MCA, I would go to Birmingham New Street Station to pick up the records we would be promoting the following week, collect replenishments for the stocks of the continuing promotions and also take in the special requests I had been asked for in the back catalogue. On one occasion a car ploughed right into the back of the MCA red Cortina, which I had parked in a bay that was allocated for me by the station attendants. The driver accused me of causing the accident because of where I had parked (!) and he came running at me. In the self-defence I had learned in the clubs and on the road I floored him and then out of nowhere the police were suddenly there. The guy's insurance company paid for the repair of the Cortina as he was one hundred percent the guilty party, but what I did not know for a long time, was that a report of the incident had been sent to MCA. I had told them of the accident, but I had not referred to the incident with the driver. They read it in the report and it would cause some fear in the office a year later.

The Crickets:

Buddy Holly and The Crickets! I had grown up on their music and the tragic story of the plane crash on 3rd February 1959 that took the lives of Buddy Holly, Ritchie Valens and The Big Bopper, all in their prime. The records, such as 'Peggy Sue', 'Rave On', 'True Love Ways', 'It Doesn't Matter Anymore' and many more have stood the test of time and sold many compilations and stage shows, such as *Buddy*. To celebrate thirty years of 'Peggy Sue', we compiled Buddy Holly and the Crickets Legend package. It had been the first time since 1965 that a new package had been put together and was a big deal. Paul McCartney was involved as he had bought the rights to the songs and had to give his permission. MCA had contact with Paul at the time because his daughter Heather had started going out with Jon Moss from the band London. McCartney had phoned and asked us to send him a copy of the London album – he obviously wanted to know who his daughter was seeing and what he sounded like, and probably, if he could play drums.

We were all excited about this package and even more so when the Crickets, who continued after Buddy Holly's death, decided to come to the UK and do promotion. For me this was incredible, I would meet and work with the legendary Crickets for a week.

To this day I am still honoured to have met, got to know and worked with Jerry Allison, Joe B. Maudlin and Sonny Curtis. Jerry Allison played drums with The Crickets and some of the most famous drum licks in the history of music are his on 'Peggy Sue' and also on 'Till I Kissed You' by the Everly Brothers, for whom he played sessions. And, Jerry was the songwriter of 'That'll Be The Day,' 'Peggy Sue', and 'More Than Words Can Say.' Joe B. Maudlin played bass with The Crickets and would go on to be a great recording engineer and producer working with Phil Spector and Herb Albert amongst others. His most famous song is probably 'Well All Right.' Sonny Curtis played guitar with The Crickets and wrote some classic songs including 'Love Is All Around', 'I Fought The Law' and 'Walk Right Back.'

With the Legendary Crickets, Martin Sattherswaite (MCA Records), Sonny Curtis, Jerry Allison, me and Joe B. Maudlin

The Legend album was to sell over half a million copies that year, go to No 1 on 11th March 1978 and stay on the chart for six months, a huge success. The biggest delight for me was to be driving Jerry, Joe and Sonny all over the UK in my Ford Cortina. We stayed in hotels together, ate together and did endless interviews in all the radio stations and six o'clock TV news programmes. They were absolutely brilliant to be with. There are some bands that have had one or two hits and think they know it all and quite frankly are a pain as they know next to nothing, yet here were legendary players with massive multiple worldwide hits under their belts and they just got in the car onto the next interview, grabbing a sandwich and keeping going – just brilliant. They told me all the stories of their tours, the struggle to get going as a band, the hits, the plane crash and their lives since – it was a privilege and one of my finest memories in the record business.

The march – and change – of time:

In 1978, winter and spring had gone and MCA had been successful. We had not had an abundance of hit singles, but the albums had sold well. Next on the agenda, in a few weeks time, was the opening of *Evita* on the West End Stage, on 21st June. Meantime, Chaplin's was still going well for me at the weekends and I finally made the pages of Blues and Soul. I had read the magazine for years – it had features on the American soul artists and was a splendid source of information about great records that might not have become great sellers, along with the out and out winners. For many years, I had seen main features on DJs at their respective clubs, stating what records they preferred, what style of music worked in their club and what their general career to date had been. I had always wanted to be featured as it gave your profile a real lift – all the DJs and programmers read the magazine. Well, finally they called. The story was all based around a visit to Chaplin's one Saturday night by local Birmingham DJ and Saturday night host on BRMB, Nicky Steele. Nicky was at Chaplin's to do one hour after the radio show and he brought along Frank Elson who wrote his weekly column, *Soul Tonic, in Blues and Soul*. We did a quick interview and photo for the magazine and Frank made references to Chaplin's trying to be like Slack Alice's in Manchester, which at the time was a famous club, mainly for the regular visits of George Best.

Chaplin's had been great for me, but the combination of losing a little interest, not being able to get a full-time job on the radio and a growing interest in the record company world, had begun to dampen my enthusiasm – only a little, but sufficient to make, no longer the 'end all' of my thoughts, which it had been. And just then, once again, the direction of my DJ life changed overnight. Dave Possall, now the former General Manager of Barbarella's, was opening his own club and wanted me there as the main DJ. The club was right next to the Holiday Inn and would be called Mr. Moons. I told Dave I would do Thursday, Friday and Saturday for the first month to open the club and then reduce the nights after that, also if I needed to do something for MCA we would use a 'fill in' DJ for that night. Dave agreed to all that and paid me well, but he could not understand why I should not give up my record company work and be his full-time DJ. I myself began to realise I had moved on and the tours and hit records I was involved with were giving me a bigger 'buzz' than just playing records, which I had now done solidly for some years.

MCA was still going well and I considered myself fortunate to work with Micky Dolenz and Davy Jones over a period of a couple of months. Both were in London to perform in Harry Nilsson's *The Point*, as the album was to come out on MCA Records, we became involved with press and promotions. Micky Dolenz had first made his name as a child actor in *Circus Boy*, a TV show I had watched at home in black and white as a kid, but along with Davy Jones, Peter Tork and Mike Nesmith he had gained international stardom in The Monkees. I loved *The Monkees* TV show and especially those hit singles 'I'm A Believer', 'A Little Bit Me A Little Bit You', 'Alternate Title', and 'Daydream Believer.' Their years of domination were 1967 and 1968, which was when the bulk of their records were sold and the TV show was at its peak. Davy Jones, of course, was English, something we were all proud of all those years ago, and the clip of him appearing in *Coronation Street* before The Monkees has been shown many times over many years. Hence, I was delighted to meet them both and do a long and concentrated promotion across the country. I got on well with Davy and he kept my number for a long time and would always give me a call when he arrived in the UK, for some years after. Micky was different and I think we just tolerated each other and professionally got the job done. He didn't want to spend any more time than he had to, either doing promotion or being with me and I felt the same. On TV, though, you would think Micky is complete fun to be with, such is the professionalism of his act.

As June 1978 came, we were invited to the press opening night of *Evita* in London, on 14th June. Sue was given time off from work and drove down to London with me. We stayed overnight at a fancy hotel in Kensington with Steve McCauphley and his girlfriend, Sarah. Cars were due to pick us up and take us to the theatre to see the opening of the show, something we had all worked on for over fifteen months. We all had coffee together and the girls then went upstairs to get ready. McCauphley had a couple of 'jazz cigarettes' – it had been with him that I had smoked my first on a stairwell of an NCP Car park in Soho some months earlier. Sue and I had a smoke of one thirty minutes before we left for *Evita*, and we had a great night, but unfortunately Steve's girlfriend didn't make the show – he said the 'jazz' had a bad effect on her and she couldn't make it. After the opening, we went to a party and met Andrew Lloyd Webber, Julian Lloyd Webber and Tim Rice, whom I already knew. All the MCA staff were there and a great night was had by all.

The following day, Steve and I had to go to a meeting at the MCA office. When I arrived, Martin asked me to come into his office and Steve went off to Stuart Watson's office. We chatted for a while and then Martin said we were going to meet with Roy Featherstone, the Managing Director. The boardroom at MCA had two doors, one from the corridor and one from Roy's office. Martin opened the door from the corridor, held the handle, I walked in, and he swivelled and closed the door – me inside, him out. Suddenly, you know all is not well. What's happening? Am I going to be fired? Then Roy's door opens and it's him and me alone in the boardroom. I now know what's coming, so I sit back in the chair and await the explanation.

To be fair, Roy did explain. Universal Pictures were the main company and it had been a bad year. The movies they had made had not worked well and so cutbacks had to be made across the film company and around the world in the record company. McCauphley was staying on – he had always been friends with Stuart Watson, who did all he could to protect him. Martin was taking on my duties and some press and A & R staff were being 'let go', as it was then, but 'made redundant', as it is today. I was shocked and completely unaware that this was coming. I sat not saying a word and watching Roy Featherstone squirm. He was clearly uncomfortable, but he was going to pay me for a month and give me bonuses for the job I had done. I could also keep the car for the next six weeks to help get myself sorted out. Finally, it was over and I could leave. I went to see Martin, but there was not much to say.

'Sorry mate.'

I replied, 'Yeh well, I'll be in touch' and started to leave. I just got to the stairs when Steve came running after me. 'Let's go', he said. We went to our jazz smoking stairwell in Soho and lit up.

'Sorry.'

'You knew and didn't say anything', I opened.

Steve explained that he had known for a week and thought he had about three months left before it was over for him too. It wasn't because of a smoke that his girlfriend was not at *Evita* that night – she could not face being there carrying out the lie and looking all happy, knowing what was going to happen to me the next day. I have respected her all my life for that. Hopefully, she got to see *Evita* sometime later. Steve also told me that the elaborate way it was set up was due to a police report that I had hit someone at Birmingham New Street Station.

'Did you?'

'I'm afraid so.'

'Well, they were on about getting someone in just in case you went ballistic; they decided not to though.'

If I had known that the police report was at the root of the uncomfortable way people were reacting, I would have made them squirm more. Stuart Watson never came out of his office or said anything. I never had much time for him from MCA onwards.

I did feel something for Roy Featherstone's family when he died years later. I think Roy had a good career and was dynamic in his early years in a fledgling industry, but by the time MCA came along I believe his power was spent, even though I know plenty of people had good words to say about him.

Steve McCauphley and I remain friends to this day and our paths would cross several times in the years to come.

So, that was it for MCA Records and me. I had left Walsall with Sue to celebrate at *Evita* and came back forty-eight hours later without a job. MCA would affect me in several ways. I had felt for the first time a little secure there and had believed all the hype that we were building a new company and I was part of it. I had also begun to look at life differently, not completely committed to being a broadcaster.

Whenever I was out of work, mother was 'on her toes' and 'on my case.' I knew all that was to come as the red Cortina was eating up the miles northward on the M1.

CHAPTER 8

RETHINK AND ALL CHANGE
1978 AND 1979

Mountain Records – and Marseille – plus a new young blonde:

My diary for the period after the return to Walsall is completely blank and this probably means that Sue and I took a few days holiday in Bournemouth. I have always gone there to sort out my head at different times over the years. I guess, as I spent so much time there growing up and it was my Dad's favourite town, I have always felt warm and safe there.

Meanwhile, as I expected, Mom asked 'How much money have you got in the bank?' Today, I cannot remember the sum, but it was enough for a deposit on an apartment. I told Mom the figure and she said 'It's time for you to leave home, I cannot take you coming in all hours of the night anymore and disrupting my life. I'll look for a flat and help you set it all up, but you're out soon.' There is not much you can say to that and I thought she was completely right. I had been on the move so much and trying to get somewhere, I had never thought of moving out. I had used the family home as a hotel for some time, but then I was used to hotels, and I had not given Mom's life any consideration. She was right, time to go. 'OK Mom', was enough.

Since February I had been working on a project on behalf of MCA named 'Battle of the Bands.' It had been put together by the breweries and they were searching for a new rock band. MCA was supposed to sign the winners and offer an album deal and tour support to get the band off the ground. This was a big operation and all the gigs were packed with radio and TV support. We started in Liverpool with Billy Butler of BBC Merseyside, Phil Easton of Radio City, Bob Mitchell a songwriter who had connections with Mountain Records and me. That night was the first time I saw Marseille, a five piece rock band that really did look the part: Keith Knowles, Drums, Steve Dinwoodie, Bass, Andy Charters, Guitar, Neil Buchanan, Guitar and Paul Dale, vocals. They played a great set and finished with a song called 'Do it The French Way', which sounded like a hit record straight off. Marseille won the first heat and went through to the quarter final; I think we all thought on the panel that we had already found something special. After that night I became firm friends with Bob Mitchell and as our friendship grew I would become drawn into Mountain Records. Marseille walked through the quarter finals again in Liverpool and during these weeks Bob Mitchell and I thought they could become an album selling rock band. Although we didn't know it at the time, MCA were beginning to get cold feet and Bob had started to talk to me about Mountain records, telling me that they were interested in Marseille. As I had become good friends with the band and believed in them, Bob arranged for me to meet Derek Nicol, owner of Mountain.

Mountain Records had grown from a management company into a record label. They had managed The Sensational Alex Harvey Band and Nazareth to worldwide success and then built the label around those artists. Derek Nicol knew what he was doing with rock bands, he was a tough Scotsman and had seen and done it all rising from small clubs in Scotland to worldwide tours. Knowing the type of label MCA was and understanding Mountain, I knew Marseille were better suited to Mountain, however, my loyalty had to be with MCA. Marseille trusted my judgment, I advised them just to keep winning in the competition and all would work out. Bob Mitchell and Derek Nicol were then constantly on my case to get the band. Fate eventually took its course when MCA made me redundant, Marseille came second at Wembley, the winners signed to MCA on a reduced deal, as MCA really wanted out of it, and Mountain signed Marseille.

During the next eighteen months I would spend a lot of my time on tour with Marseille. We started in some clubs and then toured their songs, supporting Gillan, White Snake and Nazareth. One night, after playing the 76 club in Burton-on-Trent, I was going back to Walsall and the boys back to Liverpool, so they followed me in the van back to the M6 service station for a two in the morning egg and chips. We arrived cursing Burton-on-Trent to an empty service café and ordered. Within five minutes another band arrived and ordered.

'Where have you played?'

'A toilet in Burton-on-Trent.'

'Where's that?' came the American drawl, 'Can we sit with you?'

'Yeh, no problem.'

The band was in from America and promoting their first single in the midst of the cold English winter. It would go on to be a No 2 single in the UK just a few weeks later and the band would become household names. Back then, en route in the middle of the night to London, they were more worried about getting warm, eating egg and chips and forgetting some toilet club in Manchester.

The single was 'Denis' (a.k.a. Denis Denee) and the band, Blondie. We ate together for an hour and Debbie Harry sat almost opposite me, a John Lennon cap pulled down almost to her eyes. She was very quiet, completely exhausted and cold. Even at that time and having had a long and arduous day Debbie had something – a real presence, pretty, blonde hair sprouting from under the cap, little make-up, and an amazing facial bone structure. We liked all of them in the band. We wished each other all the best and hoped we would meet again on *Top Of The Pops*; they were only weeks away from achieving that performance.

A flirt with EMI:

I had decided that I wanted to find a couple of bands, manage them, direct them on songwriting and recording and try to get a hit record. I figured I knew all the radio, press and TV people and that would be a way of obtaining exposure and moving forward. My pal, Don Evitts, ex of Pinnacle Records, had been thinking along the same lines and so we were talking about working closely together. Our discussions went on for a few months while we went to club after club searching for possible bands to work with.

Mr. Moon's was working fine for me and Dave Possall started upping my evenings at the club, hoping I would not return to working with record companies and would just work with him. At the time I was thankful he just upped the work, exactly at the right time. Disillusioned by MCA, I was not keen on working for anyone else full-time, and then just as I had made the decision not to, the phone rang and it was Roger Upright of EMI Records. Roger wanted me to join EMI and work on his sales team visiting record stores all around Birmingham, promoting to the stores and then taking orders for the records that were selling. This was definitely not a team of salesmen, he said, but of promotion men. Promoters to radio and TV in those days did not visit record stores, there was some snobbery: the record stores were for salesmen, whereas the radio stations were for promoters and artists. In any case, I explained to Roger that I really did not see my future working for a record label full time, I was disillusioned after MCA and thought the best way forward was to become a manager, find some artists and coach them with the knowledge I had gained so far, then make records and either sell the records to a label or start a small label. Roger felt this was a good opportunity to begin with EMI and if I helped with the launch of this new styled team he would then help me move within EMI to work in an area that would be better suited to my design for my future. He did a good job turning round my fears – I drove to London to discuss the situation further at the EMI office and this time I didn't need to visit the Beatles stairwell.

The office was buzzing at EMI, they had a lot of hit records that just kept on coming from all their various labels both here and in America. I still didn't really want to visit eight to ten record stores a day around the Midlands, so we agreed that I would do the job for three months and then we would review the situation.

I was flattered that EMI were so determined that I should join them, but right from the off I was uncomfortable. I had never worked for such a large and impersonal company. After a couple of days on the road I knew I had made a mistake, this really was not for me. Although Roger had tried to make his group resemble a promotional team, it was just a glorified salesman's job. I believe Roger had seen the future and was heading in the right direction of what was to come in the record business, but he had not been able to go the whole way and had somehow got caught in the middle. I had, however, committed to at least three months and would have seen it through, but circumstances changed. In my second week Roger Upright was fired and replaced by Pete Rezon. It turned out that he and I got on well, but I had made up my mind, I was off. I agreed to call on a percentage of the stores, just the main ones Pete needed covering over the next four weeks until he found a replacement. I think, because we were so honest with each other on that first day, over the next fifteen to twenty years, when our paths crossed, we always had a warm and friendly chat.

Record Sales – an innovative company:

Only having to work part time for EMI for the next four weeks enabled me to start organising other things. I was still doing gigs at Mr. Moons and meanwhile Don Evitts and I were out looking for bands to invest our time. During the course of the year we found two we felt we could move forward with: a Birmingham group called Video and a Liverpool band titled Eat at Joe's – more about them a little later. Meanwhile, I received a phone call from the radio promoter Lou Goodridge who told me she was now working for a promotion company called Record Sales. They worked independently for any record label that wanted to hire them, they had an eighteen strong team and Lou said she really enjoyed working with them. Would I like to join and help her run the radio team? I told Lou I was not interested in working full time, I was starting a management company, working with Mountain records and still DJing, so I could only work maybe two or three days a week. Lou said the owners Richard Jakobowski and Alan Wade knew of me and were really keen that I should join, so believed I could make a deal however I wished. I also suggested I would not work at store level, it was radio or not at all.

Off I went to London to meet Richard and Alan, both of whom I liked. They were operating the company more or less out of a corridor at 115 Parkway, Regents Park. It may only have been a corridor but the place was buzzing. There were records everywhere, and they had hit upon an idea that would eventually change the way records were promoted at store level – it would be an integral part of the industry for the next twenty years. As I walked into the chaos that day in September 1978 I was excited about what I had seen. Richard and Alan had big plans and believed in what they were doing, their passion was undeniable and it was mixed in with fun and humour. I explained my past and where I was, how I saw the future in my own management first and then a label, and they too wanted to go that route, but coupled with a strong promotion force that could deliver their own records while working for all the other record companies. It was music to my ears. Sixteen of the company's representatives called on stores and radio stations around the country, Alan and Richard took care of the clients and the store promotions, and Lou and I would take care of the radio side, promoting and collecting the information and then reporting to Alan and Richard and increasingly the clients.

Record Sales' original idea was brilliant: sixteen reps on the road all over the country, each calling on thirty to forty stores a week and the local radio stations. At that time the record charts were compiled by a 'book system' and only from independent retailers. Hence, when a record was sold the dealer would write the number of the record in a book and at the end of Saturday after a week's sales those books would be sent to London. All the numbers of sales would be added up and then on Tuesday the chart would be published based on those numbers. Not a sophisticated system, most record companies at the time concentrated only on radio, TV and press promotions and the stores were just serviced by salesmen who would take orders and replenish stock to accommodate demand. The stores that were on the 'book system' were supposed to be a secret in those naïve days, but the dealers who were on the system needed the book by the till to register the sales and so it was quite easy to find out who was and was not on the system.

Record Sales had painstakingly been around the country and visited all record stores. They found a definitive list of dealers on the 'book' and these became the only stores they visited. The distribution of records to stores in those days was by order only, therefore, if a dealer did not order your record the public were not at risk of buying it. Being such a fast moving industry with a hundred releases a week, if you missed those early sales that gave a record momentum, your record was lost and over.

Record Sales convinced the record companies, starting with the independents, to give them fifteen hundred records they would supply free to the dealers, and this meant three records per store to all the 'book' or 'chart return' stores. This did two things: i) your record was in exactly the right place and if a sale occurred it registered for the chart; ii) the public got wise very quickly and if they knew a store that was more likely to have the record they went there first, so it drove public traffic into the 'chart return' stores. This made the dealer incredibly happy, with more punters and free records that they could sell at full price. Record Sales began to be welcomed everywhere. If local airplay was achieved, no matter how small, it would drive those few copies out of the 'chart return' stores and if by magic it appeared on the lower reaches of the Top 75 national chart, all of a sudden, your record was moving with no wastage of sales in non-'chart return' stores. Brilliant. Excited, you bet I was.

The representatives were not really record company people, they came from management, publishing and stores. Most had probably applied to work for record companies but had not succeeded. One thing was for sure, they all loved music and records, the company gave them a route into the record business and they were taking it with both hands. People like Paddy O'Connell in Scotland, George Carr in the North-East who was the manager of the band Prelude, and Paul Birch in the West Midlands, would go on to run agencies and have several record labels. Steve Sheen and Paul Stephens in London, Keith Connor in the North-West, and John Payne in Brighton were a few of that original team that changed the industry. I loved their enthusiasm and was pleased to be with them when I joined Record Sales.

DJing – the Twilight Zone:

I was beginning to be disillusioned with my DJ career. The club work was still great, entertaining and financially rewarding, but no matter how I tried I could not get that show on radio. I had been trained on the desk at Beacon Radio and for a while was close to achieving the goal, doing voice-overs for adverts and almost 'filling in' on air, but it had not happened. That, coupled with an increasing desire to play record companies, made my decision to leave Hospital Radio Stafford and so, on Sunday 17th September 1978, I laid down the HRS headphones, sadly, for the final time. Anton Emery would take over the show and I would return to that building to be interviewed twenty nine years later by the Station Manager – Anton Emery.

Mother was quite happy at this stage about her son's activities. I received major brownie points for working incredibly hard at all sorts of jobs to do with records and never giving in, no matter what. Jonathan King would help me no end with dear old Mom, even though he didn't know it. Jonathan was a celebrity at the time having hit records and appearing on lots of TV shows, and Record Sales delivered him a hit with 'One For You, One For Me', which was in the Top 10 in October 1978. Jonathan, he of boundless energy, would phone all the team at night and 'gee' them up to work on his record. Jonathan phoned Regina Drive and Mom answered. He chatted with her for a while and when I arrived home later Mom was all over the place. 'Steve I've been talking to Jonathan King, he phoned here for you, what a nice man.' Mom thought I was on my way; celebrities were phoning up, this Record Sales must be OK. Mom was still looking for an apartment for me and I was only months away from getting the boot out of the nest.

On the DJ front, out of the blue came a new offer from Gerry Foley, ex-manager of Chaplin's. He had been offered a club to run in Weston Super Mare, and Gerry asked if I'd come down to play weekends, Friday and Saturday, for him. So, I left Mr. Moon's after some great times and opened at Sloopy's, Weston Super Mare on 30th November 1978. We ripped that opening night with four hundred people and the place was rocking. I began with the 12-inch LP version of 'Can You

Feel The Force' by my old friends The Real Thing: there is a long and complicated introduction to the song on the full version, but when the drums and horns sound off really loud to kick the groove in, there is amazing attack. During the introduction people were just standing around and we made a marvellous effect with the lights, but then when the groove kicked in the audience could not wait to get on the dance floor. I then mixed that with a Boney M 12-inch LP and it was game over – four continuous hours of great sounds. I didn't know it that night, but a few months later at Sloopy's in Weston Super Mare I would play my last ever DJ gig.

Record Sales – hit machine:

1978 was coming to a close and after the stability of the first six months at MCA, the second six months had been constant change at Record Sales. We even achieved some obscure hit singles which helped promote our image as hit makers. Sally Oldfield, sister of Mike, had her one and only hit with us, a song called 'Mirrors' on Bronze Records. I did a few interviews on radio with Sally, who was a strange one. The interviewers and I had no idea what she was talking about most of the time – a straight 'What's your favourite colour?' would turn into a long speech about the universe. We also achieved hits with Lindisfarne, who were a truly great folk-rock band, hitting with 'Run For Home' and 'Juke Box Gypsy', and we were really delighted with two obscure hits we had with Logo Records. We did exceptionally well on radio with these two singles almost immediately after I arrived at Record Sales and not least because in those days radio stations would take a bit more of a chance and allow a little more fun for everyone than they do today. The Streetband were a very good group and their lead singer Paul Young would find fame a few years later as a solo act, but when we first went to radio with a song from them titled 'Hold On', we were getting nowhere. However, after recording the single, the band had messed around in the studio and come up with a track called 'Toast', which we loved playing in the office. As 'Hold On' wasn't going anywhere, we played 'Toast' to a few DJs who agreed to give it just an occasional spin. But, from acorns do oak trees grow and the public embraced 'Toast' giving us a Top 20 record. Paul Young who was already a great singer back then, took it all in his stride – he and the band were a little upset that after all those years of gigging and becoming a marvellous band success had come with a novelty record, but that was the way it was and they just got on with it. Paul was a down to earth lad and I was delighted years later that he became a huge success.

The other obscure hit, 'Car 67' by Driver 67 was another 'off the wall' single when, again, only the odd play here and there led the public to embrace the record and, again, we ended up in the Top 10. These unfashionable, oddball records would build the reputation of Record Sales and catapult us into the area of mainstream record companies who wanted to get in on the action. Logo Records' General Manager was to become a lifelong friend and we would work together a lot of times over the next thirty years – he was the one and only, Keith Peacock.

Meanwhile, Don Evitts and I formed our management company in November and the bands Video and Eat at Joe's signed their contracts with us. We were getting ready to record them. At the same time, Sloopy's in Weston arranged that I was hired at Sloopys in Birmingham and at the end of the year my diary was full of well paid gigs. After the sudden MCA experience, I had made it through the year as a freelance independent and was still in the business, excited and passionate about what would come in 1979.

Stepping Out:

Record Sales was a vibrant place. The constant banter and belief that we were doing something different made us completely unaware of the cramped workspace we had. We moved to 72 Newman Street in February, which was a little better, but was still only a three room operation. The off the wall hits in late 1978 had registered at all the major record labels and the phone was now constantly ringing. Alan and Richard were selling our radio operation on the back of Lou Goodridge and my name and if any record company checked across the country with radio stations they would all know one of us or both. There were still a few radio pluggers and the ones that had been there from the start were held in high regard.

We started to develop relationships with all the record companies and started to be successful with a multitude of artists: Paul Stanley of Kiss working on his solo singles, dance records that are still played today, 'Shame' by Evelyn 'Champagne' King, the No 1 classic 'I Will Survive' from Gloria Gaynor, the Odyssey Top 5 single 'Native New Yorker', The Jacksons' 'Even Though You're Gone', Johnny 'Guitar 'Watson's 'A Real Mother For Ya', Phil Lynott and my old friend Gary Moore's 'Parisian Walkways', Eddie and the Hot Rods' 'Do Anything You Wanna Do' – and not forgetting The Kinks, Phil Hurtt, 'The Dr Who Theme' and even Bernie Flint, the Opportunity Knocks winner. The records were so diverse that I loved every minute of it all and indeed the theme of the company was 'The Hits Just Keep On Coming' and 'It's Not Easy Havin' A Good Time.'

I started to deal directly with a lot of the companies and slowly through the year built relationships with everyone while I began to bring in work to the company. If I was in London for two days Richard or Alan would take me with them to the record companies so I could sit in on the meetings and watch how they set up the records and the deals. The other parts of the week were built around visits to radio stations, mainly back in Liverpool and Manchester as Lou was covering the Midlands. This caused me no problem as I would stay overnight in Liverpool and work with Don and Eat at Joe's, as we were either in rehearsal rooms working on new songs or playing local gigs.

Eat at Joe's, when Don and I signed them, were a five piece band: Colin Frost, guitar and writer and leader of the band, Les Rogers on fretless bass and violin, Derek Lovelady 'Degs' on Fender Rhodes, a fill in drummer, various when we gigged and Joanne Ellis on vocals. This band were all great players and Colin was a talented writer with an abundance of songs that, as his confidence grew, would keep coming at an alarming rate. What's more, he discarded many of his ideas and only presented the best ones. In terms of style, they came from Steely Dan, Joni Mitchell and James Taylor, touched with guitar chords from Lee Ritenore and Larry Carlton. They were different, but very good and did deliver choruses, while Joanne gave them a commercial look. Their audience was certainly growing around Liverpool.

Don and I set about working on the show and as we got to know the songs and watch the gigs, we rearranged the set, dropped some songs and put in new ones while we generally tightened up the show. We then spoke to the band about rearranging some of the songs, which we did by choosing songs from my now vast record collection and spending afternoons playing them and discussing why they were successful and attractive. If you manage a band it is your responsibility to move them forward – this involves instruments, backline amplifiers, transport, dealing with agents to get the gigs and club owners to get the money, and topping up living expenses. And for recordings, it means choosing the songs to record, booking studios, finding engineers, and organising the breaks and the food – all to get what you want coming back though the speakers and, back in those days, onto tape.

Don and I were further ahead with the Birmingham band Video. They were a six piece group with two guitars, bass, drums, keyboards and, again, a girl singer, Jayni. Don was really the driving force behind the first single we would produce, he came up with a song 'Just Might Happen Again', which had all the hallmarks of a hit tune and was definitely of the day. That style was happening then – guitar driven pop songs with groups now evolving from the thrashing aggression of punk. Punk had changed the business, but now, after bands had established the new market of youth, they had to take it somewhere. In pursuing that, they were returning to better structured songs and more organised content, though with raw backing vocals and softening the delivery by adding keyboards. In terms of music, in the 1979 marketplace, it was a logical move and with Video we tried to ride alongside that musical movement.

The first record I ever produced:

Don had a friend, Brian Hutch, who owned Berry Street Studios in London. Brian was an ex-record man at Warner Brothers, and we arranged with him what they call 'downtime' in the studio: that is, when the studio is not booked, you can pay a nominal fee, pay the engineer and record for a fraction of the cost. Don and I were paying for everything so we had to keep it tight, this was money earned from many miles on the motorways, endless tours, radio and TV stations and, on my part, many nights in nightclubs playing until two in the morning. We recorded on the 6th and 7th of January, the 'A' side 'Just Might Happen Again' and a Jayni and Bob Monk song 'Who The Hell Are You' for the 'B' side. We all enjoyed the days, exhausting as they were – up early in London by 9.00am, breakfast, set-up in the studio, mike up the drums (which takes forever), balance the guitars, bass and keyboards and eventually start to record. Dave Hunt engineered and Don and I made our first recording production, which in itself was a great moment – someday soon it would even be a record.

I returned home that weekend feeling that all that effort to promote records for companies, do all that touring and deal with all those artists, had finally put me on what I thought to be the right path. I felt I had enough knowledge to pull through and certainly more knowledge than some managers I had met with up-and-coming bands. I felt there was a chance. I had great confidence in Don, he was not a musician, but had a great ear for songs. On top of that he was a good lad, great company, always pulling jokes, winding up and generally enjoying life around the work.

A new consciousness:

The DJ gigs were still coming in Weston Super Mare, but the DJ career was beginning to lose its appeal to me and also the clubs were changing and adapting to new sounds. I was beginning to fall off the scene. I began to listen to records in a different way: instead of listening to see how I could work them into my DJ set, I began looking deeper into what made the record sound great and how might that have been recorded. To do that, I needed to sit and concentrate and not be worrying about cueing the next record or finding it in my box, dealing with requests and working them into the set at the right time. I was becoming hooked on the business of records and just playing them didn't 'cut the mustard' anymore. It was still fun, but the joy was beginning to fade.

Don, through his songwriting, knew someone at LWT who were filming a new comedy series in front of a live audience with, the then very popular, Maureen Lipman, a show called *Agony*. Maureen comes home one day to find a band rehearsing in her lounge – a three piece set-up, all boys. It sounded just like a job for Col, Les and Degs, in which case, Eat At Joe's would be on television and paid well. We told the boys, they were up for it and off we went to LWT. The three lads became one-day thespians and Maureen Lipman was a lovely host.

1979 was a great learning experience in terms of being a manager and record producer. Eat at Joe's and Video were constantly recording demo's as we searched for tracks that could become singles and albums. They also gigged every week and were in rehearsals at least twice a week. Slowly we were getting the bands ready to go and sign to a record company and in the summer we had our first attempt at obtaining deals for our groups. As always, something happens, and Eat at Joe's vocalist Joanne was about to leave the band – we believed it was envy on Colin's part, as he owned the band and Joanne was always in the limelight with the public. So, Eat at Joe's became a four piece band and we decided to look to record Joanne as a solo artist. Colin took over the vocals and although he was a decent singer, something was forever lost in Joanne's departure. Don wanted to drop the band because of this, but I was very into the 'Joe's' sound and wanted to give the boys a chance. This would cause problems between Don and me further down the line.

My DJ career was now to come to its end – on 28th April 1979. Sloopy's in Weston Super Mare had been very successful in the time I had played there and the crowds were still at their maximum of four hundred people, but Gerry and Steve were falling out with the owners and I was now being booked by the owners, not Gerry. I could tell it was only a matter of time before Gerry and Steve would leave and their presence was a major part of the attraction to me of playing in Weston. When I finished at the club on Saturday the 28th, I was due to return at the end of May, but that never happened as Gerry and Steve left at the start of May and I decided it was time for me to go too. I had enjoyed being a club DJ, and although DJs today have a 'medallion man' image and are sometimes thought of as not being that bright, back then, we were entertainers, speaking after every record, communicating with the crowd and leading the ensemble. Today, there is little communication, just mixing and scratching, and I believe the art of the DJ entertainer is committed to history.

Pete Waterman has always maintained that the reason he and I were successful in the music business was that we spent so much time in clubs in our youth playing records. The job taught us instinctively what record would work and sell and what record would not. I believe what he believes is true, I also believe that to be in the record business and be successful you need to have been a musician and worked on stage, a DJ in the clubs controlling a crowd or worked in a record store selling to the public. That interaction teaches you more about what will appeal and sell than anything else and one thing is for sure: if you want to be exceptional in the record business you can't learn it at college.

The summer of '79 rolled in and I also decided it would be my last season as a broadcaster at Walsall Football Club. I was sad to leave Walsall, but with recording and rehearsing our bands and 'downtime' in the studios mainly available at the weekends, I had to prioritize. I would continue going to Walsall Football Club games to this day, season after season, and I still spent a lot of time at the club as my great friendship with Tom Edmunds grew. The players, especially the reserves, at the time, were great friends of mine, and I played a few games and socialized with them when possible. They would go on to have long professional careers – Ron Green, Ian Paul, Kenny Mower, John Horne, Kelvin Clarke, Mark Rees, Don Penn, David Preece and Paul Waddington, along with first teamers Brian Caswell, Mick Kearns, Alan Birch, Alun Evans, Roy McDonough, Jeff King and Alan Buckley.

The dream of becoming a broadcaster was now on the wane. All these years later I still harbour thoughts of being on the radio, playing records, talking about the day's matters and interviewing guests. I see it as a night-time show and I would certainly have a lot of famous people that would come along, talk and play some records. That may never happen, but I still feel good that it was my first love and some of that love remains to this day.

Making Deals:

Record Sales were building hit record after hit record, all of which I became involved in, and the summer season brought hits with The Electric Light Orchestra's 'The Diary Of Horace Wimp', 'Don't Bring Me Down' and 'Last Train To London', The Tourists' 'I Only Wanna Be With You', Bob Seger's 'We've Got Tonight', The Doobie Brothers' 'What A Fool Believes', Steely Dan's 'Rikki Don't Loose That Number' and hits for Nick Lowe, The Members, The Undertones, Motorhead, Lene Lovitch and even, Kenny Rogers. I was getting to know everyone at almost all the labels and I believed this would be key when we were ready to sell our acts to the labels. In working with Barn and Cheapskate Records, I met Chas Chandler, legendary bassist with The Animals and manager of Jimi Hendrix and Slade. Chas now owned Portland Studios and would give me great support in the following year. I also reassociated with Noddy Holder in promoting new Slade releases and got to know Jimmy Lea, Don Powell and Dave Hill well.

During Record Sales' run of hits with Logo Records, my friendship with Keith Peacock had grown and I became his Record Sales contact. I told Keith that I was making records and he asked to listen to our first set of demo's with Video. Keith instantly liked 'Just Might Happen Again', and after several meetings we signed the band to Logo Records on a singles deal, with an option for an album if successful. It was Don's and my first attempt and we had got off to a flyer. Alan Wade, at Record sales, was supportive and we made a deal with the company to promote the single at a reduced rate for Logo. Build up now began. We increased our gigs around the Midlands and the odd one in London to help with awareness and Don and I used all our contacts at radio and TV to get the promotion going. I worked well with Keith at Logo and began to understand the machinery involved in setting up a record from scratch: the master tapes, cutting the single so it could be pressed onto vinyl, the label copy or information, the co-ordination of the photos and information for the picture bag, the posters, the adverts, the promo copies, the finished stock, the co-ordination and distribution of stock to the distributor, the sales of records and promotion to BBC Radio One, commercial radio, TV, press and all the people that are involved. It was the first time I had been involved in that way from beginning to end, and I experienced how every day a new problem was born and how the entire operation was under an intense time structure. Don and I were delighted, it seemed we were getting somewhere, and our first release was scheduled for 24th August 1979. The band started to play better gigs as their confidence grew from feeling like a recording band, with a record coming out and demand coming in for interviews.

The build up to release was reasonably good, but after being involved in so many records I knew it was not good enough. The plays on radio were spasmodic, we got all the evening play, but this was a commercial record and if you didn't receive daytime airplay you could not sell enough copies to break the record into the Top 75 singles chart, which you needed, to breed more confidence and give you more time to get more airplay and move the record up inside the Top 75. 'Just Might Happen Again' by Video on Logo Records charted outside the Top 75 at No 83 and although we tried for a couple of weeks to push the record forward it just could not crack the Top 75. It was to be Video's only release and would also be the only single Don and I would put out together, yet at that time, it felt like the start of things to come. Logo Records subsequently declined the option to record a further single and the deal was over by November.

Marseille were now coming towards the end of their album with Mountain Records and were getting in touch far more often as they asked what I thought about certain situations that would arise. Derek Nicol and the General Manager at Mountain Records, Jim White, kept me involved with anything and everything to do with Marseille and especially the tracks that would be included on the album, singles choices and touring. I brought Record Sales in to do promotion for them and began to set up essentials for the next stage of Marseille's career. I had come a long way with them and my belief that one day they would become a major selling rock band encouraged Mountain Records to make an approach to me. As well as Marseille, they had a new Nazareth album nearing completion which had to be a big seller to guarantee the forward movement of the company, and so Jim White asked me to join them and take care of the promotion and tour with both Marseille and Nazareth, so that both acts would have their best possible backup in their shot at success. I was happy at Record Sales and they were a big part of the promotion that would assist both Marseille and Nazareth, so there was no way I could upset Richard or Alan. I said I would think about it.

There was a lot to consider: Video, Eat at Joe's, Don Evitts, Record Sales, and going on tour again – but – the magic pronouncement from Jim, that actually would prove to be not entirely true, was that I would be able to sign acts to Mountain and help build the label, while working especially on Marseille, Nazareth and another signing, Voyager. I went back to Birmingham and spoke with Don who thought it may work out for us and help us in putting out our own records; also, if I was a major part of the label and in control of sales and promotion, it could be a winner. Over the next couple of weeks we made the decision that Don would cover for me when I was on tour with our management company and I would firm up the ability to sign artists to Mountain and see where it took us. All went well on my next visit to Mountain and we were able to make a deal in our belief that putting together the company's ability in touring and my knowledge of promotion and sales could work all the way round.

In several discussions with Alan Wade during October I handled the delicate situation of leaving Record Sales, which they did not want me to do. Alan and I had become good friends and I had done a good job in raising the company's profile, both in terms of promotion through radio and TV and also, in respect of its position with the record companies, with whom I had very good relationships. I guaranteed the Mountain Record's singles and albums for Record Sales to promote and would still be in touch on a daily basis, so if there was a problem with the radio promotion I could step in and help. I slowly began to ease myself out of Record Sales and I officially started working for Mountain Records on 1st November 1979; this upped the pace again in my life and increased the days I spent in London. The work was intense: Marseille single, album, club tour and Gillan support tour; Nazareth single on 28th December with the album to follow on 1st February and then a UK and worldwide tour; a Voyager single at the end of January and the album to follow at the end of February. Everything Mountain had on the books was being released and toured in the coming four months.

Marseille started the club tour in Swansea at The Circles Club on a cold winter's night. We were all excited at being back on the road and there was a good crowd. I didn't attend all the Marseille dates as there was much to set up: records to all the radio stations, co-ordinating Record Sales, working on Nazareth and Voyager, plus the gigs with Video around Birmingham and Eat at Joes in Liverpool. I also had to finish some work with Record Sales: Chas Chandler and Slade were out on tour and I had committed to going on the road and handling the promotion for them on behalf of Record Sales. This was all an extremely demanding schedule, but at least I was back where I thought I should be – working with artists.

I had a great time being part of the Slade tour, they were local heroes to me and, after all those years on the road, they were a polished rock band with a catalogue of hits in the show. The year ended with a few more Marseille dates with Gillan and a few Eat at Joe's dates around Liverpool and Manchester. But our management company finished in not such good shape after originally showing so much promise. Don was unhappy with the Eat at Joe's situation, believing that Joanne was the key to their success. Video were also a disappointment in getting signed and then losing the deal, but Don felt they were a better bet than Eat at Joe's. I disagreed.

My days were now filled with Mountain Records, Record Sales and keeping Eat at Joe's moving forward, while Don spent his time looking for Video's next single and working with Joanne on some new songs. Don and I were true friends, but looking back now I see the cracks that were beginning to appear in our management company and how we were both seeing a different route for the future.

The New Year was going to be busy from the off in January, February and March and I spent the Christmas and New Year period at an Eat at Joe's gig, having festive celebrations at home and with Sue and taking a trip to see Blondie at De Montfort Hall, Leicester, just for old time's sake. They had come a long way since The Hilton Services on the M6.

CHAPTER 9

CONSTANT CHANGE AND CONSTANT
DEVELOPMENT: 1980 AND 1981

The continual learning curve:

Sometimes in life it's one step forward and two steps back. A career in the record business will always be that way, so if you are thinking of dedicating your life to records, songs and artists you will have to get used to that rhythm and accept it. When I was going through it, I didn't realise it and got through it all by 'staying in the moment' and trying to make the best decision possible with the facts as they lay.

January 1980 started quickly with a Record Sales conference at the Holiday Inn at Heathrow on the 3rd. I was always warmly received by everyone at Record Sales and I was still one of the team even though I had left my position and was working full time at Mountain. Jim White and Derek Nicol gave me full support in setting-up our records for promotion. Record Sales were about to start work on the Marseille single 'Kites' and Alan and Richard also knew that Voyager and Nazareth would be on their schedule in the coming couple of months. I had gone from employee to client, but I was always interested in what was happing record-wise with the team.

Eat at Joe's were recording and I spent many days in the studio working on Colin's songs 'Watch Out Brother', 'Dig It', 'Silly Murders' and 'What Do You Expect?' Don was still involved at this point, but just a few weeks later he quit the Eat At Joe's camp, the choice of single being the big issue. Don was convinced that 'What Do You Expect?' was the commercial chance whereas the band were committed to 'Watch Out Brother.' I felt all the discussions and arguments were premature. We needed to achieve interest from record companies so I was more interested in seeing if these songs could get the band a deal. During that journey the single would move itself forward whatever its final outcome – I would worry about it later. My viewpoint did not please Don as he wanted my undivided support and his argument with the band, along with Joanne leaving, was all too much for him: in his mind it was too many negatives.

So, I was now on my own, taking meetings with several record companies to try and obtain a deal for Eat At Joe's. Most were unsuccessful, and when Mountain decided not to sign them I was particularly disappointed, considering I had already provided them with Marseille and thought we had agreed I would bring new artists to the label. A & R men from many record companies did make a journey north to see the group play gigs, but I realised now, that to obtain a commitment from a record company, Eat At Joe's, being an album band rather than an explosive hit-single band, would first have to attain on-going success by building up their audience with constant gigs. I already knew at this time that the essence of this business was about sustaining a loyal fan base that would buy album after album. You could not achieve that without a long apprenticeship in clubs and university gigs.

Meanwhile, with Don's outlook that our attentions should now be concentrated on Joanne as a solo artist and on Video, I was forced to review our management company, which I really did not want to do, as my great friendship with Don was intertwined within it. After a couple of weeks, I made my decision. I still believed that Eat at Joe's were a great band, I thought they were different and had a great songwriter within their ranks. I just could not let go of them after all the work we had put in. So, gently and delicately Don and I parted, but we did not lose our longstanding friendship. Don took Video and Joanne and I continued alone with Eat At Joe's. We sold the car we owned jointly and paid up any debts on a 50-50 basis. It was all put to bed on 1st March 1980. As split ups go, this was calm and protective of a true friendship and handled as gentlemen.

Touring with Nazareth:

The promotion of an upcoming tour by Nazareth had been on my agenda for the whole of February and now, in March, I was with them on the tour. Nazareth was Mountain's biggest earner and this tour had to be very successful for the health of the label. *Malice In Wonderland* was the title of the album dreamed up by drummer Darrel Sweet. The band were spectacular live and they had already been on the road for years playing with perfect Rock 'n' Roll aggression. Dan McCafferty was on vocals, the brilliant guitarists were Manny Charlton and Zal Cleminson and the solid Pete Agnew was on bass. Jeff Baxter, ex of Steely Dan, had produced a fantastic album which would catapult the band into big arenas around the world. On the tour, I would take mainly Dan, but occasionally Zal and Manny, for interviews in each town that we performed in. It was well and truly back to Rock 'n' Roll touring.

We opened at the East Anglia University and I did local interviews with Manny and Zal, then on to Dunstable Civic Centre before heading north to the Newcastle Mayfair. The band had spent their whole life playing gigs and were on a constant cycle of gigs, rest, record, tour, gigs, rest, record and tour again. In the early Eighties this constant movement led a lot of bands to use all sorts of drugs to help them cope with their unusual way of life. The knowledge that has since developed over a long period of time was not available then and drug and alcohol use was perceived to be OK, as long as it helped to get the job done and kept the band on the road. The tours were like a circus travelling daily from town to town and you lived in your own bubble. As I spent only a month on tour at a time I never really lost my involvement outside of the bubble: I would be out of it for some time after a month, but the boys in the band only spent a few weeks each year out of the touring bubble and that became their main life.

On the night in Newcastle Pete Agnew was playing the bass perfectly, under the influence of a good session. One step too far backwards and he suddenly disappeared. He fell four feet from the back of the stage and landed on his back, but he went on playing. Laying there, he hardly missed a note. The crew grabbed him and lifted him back onto the stage and in great pain he played on. After the gig the left leg of his trousers was covered in blood – as he fell he had ripped the skin off from his ankle to his knee. We took him to hospital, where they dressed the leg that was now causing excruciating pain both from the injury and the drugs wearing off. The hospital gave him some painkilling drugs, which Pete loved, and the following morning we were off on the road again.

After the traditional end of tour night at London's Hammersmith Odeon, which spawned the Rock 'n' Roll mantra No Sleep Till Hammersmith; we were all delighted with the great success of the entire Nazareth tour. The album would go on to be an even bigger success and when the band went to America it became a big breakthrough record for them and took them on to bigger venues and much more success. I liked the boys, they were good, hard-working musicians, they made me feel part of it all, and they did everything that was asked of them. Hopefully they remember me as an alright guy and a professional.

Nothing in life stays the same:

Straight off the tour, I came back into the office, immediately setting up the Voyager release for Mountain and meeting at Logo Records and RCA Records on behalf of Eat at Joe's. Although I liked Jim White at Mountain, he was always a 'bottle of pop': if you shook him, he exploded all over the place, at any time. After Mountain, he would set up a company called Irate Management, which sort of summed it up. Jim decided that, as the promotion had gone so well outside London, I should now become the company's London promotion man as well. I had always resisted becoming a Radio One and London promotion man, I felt once you started doing that it became your life's path and I didn't see my life that way. When I had brought about the hits with Logo Records and signed Video to the label the previous year, Keith Peacock had made a real attempt at persuading me to become their London plugger. I did not want it then and I did not want it now. However, Jim simply insisted. Reluctantly, I agreed to go to Radio One with RCA records plugger Phil Patterson. Without my knowledge, Jim had told RCA that I would be taking over from Phil to promote Mountain Records, licensed to RCA, in London, and all Phil had to do was take me around for a couple of days and introduce me. Phil, a great lad, did as he was asked and I went along with him. In short, I hated it. Radio One producers and the people in the offices in London were all big on themselves. In the Midlands, we have a phrase that sums it up: 'They think their shit doesn't stink.' Well it was certainly not going to be for me, whether Jim White liked it or not, I was not doing that. I told Phil Patterson, 'believe me, I'm not doing it, so the promotion will probably come back to you.' I felt that was fair as Jim had similarly acted without asking me first. This was to be the start of a widening distance between Jim and myself.

We were set with an important schedule for Eat At Joe's in April. We would record for a week at CCS Studios in Manchester, living on kebabs, after which we had a good gig sheet, which included five nights in Blackpool and appearances in Manchester and Liverpool. This would be followed by more record company meetings for me in London. Meanwhile, Mom after looking around for over a year at properties arrived home one day and said 'I've found you a flat.' The following day we went to Arboretum Road, a road that cuts into the park not far from the town centre. The apartment was on the top floor, the second floor, and the large lounge looked out over the Arboretum Lake and bandstand and where the band played on Sunday's in the summer. Kitchen, bathroom and two bedrooms, I loved it – Mom had done a fantastic job in finding the perfect apartment. All those tours and jobs at record companies had somehow paid off, here was a great apartment and I was not going to leave home and live in a bedsit. Addison Cooper and Jesson, the family lawyers, worked out all the paperwork, I provided the money for the deposit and furnishings and Mom spent it on furniture; all the things necessary in the kitchen, beds, towels and everything a Mom knows how to do and things I would not have thought of. I moved a few weeks later and began four happy years in Arboretum Road. A couple of years later Mom was to sell 26 Regina Drive, and already, she was preparing to change her life.

5th April 1980 came and with it my last ever gig as a DJ. My friend, constant supporter and believer John Oebel was to marry Colleen that day and he had always said that when he married I would be the DJ. So it came to pass. The two records he insisted that I played that day were, Thunderclap Newman's 'Something In The Air' and Syl Johnson's 'We Did It', and, whenever I hear them on the radio, they remind me of John. It was a great day, John and Colleen were happy and I was happy for them. Looking back now, this was the only place I could finally lay down the headphones, records and microphone. John had been my greatest friend and supporter from when we were eleven years old: we played all our sport together and sat next to each other in school. We went through our teens together, drank together, smoked together, learned to drive, got our first cars, went to nightclubs for the first time, chased girls together, worked together and it was his 'crossed line' phone call that got my career going. John Oebel is a big part of my history. Tragically, he died in 2002, but he lives on in the minds of his wife and daughters and on the pages of this book. I will always have the greatest respect and love for him. Thanks John, 'Go Johnny Go.'

Plus ça change plus c'est la même chose? Not when you meet a Beatle:

The year of constant change was here. When you have lived for a considerable amount of time, it seems years pass and everything remains at least similar and then all of a sudden everything is in constant change. 1980 was one of those years.

Marseille were back on the road and I accompanied them through a UK tour supporting Whitesnake. David Coverdale was then lead singer and a fine one too, John Lord was on keyboards and they were the two members of Whitesnake I got to know well. They were perfect professionals, the show was perfection, and Coverdale even threw his empty coke can into the audience at the same moment every night – nothing was left to chance.

At the end of the tour the party for the band and crew was to be at Jon Lord's mansion near Reading. Marseille and I were generously invited and off we went there the Saturday after the tour. The house was fantastic, the party just casual, with everyone pleased that the tour was done and had been a success. The boys and I were delighted to be there, we felt like we were part of the Rock 'n' Roll scene. The kitchen had all sorts of food, drink and an abundance of 'jazz cigarettes' for anyone who wanted to partake, and we were given a free run of the house, enabling us to wander from room to room just bumping into people and joining in conversations. On one of my wanders I went down a hall passage and opened a door. Inside were three people I didn't know lying on the floor and someone else sitting in a chair. As I came in everyone turned to look, feeling embarrassed that I had intruded I quickly said sorry and went to close the door and leave. The guy in the chair said 'No problem, you can come in if you like.' Well, I couldn't get in quick enough and immediately sat on the floor with the other three. In the chair was the one and only George Harrison. For a huge Beatles fan like me, it was like meeting God. The other three on the floor were just asking George Beatles questions – 'what was it like when?', 'how did you record that?', etc. There was an endless stream of questions and George was relaxed and up for entertaining and talking about it all. I couldn't believe it was happening and I was there, with George Harrison. Jon Lord told me George lived down the road, and he had said he might just come over later, which thankfully he did. I must have spent 40 minutes listening to George, then he just got up and said, 'Thanks, I enjoyed that – see you around' and off he went. I couldn't wait to see the Marseille boys to tell them of my fortunate moment.

Later in the evening two or three strippers arrived and performed their show in the middle of the living room with everyone standing or sitting in the chairs pushed back to the walls. Midway through, one of the girls made a beeline for George who was sitting in a chair by the fireplace. She rubbed her assets all over him while we did a great rendition of 'She Loves You, Yeh, Yeh, Yeh.' After the show, a little while later, George just disappeared into the night, but it was a night I would always remember.

Back to Record Sales – with a New Label:

At Mountain Records I was beginning to feel strained. I had already decided I was not going to promote to Radio One and, as Marseille were now off the road and I couldn't sign new acts to the label, it seemed it might be time to move on. Record Sales was still doing well and Alan Wade asked if I wanted to come back: Lou Goodridge had left the business and they were looking for a new Head of Promotion. What finally led to me to accept was an unrelated new development that had been brewing with Tom Edmunds of Walsall Football Club, who had over a period of a couple of years become one of my best friends. He had raised a lot of money for the club and had swiftly become a director and, in arranging fundraising, his company, Goldliner, had become involved in a few events related to the music business. We had discussed my ventures and Tom had come along to see Video and Eat at Joe's play. Slowly we began to envisage a label that would release Eat At Joe's records, with Goldliner financing the operation and myself using my contacts and knowledge to set everything up. We agreed that we would start the label on a 50-50 deal and this created an ideal position of strength with which I could then operate at Record Sales. I discussed Alan Wade's offer with him and stipulated my conditions of agreement: I would promote personally to BRMB, Beacon and Central television and manage the other members of the team, and I would have my own records promoted and prioritised when released, for a nominal fee. Alan agreed and asked if I would also help with Record Sales' own artists as they were beginning to sign and record their own acts. So, on 1st May I left Mountain, came back to Record Sales with my new post of Head of Promotion and combined this with setting up Goldliner Records.

More radio stations had been opening steadily all over the UK in the past couple of years and so Record Sales now had a larger area to cover. They had seven other staff promoting nationwide and I covered Birmingham, with trips to the London office. Tom moved his offices to Halesowen in Dudley, so I had my own Goldliner Records office there and could also do the Record Sales job from a Birmingham base. The summer months were spent organising the label and meanwhile Eat at Joe's had been gigging and recording. Within the schedule we had made what would become our first single on Goldliner: 'Watch Out Brother.' Record Sales was busy too, and we had a happy collaboration preparing Goldliner's launch – Lindy, Alan's wife, helped me with getting the labels and sleeves together, and Sue Pearson, who had also joined Record Sales as a highly professional assistant to

Alan and Richard, became a good friend and helped me enormously with both Eat at Joe's and the reporting for Record Sales.

At Record Sales we obtained a No 1 hit with Olivia Newton John and the Electric Light Orchestra's 'Xanadu', we worked with The Police on 'Six Pack' and another No 1, 'Don't Stand So Close To Me', and we had big successes with Justin Hayward's 'Night Flight', Queen's 'Another One Bites The Dust', the final Sex Pistols record 'I'm Not Your Stepping Stone', Slade's 'Slade Alive at Reading', Eddie Grant's Top 10 single 'Do You Feel My Love', made for my old friend Tony Calder, and a really off the wall hit by Splodenessabounds, 'Two Pints Of Lager And A Packet Of Crisps', which became a Top 10 record in June. We also had a No 11 hit with The Regents' '7Teen', which was important as these were our own artists. The single had been put out on Rialto Records, but was owned by Record Sales, and while primarily being Richard's project, it gave all of us faith that we could start having hit records of our own. It definitely made me feel I had made the right moves. Now, as a label owner with a deal at Record Sales, the best promotion company in the UK, maybe just maybe, I could get a hit single for my label and be on my way.

By mid-July, I had physical copies of 'Watch Out Brother' by Eat at Joe's on Goldliner Records. We started promotion with Brian Haynes as our London plugger and Record Sales handling regional radio under my direction. Getting records played on Radio One in those days was unbelievably difficult, in fact, it has been in all the years I have been in the industry. As Radio One is national, they receive every record that is released and a single can usually only be played during the week if it is selected by the music director and his playlist panel. The weekend shows and evening shows used to have a little more available airtime for new releases and if you could get on these shows, which was still difficult, you could get support and have a few 'yes's' in the weekly playlist meeting when your record came up for consideration. Well, Eat At Joe's 'Watch Out Brother' leapt onto the radio as Tommy Vance played it one Saturday afternoon. The record finished and Vance said, 'That is just brilliant, so brilliant I'm going to play it again.' I have never known that happen before or since on Radio One. Slowly, through that first week, we picked up three or four plays and were up for the Thursday playlist meeting. We didn't get on, but the weekend and evening play continued. Then, on Tuesday, Muff Winwood of CBS Records called me and asked me to go in and see him on the Friday when I was in London. I duly went, and Muff said he had heard Eat at Joe's on the radio and wanted to buy the single from me. His first offer was £7,500, but it went to ten thousand before the end of the meeting. I said I would make a decision over the weekend and call him Monday. Tom and I met on the Saturday and as Tom was against selling, come Monday I told Muff Winwood, thanks but no thanks, we were going it alone.

The fickle record business:

As it turned out, despite good early sales taking us up to No 79 on the chart, our problem now was sustaining the airplay and, after an unbelievably good start, 'Watch Out Brother' went no further. We felt, though, that we had illustrated the potential of the band and the label – we had only just fallen short of breaking the Top 75, which in those days, would have breathed confidence and in turn increased the airplay. Tom Edmunds was happy with our first attempt on Goldliner Records, more gigs came in for Eat at Joe's, and I started to plan our next recording session. I had heard from Marseille about Sawmills Recording Studio in Cornwall. It sounded like a special environment in which to create a recording. It was only accessible by boat and, when you were there, you stayed on the complex in wooden chalets around the main house, which included the studio on a lower level. Simon Fraser was to be our engineer for ten days, during which we would work twelve hours a day. This I felt would focus everyone, and it was right, because the band were now ready to go one step further, they and we had confidence from our near miss. We experimented with a cover of Roy Orbison's 'Pretty Woman' and a song Colin had written with a more commercial edge, called 'Swingin' The Lead.' We also worked on 'Man On The Radio' and a Christmas song, all of which we considered possible singles. The idea was to see if when we recorded them one song would rise up and become our next single. It was all quite an experience being out in the middle of nowhere, where the only other way to the studio was to walk down a disused railway track. We only left the place once in the ten days to take a break at the village pub one night, which left a scary walk back down the railway line in the pitch dark. Everybody worked and worked with no real sense of time: sometimes it was four or even five in the morning when we finished, starting again at midday the next day.

We returned from Sawmills with 'Swingin' The Lead' as our second single and I immediately started to prepare to release it in October so as not to lose the momentum we had built so far. I always 'cut' our records from tape onto acetate so they then could be pressed onto vinyl at Portland Studios with Porky Prime Cuts, as he was known, who had cut all the Beatles albums – if his recorded quality was good enough for them it was good enough for us. We had also decided to press on with the album and Portland Studios in London was the chosen location. Chas Chandler owned it and, through my work with Record Sales and Slade, we were now business friends. Chas liked the band and made great deals for us to complete the album, which took the remainder of the year.

The first session at Portland included a Christmas record that Colin had written and we were contemplating just issuing it to keep our name around and get some Christmas plays on radio, so as to help build momentum for the New Year. We didn't expect it to become a hit single, but if it got a few plays and sold a few copies it would make the exercise worthwhile. I worked with the boys on this in the studio and also worked at Record Sales setting up the promotion on 'Swingin'

The Lead.' Radio One did not embrace it, we received only a couple of plays and it was not looking good. The regional pick up on the single was poor too, so I took the decision not to release it, put out the Christmas record and continue recording to start with a new assault in the new year.

The work started all over again to set up the new record, 'Last Year's Resolution.' It did what it was meant to do: without selling many copies it was playlisted on the radio stations' Christmas lists, then known as 'sleigh lists', and we received decent exposure. We did the usual gigs that came with more awareness and started to spread out to York, Birmingham, Wales and London. To play in London in those days was tough, there were queues of bands trying to get a gig in the hope a record company might spot them. We also had a final blast of recording in 1980, making a couple of singles for Neil Rushton, who was still operating his own labels Network, Champagne and 69 Records, and wanted a couple of jazz/ dance type instrumentals. Eat at Joe's always had a passion for that style of music and would warm up by playing in that vein, so I made a deal with Neil to release two singles on his Champagne label: 'Six Nine Shuffle', by Altitude, and 'Rhythms In Blue', by the EAJ Allstars. Both were hits on the dance charts at the beginning of 1981 and we were to start our year off in style.

Reviewing life this Christmas of 1980, the label had come together and I was earning enough money to get me by: less than before, but enough to cover all my expenses and I was doing something I believed in. I was also helping Record Sales with their own recording artists and getting the parts and records together, assisting Alan more and more as Richard was beginning to go on the missing list. It had been a very successful year for Record Sales and Richard had begun to buy flash cars, houses, motorbikes and finally an aeroplane. He was coming into the office later and later after partying night after night. When he was there he did a good job, but he was beginning to be around less and less.

1981 – Promopeople:

Eat at Joe's and I thought this might be the year that it would happen. We set about a recording process that would take us through January and February to finish our debut album. While I was in London I continued with Record Sales, but mainly in the London office. Alan and I were becoming good friends and enjoyed working together and he confided to me that his partnership with Richard was waning. I spoke to Tom Edmunds about the situation and, as he recognised the important work Record Sales had achieved, he began to become interested in working on a new company with Alan. Slowly through January, February and March we had several meetings and discussed what the shape of the new company would be, how it would work and what each of our responsibilities would be. Personally, I was delighted that the new company may get formed: I would be involved from the start and help to build it, but more importantly, Goldliner Records would be able to put out more records, have some input into their promotion and derive benefit from the support of a very large promotion team. At this time, it seemed to me the small 'one man band', Goldliner Records, would be able to compete with much bigger labels and thereby give the Eat At Joe's album its best opportunity for success.

Finally, by the end of March the new company, Promopeople, was formed. Tom Edmunds owned fifty percent, Alan had forty percent, and I was a director owning ten percent. Lindy, Alan's wife, began looking for offices, in due course settling for 9 Paddington Street, W1. The edition of the journal, Record Business, on 27th April 1981 ran a story under the title 'Record Sales duo splits up', stating that a split had occurred between Alan Wade and Richard Jakubowski, resulting in Wade's departure to form his own competitive operation, Promopeople. The first two assignments were to work on the Gem Records single by the UK Subs and 'Dogs Of War' by the Exploited on Secret Records, as well as a deal with MCA Records to promote both Tom Petty and Andrew Lloyd Webber. The new company would be active in sales promotion with a team of eighteen people, but would also offer broader marketing and promotion services with a radio promotion department headed by Steve Jenkins and print services available through Goldliners own printing works.

While this was all going on in London I was in Bristol, Reading and Newcastle recruiting the first of the new reps that would build the eighteen strong team. My most pleasurable moment of recruitment would come in May – Sue Parsons, who had pushed *Music Week* at me in the Graduate Records store in Walsall and said 'You should work for a record company and when you do, get me in', was about to be in. I spoke with Alan and told him we must employ her and so it was with great joy that I could offer Sue the job of Midlands's representative for Promopeople. It had taken me six years to complete the promise I had made to her and I was proud of her as she joined us.

The team was made up of nearly all the Record Sales representatives and our new recruits. Record Sales would close its doors within a month as it was impossible for Richard to recruit a whole new team and Promopeople had experienced reps, was bigger than any other promotion force and had a relationship with the clients that had been built over the past year while Richard was partying. There was no stopping the new company. We also had a new representative for the London area: Shaun King had joined Record Sales to help with the distribution of records to the reps and during my many hours in the office Shaun and I became friends. A great drummer, he had travelled to London from Folkestone for tuition, bitten by the record business and he became a very good rep in the London area.

Eat At Joe's album launch:

The Eat at Joe's album was now complete and ready for release on Goldliner Records. We had toiled to get the album ready for release, but were very happy with the final result and we intended to bring it out in May. The album was entitled

Ghost Hobbies, with 13 tracks, and we began to prepare for release off the back of the single 'To Move Your Feet.'

Colin was interviewed by Melody Maker and they reviewed our progress as follows:

> *Colin Frost, lead vocalist, writer and lead guitarist with Liverpool band Eat at Joe's has every right to be bitter. Despite the release of three excellent but highly underrated singles and a lot of hard work in the studio, Eat at Joe's are a long way from the fame and acclaim they deserve.*

> *Most of the work has gone into their debut album* Ghost Hobbies *available soon on the small Goldliner label. It's a fascinating work, taking cuts like the strong, heartfelt beautifully constructed ballad 'I'm Falling' and mixing it with the endearing studio experiments of 'To Move your Feet' and 'The End.' Then there's the straight commerciality of 'The Man on the Radio' and the unrelenting moodiness and tough riffing of 'Walk on Water.' Variety is definitely a spice used often in the Eat at Joe's kitchen. If you play someone 'God Save America' and then play 'Hungry As I Was' they would not think it was the same band, and that's what Eat at Joe's is. The other cooks at EAJ's are Les Rogers (Bass), Derek Love (Keyboards) and John McQueen (Drums). The current line-up has been together for two and a half years, doing gigs and looking for a deal. The same old story: nobody's interested; the A & R men cannot see their talent and it's left to Goldliner, a company more associated with lottery tickets than record companies, to pick them up and put out the goods. They have three minute pop songs of exquisite beauty, it's an album of substance power and professionalism and you should catch the band live. Come on in – Eat at Joe's have just opened.*

We issued 'To Move Your Feet' as the single and were frustrated yet again: it moved up the chart and stalled again at No 82, just outside the holy grail of the Top 75. After all the belief and hope that 'To Move Your Feet' had shown in the early promotion days of its life this was a bitter blow as it left us with no momentum to launch the album. So, we decided to hold the release and look for another single that would give us the push that we needed for *Ghost Hobbies*.

Once you have to take a step backwards in your release programme, it is always another three months before you can release another single. It would be September before we could bring another single out, so we started gigging and rehearsing again and Colin went back to writing. We needed a sure fire hit, we were running out of time and support, our bill for wages, recording and promoting was growing bigger by the month, our income from gigs was nowhere near covering our expenses, and our income from records was also not enough to make a dent in our recording expenses. Tom stuck with it and we set up two sets of recording sessions, one at Portland studios where we would record 'Don't Run Away.' I called in Steve Colyer, a well known promotion man and producer, who had released records himself and had a big part in David Essex's career. I felt that an outside influence may help the boys next time they were in the studio and we might find that elusive piece of magic. The other set of sessions were scheduled at Sawmills in Cornwall. I felt that the boys deserved one more chance at coming up with another track that might just get us into the Top 75.

Tom and Alan at this time were in daily contact as to how Promopeople was doing, which was well, as the workload was increasing. My role in the company was part time: two and occasionally three days a week – the same as it had been at Record Sales. I was in the office when I was not working with Eat at Joe's, although I still saw the band and the record company as my main priority. Alan had told Tom that he needed me in the office full-time as the workload was too much, he had also said that because we worked together well, he wanted me and would rather not hire anyone else. I also think the failure of 'To Move Your Feet' as a single did not help my cause and so it was Tom who called me to a meeting to discuss my working at Promopeople full-time. I was not in favour of this move, but, in due course, Alan and Tom made me an offer I could not refuse: if I did the job at Promopeople I could run Goldliner Records from the London office and Tom would continue in the short-term to finance the band and our recording. Promopeople would continue to promote my records, I would be paid a wage from Promopeople, which would take my wages out of Goldliner Records and help with reducing the costs and I could also have a car of my choice. I would not have to leave Walsall, a vital matter for me, and so when in London, I would stay either with Alan and Lindy or at the office where a bedroom was set up for me. Soon, I was on my way to London to become a full-time member and second in command at Promopeople.

Promopeople and the heydays of the Independents:

The company was going from strength to strength and quickly. We handled all of K-Tel and Ronco's compilation albums and had many No 1 albums – these were the days before compilations were excluded from the national album chart. Unbelievably, these were also the days before record companies compiled their own catalogues. They would simply license recordings to K-Tel and Ronco, somehow believing it was not the real record business and they needed specialist TV advertisers to compile albums. Promopeople was in the right place, putting compilations into the independent stores, which made their registered sales increase, and we could sell bucket loads off the cars. The TV companies loved us.

The independent record companies could now compete on a level playing field with the majors by simply hiring the largest promotion team in the country for a month. I must admit, that even though we worked for the majors as well, I loved being involved with the independent labels – these were the hustlers, believers and lovers of the record business. Successful or unsuccessful, they put their money where their mouth was and hustled the dream and I related to them. The major companies in those days did wise up and hire or buy these small labels to get the important act or the operator behind the label, but nine times out of ten they then stifled them and made them unsuccessful. Promopeople enabled these creative, passionate labels to compete and survive. During 1981, we had several independent Chart No 1 singles: John Craig's Safari Records benefited from Promopeople with Toyah Wilcox's No 1 indie singles 'I Wanna Be Free' and 'Four More From Toyah', an EP (Extended Play 45rpm, in case you are too young to remember). John remains a great friend to this day after a forty year career in the music business. 'Don't Let Them Grind You Down' by The Exploited on Martin Hooker's Secret Records gave us both another No 1 Indie single, but the best one for me and my old friend Don Evitts – we used to play it in our cars on nights out laughing – was 'Too Drunk To Fuck' by The Dead Kennedys. The national chart also gave us some No 1 Records: Joe Dolce's 'Shaddap Ya Face', The Specials' 'Ghost Town', Soft Cell's 'Tainted Love', Dave Stewart and Barbara Gaskin's 'It's My Party', and to end the year The Human League's 'Don't You Want Me Baby?'

Shaun King brought in The Human League record early in its release and we phoned Virgin Records to become involved. Shaun also found a record that was selling in a few London stores and said we should get on it. That record was Haircut 100, Nick Heyward's band with a song entitled, strangely, 'Favourite Shirts.' It would go on to become a No 4 hit. We encouraged all the reps to make us aware of any singles that were beginning to make a move, even if only in their area, believing that if we could strike a deal with the label the single was owned by, just the strength of our large promotion team would spread both the distribution and the sales across the country and make it into some kind of Top 40 hit. This would then guarantee us the follow up, more income and opportunity.

In August, Promopeople struck a deal with Woolworths to promote to their top two hundred stores. It meant that if record merchandisers who bought records on behalf of Woolworths did not buy your record then the only way into the huge sales of Woolworths was through Promopeople. This also made us more powerful with the independent dealers, since if they did not promote the records we were working and give us display space, we dropped them from the call pattern. The amount of singles and albums we were carrying on the cars meant a serious loss of income for those dealers, as we were now the most awaited call for most dealers, as we had independent records, major company records, huge selling compilations and now Woolworths.

By the end of 1981, Alan and I no longer needed to visit record companies and hustle for work. We waited for the phone to ring, which it never stopped doing, and then chose the singles and albums we felt confident about, thereby raising our hit ratio even more. Meanwhile, with the company growing, we made some changes to the team. Alan and I needed more help and Peter Todd, who had impressed with his work in East Anglia, became team leader and spokesman for the team. We also brought in Paul Dale, who had been the lead singer in Marseille before he and Neil Buchanan left the band. He took charge of our distribution, which was by now massive on a weekly basis. Paul was always a good laugh to have around and did a great job in getting the stock out to the reps; it was probably the fittest he ever was in his life with all that carrying of boxes. I was glad to help out an old mate.

Eat at Joe's – Goodbye:

Eat at Joe's had finished 'Don't Run Away' at Portland Studios and we hoped this might be the one to crack the Top 75 and get the band moving, especially as Promopeople were even more powerful now. We released the single in September and yet again we were destined to just miss out. This time we achieved No 78 and were in what they then called the breakers section in the chart. This normally meant that the record would chart in the Top 75 the following week. We tried everything we could to promote it, but for three weeks we stayed just outside the 75. It was unheard of for a single to stay in the breakers for that long. Everyone at Promopeople tried their best for me and the boys, but the record just would not go.

The failure of another single had serious repercussions and again we delayed the album. Eat at Joe's had now released five singles on Goldliner and although we had been the 'five minute darlings' at Radio One and had increased our audience steadily over three years through all those gigs, we just couldn't get to the next stage. For the band and me it was heartbreaking and shattered our confidence.

Tom called me to a meeting at the Birmingham offices of Goldliner to discuss the situation. I couldn't blame him, we had been paying the band's wages, we had paid for all the recording and promotion before Promopeople arose, we had paid for all the pressings, artwork and everything that goes with running a label and we were in serious debt on the entire project. Five single releases without making the Top 75 suggested in Tom's mind that the public just did not want our style of music. I really had no defence at this point. Tom wanted the running expenses cut back and a review of where we were going with the label. I thought it was a fair comment and I knew I had to come up with a fresh plan of action or probably lose the label. It was a painful situation. I still believed in the band and they were real friends of mine, we had come through a lot together and had all given everything we had, but it seemed my only option was to stop paying their wages. I might, perhaps, still be able to keep Colin on some sort of wage, then make a record with Colin and if we got a hit, bring the band back. If I could sell Colin's publishing I may be able to finance this next move and also, if I could get a record company interested, sell Ghost Hobbies to them and move forward in that way. The whole thing was a risk and could fall apart at anytime, but I was determined to give it the best shot I could – I couldn't just give up.

I went back to Tom with probably the only route left in the book and asked if he wanted to stay in under these circumstances. He agreed to finance Colin for a while longer and also agreed that I should try and sell the song publishing and album to refinance the next stage of recording. I was not happy with the outcome but could blame no-one, least of all Tom Edmunds. A meeting was set with the boys in Liverpool. It was a horrible day. I laid the facts out as they had occurred and gave them the only option I had. If they had a better one I was in. Unfortunately, they did not, and I think they were still reeling from the failure of 'Don't Run Away.' I left that day saddened, the band I truly loved were not going to survive this setback. They were very good at what they did, but life had gone against us and we were not going to make it. Our dream died that day.

The boys decided between them that Colin and I would give my last resort a go and I would use them as session musicians when we recorded, while I would set about selling the publishing. After a few attempts with different publishers I eventually received interest from Warner Brothers Music, who could see Colin's songwriting ability. On 17th December 1981 Colin and I signed the agreement at Warners for an advance of £3,000. We had refinanced the wages situation for Colin and early in 1982 we would record our next single. Meanwhile, amid dealing with all the record labels at Promopeople, I tackled the next part of the agreement, to sell *Ghost Hobbies* to another label. This task was to go on for four months as I tried everywhere to get a deal and with it the possibility of reforming the group. Unfortunately, it would all be to no avail; I received a constant stream of 'no thanks' letters from many record companies, even though they had begun with a lot of interest.

A sort of "Normal" Life:

Alan, I think, was not unhappy that Eat at Joe's had failed. He wanted me to concentrate solely on Promopeople and I believe Tom felt the same. The company had been a big winner in its first year and come Christmas we were on top of our game, with No 1 records everywhere and our position as holder of the only alternative route into Woolworths. We were indeed the leading and most popular music record promotion company in the country. Personally, I was delighted at Promopeople's success and I was enjoying being a major part of the whole operation, but equally I was greatly disappointed that Eat at Joe's were really no more.

In the meantime, Tom and I decided to suspend the Goldliner Records operation at the end of December while starting a new label that was owned by Promopeople. This was initially to accommodate a record that Alan was very keen on: 'Jingle Bells Laughing All The Way' by The Hysterics would make the Top 40. We released it on the Ka Label, the name coming from a book I was reading at the time entitled *The Ka of Gifford Hillary*. It would be the only record we released on that label, but the success of it made Alan feel he had become a hit maker. He dished out a lot of stick about how I had spent a whole load of money on five singles and yet he was one out of one. Personally, I hated the record, it was just a clown laughing over a backing track of jingle bells, but a hit is a hit and I had no come backs. At Christmas, records sell better than at any other time of the year and so a Top 40 record in December was worth a Top Ten at any other time of the year in terms of sales. It was a hit and made money, end of story.

I was now firmly in place at Promopeople and had grown used to my working week of spending four nights in London and then three nights in Walsall. I was always relieved to be back in Arboretum Road at the weekend, it was a peaceful haven. Sue was always there on Saturday and Sunday, she had a fulltime job during the week and worked a couple of nights as a barmaid. I would go and see Mom on Saturdays, Sue would come for lunch and then we would go to Walsall Football Club if they were at home, meet Tom and watch the match. Tom could catch up on the week's London news and then we would usually go to the movies. Sundays I would play football, see Sue later and then prepare for the trip back down to London. I was into a routine for a while and was no longer working nights. The transition into working in an office was difficult to start with, but because Promopeople was so fast moving and so exciting, I managed to settle into the way of life. With no gigs to attend and no direct responsibility to a record label and their touring acts, for the first time in years I began to lead a more normal existence, one might say. It all made my mother feel more relaxed: I was working in the day, which she thought was more proper, and as I had my own flat and was no longer upsetting her routine, for the moment, Mom was contented with the life of her wayward son.

CHAPTER 10

ONE STEP FORWARD,
TWO STEPS BACK – 1982

1982 started full of promise and hope. Promopeople was on top of its game and its first eight months had been an unbelievable success with a pre-Christmas couple of months that had seen us work for more or less every record company in the UK. We had become a 'must have' industry tool and everyone in the industry knew Promopeople, Alan Wade and Steve Jenkins.

Our success had brought a competitor in Bullet Promotions, set up by two ex-Phonogram Records Marketing Managers, Stewart Coxhead and Barry Evans, assisted by Henry Semmence. They had added more sales into their operation, intending to reduce their fees and give something back to the labels. Their representative field force was smaller than Promopeople's, but they were surviving and occasionally taking a small amount of work from our activity. Even so, Bullet Promotions had little effect on what had become a juggernaut of promotion at Promopeople. Meanwhile, my daily routine of working on the main promotion force and radio had to change and Austin Powell, ex of Warner Brothers and a longstanding radio promotion man, joined the company to take over my radio promotion role so that I could concentrate on the main clients and mainstay of the company.

My first song:

We were still working on our own records and the first to be released in January of 1982 was 'Alright On The Night' by the Paul Dale Band. Paul had become very friendly with Alan, who took him around to many meetings in town, and he became Alan's driver and personal 'gofer' on the days when the distribution department was quiet. Paul and I had spent many hours in the office after work writing songs together. At that time my guitar, which I had bought many years earlier, was a constant companion and although I never became a good guitar player I was always playing it in any free time and took it everywhere. We wrote together for fun and then one day Alan said if we came up with a good song the company would finance a single with Paul. This intensified our attempts and we came up with 'Alright On The Night.' We recorded once again at Portland studios, using a few musicians we knew to give it all a band feel. Everyone was up for the single and we pressed it in clear vinyl, which would make the record a collector's item and guarantee a few more sales.

We released in early January, when traditionally there are fewer new issues, and we began to get some airplay at Radio One and on commercial stations. It was fun to hear the record on the radio, especially being the first song that I had published, it was most unexpected and a delight. The record made it into the Top 75 for two weeks but never reached higher than 65. This was a little disappointing for everyone, but I was happy that for the first time I had made the Top 75 on one of my own records and a bonus that I had written it.

K-Tel, then kings of TV Compilations, approached us to include the track on their *Hungry For Hits* series that had been selling great quantities. Again, we were delighted and again success came unexpectedly. The album would go on to be No 1 and sell 400,000 copies. Both Paul and I received Platinum Discs for our song, in recognition of sales of over three hundred thousand copies. I knew I was not a talented songwriter, but pure passion and belief had brought about a song release and to win a platinum disc for our efforts was incredible. Most important of all, for the long-term, I was learning more and more about the workings of the music industry from all sides.

During January, I also finished the first solo single with Colin Frost. We had used the boys from Eat At Joe's to play as session musicians, bumped up by a few guest players, and all had gone well, but we were not happy with the drums. John McQueen had put down his always steady beat, but we felt we needed a little more life and drive in it. I arranged for Shaun King to come into Portland one night after work and set up his kit for an attempt at livening up the track. Shaun was a great drummer and put down a superb track, which we used on the final record.

Hits, Hits, Hits:

Promopeople continued where it had left off in 1981. We hit No 1 in January 1982 with Tightfit and 'The Lion Sleeps Tonight.' It was only the second release on a small independent label, Jive Records. Barbra Streisand's 'Memory' became a Top 40 hit – it would be her last single for six years. I was delighted to be involved in just a small way with Barbra's career: my father, many years before, had told me what a great talent a then very young Streisand was and here I was years later personally involved, he would have been truly happy. We had Top 10 hits with The Piranhas' 'Tom Hawk' and The Mobiles' 'Drowning in Berlin', and a Top 40 hit with 'Mirror Mirror' for Diana Ross, another artist I had been a huge fan of for years since the early Supremes days. Meanwhile, in contrast, we started working on an unknown band named The Smiths from Manchester.

Working on all these artists for many different record companies and making a few records of my own was all I could ask for. I felt as though, finally, I was in the right place with a lot of opportunities ahead of me. All we had to do was keep going and surely over the next year those elusive hits of my own that I had been searching for would finally come along. At this time, I was working with all the major people who would be involved in the popular music record business during the coming two decades: Robert Lemon at Bronze Records, Ted Carroll at Chiswick Records, John Preston at Decca Records, Steve Weltman at Charisma Records, my old friend Martin Sattherswaite at MCA, Tilly Rutherford at Red Bus Records, Ray Cooper at Island Records, Brian Yates at Arista Records, Frank Lee at Cheapskate Records, Martin Hooker at Secret Records, Scott Peiring at Rough Trade Records, Nick Raymonde at DJM Records, John Cokell at A & M Records, Bruce White at Creole Records, John Aston at CBS Records and Adrian Williams at Jet Records.

The Godfather of Rock:

It was Adrian Williams who phoned one day and said 'The old man wants to see you!'

This was not what you really wanted to hear and it instantly struck fear into the toughest of hearts. 'The old man' of Jet Records everyone knew was the legend that was Don Arden.

Don had begun his career as a singer and had toured the country, becoming an agent and tour promoter in the late '50s and early '60s. He had organised tours in the UK with the early legends of the popular music industry: Sam Cooke, Little Richard, Chuck Berry, Jerry Lee Lewis and Gene Vincent. Don's career then went into artist management where he discovered the Small Faces, The Animals, The Nashville Teens and Black Sabbath. Eventually, he started his own label, Jet Records, which most famously was the home of the worldwide selling Electric Light Orchestra.

There were many stories about Don Arden. The most famous was the one about Don and his 'boys' hanging Robert Stigwood, manager of The Bee Gees and eventually producer of the films *Saturday Night Fever* and *Grease*, out of his office window by his feet four flights up in an argument over The Small Faces. Don always denied this happened, but admitted to going to Stigwood's office and explaining what would happen to him if he messed with Don or The Small Faces. Evidently, Don did show Robert the pavement four flights below from the window, but suggested it was 'the boys' having fun as they lifted him up and headed for the window. There are many more stories about Don and 'the boys', but in his defence, the music industry of the Sixties was a young industry that The Beatles had changed forever. The contracts were prison sentences, the record companies paid the smallest of royalties and it would take another ten or 15 years for the lawyers to finally work it all out and bring respectability to the business. There was a price for that respectability, though: the originality and creativity somehow lessened over the years.

On the appointed day that I was due to meet 'The Don', I went just two hundred yards down the road to his offices. Alan had ducked the meeting and it was left to me. Adrian Williams met me and took me upstairs to Don's suite of offices, where there was a secretary outside two huge double doors and one of 'the boys' standing guard outside. Adrian said 'sit in the chair' just outside the office and the secretary made me a cup of tea. I said hello to the heavy, but he just looked at me as if I was something the dog had brought in and didn't reply. I sat there for a very long time, maybe half an hour. The door finally opened and another heavy said, 'Mr. Arden will see you now.' I walked into a large room with sofas arranged around a table and at the end of the room a huge desk with Don sitting behind it. Two heavies positioned themselves behind Don, either side of his chair, and the one from outside walked in the room after me and stood behind the chair Don had motioned I should sit in. Don was not a tall man, but was built almost as wide as he was tall. He was not fat and had huge shoulders. He had a powerful presence. Here I was with the Godfather of Rock and the show of force had been impressive, but I thought unnecessary. Even though I was a little intimidated, fear was beginning to leave my body and brain. I had been through a lot in my years since my father had died and was not about to be frightened by the show.

As I sat down Don opened with, 'So you're the new bread of Chart hyper, are you?'

'No, I'm not Mr. Arden, the industry has grown up and I don't think you can do what you could all those years ago.'

'So, if you can't put my record on the chart what are you doing here?'

'I'm here because you asked me to come; do you want me to leave?'

There was a little shuffle from the heavies, but Don just raised his hand and they stood at ease. From that moment on Don and I got on well. He spoke to me about how it worked in the early Sixties and the way he promoted his acts. I loved the stories, I am a student of the recording industry and I still find the history of it fascinating.

I explained to Don clearly what could be done to assist his records and what could not. I was nothing but totally honest, I think he recognised that and we would work on records together for a number of years. When he bought Portland Studios from Chas Chandler, he always allowed me to make records there. David, his son, became a good friend of mine, and I was invited to the house in Wimbledon for evening meals with Don and Paddles, his wife. Later, when I arrived in Los Angeles it was to Don's office I went and he made a few calls on my behalf to introduce me to people in that town. We both treated each other with a great respect and I had not a moment's trouble with 'The Godfather.' I am pleased to have known him.

Bigger and Bigger Names:

February brought more hits to the company and even bigger names: Barry Manilow's 'I Made It Through The Rain', a Top 10 record for The Nolans called 'Attention To Me', and a Top 3 for a favourite record of mine by Pigbag called 'Papa's Got A Brand New Pigbag': I still have no idea what it means, but delivering quirky records from nowhere is how reputations are built. I met and said 'Hello', but only briefly, to Marc Bolan, when we were discussing an EP, which eventually we worked on and had a minor hit with: 'The Return Of The Electric Warrior.' Marc was quiet and shy that day and seemed to lack confidence, but it was a special moment for me, as I had loved the T.Rex singles 'Hot Love' and 'Get It On.' Elton John's record company Rocket Records also came to Promopeople and we worked the single 'Blue Eyes' and the album *Jump Up*. It would be sometime later that I would eventually meet Elton. I also met for the first time that month Tom Bailey and Alannah Currie. I liked them both and they were very keen that Promopeople should get involved in their band and try to move them forward. Occasionally, we would take on bands and spread the word around record stores to get them involved in the demo's, so that when the records were eventually released the dealers felt part of it and would push the new record onto their regular customers. It would work a treat for Tom and Alannah, they would become world famous a year later with numerous hits as The Thompson Twins.

Colin's first solo record was ready. 'Ace Of Hearts' was to be the debut release on the Promopeople label After Hours. We decided to go for the valentine market and press the single in red vinyl. The sleeve was the Ace of Hearts playing card with the heart cut out to show the red vinyl inside. The record again started well and was the most successful of the discs I made with the boys from Eat at Joe's. It was yet again to stall just short of the Top 75, but became the 'No 1 breaker', a position it held for two weeks. Everyone thought this was the record that would work, but once again we fell at the final hurdle. This failure brought me more problems within Promopeople: Alan thought it was all a waste of time and the band had really had enough chances and Tom was also beginning to think this really was never going to work. It would be some time before we could record again and history now shows that it was our last single release. I shelved the project for a while as I could no longer get support to move forward, but I still believed at this time we would succeed in the future.

Meantime, the hits just kept on coming: 'Don't Walk Away' by The Four Tops, 'Haven't Stopped Dancin' Yet' by Gonzalez, the *Baal* EP for David Bowie, A Celebration and the album *October* for U2, Meat Loaf's album *Dead Ringer*, *Chase The Dragon* for Magnum, and two from a band we would do all the ground work on, just because we liked them – Scritti Politti: 'The Sweetest Girl' and 'Faithless.'

The cracks appear:

Problems were beginning to arise within the walls of Promopeople. Alan had begun to have darker moods and this really had started happening in the latter months of 1981. Following Christmas and the New Year festivities, Alan had returned to Promopeople a different man. Looking back now with the benefit of recalling what was to come it is a little easier to see why, but living it at the time was a confusing experience. My view was that Alan and Lindy's marriage was beginning to fail. I did not know the 'ins and outs' of what was happening, but we all know this is a complicated arena that brings with it a multitude of problems. Alan seemed to go within himself and that kind of situation brings insecurity and a loss of self-worth. The counterbalance to that in life is always best explained as 'I, me, mine.' Alan began to separate himself from everyone else at Promopeople and the situation was felt across the company, more so because of the way it had been set up: everyone had left Record Sales en masse to start a company that we all believed in and everyone felt that they had a share in the company. It was built on belief, passion and togetherness and a conviction that we would all succeed together. Alan's new way of operating was destructive to that movement.

At the time, Alan was very private as to what was happening and it felt that he was taking out on everyone whatever it was that was troubling him. When divorce looms there is always the financial situation that appears soon after and the 'I, me, mine' state of mind increases. This again brought problems. Our reps were self-employed on low basic wages, but they took large bonuses for successes, which were judged on chart positions. If they were successful, the team earned a good salary. Now, sometimes these bonuses did not appear and on occasions records appeared on the weekly sheets with no income attached. Promopeople had probably 25 people working at the time, it was a small company on the scale of things and so everyone became aware quite quickly that matters were different. The success of The Hysterics record on our own label, entirely Alan's project, and the continuing huge overall success of the company had added to Alan's great confidence in his position in the industry, and the stark contrast of his low confidence associated with his personal life made for a roller coaster ride. I could no longer communicate in the same way with him.

I was in an uncomfortable position. I had Tom Edmunds who had financed the whole operation, and I was sensitive not only for business reasons, but because of our longstanding friendship – Tom would not have been in the record business if it was not for me. Then there was the situation with the team: I was considered one of them and although I assisted in the running of the company, I had grown up with the entire team, they had total faith in my honesty with them and I was proud to be thought of in such terms. Regularly and, increasingly, intensely I was cornered by members of the team asking, 'What about this? Why is that? ...' It became more and more difficult to operate. Peter Todd was now team leader and through his nightly calls to the reps he knew the feeling of the team intimately. He was constantly seeking information and reasons for what seemed like wrong turns being taken for the company's health. During the first three months of 1982, as the problems below the surface of a successful company began to rise, I tried hard to discuss all of this with Alan, but he was well inside himself at this time. Increasingly, he took the attitude 'if anyone doesn't like it, then leave.' Consequently, the whole passion of the company was eroding. It was a gradually building problem, but it was becoming chronic. I felt I had no choice but to alert Tom to the change that was taking place in the company's operations and slowly he began to exert some pressure, albeit from afar – his operations were in Birmingham and Luton and he rarely came to London.

It seemed especially inappropriate that the team of Promopeople should be put at risk when the hits were coming in more than ever: MCA's Don Williams album *Listen To The Radio*, for the promotion of which we reissued the classic 'Gypsy Woman', 'Ticket To The Moon' by The Electric Light Orchestra, provided by Don Arden's Jet Records, and 'D.Days', a Top 10 single with Hazel O'Connor for Albion Records and Alan Belman. We hit with the great Rock 'n' Roll number 'Shout, Shout, Knock Yourself Out' by Rocky Sharpe and The Replays on Chiswick Records for Ted Carroll, and the enthusiasm Shaun King and I had for Kid Croele and The Coconuts impressed Ray Cooper at Island Records sufficiently for a relationship that led to the Top 5 hit with their 'It's A Wonderful Thing, Baby.' As well as this, we worked the reggae band Black Slate, who had achieved a big hit a year or so earlier with 'Amigo' and were releasing their long awaited album on Ensign Records.

These days, I was welcomed to all record company offices to discuss projects – a long way from past times of not getting past the reception to obtain a few free promo records. Now I could get as many as I liked and also charge the companies a lot of money on a weekly basis for Promopeople's service. We had always turned down projects during the first eight months of the company, to make ourselves more exclusive and to maintain a high hit ratio from the projects we took on. Alan's new purpose was to take on anything that came through the door and increase the turnover as much as possible. I thought this was a really short-term view and Alan and I fought long and hard about the records we took on. It damaged our relationship, as most times I was overruled, and we worked some absolute stinkers just for the weekly income. At times, I completely refused to deal with some records: when you could see that they would not work from the outset, I much preferred to tell the label 'No not for us, but bring us the next one.' This I felt kept us in the game with whichever label it was and they would begin to believe in our judgement. If they did not agree, then they could always use our competitor Bullet Promotions who at that time would take on anything. I felt if the label chose that route, then they would soon be back, without a hit and a few pounds less in their pocket. To me, the strategy made us look true, honest and knowledgeable about what we were doing. But now, 1982 was not going to be like that: take everything was the command and I knew that by operating in this way our power would diminish.

By Fridays I was glad to be back in Walsall. Working closely with Alan was becoming unbearable and he became more and more secretive about his movements. He was, in fact, seeing another woman whom he would eventually marry. Lindy was also in another relationship with our own Paul Dale and they would later marry: I did know about it and that made my position again uncomfortable. The team was up in arms about several issues and Peter Todd was, rightly in my view, insisting I should do something about it.

Tom had tried to put a tighter reign on Alan as we went through April and into May, but this was causing even more problems. Alan no longer trusted anyone, including me, and I was definitely and rightly seen as being in Tom Edmunds' camp and also representing the problems for the reps. Alan, in his state of mind, saw this as disloyal and set about making life as difficult as possible. I was removed from certain client calls and reports as Alan tried to gain more and more control. Finally, everything came to a head at the beginning of May. Tom had reluctantly decided to sell his shares. Alan had seen this coming and had up his sleeve a financier in the form of Steven Bentink, whose family had a fortune. In what seemed like days, but was probably a month, a new deal was struck and we were in partnership with the Bentinks. I was never invited to any of the meetings; somehow, I retained my ten percent shareholding, but I was no longer a voice at the company. Alan ran the whole operation and I cannot remember ever speaking with Steven Bentink. Furthermore, Alan now arranged everything through Paul Ridout, a lawyer and apparently a new dinner partner, who seemed to be on the phone every day.

Through all of this our hits continued: 'And All That Could Have Been' with 9 Below Zero on John Cokell's A & M Records, and two hits – 'I Ran' and 'Space Age Love Song' – by A Flock Of Seagulls, who, if you remember, had those incredible haircuts. These were released on Jive Records, a company I was fond of for their straightforward and non-emotional approach to records. Rory Gallagher, my old friend on Chrysalis, got us involved in his *Jinx* album and CBS brought us Jeff Wayne's follow up to *War Of The Worlds*, a project entitled *Matador*, which had taken forever to produce and cost CBS a fortune to record. I think John Aston gave us that one as the staff at CBS were not enamoured with Jeff at the time. The real joy for me was Joe Jackson's album *Night and Day*, a fantastic piece of work that included the big hit single 'It's Different For Girls', again, on John Cokell's A & M label.

But in contrast to the excitement of all this, Promopeople's first birthday had come and gone in April without internal fanfare and we were now in turmoil with new owners, representatives pulling in different directions and Alan and I just not getting along. Promopeople had become a bull riding contest at the rodeo and all I was trying to do was to stay on the thing and not fall off. I needed a break. Corfu was the desired destination, so Colin and Claire, Degs and his girlfriend, and Sue and I headed off to the island for nearly two weeks. Sue and I were getting along just fine, we had been together for almost seven years and were accustomed to each other. Sue always worked at night as a barmaid and in the week as a secretary, so we got together at weekends when I returned from London. Was it a normal relationship? Probably not. In today's world it has become more acceptable as people go where the work is, but back then, and especially in a place like Walsall, you grew up and could spend your entire life in the same town. We seemed solid together, though, and I for one never felt the reason to split up. I admit I never thought much about where we were going together: I was completely obsessed with making a career in records and chasing my dream.

I returned to Promopeople on 21st June, it was that year's longest day – and so it was to be in all senses. Alan had assumed complete control, backed by Bentink, the reps were up in arms over bonuses and Alan's treatment, and they were threatening to strike and come off the road. Peter Todd had listened to them and organised the team into 'things must change', while Alan's relationship with them was at its lowest ebb. I had now been removed from frontline work with the record companies and was instructed to work back on the radio singles that came through the company with Austin Powell. I was no longer involved in making the deals with the record companies, and the team sheets and instructions were done with the secretary and Lawrence, our on-site accountant and helper, who was firmly working for Alan. I really had little to do except on a Friday when the workload became greater. By the end of my first week back, I knew this was not going to work much longer. I still believed in the Promopeople we had set up, but over the past two months it had become unrecognisable internally. It was now a fast money machine for Alan.

Peter as team leader was under pressure and pushing me, along with Paul Stephens and John Payne, senior members of the team, all in full agreement that they were going to strike for missing bonuses and poor treatment. The rest of the team fell in behind them. I explained I had no relationship with Bentink and could not even get to speak with him. I tried to talk sense into Alan for nearly two weeks, but his attitude was that the company was his and if anyone wanted to leave then they could do so and that included me. Alan believed that I would sell the team down the river and look after myself by subordinating to him. In the years of experience that I have since accumulated, I can understand his reasoning. If one is married with children then you have almost no choice but to tow the Managing Director's line. But I wasn't. I also thought, if we could have a discussion with Bentink we could put this whole organisation back together. Surely, as it was his company, he would be looking to the future and the opportunity and health of a company with so much promise.

At 27 years old, I was naïve. I had only been in London working full-time for just over a year and I still thought like, and indeed was, a boy from Walsall. I still thought that people told you more or less the truth when you had a conversation with them and if they were about to make a stand they were committed to their stance, come what may. As the hits in early July continued with Elkie Brooks' 'Fool If You Think It's Over', the album *Pearls II*, Chas and Dave's 'Margate', and the *The Antmania* EP, the last single from Adam and The Ants, war broke out within the walls of Promopeople. On the evening of the 7th, I headed home feeling very despondent. During Thursday and Friday of that week all the team phoned me at home pledging support if I would go to Bentink and address the problems at the company. Pete was on the phone constantly and so were Paul and John. At first, I did not want to go to Bentink as I thought it would be fruitless. Alan had made the deal with him and I could not see Bentink changing sides or presiding over a meeting with a lot of people that he did not know. Peter, whose father was Ron Todd the General Secretary of the Trades Union Congress in the UK, believed differently and had witnessed his father change many impossible positions with the Government at a very high level. He organised the team to effectively strike on Monday 12th July for unpaid bonuses and general poor treatment by Alan. The team wanted me to be the point of negotiation with Bentink when the time came. My choices were to 'swallow' and be a 'gofer' for Alan, just walk away and leave or support the people I had grown to be successful with over the past four years and try to sort out the mess. I agreed to lead the negotiations on behalf of the team that weekend and come Monday 12th July Promopeople were not on the road promoting to record stores and radio. As Monday morning dawned, I had no idea of the consequences that our action would bring.

CHAPTER 11

IT'S ALL OVER – FOR NOW – 1982

An important lesson:

Monday 12th July 1982. The phone rang continuously from Peter and all the team. They were expecting Alan to contact me – but no call from London came. For my part, I really had no idea what would happen next. I presumed I would be called to London at some point and we could begin to repair the damage that had been done. Hopefully, we could then put the company back together in a proper manner and continue.

Peter and I spent time on the phone on Monday evening, but all we could was wait. Meanwhile, Alan was trying to contact all the other members of the team, but they were not answering their phones and were only in contact with Peter and me. Tuesday came and I could only guess at what was happening in London: with no reps on the road, news of the trouble would soon get back to the record companies and Alan would soon be under pressure. Eventually, the phone did ring from London on Tuesday afternoon: it was not Alan, but his new confidant, lawyer and dinner partner, Paul Ridout. He asked me what was happening and why the reps were not out on the road. I calmly told him that they had decided enough was enough: some of their promised bonuses had gone missing and they were unhappy with the way Alan was running the company and treating them. They had decided not to work in order to bring the situation to a head and they wanted a board meeting convened so that everyone could try and sort out the way forward. I had decided to represent them in an orderly fashion and I hoped the situation could be resolved quickly without further damage to the company. Ridout listened, we signed off, and then an hour later he called back and said that a board meeting would be arranged for this week. He requested I ask the reps to go back to work the next day in the good faith that the meeting would happen. I said I would call back in an hour and let him know.

I spoke with Peter, who contacted the senior reps, and they then spoke to the others. Within an hour it was agreed that everyone would go back to work, but only those within driving distance to London would be present on the day of the board meeting. I phoned Ridout and told him work would resume the following day if he called back with the time and place for the board meeting, which he did half an hour later: it was to be on Friday at noon. The week was set and I had a couple of days to kill. I had no intention of going into the office, but I would prepare for Friday, so I went to Northampton to discuss matters with Pete.

At this stage of the week I think all the team believed that all would be well on Friday. I do not think anyone believed the missing bonuses would appear, but they were confident that the future would bring bonuses when promised and they looked forward to a better working relationship with the management and hopefully, a return to the positive and indeed passionate feeling that had surrounded the company in its first eighteen months.

On Friday morning the reps drove to London and, in fact, they turned out from all around the country: Liverpool, Nottingham, the West Country, East Anglia, Birmingham, the South Coast, Devon and, of course, all the local London boys appeared too. We assembled in one of Bentink's offices in the West End and waited for the meeting to begin. Just after midday, Ridout came into our room and asked me to join them in the boardroom. As I walked in, there were people present whom I had never seen before. As well as Wade, Bentink and Ridout, who I expected, there were three others who I assumed were lawyers and accountants. They all sat behind a long table that faced me. I stood dead centre of the room and faced them. Behind me the room was empty. It was scary, but I was not going to show any fear or intimidation. I stood and looked at them all.

Ridout was in control of what would become his show: he was working for Alan and they were now both working for Bentink, who never spoke. Ridout began:

'We have to set out some rules and clarify the situation first. Are you representing the team of Promopeople reps?'

'Yes, they have asked me to represent them in this matter.'

'Are you aware that you cannot represent the team if you are a director of the company?'

'No, I was not aware of that.'

'Well, you can either leave the room and not represent the team or resign as a director and represent the team in this negotiation.'

'I will talk to them and come back in ten minutes.'

'Fine.'

I went back into the reps' room in a bit of a daze. I had not expected that and had no idea what it all meant. I thought we were going to talk through the problems and come to some agreement to move forward. I now knew that was not going to happen. I should have stopped everything and walked out with the reps, but I was naïve, I had never had a lawyer in all my years except when I bought the flat in Walsall and, in that instance, the family lawyer had done the paperwork. I had no experience with lawyers being used to negotiate deals, my view of them was they were 'pen and paper' boys. You talked through the deal and then they wrote it all down and only became involved at a point of law if things were not quite legally right. I had never thought of a lawyer being in charge of a situation. In today's world we are all used to that scenario: even if we have not been personally involved we have all seen it happen in movies and on TV, in *Eastenders* and *Coronation Street*. Back in 1982 it was not the case around the country, but in London it had already started to change.

I told the reps that I had to resign my directorship to represent them in this situation.

'Are you sure you want to go through with this? Are you sure you want to stick together as a team? Are you sure you want to fight on?'

Immediately, after I had put this to them and was deciding what to do next, Peter was talking to everyone and pulling them all together. After a few minutes, they all decided they wanted me to speak on their behalf and that meant I would have to resign as a director. I did not have a good feeling about resigning as a director of the company, but I thought that with a unified team behind me it could not get that bad. Here now was a harsh lesson to learn in life and one that would leave a scar forever. I walked back into the room of suits.

'Are you resigning as a director of the company to represent the team?'

'Yes.'

'Thank you, you can now leave the building, we have no need to talk with you.'

There was not much else to do but leave. I looked at Wade who just looked down. I really wanted to run and punch everyone's lights out, but I quickly decided to leave with some dignity. I had been easily outmaneuvered and had to take it on the chin.

I walked into the reps' room and told them I had been asked to leave the building. I had no idea what would happen next, but I was out of it. We quickly arranged to reconvene at a restaurant just around the corner from Promopeople's office in Marylebone High Street when it was over. I left and drove straight to the restaurant to await the team. Within half an hour of my arrival at the restaurant the team started to appear. The upshot was that Ridout had called them in en masse to the boardroom and had told them it was business as usual. They could all return to work on Monday if they called Alan at home over the weekend.

It was depressing in the restaurant. I listened to the team's reasoning and comments and then stood to address them all.

> *'We have put up a good fight, but have been defeated. It is not fair and probably should not have happened in this way, but nevertheless, this is now the situation. My belief is that you all should accept your invitations to return to your jobs, at least in the short term, it will keep you in the industry and maybe you can apply for other jobs within the industry at a later date, as I think we all know, Promopeople will never be the company we had hoped it would become. It will be difficult for you to phone Alan, but I'm sure it will only be a short call. He needs to get you back on the road and limit the damage to the company before it spreads around the industry. Think of yourselves and don't worry about me, I've had worse occur in my life and it will just be something I have to overcome. I thank you for your support over the past eighteen months and your assistance in the building of Promopeople, I wish you all the best of luck.'*

Slowly the reps began to leave and make their journeys home and their own decisions. Soon there was only Peter Todd and I left. I encouraged Peter to go back to Promopeople, he had a wife, Jean, and two daughters I had come to know well during my visits to his home in Northampton. Peter said there was no way he would return to Promopeople, it was done as far as he was concerned – he would take his chances and work with me on whatever I did next. I told him I had no idea what to do next and that he should talk with Jean and there would be no hard feelings should he return to Promopeople. Peter insisted he was not going back and would stand by his word in the coming weeks.

I left to drive home in the Ford Mexico, my pride and joy that soon would not be mine anymore. The drive went by in a blur and I arrived home late on that Friday night, shattered. And the worst was still to come. Saturday morning at Mom's was not pleasant. I explained what had happened and that now I was out of work, with no company to run and no record label. As I was explaining to Mom, it was dawning on me that my life that had been going so well was now in tatters. Mom went immediately on the offensive: 'I think that's enough now Steve, it's time to quit on all this music business and think about getting a proper job and starting a proper life. You've had a good time, travelled the country and been involved in a lot of hit records, but enough is enough. You have gone further than I thought was possible and I'm proud of your determination and drive, but it can be put to better use now. Stop, look at other things and lay the music to rest.'

It was a heartfelt felt speech from a constantly worried Mom. Her 28-year-old son had been at the record business since his 21st birthday, and for years before as a DJ, and she was getting to me – and yet I could not extinguish that little burning flame of hope that was still alight inside me.

I also had to tell Sue that my involvement in Promopeople was over. Sue always took it in her stride and asked what I was going to do. For the moment, I had no idea. I told Tom the outcome of it all and had dealt with the closest people to me by the end of the weekend.

Ridout called on the Monday and apologised for what he had done, but business is business and he wanted no hard feelings. I had to find a lawyer to wind up the paperwork and sort out the small pay off and the return of my Mexico car. Nick Kanaar, my first lawyer, took care of all that for me and that week it was all done. I returned the Mexico and, this time, I returned to Walsall on the train and walked back to the flat.

The reps went back to Promopeople and their jobs. They phoned and said it had not been a pleasant experience, but they were all back at work with a now powerful and dominating Alan Wade – all, apart from one, Peter Todd. Peter would always have a coveted place in my heart and mind for not returning to Promopeople. I could offer him nothing but talk and dreams and, at that moment, not even that, yet still Pete had a faith in me, faith that I really did not have in myself.

Out in the cold:

That weekend, I met Colin and Degs in London and we caught the boat to Amsterdam. We were going to see Warner Brothers to try and obtain a record deal after they had shown interest. Eventually, it would come to nothing, but it took me out of England and away from the phone. I was unhappy and couldn't sleep. The boys rallied around and we got drunk and smoked marijuana for four days through Amsterdam, Brussels and Paris, wandering the streets at night as they tried to lighten my mood and talk me into getting back into the studio and recording.

In what seemed like a flash I was back in Walsall and reality began to hit home. My first task was to sign on the dole, do the interview, go to the job centre and then every Tuesday at different times each week queue up to sign on. The gyro cheque came in the post on Thursday mornings. I did not want to do this but Mom insisted, I think it was part of her grounding plan to stop the dreaming. Mom was particular that my stamp would be paid and thus my pension would not be affected. A pension was not top of my list, just getting out of bed in the morning was tough enough, and by mid-August I was in a state of depression.

I had never suffered with depression and even at this time I did not fully understand what it was. I had lived my whole life with hope and passion and now, with its disappearance, there was an overbearing feeling of sickness, no wish to get out of bed and no drive to do anything. I went to the doctor, but as I had been so fit he thought there was nothing wrong. Small things raised my spirits, such as, when

I read George Martin's book *All You Need Is Ears* – George had produced all those Beatles records and finally written his autobiography. I also watched Rocky I, II and III, once again it revived my weakened will, but it really was one day at a time. My confidence was shattered.

I was used to my phone going all the time from people at record companies, even at the weekends the calls would come as they tried to get information on the sales of their records. As soon as my Promopeople days were over, the phone stopped. It takes a while to get used to not speaking to people you have dealt with for the past few years, but the record business is like that. It is best explained with the saying 'When you're hot you're hot and when you're not you're not.' That was and still is a record business mantra, so if you want a career in this business you have to accept that this will happen should you fall from grace. And if you choose this business, at times you will fall from grace, it's a guarantee. You will have to start all over again many times. It can be a gut-wrenching experience. I was back in Walsall and London seemed a million miles away. I was signing on the dole and had no car. If I went to Liverpool to work with the band it was by coach with a change at Birmingham.

We recorded three new songs in a small studio in Manchester with Colin: 'Heart Of Fire', 'Dancing In The Dark' and 'Angel Eyes.' Armed with our tapes, Colin, Degs and I had decided to go to America and seek a deal with the US homebase division of Warner Brothers. They were still our publishers and had suggested this would be a good idea to try out, so we just fell in line as we wanted to get away from England. The following three weeks were about setting up the trip to Los Angeles, where Warner Brothers were setting up introductions for us to pursue when we arrived. I organised another two days at Sawmills in Cornwall and Colin, Degs and I went off in a hired van to record another couple of songs for America.

I arrived home to bad news. My sister Helen had lost her baby, but she was OK: it was a blow, but at least Helen was going to be well. Sue also greeted me with a good talking to, the upshot being that she had really had enough of my ways with constant travelling and now heading off to Los Angeles. I really could not blame her, I was still dreaming my life away and we were getting older.

A surprise call came through in early September: Richard Jakobowski, ex-owner of Record Sales, said he had raised the money from Jet Records to start another promotion company and would I be interested in running the operation with him. I phoned Peter Todd and we discussed the offer in my flat. We were getting our minds around setting up our own promotion company and record label and we knew we were not going back into Richard's kind of arena without being in control. I played Pete the new songs I had recorded and Sue Parsons came around for a listen too. Sue said she would leave Promopeople tomorrow if we put a new company together, Shaun King also said the same and Kevin Rea, who had just resigned from Promopeople, said, 'When you get it together, I'm in.'

Peter and I decided we would be 50-50 partners come what may. He would run the team and make sure it all worked, I would get the work from the record labels with all my contacts and all we needed to do was raise the money. How we did that we didn't know, but we would put the wheels in motion before I left for the States. I sat with Tom Edmunds, played him the new songs and told him about our idea, mentioning that members of the old team seemed willing to try again with a new company. He said he would think about it all and we would speak on my return.

California here I come:

Suddenly, here I was ready to head for the promised land of Los Angeles, the city of angels, where dreams come true or you get a good ass kicking. I said my goodbyes to Sue, who had not been that friendly over the past month. She had told me she had been out with someone else and I think she was just waiting for me to leave for America – as I now was. Helen drove me to Walsall station, from where I was to go to London and then a hotel in Crawley to meet Colin and Degs. Mom had given me a good lecture to be careful. Helen just smiled as she dropped me off and said 'take care and go get 'em.' I told her I didn't know when I would be back, something I had not told anyone else, but I assured her I would be back.

I had dreamed of going to California and Los Angeles all my life. The music that had come from that area had always been on my list of favourites. I guess the Beach Boys records of the sixties started my fascination, along with the imagery of Thunderbird cars, the beaches and the movies. As a child, I had watched *77 Sunset Strip*, the hero being Cookie, and then all the stories of the building of Hollywood. And the great stars of the era: Marilyn Monroe, John Wayne, Clark Gable, Robert Taylor, Spencer Tracy, Mickey Rooney, Peter Lawford, Greta Garbo, Jean Harlow, Joan Crawford, Lana Turner, Judy Garland, Ava Gardner, Grace Kelly, Elizabeth Taylor. And then the rise and fall of MGM with Louis B Mayer and Irving Thalberg, Bob Hope and Bing Crosby, the Rat Pack: Frank Sinatra, Dean Martin and Sammy Davis Jnr. The record labels that had grown in L.A. from early Sam Cooke days through to the glory years of the '70s at Warner Brothers with James Taylor, Bread, America, Joni Mitchell and Crosby, Stills, Nash & Young. Everyone and everything seemed linked with Los Angeles and now, here at last, was my chance to experience some of it. Just to drive down the same streets as all of those people was going to be a thrill in itself.

On 21st September, we were air-bound for Los Angeles and full of excitement. When we landed we hired a car and headed for Santa Monica. We decided on a couple of days sightseeing to get over the jetlag and settle in, so we went off like kids to Universal and then to Malibu, driving around looking at the stars' homes and trying to get our bearings. We went out in the evenings to a couple of bars and after two days my diary says:

> "LA. No-one does anything here but look at the sea and the sun, go on health trips, keep fit and try to be a star. I think I'm homesick and need a little security, it's hard to keep going, you seem so close to the dream here and yet you may as well be 6,000 miles away. LA people are full of shit, I've been here two days and I know why everybody needs an analyst."

By the Saturday we were off to Santa Barbara about a hundred miles north of LA. We had met some students on the plane who had invited us up to the University of California, Santa Barbara and we spent three days there playing a couple of gigs at the student parties to pay for our keep. It was a great experience living on campus and it was just like the movies: the students never seemed to go to lessons and their prime motivation was to have a good time and party. We got to know lots of students as we were soon famous on campus by playing at the parties. We received invites to the beach and the homes on campus and the worries of England did melt away – for a time.

We needed to work, so by Tuesday we headed back to LA and fixed up meetings at Warner Brothers and PolyGram Records to try for a US record deal. The first meeting was with PolyGram's Mike Sanderval. We spent an hour or so with him playing our songs and talking, but he more or less told us we had no chance with PolyGram. Felix Chamberlain was next on the list at Warner Brothers: again, we had an hour's meeting and he liked the songs but admitted he was not going to sign us.

We drove back to our Westwood motel in silence. Everyone was feeling beaten and homesick. Colin just could not get moving and stayed in, but I wanted to go out, so Degs and I headed into Westwood, visiting Dillon's and Caesar's Palace. It relieved our disappointment and we had a good time.

Over breakfast on Friday morning we all took a vote of 'Vegas here we come!' Las Vegas was a different place in 1982 to the city we now know. For several years it has been the No 1 city for expansion in the whole of America, but then, it was more or less two main streets: the old town and the new strip that was just beginning to be built. We stayed at the end of the new strip on the edge of town, at the Jamaica Inn. We could walk to the casinos and did so straight away on that first night. Colin believed that you could win thousands of dollars for just a few dollars gambled and I think he thought that might be his chance to stay in California. He was convinced it would happen and so we went to gamble a little. Suckers – we all lost and returned to the hotel in worse shape than we had started the evening.

The following day was spent around the pool at the Jamaica Inn and the rejection by the record companies was beginning to take root. The loss of some valuable dollars in last night's gambling venture had also hit home. I read George Best's book *Where Do I Go From Here?* from cover to cover in a day and I was also beginning to ask myself what the hell was I going to do? My diary notes for that day were:

> '*Stay or leave Sue? Stay or leave the band? Get a job? Motorbike across Europe?*'

I don't know where that came from – I couldn't ride a motorbike and didn't like being on one. And look at this one:

> "*Or open a post office in Cornwall?*"

I must have been high to come up with that.

Sunday, our last day in Las Vegas, was mixed. We split up for a while to give each other a break and wandered the streets on our own. The dawning that we had overspent and were running out of money and the disappointment of the first record company responses was getting to us all. Colin and I went to North Vegas in the evening for a look around old Vegas; Degs was not so well and had become ill while we were sunning ourselves at Caesar's Palace.

Monday comes, as it always does, and we headed back to LA but drove a little further south to Redondo Beach. The money situation was going to get bad, it was not critical yet, but it soon would be. I had to do some work, raise some money and try a couple more companies. I went back to Warners to use their phones and called Robin Godfrey Cass in the UK. I told him we were doing well and had lots of interest from American labels (Sorry, Robin), but we needed more money to stay in the US a while longer to see it through. Robin said he thought it would be OK, but said I should call back in a day. I made a few more calls and got interest from Arista and Chrysalis in LA, also, I spoke with Epic and Atlantic in New York. It was all pretty desperate stuff, but I needed to at least make sure the money came from Warners Publishing and I needed some real contacts to ensure it happened.

Colin and Degs could no longer face the rejection of record companies, so I was off to Arista and Chrysalis on solo ventures. The meetings were fruitless. Despite this, I managed to get Warners in England to send tapes to Atlantic and Epic in New York, and after three days Warners sent me $500. We regrouped in Redondo, didn't dwell on the Arista and Chrysalis failure and decided we would go north to Ventura and then onto San Francisco since the boys had met some students who had invited us up there.

Ventura, north of LA, brought one of the moments of the trip I will never forget. Written in paint on a board by the side of the road was 'Beach Boys here tonight.' We drove straight in without discussion. It was Ventura County Fair and we spent the day walking around the fair until evening came and we went to watch

The Beach Boys play, on the beach. It doesn't get much better than that for a Walsall boy: Ventura County Fair, The Beach Boys playing on the beach and watching the sun go down over the back of the stage. Magical.

All this time we were just making the most of a short unreal dream. We moved on to Palo Alto, just south of San Francisco, where Degs met a girl called Jennie and fell in love. Then on to San Francisco, where the streets were just as we remembered them from the car chase in the film *Bullitt* with Steve McQueen, after that, re-visits to Palo Alto, Santa Barbara and Los Angeles, where, after further failed meetings with record companies, we went to San Diego. We visited SeaWorld as tourists do, spent the day there and then went north to La Jolla, where we found a cheap motel, bought a couple of bottles of wine and set about our planned evening. The band were not druggies and neither was I: yes, we sometimes smoked marijuana when it was available, but we never carried it around. At UCLA one of the gang had given us some 'magic mushrooms' and we were trying to talk ourselves into taking them. We stayed at a motel right opposite the beach, checked it out during the day to give us security, and decided that tonight was the night. We went out and ate then went back to the motel. Our plan was to drink some wine, wash down the mushrooms and then go to the beach when it was dark.

All went well, this was our first time, and my one and only time, and we went out to experience as much as we could under the influence. My memories of that night are of great laughter and much fun, followed by quiet, inward moments where time stood still and nothing around was moving – a feeling of being suspended. We made our way to the beach, but pretty soon we were all in our own worlds. I must have spent what felt like hours looking at the rainbow of light coming from a street light. I have never seen a street light like that before or since, the colour was truly amazing. I caught up with the boys on the beach and stood watching the waves – I could see them coming into the shore and then reforming before hitting the shore again, it was mesmerising. The sand, the sea and the wide open space of the shore was intoxicating and as it turned colder – who knows what time it was – we lit a fire on the beach and sat around enjoying the moment.

All of a sudden, there was incredible noise, made earth shattering by the mushrooms. Above, was a police helicopter shining one of those lights right at the bonfire. We were rigid with fear. We stood and Degs said:

'Let's run.'

Instantly, I say, 'Don't run.' I am trying desperately to regain my sense of reason. 'Slowly, put the fire out.'

I started and the boys followed. The helicopter just hung there.

'Let's casually walk away.'

Again, we just started to move along the beach, the big light went off and moments later the helicopter went back over the cliffs.

'Now run, in case they're landing.'

We bolted along the beach and up onto the cliff top. I then made the boys go on a long detour to come back to the hotel from the other way. I was not going to get 'banged up' for one night. We breathed a huge sigh of relief when we finally got back to the room. Everyone was silent, the wine started to flow and as our confidence in our near miss and escape grew, the funnier it became. We had a great time, but I would not advocate that anyone should try this stunt. I know little about the magic mushrooms and have never bothered to find out or try again – for me it was a one off moment. What I have heard is that the 'mushroom trip' can be wonderful or an absolute nightmare and that depends on your metabolism and mentality. Any two people will experience something different. Take my advice, it's not worth it, there are better things to do in life.

The final day of my 28th year had come and I spent the evening at a party in UCLA Santa Barbara, where we were back living for free. My diary notes about my birthday say, "A great birthday when it looked like it maybe was a bad one, 29 makes me smile rather than be depressed." We continued to spend time in Palo Alto and Santa Barbara. I would not visit anymore record companies in the US on this trip and sooner rather than later I had to face up to reality. I made my way back to meet the boys in Redondo Beach and my mind started to think about England and what I should do. It was not a pretty picture: 29 years old, out of work, back on the dole in Walsall, no record company, no promotion company, no car, no contact with the record business, Mom would be right on my case and Sue may be gone when I get back. The band are absolutely nowhere, we have been turned down in England, Europe and America; we have put out seven singles that missed and an album that has not even been released. It was all so bad that it made me smile: it really just could not get any worse. The longer I sat there the more I became determined to return to England and give everything one almighty go. I had searched my soul over the past weeks in America and had come to the conclusion I was not finished. Come what may, I had to try again. I belonged in records, it was all I knew and all I had been interested in for years.

Having made that decision, I now had to decide upon the route. With the boys still not appearing, I continued the train of thought. It seemed to me that a promotion company right now was what I knew best. The members of Promopeople would certainly follow me and Peter if we could pull it off and this would also go some way to relieving the injustice I felt I had experienced at Promopeople. If we could get that together and the team came to our new company, we would close Promopeople in a week, returning the favour so to speak by taking over their work and then building a strong operation in our own design. If we could be successful at that, then making records of my own would follow.

What happened in Redondo Beach that day was the turning point in my life. I was still nowhere and it was all just thoughts and talk, but from somewhere deep inside my soul, belief passion and determination started on an upward curve.

The boys arrived. I told them: 'no money from Warners, I have changed the flights and we are off in two days.' They would have no option but to return to England. They did discuss it all to see if there might be another way of staying, but I told them I was not up for the idea and I was going to go back to start my own promotion company, I did not know how, but I was going to do it. 'So if you stay, good luck, but I'm out.' Colin and Degs spent a lot of time in the next couple of days just talking together while we went around Redondo. I was pretty much on the outside of it all now, I had stated what I wanted to do and they were deciding on their next moves together or apart.

We made it back to LAX airport and returned the car to the hire company. We owed ten dollars, but only had one left. Fortunately, they let us off. The following day we were back in England: Gatwick, Victoria, Euston and 'bye, bye boys.' Arriving in Birmingham, I phoned Mom and she picked me up in Walsall and took me to her place to be fed while she listened to my adventure. Then she took me back to the flat where I slept for 20 hours, not waking up until five in the afternoon and, for a moment, not knowing where in the world I was. The hopes and dreams of America were over and the reality of my position was just arriving. It was November and it was bloody cold.

CHAPTER 12

THE DARKEST HOUR IS JUST BEFORE
DAWN 1982 – 1983

In the midst of the night:

Walsall in November is not California. I was back and straight into the reality of my life. My main motivation was to get back into the record business and try to form my own promotion company – either straight away or as soon as possible. Eat at Joe's, or the remains of, were now purely business and there was no more dedicating my life to the band's success. Both Colin and Degs were in touch to say they were home, but we all had little to say to each other. The dream had died in California. Sue came around, but was clearly unhappy: she said she was fed up with the situation and I could hardly blame her. Still, neither of us went as far as saying 'it's over', although it was close.

I signed back on the dole and every Tuesday morning was the same: up, down the dole office, queue up and sign on. The spare time I had was filled by reading books and watching films, anything to change my frame of mind. My time clock was off. If it was a bad day I might not get up until one in the afternoon and sometimes it could be even later. Other days, I would try to fill with small jobs: cleaning Mom's car, going to see Helen, pretty much anything to keep going.

Peter Todd was round the flat within a week and we started to discuss the way we might set up a promotion company. Richard Jabokowski's idea of a possible promotion company if Jet Records were to fund it was a non-runner for us and an approach Peter had made in my absence to Kevin Rea's father-in-law, who had originally expressed interest in putting up money, came to nothing. There is no doubt that Peter had more belief in me than I had in myself during this crisis of confidence. He was supportive and just kept quietly pushing me to come up with a plan. I owed him a lot, as he had walked from Promopeople when he could have gone back and continued working there, instead, he waited for my return from California. His driving force that we should now both move forward was vital sustenance for me.

My plan was that we should have a partnership deal with a record company that would provide a steady through-put of records as a basis to the operation and then, on top of this, I would obtain work from the other labels to enhance the company. I also felt that the reps should be employed by us rather than be self-employed and we should provide them with company cars. In this way, ours would be the first promotion company that was legitimate, in contrast to the rather gung-ho promotion operations we had been involved in before. To enable this to happen, we would need a partnership with an independent label that was not only well set-up, but which also wanted to go somewhere – a label that wanted to expand and had the confidence to do so and a label that thought it was making hit records and would continue to do so. This was not going to be that easy to find.

Peter and I talked for hours, day after day. We looked at all the independent record labels and we knew we had to get out there in London and pitch our idea in person to see if anyone was interested. We decided to try three: DJM Records, as I knew the manager Stephen James (son of the label's founder Dick James), Bronze Records, as again I knew the Managing Director, Robert Lemon, and the owner, Gerry Bron, and the company that I said to Peter was the one that we wanted most of all: Jive Records. Jive had impressed me while I had worked on their first records at Promopeople. There was a vibe about the company, one which we had shared with them and contributed to, with a No 1 record, a Top 10 and a Top 30. We had also had a couple of misses with them and I had been impressed with their reaction: it was the same whether there was a hit or a miss – non-emotional, amounting just to "why didn't it work?" and "what are we going to do next?" They were ready to listen to ideas and I believed that was the recipe for success. Their General Manager was Bob Nolan, whom I had spoken with many times during the working of the records, and I liked him and the way he operated. I had no clue who owned the company, but I thought if we could convince Bob, we could access the owner and see if he believed in our idea.

I set all the meetings for one week, beginning with Bronze Records, followed by DJM and concluding with Jive. I felt if I could hear our pitch out loud to the first two record companies then that would give us the best shot at attracting Jive Records and I would learn in these rehearsal meetings the areas not to go near when it came to Jive. At the same time, if Bronze or DJM wanted to be involved that would give us more options.

We went to Bronze Records for our first attempt at selling the new company. Robert Lemon was a very good man and we talked through everything. His conclusion was that if we were to get it together he would definitely use us, but Bronze was not in an expanding situation and therefore could not get involved financially as a partner. Peter and I were happy with the result of the meeting and, even though Bronze was not going to fund us, Robert was positive and there was a chance of work there if we were up and running.

Next, DJM. Stephen James had put out the records I had made for Neil Rushden with Altitude, our alter ego title for Eat at Joe's, and I had also worked a lot of DJM Records with Record Sales and Promopeople. Stephen listened to our proposal, which I thought was better than the one we did at Bronze, and like Robert Lemon he thought our concept was very good, but he was just licensing his label to CBS and therefore, could not become involved. Stephen, as always, was charming and a pleasure to deal with and Peter and I thought this meeting had also gone well. We were now ready to go to Jive Records: if they passed we were back to square one. The following day arrived and that afternoon was my first visit to Willesden, the home of Jive Records.

Bob Nolan handled the meeting calmly and professionally, while our presentation, without doubt, was the best of the three and went incredibly smoothly. Bob most certainly liked the idea and saw what an opportunity it might be for Jive Records. He said he would talk to his boss and come back to us. Peter and I now thought that something really might happen with Jive. I returned to Walsall via train the next day, just in time to get to Walsall Football Club and see The Saddlers play. Afterwards, I took the opportunity to tell Tom Edmunds of our plan and ask him if he was interested. He said he wanted to look at the figures but he would want sixty-six percent of the company. I said to Tom we should talk again when I had all the final figures.

Back on the roller coaster:

After what had been a good week, the following one was a stinker. I signed on the dole and struggled to get out of bed. I forced myself to run every day and try and keep my fitness levels up. Meanwhile, the films of the day occupied my time. *Who Dares Wins* with Lewis Collins, *The Best Little Whorehouse in Texas* with Burt Reynolds and Dolly Parton and others came on Channel Four as it started broadcasting on our TV screens. On the Monday morning of this week and the following one, I disciplined myself to get up and consciously start the week running in my attempt to clear my mind and try and push my career forward for a return to the record business. At last, two weeks after our meeting with Bob Nolan, Jive Records called and set a time for Peter and I to meet Clive Calder, the company's owner. I borrowed Mom's car and went to Peter's to work out the real finances for the promotion company. Peter had an accountant who was helping us with it all and that very day he delivered the news that another one of our finance schemes, a government grant, had failed. It had been a long shot, but we were trying all thinkable angles. Meanwhile, possibilities at Jive remained and we had another chat with Tom Edmunds. Two days later I was on the train to London to meet with Clive Calder. Peter drove from Northampton and picked me up at Euston. Willesden again, and straight into the meeting with Clive. My first impressions of him were good. He was articulate, had a good feel for the business, understood completely what Peter and I were trying to do and recognised that Peter and I had the experience to pull it off. He seemed committed to moving the idea forward and becoming involved and another meeting was set for two days time, in which Clive and his accountant would go through the figures with us.

The following day, Peter and I spent the evening going over and over the figures to make sure they were perfect. At the end of our session we felt the figures made so much sense that this was a viable situation and one that should enable us to make a deal and get us moving again. Friday came and we set off for London. Clive Calder and his accountant Keith Swallow went over the figures many times in great detail, and they asked many questions, all of which we answered with ease as we knew this operation inside out after all the times we had gone over it. Our figures were accepted, and Clive finished by saying he needed to give consideration to a couple of matters. On Tuesday we would be 'in or out.'

The 'out' word nearly destroyed us. Peter and I had been sure we had cracked it, but now it would be a few more days before we knew. The ride home was a long one. The weekend also dragged: I spoke with Tom and brought him up to speed, he said I should not sign anything and should let him know after Tuesday what the result was. Sue came over just once and I played terribly in my Sunday football match – my mind was elsewhere.

Christmas was almost upon us and I knew if we did not receive an answer before Christmas it might go cold by the time the New Year came. Jive phoned on Monday and delayed the decision until Friday. That set the tone of disappointment and apprehension for the week – struggling to get out of bed and back to watching movies: *Enter the Ninja* and *Amityville II: The Possession*.

Friday came and went without an answer and the following week was the same. It was turning into a huge disappointment when finally, we were called to Jive just two days before Christmas.

When we arrived, Clive and Keith said they wanted to hold off until mid-January as there was to be a chart investigation early in the New Year. However, they would commit to the new company with a clause to pull out if the investigation went badly and as a sign of good faith they would pay Peter and I eight hundred pounds each for the Christmas and New Year period and up to mid-January. Then everything would be reviewed. Not quite what Peter and I wanted, but at least a show of faith and a few quid that would come in quite nicely for Christmas.

From the ashes, the phoenix begins to try and rise:

The day before Christmas, I bought myself a small Yamaha piano and Sue a bike and Tom phoned to say he wanted to move forward with the promotion company idea and would accept a 50/50 deal. At long last the New Year had promise and I felt I could enjoy the Christmas and New Year period knowing something could well be happening. 1983 must be better than 1982, it just couldn't get any worse.

As the New Year working week began, we began making ourselves ready for the expected call from Jive in mid-January. Finally, Jive phoned and we were again off to London. This time Keith Swallow said all looked good and we should start putting everything together. We went straight to Shaun King's flat and offered him a job, which he accepted immediately. Tom Edmunds had me go to Leeds to pick up a car he had bought and said if I did so I could use it for a month. Now I was even back on the road. Peter and I then travelled for a week around the country. In London, we offered Phil Tomkins a job and in East Anglia we recruited Stuart Wickland. Sue Parsons had already accepted in Birmingham, Andy Richmond accepted in Wellingboro and then back in London, we were hoping Sue Pearson, whom we had worked with at Record Sales, would be our secretary. At Sandbach services on the M6 Kevin Rea decided to join us. By the time we had travelled for a week we thought we were getting somewhere, but then Phil Tomkins phoned back to say he would not feel able to come until he had seen how the operation was progressing a couple of months down the line and we heard from Sue Pearson that she had accepted another job. This brought a blow to our fragile confidence and caused a depression for a couple of days, but we were up and at it again soon after.

Tom Edmunds was kept abreast of all things Jive, as we still had not signed a contract and might still be starting the company with Tom if he wished, all depending on the next few weeks. I was offered a job by Spartan Records to start a promotion company with them, but I was committed to starting our own company and so I declined the offer. Mom thought I should take the job, stating 'A bird in the hand is better than two in the bush', but I had to press on down the road I was committed to. And that meant hanging on right now – at all costs, even when, by the beginning of February, Jive were no longer taking our calls. We could get no response from them at all, and the waiting, the not knowing and the calls to Peter to see if he had heard anything were taking their toll. I was still signing on the dole and beginning to get up later and later in the day as it all seemed to be falling apart again.

Jive set a meeting – and then cancelled. Following that, we could reach no-one from the company on the phone. Finally, on 10th February we just turned up at Jive and asked for Keith Swallow. We told him we could not go on like this, we needed to know if the company was to be financed or not. Keith said he would talk with Clive in America and obtain a final decision. I also went, in the meantime, to Warner Brothers to discuss Colin's contract option, but Warners declined to extend. The following day, Keith Swallow called to say he thought it was on and would send one thousand and six hundred pounds to both Peter and I to keep us going until Clive returned to England. We still did not know the final outcome, but a least we had a few pounds to ease the depression – hope was still alive.

I phoned Colin to tell him the bad news about Warner Brothers and he threw a fit. The reasons he had not become a star were all my failings – and our relationship and friendship during all those years of trying together ended at one go when he slammed down the phone. A few days later I received a lawyer's letter claiming that all the recordings that were owned by Tom Edmunds, which yielded fifty percent to me when they recouped money from sales, were Colin's. I waited two weeks before replying and basically told the lawyer to get lost. I never heard from them again and I would only see Colin once more, many years later. It had been very unpleasant, but I felt a sense of freedom after receiving the lawyer's letter: the Eat at Joe's years were finally over. The experience had dented my belief in my own record making, something that would last for a few years, but like everything, the pain eases. You get up and get on with life.

With the new company seeming to be on the cards, Peter and I started seeing a few other reps to ask if they would join us: John Payne on the south coast and Austin Powell, to help with radio, accepted. Some others declined to commit, but they sent us their call patterns and stores visited and painstakingly, Peter and I put pins in a map of the UK and began to plot our call cycles. But the weeks continued to drag by. Jive gave us more snippets of hope but never committed and then they would be unavailable for ten days. Peter used to phone and phone them, but I could not generate the drive to keep calling. Mom was seriously on my case as I had now been out of work for nearly seven months. I applied for a product manager's job at EMI just to show her I was trying to move forward – I had no intention of even going to an interview, but it could just buy me another three weeks of relative peace.

March had gone and April had begun. Three months had passed and Peter and I were now seriously doubting we would be able to start a company with Jive. We had also lost our general confidence and did not think we could pull the company off with Tom, as we would have no banker for regular contracted records coming into the company. We were in bad shape. By 8th April, we decided we had reached the end of the waiting road and needed a final and definitive decision from Jive. We decided to bluff the whole thing: there were no mobile phones in those days, so we stationed ourselves at Peter's mom's and phoned Keith Swallow. We gave them fifteen minutes to say 'in or out' or we would go with the other offer. There was of course no other offer. It was the longest 15 minutes of our lives. Keith phoned back and said it was a yes.

The Phoenix flies again:

On Monday 11th April, Keith Swallow approved the initial money for stationery, cars and a temporary office. Finally, we were getting somewhere. I stayed in London that week at Shaun's as we buzzed around London organising stationery, ordering cars and visiting our first temporary office, which was at the premises of Jive's main accountant, David Sloane, in High Street Kensington. Clive had spoken with us and said that David Sloane would become our personal accountant and would also provide us with an office for six weeks until Jive made one for us on site.

We called to Jive on 14th April and from not being able to get them on the phone we now moved to being there every week. We were to meet John Fruin and explain how and when we were going to launch the company. John Fruin had been an advisor to Clive Calder for some months, a relationship that had grown since a meeting in South Africa many years before.

Fruin had been the top executive in the British recording industry for many years: starting at EMI, he had risen to General Manager under Sir Joseph Lockwood in the Sixties and had been responsible for The Beatles and the growth of a then small label Tamla Motown. There are many photographs of John Fruin on behalf of EMI sitting with John, Paul, George and Ringo making plans for releases, especially after the death of Brian Epstein. John had then gone on to be Managing Director of Polydor Records, handling The Who, The Bee Gees, the meteoric rise of Slade and The Osmonds. This would lead to his occupying two prestigious positions at the same time: while continuing as Managing Director of Polydor he also became President of MGM Records in Los Angeles. He would have five days in England and then five days in Los Angeles, a schedule he managed to complete for eleven months before flying and fatigue made it impossible to continue. He then formed Record Merchandisers, which was owned by the major record companies and sold records to all the main high street stores on behalf of the labels. This eventually became Entertainment UK, which later chairmen of record companies foolishly sold to Woolworths. He was Chairman of The British Phonographic Industry, the governing body of the record business, and also became Chairman of Warner Brothers Records in their glory days of the Seventies when they rose to be the No 1 popular music company in the UK.

Our meeting with John was a little frightening. He was such a big name and knew all there was to know about the record business and how it worked. He definitely had Clive's ear and this was another test we just had to pass. I never liked being intimidated and would always put on a front to overcome that fear, so that you just would never know from my actions that I was not one hundred percent confident. I decided the best way to deal with John Fruin was to attack – this being the best form of defence. I went straight after John, explaining how people had failed before, himself included, and how we were not going to fail. We could guarantee the outside records and turn Jive into a hit making machine that would be driven by the promotion company. John patiently asked questions and sought his answers and reassurances under my 'full on' attack of bravado. Never once did he get close to losing his temper with what was really a young upstart who knew very little.

When we left and got out into Willesden High Road, Peter exploded.

'What the hell did you do that for? You went after him, you could have

blown the whole thing.'

'No, I had to let him know I am my own man, not to be intimidated and, win or lose, I'll stand up and take the blame.'

Peter was not happy with me, but it did work. John Fruin recommended to Clive that he should back the two of us and give the operation a shot, as he believed we had the passion and commitment to pull it off.

I look back on that meeting with total embarrassment. I should never have spoken to such a shrewd record business operator in that fashion. My only saving grace is that John Fruin saw in me someone who would never give in and would always work hard and play hard. I was either going to win or the destruction left behind would be too much for anyone to bear.

Impulse it is:

Peter soon forgot about my attack that day and we got on with building the company and organising everything that needed to be done to open the doors. We agonised for months over the name of our company. Sometimes we had fun coming up with stupid names: our favourite at the time was Peter Brady Enterprises. Peter Brady was the Invisible Man and somehow it appealed to us as we drove around the country trying to recruit the reps that had been so disappointed in those Promopeople days, all under cover. Finally, we agreed that the company name would be, The Impulse Promotion Company. We took a little stick from people who said we were running an underarm spray business, but I loved that word Impulse – it reincarnated how Peter and I had acted impulsively while we were at Promopeople. It was a name we were proud to stand behind and speak out loud. When that name came to us, we would never consider calling the company anything else.

Jive agreed that Peter and I would start on the payroll on 1st May 1983. I signed on the dole for my final time on 26th April and we picked up our new Ford Escort 1.6 Ghia's from Woking on the 29th. It had been a long hard road: ten months since we had left Promopeople in which I had seen the depths of no confidence, fought against looming depression, but managed somehow to hang on to the dream of remaining and building a career in records. My Mom had wanted me to give up and find a 'proper' job and Sue and I were almost at the end of our relationship, although somehow, we had managed to hang on. My sister Helen had constantly been supportive and always told my Mom 'just leave him alone, he will eventually work it out.' Peter Todd had also suffered throughout those months and I had kept him going when it got bad, but I believe that it was Peter who had to prop me up more. He hung in there when it looked like I was going nowhere and he had a greater belief in me than I had in myself. As we drove off the courtyard in Woking that day with brand new cars to head north and home, the smile that passed between us was one of true faith, hope and belief. We were back.

CHAPTER 13

IMPULSE – THE BEGINNING – 1983

Revenge is Sweet – or Returning a Favour:

The Impulse Promotion Company commenced work on 31st May 1983. As the next month began there was plenty of work for Peter and myself. Having promised Peter fifty percent of my next venture, I duly agreed that Zomba Records, owner of Jive Records, would have a fifty-one percent share of The Impulse Promotion Company, and Peter and I would own twenty-four and a half percent each.

Our jobs were clearly defined and they remained so for a long time in the building of Impulse. Peter organised the team, dealing with their notice periods from Promopeople, arranging the company cars and sorting out their PAYE tax, the petrol cards, our phones, photocopier, the boxes for distribution, the call cycle, in fact, everything to do with the day-to-day running of our operation, which included putting together our first meeting at the Holiday Inn in Birmingham on 28th May.

My job was to obtain the records we would be working. I remember sitting in our first office at David Sloane's just staring at the phone: would anyone respond to my calls, would anyone be interested that we had started a new promotion company, would I be able to get any records for that all important first week when we had to give the reps something to promote when they went in store? I had to walk out onto Kensington High Street to smoke a cigarette in solitude and build up my confidence to put in that first call. As with most things in life that you have done many times before, once the first call was over, it was just like riding a bike.

I started by visiting a great friend first: John Aston at CBS. After that, Robert Lemon at Bronze Records, Rough Trade Records and Geoff Travis, Tilly Rutherford at Red Bus Records, Ray Cooper at Island Records, Laurie Freeman at Ronco Records, Howard Berman at A & M Records, Graham Mabbutt at Magnet Records, Tim Reid at Polydor Records, Tim Heath at Rialto Records, Phil Cokell at Chrysalis Records, Alan Belman at Albion Records, Bill Stonebridge at Riva Records, Steve Weltman at Charisma Records, Jim Doyle at Rocket Records, Brian Yates at Arista Records, David Arden at Jet Records – well, just about anyone I knew at any record company. Peter mailed shots to every publisher we could find as they would have interests via song ownership with many records and might recommend us. We were ruthless in our pursuit of records to work and in establishing relationships that would bring records in the future. We were determined that Impulse would work.

Fortunately, the reaction to Impulse was good. The recording business has always been a small village industry where everyone gets to know everything: it is riddled with rumour and speculation and the trading of information has always been high on the list of day-to-day agendas. Most of the marketing directors had known about the staff revolt at Promopeople eleven months previously and they had been sympathetic to what I had tried to do at that company. This did surprise me, as I thought I had been totally forgotten after the embarrassing outcome of that day. Alan Wade had also not done himself any favours in the eleven months that had passed: companies had continued to use Promopeople, but with less and less success, and I believe that this was mainly because of Alan's insistence that any record offered was taken, just for the money. It meant that the company's hit ratio had increasingly diminished. Thus, the main competitor Bullet Promotions had seized the opportunity and gradually begun to take clients away from Promopeople. Bullet at that time looked fresher and more organised: Stewart Coxhead and Barry Evans had come out of a major label and were driving forward to assert themselves in the marketplace.

Word was now spreading that the Impulse Promotion Company was coming and our chosen reps from Promopeople were handing in their notice periods: Andy Richmond, one month, Kevin Rea, one month, Sue Parsons, two weeks, Shaun King, two weeks and so on. As each week went by in May, Peter and I handed a blow to Promopeople as we marketed Impulse with its already trained and experienced staff. Record companies began to stop putting records with Promopeople, trying Bullet or putting releases back to wait and see what would happen. They increasingly came to us instead. Peter and I were relentless in our approach and there is no doubt that we intended to close Promopeople, take their staff, take their work and leave Alan Wade, Steven Bentink and Paul Ridout wishing they had never heard of us. This determination and drive powered us through every day.

The First Hits:

A development in the record industry the past Christmas had delayed Jive Records from confirming our partnership: Gallup would take over the chart and start to compile it in a different way. This marked the beginning of barcodes and the magic wand that registered a sale and it was an attempt to legitimise the record chart and obtain truer information with a better sample of sales. This way a more accurate and representative UK record chart would be made. All of this was well and good when written on paper, but the change over and the communications with the stores that would be involved took a little time. There was also the question of budget, which would be paid for by the record companies themselves via the BPI

(British Phonographic Industry). In effect, and at just the right time for Impulse, due to the equipment and cost the panel of stores quickly reduced from 1,000 to 500, and by May of that year, 1983, there were only around 250 remaining. This enabled the Impulse Promotion Company to start with less than half the number of representatives that Promopeople operated and keep our costs low. Meanwhile, Peter was a master at finding each store as one by one they began to be awarded with their wand.

Peter and I discussed Gallup and we decided the best way forward was to open our books and build a relationship with them. We would tell them what records we were going to work, have an open dialogue with them and give them information we came across that would help them as they provided a chart for the BPI. We emphasised that we were also an independent that worked for all the record companies and, as we were in the same business of 'the chart', we suggested that we should be close and help each other. Over the coming years either Peter or I or both of us would visit Gallup's offices every month and we would trade information. Gallup kept Impulse legal in their eyes and we informed them of irregularities that we might find or stores that deserved and should be on their panel. This was a completely different approach from all the record companies, most of which had to deal with internal politics and blame for a record not becoming a hit. Their reaction every Tuesday was to phone Gallup and lambast the staff at their wrongful collection of data and poor effort at compiling a chart. In the early days of Impulse our strategy was a masterstroke.

The week before we opened, we moved into our first proper offices, in buildings rented from Jive. They were two rooms in Chaplin Road, Willesden. Steve Skinner, a bass player and friend of Shaun King, joined us to take care of the distribution of records to the reps, and Helen Tyler came on board as a secretary. Saturday 28th May came around and we all headed to the Holiday Inn in Birmingham for the first team meeting of Impulse. The team were raring to go: Davy Pritchard had not liked Polydor and he joined us for Scotland, Andy Richmond and Kevin Rea were operating in the East and West, Sue Parsons in the Midlands, Shaun King and Ken Spencer in London, Guy Hague in the West Country and Phil Tomkins in the South. They were full of positive energy to be with us – at last, they were employees of a company and they had company cars.

Peter and I had pulled Impulse off from nowhere and we were all determined to make it work and get hit records. I presented the first week's work. Roman Holiday were a young band signed to Jive Records and the single 'Don't Try To Stop It' was destined to be a hit and break the band. On that first Saturday we had no idea if it would become a hit, but we liked the single and it had a special cache as it had come from our backers. A Flock of Seagulls were making a name for themselves and would later be successful in America: 'I Ran', 'Space Age Lovesong', 'Wishing', and 'Nightmares' would all become hit singles and, again, they were products of

Jive Records. My old friend Tilly Rutherford was working at Red Bus Records and provided us with a single by Push that would not become a hit. Finally, there came an album from Ronco Records that would establish Impulse in its first week. Laurie Freeman was someone I had known at Ronco, having worked with him during my time at Promopeople, and I particularly noticed his *Close Encounters Of The Hit Kind*, a title play on the movie, which had been at No 2 on the album chart for two weeks. I asked Laurie if we could make an arrangement whereby we would work the album free of charge, but if it went to No 1 then he would pay us our full fee. It was an offer he could not refuse. The following Sunday, after one week, Close Encounters, as a compilation of hits, would stand proudly as the UK's No 1 album and along with it Impulse. We were No 1 – and we were getting paid!

The benefit of having Jive Records as our backers in that initial period was immense. It gave the team the feeling they were part of something bigger than a promotion company and could be part of building a label as well. After the No 1 album with Ronco in our first week we felt we wanted to send out a signal that this new company was something special, so we started work for Island Records, with Joe Cocker and Robert Palmer, and Red Bus gave us what would become a hit with Imagination's 'Looking At Midnight.' The breakthrough record on the singles chart came courtesy of Malcolm McLaren: a No 3 record with 'Double Dutch.' The third week of Impulse brought an album from Uriah Heep for Bronze Records and The Crammps' *Off The Bone* album. The biggest news of the week for us, though, was that Promopeople had closed its doors. Just three weeks short of twelve months since Peter and I had left Promopeople we had returned with our own company and blitzed Promopeople out of the marketplace.

As the weeks went by we started to work for all the record companies. My main responsibility at this time was to get discs from record companies for the team to work; it was a big responsibility as everyone's livelihood now rested firmly on my shoulders. Jive Records and Clive Calder expected Impulse to be successful on its own merit and also bring hit records to Jive. Peter and the team had backed me on this venture and their hopes and dreams rested on my ability to recognise potential hit records, obtain them from the record companies, make them into chart hits and thus bring in income for everyone. This was the first time in my life that I had trouble sleeping. I just kept waking up at three in the morning wondering if I had forgotten something, was there anything else I could do, where could I get a guarantee of more records, what were our competitors working and why were their clients not using Impulse. I was also learning to balance the books of the business: Keith Swallow, Jive's accountant, taught me a lot in these initial stages and fortunately, I found it all interesting and had a good head for figures and money. But, it still all kept me awake at night, and that would last for almost the first year until the repetition and increasing income brought more confidence that the company would not go under.

There is no such thing as bad publicity except your own obituary:

Bullet Promotions were now our only competitor in the marketplace. We had made a marketing campaign under the heading 'Act On Impulse', which we had run for a couple of weeks in *Music Week*. Bullet responded with a campaign that said 'Don't Act on Impulse, Wait, Think for a Moment and Choose Bullet.' Peter was upset about them having a go at us, but I was flattered. Here was Impulse, a small company only just in the marketplace, and the firmly established Bullet mentions us in their advertising. I suggested to Peter that they were worried and had given us free advertising – we must now attack their clients and steal them. Peter was in, so we set about talking to the labels that gave Bullet the most work and offered introductory deals with Impulse. Daniel Miller was a Bullet client as owner of Mute Records and as Clive Calder knew him well he arranged an entrée for me. Out of it came a relationship with Dépêche Mode and an immediate hit with 'Everything Counts': the first of many Dépêche Mode singles we were to work over the coming years. Bullet were furious. Next, we went after Dave Robinson, owner of Stiff Records and someone who had suggested he would use no-one else. I almost forced my way into Dave's office one day with Peter. We started to do our pitch for Impulse, whereupon Dave stood up, picked up a cricket bat and started to practice his forward defensive stroke. That he continued to do throughout our twenty minute presentation. Peter never liked disrespect and he wanted to just 'chin him' there and then, however, he refrained and we finally left peacefully. Just four weeks later we were working for Stiff Records on the Belle Stars and Dave Robinson would become a lifelong associate. I think Clive had again intervened and convinced Dave we were the right people to work with. My only comment was that Dave needed to keep his left elbow up higher on the forward defensive stroke – I would have got him out easy with a couple of normal balls.

It was not long before Impulse was attracting a huge number of small independent labels and, in particular, their managements wanted to taste the success they saw that we had achieved with Jive: Elton John's Rocket Records, Daniel Miller's Mute Records, Wham's Innervision Records, Martin Mills' Beggars Banquet Records and Chris Hills' Ensign Records were just some of the luminary labels that very quickly came to Impulse and enjoyed hit records with us. Our reputation was growing week by week and in the fourth week of our operation Nick East and Barry Evangeli came to Impulse with a record on Proto Records by Hazel Dean. The single was 'Searchin' (Gotta Find A Man)', and although the record initially would not be a hit and would take almost a year to become one, it started a long and fruitful relationship with Barry and Nick and also put me back in touch with Pete Waterman – more on that later.

Impulse's two room office became a place where recording artists would turn up to say 'Hello.' Peter and I loved it that artists thought Impulse was important enough to drop by, vibe us up about their single and encourage us to work hard for them. In those early months, Hazel Dean, A Flock Of Seagulls, Roman Holiday, Imagination, Oliver Cheatham, Julie Andrews, Chris Rea, Gary Numan, The Belle Stars, Wham and Snowy White were visitors to our two rooms.

The team had decided that they wanted monthly one day meetings, which was important to keep them in touch both with what was happening in the office and also with the labels we were talking to. This also made everyone feel a part of the company as a whole, as we discussed everything openly at those meetings: what other record companies were doing, what marketing and deals were being done at store level, what new shops we could forward to Gallup, etc. Each week Peter put together the team sheet with information about every record we worked, what was expected, where the bonus payment would be paid and at what chart position. All of us knew everything about what we were doing and Impulse was an immaculate machine.

Building a power base:

After a month of business we opened The Impulse Radio Promotion Company. Austin Powell joined us, which I was particularly pleased about, as he had been Warner Brothers promotion man in their heyday under John Fruin. I had desperately wanted to join Warners, but Austin always blocked the way. I believed that Austin was the best promo man on the road during the '70s, along with Bob Hermon from CBS. Granted they were working for the biggest companies with the most hits, but they were both no-nonsense promo men who knew radio and the game. Austin brought in Julie Griffiths, who had worked for many years at EMI, and I believed we had recruited the two most experienced radio promotion people in the country to join the company. Many record companies believed the same and it became an easy job to get a record for the reps and Austin at the same time. Austin and Julie built that arm of the company almost on their own and although Peter and I got records for them to work, they both had their own contacts and brought records in for the reps as well. Now we had four people bringing in work and from different angles.

We soon moved offices to Maybury Gardens in Willesden, right next door to the Jive Offices. Meanwhile, Jive Records had just opened a small office in New York with three or four people, including Barry Weiss. We started to receive records from New York and they were this new sound called Rap. Impulse started to work records like 'Magic's Wand' by Whodini and 'Go See The Doctor' by Kool Mo Dee. These were not hit records in the usual sense, but we were obtaining night-time radio play and beginning to see an underground swell with kids buying them – that was not enough to make the discs hits, but it was sufficient that we could break even at the outset and then increase income with every subsequent release. The age of Rap was beginning and Impulse was right there in the middle of it.

Pinnacle Records, the label and distributor, had been recently purchased by an exporter, Steve Mason. His Windsong export company had done well and he had invested his profits into the independent distributor. Pinnacle would be a part of my life for the next 27 years and Steve Mason was a close friend while we shared multiple hit records together. At that time, I had no idea who Steve Mason was, and our relationship did not get off to the best of starts. Steve also wanted to have hit singles and albums on his own label and his first offering was The Nick Straker Band. Steve contacted me and we talked through the record and how we would approach the promotion. The first week went OK, but we came up one short at No 76. This is the most frustrating number on the chart: everyone published the Top 75 at the time, so if you were No 75 you would expect an order of 8,000 records from Woolworths and large chain stores, but if you were 76 there were no orders at all. Radio also only took notice of the Top 75: hence, No 75, some radio play, No 76, no play. Impulse set about week two on The Nick Straker Band and we were confident that the record had momentum and would go into the Top 75 the following week. Not so, Nick Straker stuck at 76. I had hardly ever known a record manage that feat, normally the record went into the 75 or dropped like a stone. The Tuesday morning call from Steve Mason was one of those that I remembered for years. Steve thought that Impulse had done an incredibly poor job and was the reason for his hit record stalling. Our conversation ended with Steve calling Impulse some expletives and me responding in kind. This was how what was to be one of the most successful partnerships in the history of the record business started. It would take a couple of years for our first encounter to heal, but I believe it had been the meeting of two people with tremendous belief in what they were doing and when, eventually, we were both able to harness that passion and drive, incredible success was to be ours.

Billy Ocean:

Jive Records during these early months of Impulse signed Billy Ocean. Billy had enjoyed hits in the mid to late '70s with 'Love Really Hurts Without You', 'Love On Delivery', 'Stop Me', and 'Red Light Spells Danger.' These had all been issued on a small independent label called GTO Records. When GTO was sold to CBS Records Billy's contract went with it and so he started to record with CBS. There was some initial success with a couple of records, but eventually his contract came to an end and he returned to club gigs to make a living. Clive Calder had heard a demo around the Jive office that people were talking about. I will always remember his comments: 'It's not the song that's good, it's the singer making it sound good. Let's get the singer in.' That singer was Billy Ocean and he was duly signed to Jive, initially on a singles deal. Billy signed because Clive had a plan that involved going to America to record and work with US producers, which was just what Billy and his manager Laurie Jay wanted to hear. The first time I met Billy was on the stairs to the Jive offices. I was just returning to Impulse after a meeting at Jive and we crossed on the stairs as Billy was going up for another meeting.

Billy has always been a pleasant and charming man. We stopped and spoke for a few minutes and that was the start of a friendship that has lasted for going on for thirty years now. Neither of us knew at that point the success that would follow with record-breaking sales and the world tours that followed. We were just trying to further our careers a little bit back then.

30 years of freindship, Billy Ocean, me in the background

Laurie Jay has also been a friend since then. Laurie started in the business in the sixties as a drummer and played with both The Shadows and The Rolling Stones as a 'fill in' when Brian Bennett and Charlie Watts were laid low with illness. He then graduated through the years from playing drums to nightclub management and publishing before starting his own management company and signing Billy Ocean. The two of them always reminded me of TV's 'The Odd Couple': constantly at odds, but very much a real team that cared for each other. The ups and downs of that relationship would rumble on for years as they began to dominate the record charts around the world.

Miss World and Mr Football:

Laurie also looked after the former Miss World, Mary Stavin. Mary was extremely beautiful and a very beautiful woman inside as well as on the outside. George Best, always a keen lover of beautiful women, had met Mary and they had begun an affair that would see them all over the newspapers, radio and TV. At that time, Jive Records were making 'keep fit' records and had great success with the actress Felicity Kendall. Felicity had just been voted 'Rear of The Year' and had talked about her training that had achieved this accolade. The album sold well and Impulse played its part in the sales of that album. In looking for a follow up to this idea, plus George and Mary all over the media, Jive, with Laurie, set about a George and Mary fitness album. George Best was my all-time footballing hero and as I had heard that George and Mary were to do a photo shoot in Covent Garden for the album, I asked Laurie if I could go and meet George. Just looking at Mary would be a bonus, but meeting George was everything for me.

Come the day, off I went to Covent Garden. There were a few people around, but George and Mary had no entourage, it was just the two of them and at that time they were extremely happy with each other. Laurie had told them about Impulse and the records we had success with and that I would play a major part in their album. The two of them were just fabulous to be with. I stayed for a couple of hours as the photo shoot went on and it was easy to see why George was in love with Mary. Her experiences from being Miss World had not affected her one bit, she was still just an ordinary girl. George was one of the most charming people I had ever met. I know all the stories of his alcoholism and have read all the books about his life, but although I would go on to meet him several times I never encountered him 'on the pop.' You could not meet a more pleasant man with such a god given talent. We talked for ages about everything and finally, I asked if he would do a photo for Impulse, a sort of 'Only The Best Use Impulse.' Sadly he declined, but he did so graciously, saying he tried hard not to use his name in advertising and if he did just one the floodgates were open. I didn't mind at all, I had my moment just sitting and talking with George, something I never thought would happen in my life and I am truly thankful that it did.

A watershed hit:

In any company there is at least one turning point when things go well and, although you don't know it at the time, it sets up what is to come. As 1983 was coming to its end, on a trip to Jive when I was under pressure and worried, a record caught my eye: Love Is A Wonderful Colour by The Icicle Works – Beggars Banquet Records release No 99. This single had hovered for three weeks around the Top 100 mark: No 121, No 95, No 109. The sales, however, had increased each week and although the chart positions were suggesting it was not going to become a hit record the sales were intimating it could. I asked Steve Skinner to get me a copy of the record and, when I listened to it in the office I liked the record and thought it was a hit. I phoned Martin Mills and said how much I liked the record and could we have a go at it. I would not charge any money initially, but if it became a hit we would need to be paid in full. Martin said he would pay some costs and full payment if we were to succeed: The Icicle Works at that time were completely unknown and Martin, who just wanted enthusiasm, was taken by our offer to even work for free.

On 24 December 1983, 'Love Is A Wonderful Colour' by The Icicle Works peaked on the UK record charts at No 15 and established an outstanding relationship between Beggars Banquet and Impulse that would deliver many hit records. Impulse now had a hit record going into Christmas and it had come from absolutely nowhere. I realised all the answers I needed were in the chart book from Gallup. For years to come I analysed that book everyday and watched sales patterns intensely. If you knew how the chart worked intimately and watched what other records did around the one you were looking at, you could, to some degree, predict a record's movement in the coming week. In today's world, record companies have teams of analysts that predict movement on the chart and collect reams of information, but in 1983 no one looked at the chart book to examine the collation of sales patterns in this way. Slowly, people did get the hang of it, but at the time of our new success this thinking gave Impulse a true head start on competitors and record labels. To me, it was no hardship to spend hours with this book: records, chart positions and sales had been my hobby for years and if I had not operated for Impulse I would have still been checking chart positions as a hobby.

1983 *Impulse advert*

Hits of the year at Impulse:

Those first seven months of Impulse brought hit records and artists through our door that I could not have dreamed of only a short time earlier. There was 'Bird Of Paradise' by Snowy White on Towerbell Records, which was No 6 on 24th December 1983. Bob England owned Towerbell Records and had built the company from the success of Chas and Dave, an act he managed. At Promopeople we had been involved in 'Ain't No Pleasing You' and at Record Sales we had worked their other big hit, 'Rabbit.' Bob brought us the Snowy White record and, although it was good, it was out of fashion for that time. Our big break came when Steve Wright, then on Radio One in the afternoon, met his future wife and associated her with 'Bird Of Paradise.' In those days, the DJs had some personal choice in what they played, unlike today, which is why every radio show sounds the same now. Steve hammered the record, playing it three or four times a week to his, then, massive audience. Impulse got the records to the right stores at the right time, our radio company began to spread the play at radio as the record started to sell and we all ended up with a Top 10 single. I don't know the name of Steve Wright's wife, but after all these years I would like to thank her for giving us that unexpected hit single: to me, she is still a 'Bird Of Paradise.'

'Club Tropicana' by Wham on Innervision Records reached No 4 on 30th July 1983. A couple of years earlier I had met Mark Dean, George Michael and Andrew Ridgeley at Innervision Records when they were setting up the label, long before they had a hit single. I had gone to meet them during my days at Promopeople and they wanted to know how we worked and how we could help. I instantly got on with Mark Dean, who had created the label at the tender age of 18, and was full of passion and commitment about his company and his friends who had formed a band, Wham. We had the initial hit together 'Young Guns' and, since my departure from Promopeople, Mark had used them on 'Wham Rap' and 'Bad Boys.' Now that Impulse was up and running, Mark, Innervision and Wham were back with us. Mark had a good sense of humour, which enabled us to get along well, and I admired that he had set up a label so early in his life and just gone for it without much knowledge. 'Club Tropicana' is still played on the radio and I still sing along: the record brings back good memories for me in the first flushes of success with Impulse.

'Waiting For A Train' by Flash and The Pan, on Easybeat Records, peaked at No 7 in June 1983. The best part for me about operating Impulse at this time was the hits we had with small independent labels. Working with the major companies brought the big stars, but the little labels, that sometimes only had one act or one hit, were the ones I really enjoyed. The operators were working on a tight budget, but they were passionate and had an inner belief that they too could succeed; to be involved in taking on the big companies via Impulse with them was a pleasure. 'Waiting For A Train' was one of those. Shaun brought the record in one Friday and said 'listen to this, it's great.' We all loved it and so we got in touch with Easybeat and made a deal to work the single. To see this record climb to the Top 10 in the UK was fantastic: we had affected the nation's consciousness with a record and forced them to dance.

'Hold Me Now' by The Thompson Twins on Arista Records stood at No 4 in November 1983.

Whilst I was at Promopeople I had been involved in the set up of this band and had got to know them a little through Brian Yates at Arista Records. They had a couple of hits with 'Love On Your Side' and 'We Are Detective', but they had slipped back with the release of 'Watching.' To make sure that the band re-established themselves Brian called me in to listen to the single. We discussed the marketing and sales planning endlessly, as this was a most important single for them: a failure and it could be over, a hit and 'Watching' was just a blip. 'Hold Me Now' eventually peaked at No 4.

'Love Blonde' by Kim Wilde on Rak Records reached No 23 in July 1983. I mention this record not only because it was a hit for Kim – and what a pleasure she was to work with briefly – but also, because to be associated with the Wilde family for just a short while was a thrill. Marty, Kim's father, in my opinion, was a pioneer of the UK recording industry. His hits 'Endless Sleep', 'Donna', 'A Teenager In Love', 'Sea of Love', 'Bad Boy' and 'Rubber Ball' were all records that I heard and liked during my early years in Walsall. Also, I met one of my heroes in the set-up to this record: I was invited to Rak Records to meet and discuss Kim's single with Mickey Most. Mickey had been an artist with his bother Dave before becoming a record producer, and his label and hits, for a while, had a huge impact on the chart, building Rak Records, which was a type of Motown in the UK, but with pop records. To me, Mickey had the key, and to sit and talk with him about arranging the promotion and sales on one of his records was another thrill. Mickey and I got on well over the years and I was to work on several of his discs, work with his son Calvin and be invited to Montebello, Mickey's house, for drinks and dinner. Mickey is an icon of the British record industry and it was an honour to collaborate with him.

'War Baby' by Tom Robinson on Panic Records hit No 6 in June 1983. Tom had left EMI four years previously after chalking up four hit records, the biggest being in 1977 with '2 4 6 8 Motorway.' 'War Baby' was his comeback release. Panic Records sent us the record and asked us if we wanted to be involved and we loved the single. For a period of time we played and played it around the office and it generated real passion amongst the reps that we were succeeding in such a big way with Tom and a very small label. The record is still a classic single today.

'IOU' by Freeez, on Beggars Banquet Records, was No 2 in July 1983. Freeez had a huge record in 1981 with 'Southern Freeze.' It had made the Top 10, and we had played that record around the offices at Record Sales when they were seen as a 'cool' band. 'IOU' was, again, a comeback record after almost two years without a release, and we were, again, under pressure as the band's livelihood was dependant on the single's success. Once again we managed to deliver our part in the promotion and our reward was a No 2 record.

'In Your Eyes' by George Benson on Warner Brothers Records made No 7 in September 1983. Impulse was trying hard to work for Warner Brothers. History shows we never did crack the Warner's account, they believed in their own way of doing things. In Impulse's early days they were, though, trying us out and George Benson was the chosen artist. George was and still is one of my favourite artists of all time and I couldn't get hold of the single quick enough. We wound up the team that this might just be our chance to get in with Warner's. They did an outstanding job and we had a Top 10 single.

'Cry Just A Little Bit' by Shakin' Stevens on Epic Records was No 3 in November 1983. At CBS, the owners of the Epic label, John Aston, had progressed to become Sales Manager and he was in charge of all sales and outside promoters. I had now known John eleven or twelve years and we had both watched each others' fortunes blossom. John called us in to work on Shaky who was in a tremendous run of hit singles that went on for years. We were delighted to be involved and John always knew I would give one hundred percent effort on his records.

We also worked with and had hits with The Belle Stars, Gary Numan, Killing Joke, Toyah, The Beat, Comsat Angels, Diamond Head, Chris Rea, Todd Rundgren, Robert Palmer, The Stray Cats, The Stranglers and Joe Cocker. They all added something special to the early days of Impulse.

1983 also brought one of those big moments that you remember all your life. My Dad had been a big fan of Julie Andrews and it was with Mom, Dad and Helen that I went to the cinema in Walsall to see *Mary Poppins* and *The Sound Of Music*. My friend Steve Colyer, who had produced an Eat At Joe's track for me, now had a label called Runaway Records and somehow had obtained the rights to a Julie Andrews album. Steve got in touch and asked if we would become involved and I said yes, on condition that I could meet Julie. Steve said it was a deal and some weeks later I went along to meet Julie Andrews. I could hardly catch my breath. Julie was brilliant that day and I spent over an hour just chatting with her. At the time, her image was of a prim and proper woman, however, she was not like that at all: she was fun, charming and enjoyed making fun just like the rest of us. I told my Mom that I had met Julie Andrews and showed her the autograph that Julie had signed on the album for me, but I so wished that my Dad had still been alive: he would have had a real kick from me hanging out with Julie Andrews.

1983 had been the year that The Impulse Promotion Company had changed my life. We had made No 1 on the UK album charts in our first week of operation in June and even though, as hard as we tried, we did not achieve a No 1 single that year, we made the Top 10 several times and achieved Nos 2 and 3. The singles No 1 slot had not been destined for us this year – but momentous times were just around the corner.

1984 *Impulse advert*

CHAPTER 14

THE FIRST FLUSH OF SUCCESS – 1984

Life in The Fast Lane:

As 1983 drew to its close, the Impulse Promotion Company stood fully established in the UK record business marketplace and we were beginning to reap the rewards of our hard-work. Even so, we never imagined what was to happen in the coming year. 1984 would be groundbreaking and set the company apart from all others, and running up to that came a milestone personal development. Pete Waterman and I had been friends from our Midland DJ days and train journeys to and from London and now that friendship was reborn in a new context, binding our relationship in a special way that has continued to this day. It arose out of the small label Proto that Barry Evangeli and Nick East were building. Barry had said he was thinking of working with Pete Waterman, who was setting up a production company with his two new partners Mike Stock and Matt Aitken, who Pete thought he could make hit records with. At that time Pete was driving around London in an old battered Jaguar and trying to persuade artists and labels to give him a shot at producing a record or two. I told Barry I knew Pete from the old days and a couple of weeks later he showed up at our Impulse offices. We reminisced about those old days and discussed what we were looking to do now.

Pete was trying to make records and I was looking for records to work through Impulse, so we casually agreed that Pete would 'make 'em' and I would 'promote and sell 'em.' Little did we realise back then that the coming years in this partnership would bring more hits than we could begin to dream of. All that mattered then was pushing for a hit with Searchin' for Hazel Dean, as it was agreed that Pete would make the follow-up single and begin his production company with Stock and Aitken. This was to take a little time to happen.

As 1984 dawned Peter Todd and I were hoping for a No 1 record, but in fact it fell to Austin Powell and our Radio Promotion Company to deliver the first of our No 1 hits from an unlikely source. 'Only You' by The Flying Pickets became the UK's No 1 and Austin delivered playlist after playlist with Julie Griffiths on its march to the top.

Our operation between Christmas and New Year brought immediate results. The huge TV show that had become compulsive viewing at that time was *Auf Wiedersehn Pet*, the story of some bricklayers from Newcastle who had gone to Germany to find work. The viewing figures were enormous and straight after Christmas we had a No 3 record with the show's theme 'That's Living Alright', by Joe Fagin for Towerbell Records. Bob England's Towerbell was an unfashionable label at the time and the success of this single brought a lot of credibility to Impulse. The major labels thought that if Impulse could do it with Towerbell then the company must have an even better chance with an established label. Our reputation was growing.

David Massey, who would go on to have a big career in the record business, was then the manager of an unknown band, Wang Chung, and he brought us a single I really liked. We worked Dance Hall Days during the Christmas period and managed a No 21 that broke the act and brought Wang Chung a fanbase and fame. Impulse and Massey were ecstatic at this result as their label Warner Brothers were struggling with the act. However, this one record was to curtail our relationship with Warner Brothers for years to come. Rob Dickens, a man I have long had the utmost respect for, was Managing Director of Warners at the time and I don't think he was ever a fan of Impulse: he believed his own promotion and sales forces were the best. He did not want to pay outside promoters for assistance even though managers of his acts always wanted him to use us, especially after the Wang Chung success. I thought this was fair enough, but I believed we were more aggressive and better. Rob always declined to comment publicly, but his then marketing director, Paul Conroy, took real offence, probably caused by internal pressure. When the follow-up single was being discussed David Massey obviously wanted Impulse to do the job and Conroy did not. History is sometimes defined in one phone call and Conroy made a call to me with a list of unjustified accusations that sparked an intense confrontation and sadly ended in a parting of the ways between Warners and Impulse. It took many years to heal the rift between us and I do believe it was Warners' loss as to this day the only hit record Wang Chung ever achieved was the one Impulse worked: 'Dance Hall Days.'

Zomba was the holding company for Jive Records. Zomba also owned Battery Studios' Dreamhire, which was a studio equipment hire company, and Zomba Music Publishing. As well as all this, Zomba was the shareholder in Impulse. A new Zomba Managing Director was now installed: David Clipsham. David had worked for John Fruin as Marketing Director at Warner Brothers when John was Chairman. In John's new role as consultant to Zomba, Jive Records and Clive Calder, John had recommended the appointment. It had come about because Zomba was beginning to grow quickly and Clive was spending more time in the United States. John Fruin had called me to his office and informed me of David's arrival, whereupon I had suggested that it meant little to me as surely this had nothing to do with Impulse.

But John said that, in fact, I would now discuss the future of Impulse with David and I was to welcome him to the company. Peter Todd was about as interested as I was in David's arrival: we thought we were partners with Clive and if we wanted to discuss anything we would do so with either Clive or John. Peter had no time at all for David Clipsham and so it was decided between us that I would deal with him, even though I really didn't want to. The only reason I did so was that I had the greatest respect for John Fruin.

Going back to school:

David Clipsham had decided that I should go on a course about management and selling. This was to be a two-week affair and he believed it would knock off some of my rough edges and bring me into line. Originally, Peter was also to participate and we would attend at different times, but he completely ignored the suggestion. This put pressure on me to agree with the proposal and so during February I attended a two-week course on sales promotion. I hated it from the moment I went into the building, it was like being back at school. The people who had designed the course were like a sect. They had received a lot of press and it was all to do with mind conditioning – part of the first phase of the eighties 'yuppies' movement. They wore business suits and insisted we did the same. Each day they had a programme to break down your own individual personality so that you all respond in the same way to the same problem. We rehearsed daily on how to obtain a meeting, how to convince someone to make a deal, how to respond when the conversation was not going your way. Test after test on the right and wrong way to respond, it was like being a part of the 'Moonies.'

This went against everything I believed in and although I could see what they were doing and some parts of the course were undeniably good, the whole concept for me took away being original, being true to yourself and being able to think for yourself. We were filmed every day and then when the film was shown back to the class you were criticised, with the class then joining in on breaking down your character and personality. That was the first week. Then, the second week was all about rebuilding you in their design, showing you how much better it was to respond in their way and cheering you on when you succeeded in their way. By the time the second week had arrived I had had enough. Whatever they were selling, I wanted no part of it. I tried to remain quiet during the classes and just get through everything, and I almost made it, but by Thursday of the second week it became impossible. One of the final tests was to address the class from the front of the hall while being filmed and when the film was then played back everyone joined in with the criticism. In my previous years as a DJ compere and my more recent years as a promotion man, I had addressed a very wide range of people in a very wide variety of situations. I was experienced in the discipline of selling a company and service and getting clients to invest in the operation, and my belief was and is that the style of this should be entertaining, but serious at the relevant moments. This had worked exceptionally well in my career and two weeks of attempted brain washing could not disturb my beliefs.

As I approached the front of the room, I started and had only completed a couple of sentences when the instructors called a halt.

'That is not how we have taught you.'

'I know that, I want to illustrate a slightly different style that I have operated over the years.'

'No. No. No! Do it how we have shown you.'

This happened again and then when I explained my problem in front of the class I was told if I did not conform to the rules I would be expelled from the course. I continued:

'Ladies and Gentlemen, I've had a great couple of weeks and have enjoyed looking at another way to do things in business. Power selling over the phone without emotion is probably the way forward for a lot of people and probably for some of you, however, it's not for me. I'd like to thank all the operators that have spent time with me imparting their knowledge and I'm thankful for being part of your class and getting to know you, the students, over the past weeks. Unfortunately, I'm about to fail the course and be expelled, so I will not be seeing you tomorrow. Thank you.'

As I stepped outside, one of the senior course executives came to me and said that he would have to report me to my company for walking out improperly ahead of being expelled. I told him he could do whatever he liked, and my return to school came to an end.

David Clipsham did call me in a few days later, having read the report of my behaviour, which had been grossly exaggerated in print. I went through what had happened with him and suggested it was probably best not to send me on any more courses. I had my particular style of doing things, for the moment it was working, and when it stopped working we could review it. Fortunately, that never happened. John Fruin laughed at the report and we never discussed it again.

In fact, a combination of the experience of being with the 'Moonies' for a couple of weeks and the effects of a situation when one of our reps took a week or two off for holiday began the germ of an idea for a telephone sales company that would be a 'bolt on' operation to the promotion force. When a rep took a holiday we would mail the records to his area and follow up with phone calls from the office. Helen Tyler, Peter and occasionally I, would talk to the dealers and find out how our records were selling. This coupled with the 'Moonies' experience gave me the idea of how powerful and quick the phone was. Telephone sales operated by record companies at that time were incoming only. The record distributers had teams of sales girls that took orders when dealers phoned in, but they were not phoning out to pre-sell. They would only pre-sell as and when a dealer called, when they would mention the new records on offer. I believed there was a gap here that we could fill. If we pre-sold on our records to the dealers, even if this was a small quantity, they would at least have stock at the beginning of the week before our reps' call cycle reached them. I could not rid this idea from my mind and during the next couple of months it would grow into a new company for Impulse.

Bob Geldof:

One day I took a call from Bob Geldof. The Boomtown Rats' glory days were over and after some time off they were beginning a comeback with a new single and album. Bob invited me to his house off the Kings Road to discuss this. The single, which was destined to be only a minor hit, was 'Tonight.' Bob had originally been the Boomtown Rats manager, but when the singer quit, Bob decided to take his place and became the vocalist for the Rats. Much like Mick Jagger with the Rolling Stones, Bob controlled the recording contracts and generally organised everything. He is intelligent, inquisitive and articulate, and he quickly grasps whatever he is involved in. We both got on well together and I taught Bob the workings of the chart from the ground up, first of all, in the meeting at his house and then over the phone. During 1984 we became friends and, at his house, I also came to know Paula Yates: we all enjoyed tea and toast many times in his lounge.

Bob was trying to get the fanbase going again and looking to tour towards September that year and so Impulse and I became very involved in the workings of The Boomtown Rats during that period. I had been experimenting with picture discs, coloured vinyl and all sorts of different ideas to make our projects become singles collectors' items at store level. I took many samples of these to meetings with Bob and told him how music fans would buy these rare and collectable items, even if they did not really want the record. Bob grasped this and later that year came up with a superb idea and one that had passed me by: in a transparent vinyl 7-inch single he wanted to put a ticket to the concerts the Rats would perform in September. Bob even drew the design and wondered if we could do it. I took his design to Gallup, the compiler of the chart, and obtained their permission and then I went to a factory to see if it was possible to seal the ticket inside the clear vinyl. The fans would then bring their copy of the single to the concert and have a free entrance. Brilliant – and all Geldof. Bob convinced Phonogram to use Impulse as the promoters and we were off. The single was 'Drag Me Down', and although it did not become a huge hit, the ticket/single concept caused a stir and generated significant interest in the tour, launching a successful return for the band out on the road again.

I met Bob all over London during this preparation and one day he called and asked me to meet him at Fortnum and Mason's. I couldn't believe it. The King of Punk wanted to meet me for cucumber sandwiches. Also, in the build up to the tour Bob would warm his voice up while we were walking down the street, explaining it was terrible until he cleared it out. I must admit it sounded like a bag full of nails in the warm up. It would be later that year that Bob phoned my house one night and said 'Did you see the programme of those kids starving in Africa? It's utterly terrible, I'm going to do something about that.' Doing something about that was, of course, Band Aid and 'Do They Know It's Christmas?', something Impulse would play its part in at Christmas, 1984.

A radical new concept:

Godfrey Rust had taken over from Graham Dossett at Gallup at the end of 1983 and Godfrey would more or less be in charge of the UK chart for the next few years. This turned out to be excellent news for Impulse. Godfrey was a tactician and I believe he loved his job of compiling the chart and trying to make it as accurate as possible each week. He would be lambasted by most of the marketing managers from major record companies if their record did not reach the position they hoped for, but dealing with Impulse was much easier for him. With him in charge at Gallup I truly enjoyed going there and seeing firsthand the way everything was compiled, and this also helped Impulse to stay one jump ahead of the major record companies. At one of these meetings Godfrey told me about Gallup trying to introduce 12-inch singles into the chart. 12-inch singles were then considered a tool for club DJs to get extended versions of hit singles to play in the clubs. They were not the mainstay of the record companies' income and some thought they were a bind and too expensive to produce in that studio time was incurred for such a small return. I had a different view, probably arising from my background as a DJ and knowing how important it was to play something known and yet new in a club, where an extended version felt special and in turn made the DJ stand out. At this time many record enthusiasts wanted to be DJs and even if they never did a gig, their record collections, which they were obsessive about, meant they felt there was potential for them to be a DJ if only someone would give them an opportunity. Each week they would go and buy the new hits and something like a 12-inch single or coloured vinyl item was a special attraction.

As soon as I knew Gallup were including 12-inch singles in the chart, something that had passed most people by, I started insisting that if we worked a record the company would have to give us six hundred free copies of the 12-inch single: not that many that the label would object and not that many that would flood the market. This one move was to guarantee the success of Impulse during 1984, as we were the only company giving one 12-inch single away to each store and, what is more, every one of them sold during the first week of promotion. So, at the very least, our record was six hundred unit sales higher up the chart than it would have been. I instructed all the reps to not make a big deal of this, as it was a key we had to keep to ourselves for as long as possible. I predicted it would probably take about eight months for everyone to catch on to what we were doing and, sure enough, during that very period we had wall to wall hits with almost everything we worked on. Slowly and inevitably record companies did cotton on and began to start labels designed at this market. In particular, Cooltempo Records, Fourth and Broadway Records, Abstract Dance Records, Ensign Records and Proto Records took on this movement, but they all came to Impulse as we were seen as pioneers and hit makers.

Battery Studios were at the back of our offices, and for the previous nine months Mutt Langer, a producer managed by Zomba, was making the album *Heartbeat City* for the American group The Cars. Mutt would go on to be one of the best producers in the world selling over one hundred and fifty million records with The Cars, Def Leppard, Brian Adams, Billy Ocean, The Corrs and Shania Twain. The lead singer of The Cars, Rik Ocersek, spent many of his days in our office waiting for his turn to sing or play guitar. Mutt was notoriously slow and a perfectionist, but it would always be worth it and five Top 10 American hits were to come from that album, including the beautiful 'Drive', probably better known as 'Who's Gonna Drive You Home?.' Mutt used our ghetto blaster to constantly check his mix on that track for weeks. In the end I said, 'Mutt, you've got it, let it go', but he was still not satisfied. Mutt also loved football and although he was South African he had somehow become an Ipswich Town supporter.

On the home front it was time now to move permanently to London. I had put my Walsall flat in Arboretum Road up for sale and it had been bought straight away. I had made an offer for 28 Roe Lane in Kingsbury and, as the year rolled into April, Sue and I left Walsall and moved to London. It was a relief not to have to drive to Walsall every Friday and back on a Monday, but, in truth, I never did want to leave Walsall and never would have done so, it just seemed that now I had no choice.

A *vision for expansion:*

Impulse scored hit after hit in those first few months of 1984. With a month or so to go to our first anniversary in June, it was clear that we were going to come away with a decent profit having already paid back all the investment. I was insistent that we keep moving forward and had several ideas that I wanted to implement. Firstly, just around the corner from our Chaplin Road base I had seen some offices for sale that had a 'drive in' entrance, which would enable us to unload and load the records that were turning up at our door with more ease. We also needed more room for expansion and I saw that, for Impulse, owning property was the right move to make at this stage of the company's career. Secondly, Peter and I had discussed the telephone sales concept and we thought the time was right to move forward on that new company as well. This also meant we needed room for ten or more staff and the new premises would be able to contain that development. Thirdly, I wanted to start a new label soon and I saw that as crucial to the future of Impulse. I wanted Impulse to be a company where I could work for a very long time and the building of different sales and promotion arms, the ownership of property and a label to develop, would all guarantee a future for Peter, myself and the staff.

Clive was spending more and more time in America, so discussions about Impulse became the workload of the accountant Keith Swallow, David Clipsham and, whenever I caused too much trouble or would not take no for an answer, John Fruin. All concerned became aware that the only one who had some kind of control over me was John. Peter and I started with Keith Swallow on the building acquisition and were told, Clive says 'No.' The label was hardly discussed but came back 'No.' Then the telephone sales became a protracted discussion piece as I threw a fit when it looked as though that would come back as a 'No' as well. It is hard to tell whether Clive was approached in a proper manner about these ideas or just casually asked over the transatlantic phone, but whatever way they had been presented to him the answer of 'No' without good reason was not good enough for me. John was always drafted in as peacekeeper and, in due course, David Clipsham did see the idea of a telephone sales company as positive: after all it arose out of my experience with the 'Moonies' under his direction and so he supported it.

I realised now that Impulse was not going to be the company I had envisaged. It could not become a new Motown, Stax or Atlantic under the restrictions that were being applied. I was very upset that I had to beg to start another branch that was completely logical and would only require reinvestment of the money we had already earned. To me this was not a discussion matter – we had proved our ability, and I knew that the new telephone sales company for one would certainly be in profit quickly. I told Peter we should leave, as any record company in the country would support us now, but this time he could not go with me as he had a family to support and it was too risky for him to walk out. I pondered life without Peter as my partner and reminded myself that Sue and I had just come to London. Maybe I needed to rethink my intention to quit. The hits were still continuing to come and I could at least start the telephone sales company. Perhaps, I could then pick off the next moves one by one as we became more successful. I did not really believe that would happen, but eventually I concluded it was worth giving it a go.

I'll give you my prime time:

The telephone sales company would be called Prime Time. I chose the name from a record I had loved by an American group called The Tubes. It had been a Top 40 hit in 1979 and not a big issue, but I had always had a great affection for the song and its title seemed to be ideal for the identity of a telephone sales company. As all Impulse paperwork and logos were in red I decided all Prime Time paperwork would be in blue. We launched in May with Jive product and Peter, Austin and I used all our contacts to promote the company and its recordings with the advantages of an aggressive telesales company. We hired Barry Cohen to head up the team and started with Steve Ayres, Colin Line, Dawn Lauder and Derek Lovelady on the phones. Degs and I had remained friends after the demise of Eat at Joe's and he needed a job, so I agreed with him that he would work hard and stay for as long as he wanted, but if a keyboard job in a band came up, then he would be able to leave.

Peter and I talked to *Music Week*, the trade paper, and asked if they wanted to do a special feature on Impulse and the launch of Prime Time. They agreed, and our clients provided advertising to surround the piece. *Music Week* described Prime Time liked this.

Prime Time has a very clear role, in the way it was planned and the way it will operate. It has been set up for boosting sales of records which are not natural big charters, but have good potential in any of the smaller, more specialist, minority music markets.

This sales service is ideal for releases which sell an initial 2,000 to 3,000 copies and need to be sold quickly into more shops to capitalise on this start' says Jenkins. 'Rather than let it wait until after release, we could even move in and sell to them before release. We feel we can reach the right shops as quickly as that and give the best service on this. So many records that are very good get lost because the record companies themselves cannot react quickly enough to things taking off in the minority music markets.

It is expected that Prime Time will develop in much the same way that Impulse developed – and for the same good reasons. When Impulse was set up it catered for independent labels, being used quite predictably and correctly by the smaller companies for their strong releases. It gradually branched out and added the majors to its list of clients. This is what Prime Time expects and what it is geared for.

But Jenkins stresses 'we have and will keep our feeling for the Indies. We know what they need for promotion and for sales and we will continue to be able to give the right service.'

The way that labels can best start using Prime Time might be to place a record with the sales force the moment it enters the lower end of the Top 75 on any Tuesday. Prime Time can start putting it across to the right selected dealers very strongly, to ensure that supplies have been ordered and delivered into the shops before the demand builds up to the usual peak weekend levels.

'Prime Time is intended to be quite separate from Impulse,' Jenkins points out, 'working in a different way for a different purpose. We have been selecting and sorting out different dealer categories for six months before putting the new company into operation. Using our own experienced reps we have devised lists of stores to sell into according to the type of music e.g. disco, and dance, heavy metal and rock. We also have lists which point out all the record shops around any given commercial radio station. This means we can check all the playlists and sell any title strongly in just the areas where it is getting I.L.R. (sic. Independent Local Radio) exposure, so that they will get the best sales chance out of the interest created by radio play.'

Jenkins and Todd are well aware that there is more to selling records than just selling the idea to a dealer. The dealer must have stock to sell to the customer as soon as the customer asks for it. To do as much as possible in helping out with this, the distribution end of things, there will be constant liaison with the manufacturers and independent distributors.

Barry Cohen, heading the Prime Time telesales operation, has good contacts with distributors, and has already been talking to them about speed of delivery.

Prime Time will send details of all orders taken each day to both the distributor and label and these daily details will be delivered by hand to both client and distributor.

'We are' stresses Jenkins, 'doing all we can do, to make sure the records we are selling in are available to go out to the dealers immediately.'

As successful directors of a promotion company, which has successfully proved its usefulness to the industry, Jenkins and Todd found that distributors soon started coming to them for guidance on how many copies of discs to ensure were in stock when the Impulse reps started promoting a title. The Industry has found that an Impulse promo means trade orders and Prime Time is an operation being run by the same directors along the same basic principles. So with Prime Time the record labels are getting a new company, which in a way already has a track record.

Advertising around the feature were Jive Records, K-Tel International, A & M Records, D.J.M. Records, Chrysalis Records, The Artful Dodgers (my old friend Keith Peacock's design company that put together many of my specialist single ideas) and Proto Records, which featured a drawing of two behinds and a title of 'Congratulations Steve and Pete for having the Bare Faced Cheek.'

The response to this supplement was enormous. Over the next few months Prime Time signed sales contracts with Arista Records, A & M Records, Virgin Records, CBS Records, RCA Records and all the independents we worked with on the Impulse side of our operation. The company was an immediate success and we were constantly increasing and interviewing for more staff. Every time I went into the Prime Time offices it was a hive of movement and noise, the telesales people that worked there were young, into the records and the radio was blaring away as they fed information about records to the dealers and took orders. Today, 'buy one and get one free' offers are everywhere, but in 1984 there was no such thing in the record business. Prime Time introduced it through telesales. The dealers also used Prime Time to send messages to our reps to call sooner or bring more copies of such and such a record. Dealers also alerted us to what new records were selling in their stores so that information could be passed on to Impulse, who could then possibly get the record to work, have success and bring in free stock to the dealer. We were now a vital part of the retail chain and were becoming an ever stronger influence in the success of any record.

Prime Time – Explosion:

The hits started to come for both Impulse and Prime Time at an alarming rate. In April, after some months of trying, we finally cracked Hazel Dean's 'Searchin' on Proto Records. This had been an enormous effort on behalf of Barry Evangeli, Nick East and Impulse. We had refused to give up and completely believed it was a hit record. Now it was a major triumph, and Pete Waterman and I believe today that 'Searchin' was the record that started the whirlwind which would grow and grow into the domination of the charts that was Stock, Aitken and Waterman throughout the remainder of the Eighties. 'Searchin' finally became a Top 10 record and the follow up, 'Wherever I Go Whatever I Do', became the first Stock Aitken Waterman production that stormed into the Top 10 in July 1984, finally peaking at No 4. Proto Records, S.A.W and Impulse followed that immediately with Divine's 'So You Think You're A Man', which also made the Top 20. It was not as big as Hazel Dean's single, but its impact was enormous. Proto Records was small and unfashionable and Divine was a transvestite New York club performer, yet this still made the chart. *Top of The Pops* were having kittens about putting Divine on the show and we all gathered around the TV as it was broadcast. It was a wonderful opportunity to laugh at the BBC Establishment.

The summer hits of Impulse continued and I worked very closely with Phil Cokell, who was now marketing manager for Chrysalis. Phil was and always has been a no-nonsense operator, which suited me perfectly. He has always been one of my favourite record executives. Phil believed in what we were doing at Impulse and we proved the point together by having two Top 10 records with Alvin Stardust. Alvin had not had a hit single for over three years and was considered to be finished as a chart act, but at Impulse we liked the new single 'I Feel Like Buddy Holly' and Phil had total belief in its potential as a hit record. Alvin Stardust was born Bernard Jewry and had hits as Shane Fenton and the Fentones in the Sixties. By the early Seventies a name change to Alvin Stardust brought hits with 'My Coo Ca Choo', 'Jealous Minds', 'Red Dress' and 'You You You', before the hits stopped again. In 1981 a one-off hit 'I Pretend' brought Alvin back again, but then he fell away from the limelight. Now, after three years, he had come up with 'I Feel Like Buddy Holly.' Phil invited me to have a lunch with Alvin, who was known privately as Shane. We had a marvellous time together and Impulse was all fired up to aim for another unfashionable hit if possible. The single eventually made No 7, and the follow up, 'I Won't Run Away', also peaked at No 7, which set up the album to sell well over the coming months. I had many more meetings and lunches with Alvin during that period and he was always charming and fun to be with.

Impulse's success with Alvin Stardust made us famous within the walls of Chrysalis and their other acts. Phil phoned and asked if we fancied working on Spandau Ballet. They were in a strong run of hits and I was up for being involved. The single in question was 'I'll Fly For You', still one of my favourite Spandau tracks. I went to Chrysalis to meet with Steve Dagger and we talked through how we would attack the promotion. We got along and the deal was made. This record was to be a double-edged sword, though. It became a Top 10 record, peaking at No 9, and although I would have liked it to do even better I thought we had represented it very well. Steve Dagger thought differently, and said he would sue Impulse because I had guaranteed him a No 1 record, which of course I would never remotely promise anyone. He never sued and we never worked Spandau Ballet again. I still like the band and was fortunate enough to meet Tony Hadley in the future many times. We had a good laugh about Steve Dagger and the single, which we nicknamed, 'I'll Sue For You.'

As Impulse was expanding at a rate of knots, I asked Sue if she wanted to be the receptionist. Her move to London had not been easy and she had been unhappy from the start, finding it hard to settle in the more aggressive atmosphere of London people at work. I suggested she might feel happier trying out being a receptionist in the happy surroundings of Impulse. I was not at all sure that living and working together would work for us both, but as she seemed so unhappy I thought we could see how it went. My mistake was to make this all happen while Peter was on holiday. I just really did not think he would mind, but when he returned there was no doubt he was unhappy that I had not consulted him. Soon, Peter got to know Sue well and it all began to work out, but I do not think he ever forgot what had happened and I think it was a factor in causing problems later on in the running of Impulse. For now, though, Sue could feel secure, and she proved to be a very good receptionist who all the reps and staff liked.

More and more expansion – The Impulse Group:

Impulse now became The Impulse Group of Companies, consisting of Impulse Promotions, the Impulse Radio Promotion Company and Prime Time telephone sales. Each company operated independently, but introduced clients to our other services across the board, so the client base was expanding weekly on all fronts and the phone was constantly ringing. During October, we managed to deliver a hit record for Jive that would set up a strong run of hits for them over the next couple of years. We had tried in the summer with 'European Queen' by Billy Ocean; the record was good but had hardly made the Top 100. Laurie Jay's assistant Val had said that 'Caribbean Queen' was a much better title with more mystic and sex appeal about it. Billy went in the studio and tried Caribbean Queen and African Queen, and Caribbean was the one that worked. Jive issued 'Caribbean Queen' in America and as the record started to bite and climb the charts we prepared to reissue the single under its new title in England. As we did so the record grew and grew in America and by the time we were ready to go it was well on its way to No 1 over there. Billy Ocean was back on the chart and bigger than before, and 'Caribbean Queen' would establish a long run of hit singles albums and tours for him, the record eventually peaking at No 6 in the UK.

I was called to Charisma Records by Steve Weltman to discuss the upcoming release of 'Too Late For Goodbye's' from Julian Lennon. Like everyone else, I was a huge Beatles fan and John Lennon was one of my all time heroes, so to work with Julian was a special moment. I loved the record and we would eventually have a Top 10 single peaking at No 6. We also worked Julian's album *Valotte*. I still have it to this day, signed by Julian, it reads 'Steve, Thanks Valotte, Julian.'

Impulse had been working a lot of records for RCA during the year and we had been blessed with good success. Daryl Hall and John Oates were a major act for RCA, but they had just flunked in England with 'Out Of Touch', the first single from a new album and a huge hit in the USA. This was extremely bad news for the executives at RCA in England, and especially as the Hall and Oates manager was the fearsome Tommy Mottola. Tommy, some years later, would become President of Sony Music, discovering and marrying Maria Carey, but at this stage he had a notorious reputation and was rumoured to be in the Mafia. I do not believe that was true, but Tommy let people think it was to accentuate his presence. I had never been to the top floor at RCA before nor seen their boardroom facilities, which were fabulous. Gareth Harris and Roger Seamen were both nervous of meeting Mottola – I knew no different and was not intimidated at all. Tommy did a good rant and rave and asked how they could lose a record like 'Out Of Touch.' There was plenty of verbal stumbling and fumbling and finally Gareth said that they were going to bring in Impulse to sort the situation out, giving a good account of the successes of our company. Tommy looked at me through the sunglasses he was still wearing almost for the first time.

> *'So what the fuck do you want to do?'*

> *'I want to get you, Hall and Oates a hit in England and I can do it if you do what I tell you.'*

> *'Ok, what's the fucking single then?'*

I had already been given a copy of the album a few days before and was sure it was 'Method Of Modern Love.'

> *'I'd put out 'Method of Modern Love.'*

> *'Well no-one's said that before, why?'*

> *'Because I know a hit when I hear one.'*

> *Tommy turned to Gareth.*

> *'I like this fucking kid, he deals with Randy Hoffman from my office personally and the next single is 'Method of Modern Love.' You better deliver it, son.'*

> *'I know I will Tommy, draw out the cash for the bonuses for when I do.'*

At that I was dismissed, but Gareth called later in the day and said 'thanks, you handled him brilliantly, but do you really think 'Method Of Modern Love' is a hit?' Yes, I did believe it was a hit and it would become so in 1985. For the five years after that, I would be Champion Entertainment's UK contact – the owner of Champion Entertainment was Tommy Mottola.

Towards the end of the year, Helen Tyler departed Impulse and headed for America. Her replacement was to stay with Impulse for a number of years and eventually become Mrs Shaun King, which I could not have known when I interviewed Jayne Fisher. Kieran Fanning also joined Prime Time in December of 1984 and would work for me for the next twenty years except for a one year period. Kieran's interview was one that was written into the folklore of Impulse. I interviewed him and thought he would be a good addition to the company, but I was travelling at such speed in those days that I did not think I could handle a name like Kieran. I suggested he could have the job if I could change his first name. Kieran asked what the new name would be, I said Kipper and, for short, Kip. To this day he is still known as Kip.

A pioneering innovation:

December brought two final moments of happiness in 1984 that stay in my memory. The first, was that Impulse had its own pages on the Teletext, which broadcast information on the records we were working each week. With this, the dealers knew in advance what records would be on the reps' cars the coming week and not one record company in the UK had this facility. I showed Mom how to flick up teletex on her TV and she would check weekly what records we were working on and then look in the paper to find out if they had become hits. It gave her much fun over the coming years.

The second happened as the fulfilment of a project that had originated when Arista had called me into their offices in October. They had wanted to see if I could come up with a marketing idea to get Gary Glitter a hit single. Gary had not been in the UK Top 10 for nine years, but he was about to make a comeback and play a series of Christmas shows. Arista played me what I thought was a hit single and the best record Glitter had made in years: 'Another Rock 'n' Roll Christmas.' This was not long after I had been trumped by Geldof and his free ticket single and as something quickly came into mind I told Arista that I would be back in a few days. All picture discs up until that point had been based on the 7-inch single and now I began to toy with the idea of a 12-inch cut out record. I went home, drew a circle around a 12-inch record and tried to fit a stand up image of Gary Glitter inside it. Seeing how good this looked, I spoke to Damont, a record manufacturer, and asked if they could cut out the Gary Glitter figure. After a couple of days they said they could and could even make the record in the middle three inches wide and in transparent vinyl. This made the Gary Glitter single look like an Oscar from a short distance. I then asked if they could make a cardboard plinth that would easily fold together and hold the statue and again they came back with a yes and made a prototype for me to show to Arista. When I showed it to Brian Yates at Arista, it was a stone-cold winner. Damont made the figure and the Impulse team assembled the copies in store and placed them on the counter. This idea caused such a stir that Gary Glitter returned to the UK Top 10, peaking at No 7 and sold out six shows at Wembley.

That idea delivered Impulse a nine-month contract with Arista to work all their records and it put me on TV being interviewed about marketing in the record industry. It was an unprecedented and pioneering new innovation in the industry and would lead to many creations by other record companies that would try and copy its success. At the time I thought so little of the idea's importance that I never kept a copy of that original stand up product, but somewhere somebody still must have the first release edition of Gary Glitter's 'Another Rock 'n' Roll Christmas.'

And now, for the record, here is a list of the discs that Impulse worked during the year of 1984. In January 1984, the Impulse Promotion Company was only seven months old but its impact on the UK record business was so immense that record labels from all corners of London made a pathway to its offices in Chaplin Road, Willesden. I believe that the team of people that started Impulse did so with such passion and commitment that we were always going to succeed and win, but we never dreamed that it would turn out quite like this.

The Impulse Group Hit Records 1984

January			
That's Livin Alright	Joe Fagin	Towerbell Records	No 3
Where Were You Hiding When The Storm Broke	The Alarm	IRS Records	No 22
Dance Hall Days	Wang Chung	Geffen Records	No 21
February			
Joanna	Kool And The Gang	DeLite Records	No 2
Tonight	The Boomtown Rats	Mercury Records	No 73
Doctor Doctor	The Thompson Twins	Arista Records	No 3
March			
Robert De Niro's Waiting	Bananarama	London Records	No 3
Glad Its All Over	Captain Sensible	A&M Records	No 6
People Are People	Depeche Mode	Mute Records	No 4
It's A Miracle	Culture Club	Virgin Records	No 4
Time After Time	Cyndi Lauper	Epic Records	No 3
Nelson Mandela	The Specials	2Tone Records	No 9
Wood Beez	Scritti Politti	Virgin Records	No 10
April			
Searchin'	Hazel Dean	Proto Records	No 6
Somebody Else's Guy	Jocelyn Brown	4th & Broadway Records	No 13
Pearly Dewdrops Drops	Cocteau Twins	4AD Records	No 29
May			
I Feel Like Buddy Holly	Alvin Stardust	Chrysalis Records	No 7
Perfect Skin	Lloyd Cole	Polydor Records	No 26
Drag Me Down	Boomtown Rats	Mercury Records	No 50
June			
Young At Heart	Bluebells	London Records	No 8
Agadoo	Black Lace	Flair Records	No 2
Heaven Knows I'm Miserable Now	The Smiths	Rough trade Records	No 10
Smalltown Boy	Bronski Beat	Forbidden Fruit Records	No 3

On The Wings Of Love	Jeffrey Osborne	A&M Records	No 11
Eyes Without A Face	Billy Idol	Chrysalis Records	No 18
Talking Loud And Clear	Orchestral Manoeuvres In The Dark	Virgin Records	No 11
Come Back	Wah	Beggars Banquet Records	No 20
July			
You Think You're A Man	Divine	Proto Records	No 16
Whatever I Do Wherever I Go	Hazel Dean	Proto Records	No 4
Everybody's Laughing	Phil Fearon	Ensign Records	No 10
More You Live The More You Love	A Flock Of Seagulls	Jive Records	No 26
Closest Thing To Heaven	Kane Gang	Kitchenware Records	No 12
August			
Ghostbusters	Ray Parker Jnr	Arista Records	No 2
I'll Fly For You	Spandau Ballet	Chrysalis Records	No 9
September			
Human Racing	Nick Kershaw	M.C.A. Records	No 19
Telsa Girls	Orchestral Manoeuvres In The Dark	Virgin Records	No 21
Why	Bronski Beat	Forbidden Fruit Records	No 6
Apollo 9	Adam Ant	C.B.S Records	No 13
October			
I Wont Run Away	Alvin Stardust	Chrysalis Records	No 7
The Wanderer	Status Quo	Vertigo Records	No 7
Skin Deep	The Stranglers	Epic Records	No 15
Too Late For Goodbyes	Julian Lennon	Charisma Records	No 7
Caribbean Queen	Billy Ocean	Jive Records	No 6
November			
One Night In Bangkok	Murray Head	RCA Records	No 12
Do The Conga	Black Lace	Flair Records	No 10
December			
Another Rock 'n' Roll Christmas	Gary Glitter	Arista Records	No 7
Atmosphere	Russ Abbot	Spirit Records	No 7
Do They Know It's Christmas	Band Aid	Mercury Records	No 1

Prime Time telephone sales achieved its first No 1 record in December 1984, to follow up Impulse Radio Promotions' No 1 in December 1983. As in 1983, Impulse Promotions had not reached the No 1 slot all through the year, even though we came close so many times. Peter and I were frustrated that we had not made No 1 with the main company – but that was to change in the coming year.

1984 *Impulse advert*

CHAPTER 15

IMPULSE – HOME OF THE HITS – 1985

Billy Ocean:

As 1985 was born, Impulse used the same work ethic as the year before: 'they are not working but we are' and again we reaped the benefits of early hits in the New Year. Thankfully, one of those hits was 'Loverboy' with Billy Ocean, for Jive Records.

Clive Calder and John Fruin had backed and believed in Impulse and were proven right to do so. Within Jive Records it was initially seen as a huge plus to have Impulse working all Jive's output, however, as time went on Jive did not have as many hit records as they had hoped, whereas Impulse began to have back-to-back hits with other labels. This caused some frustration on both sides. Bob Nolan, General Manager of Jive, was a calm and rational man, but some of the people that worked beneath him in sales and promotion wanted to blame Impulse for their lack of chart success, rather than think they themselves just might be at fault or may have put in a poor performance. So, whenever we got a big record with Jive I was delighted, as for a few weeks I would not have to listen to the rubbish some of the staff at Jive spoke about Impulse. For my part, I ignored most of it, but Peter always liked a bit of a dig and the Jive staff were no match at all for him when he wanted to have a go. Quick in thought and mind, he normally reduced them to a crumbling wreck with only a sentence or two and it always made me laugh.

Billy Ocean had followed up 'Caribbean Queen' successfully with 'Loverboy' and we started to work the first album, *Suddenly*. Billy Ocean had originally been signed to Jive Records on a singles deal, which means the artist is signed for one single with an option for a second single, and in some cases the contract may then have an option for a third single or a first album. This is a normal deal structure if the record company does not commit initially to an album. Madonna was originally signed on a deal like this and many major artists' recording careers grew from this kind of arrangement. Today, most artists want a firm album deal at the start and are insulted if they are offered a singles deal. I do not agree with that theory and believe an opportunity is the most important event. If an artist signs the singles deal and gets a hit, the record company will not be able to sign an album quickly enough, but you need to make a hit first.

197

Billy Ocean, as ever a charming and reasonable man, thought little about whether Jive had signed him on a singles or album deal. Billy thought he would get hits and only a few weeks after signing the singles deal he wrote the song 'Suddenly.' When Clive Calder heard the demo of 'Suddenly' with just piano accompaniment he remarked 'This is an album deal now.' That is how confident we all were about the song 'Suddenly', which became the album title too.

America calling:

Personally, I was up to my eyes in Daryl Hall's and John Oates's failing album at RCA. I had chosen the single and done all the set-up marketing, insisting on a gatefold 12-inch single, extra tracks on the 12-inch version, another 12-inch single held in reserve with three past hits on it to boost sales if necessary, in fact, all I could think of to make sure that 'Method Of Modern Love' was a hit. I definitely did not want to be found at the bottom of the Thames wearing concrete shoes, which may have been fitted, had the rumours that Modern Love was not a hit been true. However, all was well, the single would peak at No 21, and it was enough to put Daryl and John on *Top Of The Pops*, make awareness for the album's release and put their career in the UK on the up and up again. So it was that I became the UK contact for anything to do with Champion Entertainment and their artists. And, if you don't own a copy of *Hall and Oates' Greatest Hits*, you are missing out.

The Impulse Group of Companies was growing at a rapid rate and, although some of the staff were changing, we never had a large turnover of people. Most people who came to work for Impulse had a long career there. It seemed they either left within six months or stayed a lifetime. Davy Pritchard only stayed for a few months before leaving the record business, never to return. His replacement, Libby McGee, did not stay long, and then, hoping to succeed her, into my office walked Kenny McCloud for his interview. Kenny was wearing trousers that should have had a little more material in them and been a bit looser, a jacket that should have had less material and been a little shorter, pink brothel creeper shoes and Elvis' early years haircut. Kenny I am sure, thought he was very dapper, and I thought, 'if someone can come to an interview looking like that then they deserve the job, as they should be working for a passionate company like Impulse.' Kenny was to work for Impulse for thirteen years and he became a most loved and valued member of the Impulse team. His long time catchphrase when he walked in a room was 'Aahh, I wandered lonely as a McCloud.'

Terry the Pil:

Around this time, Impulse was contacted by Fanfare Records. Iain Burton was the owner and his General Manager, A & R director, promotion man and helper, was Simon Cowell. Simon and I worked together on Fanfare Records trying to get a hit record, which took almost a year, and then was massive. Simon became part of our personal group consisting of Barry Evangeli, Nick East, Tilly Rutherford, Pete Waterman and me. Meanwhile, we arrived at our offices one day to find them all daubed in red paint with a 'Ban the Bomb' sign that everyone recognised at the time. The staff were not sure what all this meant and thought it was some lunatic that had gone wild during the night. Peter Todd and I knew better: it had to be 'Terry the Pil.' Back in those days, if you wanted any posters put up around London you had to hire Terry the Pil and the penalty for putting posters up yourself or hiring anyone else was to have your house or offices painted red and, somewhere, a 'Ban The Bomb' sign would be featured.

Terry the Pil had controlled his empire and 'patch' for many years by this kind of behaviour. The painting of the offices was a warning and worse was to come should you not take heed. In today's London all poster advertising is worked out by the local Council, who decide where and how advertisements are displayed. In 1985, you would see independently commissioned posters all over bridges or on busy street corners and Terry the Pil had long dominated this tough world. He was not to be messed with. His men were used to working at night, operating quickly and sometimes coming under attack, and it is safe to say they were not shy lads. They and their boss did very well out of their operation. A poster cost about a pound to buy and a further pound to put up, and some companies would have two to two and a half thousand posters put up, making a five grand fee for Terry and his boys. The Pil himself kept a low profile and this added to his mystique.

Now, when I saw Impulse offices daubed in red 'Pil' paint, to say I was not best pleased was an understatement. Impulse was not in the poster business and we had no need or desire to be so. We did use posters, but not the large ones you see on the street, which would not fit inside small independent record stores. We used smaller copies, but the 'Pil' did not work inside stores.

Pete said we should think about this and be careful, he was right to be that way, but I was wild.

I managed to find Terry's phone number, although I knew I was taking a risk, he had to be confronted. We discussed what Impulse did and why Terry had been upset, and, eventually, it was agreed that we had a misunderstanding. We also agreed that should a potential misunderstanding occur in the future, we would discuss it before any painted warnings were issued. I had to engage a company to repaint the outside of our building, but I refrained from sending the invoice to 'The Pil.'

Busier and Busier:

January 1985 also brought Peter's and my first visit to Midem. This is the huge music and record business festival held annually in Cannes and, for us, it was to be the first of twelve or thirteen consecutive years of visits. The festival is attended mainly by small companies, for which I believe it was designed, and they buy and sell products. A lot of deals are struck and for a small record label these can keep them going for the year. The most exciting part of it all for me was that it was here that you could buy a record outside the UK and return with a hit. For Impulse, we could find records we liked, make deals to work them and make new contacts that would bring records and work to the company later in the year. It was Midem that spread the name Impulse across continental Europe. I would later work out that in that first year we made fifty thousand pounds from the work and contacts we made at Cannes.

Midem in those early years was fun. Most of the independent record business would travel to Cannes and you would just bump into people all around the town and go off for dinner or arrange coffee or lunch for the following day. The major UK labels did have stands in the main hall for show, to have a presence there, but the major hub of activity came from the independents. Impulse became most famous at Midem for the success it was having on the singles chart, but in the meantime we were being equally effective on the albums chart. Every week we were in business we worked on albums and we would receive many platinum, gold and silver sales awards for our work and sales on the album chart.

In the first six weeks of 1985 we worked *The Everly Brothers Greatest Hits*, an album with Barbara Dickson, who I had known years before from MCA Records, the *Evita* soundtrack and *Gilbert O'Sullivan's Greatest Hits*. I had been a big fan of Ray O' Sullivan for a long time and I would later meet him and find him to be rather shy and very quiet, but he had warmth about him that you could feel while you were in his presence. *The Best of Sandie Shaw* was also on our Impulse team sheets early in 1985. The records were marvellous: 'Always Something There To Remind Me', 'Girl Don't Come', 'I'll Stop At Nothing', 'Long Live Love', 'Message Understood', 'Tomorrow', these were the bulk of Sandie's hits that came between 1964 and 1969, a great five year run and it was a great feeling that Impulse could work on those hits in the Eighties.

Bob Geldof was still regularly in touch after the Band Aid single and was now beginning to work on the Live Aid idea. Bob had realised that even though the Band Aid single had been an enormous success, in financial terms, it would mean very little to the weight of the problem in Africa and something bigger needed to be done. Bob was also trying to keep his band, The Boomtown Rats, together in the middle of all this, and we were talking about doing *The Rats' Greatest Hits*. In those days, major record companies did not think highly of greatest hits packages, a form of snobbery I suppose, and so 'As Seen on TV' companies such as K-Tel and Ronco existed to fill this gap in the market. It was these companies that major labels licensed their product to, and Ronco and K-Tel marketed Greatest Hits and Best Of's to the public. The major companies were extremely foolish to do this, as they consistently have been with some of their decisions over the years. The amount of revenue lost through egos and snobbery has been immense. No problems for us at

Impulse though, and as we worked weekly with both K-Tel and Ronco I spoke with the people I knew at these companies to get Bob in there to discuss the possibility of a Boomtown Rats Best Of.

Steve Mason of Pinnacle came back to Impulse around this time. We set up a short-term deal with Pinnacle to service and sell into the chart return stores, and this was the start of a friendship between Steve and I that lasts to this day, coupled with a tremendously successful business relationship in which we achieved an unbelievable amount of hits together over twenty years.

Expanding Impulse:

Impulse was looking to expand again through 1985 and we believed that the next area should be club promotion, since dance records were beginning to feature more and more on the Top 40 chart – this was a direct result of Gallup enabling 12-inch singles to qualify within the collection of sales data. The top company at the time was Rush Release, operated by Ian and Nick Titchener. Peter and I had known them both for some time and our relationship had developed, with Impulse recommending Rush Release and, in turn, Rush Release recommending Impulse on the records they worked. We could see there was a very good business here and it was time that Impulse was involved in the financial rewards. We invited Ian and Nick over to Impulse and opened talks about a future company operating on a 50/50 basis, but although I believe Ian saw the possibilities of what we were talking about, Nick was almost offended and thought we were trying to take away his business. Peter and I now felt we had no alternative but to start The Impulse Club Promotion Company on our own, which we eventually launched in June. Justin Lubbock, an experienced club promoter, joined and he was assisted in the set-up period by Colin Line, who worked for Prime Time. By the end of the year, with the increase in business, Colin had become a full time club promoter.

Impulse also started a programme of Rep Holiday Relief. There were still a few record companies we were not working for, and in an attempt to get in the door with those companies we started Holiday Relief for those businesses that had their own sales forces. We would hire out our rep, say for the north east, to EMI when their own rep went on holiday for a week or two weeks. The Impulse rep would present all the records we were working and when finished would start again presenting EMI product for that two weeks. The record companies saw this operation as incredibly supportive and the project built our contact with companies that were not using us regularly.

Champion Records:

At this time, June 1985, coming to fruition was a project that had begun at the start of the year when we had been approached by Mel Medalie with a proposal that we start a record company in partnership with him. Initially, we were not interested, but after several meetings we realised that he had happened upon what would be a foolproof way of delivering records that would sell consistently and eventually bring real hit records at somepoint. Mel knew Ron Boulding, who was an importer of American records. A lot of small independent record labels had been springing up all over America, notably in New York and Los Angeles, but also, importantly, in Florida and the Mid West. Ron was importing a small quantity of 12-inch releases from these sources and selling them into the London independent record dealers. He was a hard worker and had built a good company with a couple of vans supplying the dealers. He himself worked one of the vans, in which he brought all the records from the US, while he had another van salesman who worked for him. After meeting Ron, with Mel, I was fascinated by what he was telling me. By the amount of re-orders that the stores asked him to obtain from America, he knew, more or less before anyone, which imported records had the chance of becoming hits in the UK. We started to monitor the records that Ron brought in from the states, the quantities sold, and the re-orders. We arranged weekly meetings to see which records then went on to sell between 8,000 and 10,000 copies and journey into the lower reaches of the chart. We also watched to see if the major record labels in the UK through their young A & R men actively went and purchased the rights to these records from the US. It was a fascinating exercise for me and I liked Ron's work ethic immensely. Mel was always a little more effort to deal with, but there was no doubt that he knew how to pull together a release with the pressing plants, labels, sleeves and do it both well and economically.

The meetings became more regular and intense and we finally formed an idea for a foolproof label. Ron would own thirty-three percent and he would tip off the label about a record that had the demand to sell eight to ten thousand copies. Mel, who owned the other thirty-three percent, would buy the record from the US label for the UK, on a purchase scale, ranging from as little as five hundred pounds to as much as two thousand pounds. Peter and I would own thirty-three percent of the label and would use Prime-Time to widen the market through pre-selling and then Impulse to put the records in the chart stores so the release would appear in the Top 100. The labels we worked with in America were delighted with their advance release in the UK that would normally achieve at least a Top 100 chart position. We agreed the label would be called Champion Records and signed the paperwork. Peter and I split our thirty-three percent fifty/fifty on the new venture. Champion would also pay Impulse and Prime Time the regular fees for pre-sales and promotion, so the operation was all above board as far as the Zomba/Impulse partnership was concerned.

Champion Records started in June 1985 and issued six singles that year. Two made the Top 50, selling roughly fifteen thousand each, and the other four were Top 100 singles selling between seven to nine thousand singles. One of Impulse's masterstrokes, and an idea I was personally proud of, was the small posters that we insisted were displayed in record stores across the country. They read CHAMPION RECORDS FOR DJs ONLY. This made the real record enthusiasts buy our singles, because record enthusiasts want to be DJs even if they have never done a gig. When they play their records to themselves they are in fact their own DJ. A simple sign like this generated massive support and we were guaranteed an amount of initial sales no matter what the record. Champion Records very soon had genuine hit records of its own.

Mel Medalie made another brilliant move in signing on Paul Oakenfold as our part time A & R man. Paul is now world renowned as one of the best ever DJs and he has played gigs and had hit records in a lot of countries. Back then he was just twenty years old, but he already had important experience as he had lived in New York for one year before returning to the UK and he knew a lot of young record people in America. He had an outstanding ear for a record and could always find the people we needed to contact to buy the rights for the records he recommended. With him and all the other members of the Champion team being specialists in their field, this label could not fail from the moment we signed the contracts together.

Operating The Impulse Group of Companies, especially with all the chart successes, gave me opportunities to become friends with some of the major artists in the world at that time. Some of those friendships have lasted my lifetime, others were fleeting associations but of no less value in my memory. Billy Ocean has remained a friend throughout my life. Daryl Hall and John Oates were friends just for a couple of years. And then there was someone else.

David Cassidy:

It was in the early part of 1985 that Arista Records had brought David Cassidy to Impulse. He had first risen to enormous fame in America and the UK in the early seventies via the TV show *The Partridge Family*. After leaving the show, David became a solo popstar in his own right with hits like 'Could It Be Forever', 'I Am A Clown' and the No 1 singles 'How Can I Be Sure' and 'Daydreamer.' The hits had stopped in 1975; February 1985 was the time for a comeback. Arista in the US had signed David and thought the UK should be where he re-launched his career because of his previous popularity here. David Cassidy made his way to Willesden to meet Impulse and we went out for lunch to discuss the promotion of the single 'The Last Kiss.' We were working on a Terry Wogan chat show appearance and performance which David seemed a little nervous about: I assured him that Terry was a good chat show host and normally did not stray into uncomfortable personal areas. All would go well. At the time Terry, was making a joke of friendly knee touching in conversation, so we got David to join in on the joke while on air. David was not sure if we were the ones who were joking, but he did the friendly 'knee touch' on Terry, which caused a laugh and the interview went extremely well.

However, the most important move in the promotion of the single was the issue of a picture disc of David and Samantha Fox in a caress pose. Sam was then the darling of the press and the top 'page three' model in the country, and the success of the picture disc was to go some way to her signing to Jive Records a few weeks later. After David's single had been released it had slowly climbed the chart, but when we issued the picture disc it rocketed into the Top 10. We realised that a huge percentage of people wanted a picture disc of Sam and I think David was just a by-product of the sales. Whichever was the reason, 'The Last Kiss' became a No 6 hit for David Cassidy in the UK and successfully re-launched his career. History now shows this would be his last hit on the UK record chart, but at the time it made David Cassidy a big name again. I met with David several times on two or three promotion trips and found him to be fun with a great sense of humour. He was not at all egotistic about his career or demonstrative of his previous huge pop star status. In the years that followed, David would again become a huge star in Las Vegas.

A hit with Pete:

During March of 1985 my long time pal had begun to find a sound that would dominate the next five years of popular music in the UK. Pete Waterman was about to become a household name. As a result of the hits we had achieved with Hazel Dean and Divine in 1984, Pete along with Stock and Aitken had been asked by CBS to work with Dead or Alive and we enjoyed our first No 1 together with 'You Spin Me Round.' Impulse followed up that No 1 with another almost immediately: CBS again was the label and the single was 'Easy Lover' by Philip Bailey, one of the vocalists from Earth Wind And Fire, and Phil Collins (his only release on CBS). Impulse had finally broken the spell preventing us achieving a No 1 record and, as is usual in life, after you can't get something then two come along at once: just like the old saying about buses. Impulse would go on to have further No 1's that year with '19' by Paul Hardcastle for Chrysalis Records in May and 'West End Girls' by The Pet Shop Boys for EMI and manager Tom Watkins in November. No, No 1 records for almost two years and then four in a year, they all gave me great pleasure, but it was only right and just that the first one should be with Pete Waterman.

Impulse was beginning to become so successful that I could now phone up record companies and ask them if we could work on certain records just because I liked the single. I was a real fan of Pat Benetar and contacted Phil Cokell at Chrysalis about her record 'Love Is A Battlefield.' We eventually peaked with the single at No 17, and it was Pat Benetar's biggest ever hit in the UK. For several years I had a signed photo from her that hung in my kitchen.

I was always a fan of records that were made in America – not all of them, but some just appealed to my ear in a special way. I really liked Tom Petty and The Heartbreakers and I phoned MCA to work a superb single called 'Don't Come

Around Here No More.' Unfortunately, my influence did not work on that single and it peaked at No 50, but I am still pleased that I chose to work on it. The record did go on to become a Top 10 single in the US and it is still played on UK radio, giving the impression it was a bigger hit than it actually was.

My favourite hits from the year were ones that I became directly involved in. I loved Huey Lewis and The News, and we worked together on the 'Power Of Love', which Phil Cokell issued at Chrysalis. It peaked at No 11, but that was enough to lead to sales of thousands of albums. My work on that record was recognised by Phil and Chrysalis and when Huey and the band came in to the UK to play Wembley, I was presented to Huey and the boys and spent hours in their company while they prepared for the gig, sitting in on the sound-check and having fun. Huey Lewis is one of the most down to earth artists I have ever met and superb to spend time with.

Phil and I worked together on another artist that I thought was a major star. We had two hits that year with Billy Idol: 'White Wedding' and 'Rebel Yell' both peaked at No 6. Billy went on to sell a lot of albums and was a charismatic performer. Off stage he knew how to have fun and was always outrageous at launch functions and parties. I used to hang out with him early evening, but there was always a moment to check out, as trouble would most certainly come the later the hour, although always with great humour.

Another record I believe wouldn't have been a hit if it had not been for the refusal to give in by the Impulse team. RCA's 'Broken Wings' by Mr Mister took weeks and weeks to get going and, on occasions RCA wanted to give up, but I always thought we had a chance and kept suggesting that it was not dead. Eventually, and only after a long time, 'Broken Wings' reached No 4 in December 1985 and it sold huge quantities.

Another pleasure that year was the rise of Supreme Records and my good friend Nick East from Proto Records. Pete Waterman and I really liked the work Nick had done on those records and when Nick decided to leave Proto Pete gave him the facility of office space to start up Supreme Records. This was an extension of the 'You make 'em and I'll sell 'em' agreement that Pete and I had made a year or so earlier. Hence, S.A.W. came up with a single for the artist Princess, Nick got it all together and Impulse then took care of all the promotion and sales. As its first release Supreme Records' 'Say I'm Your Number One' by Princess hit No 7 in the UK charts and we had another label that could deliver the records of S.A.W.

It was always good to be in at the start with a new label or new act and Impulse achieved that double simultaneously with Elektra Records UK and Simply Red in June of 1985. Simon Potts was a successful A & R man I had got to know through the Impulse deal with Arista Records and we became good friends. Simon's first signing to the label was Mick Hucknell and Simply Red. He had played me their demos some weeks before and was completely convinced that this was a hit band. He and I worked on the marketing together as at the time the label had hardly any staff at all, and we had a hit straight away when 'Money's Too Tight To Mention' peaked at No 13.

Dusty Springfield:

In July, I met one of my all time favourite artists. Peter Stringfellow had become very successful with his London nightclubs, Stringfellow's and The Hippodrome, and he had decided he wanted to be in the record business. As he had created Hippodrome Records, he came to Impulse and we helped set up the label for him and made it ready to put out product. One of the first signings was Dusty Springfield. Dusty had made some of the most justly famous of all records during the sixties, especially 'I Only Want To Be With You', 'I Just Don't Know What To Do With Myself', 'In The Middle Of Nowhere', 'Some Of Your Lovin'', 'You Don't Have To Say You Love Me', and 'Son Of A Preacher Man.' The album *Dusty In Memphis* is a classic and everyone should have a copy in their collection, it is simply outstanding.

The day arrived when I went to the Hippodrome offices in Leicester Square to meet with Dusty and prepare her for the promotion of the first single. You would expect an artist who had been so successful, appeared on numerous TV and radio shows and thrilled audiences at concerts throughout the world, to be worldly wise, confident in herself and ready to go. Unfortunately, that was not Dusty at that time. I was surprised by her chronic lack of self-confidence, and she really did not want to do interviews: it was a total opposite to what I expected. I left that day feeling very sorry for Dusty. We had a great chat and after a short while she became more confident and at ease with me, but it seemed the world had treated her poorly and the years since the 1960s ended had not been kind. I liked her and was honoured to meet her, but the record did not become a hit single and I still think she was not ready for the demands that were being placed on her. She was to make a comeback a few years later on two great singles with The Pet Shop Boys, and by then she looked much fitter. I was pleased that success came back in the end. I shall always remember my meetings with Dusty, I just wish I could have brought her a little more success at that time.

Bigger and Bigger:

Jive Records were beginning to grow with the success in the UK and America of Billy Ocean. David Clipsham left the company and John Fruin was made Managing Director of Zomba, which meant he was in charge of Jive Records, the recording studios, publishing, Dreamhire and Impulse. This was a splendid move as far as I was concerned, as my relationship with him had grown ever since our first meeting. He was a strong supporter of Impulse and I believe he saw in me something from his own past youth, with the drive, passion and a real will to win.

Furthermore, the growth of Impulse's success, being a company he had initially consulted on for Zomba and Clive, was a feather in his cap – we had surpassed everything that had been hoped for. We by now had a special friendship that would last through John's lifetime.

During the final months of 1985, Nick East made a record with The Three Degrees, always one of my favourite groups from the Philadelphia Records explosion in the seventies. 'The Year Of Decision', 'When Will I See You Again', and 'Take Good Care Of Yourself' had all been massive hits for the band and at one time they were the favourite group of our own royalty, when Prince Charles took part in many photo opportunities with the girls. It was such a pleasure to meet a band whose records I had bought back in the days of Walsall, when I had played them many times at my gigs as a DJ. Sheila Ferguson, Valerie Holliday and Fayette Pinkney were great fun to be with and fabulous at launch parties for the single, TV appearances, and radio. They were full of laughs, but always-complete professionals. 'The Heaven I Need' reached its peak at No 42, but we all had a wonderful time with this near miss.

In November, Impulse expanded yet again, this time into Northern Ireland. Godfrey at Gallup had told us that they now were taking data for the chart from Northern Ireland and so Impulse were straight onto hiring someone to work that area for us. It was Joe McMurray that we chose and he became a real asset. Gallup in those days used a weighting system and because of the amount of people in Northern Ireland and the few record dealers contributing to the chart, they weighted sales upwards. In other words, a sale in Northern Ireland was up-weighted maybe three or four times, and if your record was in those stores then it could make a difference of three or four places on the chart by the end of the week. This could be crucial. A record that might be 78 without Northern Ireland sales would be 73 or 74 with them and a record that might be 42 without Northern Ireland might be 39 with Northern Ireland sales. Impulse was the first promotional company to employ someone in Belfast and, again, we had a head start over all the other UK companies and better chart positions for our records because of it.

On Wednesday evenings all our reps would phone in and let us know how each of our records was working in their area. This would enable those of us in the office to form some kind of a picture on how the records would perform on the chart by the end of the week. In today's computerised chart, daily chart positions are issued to the industry, but in 1985 one of the only indicators was the guesswork performed by our office based on information from our reps. We became amazingly accurate with these calculations and our Thursday phone calls to our clients were readily accepted.

We finished 1985 with Top 10 albums of *The Best Of George Benson*, The Nolan's, Shirley Bassey and Barry White – a marvellous climax to another fantastic year for The Impulse Group of Companies.

The Impulse Group Hit Records 1985

January			
This House	Big Audio Dynamite	Source Records	No 21
Loverboy	Billy Ocean	Jive Records	No 15
February			
Method Of Modern Love	Hall & Oates	R.C.A Records	No 21
We Close Our Eyes	Go West	Chrysalis Records	No 5
The Last Kiss	David Cassidy	Arista Records	No 6
March			
Could It Be I'm Falling	Jaki Graham	Chrysalis Records	No 5
You Spin Me Round	Dead Or Alive	C.B.S Records	No 1
Welcome To The Pleasure Dome	Frankie Goes To Hollywood	ZTT Records	No 2
Love Is A Battlefield	Pat Benatar	Chrysalis Records	No 17
Black Man Ray	China Crisis	Virgin Records	No 14
Easy Lover	Philip Bailey & Phil Collins	C.B.S Records	No 1
Spend The Night	Coolnotes	Abstract Dance Records	No 11
Kiss Me	Stephen Tin Tin Duffy	10 Records	No 4
Everytime You Go Away	Paul Young	C.B.S Records	No 4
April			
Walk like A Man	Divine	Proto Records	No 23
Love Don't Live here	Jimmy Nail	Virgin Records	No 3
Don't Come Around Here	Tom Petty & Heartbreakers	M.C.A Records	No 50
May			
She Sells Sanctuary	The Cult Beggars	Banquet Records	No 15
19	Paul Hardcastle	Chrysalis Records	No 1
Suddenly	Billy Ocean	Jive Records	No 4
The Word Girl	Scritti Politti	Virgin Records	No 6
June			
Money's Too Tight To Mention	Simply Red	Elektra Records	No 13
July			
White Wedding	Billy Idol	Chrysalis Records	No 6
In Between Days	The Cure	Fiction Records	No 15

Your The One For Me	D Train	Prelude Records	No 15
August			
I Can Dream About You	Dan Hartman	M.C.A. Records	No 12
The Power Of Love	Huey Lewis & The News	Chrysalis Records	No 11
Say I'm Your No 1	Princess	Supreme Records	No 7
September			
Rebel Yell	Billy Idol	Chrysalis Records	No 6
October			
Lipstick Powder & Paint	Shakin Stevens	Epic Records	No 11
Slave To The Rhythm	Grace Jones	ZTT Records	No 12
November			
We Built This City	Starship	R.C.A Records	No 12
Secret Rendezvous	Rene & Angela	Champion Records	No 54
Sisters Are Doin' It	Eurythmics	R.C.A Records	No 9
After The Love Has Gone	Princess	Supreme Records	No 28
West End Girls	Pet Shop boys	Parlophone Records	No 1
December			
Girlie Girlie	Sophia George	Winner Records	No 7
Inspector Gadget	Kartoon Krew	Champion Records	No 50
Broken Wings	Mr Mister	R.C.A Records	No 4

In 1985, Impulse finally achieved the No 1 records that we had been searching for, scoring four in the year. Two were with CBS Records for John Aston, one with Chrysalis Records for Phil Cokell and one with Parlophone Records owned by EMI, although we were hired by the Pet Shop Boys management on that one and delivered for Tom Watkins.

Again, we worked in between the Christmas and New Year period to try and start the year quickly, and Sue and I were only back in Walsall for a couple of days before the Impulse machine set about 1986 with gusto.

1986 Impulse advert

CHAPTER 16

IMPULSE – THE UK's No 1 POPULAR
MUSIC PROMOTION COMPANY – 1986

New ideas, New concepts:

1986 would be the year when the Impulse Group of Companies' success and influence would surpass all other promotion companies in the history of the UK record business. The main competitors, Bullet Promotions and First Strike, would capitulate under the increasing pressure from our company's continuing growth.

Impulse expanded once again in 1986 and although we failed to sell to the major companies our first idea of a van sales company that had the working title of Impact, our second idea did work. We began the Impulse Weekend Team, which was a team of part-time reps that joined the company and worked for two days a week on Friday and Saturday. Our Impulse team members recruited the new people who were individuals that wanted to be reps in the record business. So, the Impulse Weekend Team became a training ground for new reps taught 'on the ground' and monitored by our experienced reps. The Weekend Team were further employed when our main reps took their holidays and this meant that we covered two fifths of our call pattern twice a week with over twenty reps working on Fridays preparing for the weekend sales and ten weekend reps working on Saturdays when no regular reps worked. It also meant that Impulse were never off the road due to holiday entitlement, something no other company could guarantee. This team was the final nail in the coffin of our competitors and was tremendously well received by all the record labels, vitally determined as they were to influence their records' chart positions at the weekend. Another 'dead bang winner' of an idea and another successful arm to The Impulse Group.

We opened 1986 quickly with hit records. 'If You're Ready Come Go With Me' was a No 30 hit for Jonathan Butler and Ruby Turner. It was produced by Billy Ocean and was a major priority for Jive Records as it made Jonathan and Ruby viable artists. They had further hits thereafter and they started to sell albums. Our first No 1 of the year came in February: 'When The Going Gets Tough The Tough Gets Going' by Billy Ocean was a worldwide hit and cemented Billy as a major global star. I had first heard the record, produced by Mutt Langer, just before the previous Christmas, and from the opening bars it sounded like a No 1. The video to the record was the icing on the cake and made sure of its huge international success. Michael Douglas, the famous Hollywood actor, and a huge music fan was on top of his game at the time and while he was making the movie *The Jewel Of The Nile* he contacted us to see if we could come up with a song that would fit the film and help promote it. After hearing 'Tough' we suggested that Michael Douglas, Kathleen Turner and Danny DeVito appear in the video as Billy's backing singers, which they all agreed to do. The original video was a masterpiece and included Danny DeVito miming the saxophone solo in the middle of the song. For this piece, we found the biggest saxophone we could get, one that was almost as big as Danny, and it was a brilliantly funny scene. Sadly, the American Federation of Musicians made us edit out that very segment because Danny was not playing but miming, and so the general public were denied one of the greatest mimed solos of all time. The backing vocal sections were included and prolonged to include a backing vocal dance, which is also good, but Danny 'playing' the sax was outstanding. Even so, regardless of the Musicians Union, 'When The Going Gets Tough The Tough Gets Going' went to No 1.

At the same time, Impulse also claimed the No 2 record for Rainbow Records after Bill Kimber had brought us a single from Su Pollard, a national star from a TV series about a holiday camp. The record was called 'Starting Together', and to this day Bill claims that I stopped Su reaching No 1 by working Billy's record harder, as I was associated with both Billy and Jive. This is not true and I would have liked to have that much influence over the UK public! Billy won the race fair and square, and we were delighted to work on both records. We took a full page advertisement in *Music Week* showing both records with their No 1 and No 2 chart positions and a strip line underneath saying 'Impulse – The No 1 and No 2 Promotion Company.' That advert was an arrow in the hearts of our competitors, especially as both Jive and Rainbow were considered small independent labels.

Samantha Fox:

Jive were now beginning to deliver more records that had the quality to become big hits. We had signed Samantha Fox after the David Cassidy picture disc had proved there could well be a music market for the country's favourite Page Three girl. In fact, the way this happened was very much in accord with the idea behind Jive Records itself, which was built on the concept of Berry Gordy's Tamla Motown. Our publishing company signed what we considered to be good up-and-coming writers and then gave them a project like Samantha Fox, in which we individually challenged them to come up with a hit single for the act. That process delivered Samanatha's debut single 'Touch', which climbed to No 3 in England and began to sell around the world. It is often thought that Sam just sold records in

England and this is not true at all. She sold records and had No 1s in America, all over Europe, India and the Far East, also selling thousand of albums everywhere, and as time went by she would sell more records abroad than in England. The rest of the world saw her as a recording artist that you could find topless pictures of and yet at home Sam was perceived as a topless model who had a few hits. I was amazed a year or so later when I arrived in Los Angeles to see posters of Samantha all over Sunset Boulevard. She had already become a big star in America. I got to know Samantha, and also her parents, very well and I liked her a lot. She is a great professional and real hard worker and we would spend the next few years working on her records and counting her as a good friend.

The Real Thing – again:

Life goes round and round and sometimes the past becomes the future. PRT Records, which were formerly Pye Records, organised themselves again, after a lull, into becoming a major distributor and record label and Impulse became their promotion company. I had worked with The Real Thing way back in my days at Barbarella's in Birmingham and was delighted that they had achieved success after years of trying in 1976 through to 1979. PRT decided to remix and re-issue their great hit single 'You To Me Are Everything' and they brought me in to do the marketing. I loved the idea and met up again with Chris and Eddie Amoo, Ray Lake and Dave Smith. Our relationship was still so good that they greeted me with 'Oh no not him, it's all over now, we thought we were making a comeback, we're finished before we've started.' 'You To Me Are Everything' was to do it all over again, selling over two hundred thousand copies and peaking at No 5. I loved it when they had to present me with a silver disc for my efforts. We then decided that maybe 'Can't Get By Without You', originally their second hit in 1976, was worth a try. It was: the remix of 'Can't Get By' would be a hit again and peaked at No 6. Following this, I was involved in getting the boys signed to Jive and we tried our luck with a new single 'Straight To The Heart', which was a good record, but our luck had run out and it only became a minor hit. The Real Thing had been part of the tapestry of my life and whenever those records come on the radio today I remember our times together with great fondness.

No 1, No 1, No 1:

Impulse hit the No 1 slot for the second time in 1986, in March, with 'Rock me Amadeus' by Falco. Howard Berman at A & M Records, always one of my favourite labels, had brought us the record, and although originally I was not so sure about it, Shaun King was very enthusiastic and later used to dance around the office singing it in a very strange voice after it had become a No 1. It just goes to show that no matter how many hit records you have, you can always miss a big one. Fortunately, because of Shaun we did not miss 'Rock Me Amadeus.'

March also brought the first big hit for Champion Records. We always knew that our system for Champion using Impulse Club Promotions, Prime Time telesales and then Impulse as the strike force would sooner or later bring big hit records, it was only a matter of time. '(Nothin' Serious) Just Buggin' by Whistle was a No 7 single in the UK and the band flew in to do *Top Of The Pops* and attend an Impulse monthly team meeting at The Holiday Inn, Swiss Cottage. The following day we all rejoiced: this little idea and company was undeniably affecting everything in the UK popular music record business.

Impulse would hit the No 1 spot another seven times during 1986. In April we made it with George Michael's 'A Different Corner' for John Aston at CBS Epic. In May, our hit was 'Spirit In The Sky' by Dr and The Medics for Steve Tannett at IRS Records. July brought us both 'The Lady In Red' by Chris DeBurgh for Howard Berman at A & M Records and 'I Want To Wake Up With You' by Boris Gardiner for Revue Records. In August, we scored with 'Don't Leave Me This Way' by The Communards and Sarah Jane Morris for Colin Bell and Roger Ames at London Records. October brought us 'Every Loser Wins' by Nick Berry, then of Eastenders fame, which was our first hit with BBC Records. I had worked hard to build a relationship with BBC Records as I could not understand why the BBC did not take their label seriously. Simon Cowell had helped me get 'in' with the BBC by recommending us, and just a few weeks before we had brought BBC Records a No 4 single with Anita Dobson. I found Anita, who would later marry Brian May of Queen, charming. She was very excited to have a hit single, as she had always wanted to sing and make a record, and 'Anyone Can Fall In Love' fulfilled many of her ambitions. And then our final No 1 hit in this bumper year of 1986 came at Christmas when we worked 'Reet Petite' by Jackie Wilson for Anne Plaxton at Scratch Records. 'Reet Petite (The Sweetest Girl in Town)' had been a No 6 record in the UK in 1957 and now, for the reissue, we accompanied it with an ingenious video of a plasticine man continually changing shape, which ensured we made No 1, where the record stayed into the New Year, making it also our first No 1 of 1987. It was one of my two favourite No 1's of 1986, the other being Billy Ocean's 'When The Going Gets Tough.'

Through its many services to the record industry Impulse now had relationships with all the record labels. Only three years earlier my phone never rang and I was visiting the dole office in Walsall. Everything can change and even when you are in the depths of despair and depression there is usually a way out. Belief is a major factor, a will to win is essential and a 'never say die' attitude is a must. If you can muster the first two and work on the third, anything can happen, just as my Mom and Dad always told me.

Tony Calder returned to Impulse during 1986 with a new company that would eventually bear fruit a couple of years later. He wanted and obtained a twelve single deal with Impulse and, as always, he asked me to go back and work with him full-time, something I never did in all the years that followed. I have always had a great affection and respect for Tony, his work in the sixties with Andrew Loog Oldham, The Rolling Stones, The Small Faces, Marianne Faithfull, The Nice, Amen Corner, Chris Farlowe, Crispian St Peters, to name a few, was exemplary. I have always felt if Tony could have controlled his incredible mind and brain he would have been one of the very top record executives the business has ever seen. He would get up at 6.00am and read all the newspapers every day, and he had such a vast capacity for retaining information.

It was Rod Duncombe and Tony Calder that gave a club DJ from somewhere called Walsall a chance in the record business, for which I have been, and always will be, grateful, and I have tried my utmost to prove their decision a correct one throughout my years. If Tony Calder wanted a twelve single deal with my company, he got one.

New York, New York:

In July of this year I made my first visit to New York. The New Music Seminar had begun and would continue for many years as a similar fair to Midem, in which all the independent labels gathered in one place to make deals and trade records. I still remember the sharp intake of breath you feel as New York looms in front of you and you go over the bridge from the airport. I would make that journey many times over the years, but never tired of that sight, especially at night. My first stay was for six days and The Sheridan City Squire on Seventh Avenue was my home. At first, I was disorientated. New York seemed a scary place, where everyone spoke and moved at rapid pace and to me appeared to shout at each other in normal conversation. I originally thought all these people were so stressed and a little bit mad, the speed of the place was much quicker than London. By the second night my fear increased. It was late and I was in my hotel room when I heard gun shots. That's a sound that you never forget, it is not at all like a firework, it is far more powerful and intense: when immediately you hear a shot you know the difference instantly. I went downstairs to the lobby and moved closer towards the entrance and about forty yards down the road were police and tape blocking off the corner: someone had been shot just moments before and only yards from my hotel. I thought 'this place is still the Wild West and John Wayne still rules', and my antenna was up for the rest of that week – I didn't know if this was a daily occurrence.

Before I had left for New York, Impulse had advertised in *Billboard*, the US trade paper, and I had also given an interview that was published that week. Our idea was to try and build a base of contacts in America so that we could work their records in the UK and we had a dream that one day we may be able to open Impulse in America. That first trip was organised to try and get a feel of how everything worked and I made some contacts who over the next few years would become friends. Cory Robbins and Steve Plotniki at Profile Records, Freddie Munao at

Select Records, Bryan Turner at Priority Records, Will Shokolov at Sleeping Bag Records, Bo Crane in Miami and Carl Strubbe in Boston were all record hustlers and gunslingers of music in those days, and we were all about the same age, had similar aims and were very passionate about our work. I began to like America and its record business.

Tommy Silverman of Tommy Boy Records had set up the seminar and we would become friends and work on many of his records through the years. He took great care to introduce me to a lot of labels, and he was a big fan of Impulse, our ideas and successes. Mel Medalie and Paul Oakenfold were also in New York looking for records for Champion, and there were also a lot of other English people there so I never felt alone. We would all meet up at Peter Stringfellow's New York club where we were made very welcome: it seemed like a little piece of England in New York. As my confidence grew after a few days, Paul Oakenfold, who had spent a year living in New York, said he would take me around on foot to see the real Big Apple. In some areas, Paul said I must not look people directly in the eye and never stop walking, just keep moving at all times. I obeyed. I was not going to mess with his instruction. It was a fascinating night, I have little idea where we went, but some of those streets were tougher than I had seen in the east end of London or Birmingham. In one square, surrounded by high rise apartments, there was a small patch of green that was a small railed park and it was patrolled by two police cars that drove around it all night long, such was the consistently expected violence. Thankfully, we moved on quickly.

Even the stone you trip on is part of your destiny:

Impulse was moving into its fourth year and could not have been in a stronger position. I was beginning to make inroads into Europe and America, we were in a year that would yield nine No 1 records and life was great. Nothing can go wrong now...can it? If you decide or are lucky enough to achieve a career in the record business, show business, the film industry or professional sport and you manage to have a long run, you will begin to understand that it is a rollercoaster ride. My advice would be to treat success and failure, the ups and downs as similarly as possible. In other words, do not become too high when all is going well and that feeling of invincibility arrives and conversely when things are going badly, try not to be too down and lose sight of your goals. Very early in my Impulse career, before we hit the big time, I was talking to Mutt Langer one day. Mutt has sold over a hundred and fifty million records with many artists he has produced and he is a down to earth man. It was Mutt that told me 'Don't bother with the parties, the press and all the show business nonsense, just get up every day and give a great day's work. If you do that, eventually, it will take care of itself.' One day at a time and give it everything you can in those hours, you can then sleep contented with yourself. Mutt also told me that the marketplace will move around on you, in other words, sometimes you can make great records, but because the marketplace has moved and fashion is elsewhere you will not achieve the hit you deserved and you must just go back in the studio and do your best again – eventually you will succeed. This struck a chord with me straight away and although I learned many valuable ways to lead my life from John Fruin and Clive Calder, this one piece of advice from Mutt stuck with me and I have lived my life trying to stay with that principle.

During July, Peter Todd became very ill. It had been coming for a while, but I do not think Peter or any of us realised it was a reality until now. Peter eventually ended up in hospital and underwent a long recovery process at home. He did not return to Impulse until January 1987, which was a major loss to all of us at the company, as Peter knew everything about how we operated – after all he had built it all up with me every day from the start. Shaun King, Jane Fisher, Austin Powell, Justin Lubbock and Kieran Fanning all stepped up their game to cover his departure, whereas the outside world may have felt little difference in our operation, internally it took a bit of getting used to. Sue and I had also had problems in our relationship and my obsession with Impulse and records must take a lot of the blame. Sue was in any case never that comfortable in London and by September, she had left to return to Walsall. Two of the major support scaffoldings of my life had disappeared within a few weeks and although I got on with the job I must admit I had a feeling of great loss. The Impulse Group, however, was a juggernaut that would not stop, so all my days were filled to the maximum, and parts of my free time were also filled with sport. I was still an avid Walsall Football Club supporter and would get to as many games as possible. Whenever they played anywhere near London, I was there and I also managed home games some weekends as I would visit my Mom and then go to the game.

Elton John:

Although I rarely went to industry parties I could not pass on the invite to Billy Gaff's country mansion for a summer party that year in August. Billy was the famed manager of Rod Stewart and his party was the kind that you see in films: there was a hot air balloon going up and down giving people short rides, a full orchestra playing all night, jugglers and circus show people doing tricks and acrobatics – I had never seen anything like it. I met Elton John that night and stood there talking with him for fifteen minutes about records and touring. Elton asked what I did and listened to my description of Impulse – and three weeks later we were working an Elton single. I also managed to talk to Rod Stewart, who was one of my favourite vocalists through his days with The Faces and his solo career.

Another run to Christmas:

In September, my sister Helen gave birth to an eight pound baby boy, David. This was great news. David was born as Impulse was flying and his elder sister

Sally had been born three years earlier at the beginning of Impulse. Our family was growing in tandem with Impulse.

Champion Records scored another Top 20 single in September with an artist who would eventually become a world movie star, a friend for a number of years and a real hit maker.

We had heard a record that Paul Oakenfold had found in Philadelphia. Mel, Ron and I loved it straight away and bought the rights for the UK. It had been made by two 16 year-olds who were still at school and they were delighted that their first record was going to come out in the far off land of England. The band was DJ Jazzy Jeff and The Fresh Prince and the single 'Girls Ain't Nothing But Trouble' peaked at No 20 in the UK charts, beginning a long career for the boys. Later Jeff Townes and Will Smith would sign for Jive Records and we would be reacquainted and score many more hits together. Whenever he visited the UK after he had become a blockbuster film star in the 1990s, Will Smith would always remind me of those early Champion days and his hit record in England during his last year at school.

During October, I was invited to EMI Records to have lunch with the Managing Director, Rupert Perry. I liked Rupert and knew that he had worked in Los Angeles for Capital Records before returning to the UK to run EMI Records, a position he occupied for a number of years. Rupert most definitely had class and style. He quizzed me about Impulse for a long time and also about the future and what I might like to do. Over the coming months we met a couple of times more in his office and had dinner together. Rupert wanted me to join EMI, but he soon realised I was committed to Impulse: it was my baby and there was no way I would consider leaving all those people who had supported me in the building of the company.

Towards the end of 1986, for the first time, Impulse suffered a couple of record companies going into liquidation. Bob England's Towerbell Records went down owing us £33,000 and Dave Robinson's Stiff Records collapsed owing us £15,000. This had not happened to us before and it was a huge blow: £50,000 gone in a moment. Zomba handled our accounts and we were too busy dealing with the records to chase the outstanding debts, which was a major mistake and one that only happens once. I do not blame Zomba or the accountants in this instance. Impulse was a fast moving company and no-one had ever before achieved our sheer volume of records and varied clients. This made me into a businessman and never again would I be unaware of what bills had been paid or what was outstanding. Impulse would have its own internal accountant from the start of 1987. Sue Knowles joined Impulse from Zomba, at first for two or three days a week, but very soon in a full time capacity. Sue met with me every week and taught me a lot about accounts. She became our credit control monitor and when she felt we were running into a potential problem she would alert me. I would then go in to get the money or stop our companies working on the labels' records, usually at a crucial time for them.

Never again would we lose a substantial amount of money and never again would I be unaware of the accounting position. Sue and I became a strong team together for The Impulse Group of Companies and we forced all the company's main players to be aware of the clients' financial positions with us.

We finally and joyously managed the big hit record 'So Macho' that Simon Cowell and Ian Burton had been looking for with Sinitta, whose career they had tried so hard to get going. Pete Waterman, Mike Stock and Matt Aitken were becoming regular hit makers and Impulse was working all their hits, such as this one for Sinitta and the fantastic 'Showing Out' with Mel and Kim (Melanie and Kim Appleby), which were signs of what was to come. 'Showing Out' was an important hit in November after being one of those records that would not go into the chart for weeks, but also would not die. Pete Waterman, Nick East and I just would not give up on this single. Initially, we could not get into the Top 75 and then it took weeks to reach the Top 40, but when that happened the record took a real grip and catapulted Mel and Kim to national stardom – short-lived, tragically, when Mel succumbed to cancer little over three years later.

John Fruin had called me to his office in late October, as he did every year, regular as clockwork. 'What are the new plans for next year? How are you going to build the company?' John never missed a beat and by 1st December I had to have the ideas and commence work on them.

Meanwhile, 1986 had been a memorable year. Impulse not only had nine No 1 singles during 1986, we also had seven No 2 singles. When I received an enormous dressing down from Jermaine Stewart's manager for only making No 2 on the chart with 'We Don't Have To Take Our Clothes Off To Have A Good Time', I thought he was joking and laughed, which induced him to lose his mind completely with me – so we never worked with him again, nor did he have any more hits. We had a great year with Chrysalis Records, Virgin Records, Supreme Records and Island Records, and finally, after three years of great effort, Jive Records had a consistent year of hits. Champion Records managed two Top 40 hits and another ten Top 100 and Top 75 hits, all of which were money makers, and the label established itself as a 'taste maker' label and one that DJs all over the country had great respect for. I became the regular breakfast partner of Gareth Harris at RCA Records, which was sometime before that kind of meeting became popular, and in 1986 we had hits with The Eurhythmics, The Blow Monkeys, Five Star and Daryl Hall, which also kept my relationship with Randy Hoffman and Tommy Mottola in the US. John Aston at CBS Records kept his faith in me and I was able to deliver some hit records for him during the year with George Michael, Cyndi Lauper and Big Audio Dynamite. On the back of the hugely popular vogue for Snooker on TV, we had a Top 10 single 'Snooker Loopy' with Chas and Dave, reaching No 6 just two weeks after its release in May, although this was one of the records we were destined not to be paid for with the collapse of Towerbell Records.

219

This year had been vital not only for the No 1 records, Champion's first couple of big hits and our attack on Europe and America, but also because major artists were now becoming aware of Impulse, its success rate and its high level hit ratio. Elton John, David Bowie, Chris Rea, The Eurhythmics, Daryl Hall, David Essex, George Michael, Bruce Springsteen, Lionel Ritchie, Aswad, The Beastie Boys, The Art of Noise, Marc Almond, Genisis, Kim Wilde, Huey Lewis and The News, Grace Jones, Chris DeBurgh, Cyndi Lauper, The Communards, Erasure, Ultravox, Debbie Harry, Billy Ocean – the Impulse Group of Companies was known to all these artists, who made up a roll call of the biggest names in the industry.

The Impulse Group Hit Records 1986

January			
If You're Ready Come Go With Me	Jonathan Butler & Ruby Turner	Jive Records	No 30
Pull Up To The Bumper	Grace Jones	Island Records	No 12
When The Going Gets Tough	Billy Ocean	Jive Records	No 1
February			
Do You Believe In Love?	Huey Lewis & The News	Chrysalis Records	No 9
Starting Together	Su Pollard	Rainbow Records	No 2
March			
Touch Me	Samantha Fox	Jive Records	No 3
So Macho	Sinitta	Fanfare Records	No 2
You to Me Are Everything	The Real Thing	P.R.T. Records	No 5
E=MC2	Big Audio Dynamite	C.B.S. Records	No 11
Diggin' You're Scene	Blow Monkeys	R.C.A. Records	No 12
Absolute Beginners	David Bowie	Virgin Records	No 2
Rock Me Amadeus	Falco	A&M Records	No 1
Just Buggin	Whistle	Champion Records	No 7
Peter Gunn	Art Of Noise	China Records	No 8
April			
Can't Wait Another Minute	Five Star	Tent Records	No 7
A Different Corner	George Michael	Epic Records	No 1
I'll Keep On Loving You	Princess	Supreme Records	No 16
There'll Be Sad Songs	Billy Ocean	Jive Records	No 12
May			
Snooker Loopy	Chas & Dave	Rockney Records	No 6

Spirit In The Sky	Dr & The Medics	I.R.S. Records	No 1
Invisible Touch	Genesis	Virgin Records	No 15
Can't Get By Without you	The Real Thing	P.R.T. Records	No 6
Sinful	Pete Wylie	Eternal Records	No 13
June			
Do Ya Do Ya	Samantha Fox	Jive Records	No 10
July			
The Lady In Red	Chris DeBurgh	A&M Records	No 1
I Want To Wake Up With You	Boris Gardener	Revue Records	No 1
Calling All The Heroes	It Bites	Virgin Records	No 6
August			
We Don't Have To Take Our Clothes Off	Jermaine Stewart	10 Records	No 2
Dreamtime	Daryl Hall	R.C.A. Records	No 28
Don't Leave Me This Way	The Communards	London Records	No 1
I Just Died In Your Arms Tonight	Cutting Crew	Siren Records	No 4
Anyone Can Fall In Love	Anita Dobson	BBC Records	No 4
September			
World Shut Your Mouth	Julien Cope	Island Records	No 19
Thorn In My Side	Eurythmics	R.C.A. Records	No 2
True Colours	Cyndi Lauper	Portrait Records	No 12
Showing Out	Mel & Kim	Supreme Records No 3	
Girls Ain't Nothing But Trouble	Jazzy Jeff & The Fresh Prince	Champion Records	No 21
October			
Every Loser Wins	Nick Berry	BBC Records	No 1
Sometimes	Erasure	Mute Records	No 2
You Keep Me hanging On	Kim Wilde	M.C.A. Records	No 2
November			
All Fall Down	Ultravox	Chrysalis Records	No 30
French Kissing In The USA	Deborah Harry	Chrysalis Records	No 8
December			
No More The Fool	Elkie Brooks	Legend Records	No 5
Reet Petite	Jackie Wilson	Scratch Records	No 1

The Impulse Group of Companies had hit the big time in 1986. We ended the year with a confidence we had not felt before. The sun was blazing down for the moment.

1986 Impulse advert

CHAPTER 17

LIFE'S DOWNS AND UPS
1987 AND 1988

Down, Down – though far from out:

Along with the highs, came the lows, and the biggest low this year was breaking up with Sue my long term partner, her subsequent return to Walsall was a great loss in my life. We had been together almost thirteen years and she had been with me as I grew in the record business. Not only was Sue my girlfriend, but also a friend who knew me better than anyone. I had bought 28 Roe Lane because of Sue and it now seemed an empty place.

Finding a new girlfriend was a difficulty. I had no interest in girls at record companies or associated with the business and I felt that one addiction to records was enough for any home. I had also made a golden rule: no female artist relationships, they could only lead to disaster. I also never visited clubs in London; I only went when there was a record or artist launch or something I had to attend for business. Clubs held no fascination for me outside the work I had fulfilled in them. Hanging around 'on the pull' was not an option. I was without doubt lonely in a crowd, constantly surrounded by a whole host of people, but most definitely alone. I didn't know at the time that this would continue for nearly two years.

And now another vital piece of scaffolding that had helped to hold me up for five years was to come down. Not long after coming back to work following his long illness, Peter Todd decided he was going to leave Impulse and, eventually he negotiated his way out, selling his shares to Zomba. Precisely why Peter left I don't know, but for sure he seemed to have become a different person. Perhaps, all those months of recuperating had brought about a feeling of wanting a change in his life and also, perhaps in a company that is so fast moving like Impulse it felt very strange returning to such an intense level of activity after months away. Maybe he felt the company had changed for him since Shaun King and Jane Fisher had stepped up in his absence. Or maybe he had really had enough of me. Whatever the reason or reasons it was painful for both of us and while his negotiations with Zomba dragged on for some months the atmosphere at Impulse was negatively affected.

In amongst all of this, and probably the final straw for Peter, was the selling of our shares in Champion Records. An accountant at Jive Records had noticed that a cheque from Champion had been paid to Impulse with my signature on it. The Champion rules were that Ron Boulding or Mel Medalie could sign cheques on the company's behalf, but they had to be countersigned by Peter or me. In Peter's absence, all the cheques for a period of time carried my signature.

Much to my surprise, Clive Calder threw a fit and instructed John Fruin to see that we sell our shares in Champion or leave and close Impulse. I decided to sell, mainly because I had a lot of people that now worked for Impulse and I had a major responsibility to them. I was disappointed, but it was not the end of the world. Peter, I think, took it more painfully.

After leaving Impulse, Peter would be successful running Swanyard Records. I think Champion had given him a taste for operating a label. He thought at this time that I was being groomed to be Managing Director of Jive Records and I always told him what a load of complete rubbish that was. I had no intention of running any label but my own and the selling of the Champion shares had put that opportunity back some way. On top of that, I was an Impulse addict, I loved that company and I believed it still had a long way to go.

Champion Records remained a client of Impulse for the next five years, and we helped them achieve many hit records before the label was eventually sold to BMG Records many years later. Of its time, Champion was the most brilliant and profitable idea for a label in a volatile industry. That it did not become part of Jive Records or did not remain part of Impulse was stupid and tragic.

When Peter left Impulse we tried hard to keep our friendship alive for a while, but I think he never forgave me for not leaving the company with him, as he had done at Promopeople with me. I felt I had greater responsibilities to the staff at Impulse and to leave now was not the right thing for me to do. Our rift was painful for me as there is no doubt that Peter Todd played a massive part in the building of Impulse and its coming about would not have happened without him. I always remember clearly how it was Peter who gave me the confidence to try again when everything had fallen apart at Promopeople and we worked together for four years at Impulse as a formidable partnership making a real mark in the UK record industry.

Impulse under attack:

In the Midlands there is a phrase, 'You couldn't pull in a brothel.' That sort of summed me up on that front for some considerable time. With the loss of Sue, Peter leaving and the Champion Records affair, I was not really enjoying life. Impulse was continuing to have hit after hit record and I was busy all day and night, then came the attack on my company. The record industry in those days was an entrepreneur's business, hence when something was extremely successful lots of people tried to copy the idea. There were always new promotion companies coming along, but Impulse had such a client base, reputation and hit ratio that we never really took much notice of them. We monitored their records, success rate and clients, but they never really threatened our position. Bullet Promotions were the only viable competition and they had long since been defeated. Then came Platinum Promotions. Duncan Robertson had worked at London Records and Polydor Records and felt that he could command their outside promotion work if he set up a company like Impulse. Robertson probably had some assurances from within the building: he had also invited me for lunch on a couple of occasions, under the pretence of hiring Impulse for Polydor, but I realised later that this was just to gain information about how we operated.

Platinum hit the ground running and had quite a few early hits. When a new company started in our area it usually tailed off after a couple of months, but this time there was one big difference: from the start Platinum were having hits with major labels as distinct from independent labels. Impulse had grown from the independent label sector to working for major labels, a complete opposite. Platinum worked hard on the insinuation that Impulse was for independent labels and Platinum along with their 'on the road' selling operation was designed for major companies. It was a good, if misleading, idea and Platinum began to eat into our major record company client base over a period of months.

This was the final nail in my fragile state of mind at this time. The Impulse team began to be concerned that Platinum was a viable competitor, and the team wanted to add sales into our call pattern as they thought that was the reason clients were moving away from Impulse. I thought about it and decided to implement the idea as the team were insistent, even though personally I felt this took away some of the mystique of our operation. I would have preferred to hold out and continue to operate our sales through Prime Time exclusively. However, I reluctantly agreed to the pressure, made a reshuffle of our team's responsibilities and decided I would 'get out there' and see as many of the marketing guys at other labels as I could.

Even with these changes, Platinum still kept moving forward and taking records I believed should be ours. Robertson was beginning to become very cocky, with a flash car and the image of a big man about town, and this was the direct opposite to how we had operated, always trying to fit in with the record company and not taking all the glory of the hit away from them. For months I toiled, out at labels every day, and in all honesty was not solving the problem. I was at a record company one day just hustling for records, talking up our recent success when an old friend said 'Let's go out for a cigarette.' We walked out the back to where they had a few tables and chairs. 'Listen', he said, 'Platinum use a kick back system, that's why they are getting the work. Now, I didn't tell you and I will always deny it.' I was always thankful for that piece of information, it stopped me going absolutely mad. When you know your company is the best and it is failing to a poorer operation it can drive you absolutely nuts.

The 'kick back' system means you charge a fee to the client company, but the operator at the company gets some reward for hiring you. Robertson turned out to be a master at the system and would reward operators in any way they wished. Under no circumstances was I going to adopt that device at Impulse to rival Platinum and although we had to wait eighteen months, they were to collapse virtually overnight through their tactic. If you play 'kick backs', sooner or later the wrong person finds out, your credibility disappears and no-one will use you. In 1988, word got to the record companies that Platinum were not playing with a straight bat and it then only needed two vital new developments at Impulse to bring all the clients back to us and bring about the demise of Platinum: firstly my old friend Pete Waterman became the hottest producer in the country, and Impulse were working and marketing all his records, and secondly, I came up with an idea with Woolworths for new singles, which made Impulse the only call if you were a major record company (more about this later). Almost immediately after this service began Platinum closed their doors. By attacking Impulse in the way they did, Platinum had in short, as the Americans say, 'opened a can of whoop ass.'

There would never be another popular music promotion company built on our designs. Slowly and gradually over the next ten years major record companies would one by one build their own promotion and sales operations. They would never become fashionable or as well known as Impulse and would never have the close relationships with record dealers. We were different.

The Impulse star rises again – and the Waterman Factor:

We had begun 1987 at No 1 with the reissue of Jackie Wilson's 'Reet Petite' that had hit the top just before Christmas, and Anne Plaxton at Scratch Records followed it up with 'I Get The Sweetest Feeling', which was a No 3 hit in March. Still, we were not finished with Jackie: 'Higher And Higher' reached No 15 in June. I loved working on Jackie Wilson records, he was a soul icon and was the most important vocalist during a time when R&B records developed into soul records in the late Fifties. He had recorded over fifty singles and I had bought a good few of them as I grew up in Walsall, so to have a run of hits with him was a tremendous honour. Not that Jackie would have known much about it. On stage in 1975 he suffered a massive heart attack and severely concussed himself as he fell. Although he survived, he lived not knowing who or where he was for another eight years: a tragic end for someone who had exerted so much influence.

Impulse hit the No 1 spot again in March with the record 'Respectable' by Mel and Kim. This is a pop anthem, not only for Mel and Kim, but also for the team of Stock Aitken Waterman, Supreme Records and Impulse. We all felt we were doing something different, together and separate from the establishment. As S.A.W had started to have a few hits they advertised in *Music Week*, and the text read:

You can love us or hate us,

You ain't never gonna change us

We ain't ever gonna be Respectable!

That advertisement was part of the lyrics in 'Respectable', a pivotal record. Mel and Kim were growing into real popstars of the day – in a pioneering way. In the video, Kim knocks the helmet off a policeman's head, and this was the girls just having fun, but when the kids of the UK saw it they responded immediately and Mel and Kim became 'Girlpower' years before we knew that phrase. 'Respectable' was the start of something huge that would become historical over the next three or four years. Stock Aitken Waterman had gone from dance producers to pop producers and the first of their pop groups were Mel and Kim. For us, they changed the world and we all remember them both with great affection.

For the first time we now knocked ourselves off the No 1 slot. After Respectable rocketed to No 1 it stayed there for one week, and I believe it would have had a much longer stay had it not been for the Zeebrugge Disaster that had occurred on 6th March 1987 when *The Ms Herald of Free Enterprise* ferry capsized and killed 193 passengers. *The Sun* newspaper had sold cheap tickets for the ferry that day and wanted to raise money for the victims' families. They contacted Stock Aitken Waterman and Ferry Aid was born. S.A.W produced a new version of Paul McCartney's and John Lennon's 'Let It Be', and an array of star artists from our industry joined in to make the record. McCartney himself took part along with Boy George, Bananarama, Mel and Kim, Mark Knophler, Edwin Star, Kate Bush, Bonnie Tyler, Alvin Stardust, Rick Astley and Frankie Goes To Hollywood to name a few. Along with Stock Aitken Waterman came Impulse, we donated our services free of charge and the record, issued on CBS, went straight to No 1, where it stayed for three weeks knocking Mel and Kim off the top spot.

The UK chart was beginning to carry several S.A.W productions: Ferry Aid, Mel and Kim, who followed 'Respectable' with 'FLM' (Fun, Love, Money), Bananarama's 'I Heard A Rumour', and Samantha Fox, whose superb single 'Nothings Gonna Stop Me Now' for Jive Records hit No 8 in May, and then Rick Astley. Pete had found Rick Astley in Newton on The Willows at a showcase gig for local bands; Pete hated the band and the songs but loved the voice of Rick Astley. Rick is a great lad and he came to London to learn his craft working in studios and recording some songs on forty pounds a week for experience. He fitted in well, stayed some of the time in Pete's flat and went back up north with Pete on Fridays. Pete organised a deal with RCA Records and work began on what would be 'Never Gonna Give You Up.' An unfinished, but good club version of the track mysteriously found its way onto vinyl and started creating a buzz in the clubs where people were asking 'who is that voice?' Legend of the record business says this was a mistake and no-one should have heard or been given a copy of this 'unfinished' track, but I know Waterman and I can assure you it is not beyond the realms of possibility that he carefully slipped it into the wrong hands to see what might happen. Pete Waterman at that time was the greatest promotion man and would try all sorts of ways to make exposure for his records.

I had a good relationship with RCA at the time and Impulse was brought on board to work the single. This normally happened with whichever label Stock Aitken Waterman records came out on: everyone knew we had success together with the records and if Impulse was on the record Pete felt he would get the best and most truthful information from me. On the rare occasion that a record company did not hire Impulse on a S.A.W record, Pete would normally phone Impulse and say 'I know you're not on it, but find out how it's doing' or if something went wrong Pete would go ballistic at the label for not hiring Impulse and we would most certainly be hired on the next one. Pete always thought his records should be higher on the chart and I thought they should be too, so it was more of a question of planning the single properly than working it 'live.' Over the next four years we perfected the system from start to finish.

The hits just kept on coming, the more artists we broke the more follow-up hits came. Rick Astley followed up with 'Whenever You Need Somebody' and 'When I Fall in Love' for Christmas, and Bananarama did the same with 'Love In The First Degree.' Simon Cowell and Iain Burton now had a hit artist in Sinitta and S.A.W produced 'Toyboy', a No 4 hit in July, and 'GTO', a No 15 hit in December. CBS brought us Terrence Trent D'Arby and we had three hit singles with him that year, Epic brought George Michael's 'Faith', we broke 'Living In A Box' and 'Letter From America' by The Proclaimers, and we continued our success with Billy Idol's 'Mony Mony' for Phil Cokell at Chrysalis. Virgin was a big client for us: they brought us T'Pau on Siren Records where we had a hit with 'Heart And Soul', No 4 in August, before achieving a No 1 single with the classic 'China In My Hand.' I met T'Pau's singer and front woman Carol Dekker a few times during that year. Carol had little time for record company flannel, she recognised I didn't care for it either and we always had a laugh during those months. I always felt that she thought it was all a bit of a dream that should really have happened to someone else. Virgin had also financed Circa Records for Ray Cooper and Ashley Newton, and Impulse was delighted to be involved in the breaking of their first act Hue and Cry, whose song 'Labour Of Love' made No 6 in June. And then closer to home with Jive Records, we had hits with Billy Ocean, Samantha Fox, Ruby Turner and Jonathan Butler.

Donny Osmond:

During August we started work on a comeback record for Donny Osmond in the UK with Virgin. The single 'I'm In It For Love' would eventually be a Top 20 hit, although it would not stimulate a massive sales base for Donny. Donny Osmond is a great guy, he is nearly always smiling, has plenty of time for everyone and having been in the business nearly all his life he knows exactly how to handle himself and gets the job done. We were all invited to a get together to launch the new Donny single and album and Donny was there meeting and talking to as many people as possible. I had previously met him a couple of times in the build up to release, but Helen, our Impulse office assistant at the time, who eventually would operate our radio promotion company, had not had an opportunity to meet him and as she thought this was just a straight record launch she never imagined that he would be there. The Impulse crew stood in a circle chatting when Helen talked about Donny Osmond being her childhood pop star, with posters on her bedroom wall. 'He's right over there' we all said. 'That's not him' said Helen, not believing Donny would have travelled all the way from America. I casually walked over a few minutes later and told him about Helen – would he come over and say hello? Sure enough five minutes later Donny came over, walked up to Helen and said 'Hello Helen, I'm Donny.' The look on Helen's face was a picture, she had suddenly lost the ability to speak and so we talked with Donny while Helen regained her composure. She gave me a good thump on the arm for that later, but I believe she greatly enjoyed meeting her childhood hero. Donny Osmond, a true class act.

A couple of surprises:

The first of the hit singles featuring Stock Aitken Waterman as artists happened in July of '87 when 'Roadblock' was released, and it is still one of my favourite records. S.A.W had been receiving appalling notices in the press, mainly born out of jealousy, so Pete decided to teach them a lesson. Mike Stock came up with the Roadblock groove when the word was fashionable at the time with the kids going to 'raves.' Pete then sent the tapes to America to be cut and pressed and leaked the record into England without any writer or artist credits. The single gathered momentum in the clubs, where it was seen as a credible dance and club record, and this coupled with 'Who is it' questions in the press brought the single to everyone's notice. One day Tilly Rutherford got hold of the record, played it to Pete and said Pete Waterman Limited should be making records like this. You can imagine how much Pete enjoyed the moment. Eventually, the single came out and Stock Aitken Waterman peaked at No 13 as artists.

Finally, in October of '87 we were given the opportunity to work on a single from Nina Simone. I always enjoyed it when Impulse was associated with history–

making artists, and to have just the briefest of moments in Nina Simone's career was an honour. 'My Baby Just Cares For Me' on Charly Records became a Top 5 single and it still stands out as a fine record all these years later.

1987 had been tough, but our hits had rolled on and on:

January			
Surrender	Swing Out Sister	Mercury Records	No 7
Coming Around Again	Carly Simon	Arista Records	No 10
I.O.U. remix	Freeez	City Beat	No 23
You Sexy Thing remix	Hot Chocolate	EMI	No 10
Love Is Forever	Billy Ocean	Jive Records	No 34
February			
I Get the Sweetest Feeling	Jackie Wilson	Scratch Records	No 3
Stay Out Of My Life	Five Star	Tent/RCA	No 9
Heartache	Pepsi and Shirley	Polydor	No 2
March			
I'd Rather Go Blind	Ruby Turner	Jive	No 24
The Irish Rover	The Pogues	Stiff	No 8
Respectable	Mel & Kim	Supreme	No 1
If You Let Me Stay	Terrence Trent D'Arby	CBS	No 7
Ever Fallen In Love	Fine Young Cannibals	London	No 9
Let's Wait Awhile	Janet Jackson	Breakout/A&M	No 3
Weak In The Presence Of Beauty	Alison Moyet	CBS	No 6
April			
Living In a Box	Living In a Box	Chrysalis	No 5
Let Yourself Go	Sybil	Champion	No 34
Let It Be	Ferry Aid	The Sun	No 1
Back and Forth	Cameo	Club	No 11
The Slightest Touch	Five Star	Tent/RCA	No 4
I Want You Back remix	Jackson 5	Motown	No 8
Shattered Dreams	Johnny Hates Jazz	Virgin	No 5
May			
Nothing's Gonna Stop Me Now	Samantha Fox	Jive	No 8
Friday on My Mind	Gary Moore	Virgin/ 10	No 26
Luka	Susanne Vega	A & M	No 23

June			
Wishing Well	Terence Trent D'Arby	CBS	No 4
Star Trekkin'	The Firm	Bark Records	No 1
Labor Of Love	Hue And Cry	Circa	No 6
Let's Dance	Chris Rea	Magnet	No 12
Higher and Higher	Jackie Wilson	Scratch Records	No 15
July			
I Heard A Rumour	Bananarama	London	No 14
Jive Talkin'	Boogie Box High	Hardback Records	No 7
I Surrender	Samantha Fox	Jive Records	No 25
Songbird	Kenny G	Arista	No 22
F.L.M.	Mel and Kim	Supreme	No 7
Somewhere Out There	Linda Ronstadt	MCA	No 8
Toyboy	Sinitta	Fanfare	No 4
August			
Never Gonna Give You Up	Rick Astley	RCA	No 1
Wonderful Life	Black	A&M	No 8
Lies	Jonathan Butler	Jive	No 18
Mary's Prayer	Danny Wilson	Virgin	No 3
I Don't Want To Be A Hero	Johnny Hates Jazz	Virgin	No 11
My Love Is Guaranteed	Sybil	Champion	No 42
Heart and Soul	T'Pau	Siren	No 4
September			
Cars remix	Gary Numan	Beggars Banquet	No 16
I'm In It For Love	Donny Osmond	Virgin	No 18
October			
Whenever You Need Somebody	Rick Astley	RCA	No 3
Love In the First Degree	Bananarama	London	No 3
Dance Little Sister	Terrence Trent D'Arby	CBS	No 20
Mony Mony	Billy Idol	Chrysalis	No 7
Faith	George Michael	Epic	No 2
Some Guys Have all The Luck	Maxi Priest	10 Records	No 12
November			
Letter From America	The Proclaimers	Chrysalis	No 3
China in Your Hand	T'Pau	Siren	No 1

When I Fall In Love	Rick Astley	RCA	No 2
Paid In Full	Eric B & Rakim	4th & Broadway	No 15
Turn Back The Clock	Johnny Hates Jazz	Virgin	No 12
What Do You Wanna Make Those Eyes at Me For?	Shakin' Stevens	Epic	No 5
December			
Heaven Is A Place on Earth	Belinda Carlisle	Virgin	No 1
Rise To The Occasion	Climme Fisher	EMI	No 10
The Time Warp	Damian	Jive	No 51
G.T.O.	Sinitta	Fanfare	No 15

Kylie Minogue:

After the rollercoaster year of 1987 I had no idea about what was going to happen in 1988 or the position we would be in by the end of the year. If I could have dreamt it, I don't think I would have believed it. 1988 would be the year of Kylie Minogue and the start of PWL Records: they would catapult Impulse to the top of the music business tree and lead to discussions that would herald a new career for me in 1989.

In the Autumn of 1987 a young actress had made the long journey from Australia with a promise of recording with Stock Aitken Waterman. She had been appearing in a weekly lunchtime soap opera called *Neighbours*, which had been brought over here from Australian television. It had been strongly embraced by children, as teenagers were a focal part of the series, and so much so that they were playing truant from school to watch it. One of the characters was Charlene, whom the kids knew of course, but as the show had not yet reached the conscience of the older generations, the actress who took the part, Kylie Minogue, was largely unknown to the generations that were not kids. In Australia *Neighbours* was a hit show and Kylie was well known there because of it, so Mushroom Records had wanted to make a S.A.W type record for Australia and had engaged an engineer from the PWL Studios to go out there to make a recording in the style of a S.A.W production. The engineer, Mike Duffy, had tried to bring Pete over to make the record, but by then the studios were so busy that he could not spare the time and, in any case, he did not have the inclination to travel to Australia to produce an actress from a soap opera. Duffy went on to make the record the best he could in the vein of S.A.W and after just two weeks on release Kylie Minogue's new version of Little Eva's 'The Loco-motion' was No 1 in Australia. It was the start of an extraordinary chain of events.

Mushroom wanted a follow-up and were working hard to get S.A.W to produce. Duffy felt he had used up his one trick of copying S.A.W with a cover and

Kylie needed new material to move forward. A deal was struck between PWL and Mushroom to produce a Kylie record and the legend goes that Kylie and her Mom pitched up at PWL studios expecting to record her next single, but no-one at the studio knew who she was or that she was booked in to record. Kylie had to spend hours in reception while it was all sorted out. Pete, constantly on the move with any number of projects in his head, had forgotten all about Kylie Minogue. Mike Stock tracked him down and asked him about a young Australian in reception waiting to record. Pete expressed his sorrow at forgetting, but, in response to being told Kylie was there to record, uttered the phrase 'She should be so lucky.' Mike liked the phrase and turned it into a title for a single – 'I Should Be So Lucky.' During the next half hour Mike and Pete worked on the lyrics and Matt Aitken started working on a loose backing track on top of which Kylie's vocals would be placed. All this had to be done at great speed as there were only two more hours available before Kylie left for the airport and Australia.

Mike and Matt recorded Kylie, who put in a great performance on 'I Should Be So Lucky', and then the track was left on the shelf as S.A.W continued with the projects that needed to be ready for Christmas 1987. By late November, the continuing promises of 'it's coming next week' were becoming frustrating for Mushroom Records and they decided to make an imminent deadline when they would fly to England to pick up the record. Pete, in a small panic, sat up all night with Pete Hammond to work on a 12-inch version of I Should Be So Lucky that could be used to promote and gauge a reaction before Mike and Matt set about working on the key 7-inch single. A couple of strokes of fortune then occurred. At the PWL Christmas party held at the National History Museum and hosted by Lenny Henry, the 12-inch 'I Should Be So Lucky' was played. Pete, working on so many tracks at the time and in a haze of enjoyment, had not recognised his work from five weeks ago and asked what the track was. In realising it was Kylie's 'I Should Be So Lucky', Pete realised after hearing it in front of a live audience that it truly sounded like a hit record. He took the record to Liverpool, where he had a Saturday morning slot broadcasting on Radio City, and it was there and then that he realised the power of *Neighbours* and understood the kids' adoration of Charlene. While talking to his radio producer, Pete said he was going to play his new production of Kylie Minogue's 'I Should Be So Lucky', and the producer asked 'is that Charlene from *Neighbours*?' This came as a surprise to Pete, but he quickly understood that the record was showing all the potential of having a great demand.

Pete now set about obtaining a record deal for Kylie. Now you would have thought that with records constantly in the Top 10, the most successful record producers in the country would have an easy job obtaining a deal. The asking price for the Kylie single was £2,500 and the great British record companies declined enmasse. So here was a single that was showing all the signs of being a hit, but there were absolutely no takers.

Thankfully, for all our sakes, the failure of record companies' A & R Departments left us with no option but to start PWL Records. Pete did not want to start a record company, his design was to make records and productions for all the labels, and he had Impulse to work and market the records and tell him honestly how his records were performing at street level. The thought of manufacturing, and putting up money for pressings, sleeves and promotions were all too much to comprehend. But, with no takers for Kylie Minogue, the decision was made to start PWL Records. Our executive team was quickly formed. Tilly Rutherford became General Manager, Impulse Promotions took its place as marketers and street promoters, Robert Lemon and Ron McCrae became our national radio and TV promoters, and slowly we set up a complete team that would work together for the next five years and bring enormous success.

'I Should Be So Lucky' was set for release two weeks into January 1988 and the idea was that we should chart the record in the Top 40 in time for Pete to do some European deals at Midem to raise the necessary money to finance the label. You would think that after all the hit records of the previous three years PWL would have money to burn, but that was not the case, as it always takes a couple of years for the royalties from hit records to filter through. This is not a case of anyone being ripped off, as the press usually states. It is just a matter of accountancy, as records are pressed, there are costs, it usually takes months for the record to become a hit after the initial pressings and then the most money is made by the sales of the following album. This could happen nine months after the initial single and accounting periods then follow, so it is not unusual for the big money to take two years to filter through. Hence PWL Records was operating on a wing and a prayer. The sale of the record into other countries would bring instant income in advances; this is what would pay for the continuing operation of PWL Records.

Pete made a deal for PWL with Steve Mason's Pinnacle Records, the largest independent distributor, and Steve and Pinnacle joined our team, where everyone was independent and worked for themselves. Meanwhile, Pete had called me over to PWL to tell me the importance of Kylie being in the Top 40 for the Sunday evening before Midem opened on the Monday. The brief was simple: put it in the Top 40 that day, so I can sell it all over Europe on the Monday, Tuesday and Wednesday. If you don't, we are all finished, we need the money urgently. I was confident that Kylie would be in the Top 40 by Sunday night and I told Pete that it would be between Top 35 and 40. Off I went to Midem on Friday, with the others following later. Sunday came and dragged on for an age and the next part of the story I was told several times by the people who were there when this happened (I was not). The PWL crew had gathered at their hotel,

Pete phoned someone in England to get the chart position, holding on the phone as the run down went on, and everyone expected Kylie to appear between

Top 35 and 40, which would guarantee signing the single to other countries. The run down began with the room in a buoyant mood. 40, 39, 38, no Kylie. A little concern began to creep in. 37, 36, concern was turning to worry. 35, 34, still no Kylie. The level of upset at this time, I am told, was immense. 33 and no Kylie, 'I'm gonna kill Jenkins at 6.30', said my lifelong friend. 32, 'I Should Be So Lucky' by Kylie Minogue. Impulse went from the worst team on the road to world beaters, PWL Records was in business and Kylie Minogue was on her way to being a pop icon.

That evening we had a great night out and the following day Pete started to sell the record to Europe and raise the necessary money to keep the label moving. History now shows that 'I Should Be So Lucky' was to make it all the way to No 1; it would make Kylie Minogue the darling of the pop business and change my life.

Sabrina – and the hits just keep on coming:

Impulse continued the year in a rich vein. We went to No 1 with Tiffany, who had risen to fame in America by performing in shopping malls and scoring a hit with 'I Think We're Alone Now.' I remembered the song from the original version some years earlier by The Rubinoos. We had No 2's with Terence Trent D'Arby, Rick Astley and Bomb The Bass, and No 3's with Taylor Dane, who had recently signed to Tommy Mottola's Champion management company, for whom I was still their UK contact, and a record by Sabrina entitled 'Boys (Summertime Love).'

Sabrina had caused a commotion in the office at Impulse. The boys loved her video that accompanied the single, in fact, I think we took the record on for the video rather than the song. Sabrina performed the song in a white swimming costume, in and out of a swimming pool, and she struggled to contain her ample breasts in a small top. It was similar to two puppies fighting their way out of a pillow case and kept the boys glued to the screen. After that hit single we got to know Sabrina as she visited Impulse on a few occasions, and we then recorded a follow up on PWL Records.

Billy Ocean scored again for Jive and Impulse with another No 3 record: 'Get Out Of My Dreams, Get Into My Car.' This was a truly great record, but we had difficulty getting Radio One to play the song. They thought the lyric of Get Into My Car was not politically correct and it took a few weeks to convince them differently. As the record began to climb the chart they forgot all about their problem and played it.

We had a No 12 record with 'Bass, How Low Can You Go' from Simon Harris, who became a regular visitor at Impulse. He told us he was also Britain's Champion YoYo performer, something we didn't really believe. One day he turned up with a YoYo and treated us to a private showing – to this day I have never seen anyone do that with a YoYo.

Woolworths – a power-house deal:

During January we had a hit with Eddie Grant 'Gimme Hope Johanna.' Eddie was managed by my old friend Tony Calder, who asked me to take care of the record for him. The main problem was getting it into Woolworths, who were proving to be the volume sellers of singles. At the time, they stocked the Top 75 singles and would only order guaranteed singles that would appear in their first week in the Top 75. I had learned previously that if you took the artist to meet the staff at Woolworths' head office a couple of months before, then they most likely ordered the single. Eddie and I went to Woolworths and had lunch with some of the staff in the canteen and they did indeed order the single on release.

I became more and more interested in the growth of Woolworths in record sales terms. Their racking of records was moving to the front of store, which they believed brought in the kids and record buyers who would then spend even more money on odds and sods and pick 'n' mix. It was working. At the same time Woolworths had become criticised for concentrating on records that were safe sales. They were constantly in the press saying they would give new artists a chance, but rarely did. This got me thinking. I felt that if Impulse were allowed into their stores and could place maybe six new records a week there, this would bring great press for Woolworths and move Impulse to the very top of the industry. If Woolworths would not buy your single then all record companies would have to hire Impulse to put the record in the Woolworths store.

I worked hard on the idea and had Jive's art department work on baseball caps with 'New music at Woolworths' slogans, badges with 'Woolies for new music', posters, stickers and any promotional material I could find. I took the idea to John Fruin and talked him through why and how I thought it would work. John knew Paddy Toomey, the head of Woolworths, very well and set a meeting for me to pitch my idea to him.

Paddy was a tough operator and I would have got nowhere near him without John. He quizzed me every which way on how this would work and then, four weeks later, he accepted the idea. Impulse were to have the bottom shelf below the Top 75 singles in 800 Woolworths stores. We would put in store six singles a week that Paddy and I would choose. They would be installed free of charge and they would be separated by Impulse advertising cards that carried our name. Paddy did not want to go for the baseball caps, badges and posters, but nevertheless Impulse was in Woolworths. It was a master stroke, and overnight all the record companies called Impulse: EMI, Warner Brothers, CBS, RCA – they could not guarantee getting into Woolworths no matter how big they were and the only way in, if Woolworths chose not to buy their new release, was via Impulse. This operation ran for three years and made Impulse £300,000 a year. It was also the final nail in Platinum Promotions and they closed within weeks.

The Psycho:

Jive Records, our partners, were still having hit records with Billy Ocean and also with Samantha Fox, Ruby Turner and Jonathan Butler, but these artists were coming to the end of their best record selling days. The new product from Jive was good, but it was not making a real impression on the sales charts. The most notable new signing to come on the scene that year was the Wee Papa Girl Rappers. Their biggest hit came in October with 'We Rule' – but, soon their success was over. Clive Calder was now spending most of his time in the USA, and I believe his focus on America was so concentrated that the UK Company was beginning to suffer. The frustrations between Jive and Impulse were growing and the new staff at Jive did not like the attitude of the Impulse staff or me in particular: Impulse was having hit after hit and perceived to be having the greatest time while Jive was struggling. Whenever Jive failed with a record this was the fault of Impulse being too busy looking after other companies' records. We were accused of dropping everything for Waterman. They suggested that if Waterman whistled, I ran, I felt I had to go where the hits were and if Jive could deliver hits then they could have more of my time, but if they didn't then I followed the hits. Jive staff did not seem to be fazed by all the hits we were having with a whole host of other companies, it was PWL that they were transfixed with.

None of this really bothered me. John Fruin was Managing Director, he was above all the companies within Zomba, and Impulse was a profit maker within the group. I was fortunate in that John liked my 'never say die' attitude and that I was always chasing the hits. John asked me several times was I doing my best for Jive and I could honestly say that I was, but the records were just not good enough. He also asked me to try and tame the uprising in Jive Records and manage the unrest. I had bitten my lip so many times during that year and put up with constant abuse from the new breed that had been hired. Their lack of success put pressure on them and they tried to divert that pressure into Impulse as a reason for their failure. I understood a lot of their frustrations. Working for Clive Calder when you are failing is not easy: he hates failure and will not tolerate it for long, so you better be doing all you can to succeed or you really did not have long left in his company.

The legend goes that, one day, I just grabbed Jive Records Sales Manger Nic Moran and threw him headlong down the corridor at Impulse. That one moment of loss of control brought with it several misconceptions. Nic Moran had been brought into Jive Records almost a year earlier and he had his own ideas on how a record should be made, promoted, sold, performed, in fact, he thought he possessed the whole nine yards. In his mind, he was above Impulse and me and should dictate how things were done, as Jive owned part of Impulse. Nic did not find great enthusiasm for his style within the walls of Impulse, and he did begin to irritate me, but as per John Fruin's request I put Shaun in charge of all Nic Moran meetings and told Shaun it was best that I was not involved. This worked for a while, but was not good enough for Nic; he had to keep on picking and laying sly remarks whenever I was in a major Jive record company meeting.

Finally, the day came, Nic had told Shaun he wanted a meeting with me and so Shaun arranged it. Nic and Shaun came into my office and Nic slowly began to warm up into his tirade about how Impulse should be run and what I should be doing for him and Jive Records. I managed about fifteen minutes of Moran talking down to me and destroying Impulse and what had been built over the past five years. The rest is a little bit of a blur. I could hear Shaun in the distance saying 'No...No...No', but it was all to no avail, I was gone. I rounded my desk, walked over to the sofa, pulled a stunned Nic to his feet, banged him against the wall, opened the door and threw him down the hallway. Helen's office was positioned next to mine and the main office and she later recalled, she suddenly heard raised voices and a big thud as Nic flew past her open door. Later that day I thought it best to own up and went to see John Fruin. I confessed to throwing his Sales Manager down the hallway and explained why I thought he was such a jerk.

That episode brought with it an industry story that became legend, a belief in people that I was capable of anything and a nickname of 'Psycho.' The 'Psycho' name lives to this day and I still believe it misrepresents the patience I have.

The year was getting better and better, Impulse was reaching greater and greater heights within the industry, my personal life was a mess and pretty non-existent, but that in itself seemed to drive me forward to work harder and harder. Meanwhile, the buzz of Walsall Football Club winning promotion and the thought of playing bigger and better teams in the second tier of football carried me through the summer. My general mental state was in the full bloom of recovery, Impulse had beaten all comers and was striding forward, Walsall F.C. were in Division Two, and if only I could meet a woman I loved and could have a meaningful relationship with, life would be a dream. My Mom said at the time, 'You know what Steve, you just can't have it all and be thankful for what you've got.' I was.

Off the beaten track(s):

Certain records always stay in your mind even if they are not big hits. I am intentionally mentioning in the list of Impulse hits for 1988 Boogie Down Productions' 'My Philosophy', which peaked at No 69. This may mean nothing to most people, but for me that record signified the underground swell of a harder rap sound that was beginning to take a hold in England. I was out one night with a few people at a reception and met Samantha King, who some years later would become a rep for Impulse. That night we spoke about the records we were working and she was not at all impressed with the likes of Kylie, Jason & Rick. I just happened to mention Boogie Down Productions and Samantha went into a long and detailed story about 'My Philosophy', telling me much more than I knew about the project. Samantha was right, and although the single only peaked at No 69, the album went on to sell over twenty thousand copies. That moment to me was important. Suddenly, I had seen the passion that even white English kids had for this style of music and I started taking much more notice of rap thereafter.

Another record that is not obvious from 1988 was the remix of 'Downtown' by Petula Clark, which would become a Top 10 hit again, 24 years after its original release. When PRT Records asked if we were interested in working the record I jumped at it: the song 'Downtown' was always great and Petula had made a great record back in 1964. At home in Walsall in my early teens I had watched the *Petula Clark Show* on TV and Petula always finished the show with three songs. For the first two she would dress in a long skirt, but for the third song she would remove the long skirt to reveal a mini skirt. This became a great moment for me in my early teens and I always tuned in for the final three songs of the show to witness the maxi to mini skirt routine. Would I like to work Petula Clark's 'Downtown'? You bet I would.

A Kylie Christmas – and some personal changes:

Kylie was to have one of her biggest albums that Christmas. *Kylie The Album* already had four hit singles from the year on it, and the album was selling well but not growing at the pace that was expected. Tilly Rutherford then came up with the idea of TV advertising in between Christmas and New Year. In those days records were not advertised at that time on TV even though the advertising spend was relatively low in cost. The advertisements were mainly about the coming sales and household goods, and there was a long debate about Tilly's idea at PWL, but we finally supported it. Tilly thought it would work purely because the album already had four hits on it and the competition would not be advertising. Pete was worried, as it was he who was putting up the money for the TV spend and we had to press a lot of records to fulfill the demand should it occur: it was a big double gamble for a small independent label. If it did not work it could wipe out PWL in one go. History relates that it did work. The album went from three hundred thousand to 2.7 million by the end of January and it was a Kylie Christmas.

The main disappointment of the year as it came to its close was that Andy Richmond had decided to call time on his Impulse career, Andy was returning to Scotter in Lincolnshire to be landlord of The Sun and Anchor. I tried hard to change his mind, but Andy was set to have a different future. The day he left, Shaun, Andy and I were holding back the tears: Andy was one of the originals, he was a fully paid up member of our team, and the disappointment of him leaving was hard for us all to take. It was also the end of my Shaun, Jane and Andy combination operating Impulse, which I thought was a world beating team.

Two weeks before Christmas Nick East and I were at a loose end for the holiday period and I needed a break to get away from the phone and records. We decided one night over a drink to escape for a couple of weeks. Nick had a friend who ran a travel agency and he arranged a trip to Maui, one of the Hawian Islands. The night before we left, some of the Impulse staff, including me, attended a Simon Cowell and Iain Burton party in a huge restaurant on the Thames. Sinitta had sold records that year and Simon and Iain were up to celebrate. As we entered the party we were introduced to the crowd and posed for photos with Iain and Simon, it was all very Hollywood. That night I met Jacqui, and she became my partner for the next four years. I saw her across the room, we smiled, a while later we danced and spent a great evening together. There was no doubt in my mind that I was taken with Jacqui and the fifteen months since Sue had left had been lonely. I looked forward to the New Year with great hope.

Impulse Hits 1988

January			
Come Into My Life	Joyce Sims	London Records	No 7
I Think We're Alone Now	Tiffany	MCA	No 1
Sign Your Name	Terrence Trent D'Arby	CBS	No 2
Tell It To My Heart	Taylor Dane	Arista	No 3
Gimme Hope Joanna	Eddie Grant	Ice	No 7
Hot In The City	Billy Idol	Chrysalis	No 13
February			
I Should Be So Lucky	Kylie Minogue	PWL	No 1
Together Forever	Rick Astley	RCA	No 2
How Men Are	Aztec Camera	WEA	No 25
Beat Dis	Bomb The Bass	Mister-ron	No 2
That's The Way It Is	Mel & Kim	Supreme	No 10
Get Outa My Dreams and Into My Car	Billy Ocean	Jive	No 3
Boys (Summertime Love)	Sabrina	Ibiza	No 3
March			
Bass How Low Can You Go	Simon Harris	FFRR	No 12
Dreaming	Glen Goldsmith	RCA	No 12
Cross My Broken Heart	Sinitta	Fanfare	No 6
Don't Turn Around	Aswad	Mango	No 1
I Know You Got Soul	Eric B & Rakim	Cooltempo	No 13
I Fought The Law	The Clash	CBS	No 29
Love Changes Everything	Climme Fisher	EMI	No 2

Prove Your Love	Taylor Dane	Arista	No 8
Ship Of Fools	Erasure	Mute	No 6
April			
I Want You Back	Bananarama	London	No 5
Who's Leaving Who	Hazel Dean	EMI	No 4
A Love Supreme	Will Downing	4th & Broadway	No 14
Let's All Chant	Pat & Mick	PWL	No 11
The King Of Rock 'n' Roll	Prefab	Sprout	No 7
Love Is Stronger Than Pride	Sade	Epic	No 44
May			
Tribute (Right On)	The Pasadenas	CBS	No 5
My One Temptation	Mica Paris	4th & Broadway	No 7
Calypso Crazy	Billy Ocean	Jive	No 35
Perfect	Fairground Attraction	RCA	No 1
Give A Little Love	Aswad	Mango	No 11
Naughty Girls	Samantha Fox	Jive	No 31
Got To Be Certain	Kylie Minogue	PWL	No 2
Blue Monday remix	New Order	Factory	No 3
Heat It Up	Wee Papa Girl Rappers	Jive	No 21
Push It	Salt & Pepper	Champion	No 2
June			
My Philosophy	Boogie Down Productions	Jive	No 69
STOP	Sam Brown	A & M	No 4
Chains Of Love	Erasure	Mute	No 11
Tomorrow People	Ziggy Marley	Virgin	No 22
Wild World	Maxi Priest	10 Records	No 5
Heat It Up	2 Men, a Drum Machine & a Trumpet	Jive	No 21
July			
The Harder I Try	Brother Beyond	Parlophone	No 2
Anything For You	Gloria Esterfan	Epic	No 2
Like Dreamers Do	Mica Paris	4th & Broadway	No 26
August			
The Locomotion	Kylie Minogue	PWL	No 2
Soldier Of Love	Donny Osmond	Virgin	No 29
I'm Gonna Be (500 miles)	Proclaimers	Chrysalis	No 11

September			
She Wants To Dance With Me	Rick Astley	RCA	No 6
Love Truth & Honesty	Bananarama	London	No 23
Nothing Can Divide Us	Jason Donovan	PWL	No 5
Big Fun	Innercity	10 Records	No 8
I Don't Believe In Miracles	Sinitta	Fanfare	No 22
All Of Me	Sabrina	PWL	No 25
Je Ne Sais Pas Pourquoi	Kylie Minogue	PWL	No 2
October			
One Moment In Time	Whitney Houston	Arista	No 1
Kiss	Art Of Noise & Tom Jones	China	No 5
We Rule	Wee Papa Girl Rappers	Jive	No 6
Harvest For The World	Christians	Island	No 8
A Groovy Kind Of Love	Phil Collins	Virgin	No 1
Missing You	Chris De Burgh	A & M	No 3
Real Gone Kid	Deacon Blue	CBS	No 8
A Little Respect	Erasure	Mute	No 4
November			
Suddenly	Angry Anderson	Food For Thought	No 3
Take Me To Your Heart	Rick Astley	RCA	No 8
Nathan Jones	Bananarama	London	No 15
He Ain't No Competition	Brother Beyond	Parlophone	No 6
Downtown remix	Petula Clark	PRT	No 10
Love House	Samantha Fox	Jive	No 25
Till I Loved You	Barbra Streisand & Don Johnson	CBS	No 16
December			
Cat Amongst The Pigeons	Bros	CBS	No 2
Buffalo Stance	Neneh Cherry	Circa	No 3
Crackers International EP	Erasure	Mute	No 2
Loco In Acapulco	The Four Tops	Arista	No 7
Good Life	Innercity	10 Records	No 4
Break For Love	Raze	Champion	No 28

Hit makers, Pete Waterman and Steve Jenkins

1988 Kylie and me

CHAPTER 18

SURPRISE, SURPRISE – 1989

Kylie and Jason – Happy New Year:

1st January 1989. Nick East and I arrived back at Heathrow Airport from our short Christmas break in Maui and as we got into a cab we asked for the radio to be put on so we could hear the chart run down. The record I most wanted to know about was Kylie Minogue and Jason Donovan's 'Especially For You.' This had been a hard record to get together and both Jason and I had argued strongly for it in the face of considerable opposition in the S.A.W camp. Back in the autumn of 1988 S.A.W had never intended to work with Jason in the first place: they were committed to Kylie and two soap opera stars on the roster did not appeal to them. Jason worked hard to convince S.A.W to produce for him and the matter was finally solved at dinner with Kylie, Jason and Pete. Pete suggested if Kylie wanted him to produce Jason then he would do it, and as Kylie wanted it to happen Jason became a S.A.W production. But, despite establishing that, when Tilly Rutherford had phoned me with the idea of Kylie and Jason doing a duet for Christmas, I had to fight against Pete's complete lack of enthusiasm. It was only when I showed him the big support at store level the Impulse reps were reporting for the idea that S.A.W reluctantly agreed to write a song, 'Especially For You', which they then hated.

The record came out and the fight was to keep it in stock across the country in all retail outlets, as it was selling everywhere. Our one problem with competition was Cliff Richard with 'Mistletoe and Wine' and we landed at No 2. Back in the cab on 1st January, I knew I would have to face the wrath of Pete and be told what he thought of me if Kylie and Jason did not make No 1. Then we heard the chart run down awaiting the No 1 single. 'Especially For You' by Kylie Minogue and Jason Donovan was announced and the cab started bouncing down the motorway as the guys in the back seats gave an impassioned rendering of 'Especially For You.' On New Year's Day 1989, Kylie and Jason were more the New Year than Cliff Richard.

Holiday on Ice:

Getting back to work, Impulse needed a little restructuring, and we brought into the London office Kenny McCloud, who had been our Scotland representative.

I also phoned Jacqui and arranged to go for dinner a couple of nights later. We had a lovely time and then went back to the flat when Jacqui said 'I now have to tell you something.' I thought 'Oh no here we go, what's coming now, given my lack of success in recent times on the relationship front.' Well, Jacqui told me she was an ice skater and had signed to do a world tour with Holiday on Ice starting in July. She was definitely going and nothing could change her plans, so if I wanted to go out with her then I should not get attached, as come July she would be leaving. I admired her honesty, and I agreed that we should just enjoy the time and see how it goes, realising what would happen in July.

The big surprise:

In February, a change occurred in my life. Clive called me to a meeting at his home, which was not unusual, and I didn't see this opportunity coming. Clive told me he was going to reside in the US full time to build up Jive there. He wanted a Managing Director to operate the company in the UK and offered me the chance to take over. I explained that I was incredibly happy at Impulse, I had never operated a record company from top to bottom and I was also flying all over the place with Pete, Kylie and Jason and really enjoying the ride: I felt I was right in the middle of the biggest pop explosion in years and wanted to see the ride through. Also, Jive was at the tail end of a phase: Billy Ocean and Samantha Fox were the big sellers, but Sam was beginning to slow up sales-wise and Billy was more or less retiring from the game. Clive was very patient, he suggested that joining Jive Records with this opportunity was the right thing for my career and would lead to better things. I asked him 'What about Impulse?' and he casually said that I would have to leave that company to operate Jive Records. That decided it, absolutely no chance, it was just unthinkable. I thanked Clive for thinking of me and declined. I was flattered, but I didn't give his offer another thought.

A month later I was invited for lunch at The Master Brewer, a favourite breakfast and lunch place of John Fruin. John went into great detail about the proposal at Jive Records and explained that he would become Chairman and I would be Managing Director. That idea I liked. John was not only a hero and friend, I thought of him as the best record company operator in the past twenty-five years. I was now interested but would only join Jive Records if I became Chairman of Impulse, Shaun King became Managing Director of Impulse and I could continue my work with Pete Waterman and PWL records. I would be operating both companies and would slowly take a lesser role in Impulse. If that wasn't acceptable then the answer was thanks, but no thanks.

It took a lot of meetings and discussion of proposals I rejected before I was finally presented with a plan I could accept. I would become Chairman of The Impulse Promotion Company and Managing Director of Zomba Records, which owned Battery Studios, the Dreamhire equipment hire company, Coombe Music (a library recording company), and the labels Jive Records and Silvertone Records. Jive and Silvertone were turned into A & R centres and would be operated by Steven Howard (Jive) and Andrew Lauder (Silvertone). They were supposed to make the records and I was to market and sell them and make them into hits, which would put the company back on track. Shaun King would become Managing Director of Impulse reporting solely to me and I would personally continue the PWL client account at Impulse. It was set, I agreed and the date of 1st June 1989 would be the start of my Managing Directorship of Zomba Records.

I had met Tina Wisby a couple of years earlier in the Zomba accounts building. I decided that I would like Tina to be the person who would help me turn the record company around; I thought that she was a strong independent individual and she would need to be, as I was definitely going to change the culture at the company. I knew it would not be an easy ride and that initially whoever worked with me would not be liked by the current staff. Tina would need to be tough to get through the initial months. She asked me what she would be doing and in my flippant way I said I had no idea, I had never run a record company before, so just watch me and copy what I do and we'll get through it together. Tina needed to think about it all, but a couple of weeks later she agreed to join me and start on 1st June.

Over the course of the next twelve months Impulse would change a lot of its staff and Shaun would begin to move forward with staff that he hired. We lost a lot of our main players during the year – they were the people who had really built the company and made it a special success, but as with everything, six years is a long time and I think naturally those peoples' lives were changing. They felt it was time to move on. For the next few years the new main players at Impulse would be Shaun, Kenny McCloud, Tony Rounce, Helen Hancock, Sue Twiggs, Sue Buckler and Kenny Spencer. Meanwhile, because of the Woolworths operation the company was expanding its client base: not only was it dealing with all the marketing departments at record companies, but now the sales departments were coming to Impulse, to get their records into Woolworths too, and the people we were in contact with at that time was a Who's Who of the UK record business.

Perspective from the past:

As 1st June approached I had been reading a lot about great record company operators and the history of their labels – how they began and how they attracted artists, made records and sold them at home and overseas. I tried to glean any information that may help in the next stage of my life. In particular, several companies were important models to study.

Stax Records, originally called Satellite Records, was created by Jim Stewart and his sister Estelle Axton in Memphis in 1957. The name Stax comes from the ST from Stewart and the AX from Axton. They started work in an old cinema, The Capitol Theatre in south Memphis. They say that the raw and exciting sound of Stax was due to the studio having a sloping floor from the theatre days where the seats originally were. The room was therefore imbalanced and it created an acoustic anomaly that translated into the recordings often giving them a big raw sound. Their artists and records scored hits around the world during the sixties. Booker T and The MG's were the house band and they played on all the Stax hits and recorded hit singles themselves. Isaac Hayes and David Porter became the main in-house writers and the team was set to make a run of hits that would make world stars out of Otis Redding, Sam and Dave, William Bell and Judy Clay, The Bar-Kays, Johnny Taylor, Rufus Thomas, Eddie Floyd, Wilson Pickett, Albert King, Arthur Conley and Carla Thomas. Altogether, Stax's sound of Southern Soul and Memphis Soul became tremendously influential.

Tamla Motown was first created as Tamla Records in Detroit by Berry Gordy Jr in 1959. The label was originally conceived with the intended name of Tammy Records, after the hit by Debbie Reynolds, but that name was already registered so Tamla Records was born. It started with an eight hundred dollar loan from Gordy's family, and the label's hugely influential sound, mixing soul and popular music elements, grew from a group of former jazz musicians called the Funk Brothers, who played on all the records. The majority of the songs were written by a team of writers, Holland-Dozier-Holland – they were Lamont Dozier and the brothers Brian Holland and Edward Holland Junior. The first act signed to the label was the Miracles, with lead singer Smokey Robinson, and they would provide the company's first million selling single 'Shop Around.' A building was purchased in 1959 that was to become known around the world as Hitsville USA and the recording studio from where all the hits came was at the back of the house. Between the years 1961 and 1971, Tamla Motown had one hundred and ten Top 10 hits in America with artists like Stevie Wonder, Marvin Gaye, Diana Ross & The Supremes, The Four Tops, The Temptations, The Jackson 5, The Contours, Martha Reeves & The Vandellas, Jnr Walker & The All Stars, Gladys Knight & The Pips, and Jimmy Ruffin. I had loved Motown as a teenager and owned many of their records. I knew the story well but researched all I could in those pre-internet days to give me even more knowledge.

Philadelphia International Records was another label I tried to find out as much as possible about. Again, I had bought lots of their records and knew their artists well. Kenneth Gamble and Leon Huff set up Philadelphia International Records in 1971 and later the label was renamed TSOP, The Sound of Philadelphia. Most of the songs were recorded at Sigma Sound Studios and the sound came from over thirty musicians who became internationally known collectively as MFSB: Mother Father Sister Brother. The Philly artists that would score hits around the world were The Three Degrees, Patti Labelle, Archie Bell & The Drells, Jerry Butler, The Intruders, The Jones Girls, McFadden & Whitehead, Harold Melvin & The Bluenotes, The O'Jays, Billy Paul, Teddy Pendergast, Lou Rawls, Bunny Sigler, Dee Dee Sharpe and finally, The Jacksons.

I was also interested in the growth of the WEA conglomerate. Those initials stood for Warner Brothers, Electra Records and Atlantic Records and each of the three labels were incredibly interesting for me. Elektra Records was formed in 1950 by Jac Holzman with an investment of three hundred dollars. Through the Fifties and until the mid-Sixties it concentrated on folk music, the label's bestsellers being Judy Collins and Tom Paxton. In the mid-Sixties the label started to branch out into pop and first signed The Paul Butterfield Blues Band from Chicago, Tim Buckley, Love and The Doors from Los Angeles and The Stooges and MC5 from Detroit. Hit records began to come thick and fast from artists such as Badfinger, Anita Baker, Jackson Browne, Bread, Harry Chapin, The Cars, Natalie Cole, The Eagles, Huey Lewis and The News, Lindisfarne, Sergio Mendes, Joni Mitchell, Linda Rondstadt and Carly Simon. Jac Holzman sold the company to the Kinny National Company in 1970, but continued to operate the label until 1972. After that, Elektra Records was merged with Asylum Records, David Geffen's company, and became the E in WEA.

The A in WEA represented Atlantic Records, another of my favourites and a constant source of information during these times. The label was set up in 1947 by Ahmet Ertegun and Herb Abramson and in the early fifties both Jerry Wexler and Nesuhi Ertegun joined the growing company. Nesuhi took care of the jazz recordings and signed both John Coltrane and Charles Mingus to the label. Jerry Wexler became famous for signing the Stax label for distribution and working with Aretha Franklin, amongst many others. Atlantic also began working in the pop field in the mid sixties, getting off to a flying start with Sonny and Cher. The label was sold to the Kinny National Group in 1969 and took its position under the WEA banner or Warner Communications Group, as it was also called. Atlantic Records artists were The Bellamy Brothers, Brook Benton, Boney M, Glen Campbell, Chic, Alice Cooper, Cream, The Drifters, Aretha Franklin, Genesis, Peter Frampton, Hall and Oates, Bette Midler, Stevie Nicks, Led Zeppelin and The Rolling Stones, to name but a few.

I was also a fan of the Warner label in the Seventies. It was operated by Mo Austin, who had originally been hired by Frank Sinatra to manage his Reprise label. When Reprise was sold to Warner Brothers, Mo Austin went with it and soon became the driving force behind Warner records in the seventies. Back in the late Sixties, Mo Austin and Joe Smith had been recording artists such as Van Morrison, Petula Clark, The Everly Brothers, Pete Paul & Mary, Harpers Bizarre, Kenny Rogers, Joni Mitchell, Randy Newman and Neil Young, along with English acts The Kinks, Fleetwood Mac and Jethro Tull. As the 1970's arrived, the label exploded with Black Sabbath, Deep Purple, Grateful Dead, Alice Cooper, The Faces, James Taylor, Seals and Crofts, America, Dion and Dionne Warwick.

As Warner, Elektra and Atlantic were all now under the Kinny umbrella, they searched for the best operators around the world to handle these labels and their hit making artists. In the UK, John Fruin was chosen as the country's leading record operator and he would become Managing Director of WEA. After I had initially entered the record company side of the business in 1974, whilst working for Nems and Immediate Records I always wanted to work for WEA, as they were the hottest label group in the world and seemed to release the most extraordinary records each week from a whole host of artists. As it transpired, I would never become an employee of the Warner Group.

I also tried to learn lessons from other labels, such as A & M Records, formed by trumpet player Herb Albert and Jerry Moss in 1962. Its offices were just off Sunset Boulevard in Hollywood, and over the next ten years the label would grow and eventually become the largest independent record company. The hits came from Burt Bacharach, Sergio Mendes, The Carpenters, Chris Montez, The Captain & Tennille, Quincy Jones, Paul Williams, Joan Baez, Billy Preston, Carole King, The Tubes, Styx, Supertramp, Squeeze and Peter Frampton. PolyGram finally bought the label in 1989 for 500 million dollars.

I also knew a lot about Chrysalis Records having worked for them in the mid-Seventies and I knew that Chris Wright and Terry Ellis had set up the company in 1969 through a licensing deal with Chris Blackwell's Island Records. The label had been built on Jethro Tull and Procol Harum and both groups were still with Chrysalis in my days there. After I had left, I had continued to be involved in a lot of Chrysalis artists and hit records through Impulse. The Art of Noise, Pat Benatar, Blondie, Fun Boy Three, The Specials, Go West, Billy Idol, Huey Lewis & The News, Leo Sayer and Spandau Ballet were some of the finest. The company was sold to EMI Records in 1991 and has since become a label imprint for the releases of Robbie Williams. One of the great UK record labels and one that I learned a lot from during my involvement with them.

Island Records was another great story of an independent record label bringing new music to the public. It was started by Chris Blackwell in Jamaica in 1959 and the company relocated to the UK in 1962. The name Island Records came from the Harry Belafonte hit, 'Island In The Sun', and the label always had an artist friendly image, being most well known for bringing Bob Marley to world fame. Aswad, U2, Jimmy Cliff, Bryan Ferry, Frankie Goes To Hollywood, Elton John, Robert Palmer, Cat Stevens and Sly and Robbie were just a few of the other artists who recorded for Island. A deal to sell to PolyGram was concluded in 1989 for 272 million pounds.

These were all outstanding labels that had made their mark in history, finding artists and generating hit records, and now that I was to be Managing Director of Zomba Records, including both Jive and Silvertone Records, my ambition was to make it into a respected label alongside these great names, with a long list of hit records and artists behind its name.

Zomba Records – a baptism of fire:

The Zomba Records press statement was to occur in mid-May and just before the announcement appeared John Fruin set about the task of telling the staff at Jive and Silvertone who would be coming in as the new Managing Director. Nic Moran, Jive Sales Manager, immediately quit his job at that meeting, stating how it was a disgrace that I would be the new MD and under no circumstances would he work for me. Nic made a good decision as on 1st June I would have walked in the building and fired him five minutes later. His resignation saved us both a little time. There were not any other resignations that day, although I was led to believe I was not a popular choice. I also felt that some of the staff had not been told of the complete control I had over all the company, something I had insisted on, and this brought about some early confusion as I slowly started to see people in the coming couple of weeks before 1st June.

I was extremely interested in the accounts, the business affairs and production. I wanted to know all I could about these areas and how they all fitted together – were we good in these areas or just average, I didn't know. I did know that some of the product managers and in-house club promoters were poor, I was not impressed by the radio promotion people, neither those hired from outside or those working within, and I felt I had a far better grasp of all that given the amount of hits I had worked on over the past six years.

The A & R departments, which had been fudged into the Jive and Silvertone labels, I think mainly to make Steven Howard (Jive) and Andrew Lauder (Silvertone) feel more comfortable with my arrival, were both in different stages of development. Silvertone Records was operated by Andrew Lauder, an old fashioned A & R executive. Andrew saw his job as a responsibility to find artists, get the best recording he could out of them and remain as friendly as possible with them. The thought of saying 'No' to one of his artists was just not in his mind. That was somebody else's job as Andrew never wanted to jeopardize his relationship. Personally, I thought that was OK, you knew where you were with Andrew, he would never support you in a conflict and would always align himself with the artists. It was not the job description of a Managing Director as far as I was concerned, but it was an honest and straightforward approach. Andrew and I would eventually get along just fine and sell a lot of records together.

Jive Records was a different label altogether. It was mainly in the business of finding vocalists or instrumentalists and then making the records 'in house' with our producers and songwriters. I was not that impressed with the new artists that Jive had been working with. Samantha Fox and Billy Ocean were both coming to the end of their hugely successful hit runs, and what was coming along behind them I felt was not good enough to keep the label operating healthily. The one A & R man that did have a clue in my opinion was Roddy McKenna. Roddy had worked his way to London from Scotland and had worked on *The Peter Powell Show* on Radio One. This had brought him to the notice of many bands across the country as they tried to further themselves and get airplay on Pete's show. I felt Roddy didn't manage his time properly, he was always worrying about the wrong thing, just little things, and then the big problems just passed him by. But he had a talent and I liked him. Andrew Lauder, over the years, has had all the praise for signing The Stone Roses when this just is not true, it was definitely Roddy McKenna who found, brought to the label and signed The Stone Roses. Yes, their records came out on Andrew's Silvertone Records imprint, but it was Roddy who signed them most certainly – I was there. Roddy was also responsible for both the Wee Papa Girl Rappers and The She Rockers, and although neither act had long-term staying power after their hit singles, Roddy had proved to me he could be around the hits if and when he wanted too.

The business affairs department was operated by Mark Furman and, here, there was a major clash of personalities. Mark set about being as awkward as possible from the very beginning. I believe he saw himself above me, both intellectually and in position, and he certainly saw his role as the great protector of his flock that previously had power. He enjoyed telling little tales to Clive, whenever possible. If he had been a great lawyer, you could have excused him, unfortunately, he was not and I was stuck with him for the time being. I decided just to instruct Mark on what I wanted done and hoped that he did it: if he didn't, I would have to find out and correct it later. That was a mistake, when I look back now.

1st June 1989 was a Thursday and that morning Tina and I walked into the record company pretty much to silence. There was a big room where the product managers, production, press, and promotion staff all had desks in an open plan space. Bob Nolan, the General Manager, had a private office across the corridor and I think the staff thought that I would have an office on the floor upstairs or in another part of the building. There was a huge surprise when I pushed two desks together in the middle of the big room, dragged two phones onto the desks and said to Tina 'that one's yours, facing me.' Just before I sat down I addressed the room. 'OK, I'm here now, so let's get the hell on with it.' I was later told it confirmed all their fears: the record company was now in the hands of a market trader.

After the first day I went home thinking I had made a terrible mistake. The people at the company hated both Tina and myself and wanted nothing at all to do with us. All day long they had ignored us both and did not want to communicate whatsoever. It was the total opposite from the warm, friendly, 'us against the world' mentality of Impulse. I phoned Tina at home and asked her what she thought. She too thought she had made a mistake and had suffered more than I had on that first day. We spoke for a while and then decided to go in again the following day. That Thursday night was a long one; I tossed and turned. I was quite shocked at the record company staff. I had at least thought that a few people would have believed in my success rate and believed I might be able to make a difference. However, that was not the case. I decided by morning that if they did not want to be part of the new company there was no point in them hanging around, I might as well find out how tough everyone was and how much they wanted to take me on.

I started by talking to Bob Nolan, who was the only one I felt sorry for. Bob had done a great job for Jive records and had been responsible for bringing me to the company and the setting up of Impulse by way of introducing me to Clive. I believed Bob deserved more from Clive than to be put in the position he was, with me coming in over him. He had no idea what was going to happen and obviously did not like the situation, but handled himself perfectly, just as a gentleman would. I went in to see him and told him he had a job for as long as he wanted it. I knew he had three children and I was not going to put him under any stress at all. I also told Bob that Tina would be my assistant and would work with me all the time, so I may want a little information from him occasionally. I was going to change everything from the ground up and it would be an 'all or nothing' regime. I then told him I wanted him to take this afternoon off as I was going to use his office to fire a couple of people right there and then. The staff did not believe that I was here to stay and was going to change everything, so the sooner I got to it the better.

Bob left for the day not long after and I told Tina what was going to happen. I don't think Tina really liked the idea. I told her to go over to her old office and speak with Susan Kennedy in accounts. She was to give her these two names and start preparing the paperwork, as I was going to send them over after I had fired them. Straight after lunch, Tina went to the accounts building and I started to call in the first two people that would be leaving that day. The first one took it reasonably well as he was no fan of mine, and he was quickly on his way. The second one had a high opinion of himself and wanted to let me know what a mistake I was making, how I had no idea how to run a record company and how no-one wanted to work for me. He finished with 'So, God help you!'

I did need a little time in Bob's office to steady myself. This was not an easy situation. After maybe half an hour I went back into the main room. Tina was sitting there with no one talking to her. I quietly asked if she was OK. She said she was. I then arranged a meeting for an hour later with the remaining staff. I told them they should think about their situation over the weekend. If anyone did not want to work for me and Tina then they should hand in their notice on Monday. That would be the right and honourable thing to do and I would have the utmost respect for the ones that did that. If, however, they chose to stay then they would be doing as I wished with no complaint. Anyone who subsequently started putting obstacles in my way in any shape or form would be fired on the spot. They could either come in on Monday to the new record company or leave with the old one.

Zomba – Building a hit house:

In amongst all the staff problems I had been trying to get a couple of records together. One of the only groups in the A & R department of Jive I liked was the act Big Fun. They had done a cover of Carole King's 'I Feel The Earth Move Under My Feet', which was supposed to be their first single. I didn't think it was the stone cold smash I needed at the time and on Thursday night I had phoned Pete Waterman to say that Big Fun were just the vehicle to carry a S.A.W production and did he have a hit just lying around for me. Pete said he would call in a couple of days and would find a hit to start off my tenure at Jive Records. I also liked a record by Damian, 'The Time Warp', which had been recorded at Jive and had been released twice but never rose above No 50 in the chart. I believed the record was a hit, it just needed polishing up a little. Damian had been dropped by Jive and I asked his manager Nigel Martin Smith if he would get Damian to re-sign as I wanted to remix 'The Time Warp' at PWL studios. Nigel responded by saying that he had been waiting for a call like this and had given up hope that it would come.

Tina worked with Mark Furman to re-sign Damian, and within a couple of weeks he was back on board.

On Sunday evening Pete phoned.

'I've got it, we cover 'Blame It On The Boogie' by the Jacksons. I played the original on The Hitman and Her last night and the crowd went wild, so that's it. I'll get Mike and Matt to do a backing track, so bring the boys to the studio on Thursday and we're off.'

Pete was on a roll and I trusted his judgment, but I still thought covering such a classic track would be sacrilege; I said I would call him first thing tomorrow after thinking about it over night.

The following morning I called Pete and asked him if he was sure, telling him my reservations. Pete said:

'You wanted a hit and here it is. If you don't want to do it then OK, but I'm going to do it with someone. You asked me for a hit, here it is, it's up to you.'

I decided there and then to go for it. Tina organised Big Fun and off we went on the Thursday to record 'Blame It On The Boogie.' While I was there I went into Pete's office to play him the version of 'The Time Warp' by Damian that had been recorded at Jive. I said I thought it was a hit just waiting to happen, but that it needed a new backing track that would make it move a little more. Pete loved the record and the idea and said he would remix the whole piece the following week. I left PWL Studios that day thinking that in just a week I had come up with two records that stood a great chance of being hits.

That week I also started on what was to become our big album for Christmas, *Billy Ocean's Greatest Hits*. Clive had said to me that this was to be the big project of the year and the sales from this album would go a long way to straightening out the finances of the label for the year. I had mentioned to him I was very scared, this was Jive's premier artist, possibly the biggest album of Billy's career – I had no experience of setting up an album of this kind with the huge TV advertising spend and if I got it wrong, it would be a disaster. Clive said that he had faith in me and he insisted that I take complete control of the project.

A few days later, having done a lot of research, I asked if I could hire a professional researcher for the project. Although Clive thought it was unnecessary, he finally agreed. I commissioned Gary Truman. Gary undertook splendid research over the next couple of months, from which I discovered who bought Billy Ocean records, what TV shows they watch and even what colour they saw when they thought of Billy. That colour, a sort of 'off-white', was then made into a suit with a black T-shirt underneath, and that became the album cover. A second colour a 'deep off-red' was made into another suit and is featured on the back cover. I was determined not to make one single mistake on this project and I employed Peter Lacy to programme the TV adverts. It had been Peter who had performed so brilliantly the previous Christmas with the Kylie Minogue album, and I intended using some of the same ideas for Billy.

That first week I also had a meeting with Andrew Lauder at the Silvertone offices, located in the cottage in the grounds of Battery Studios, and we went through the artists that were due for release: the rock band Mary My Hope, The Men They Couldn't Hang, Loudon Wainwright and Sonic Boom. I liked what Andrew was trying to do at Silvertone: the artists were average sellers in terms of numbers, but I thought the label augmented Jive Records perfectly. I was just about to leave when Andrew mentioned The Stone Roses. The band had been signed to Silvertone and their debut album of the same name had been released. The sales were coming mainly out of Manchester, but the album had already accumulated almost thirteen thousand units with almost no investment in promotion. This stopped me in my tracks. I knew from all my chart experience at Impulse that if thirteen thousand people went out and bought a single in six days it would be close to the Top 40 in sales. A Top 40 single for The Stone Roses would be the best promotion the album could get and it may double the sales of the album the following week. I took the album and said I would listen to it and come up with a plan.

I believed that things were really going my way. Within a few weeks of joining Jive Records, Big Fun and Damian were recording with what I thought were real shots at the chart, I believed Billy Ocean could have one of the big Christmas albums and out of the blue The Stone Roses were showing signs of possibly having the chance of selling records. Maybe I could be good at running a record company.

It was a surprise and disappointment when Keith Knowles, whom I had taken from Impulse and installed as sales manager for Jive and Silvertone, decided to join Swanyard Records along with Kevin Rea one of the original Impulse reps, but this enabled Andy Richmond to return to the record business. He had asked me if there were any openings just before Keith announced his departure and now he could join Jive as Sales Manager, just in time for a good run of hits.

Tom Jones:

Tom Jones was signed to Jive Records when I arrived at the label. The year before, Impulse had been involved in his comeback hit single 'Kiss', with the group The Art Of Noise. Jive had moved swiftly and signed Tom, licensed the hit single to put on his album and recorded a soul type album entitled *Move Closer*. I think the whole operation had been put together too quickly without enough thought: the album sold OK, but was not the winner Tom, his manager Mark Woodward and Jive had hoped for. Now, the rise in video sales and a conversation with Mark brought an idea that as there was no footage of Tom's live show for sale, a video of the show with all those hits could be a big seller as a piece of history the fans should own. So, on Tom's next tour we shot footage at the Hammersmith Odeon, followed by some further bits and pieces around London and the Albert Hall. Tom's performance at the Hammersmith Odeon was superb and this was the beginning of a friendship with Tom and Mark that lasts to this day.

We spent a hundred thousand pounds making the video, which we released at Christmas. The sales were slow rather than exploding and it looked like a long hard road to recoup our money, so at that time it was considered a failure. Some years later we reviewed the video and found it had sold consistently every month from its time of release. Over time, it would not only recoup its investment but make a huge profit, and it remains one of the best Tom Jones concerts available on video and DVD. I was proud to have been involved with such an iconic artist.

A Top Ten double for Jive:

Meanwhile 'Blame It On The Boogie' by Big Fun was released in August and it peaked at No 4 on the UK charts, staying in the chart for eleven weeks. The boys had gone from nowhere to being unable to walk down the street in privacy. They were featured on all the Saturday TV shows, *Top Of The Pops*, and on tour with Pete, Kylie and Jason. They were suddenly living the life of pop stars.

August also saw the remix of 'The Time Warp' by Damian. Jive had put their recording out in December of 1987 and it had peaked at No 51. When it was reissued in August 1988 it reached No 64 and Damian was dropped from the label. Now, the reaction to Mike and Matt's remix across the clubs of the UK was phenomenal. The single started to build pre-orders and Damian started to appear on the Saturday morning shows and get a little airplay. 'The Time Warp' eventually peaked at No 7 on the chart and its lifespan would be 13 weeks. This coinciding with Big Fun's Top 10 appearances meant Jive Records was claiming two singles in the UK Top 10 for the first time in its history.

As Jive hit the Top 10 I was contacted by the BBC Saturday morning TV show *Up to You*. As we had so many artists on Saturday morning TV, through PWL with Kylie and Jason, and with Jive's Big Fun and Damian, the show had got to know of me and I was invited to come on and talk about how we were getting so many hit records. I was interviewed by a very young and pretty Anthea Turner who was making her way as a TV presenter. The show was broadcast from Manchester and watched by all the Impulse staff, who lined up to give me some enormous stick the following Monday.

Those two singles by Big Fun and Damian established me at Jive Records. The old staff that remained from before became stimulated both by the enthusiasm of the new people I had taken on board and by the Top 10 records. Even so, there was no time to waste, as we had to come up with quick follow-ups. In this, my friendship with Pete counted for a lot, and the power that Impulse had with Stock Aitken Waterman was a huge plus factor. S.A.W also wanted me to have hits, it was another label that was true to them and, indeed, the next Big Fun single was a good one: 'Can't Shake The Feeling.' The pressure at PWL Studios meant we were not going to have an album ready for the Christmas market, so we agreed to go with 'Can't Shake The Feeling', complete the album through late December, January and February and put the finished album out on the third single around March. We believed that we could then sell records through the whole year with a fourth single in the summer of 1990. The single was released in November and very soon it was all over Capitol radio and spreading in the clubs. The pre-sales were enormous and we knew it was going to be a hit single for Christmas. Its highest position was No 8 and its lifespan was nine weeks.

The next Damian single was scheduled for Christmas and we decided on a cover of 'Wig Wam Bam', the single recorded by Sweet that had been a No 4 record in 1972. S.A.W made the record and Damian did a good video dressed as an Indian. It was released on 16th December, but in hindsight all these years later I should have waited ten days and put it out on 26th December. The sales Damian achieved in the week before Christmas would have put him in the Top 20 just ten days later, whereas in the chaos of Christmas sales the single entered the chart at No 49, even though it sold well. No matter what we did in the following three weeks we could not get the record to go. We had lost the momentum and with it Damian's chance to have a run of hit singles.

Liza:

Top of The Pops always liked an 'up' record to open the show and if Big Fun were on they normally opened. Traditionally, I would always go to 'The Tops' for any of my artists' first appearance, but thereafter I would only go on occasion as I always had a lot of things to do at the office. One night Big Fun were in their usual slot of opening the show and I had managed to arrange that Tina and I would attend the performance after a day at the office. I was standing at the side of the stage waiting for the show to begin so I could catch their performance when I became aware of someone next to me smoking, which was normally not allowed in the studio.

I was not offended and casually turned to see who it was, thinking it was the producer or director. As I turned she smiled and said 'Hello.' It was one of those unexpected moments in your life that you never forget. There smoking a ciggie and saying hello was Liza Minnelli.

Liza was beautiful that close, she was obviously nervous as she was following Big Fun with her current hit record 'Losing My Mind.' She was appearing on *Top Of The Pops* for what was to be her one and only time. Liza told me she had met Big Fun earlier in the day and they had been lovely and were fans of her. She had promised them she would come and watch them perform. I informed her that I was the Managing Director of the label they recorded for and if she ever wanted to change labels, I would be delighted to sign her to Jive. Liza gave me a huge smile and said she would bear it in mind. She handed her cigarette to her assistant, walked onto the stage and gave the most flawless rendition of 'Losing My Mind.' As she finished, the technicians, staff of TOTP's and the audience gave her a standing ovation. She bowed, thanked everyone and walked off, and as she passed me she waved and said 'Bye.' A class act, that's Liza with a Z.

The Stone Roses – The Legend:

The Stone Roses' rise to fame also occurred during the first seven months of my term as Managing Director. Following that early meeting with Andrew Lauder we decided to release a single and film a small budget video to accompany the release for July. I liked a song 'She Bangs The Drums', Andrew spoke with the band, and everyone agreed to the release and filming. We could never have foreseen that the album we were working would in all the years that followed be ranked in the Top 5 of all time best ever albums.

Zomba, Jive, Silvertone and Impulse all played their part to perfection and within six days the single propelled into the Top 40, charting at No 38. Two days later *Top Of The Pops* had committed to showing just twenty-five seconds of the video as a new entry in the Top 40. Those twenty-five seconds were the most important in the Stone Roses' history. The single did not progress up the chart, but the album started to sell immediately after the Pops and would not stop selling in volume for the next couple of years. From then on it sold regular quantities in each of the following twenty years.

Although today The Stone Roses story is held up alongside stories of The Beatles and The Rolling Stones, we really had no idea that we were making history. We were just trying to get a hit record and sell a few more albums to reach the next level. I was experienced in the new wave of marketing records, but not as a Managing Director of a record label. I did everything by gut instinct and I had no real concept about building an artist's career. I just concentrated on achieving the hit and I reckoned we would worry about what to do with the artist once we had achieved the hit. It was naïve thinking, but it enabled us to focus and not be troubled by internal record company politics or accounts. We were raw, but focused on driving the company, the records and its artists forward.

On Saturday 12th August 1989, Tina and I drove north on the M1 and M6 heading for Blackpool. The Stone Roses were playing the Empress Ballroom that evening and this gig is now written into history. Over the years so many people have told me they were there. As Tina and I made our way back to London, we were looking for further singles and working on marketing ideas to keep the album selling, still blissfully unaware that the press would soon be calling it the second coming of The Beatles. As each week went by the album began to sell more and more copies. It is a little known fact that the highest chart position for the Stone Roses album in 1989 was No 19 – there was no explosion of sales and a Top 3 chart position, the band just steadily grew and grew its sales and fan base as each week went by.

Capitalising on its success and a new confidence, we put The Stone Roses back in the studio to record a couple of new songs with John Leckie producing. Those new songs would become the next single release for November. 'What The World Is Waiting For' was Side A, and 'Fools Gold' was on the reverse. As we listened, we realised that 'Fools Gold' was an enormous hit record, completely different sounding and unusual. I believe the freedom and style of playing on that track was achieved because the band knew it was only the B side in their minds. I could not convince the band or Andrew that 'Fools Gold' should be on Side A, so I suggested we issue two separate 12-inch records to the clubs. 'What the World Is Waiting For' pleased all Roses fans and was accepted immediately, while 'Fools Gold' spread the Stone Roses' name to more mainstream clubs. The drums and bass line made the record into a traditional dance hit single with a twist.

We made our living out of being able to hear a hit record when it came along. 'Fools Gold' was a hit as soon as it left the studio and the reason the record finally came out as a double A side was because the argument about A and B sides was still going on while we were pressing the records. A double A was the only way to compromise the situation. The boys were still unhappy about the double A side when we released it, but as the public went crazy for the record the argument slowly faded away until it was never mentioned again. History has since been rewritten. Even the band's manager, Gareth Evans, now insists that he was adamant that

'Fools Gold' should be the A side. Had that been true we of course would not have had to issue two 12-inch singles as promotion, just to prove the situation. Ah well.

'Fools Gold' remains the classic Stone Roses track. The single peaked at No 8 on the UK chart in December and had an initial lifespan of nineteen weeks. It catapulted the Stone Roses to fame and the album began to increase its momentum. Within five months sales had gone from thirteen thousand to nearly two hundred thousand. All the single and album sleeves were designed by John Squire and for the 'Fools Gold' cover he made a painting of dolphins on a splattered background and photographed it through a pain of frosted glass. John called it Double Dorsal Doppelganger.

Jive – New Artists:

Jive Records had a few other artists signed to the label in 1989 when I arrived. Our American label was discovering rap, the new music of America, and we had a couple of new singles that would sell small quantities, but make a mark on the landscape. 'Go See The Doctor', by Kool Mo Dee, did not become a hit but it was one of the first rap records to make a mark and Kool Mo Dee became a well respected rapper. Similarly 'Magic's Wand', by Whodini, was close to being a hit. The band came from New York but had never been on a plane before, and they travelled to England to record in our Willesden studios. Strange to think the cool American rap sound was made in North West London and very nearly became a hit record. 'Magic's Wand' would sell for years and be reissued and remixed on occasions.

Other artists Jive had signed that I really liked were Romeo's Daughter, Dina Carrol and Lisa M. Somehow we couldn't get the public to take to Romeo's Daughter, but Dina Carrol and Lisa M showed great potential for success and it was a big disappointment for me that Clive Calder and Steven Howard dropped them, thinking they were too lightweight. Dina went on to have a string of hits and become very successful with A & M records while Lisa M eventually had a couple of Top 40 records with Polydor Records. I think because of the successes I had achieved with Big Fun and Damian as new Jive artists, Clive and Steven thought some of the ones they had previously signed were just not up to the task of the new hit standard we were setting. They were wrong: it was the staff not making the right record or putting those artists with the right people.

The Waterman Explosion:

Pete Waterman was by now a TV personality with the late night/early morning cult TV show *The Hit Man and Her,* which he had created in September 1988. Pete was the host, and his co-host was Michaela Strachan. I went to, and also saw on television many of these shows and Pete was in his element as conductor of proceedings. There was much concern and worry over him at the time, he was working all hours and was continually exhausted. Driving on long night journeys was a clear mistake and an accident through tiredness was just waiting to happen, but he was at the top of his game and success is a drug fuelled with adrenalin.

The Hitman Roadshow was also in operation, which had started from the radio show in Liverpool when Pete took two thousand kids on a ferry across the Mersey for the price of a pound and they danced away a couple of hours. This expanded into touring – The Hitman Tour/The PWL Tour/S.A.W Tour, it became known by many titles but was all the same. Pete conducted the shows and the tours grew and grew until there were thirty-seven shows, with eleven acts performing and probably five or six that were currently on the chart. It was a not-for-profit tour, financed by Pete, Coca Cola and Iceland Frozen Foods, so the kids paid just one pound and were given a free coke and hamburger. The tours went to unfashionable places like Barnsley, Wigan, Rotherham, and Leicester, places where big artists didn't travel that often, and the kids went crazy when the likes of Kylie and Jason were in town. It was like the heyday of the Beatles, with screaming kids everywhere and the local and national news reporting the tour's travels and appearances. My act, Big Fun, did the tour with their two hits and to promote their upcoming third single I went to several of the dates, had my burger and coke, but fortunately stayed backstage most of the time with the artists.

The tours were based on the Motown revue of the sixties when Diana Ross & The Supremes, Smokey Robinson & The Miricals, The Four Tops, Martha Reeves & The Vandellas, Junior Walker & The All Stars, The Temptations and Stevie Wonder all hit the road together as the stars of Tamla Motown. The Tamla logo included the slogan The Sound of Young America, which PWL copied for these tours with The Sound Of Young Britain. I remember being in Edinburgh and watching the show from the side of the stage when Kylie was topping the bill. This was years before she became known as 'rear of the year.' I did watch that bottom perform many songs: well, I was backstage and Kylie was facing the audience.

Jacqui and I also went to Brighton for a show and met up with Pete and Denise, Pete's future wife. We had a Chinese meal after the show, a dinner to remember. Pete and Denise's relationship was always volatile and loud, although they were a definite couple.

1989 Summary:

By the end of the year the Impulse Promotion Company had gone through enormous change. Most of the original staff that had started the company had now, for one reason or another, moved on, but Impulse at almost seven years old with Shaun as Managing Director was unbelievably successful. Through 1989 it was the marketing and sales arm of the biggest explosion in pop music since the Beatles: with Stock Aitken Waterman, Impulse hit the No 1 slot thirteen times.

My personal life in 1989 came almost exactly in two parts. For the first six months Jacqui and I enjoyed each others' company, and because we were not supposed to become attached as Jacqui was leaving to go on tour, we obviously became incredibly attached. Jacqui left in July for rehearsals in France and commenced the tour in August and my life took a different turn: I would work all hours for three or four weeks and then fly to wherever the tour was stationed for a week and spend three or four days with Jacqui. That year, I was with Jacqui in Paris, Cannes and Lyon as *Holiday on Ice* played those cities, performing to around eight thousand people several times in a week. I watched the shows many times in many cities and was very proud of Jacqui and her talent as a skater.

As Christmas approached, I was exhausted, but overjoyed with an incredibly successful year to look back on: running a major recording company for the first time, bringing it new kudos, and seeing the promotion organisation I had created scale even greater heights. 1990 was looking to be the rosiest New Year. One must always be vigilant, though, most especially when the sun is blazing down.

Impulse The Hits 1989

January			
Especially For You	Kylie & Jason	PWL	No 1
Something's Gotten Hold Of My Heart	Marc Almond and Gene Pitney	EMI	No 1
Respect	Adeva	Cooltempo	No 17
Get on The Dancefloor	Rob Base & DJ E-Z Rock	Supreme	No 14
Where Is The Love?	Will Downing and Mica Paris	4th & Broadway	No 19
I Only Wanna Be With You	Samantha Fox	Jive	No 16
Cuddly Toy	Roachford	CBS	No 4
February			
Belfast Child	Simple Minds	Virgin	No 1
Looking For Lynda	Hue & Cry	Circa	No 15
Blow The House Down	Living In a Box	Chrysalis	No 10
I'd Rather Jack	The Reynolds Girls	PWL	No 8
This Time I Know It's For Real	Donna Summer	Warner	No 3
March			
Too Many Broken Hearts	Jason Donovan	PWL	No 1
Wages Day	Deacon Blue	CBS	No 18
Beds Are Burning	Midnight Oil	CBS	No 6
I Haven't Stopped Dancin' Yet	Pat & Mick	PWL	No 9

April			
Eternal Flame	The Bangles	CBS	No 1
Move Closer	Tom Jones	Jive	No 49
May			
Ferry Cross The Mersey	The Christians, Holly Johnson, Paul McCartney	PWL	No 1
Every Little Step	Bobby Brown	MCA	No 6
Manchild	Neneh Cherry	Circa	No 5
I Drove All Night	Cindy Lauper	Epic	No 7
Hand On Your Heart	Kylie Minogue	PWL	No 1
Funky Cold Medina	Tone Loc	4th & Broadway	No 13
June			
Sealed With A Kiss	Jason Donovan	PWL	No 1
I Wanna Have Some Fun	Samantha Fox	Jive	No 6
Pop Musik remix	M	Freestyle	No 15
Right Back Where We Started From	Sinitta	Fanfare	No 4
Don't Make Me Over	Sybil	Champion	No 19
July			
You'll Never Stop Me From Loving You	Sonia	Chrysalis	No 1
Don't Wanna Loose You	Gloria Estefan	Epic	No 6
Days	Kirsty McColl	Virgin	No 12
She Bangs The Drum	Stone Roses	Silvertone	No 34
Toy Soldiers	Martika	CBS No 5	
August			
Swing The Mood	Jive Bunny & The Mastermixers	Music Factory	No 1
Blame It On The Boogie	Big Fun	Jive	No 4
The Time Warp	Damian	Jive	No 7
Wouldn't Change A thing	Kylie Minogue	PWL	No 2
I Just Don't Have The Heart	Cliff Richard	EMI	No 3
September			
The Downtown Lights	Blue Nile	Linn	No 67
Everyday I Love You More	Jason Donovan	PWL	No 2

October			
That's What I Like	Jive Bunny & The Mastermixers	Music Factory	No 1
I Thank You	Adeva	Cooltempo	No 17
Love On A Mountain Top	Sinitta	Fanfare	No 20
Can't Forget You	Sonia	Chrysalis	No 17
November			
Can't Shake The Feeling	Big Fun	Jive	No 8
808 State	Pacific State	ZTT	No 10
Never too Late	Kylie Minogue	PWL	No 4
Get Busy	Mr Lee	Jive	No 41
December			
Let's Party	Jive Bunny & The Mastermixers	Music Factory	No 1
When You Come Back To Me	Jason Donovan	PWL	No 2
Touch Me	49ers	4th & Broadway	No 3
Listen To Your Heart	Sonia	Chrysalis	No 10
Do They Know It's Christmas?	Band Aid II	PWL	No 1

CHAPTER 19

THE SHAPE OF THINGS TO COME
1990 AND 1991

If the shoe fits:

The hits of Big Fun, Damian and The Stone Roses, and the blossoming artist roster at Silvertone had given me some confidence that I may just be able to be a Managing Director of a successful record label. I had dreamed of a label from all those years ago and here I was, in the chair, a great start, but with a lot to learn.

We had doubled the turnover from 1988 by the end of 1989, there was clearly all to play for in the coming year. Just when you think you are getting on top of it all and the shoes are beginning to fit a little easier, something always comes along to change the prospective, known commonly as 'sod's law.' One Friday afternoon early in 1990 John Fruin told me that Clive had said I now had to decide on whether I wanted to be at Impulse or wished to continue working at Zomba. There would have to be a straight choice as he was not prepared to continue with me working in both companies. I was distressed and annoyed with this after we had made an agreement nine months before with my sole condition that I operated both Zomba and Impulse. Not only that, Zomba Records and its labels Jive and Silvertone were having their best run in years and that had commenced shortly after I began as Managing Director. The final blow was that I had to decide and let John know before I left for the weekend. If it were to be Impulse then I would leave Zomba that night. John suggested I take a couple of hours and think it through. My mind was in a spin. I truly loved Impulse and its staff and all that we had achieved together, and there was also my PWL connection, which would also have to go should I choose Zomba. Within Zomba I had gone a long way to setting up a team and had provided hits that had given them confidence: I thought I would have been applauded at this time, not threatened with change.

Two hours later, I went to see John and said I could not make a decision today, but I would do so over the weekend. On Monday I would start the normal planning meeting, set the company off for the week and come in to see John with the decision around 12.30. John agreed to let Clive know and I left for the weekend.

Jacqui was on tour in Germany so I headed up the M1 to Walsall, for me the land of the sane, although most would disagree. Mom was now living in a bungalow that I had managed to contribute to, as I had collected the money from my bonuses at Impulse and paid off the mortgage on my house at 28 Roe Lane. Now, she could spend her final years in a bungalow in a quiet cul-de-sac with a little garden she loved. I was not looking forward to telling her of my latest dilemma, I knew the analysis would be long and arduous, but nevertheless it had to be done. We discussed it most of the day, and by Saturday night mother had convinced me to stay at Zomba and let Impulse go. She felt that I had been given an opportunity by Clive and that I should do as he wished. Mother also felt that I had now achieved the position I had hoped for all those years and it might not come around again: Impulse had been wonderful, but maybe Zomba was what I was meant to do. It was all good logic and so, before we retired that evening, I said Zomba it would be and I would sell Impulse with a heavy heart. I remember I did sleep well that night as opposed to the night before. When I woke and my mind opened, the first thought that came into my head was *I'm not selling Impulse, if they want me to leave Zomba Records and all that I've achieved in such a short time is not good enough, then so be it. They obviously do not think highly of my ability or me, so they can get someone else.* I explained my reason to Mom and made sure she knew that was my decision and come what may that was what I was going to do. Mom said if I could live with the consequences and never have regret then that's what I must do. I drove back to London and no matter how many times I revisited my decision it never changed. I was most definitely ready to leave Zomba at lunchtime on Monday: I knew my decision was final.

Monday came and I started the working week at Zomba with the planning meeting and set the week's tasks for each department. Then I went to see John. I don't think he or Clive were ready for what was going to happen. I explained my reasons to John and asked should I clear my desk and go to Impulse. John was calm. He definitely had not expected my response, but he told me to stay at the label and he would talk to Clive when New York woke. Then he would let me know what was to happen.

Before six o' clock I was back in with John. He simply said 'OK, carry on as normal, it's over.' I had scored a moral victory, I was not to be pressured, I was and always would be my own man and only do the things I believed in regardless of the consequences. Even so, for those who would like to be Managing Director of a record label, if you find yourself in those kinds of positions, I would not insist that you take my style of play or route in life – it does make your job more difficult, and to snub the owner or the boss is not the brightest way forward. Today's record companies are more about the company politics and the shareholders than they are about the music or the people that find it, make it and sell it, and there is little room for the maverick style of swashbuckling.

Charting the future:

After my near loss of Zomba I returned to the jobs at hand. Pete was nearing the conclusion of the Big Fun album and we planned for an Easter release. 'Handful of Promises' would be the third single and *A Pocket Full Of Dreams* the album to follow. The Stone Roses were preparing to record a single at Rockfield in Wales, although their output was slow and laborious, and the single would take almost seven months to be delivered. I was at home one night thinking about The Stone Roses, how I would keep up their momentum and how the press had been suggesting they were the second coming of The Beatles. Having lived through the Beatles, they were most definitely not the second coming, but a lot of people believed that they were, because of the continual claims in the press. That started me thinking about The Beatles and how the chart sometimes had three Beatles tracks in the Top 20 at one time: a new single, a single on its way down the chart and then an EP which carried four songs from an album. Hence, when you looked at a chart from say 1965, the Beatles were all over it, generating radio play and press which just kept their albums selling. This led me to imagine that maybe I could issue an EP in the old fashioned style with The Roses. Then, when Andrew made me aware that they had made a couple of promo singles that had gone to radio before I joined Zomba, in one moment it dawned on me that if the press and public believed it was the second coming of The Beatles I should not disappoint them and we could make a bonanza release issuing the two promos, 'Elephant Stone' and 'Made Of Stone', and reissuing 'She Bangs The Drums.' 'Elephant Stone' would come out on 3rd March, 'Made Of Stone' two weeks later on 17th March, and the reissue of 'She Bangs The Drums' another two weeks down the line on 31st March. I asked John Squire to provide artwork for 'Elephant Stone' and 'Made Of Stone', which he did.

Ironically, the success we savoured from this three single strategy was to be a catalyst for increasing trouble that, unknown to me then, had already been brewing with The Stone Roses' recording contract. A catalogue of mistakes would lead to a court case and me standing up in the dock a year later. Back in the Eighties, recording contracts followed a pattern of negotiation that at the time seemed acceptable. The company would decide to offer a contract to an unknown band, and the band would hire a lawyer who would then renegotiate the majority of the points in the contract. Hence, record companies would offer poor contracts in anticipation of negotiation. If all the rates were low, then the band lawyer could negotiate up and an agreement would be made. There was never any point in offering a great deal at the start because the band lawyer would always have to prove himself and obtain more. This had developed over the years and was the acceptable way to do business. Unfortunately, at Jive, as we were a developing company and did not yet have the finances to hire a top of the range company lawyer, our legal man was inexperienced, at least to me. The contract for the Roses was offered and came back signed with no negotiation. Wrongly, our lawyer deemed it a fait accompli and put it in the drawer with no further thought. At the time, the Roses may never have had a hit single, they could have been like many artists who are signed and do not sell records, but in this instance our lawyer's work was about to blow up in his face. As the records began to sell and the band became more and more successful, the contract came out of the drawer – to the horror of Jive. We had a successful band with a poor contract – they had the upper hand. Before long we had a battle, with our lawyer getting nowhere, and I was brought into the battlefield not long after the three single chart attack. We should have stopped recording and issuing singles until it was all sorted out, but instead, as the arguments dragged on for months and months, we continued to nurture an animal that would eventually bite us all.

Meanwhile, Impulse had continued in the vein in which it had left off at the end of 1989. Kylie had a No 1 with 'Tears On My Pillow', a great band Del Amitri had a hit with 'Nothing Ever Happens', Champion had a hit with 'Raze' and PWL International scored with Sybil's 'Walk On By', an act that Pete had asked me to help get signed from my old label Champion. The Woolworths deal was still at the centre of our services, and they said that although it would have to end one day, it would continue for now into the foreseeable future. All in the garden was rosy.

Nick East had found a vocalist Lonnie Gordon, but had fallen out with Pete Waterman. I convinced Nick that Lonnie should record with Matt, Mike and Pete and I set about putting Pete and Nick back together. It worked, we recorded 'Happening All Over Again' and Lonnie scored a No 4 record for Supreme Records.

John Lee Hooker – and J. J. Cale

During late 1989 Silvertone had signed two legendary guitar players who would become fixtures on the label for the next few years. We had issued both their albums and they began to gather momentum during the early part of 1990.

John Lee Hooker had made an album in San Francisco where he spent his later years opening and running his club The Boom Boom Room, named after one of his biggest hit records. The album, *The Healer*, is now a blues classic. Back then, before it was to go on and win a Grammy Award, we just liked the record and were honoured to be involved with such a famous musician. We started promoting anywhere we could through blues and guitar magazines, as well as specialist radio plays, and eventually we were to sell nearly 200,000 copies, an unprecedented sales figure for a blues album in the UK. After nearly twenty years people still mention the album to me and are happy to say that they bought a copy back in 1990. I had the pleasure of talking with John Lee many times over the phone to his home in San Francisco. I would receive a message from his manager advising me at which time to call and that had to be kept to most precisely. John Lee would deal with the phone for about an hour a day and if you missed the time slot then your call would have to wait until another day. The first time I called I was quite nervous of talking with an artist of such stature and great fame. John Lee Hooker had fought his way through the record business from fifteen years of age when he ran away from home after his father died, after which he never saw his mother again. He recorded for many labels and was ripped off by many people, but just kept on writing and playing all his life, regardless of the setbacks. John Lee had my admiration. As our phone calls continued he was still excited about the sales of his records and delighted that the UK had embraced his album. He had a dry sense of humour and I believe we got on very well: I was always 'That boy from England.'

It was Andrew Lauder who had made the John Lee Hooker deal, and he set off to the USA to find J. J. Cale, another laid back blues guitarist who throughout his career has managed to maintain his cult following. J. J. is probably best known for writing a couple of hits that Eric Clapton covered and made famous in the popular world: 'After Midnight' and 'Cocaine' were both J. J. Cale songs. J. J. had not recorded for six years and was known to be a recluse. Andrew found him holed up in a trailer in California and managed to persuade him to record with Silvertone Records. His first album for the label was *Travel Log*, and we set about building up the record through the same avenues that we had taken with John Lee Hooker. *Travel Log* never achieved the sales figures of *The Healer* but it did well enough for J. J. Cale to come to England and play a few sold out dates. I met J.J., or John as we knew him, at the opening night in London. We had a great few minutes together, he was delighted to be recording, selling records and playing back in the UK.

We were also able to publicise this coup in J. J.'s own country as our small New York office was beginning to grow. Barry Weiss was the main operator, he would eventually become President of the label, and our relationship began to flower from this year of 1990. I was always looking for records and especially hits, Barry had the same mentality and so we became good friends over the years that followed, especially as the UK would eventually have many hits with US artists.

Esther Rantzen:

Jive Records now launched Big Fun's 'Pocket Full Of Dreams.' This was the band's third single and it peaked at No 21. It was the beginning of the pop backlash that would all but end pop music in the coming years. The band was still popular and their album sold 120,000 copies very quickly, but the failure in not reaching the Top 10 with their single was ominous. Nevertheless, my Stone Roses releases began to come out during March and it was to send the album into a sales spin. 'Elephant Stone' peaked at No 8, 'Made Of Stone' at No 20 and 'She Bangs The Drum' at No 34. We had achieved three singles in the Top 40 and given the public and the press 'the second coming of The Beatles.' The Stone Roses album was on its way to half a million copies.

At this point, I received a call from Esther Rantzen. Esther's TV show *That's Life* was the nation's Sunday night viewing, regularly reaching 10 million viewers. She was a national treasure and one of my Mom's favourite people, along with The Queen and Margaret Thatcher. I always joked that The Queen, Thatcher, Esther and my Mom were 'The gang of four.' Esther asked me if I was aware of Childline. I was, I knew from *That's Life* that Esther had set up Childline, where kids who were being abused could call in complete confidence and obtain help and counselling, and I also knew that Childline had made a difference to kids who had nowhere to turn. Esther said that Childline was always in difficulties through being under financed and would I consider making a record and giving the profits to Childline. I said I would try and come up with an idea and Esther invited me to come and see the operation and premises.

The company was situated in an old post office building that Esther had managed to convince them to lend her. The staff I met that night were really caring human beings trying to do something to help unfortunate kids. It made a huge impression on me. At Childline you are not allowed to listen in to the calls from the kids, they are private conversations between them and the people manning the phones, any interruption could lose the child's confidence. However, Esther had made a tape for me to listen to, so I could appreciate the despair that some kids live with. It was not long before I asked her to turn off the tape. I agreed to come up with a record and to cut all the costs so as to make the single as profitable as possible. There was just one sole condition I made: Esther would never play me any tape again.

Over the next two weeks Pete and I worked on getting a record that would sell and raise some money for Childline. We came up with a fitting title: 'You've Got A Friend.' Mike, Matt and Pete wrote the song, we put Sonia, whose No 1 record on Chrysalis had been 'You'll Never Stop Me Loving You', and Big Fun together and made the record. The single came out in June, just eight weeks later, and peaked at No 14. Because everyone had donated their time and efforts free of charge, the record was very profitable and enabled Childline to continue their valuable work.

Esther Rantzen and I became firm friends during the process of recording and promotion and I would go on to make more records for her over the coming years. My mother never quite believed I knew Esther, it was too much for her to believe having seen her on TV all those years, from the *Braden Beat* through to *That's Life*. Some years later, on one of Mom's trips to London to see if her son was eating properly, we had stopped in Highgate at a brassiere to have lunch. We took our seats by the window and only a few minutes later Esther and her daughters came in for lunch. I said to Mom

'Oh there's Esther, do you want to say hello?'

Mom scolded me with *'You don't know Esther, don't be silly.'*

I said *'OK but you better prepare yourself because she will come over and say hello and I'm going to introduce you.'*

Later, Esther did come over to give me a kiss and a hug and I introduced my Mom who, bless her, was speechless. Esther made my Mom's world that day, it was really true that her son was friendly with Esther Rantzen. She still scolded me later and insisted I never embarrass her again, but I knew she loved it.

Jacqui had now returned from the Holiday on Ice tour, and she began to educate me in the world of dance and ice-skating. We went to the ballet and saw Torvill and Dean and The Russian touring ice show, they were truly amazing. Jacqui also went with me to the, now legendary, Spike Island gig by The Stone Roses, and afterwards she accompanied me to Jason Donovan's party when he kindly invited us. We were in the middle of a wonderful summer.

The Stone Roses at last had a No 4 record with 'One Love.' It had taken months for them to finish, but it was worth the wait, as on release it catapulted into the chart.

Sometimes, when you will not do what the owner or Chairman of a record company wants you to do, there is a penalty to pay. My penalty was Charlie Eyre. Charlie had been an A & R man at MCA and Phonogram Records, where he had signed a few acts that had some success, but never achieved really big sales. In my absence on a two week summer holiday I had taken with Jacqui in Florida, Charlie had been offered a good contract at Jive Records by Clive Calder and Steven Howard without consulting me. I believed that this was a payback for my refusing to leave Impulse and I was appalled and disgusted it could happen. I appreciated we needed to move on and obtain A & R people who could move with the marketplace, and my chosen people for that were Paul Oakenfold and Nick East. I believed they would lead us into the now more popular dance and indie world, but instead I had to contend with a mainly rock orientated A & R executive. I neither understood nor wanted this decision, but I was lumbered with it. From that point I became less interested in Jive UK's A & R strategy. I immersed myself mainly with Silvertone and the US product coming out of New York, where the records were rap and the beginning of R & B. Kids loved this new style and I could tell it was the music of the future.

The history of the record business shows that music that has been incredibly popular in a space of a few years suddenly stops selling almost overnight as the buyers grow up and start thinking about paying the rent, buying a house, getting married and having kids. The next generation of buyers do not like what their elder brother or sister liked and want their own style of music to go with their teenage years. This movement has always happened and will always do so. In mid-1990 one of these changes occurred and Impulse, as always, followed the musical style. We started working on acts such as The Happy Mondays, Betty Boo, The Charlatans, The Inspiral Carpets, The Farm, The Pixies, EMF and The La's – all a complete contrast to Kylie, Jason, Sonia, Big Fun and the pop phenomena that had gone before and those records almost fell off a cliff.

Jason's records started peaking at No 18 with 'Another Night', No 9 with 'Rhythm of The Rain' and No 8 with 'Hold Onto Your Love.' Although Kylie was now a massive star, she was peaking at No 4 with 'Step Back In Time', and her only record that bucked the downward trend was a classic, 'Better The Devil You Know' which peaked at No 2. Mike, Matt and Pete had written and recorded this song after a discussion with Kylie. Jason and Kylie's relationship was now in trouble as they grew from kids through their teenage years and into their twenties. Kylie had met Michael Hutchence and was on the verge of starting an affair. She had asked her friends who had recorded and supported her over the past few years their thoughts: S.A.W's response was 'better the devil you know...'

I remember being at PWL Studios with Tilly Rutherford one afternoon, talking over releases and projects that were coming up, and as the meeting wound up Tills played me the new Kylie single 'Better The Devil You Know.' It sounded like another in the line of No 1 singles, but it peaked at No 2 and was beaten to the No 1 spot by the acid house producer Adamski's 'Killer' featuring Seal. We had a lot of No 1 singles and I always believed that 'Better The Devil' should have been one of them.

Pop was beginning to come to a close, and indie, rap and dance were on the way up, but for now, at Silvertone Records, we decided to sign more historical music greats in Del Shannon, Willie Dixon and Buddy Guy, who was beginning to enjoy a comeback with the revival of interest in blues music. Buddy Guy arrived in England to commence recording *Damn Right I've Got The Blues*, an album that would eventually become a Grammy Award winner. Buddy had not recorded for over ten years and Andrew Lauder asked me to try to impress upon him that in today's world tracks on an album were usually about four minutes long. Having been away from the recording studio for the best part of two decades and only playing live during that time, Buddy had become used to a song being eight or nine minutes long. I walked over to Battery studios to meet this legendary guitar player and we talked for half an hour or so before I attempted the conversation about the length of recorded songs. I said that we, and also the public, expected that the new recordings would be around four minutes long – with a couple of songs we could stretch that to four and a half or five minutes. Buddy smiled and said 'I won't have got to the guitar solo by four minutes.'

Buddy Guy is a great artist and a fine man: we got along well and were to have some incredible success together in the coming years. He told us his favourite food is steak, so Andy Richmond and I took him off to Craigs in the West End for dinner. We were eating and chatting when two ladies walked by after completing their dinner. They were obviously going out on the town – well dressed, high heels, hair done and pictures of beauty. Buddy, not taking any notice of Andy and me, and somewhat in his own jetlagged world, stopped eating as he watched the girls pass and just said 'Praise The Lord.' Then he continued eating. This now became Andy's and my catchphrase. For many years to come, when a pretty woman went by we would always say 'Praise The Lord.'

Impulse was still doing well as Shaun and Kenny were growing in their positions and guiding the company into the new wave of hit singles. It was a difficult period as the artists that we had such success with were beginning to end their hit making runs. Indeed, some of the labels, such as Simon Cowell's Fanfare Records, were beginning to have financial difficulties, as they were not set up to move into the new sounds of music that were starting to dominate.

A huge blow to Impulse came in November when Woolworths decided that our two and a half year run as the only company that could place new singles into their stores would finish in January 1991. The deal had been a huge financial earner for the company and its end was dramatically to contribute to a drop in the volume of records going through the building. But, it was not the only reason for this. The chart landscape was changing and Prime Time had been copied by most labels, who were now pre-selling their own products. In 1991, our eighth year of business, we would once again have to reshape our company and it was to be a very challenging time.

Impulse The Hits 1990

January			
Tears On My Pillow	Kylie Minogue	PWL	No 1
Nothing Ever Happens	Del Amitri	A & M	No 11
Happening All Over Again	Lonnie Gordon	Supreme	No 4
Break For Love	Raze	Champion	No 30
Walk On By	Sybil	PWL International	No 6
February			
Nothing Compares To You	Sinead O' Connor	Ensign	No 1
Dub Be Good To Me	Beats International	Go Beat	No 1
How Am I Supposed to Live Without You	Michael Bolton	CBS	No 3
Enjoy The Silence	Depeche Mode	Mute	No 6
Lily Was Here	Candy Dulfer and Dave Stewart	RCA	No 6
March			
Handful Of Promises	Big Fun	Jive	No 21
Elephant Stone	The Stone Roses	Silvertone	No 8
Made of Stone	The Stone Roses	Silvertone	No 20

Blue Savannah	Erasure	Mute	No 3
This Is How It Feels	Inspiral Carpets	Cow	No 14
April			
Hang On To Your Love	Jason Donovan	PWL	No 8
She Bangs The Drums	The Stone Roses	Silvertone	No 34
Step On	Happy Mondays	Factory	No 5
Use It Up, Wear It Out	Pat & Mick	PWL	No 22
Hitchin' A Ride	Sinitta	Fanfare	No 24
May			
Better The Devil You Know	Kylie Minogue	PWL	No 2
Doin' The Do	Betty Boo	Rhythm King	No 7
I Still Haven't Found What I'm Looking For	The Chimes	CBS	No 6
Angel	The Eurythmics	RCA	No 23
June			
Close To You	Maxi Priest	Ten	No 7
Another Night	Jason Donovan	PWL	No 18
You've Got A Friend	Childline	Jive	No 14
One Love	Stone Roses	Silvertone	No 4
The Only One	Charlatans	Situation Two	No 9
July			
The King Of Wishful Thinking	Go West	Chrysalis	No 18
She Comes In The Fall	Inspiral Carpets	Cow	No 27
Mona	Craig McLachlan	Epic	No 2
Velouria	Pixies	4AD	No 28
August			
Hey There Lonely girl	Big Fun	Jive	No 62
Let Love Rule	Lenny Kravitz	Virgin	No 39
Silly Games	Lindy Layton	Arista	No 22
Bonita Applebum	A Tribe Called Quest	Jive	No 47
September			
Rhythm Of The Rain	Jason Donovan	PWL	No 9
Vision Of Love	Mariah Carey	CBS	No 9
Groovy Train	The Farm	Produce	No 6

It's a Shame	Monie Love	Cooltempo	No 12
Love And Affection	Sinitta	Fanfare	No 62
October			
I'm Your Baby Tonight	Whitney Houston	Arista	No 5
November			
King Of The Road	The Proclaimers	Chrysalis	No 9
Step Back In Time	Kylie Minogue	PWL	No 4
Unbelievable	EMF	Parlophone	No 3
Kinky Afro	Happy Mondays	Factory	No 5
Island Head	Inspiral Carpets	Cow	No 21
There She Goes	The La's	Go discs	No 13
December			
Gonna Make You Sweat, Everybody Dance Now	C & C Music Factory	CBS	No 3
All Together Now	The Farm	Produce	No 4

A year of change:

We kicked off 1991 with a No 1 hit right away. Towards the close of 1990 Zomba had bought a share of Sanctuary, best known then for the management of Iron Maiden, and with both my Impulse and Zomba hats on I had been to meet Andy Taylor and Rod Smallwood a few times. They were interested in getting a huge hit for Iron Maiden. The band was on a good run of Top 5 singles but found the No 1 position impossible to achieve. Rod and Andy asked me if I had an idea that might deliver a No 1 record. I knew exactly how to deliver a No 1 record and suggested they released the single in between Christmas and New Year when no-one had new records out. If we alerted the fan base to buy it in that week the numbers would propel the record to No 1 with no new competition in the marketplace. It would take a huge set-up and persuading EMI's distribution department to make facility for shipping, as corporations are governed by overtime and complexities. Andy assured me he could do the job, but the idea at the time was so new to everyone that I had to present the figures and reasoning to Bruce Dickinson, Iron Maiden's lead singer. Bruce and I became friendly in the set up and execution of the plan. I had expected it to be hard to explain the mathematics to an artist, but I quickly realised that Bruce is no usual artist, being knowledgeable about the whole recording industry and possessing a complete grasp of what we were intending to do. He took on board my plan, Impulse once again set about working through the Christmas period when the competition did not, and we opened our doors in 1991 at No 1 with 'Bring Your Daughter To The Slaughter' by Iron Maiden.

The national average time in the job for a Managing Director of a record label back then, and not much has changed since, was two and a quarter years. One year to have a look at the company, one year to make it work and, if it doesn't, three months later you are gone. This brings intense pressure on getting hit records, hit artists and hit projects. The focus becomes very much hit driven and maximising the sales of everything that is selling – in other words, it is not good enough just to get the hit, you must then control the expenditure on marketing and promotion, to maximise the profit. This brings conflict with the artist and the artist manager: they want expenditure at the maximum, and as marketing and promotion are not recoupable from the artist, they do not care how much is spent. The expenditure does not affect their royalties, in fact, the more that is spent can only add to their royalty count. Hence, conflict. Music and business in different corners, and it takes a smooth operator to overcome this basic problem and maintain a relationship with both the artist and the manager. If you do not, then nothing works.

Nick Howe was becoming a major force within Zomba and I must credit him with eventually putting the company on a solid financial footing over the coming years and teaching me the accounts side of a label. It was a painful process for both Nick and I as we came from different sides of the track, we were both determined in our personal views and our relationship would explode many times over the next ten years. However, underneath all that was a respect for each others' abilities. When Nick was eventually named Financial Director of Zomba, my opening salvo, which I remember now with some embarrassment, was 'I don't mind what you have to do, but don't screw with me or the records.' Not quite the way to address an intelligent man who was 'first pick' from Cambridge University.

Nick started by organising meetings, which at first I dreaded, but eventually he taught me accounting and the running of a label in a true financial way: un-recouped artists, promo expenditure, marketing costs, staff costs, A & R costs, release date planning costs – all reviewed each month in the accounts. Before Nick, I had a rough idea where we were in my own mind: some of it was guesswork and some of it I knew nothing about, such as hidden costs within the labels. Nick's regime documented it all: we went from being an artistic accounting company to an artistic company with proper business accounts.

Change for Pete:

On 29th January Pete Waterman and I had dinner, and this was not my pal in his usual state of positivity. Pete keeps a lot to himself, but I knew he had problems and was falling out of love with his empire. Poor management by others in the group was coming home to roost and laying itself firmly at his door. The unbelievable success that had arrived at PWL five years earlier and had continued growing had camouflaged all the mistakes that had been made during that period. It is easy in hindsight to point the finger. Never before had a production team and a small independent label had so much success in the UK, it was unchartered territory. The people that Pete had put his faith in were probably not of the calibre that was required for that much growth and success. Pete, like me at that time, had a gut feeling for what was being spent and what was coming in, and he had felt confident enough to invest in one of his passions, cars. He had bought plenty of them and at one point his collection included eighteen Ferraris. It was David Howells, then Managing Director at PWL, who first confronted Pete with the idea that there may be a problem between his car collection and the cash flow at the company. Pete did not relate the two as he had bought the cars with personal bank loans – however, the red danger flag was being raised.

During the following months new accountants were brought in to PWL and assessments were made. Contracts were checked and found to be poorly negotiated. The lifeblood of the company, the artists, were on poor contracts from a PWL point of view. Finally, the accountants announced that PWL owed 8.9 million pounds; personally I believe this was not a thought out figure, but not surprisingly it resulted in a staff cutting exercise and a belt tightening operation. The company had become too large for what it was doing and the artists it had on board, but the influx of money had made everyone, including Pete, feel that PWL was invincible.

This would result later in the year in the sale of PWL Records to Warner Brothers International, but, for now, Pete rallied the troops and we pushed for hit records and bigger sales.

Pete and I have been pals for as long as we can remember and it will always be that way until this mortal coil ends. Over the years, I have been privy to many Watermanisms: I guess coming from the same part of the world we both have similar memories and the same local descriptive language, which when used on London or southern English people usually leaves the victims with puzzled looks on their faces as they try to keep pace. I was at PWL with Pete for a meeting with a corporate, major label A & R guy. His job was to convince Pete that the record he had was a hit and that Stock Aitken Waterman should produce the follow-up. The man played the record amidst cries of 'It's hot, it's hot.' I knew he was already in deep trouble: with Pete it is best to let him form his own opinion and concentrate on his job, which he takes seriously.

The record ended and the man said;

'*I told you it's hot and a hit!*'

'*Hot!, Hot!, it's as cold as a witches tit!*', Pete retorted.

The look on the man's face was a picture, it showed how hard he was thinking about the coldness of a witch's tit. He finally left with no S.A.W. production. Pete looked at me and said

'You see Steve, major label A & R guys are about as much use as a chocolate wristwatch.'

It was then me picturing the mess caused on my arm by a chocolate wrist watch.

Years later, when Pete's marriage to Denise was in the past, I asked him if he would consider marriage again. 'I can't', he said. 'The problem is when I can't sleep, which is often, I like to watch old war documentaries in my trolleys with a lardy on.' To me hilarious, but to the vast majority, what does that mean? It means sitting up in the middle of the night, watching TV in your underpants with a huge cigar on the go. Not a pretty picture, but I guess the ultimate in relaxation. Pete added 'No woman will put up with that.' And he's probably right.

Hit of the Year:

Jive's major hit in January 1991, and one I considered a real result, was 'Can I Kick It', by A Tribe Called Quest. This would be the final ATCQ record that I was allowed to remix. Q-Tip, still my favourite rapper and leader of the group, was incredibly upset that I had reworked his record in the studio. I had made the most of the hook line 'Can I kick it? Yes you can!', something that is still a huge phrase in the UK today. Try it in a group of people: 'Can I kick it?' The group will answer 'Yes you can!' We did not change the version on the album, I felt their album should be presented in the way they had made it, but the single remix could bring us many album sales and break the group nationally, and it did. 'Can I Kick It' reached No 15 on the chart and was all over the radio. Still, when I next saw Q-Tip, he was not happy and spoke with Clive and Barry, who reluctantly told me 'no more remixes on A Tribe Called Quest.' Over the years we would put out four ATCQ albums, but they would never again feature in the UK's Top 40 singles chart. 'Can I Kick It', the remix, however, lives on.

Raising my right hand:

The problems with Silvertone and The Stone Roses now began to gather steam. The band were now considering that their contract was null and void and were wanting to sign to a major company, primarily, for what would be a huge advance. After almost two years of trying to renegotiate the contract to no avail, lawyers were circulating and there was no way forward but to go to court and defend the label's position.

We knew that our contract was not good and we were not surprised that the way in which the band had signed their deal was coming back to haunt us. The immaturity of our in-house lawyer was now about to cost us dear. I admired Clive Calder at this point. He knew we were in a poor position but told me no matter what, after all our exceptional work to break the band and make them successful, we just would not lie down and take it, and we would fight it all the way.

We began to prepare our defence, with Anthony Jay of Gentle Jays, on Wednesday 27th February. I attended the first meeting and realised for the first time that I would have a major part to play in the forthcoming court case. I had not anticipated this situation, as when The Roses had been signed to Silvertone I was not Managing Director of Zomba Records, so I somehow believed I would not be involved.

Most of the attempted renegotiations had been handled by John Fruin or Mark Furman and I had only been brought in late in the day as I had a good relationship with the boys' manager and the band, primarily because of our success together. My final attempt at a renegotiation had failed, and Gareth Evans, the band's manager, had said, 'We like you Steve, but their ain't no way we are re-signing or re-negotiating.' After that comment everybody knew we were going to court.

Anthony Jay explained to me how I would eventually end up 'in the box' and my comments would be critical to the defence. On 8th March 1991 I attended Court 49 at The Queens Building, and the case began. It was a day or so before I was summoned to 'the box.' I don't remember being that nervous, I had been on stage a lot and just imagined it was an audience that I had to address. I was also confident in the job I did as a Managing Director – I had already been involved with a huge number of hit records and the breaking of The Stone Roses was my work: no one could get the better of me in that situation.

The Judge was to my right and nodded politely to me as I entered the box. Our defence team was in front of me and the Roses team was slightly to my right. Their leader was John Kennedy, a well-known music lawyer with a list of victories for artists and companies behind him. The band were at the back of the court watching the proceedings. I had been sitting not far from them for a day or so, we had nodded and smiled at each other during the proceedings but had not spoken. I think they, like me previously, did not expect that I would be called; I remember their surprised look as I made my way to the box.

The QC began his questioning in the usual polite way QC's usually do, but you know that pretty soon the sting is coming. I concentrated hard and listened to every word. This well educated man in his own familiar surroundings was not going to intimidate me or trick me into some corner. His main objective was to prove that we had in some way poorly promoted and poorly distributed the single 'One Love' by The Roses and this was a big mistake on his part. He had now put himself in my world and believed the emotions of the band and their manager. Every artist I have ever known blames the record company for their single not appearing at No 1 when it debuts at No 2, 3 or 4.

The QC went into an enormously long speech of how Silvertone had sabotaged the success of 'One Love.' I stood and listened, waiting for the question that would allow me to respond. It came.

'Is that not true Mr. Jenkins?'

'No, it is not true and I believe that neither you nor the band nor the management have full understanding of the British record charts. They are and always have been popularity charts, hence the No 1 record is the most popular and the No 10, the tenth most popular.'

At this point the QC jumped in, seeing it was going the wrong way.

'Ah, but would you not say that the distribution was at fault, Mr. Jenkins?'

'No Sir, I would not. The record entered the chart at No 4, so, was it the fourth worst distributed single that week? What about the No 20 record? Was that the twentieth worst distributed record of the week?'

There were smirks and sighs around the court room, the QC wobbled and shuffled some papers to steady himself and played for a moment to regain his composure. There was one of those pregnant pauses. The Judge stepped in:

'That is all for today, Gentlemen. Mr. Jenkins, I might remind you that overnight you are still considered to be in the witness box. You will not speak to counsel, you will not talk to counsel on the phone, in fact, I expect you to go straight home, stay in, and return to the box at 9 am in the morning, having spoken to no-one regarding this case. Do you understand?'

'Yes Sir, I do'

To be 'In the box' overnight is a strange situation. You feel totally cut off from the rest of the world, even in your own home. I knew I had won a small victory in the court that afternoon and made their QC look a little foolish, and I was sure that the coming morning would bring a revenge attack.

The following morning arrived and I once again entered the box. The Roses QC stood and said

'No further questions for Mr. Jenkins your honour.'

'You can step down Mr. Jenkins', the Judge smiled. *'Thank you.'*

That was the end of my involvement with The Roses versus Silvertone court case. We lost the case and The Roses contract with Silvertone was over. We appealed the verdict, which took another year, and we were unsuccessful. Silvertone retained all the recordings we had made with The Stone Roses and the band signed to Geffen Records for a two million pounds advance.

Looking back, the court case did none of us any good at all. The delay in the release of the second Roses album, titled *The Second Coming*, meant that it finally came out nearly four and a half years after the first album, during which time the market and generation had moved on. The 'top of the wave' had been missed. I have always believed, and continue to do so, that if The Roses had stayed with Silvertone, taken the renegotiated offers, recorded their second album and released it a couple of years after the first album, they would have become one of the biggest grossing bands of their generation. The wave of support for The Stone Roses in 1990 and 1991 was immense, they had the country and possibly the world in the palm of their hands, and I remain disappointed that none of us got to take that worldwide ride.

Keep on movin':

With that debacle behind us, Silvertone worked on the new signings of Brendon Croker, The Men They Couldn't Hang and Loudon Wainwright. Impulse was still at the very top of its game, hired by all the record labels and now considered part of the industry and it brought further No 1 records for Chrysalis and CBS: 'The One And Only', by Chesney Hawkes, on Chrysalis, and 'Should I Stay Or Should I Go', by the Clash, on CBS. Records and memories at certain times can make you feel old and the Chesney Hawkes record did that for me. When Chesney came to Impulse to make a promotional visit, I nipped in to say hello, and all I could think of was that his Dad was a hero of mine: Chip Hawkes had been the bass player and lead singer for The Tremeloes on all their hit records, 'Silence Is Golden' being their biggest hit in 1967.

The major frustration of my job at this time was the state of A & R at Jive Records. Steven Howard, Charlie Eyre and Roddy McKenna were the team, and I had little problem with Roddy as he had his own way of doing things and had found The Stone Roses, but in my view, Steven's and Charlie's roster of artists was poor, and I could not see hit records coming from that area.

Worse than that, Steven and Charlie blocked my initiatives and took their opposition to Clive. This became a particularly serious issue over the signing of Take That, who had made a big impression on Pete Waterman's TV show *The Hit Man and Her*. For some time I had been desperately keen to make a deal with Take That. Regarding A & R, I had worked out a first class arrangement with Paul Oakenfold, who trusted me from our days together at Champion Records, also with C. J. Mackintosh, one of the best DJ remixers of the day, who would go on to produce many hit records. Steven and Charlie dragged their feet on these issues and finally decided to pass on the group, to my fury. Despite this, the opportunity remained on the table and as I could get absolutely nowhere with Steven and Charlie, I took the matter to John Fruin. He spoke with Clive, and I believe when this happened Clive decided to support his A & R team. I also learned through Impulse that Kitchenware Records were reaching their end of contract with CBS: my favourite act of theirs was Prefab Sprout and they would also have hit records with The Kane Gang. I wanted to break the bank to sign that label – again to no avail.

I still wanted to employ Paul Oakenfold, who would become a world renowned DJ and producer in the years that followed. I also wanted to employ Nick East from Supreme Records, who I had been involved with in our collaborations with Mel and Kim, Lonnie Gordon and Princess. These were the new breed of A & R guys in the UK, but Clive had a problem with them. He claimed they did not understand the bigger picture of albums and US sales, because they were too focused on hit singles. I believed that we as Zomba had exceptional management skills and would have been able to bring them forward in a true business fashion. The mistakes we made by not signing all these deals in 1991 would haunt me for years, and over the next two years they would nearly cost me my position as Managing Director of Zomba Records.

During May, the Holiday on Ice Show finally came to London's Wembley Arena. Jacqui and I had been in touch by phone and letter during her nearly five months away on tour. We were still trying to make our relationship work, it was a struggle, but the summer was coming and Jacqui would be in England, keeping fit, but at least not on tour. We decided to spend most of the summer together and see what happened, although it was almost a certainty that Jacqui would return to touring. Ice skaters, like footballers, have a limited career span and if they don't do it during their fittest years it is not something you can do later in life. I understood totally that Jacqui had to do it then or not at all and I did not want to be responsible for regret later in her life.

Mariah Carey:

For Impulse I was still handling Champion Entertainments artists' representation in the UK, and 1991 was a busy time on that front with Mariah Carey coming to England, Daryl Hall and John Oates releasing their Greatest Hits album, and a new signing to Champion in the form of John Cougar Mellancamp, who released new singles and an album. This kept me involved with Sony Music Entertainment (which had now acquired CBS), RCA and Phonogram for most of the year.

Mariah Carey was, at the time, a valuable asset to Sony. Not only was she a huge debut-selling artist with US No 1 singles and an album but she was also the girlfriend and future wife of President Tommy Mottola. Mottola also owned Champion Entertainment, which was responsible for managing Carey, and as a long time UK aid this put me in the pressure cooker of Mariah's success in Britain. John Aston at Sony, also being a lifelong friend, made the situation much easier and we all worked hard on Mariah records.

I liked Mariah. She knew she was in a privileged position and was completely protected and she knew that all those surrounding her were seeing to it that not a stone was left unturned. At the time, I believe that Sony, Champion and Mottola thought that Mariah should be obtaining better chart positions and in turn more sales in the UK. Hence, I was an important member of the group to make sure all that could be done was being done. The reality is that Mariah was destined to be a world star and just because her records were No 1 in America at that time was never 'a given' that they would repeat the same feat in the UK. It was hard work for us, and we achieved hits, but not in as big a way as in the US I attended Mariah's appearance on the Terry Wogan show when she and the group performed 'Emotions', which would change the fortunes of her singles in the UK. After the first single 'Visions Of Love' had peaked at No 9, Mariah's next three records had peaked at No 37, 38 and 54, giving us cause for concern. 'Emotions' reversed the trend and peaked at No 17. After that, Mariah's singles would all be Top 10 records for a seven year run, right up until 1998, when for just one record she was outside the Top 20.

Impulse gained a lot of credit for the work on Mariah Carey and we went on to have a great year with Sony, No 1 records coming with The Clash's 'Should I Stay Or Should I Go' and Cher's 'The Shoop Schoop Song.' We started to work more and more albums during this year and promoted *The Stranglers Greatest Hits*, *Fellow Hoodlums* for Deacon Blue. and Michael Bolton, all big time acts for Sony.

R. Kelly:

I was off to New York in July, as I was most years now, and very late one night Clive said he wanted me to meet R. Kelly, as he had just signed him and he was working on the tracks for his first album. That would be the first of many meetings around the world that I had with Robert Kelly and it was the start of a relationship that would last for thirteen years. That night, at about 1.00 am, there were just Robert, Clive, me and a studio engineer. Clive introduced Robert to me and soon disappeared to his office on another floor. Rob and I got along straight away. I stayed in the studio until around 3.00 am and we got to know each other well in that short period of time that night. He was working on a track called 'Definition Of A Hottie', and the song would end up on his first album *Born Into The Nineties*.

I could not possibly know at the time, of course, that Rob was to become the artist I was to have the most number of hit records with. Over the next thirteen years we would chalk up twenty-seven hits together and Rob's first hit single and first concert dates would be in England rather than the US. He would forever have a fondness for the UK, saying that Britain recognised his talents before his home country and started off his career. Personally, I always thought that Rob was the most complete talented artist I ever worked with. He wrote all the tunes and the lyrics for himself and other artists, did the vocals, played the instruments, recorded the songs, produced them and then was a complete performer, completing many world tours in the years that followed. A lot of water has passed under the bridge in nearly twenty years since that night, but I can still remember the evening clearly, the discussion and the hopes and dreams of a then unknown R. Kelly.

A new kind of rap:

I returned to the UK knowing Jive Records had a big hit single coming with Jazzy Jeff and The Fresh Prince. Jeff and Will Smith had been in New York and I had met up with them, along with Barry Weiss. I had known Jeff and Will from their first ever release that we had signed at Champion Records, 'Girls Ain't Nothing But Trouble': the single had been a hit for us in the UK while the boys were still at school in Philadelphia, and the next year we had issued the album *Rock The House*. It had been all quiet for them in the UK since then, and when Barry played 'Summertime' I knew at once it was going to be a hit record across the world. People still talk to me today about that record and what a favourite it is of theirs. I guess it's one of the best summer records ever made, it's fun, it's up and it's relentless in its joy, you cannot help but sing along and be happy with it.

I think that single gave Jive Records a real boost. It was a pop rap record when rap was pretty tough, dark and street, being the genre's attraction to the youth of the day. 'Summertime', especially in the UK, widened the base of people who now liked rap – it could also be up, happy, commercial and pop. I think that is why so many people remember that record with such fondness. That record of Jeff and Will lives with me forever: the UK A & R was failing and frustrating, and then seemingly out of nowhere came a record that gave us all hope. The single eventually peaked at No 8 and became a Grammy award winning song in the US. It is no surprise to me that Will Smith has become one of the biggest film stars in the world. He works harder than anyone and he deserves all he gets.

Children in Need:

As August came in 1991 we had no idea of the changes that were about to be made in the final months of the year. For now, it was very much business as usual: we set about organising the release of Buddy Guy's *Damn Right I've Got The Blues* album and tour, our big hope YoYo Honey were about to release the first single from their forthcoming Mike Peden produced album, and I was becoming more involved in Battery Studios, not really an area that I had been instructed to get involved in, but the studios were not as full as they should be. I was also working with Children in Need: they wanted me to make their end of year fundraiser have more profile with a hit single. Bruno Brookes and Liz Kershaw had a Saturday morning radio show with a very strong following and were making several TV appearances at the time, and Bruno asked if I would make and issue the record, a duet of 'Come Outside' with Liz Kershaw.

We then got together several times to come up with an idea that would be both entertaining and possibly sell some records with the proceeds going to Children in Need. We thought of a video with as many people as we could put together and eventually we settled on a big part for Jive artist Samantha Fox, who was preparing to re-launch her career in the coming year. We also brought astronomer

Patrick Moore to play the part of the moon in 'Come Outside, There's A Lovely Moon Out There.' Patrick was great fun and played his part well. He enjoyed being in a pop video and helping Children in Need and I will always remember that distinctive and so familiar voice saying 'and what is it that you want me to do Steve?' Additionally, we wanted national boxing hero Frank Bruno to play a part on the record and video in a sort of 'Blues Brothers' fashion, complete with a dance and sunglasses. We eventually filmed his part of the video and it was a pleasure and privilege to work with him.

Temptations:

RCA contacted me at the start of September with an invitation to be the Managing Director of Tamla Motown. A meeting was arranged, and I left it with a huge dilemma. I was unhappy with the A & R situation at Zomba/Jive/Silvertone and Tamla Motown was always one of my favourite labels. Since my young years I had always dreamed of working for Tamla Motown – Motown, Motown, Motown, it rolled round and round my head. After a couple of weeks, I declined and gave up on my youth's dream. The reason: my loyalty to the staff of Impulse. Leaving Zomba and operating Motown would have severed my links with Impulse and that was too much for me to bear.

Later, in the same month, Rupert Perry, Managing Director of EMI, Records called and invited me for dinner. He was in the market for my services but with no clear picture as how we would proceed: it was more of a sounding out meeting. After turning down Motown I knew I had to explain to Rupert that now was not the time to give up on Zomba or Impulse. I thanked him for his interest and was honoured that he thought of me so highly, but declined further talks at that time.

Although Zomba was not working in the way I wanted it to, outside the company my work was being noticed and monitored. In our quest for new areas to find the next records that might become hits, we invested in a small studio operation in Chicago and hired Wayne Williams who would over the years be involved in many of our hit records. Meanwhile, Roddy McKenna, as ever hustling around, found The Lost Soul Band in Scotland, an act we would eventually sign to Silvertone.

In October 1991, as I reached thirty-eight years old I was invited to Number 11 Downing Street to have afternoon tea with Norman Lamont. My work with Childline, Children In Need and Comic Relief had brought about this invitation, and frankly, it all passed very quickly with just an exchange of a few words with Norman Lamont. The best part for me was that my Mom was impressed: her son had been invited to Number 11 Downing Street and I tried to drink it all in on the day.

Goodbye PWL and all that:

October brought Silvertone's best sales month in its history – and the sale of PWL Records to Warner Brothers. I think the PWL sale came as a shock to a lot of people, especially as we were still riding high, although not as high as we had been, with both Kylie and Jason. In hindsight, which is always 20/20 vision, Pete did not need to sell, but the advisors at the time were pushing him to do so. The deal was made not with Warner Brothers UK under Rob Dickens, but with Warner International, and although this looked good on paper, PWL was not directly represented in its own country where its successes had always started, and because of this it would drop down the pecking order of priorities at the drop of a hat. Even so, as the deal was signed we stood at No 2 on the chart with 'Get Ready For This' by 2 Unlimited. 2 Unlimited would go on to sell millions around Europe, yet neither Warner's nor PWL would benefit from those sales, as Warner's passed on a worldwide license. That was how the deal started and would continue. Warner's could not react to market changes as quickly or sharply as an independent PWL. Within time, Matt Aitken would leave S.A.W and split up one of the greatest ever UK production teams and, months later, Mike Stock would also leave. I remained as marketing and promotion to PWL and Pete Waterman through Impulse, and we would continue to have hit records although not the Stock Aitken Waterman pop masters we had been used to over the past eight years.

Perseverance – and destiny:

One of the records that I will forever be associated with is R. Kelly's 'She's Got That Vibe.' From the moment I heard this record I was completely convinced it was a hit. Little did I know it would take me years to prove the point. We first issued the record in November 1991 and it completely died. I was determined I would re-issue the record and was sure it would become a hit then. My first attempt was six months later in May 1992 and it did better, but stalled at No 57. A year later in the Summer of 1993 we were not third time lucky – the record didn't make the Top 75. In 1994, we had scored two R. Kelly hits from his second album: the single 'Your Body's Calling' which peaked at No 19, and 'Summer Bunnies' which became a No 23 hit. I just would not give up on She's Got That Vibe, even though the staff at Jive always said 'not that again' whenever I mentioned it. I asked Steve Jervier in the studio if he could take a look at remixing it or coming up with a couple of ideas for me. A couple of weeks later when we were in the studio together Steve said

'I've found something brilliant but you ain't ever gonna get permission to use it.'

'What's that then?'

Steve then told me that a Michael Jackson track fitted perfectly under 'She's Got That Vibe.' In the studio they had discovered this accidentally when playing a few records to come up with an idea for the track.

'OK do it and let me listen to it,' I said.

'I'll pay you even though I might not be able to use it.'

We agreed, and two weeks later Steve delivered the track. I said to Steve that it was probably best that he denied all knowledge of the track. I played the record to Tina who saw the possibility straight away, but we would have no chance of clearing the sample through Sony or with Michael Jackson. I also spoke with Graham Stewart and asked him if he could press one thousand promo copies outside of England with no prefixes or markings on the vinyl to associate it with Jive Records. Graham was the greatest 'fixer' I have ever met: within two weeks I had my thousand copies manufactured out of the country with no trace of Jive Records. Tina and I devised a plan where we would just let twenty promo copies escape into the London area and then a week later do the same in Birmingham and then Manchester. After three weeks, the record was having enormous club play and appearing in all the dance charts. We then mailed the rest of the stock to secondary clubs and DJs. The record started to explode. We got together the single for release including R. Kelly's 12-inch mixes and the original single, but minus the new promo mix.

On 22nd October 1994, R. Kelly and 'She's Got That Vibe' peaked at No 3 on the UK chart. It remains one of R. Kelly's biggest ever UK career hits.

I could never really enjoy the hit at that time, I was always worried that someone would come knocking on the door about the Michael Jackson sample. I also thought that the public would be disappointed at not having the sampled version with their purchase and I expected bad press. Nothing ever happened, no one complained, I think the buyers realised what a great record it was in its original version. I had escaped cleanly, and all Clive and Robert Kelly knew was that they were Top 3 in the UK with a record that was three years old.

For the third time in three months I was headhunted with an offer to run another record company. Gary Ashley of the Australian based Mushroom Records, home of Kylie and Jason, wanted me to become their new MD. I liked Mushroom and we met several times, but for the same reasons as before I declined their approach.

Cabinet reshuffle:

Andrew Lauder decided to resign from Silvertone. The reason given was artistic differences and Andrew would leave as the year ended. I liked Andrew and thought it was disappointing that he should decide to go. I think the tighter controls that were now in place at Zomba regarding expenditure had made Andrew feel as though he was working for a major and thus could not spend money exactly as he wished. I was immediately called to New York to meet with Clive and discovered that Andrew's departure and my lack of interest in Jive UK's operation had heralded change. Steven Howard was to become Managing Director of Zomba Publishing, so he was leaving Jive Records, and Charlie Eyre was also leaving Jive. For the first time, I was asked for my views on the structure of the company. Thus, we decided Roddy McKenna would become A & R for Silvertone to finish off his work with the acts he had signed to Jive, and Michael Tedesco would move from Jive US to a new Silvertone US office where he would be A & R for the US based acts. I thought this gave Silvertone an international appeal and would look like growth after Andrew's departure. Clive was keen to give Mike Pedan a shot at A & R for Jive – and I was to become Managing Director of the group comprising Zomba, Jive, Silvertone, and Coombe Music, also having some responsibilities for Battery Studios. The new deal was entirely done in one afternoon and I left New York with renewed vigour: the labels would be a different place in 1992.

In 1991 Impulse had once again delivered the goods, hits and profits.

January			
Bring Your Daughter To The Slaughter	Iron Maiden	E.M.I/Sanctuary	No 1
Get Here	Oleta Adams	Fontana	No 4
Got The Time	Anthrax	Island	No 16
Cry For Help	Rick Astley	R.C.A	No 7
Coming Out Of The Dark	Gloria Estefan	Epic	No 25
Can I Kick It	A Tribe Called Quest	Jive	No 15
February			
In Yer Face	808 State	ZTT	No 9
The One And Only	Chesney Hawkes	Chrysalis	No 1
What Do I Have To Do	Kylie Minogue	PWL	No 6
March			
Ever Rising	The Charlatans	Situation Two	No 15
Human Nature	Gary Clail on U-Sound System	Perfecto	No 10
Should I Stay Or Should I Go	The Clash	Columbia	No 1
Sit Down	James	Fontana	No 2
Can You Dig It	The Mock Turtles	Siren	No 18
Sailing On The Seven Seas	Orchestral Maneuvers In The Dark	Virgin	No 3
April			
Ring My Bell	Adeva	Cooltempo	No 20
Love Is A Wonderful Thing	Michael Bolton	Columbia	No 23
The Shoop Schoop Song	Cher	Epic	No 1

Promise Me	Beverley Craven	Epic	No 3
The Whole of The Moon	The Waterboys	Ensign	No 3
May			
Recipe For Love/ It Had To Be You	Harry Connick Jnr	Columbia	No 32
R.S.V.P.	Jason Donovan	PWL	No 17
Get The Message	Electronic	Factory	No 8
Gonna Catch You	Lonnie Gordon	Supreme	No 32
Baby Baby	Amy Grant	A & M	No 2
June			
There's Nothing Like This	Omar	Talkin Loud	No 14
Planet Of Sound	Pixies	4AD	No 27
Rush Rush	Paula Abdul	Virgin	No 6
Hey Stoopid	Alice Cooper	Epic	No 21
Real Love	Drizabone	4th & Broadway	No 16
Chorus	Erasure	Mute	No 3
Damn Right I Got The Blues	Buddy Guy	LP	No 43
I Like The Way (The Kissing Game)	Hi-Five	Jive	No 43
Always There	Incognito	Talkin Loud	No 6
It Ain't Over 'Til It's Over	Lenny Kravitz	Virgin	No 11
Shocked	Kylie Minogue	PWL	No 6
July			
Bring The Noise	Anthrax	Island	No 14
Time, Love and Tenderness	Michael Bolton	Columbia	No 28
Things That Go mmmmm	C & C Music Factory	Columbia	No 4
I like It	DJH featuring Stephy	R.C.A.	No 16
Go	Moby	Outer Rhythm	No 10
Pandora's Box	Orchestral Maneuvers In The Dark	Virgin	No 7
I'm Too Sexy	Right Said Fred	Tug Records	No 2
Move Any Mountain	The Shamen	One Little Indian	No 4
August			
Summertime	Jazzy Jeff & The Fresh Prince	Jive	No 8
Happy Together	Jason Donovan	PWL	No 10

More Than Words	Extreme	A & M	No 2
Saltwater	Julian Lennon	Virgin	No 6
Set Adrift On Memory Bliss	PM Dawn	Gee Street	No 3
September			
I Wanna Be Adored	The Stone Roses	Silvertone	No 20
Everybody's Free	Rozalla	Pulse 8	No 6
Such A Good Feeling	Brothers In Rhythm	4th & Broadway	No 14
Love Your Life Be Free	Belinda Carlisle	Virgin	No 12
Homebase LP	Jazzy Jeff & The Fresh Prince	Jive	No 53
Greatest Hits	Jason Donovan	PWL	No 9
Love To Hate You	Erasure	Mute	No 4
Mr. Lucky LP	John Lee Hooker	Silvertone	No 3
The Word Is Out	Kylie Minogue	PWL	No 16
October			
Emotions	Mariah Carey	Columbia	No 17
The Best Of Daryl Hall & John Oates	Daryl Hall & John Oates	Arista	No 9
Always Look On The Bright Side Of Life	Monty Python	Virgin	No 3
The Low End Theory LP	A Tribe Called Quest	Jive	No 58
Get Ready For This	2 Unlimited	PWL Continental	No 2
November			
Active 8 (Come With Me)	Altern 8	Network	No 3
The Square Root Of 231	Anticapella	PWL Continental	No 24
Playing With Knives	Bizarre Inc	Vinyl Solution	No 4
When A Man Loves A Woman	Michael Bolton	Columbia	No 8
Ring My Bell	Jazzy Jeff & The Fresh Prince	Jive	No 53
No Son Of Mine	Genesis	Virgin	No 6
If You Were With Me Now	Kylie Minogue	PWL	No 4
Let's Get To It LP	Kylie Minogue	PWL	No 15
December			
Keep On Pumping It	Kylie Minogue	PWL	No 49
Don't Talk Just Kiss	Right Said Fred	Tug	No 3
I'll Be Home This Christmas	Shakin' Stevens	Epic	No 34

Impulse had also worked on albums throughout its history. Although I do not have details of every album we worked, I do have a list for 1991, and here are some of the successful albums of that year.

Love Hurts	Cher
Greatest Hits	Eurythmics
Greatest Hits	The Stranglers
Fellow Hoodlums	Deacon Blue
Stars Crash Down	Hue & Cry
Best Of Dexys	Dexys Midnight Runners
Mama Said	Lenny Kravitz
Ultimate Collection	T.Rex
Singles Collection	Paul Young
Worldwide	Everything But The Girl
Timespace	Stevie Nicks
Greatest Hits	Elton John
Greatest Hits	Barry White
Greatest Hits	Jason Donovan

The Impulse hits that year were plentiful, including four No 1 records, two of which were for Sony and John Aston. I enjoyed the big name artists we worked for, including Gloria Estefan, whom I met backstage at Wembley. I loved 'Sit Down', by James, and 'Can You Dig It', by The Mock Turtles. Beverley Craven's 'Promise Me' was beautiful and so was she, a charming lady. 'The Whole Of The Moon' by The Waterboys is a great record to get you down the M1 late at night when you are flagging. 'Baby Baby', by Amy Grant, 'There's Nothing Like This', by Omar and 'Always There', by Incognito, remain favourites of mine to this day. 'Set Adrift On Memory Bliss', by PM Dawn, lifted me out of my seat the moment I heard it, and 'Summertime', by Jazzy Jeff and 'The Fresh Prince', will always make the world feel a better place whenever it comes on the radio. A good year for songs to remember, and a pleasure to have played a part in their success.

Jazzy Jeff and The Fresh Prince

Thank you for helping us answer
so many more children!
To Steve

with thanks

and love ChildLine
+ Esther Rantzen

Esther Ranzen Original Drawing

CHAPTER 20

THE WIND OF CHANGE – 1992 AND 1993

Watching the wheels:

A life in the record industry, as in show business, is always up and down. Some years you can do no wrong, others you can do no right, and it seems there is no rhyme or reason to the results of your efforts. Zomba, Jive and Silvertone were entering a cold period and it would last for nearly two years.

The change in the staffing of the company was continuing. The failure of Jive's A & R and the departure of Andrew Lauder from Silvertone had changed the working of the entire company and my job as well. Jive and Silvertone were now labels devoid of A & R, apart from Roddy McKenna, and as my attempts to employ people in that area had been dismissed, 1992 began with a gaping hole. Furthermore, as Andrew Lauder and Steve Howard were no longer around, the clean-up of the roster of artists was now my responsibility, hence for months I was delivering bad news to a list of artists we no longer had faith in.

The market was worsening as dance records exploded. You could have a No 1 record with a dance single, but very few album sales. They were mainly one off explosive records. Most of these records were licensed territory by territory, so there was no long-term ownership and no album reward. Clive believed we should stick to the principles of the proper record business, look for artists who could succeed in the long term, own the product for the world, and, if successful, receive the rewards from the album sales. I cannot fault that thinking, it is right and proper, but when you are struggling to get a hit record, you will take one from anywhere. I believed we should have been dabbling in the dance market to bridge the gap while we were looking for artists with album potential, and I believed the lack of confidence caused by few hits was damaging to the staff and the company as a whole. Furthermore, I believed it made us unattractive to artists we may be chasing, as we were not on the chart frequently. This argument would rage on for eighteen months and it was an argument that only the owner could win.

They say that if you are to succeed you learn more from your failures than your successes, and I believe that to be true. During the next eighteen months I would learn to become a proper Managing Director, understanding business affairs, contracts, accounts and staff issues, trimming the roster, operating Zomba, Jive, Silvertone, Impulse, Prime Time and Coombe Music, and additionally, a classical company we purchased, Conifer Records. All this came under my management. I could really have done without Coombe and Conifer, as the learning curve I was going through and the endless search to find A & R for the company, plus trying to prop it up with any record I could find to sell, was more than enough to cope with.

The US division of Jive had found hip hop and rap, which did not operate on radio play, and so these sales increased more by word of mouth. The records had a huge black base and this was now spreading to the white kids of America: it was youth music across the board. However, the records did not travel well into the UK, where there was a small base. Although it was growing, the UK was slower to embrace this sound and it could not deliver massive album sales at that time.

Zomba UK had to exist on selling twenty thousand of this and ten thousand of that, as well as building up sales overall by a lot of small selling records. The worst part of all of that is you put as much effort into selling twenty thousand as you do into a three hundred thousand seller. They both start off in the same way with extremely hard work, and whereas the three hundred thousand seller at least brings some comfort and joy as the record increases its sales base, bringing added radio, TV and press, which in turn delivers even more sales, the twenty thousand seller remains hard work until you have milked every last sale. The ten and twenty thousand sellers we started with that year were US artists Fu Schnickens, B. D. P with KRS One, Sonic Boom, Robert Ward and Del Shannon, J. J Cale and the bigger selling Buddy Guy. Apart from Fu Schnickens and B. D. P with KRS One, all the artists were with Silvertone.

All we could do was to clean up the labels, look for opportunities and sell what we had.

John Lee Hooker had come to the end of his two album deal with Silvertone, and after bringing him back to the centre of the business with the huge selling *The Healer* and *Mr. Lucky* albums, we wanted to re-sign him, having to take on board that he now could command much bigger fees for his services. We worked hard on three deals for him – 1) The World, 2) UK and Europe as a single deal, and 3) UK and Europe for the coming album and the follow-up greatest hits album.

One of our main problems was that the rise of Silvertone and Blues music had inspired Richard Branson to start a blues label called Point Blank. To establish Point Blank quickly the label needed to sign the King of the Blues, John Lee Hooker, and they would eventually pay a fortune to obtain him, which they would never recoup. John Lee's manager was Mike Kappas, a truly unpleasant man. Kappas had been upset at the departure of Andrew Lauder and who knows what Andrew had said to him. Kappas was unbearable, he knew he had a valuable artist and had suddenly hit the big time after years of scraping around with very little. The re-negotiation took over six months while Kappas was just upping the price with Point Blank and finally, I said to him 'Is there anything we can do to make this deal?' 'Yes. You can die' was his reply. That was the end of John Lee Hooker and Silvertone.

Andy Richmond and I milked every sale we could out of the Silvertone catalogue during the year. We released a 12-inch box set of Stone Roses singles and re-mixes, two single releases, 'I Am The Resurrection', which was a No 33 single, 'Waterfall', a No 27 single and an album of tracks and 'B' sides titled 'Turns Into Stone', which would peak at No 32. We made sales out of anything we could.

In January, Peter Caisley had joined our Business Affairs department, and in February, after much effort, Mushroom Records conceded defeat in trying to obtain me as MD of their company. Even though Zomba, Jive and Silvertone were in for what I thought would be a difficult year, I felt I was in the right place, and to work with John Fruin and Clive Calder was the best possible learning curve. To my mind, they were the best teachers in the business and whatever happened I believed it would be an advantage to work and just listen to those two.

By March I was rearranging the company and I moved Zakes Gordon into A & R to look after the US rap and hip hop product. 'Zakes E Boy' as he became known was the right person for that product, in terms of age and knowledge. Zakes would listen to the albums and pick three tracks that he would then play to me, the US single and the possible follow-ups. I could then quickly get a handle on which track to spend the most money on in terms of success and reward. Zakes would become my right hand man on all this product and I was miffed when my great mate Pete Waterman nicked him a year or so later as A & R for PWL. I maintained that Zakes was not an A & R man in the true sense of the phrase, but was fantastic with our US product. PWL offered him a lot of money to go and you really have to let people go even if you know it is not a good move. Pete thought he was something more than what he really was and the PWL job did not last long. Pete and I never spoke about the move of Zakes E Boy, as Pete would never hurt or harm our friendship and he genuinely thought that Zakes could assist in the rebuilding of PWL.

I hurtled into April in a bit of a mess. My diary at the time was just full with page after page of company issues that I really had never dealt with before, each taking up ages of my time as I learnt on my feet. Tina was with me all the way and protected me as much as possible, although she was now growing from being my personal assistant to dealing with the records as they came down the track. Jacqui got a break from Holiday on Ice and we headed for Madeira, a lovely island in the Atlantic where The Beatles once escaped the pressures of the world many years before. The Beatles boat was still moored in the harbour and is a tourist attraction for the island. If you had said to Jacqui or me that when we returned to England it would be the last we would ever see of each other, I don't think either of us would have believed it. But when Jacqui returned to the tour and I returned to Zomba, our relationship could no longer continue with each of us in different parts of the world all the time. Jacqui returned to the UK for a short while in the summer, but then left for America as an offer had come in from Disney on Ice. We still spoke at times on the phone until about a year later, when she called to say she was going to get married to a skater from the tour. It was our last phone call. I hope she is having a fabulous life as for some years Jacqui enriched mine.

Kylie Minogue and Jason Donovan depart:

More changes came as Jason Donovan left the company and signed to Polydor. Kylie Minogue decided that 1992 would be her last year with the company too. Her association with us ended at the close of 1992 with a No 1 greatest hits record, bringing to a close a run of twenty hit singles that had started in 1988. They included four No 1 singles – 'I Should Be So Lucky', 'Especially For You', 'Hand On Your Heart', and 'Tears On My Pillow' – and three No 1 albums – *Kylie*, *Enjoy Yourself* and the *Greatest Hits*. We would also have six No 2 singles during that run of hits.

For nearly five years of my life I had been involved with Kylie and her manager Terry Blamey, who remain a partnership to this day. Kylie's work ethic is second to none, her effort in everything she does has to be admired and she deserves to be the icon of popular music she has become. In the years that have passed I have met with Kylie a few times and I tried to sign her to Jive Records in 1993, but I believe my close relationship with Pete, as well as Kylie's desire to work with dance producers, went against us. The last time I saw her was at her final concert of the UK tour at Earls Court before her illness, which was announced only a week later. Mike Stock, Matt Aitken, Pete Waterman and I were invited to the show, which was a nice touch after all those years. Kylie was in her room after the show eating the smallest bowl of spaghetti I have ever seen, it was in one of those tiny desert bowls. She was charming as ever, but both Pete and I remarked afterwards how tired she looked. When her illness was announced it was difficult to know what to do, we decided just to pray for the best and send her all the positive thought we could. Fortunately, all has turned out well and hopefully will continue to do so for many years to come.

A taste of BMG:

I was on the move again in May to Austria for a BMG international meeting where I was presenting our product to BMG for Europe. BMG or The Bertelsmann Group were now the owners of RCA and Arista Records. I never really enjoyed corporate conferences and to my mind as the years went on they just got worse and more corporate with each passing conference. Record companies were being bought by corporate businesses and entertainments, in their portfolios, were seen as exciting vanity opportunities – the directors could show off photos of themselves with celebrity artists. Bertelsmann being German were more regimented than most and everything was run very tightly, with time allocated to the minute. I never had a problem being on stage or speaking to a room of people, I guess all those years on stage in my youth had done away with any fear I might have, so I did my piece, advised the group of our up-and-coming product and was pleased to leave the following day and return to England.

I was now the subject of an offer from Chrysalis to join their company. I nipped it in the bud over a lunch, as I could not go through the whole thing again after the three offers in the past nine months. It did make me feel that I was doing something right, even though I found the Zomba transformation tough going.

Yazz and John Mayall:

I was still in touch with Jimmy Nail, completing the publishing deal we had agreed, and found myself at Laurie Jay's office. A voice came over my shoulder and said 'Anyone fancy a cup of tea?' I turned to see Yazz who was having a lot of hit records at the time, the biggest of which was 'The Only Way Is Up', which had stayed at No 1 for six weeks a couple of years earlier. Laurie had started to manage her career and next album, we sat and drank tea, and we began a friendship that has lasted to this day. Yasmin Marie Evans and I would work together in the coming years on three of her albums including *The Best of Yazz*.

By October, after many frustrating months trying to sign many artists without success, I had managed to sign Rory Gallagher to Silvertone, I had re-signed Sonic Boom, and I now signed John Mayall of the Bluesbreakers fame. We had a hit with 'Sonic The Hedgehog', something I must be forgiven for as I was looking for a hit anywhere I could find one. In my saving grace I did create a label for it entitled Internal Affairs, as I just could not put it out on Jive Records – that was not in my vision. I also signed The Time Frequency to Internal Affairs, as I liked a track they had called 'Real Love.' We first issued it in 1992 but it would take eighteen months before it became a Top 10 record. We also recorded Tom Jones with Dave Stewart on 27th November and the record was earmarked for the following year's schedule.

A trip to No 10:

November also brought an invitation to Number 10 Downing Street, which had come around for my continued work with Childline and Esther Rantzen. I was to have tea with the Prime Minister John Major and, Norma Major, his wife. When I first received the invitation I was due to go to Walsall that weekend both to see Mom and to watch the mighty Saddlers play. I thought I would take the invitation and show Mom that her son, who had shown real signs of becoming a waster in his teens, was now invited to have tea with the Prime Minister. None of my achievements so far had impressed her much, at least on the surface. At thirty-eight years old I was still being driven to succeed with what felt like a trail of failures behind me. Surely, this would win her over. I walked into her bungalow, produced the invitation and enquired 'What you think of that then?' My Mom calmly took the invite, put on her glasses, studied it for what seemed like five minutes, and then said 'So where have you had that printed then?' You can't make it up, can you. No one could have predicted a statement like that. I responded with 'See the date and time on that invite, when that day comes, wherever you are, just remember I'll be chatting with John Major!'

But that invite was a turning point in my life. A couple of weeks later when I told Mom what it was like inside Number 10 and described my conversation with John and Norma Major, I was finally off the hook. I think my Mom had decided that whatever I went on to do, I had not soiled my father's name and was now worthy of some respect for my achievement. The invite was framed and hung in her hallway. Number 10 also felt like some kind of achievement for me. Esther Ranzen, who had become a good friend, had set up the whole affair and was probably lobbying the Government to come up with funding for Childline. Esther in those days was a whirlwind of activity and moved heaven and earth to get what she wanted for her TV shows and projects, no stone was left unturned. I entered Number 10 and went into a huge banquet room where I would imagine these things go on every week. Drinks, waiters with trays of food and general chatter for about thirty minutes. Then John and Norma Major moved into a smaller room with a few chairs and in a very organised way we were manoeuvred into our few minutes with the PM. Esther must have told the PM about me and we spoke for a few minutes about the record business.

R. Kelly – The Beginning:

The year was coming to a close, we had been working hard for almost eighteen months on our R. Kelly project, and we had, through Choice Radio and the black press outlets, built a strong following for Robert's music. It was mainly in London, but had also spread to Birmingham. It was a totally black support, but it was passionate. In chart terms all we had was a No 57 position for the first release of 'She's Got That Vibe' and we had just scraped the Top 75 with the release of 'Sex Me.' The latter had caused a storm from plays on Choice Radio, but was not selling in enough quantity to move up the chart. The album *Born Into The Nineties* had only stayed on the chart for one week on release in February but it had continued to sell throughout the year – just a trickle of sales each week, but the album total was about twenty five thousand. We then had an offer from Barry Marshall to stage two gigs at Hammersmith Odeon for R. Kelly. It was a nervous time, we were not confident about sales, and on top of that Robert had never done a gig with a band, he had only done track dates in America where he would sing to backing tracks. But, I knew that this was our chance.

Until then, Radio One had completely blanked R. Kelly, with no interest at all, and Nick Fleming did a marvellous job in getting the radio producers and DJs to Hammersmith Odeon. We sold the event to them as a happening – if they didn't go they would miss the gig of the year and the birth of a star. Frankly, I had no idea if Robert could put together a show and pull it off when he had never done it before. I should not have worried. The Radio One people arrived just before he went on and then the start of the show was so electric that the audience went wild. The screams were so loud you could not hear your own voice. Robert was amazing and did his Bump 'N Grind to perfection. By the end of the evening, I knew I had Radio One's support on the next single release and we had a chance to break R. Kelly in England.

A tough year:

The final meeting of the year in the Zomba offices in Willesden was with Clive, John Fruin, Barry Weiss, Bert Meyer and myself. We discussed the record business, our business, the effect of the recession, the artists, the financial state of the company and every aspect we could think of. We decided to operate the company as one worldwide office: the lack of artists coming from the UK and Europe and the growing list of artists from America would mean that 1993 was to be a year working what we had. A & R acquisition was on the back burner and it was felt we would turn our US artists into worldwide artists rather than push new European artists. Although this made great sense to me, it was a disappointment.

Impulse, on the other hand, was recession proof, the team went from strength to strength and had another great year. Major record labels were starting their own teams, but using Impulse as their back-up and overflow operation. No 1 Records came from Right Said Fred, Erasure, Boys II Men, KWS and The Shaman, and the year finished with a No 1 greatest hits album from the departing Kylie. Impulse had continued its work as a champion of the independent labels – Mute, China, M & G, Living Beat, Cow, Tug, Cat, Slash, Vinyl Solution, Network, Ritz, One Little Indian, Jive, Silvertone, and PWL, while it still worked with the big corporates Columbia, Epic, Virgin, Chrysalis, A & M, Fontana, Motown, Island, MCA, RCA and Arista.

Impulse 1992 Hits

January			
Take Me Away	Cappella	PWL Continental	No 25
Can't Let Go	Mariah Carey	Columbia	No 20
I Can't Dance	Genesis	Virgin	No 7
Take Me Away	Loleatta Holloway	PWL Continental	No 25

Gimme Just A Little More Time	Kylie Minogue	PWL	No 2
We Got A Love Thang	Ce Ce Peniston	A & M	No 6
I Wonder Why	Curtis Stigers	Arista	No 5
Waterfall	Stone Roses	Silvertone	No 27
Twilight Zone	2 Unlimited	PWL Continental	No 2
February			
Dragging Me Down	Inspiral Carpets	Cow	No 12
It's A Fine Day	Opus III	PWL International	No 5
I Love Your Smile	Shanice	Tamla Motown	No 2
March			
High	The Cure	Fiction	No 8
Rock Me Steady	DJ Professor	PWL Continental	No 49
Breath Of Life	Erasure	Mute	No 8
Every Kinda People	Robert Palmer	Island	No 43
Deeply Dippy	Right Said Fred	Tug	No 1
Human Touch	Bruce Springsteen	Columbia	No 11
Get Ready LP	2 Unlimited	PWL Continental	No 37
April			
The Days Of Pearly Spencer	Marc Almond	Some Bizarre	No 4
Every Day	Anticappella		No 45
Make It Happen	Mariah Carey	Columbia	No 17
The Only Living Boy In New Cross	Carter The Unstoppable Sex Machine	Big Cat	No 7
Hold On My Heart	Genesis	Virgin	No 16
Pretend Were Dead	L7	Slash	No 21
Finer Feelings	Kylie Minogue	PWL	No 11
Too Good To Be True	Tom Petty and The Heartbreakers	MCA	No 34
I Am The Resurection	Stone Roses	Silvertone	No 33
Am I The Same Girl?	Swing Out Sister	Fontana	No 21
Please Don't Go	KWS	Network	No 1
May			
Friday I'm In Love	The Cure	Fiction	No 6
Always The Last To Know	Del Amitri	A & M	No 13
Love Makes The World Go Round	Don E	4th & Broadway	No 18

Two Worlds Collide	Inspiral Carpets	Cow	No 32
Jump	Kriss Kross	Ruff House	No 2
15 Years EP	The Levellers	China	No 11
Workaholic	2 Unlimited	PWL Continental	No 4
June			
Heartbeat	Nick Berry	Columbia	No 2
I'll Be There	Mariah Carey	Columbia	No 2
Abba-Esque EP	Erasure	Mute	No 1
Real Love	The Time Frequency Internal	Affairs	No 60
July			
All I Want Is You	Bryan Adams	A & M	No 22
Damn I Wish I Was Your Lover	Sophie B Hawkins	Columbia	No 14
I Drove All Night	Roy Orbison	MCA	No 7
LSI	The Shamen	One Little Indian	No 6
Love You More	Sunscream	Sony S2	No 23
August			
The Best Things In Life Are Free	Janet Jackson & Luther Vandross	Perspective	No 2
Crying	KD Lang	Virgin	No 13
What Kind Of Fool	Kylie Minogue	PWL International	No 14
Turns Into Stone LP	Stone Roses	Silvertone	No 32
The Magic Friend	2 Unlimited	PWL Continental	No 11
Baker Street	Undercover	PWL Continental	No 2
September			
End Of The Road	Boys II Men	Motown	No 1
Number 10 LP	J.J. Cale	Silvertone	No 58
Its My Life	Dr Alban	Logic	No 2
Generations	Inspiral Carpets	Cow	No 28
Greatest Hits	Kylie Minogue	PWL International	No 1
I Just Wanna Dance With You	Danial O'Donnall	Ritz	No 20
Ebeneza Goode	The Shamen	One Little Indian	No 1
Metal Mickey	Suede	Nude	No 17
October			
Supermarioland	Ambassadors Of Funk	Living Beat	No 8
People Everyday	Arrested Development	Cooltempo	No 2

Erasure-ish	Bjorn Again	M & G	No 25
Faithful	Go West	Chrysalis	No 13
She's Playing Hard To Get	Hi-Five	Jive	No 55
No Ordinary Love	Sade	Epic	No 14
Love Song	Simple Minds	Virgin	No 6
November			
Your Town	Deacon Blue	Columbia	No 14
Who Needs Love Like That	Erasure	Mute	No 10
Temptation Remix	Heaven 17	Virgin	No 4
Bitches Brew	Inspiral Carpets	Cow	No 36
Celebration	Kylie Minogue	PWL International	No 20
Never Let Her Slip Away	Undercover	PWL Continental	No 5
December			
Boney M	megamix	Arista	No 7
Supersonic	HWA Featuring Sonic The Hedgehog	Internal Affairs	No 33
Boss Drum	The Shamen	One Little Indian	No 4
Check Out The Groove LP	Undercover	PWL Continental	No 26
Slam Jam	WWF Superstars	Arista	No 4

The Break-up of S.A.W:

Pete Waterman started 1993 with his usual gusto and we celebrated with PWL and Impulse the No 1 single 'No Limits', by 2 Unlimited. This record going to No 1 was a general surprise to the industry and we quickly followed it up with Sybil's No 3 record on PWL, 'When I'm Good And Ready.' On the surface, in the PWL camp, all looked well, but underneath it all the huge hit machine that created havoc on the UK record chart was coming to an end. Matt Aitken had already left the company and although Mike and Pete had continued to produce records together for a few months, the finish was near. 'All That She Wants', by Ace of Base, is credited with the final huge argument between Mike and Pete that brought the S.A.W partnership to its close. Mike hated the record and decided that he could not accept Ace of Base and their sound whatsoever. After leaving Pete and starting his own company, it was not long before he joined forces once again with Matt. Pete found this hard to take and was even more disappointed that what he thought had been a very personal relationship was, in fact, basically a business relationship for the others. His feelings were to be dramatically compounded when Mike and Matt embarked on years of litigation against him over copyright. It was

1999 before the whole issue came to court and, although ultimately Mike and Matt dropped their claim for hundreds of thousands of pounds, the wounds penetrated deep and the scars have never healed.

Childline – with Tom Jones:

I was back working with Esther Rantzen and Childline. The charity needed an influx of money and I needed a hit even if we did not earn any money from it. Our idea was to record the Lennon and McCartney tune 'All You Need Is Love', and we were deciding on whom to work with. I had said to Esther that I knew Tom Jones and maybe he would be interested. Esther liked the idea of Tom and so I contacted his manager Mark Woodward and explained the plan. Mark was supportive and thought Dave Stewart would be a good producer for the project and within a few days he came back with a yes from both Tom and Dave.

During January we launched the single for Childline. The press gathering was in Kensington and Esther, Dave Stewart, Tom Jones and I were there to answer questions from the press. Shortly after, we went outside into the park to have our photographs taken together and to this day it remains one of my favourite photos, with Esther in front, Tom and I together, and Dave fooling around. 'All You Need Is Love' went to No 19, with our label Internal Affairs and Childline scoring their first joint hit record. As everyone had given their services free of charge, it was a very profitable record. Childline again had an influx of money to continue their great work with children and Tom Jones was back in the UK Top 40 for the first time in five years.

An album from Yazz:

Yazz, who had become a good friend over the past year, asked me to help her with the launch of the album *One True Woman*, my old friend Nick East took over as her manager and we all worked on providing new tracks for the album. Another friend, Albert Hammond, provided a couple of songs and we recorded 'How Long' with Aswad. 'How Long' by Ace, has always been one of my favourite songs and the reggae version with Yazz and Aswad would go on to be a hit record in the summer. That single launched the album, and it put Yazz all over the TV and newspapers and back on *Top of The Pops*. We had a huge launch party in Camden that July on one of those balmy summer nights, it seemed that about three thousand people turned up.

Billy Ocean – End of the Road:

Jive Records' big hope for the first quarter of the year was a single and album from Billy Ocean, who had not released a new album in nearly five years. Bill had decided to record a lot of his songs for the album in the Caribbean and he had then gone to Chicago to work with R. Kelly on four more tracks. The single entitled 'Pressure' was launched in February and although it was played regularly on radio and supported at retail, the public did not go for it. 'Pressure' became no more than a Top 50 single and with that poor performance the album sold only small numbers. Sadly, this was to bring to a close the recording career of Billy Ocean for several years to come.

Billy had spent many years on the road and was missing the growing up of his children before they got too old. He gracefully retired to bring up the kids and see more of his family and wife, Judy. I have always admired Billy for making that move. I became his main contact with the label over the next eleven years, although I have to admit there was very little contact from Billy. I would call about once every three months and check all was well, and Billy's recording and publishing contract with the company remained intact throughout all that time. We all felt that the success of Jive Records had originally been built mainly on the sales of Billy Ocean records and consequently Billy and his manager Laurie Jay were considered unofficial Members of the Board and were always treated with the utmost respect.

Mayall can cook too:

Silvertone's signing John Mayall brought him to England for the release of his first album on the label, entitled *Wake Up Call*. I was excited to meet the great John Mayall of the Bluesbreakers fame. John had become a legend of the record business for the band that had given a start to such artists as Long John Baldry, Eric Clapton, Jack Bruce, Peter Green, John McVie, Mick Fleetwood, Jon Hiseman, Andy Fraser, Walter Trout and Mick Taylor, all those years before.

John arrived in the UK and we went straight to Andy Richmond's flat. He was to cook dinner for a magazine and reminisce whilst doing so. We brought in all the ingredients and John started cooking and talking, it was a fantastic couple of hours: the stories from a life on the road gigging were amazing and, what is more, John could cook too. John always had his year in order: he would perform one hundred and twenty nights a year with his band, every year and always. The discipline and passion to continue doing so after thirty years was amazing, and he knew everything about travelling, what to eat, how to look after yourself, what comforts you needed to be away from home for long periods – he was the ultimate professional touring artist.

Wake Up call was released in the UK in late April, and John would be back later in the year to perform some UK gigs before heading off to Europe. The album was to achieve over a hundred thousand sales around the world. For me it was a great honour to be involved with such a legend, if only for a short while.

More change:

The summer brought a change in UK distribution for Jive Records, which I had been working on for some time: we left BMG by buying out our contract for fifty thousand pounds and I remember the delight as I signed the paperwork. Jive Records, along with Silvertone Records and Internal Affairs Records, would now be distributed in the UK by Pinnacle Records. BMG would still be our distributor throughout the rest of Europe and so would still be involved, but we had escaped them in the UK, I would continue to spend a little more time in Europe during the year to calm the BMG people. The meetings were always stiff and rarely about music, more about how this or that would look in the eyes of the masters of BMG. This was the political outlook of a major record company owned by a corporation.

Tina and I had been at *Top of The Pops* for the Tom Jones Childline performance and we found ourselves back there again in June with The Time Frequency. We had signed them to Internal Affairs, and their EP single 'The Power Zone' had become a No 17 hit. Bill Grainger, the manager of Big Fun, had brought the Time Frequency to Jive records, but had soon been fired by the band's leader John Campbell. The new manager, Deke Primo, would work off and on with John for years. As the group's popularity was growing, I knew it was time to re-issue the record I had originally signed them for, 'Real Love.' It was fraught with problems as John had fallen out with the vocalist Mary Kiani. This made life difficult and I had to come to some arrangement with her on the record, which John was not happy about, but I convinced him that this was the moment to break the band nationally. I got John to remix and freshen up the record, but retain Mary's vocals, and we set about getting the single ready for release. During November, 'Real Love' by The Time Frequency would become a Top 10 record, finally peaking at No 8. Such was the swell of support north of the Border, where the greatest fan base for the band lay, that when Prince's UK gig in Edinburgh was undersold the promoter contacted us to have The Time Frequency support Prince and sell out the tickets. John and TTF performed brilliantly that night and we had our few moments with Prince backstage before he went on and really wowed the crowd. The Time Frequency had come a long way in a short time and I was most pleased to see Scotland embrace one of their own so fully.

Esther – and a piece of history:

Esther Rantzen was again on the phone and asked me if I had seen her Hearts of Gold feature on *That's Life*, which was supported by Princess Diana. I said I had not and she asked me to watch the upcoming programme on Sunday. That Sunday Esther relayed the story of thirteen year-old Amanda Thompson, an excellent piano player who had been struck down with cancer. Following chemotherapy sessions, which had cost her the loss of her hair, she was playing again. Amanda's dream was to make a record and the day after the show Esther phoned to explain she wanted to record Gounod's arrangement of Bach's 'Ave Maria' with Amanda Thompson playing the piano and Lesley Garrett singing. We agreed I would record and issue the record, Esther would engage Lesley and the proceeds would go to the Malcolm Sargent cancer appeal fund. 'Ave Maria' was released and became a Top 20 hit peaking at No 17 for Amanda Thompson and Lesley Garrett. This record, which we issued on Internal Affairs, would be the only hit single in the long and celebrated career of Lesley Garrett.

I spent a lot of time with Amanda and although part of that time was tragic, I was amazed at her view on life. She had been through so much so young, but lived with a constant smile. She added to my life. I have always felt delighted that I could make her dream come true. I would see Amanda again in November where I was presented to the audience, with thanks by Esther, at The Childline Christmas Ball.

Boom Boom Shake The Room:

I had made my yearly trip to New York for the new music seminar that summer when Barry Weiss had played me the new track from Jazzy Jeff and The Fresh Prince entitled 'Boom! Shake The Room.' The US division of Jive was not sure about the record, as the US rap records were then a much tougher sound, where as 'Boom! Shake The Room' was a rap pop record. Barry and Clive asked me what I thought and I told them I believed it was at least a Top 10 single in the UK. Will Smith had been arguing with the company over the video investment that had been proposed, as he wanted a big budget video and Jive was offering a smaller package. After my positive response the budget was increased and Will got his way. Will and Jeff made an explosive video and the single and video formed an explosive package. I then returned to England and started to wind up the company on 'Boom! Shake The Room.' We worked through the remainder of the Summer on setting up the single, as I saw it as a real chance to have a huge hit and generate some much needed sales for Jive while building confidence with our US company. We had been through a major struggle in the last eighteen months and for me the success of this new single was critical for Jive's future.

We came to the start of September in good shape with the record, all the pre-sales were done and the release date was set. I thought there was a genuine chance of a No 1 record, but timing was crucial. Despite excellent pre-sales and first class radio and TV coverage, I decided to delay the release for just one week, much to the chagrin of my staff who did not agree at all. I stuck to my guns and told the staff that should it all go wrong I would take full responsibility on my own shoulders, it was my decision and mine alone. It was a tough week – I had calls from radio, TV and retail, how could I do such a thing. Finally, 'Boom! Shake The Room' hit the stores and through the midweek sales checks we had, we knew we had made it. Jazzy Jeff and The Fresh Prince would be the UK's No 1. I breathed the most enormous sigh of relief; we were back from the dead.

'Boom! Shake The Room' will always be one of my favourite records. It was a watershed release because had that record not come along at that time and had we not risked manoeuvering the release in the way I did to maximise its chart potential, quite possibly my career at Jive would have ended, and I would not have been part of what was to come. The single was a lifesaver.

Jive Records had not had a No 1 single since January 1986 when Billy Ocean's 'When The Going Gets Tough' had managed that feat – it had been a long gap of nearly eight years.

As we needed to capitalise and make as much money as possible from the hit record, I chose to license the single to as many compilations as possible. It was coming into the Christmas period, and there were many to have. I charged three thousand pounds a license, plus royalties, and built as much income as I could. It was not the way I would normally do things, but we were in trouble and needed the income. It was not good to hear Steve Wright on the radio expressing his distaste that every compilation in the market had 'Boom! Shake The Room' on it. Sorry Steve, but needs must.

R. Kelly explodes:

BMG were not pleased. We had moved to Pinnacle and scored with Amanda Thompson, The Time Frequency and now Jazzy Jeff and The Fresh Prince, and worse was to come as R. Kelly's album *12 Play* would be Top 20 for Christmas. I did smile. We had worked R. Kelly's *Born Into The Nineties* album for the whole year in an attempt to build the fan base for the new album. Our disappointment was that Jive US had chosen 'Sex Me' as the first single, there were far more commercial tracks on the album and we had Radio One positioned to go with full support on a genuine contender of a single. 'Sex Me' was not that. I argued our case in America, but to no avail, however, I would be able to influence the following single release. Radio One did play 'Sex Me' a couple of times, but they were uncomfortable with the title and lyric. The single just popped into the Top 75 for a week and then disappeared, but the album *12 Play* was a must-have item and charted in the Top 20 albums. This success brought a much more confident Robert Kelly to the UK to perform a short tour of large gigs – just five dates, but the fans went wild and we knew, with the right single, R. Kelly would be a hit maker in the UK.

A year of progress and novelty:

At our end of year it was decided that we would sell Conifer Records, which I was pleased about as I did find that company a distraction, being old-fashioned in its approach and with no will to change. I had also had enough of Coombe Music and made it known it was not what I should spend my time on. Although I would still be in charge of it for the coming year, by the Summer of '94 Coombe would come under the direction of our European operation in Holland, under Bert Meyer. Jive Records ended the year with great credibility in the black music field and our rap artists and R&B artists were the backbone of that credibility, but more important for me were the shoots of big selling records. 'Boom! Shake The Room' had proved we could take a record to the top and handle it and the two years of effort on the R. Kelly project were beginning to pay off. Silvertone Records was still continuing in its low key way. The constant working of its catalogue, especially The Stone Roses and albums coming in from John Mayall, Buddy Guy, Walter Trout, Co Co Montoya, Tupelo Honey, The Lost Soul Band and Whiteout, made the future look steady rather than promising. We needed another Stone Roses, but they are not that easy to find. Internal Affairs Records had a good year, even though it was overshadowed internally by both Jive and Silvertone. A label that had put out hit records and worked with the likes of Tom Jones, Dave Stewart, Lesley Garrett and established The Time Frequency had done well. The Impulse Promotion Company had another profitable year, with five No 1 records making sure we remained the undisputed No 1 company in our field. We had achieved the No 1 with 2 Unlimited's 'No Limit' for PWL, Shaggy's 'Oh Carolina' for Greensleeves Records, the life saver 'Boom! Shake The Room' from Jazzy Jeff & The Fresh Prince for the Chairman of Impulse and Jive Records, Meat Loaf's 'I'd Do Anything For Love But I Won't Do That' for Virgin Records, and finally, 'Mr. Blobby' for Destiny Music rounding off the year.

Impulse was under some pressure as the record labels had finally seen the benefit of their own promotional telephones sales operation and set up their own. Prime Time had suffered from the reduced workload and slimmed down accordingly. It now operated for Jive, PWL and a range of independents, and its glory years of working for all the labels were now over. Similarly, the upsurge in dance music had brought into the marketplace many dance promotion companies. I believe they were better than Impulse Club Promotions, as they were dealing solely in that area, whereas for us it was a bolt-on operation.

A similar circumstance happened to our Radio Promotion Company. Our competitors had to survive on that operation alone, whereas we always had the mainstay of our group in the strike force store operation. We re-arranged the Company for 1994 by merging Prime Time and the main strike force into one. This enabled us to grade the independent stores and become more focused where the bigger sales were. Millward Brown had taken over the chart from Gallup and had changed and upgraded the chart. We had to alter our operation accordingly.

The major labels had all copied Impulse's ideas and that too had reduced our intake of new records. We countered this by the main team pre-selling and operating its usual promotions when the record became 'live.' The team on the road operated what we considered to be our 'A' grade stores and the 'B' grade stores were handled by the new Impulse telephone team.

If there was any real competition in our marketplace before, there would be none after. We gathered all the available records to work and remained the No 1 call for all record companies. Impulse was now a smaller company in terms of staff, but it was still viable and profit making.

The Roll Call of Impulse hits for the year 1993 was as follows:

January			
She Sells Sanctuary	The Cult	Beggars Banquet	No 18
Show Me Love	Robin S	Champion	No 6
The Love I Lost	Sybil	PWL Sanctuary	No 3
New Emotion	The Time Frequency	Internal Affairs	No 36
No Limit	2 Unlimited	PWL Continental	No 1
February			
I Feel You	Dépêche Mode	Mute	No 8
All You Need Is Love	Tom Jones	Internal Affairs/ Childline	No 19
How Can I Love You More	M. People	Deconstruction	No 8
Pressure	Billy Ocean	Jive	No 55
Oh Carolina	Shaggy	Greensleeves	No 1
I Wanna Stay With You	Undercover	PWL International	No 28
March			
Alone	Big Country	Compulsion	No 24
To Young To Die	Jamiroquai	Sony S2	No 10
Mr. Loverman	Shabba Ranks	Epic	No 3
Animal Nitrate	Suede	Nude	No 7
When I'm Good And Ready	Sybil	PWL International	No 5
Feels Like Rain LP	Buddy Guy	Silvertone	No 36
April			
We Got The Love	Lindy Layton	PWL International	No 38
Copacabana	Barry Manilow	Arista	No 22
Wake Up Call LP	John Mayall	Silvertone	No 61
May			
Ships Where Are You	Big Country	Compulsion	No 29
Jump around	House Of Pain	Ruffness	No 8
The Jungle Book Groove	The Jungle Book	Hollywood	No 14
The Love In Your Eyes	Danial O'Donnell	Ritz	No 47
House Call remix	Maxi Priest	Epic	No 8
Bullet In The Head	Rage Against The Machine	Epic	No 16
Tribal Dance	2 Unlimited	PWL Continental	No 4

June			
Human Behaviour	Bjork	One Little Indian	No 36
What Is Love	Haddaway	Logic	No 2
Tease Me	Chaka Demus & Pliers	Mango	No 3
Beyond Your Wildest Dreams	Sybil	PWL International	No 41
The Power Zone	The Time Frequency	Internal Affairs	No 17
How Long?	Yazz & Aswad	Polydor	No 31
July			
Insane In The Brain	Cypress Hill	Ruff House	No 32
Can't Get Enough Of Your Love	Taylor Dane	Arista	No 14
Belaruse	The Levellers	China	No 12
Down That Road	Shara Nelson	Cooltempo	No 19
Luv 4 Luv	Robin S	Champion	No 11
Energize	Slamm	PWL International	No 57
August			
Nuff Vibes EP	Apache Indian	Island	No 5
Cannonball EP	The Breeders	4AD	No 40
Dreamlover	Mariah Carey	Columbia	No 9
What Happened To Old Fashioned Love	Daniel O'Donnell	Ritz	No 21
Right Here	SWV	RCA	No 3
September			
Venus As A Boy	Bjork	One Little Indian	No 29
Love Scenes	Beverley Craven	Epic	No 34
She Don't Let Nobody	Chaka Demus & Pliers	Mango	No 4
Boom! Shake The Room	Jazzy Jeff & The Fresh Prince	Jive	No 1
Life	Haddaway	Logic	No 6
I'm In A Philly Mood	Daryl Hall	Epic	No 52
Move	Moby	Mute	No 21
October			
Please Forgive Me	Bryan Adams	A & M	No 2
Never Gonna Give You Up	FKW	PWL International	No 47
I'd Do Anything For Love	Meat Loaf	Virgin	No 1
Joy	Staxx	Champion	No 25

November			
Music Is A Passion	Atlantic Ocean Eastern	Bloc	No 59
I'm Looking For The One	Jazzy Jeff & The Fresh Prince	Jive	No 24
Ave Maria	Lesley Garrett & Amanda Thompson	Internal Affairs	No 16
Sex Me	R. Kelly	Jive	No 75
12 Play LP	R. Kelly	Jive	No 20
Real Love	The Time Frequency	Internal Affairs	No 8
Maximum Overdrive	2 Unlimited	PWL Continental	No 15
Midnight Marauders LP	A Tribe Called Quest	Jive	No 70
December			
Big Time Sensuality	Bjork	One Little Indian	No 17
Seize The Day	FKW	PWL International	No 45
Mr Blobby	Mr. Blobby	Destiny Music	No 1
Code Red LP	Jazzy Jeff & The Fresh Prince	Jive	No 50

To Celebrate
The 6th Birthday of ChildLine

**The Prime Minister
and Mrs John Major**

request the honour of the company of

..........Mr Steve Jenkins..........

at a Reception at 10 Downing Street, Whitehall
on Wednesday, 25th November 1992 from 6.00 p.m. to 7.30 p.m.

An answer is requested to:
The Secretary (Invitations),
10,Downing Street, Whitehall
London SW1A 2AA

Dave Stewart, Esther Ranzen, me and Tom Jones

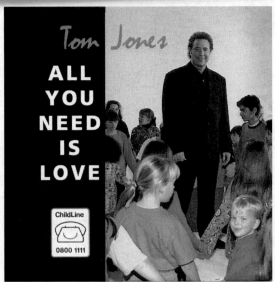

Child Line single

CHAPTER 21

JIVE TALKIN' – 1994 AND 1995

The upward curve begins:

After almost three years of unbelievably hard work and realigning our labels at Zomba to suit different parts of the marketplace, we would finally see some reward. When you are working in a record company on a day to day basis you never know if it will work or when the hits will come. Hope, desire, passion and a strong will become your allies, and a complete refusal to give in is a must. Fortunately, I was blessed with that kind of will.

I had started Internal Affairs to protect the credibility of the emerging Jive Records and our plan to reinvent Jive as a black music label came to fruition during 1994. I agreed to my first magazine interview in ten years in November '94, my reluctance to be interviewed going back to early experiences at Impulse. When the interviews were printed they always had the writer's inflection. It seemed to me that no matter what I said it was printed in a different way, always leaving out a few words that I had spoken in a sentence or adding one or two words, which changed the emphasis. The writers, it seemed, all had a pre-conceived idea of the story they wanted to publish and by interviewing me they could prove their theories correct. This style of writing infuriated me and I was very careful in my responses to say correctly how I saw things and protect Jive at all times. In due course I would ask for editorial approval, which press people detest, and so they began to decline interviewing me. I was not at all unhappy about this and for years I did not do any publication press interviews. I only agreed radio and TV because that was normally live and could not be edited.

Hardcore Magazine, a black music publication, came with their request in late 1994 and I believe they thought I was black. Their headline for the three-page spread read

Jive Talkin'

'Steve Jenkins is sitting pretty. As Managing Director of Zomba Records,
he has some of the most sought after acts in black music; R. Kelly, Aaliyah,

Jazzy Jeff & The Fresh Prince and A Tribe Called Quest. For the first time in ten years, Steve Jenkins gives an exclusive interview about his successes as MD of the largest independent and his passion for black music.'

It had taken five years of being Managing Director of Zomba to look like I was sitting pretty and on the outside it did look that way: we had brought R. Kelly and Aaliyah through to chart success, we had not given up on Jazzy Jeff and The Fresh Prince and we had stuck with A Tribe Called Quest through three albums. On the inside we were not out of the woods: these artists were still in the early years of their record sales and, although they were winners, they were not yet half a million sellers. The books were still not balanced.

The success of the R. Kelly album *12 Play* meant that Rob would tour England twice in 1994. During February, he played dates at the Hammersmith Apollo before returning at the end of the year to play the NEC in Birmingham and Wembley in London. The growth of the venues for Rob was about single success and finally, after nearly three years of trying, we made the Top 20 singles chart. The record that did it is still one of my favourite R. Kelly tracks to this day, 'Your Body's Callin.' ' I loved that record from the first time I heard it and I influenced the US division of Jive to issue it as a single. We had first class support from Radio One with Ivor Etienne and Paul Robinson and that, along with the continuing support of Lindsey Wesker at Kiss Radio and Merritt Crawford at Choice Radio, brought Capitol Radio to the party and R. Kelly was a national star. The single peaked at No 19, but the sales of the album began to explode week by week and it worked its way first to gold status and then platinum.

Clive Calder would always credit me with spotting a true star in R. Kelly from the day we signed him. It had taken three years, but I always maintain that Rob is one of the most talented artists I have ever worked with.

In late August we issued the next R. Kelly single, 'Summer Bunnies', just catching the last few days of summer. The record, again, was all over the radio and peaked at No 24. As with 'Your Body's Callin'', this may not seem like a massive hit, but once again the album took a huge surge in sales and headed towards platinum. By this time I was extremely confident that we had a huge support for R. Kelly and when we found the sparkling remix of 'She's Got That Vibe', I was determined to reissue. I had some resistance from my own staff on this, but I totally believed that it was a huge hit single and had done so for three years. This time, and at last, it all happened. Just prior to the huge Wembley and NEC gigs in October 1994, 'She's Got That Vibe' peaked at No 3 on the UK chart. The American company was amazed: how can a small US hit that is three years old be Top 3 in the UK? Fortunately, they didn't find out for a long time. Barry Hankerson, Rob's manager, Robert, Tina and I celebrated well on the huge UK gigs at the end of the year. R. Kelly was here to stay.

Aaliyah:

1994 was also the year that Aaliyah became a name known to the world. She was the daughter of the sister of R. Kelly's manager, Barry Hankerson. Rob had met Aaliyah at her home with Barry and they had started to work on an album together during 1993. The result was *Age Ain't Nothin' But A Number*, an album completely written and produced by R. Kelly for Aaliyah. The album was outstanding and Aaliyah was already a charismatic fourteen year-old with a fine voice. The ground swell of support for R. Kelly made me believe that this Aaliyah album could do great business, and indeed the album was instantly more commercial than an R. Kelly album, as the fantastic youth style that Aaliyah brought to the album was undeniable. The first single 'Back And Forth' had hit written all over it.

Tina and I decided we would go all out for Aaliyah, bring her in for interviews, radio and TV appearances, and capitalise on our three years hard work with R. Kelly. It could not have worked better. Straight out of the box 'Back and Forth' was in the slot, radio came on board instantly, and only weeks after delivering her first album Aaliyah was a UK national star.

I spent a lot of time with Aaliyah, as Barry Hankerson and Liyah's father had both called many times insisting that I take care of this fourteen year-old girl on her first trip outside of the US Tina and I took Aaliyah under our wing and what a great time we had. Liyah was great fun, intelligent and articulate, and even at such a young age it was obvious we had unearthed another world star. There were no tantrums, no fear of being far from home and the radio, press and TV fell in love with her. During her interviews she talked about R. Kelly and that in itself was worth their time as Rob was always too shy for interviews.

Before Aaliyah left the UK after her first time here, she had recorded an appearance on *Top of The Pops*, and she came to see me in my office just before her flight.

> *'Steve, I've had a great time and I just wanted to say thanks. I've got nothing to give you for your support so please take this photo.'*

She had written on a press photo

> *'Steve, many thanks and stop teasing me all the time, Love, Aaliyah.'*

I still have that photo to this day.

It would be a superb year for Jive Records and Aaliyah. 'Back And Forth' peaked at No 16 in July, and the follow-up 'At Your Best You Are Love' reached No 27 in October. The album *Age Ain't Nothin' But A Number* peaked at No 23 in August, but it would continue to sell well thereafter for over a year. Meanwhile, Jazzy Jeff & The Fresh Prince continued their hit making run. 'Can't Wait To Be With You' topped at No 29 in February and 'Twinkle Twinkle' hit No 62 in June, both of which kept the album *Code Red* selling through the year. A Tribe Called Quest led our rap artists, of which there were many, and the album *Midnight Marauders,* outsold them all and established 'Tribe' as an album selling act. Jive Records had gone from no real hit artists to four hit artists in the space of a year. It seemed as if they had all come out of nowhere, but we had been working on R. Kelly, Jazzy Jeff & The Fresh Prince and A Tribe Called Quest for three years. Aaliyah was the only real surprise package that came out of nowhere and even that project had the benefit of the years of hard work on R. Kelly. It seemed that our decision to become a company driven by worldwide A & R, and promote those artists worldwide in terms of marketing and promotion, was finally working.

Nashville:

The following month I was off to Nashville. Clive had bought Brentwood Music in Nashville and it was another move that I thought was a stroke of genius. Slowly, we would build up our Christian music catalogue by buying Christian record companies. The sales of these albums were huge in America, they were cheaper to make in recording cost terms, they had a huge fan base and the marketing was tiny compared to the pop world. John Fruin, Bert Meyer and I headed for Nashville, and I was really up for this trip, as the songs, records and artists that had come out of Nashville made it the music capital of the world for country music.

The Rednex:

The travelling continued as I went around Europe selling our artists and obtaining release dates from BMG. The main thrust of my visits, to Amsterdam, Berlin, Paris and Madrid, were on behalf of R. Kelly, Aaliyah, Buddy Guy and The Rednex, whose 'Cotton Eyed Joe' was a record that everyone had an opinion about. I have always thought that if a record generates opinion it has something going for it even if that opinion is a bad one. 'Cotton Eyed Joe' generated some terrible reactions all over Europe, but the record was without doubt one that had a chance and probably a big chance. We felt that if it became a hit in Europe we could push the record into England with a hit pedigree and obtain a hit. It took some convincing for the European countries to give it a go, but when they started to set up the record they all became surprised at the reaction they were receiving and the demand that followed.

The record had been discovered by Martin Dodd, who had joined Jive a year earlier from Mega Records. Martin had been very involved in the huge selling Ace of Base records and had come to the attention of Bert Meyer, who in turn had persuaded him to join Zomba in an A & R capacity. Martin's arrival added to our theory of worldwide A & R. Shortly after his arrival we began to manage and publish the producers Dennis Pop and Max Martin, who had previously worked with him. This move would bear tremendously successful fruit in the coming years and provide us with a hit factory of songs and productions from Stockholm, their base and studio.

Europe began the push for The Rednex and, during late 1994, 'Cotton Eyed Joe' would become No 1 in Austria, Holland, Germany, New Zealand, Norway, Sweden and Switzerland.

This gave the UK Company the ammunition to launch an attack on the media. Radio really did not want to know, but we pushed the press to write about this record that had been No 1 all over Europe. TV did come on board and whenever the video was shown there was a surge in demand. Slowly, we kept building and building the demand before launching the record in December – we felt that at Christmas time different fun records have a chance, as the party season gets under way.

The record charted in the Top 10 and began to sell more with the added chart run down plays on radio. Slowly, the country was becoming aware of 'Cotton Eye Joe' and The Rednex, and there were also country line dancing clubs and venues in the north of England that embraced the single as it became the fun tune for Christmas. It was played and played all over Christmas and the New Year period and came out the other side into the New Year, eventually going to No 1 in the UK on 14th January 1995, staying there for three weeks.

A new discovery:

During 1994 we signed a new band. The Backstreet Boys had been formed one year earlier in Orlando and consisted of Nick Carter, Brian Littrell, A. J. McLean, Howie Dorough and Kevin Richardson. Their manager, Lou Pearlman, had been infatuated with the rise of New Kids On The Block a few years earlier and felt he too could manage a band to worldwide success. The band had recorded a few songs for Phonogram Records, but they were soon languishing on the roster with no real commitment or direction from the label. We learned of their plight and approached Phonogram to obtain their release, which they soon agreed to, surprisingly with no override and a small payment to recover some of their costs. The Backstreet Boys were now a Jive act and began recording during 1994 for their debut album. In time they were to become superstars.

The Impulse tally for No 1 records during 1994 was five. Two No 1's in April and May came for Tony Di Bart, on Cleveland City Records, with 'The Real Thing' closely followed by Prince's only UK No 1 in a long career, 'The Most Beautiful Girl In The World', on his own NPG label. In July, we hit the No 1 album spot with *Real Things*, by 2 Unlimited for PWL, and towards the end of the year 'Saturday Night', by Whigfield, for Systematic and 'Baby Come Back', by Pato Banton, for Virgin Records.

The full list of hits follows:

January			
Autumn Leaves	Coldcut	Arista	No 50
Stop Loving Me Stop Loving You	Daryl Hall	Epic	No 30
Whoop There It Is	Tag Team	Club Tools	No 34
Dis-Infected EP	The The	Epic	No 17
February			
Waterfall	Atlantic Ocean	Eastern Bloc	No 22
Linger	The Cranberries	Island	No 14
Can't Wait To Be With You	Jazzy Jeff and The Fresh Prince	Jive	No 29
I Love Music	Rozalla	Epic	No 18
Spoonman	Soundgarden	A & M	No 20
Stay Together	Suede	Nude	No 3
Let The Beat Control Your Body	2 Unlimited	PWL Continental	No 6
March			
Violently Happy	Bjork	One Little Indian	No 13
Jingo	FKW	PWL International	No 30
Whispering Your Name	Alison Moyet	Columbia	No 18
I'm Outstanding	Shaquille O'Neal	Jive	No 70
April			
Light My Fire	Clubhouse	PWL Continental	No 7
MMM MMM MMM	Crash Test Dummies	RCA	No 2
You Gotta Be	Des'ree	Dusted Sound	No 20
The Real Thing	Toni Di Bart	Cleveland City	No 1
Sweets For My Sweet	CJ Lewis	Black Market	No 3
Let The Music	Loveland	Eastern Bloc	No 16
Singing The Blues	Daniel O'Donnell	Ritz	No 23
The Most Beautiful Girl In The World	Prince	NPG	No 1
May			
Reach	Judy Cheeks	Positiva	No 17
Slave To The Rhythm remix	Grace Jones	Zance	No 28
Your Body's Callin'	R. Kelly	Jive	No 19
Julie EP	The Levellers	China	No 17

Set You Free	N Trance	All Around The World	No 39
Get-A-Way	Maxx	Pulse 8	No 4
No Good	Prodigy	XL	No 4
Such A Phantasy	The Time Frequency	Internal Affairs	No 25
The Real Thing	2 Unlimited	PWL Continental	No 6
June			
Everybody's Talkin'	Beautiful South	Go Discs	No 12
Baby I Love Your Way	Big Mountain	RCA	No 2
Two Can Play That Game	Bobby Brown	MCA	No 3
7 Seconds	Neneh Cherry	Columbia	No 3
Twinkle Twinkle	Jazzy Jeff & The Fresh Prince	Jive	No 62
Dominater LP	The Time Frequency	Internal Affairs	No 23
Oh My God	A Tribe Called Quest	Jive	No 68
Real Things LP	2 Unlimited	PWL Continental	No 1
Feel What You Want	Kristine W	Champion	No 33
Shine	Aswad	Bubblin'	No 5
July			
Back & Forth	Aaliyah	Jive	No 14
Age Ain't Nothin' But A Number LP	Aaliyah	Jive	No 23
Lets Get Ready To Rumble	Ant & Dec	XS Rhythm	No 9
Body In Motion	Atlantic Ocean	Eastern Bloc	No 15
Meet The Flintstones	B-52's	MCA	No 3
Searchin'	China Black	Wild Card	No 4
Living In Sunshine	Clubhouse	PWL Continental	No 21
Regulate	Warren G	Death Row	No 5
August			
Everything Is Alright	CJ Lewis	Black Market	No 10
No More	Maxx	Pulse 8	No 8
Caught In The Middle	Juliet Roberts	Cooltempo	No 14
September			
Atomic remix	Blondie	Chrysalis	No 19
Summer Bunnies	R. Kelly	Jive	No 23
Girls Just Wanna Have Fun	Cyndi Lauper	Epic	No 4
Stay	Lisa Loeb	RCA	No 6

Voodoo People	Prodigy	XL	No 13
Saturday Night	Whigfield	Systematic	No 1
Detroit	Whiteout	Silvertone	No 73
October			
At Your Best You Are Love	Aaliyah	Jive	No 27
Baby Come Back	Pato Banton	Virgin	No 1
Turn The Beat Around	Gloria Esterfan	Epic	No 21
Total Eclipse Of The Heart	Nikki French	Bags Of Fun	No 5
Space Cowboy	Jamiroquai	Sony S2	No 17
She's Got That Vibe	R Kelly	Jive	No 3
Best Of My Love	CJ Lewis	Black Market	No 13
Dreamscape	The Time Frequency	Internal affairs	No 32
No-One	2 Unlimited	PWL Continental	No 17
Some Girls	Ultimate Kaos	Wild Card	No 9
November			
All I Wanna Do	Sheryl Crow	A & M	No 4
Shining/ Hope	Loveland	Eastern Bloc	No 37
What's Going On	Music Relief	Jive	No 70
Small Bit Of Love	Saw Doctors	Shamtown	No 24
December			
Yabba Dabba Doo	Darkman	Wild Card	No 37
Hold Me, Thrill Me, Kiss Me	Gloria Esterfan	Epic	No 11
When I'm Cleaning Windows	2 In A Tent	Love This	No 25

The politics of companies:

Zomba Records entered 1995 in good shape. After my instant and early success in 1989, 1990 and 1991, the years following had been a long road and it had been tough going. There is no doubt that you learn much more from hard and traumatic times than successful years, that is if you are prepared to learn, and I knew by the start of 1995 that I was a better Managing Director of a label than I had been through those early successful years. Finding the way through 1992 and most of 1993 had taught me a lot and, finally, the successes of 1994 had given the staff confidence. I felt we had the right people in the right place and they now had a deeper knowledge of the business.

Our worldwide A & R strategy had worked and looked like it would continue to do so. Martin Dodd was influential from our Dutch office and the US product was becoming more commercial and giving us a better chance of success in England. Still, the A & R within England had not reached the levels required and when Clive came to visit in January '95, it was time to set the structure for the coming year and beyond.

Clive arrived with Zomba in full flow. R. Kelly was in town for gigs at the N.E.C and Wembley and pre-recorded 'Bump N' Grind' for *Top of The Pops*, two weeks before the single peaked at No 8 in the UK Top 10. The Rednex's 'Cotton Eyed Joe' raced to No 1, beautifully timed for Clive's arrival, and it remained there for three weeks – a great start to the year. Clive, John Fruin and I sat down to discuss the way forward and I put forward my requests and designs for the coming year. Tina Wisby had done so well, it was time for her to move on and take sole responsibility for the US artists, and as Andy Richmond had also done a magnificent job I wanted him to remain as sales manager, but have responsibilities for Silvertone and look after our new and upcoming artists too. Clive agreed to all of that and I felt I had rewarded both Tina and Andy for outstanding effort and hard work. But the next part of my proposal became an issue. I felt I had earned the right and opportunity to appoint the A & R team that I wanted, one that I felt good and confident about. It was a great disappointment when this did not work out the way I had hoped.

Although Steven was now operating Zomba Publishing, behind closed doors both Clive and he still wanted control over A & R, seeing that part of the company as all-important. I wanted to sign Ken Greenbaum from Cooltempo, who had created a long list of hit singles for that label and was beginning to sell more and more albums, and I also wanted Steve Wolfe from MCA, again another A & R man who had commanded respect at MCA and brought hit records to the company. Clive could not have known these players, but Steven certainly would. They decided, irrespective of me, on Mike Pedan and Max Bloom. Mike Pedan had scored a huge hit with The Chimes' 'I Still Haven't Found What I'm Looking For' in 1990, a truly great record, and he had also produced our *Yo Yo Honey* album, which still to this day is a favourite of mine, but he had singularly failed to deliver a hit single from the album and consequently poor sales followed. Mike had insisted on the title of Creative Director at Jive and it seemed this was again another done deal. Mike is a pleasant man, but I had little confidence in his ability to bring us hits.

I then had to battle with Clive over the rising dance area for singles. It was beginning to sell albums and to my mind, although Portishead and Massive Attack had grown up in a dance based marketplace they were turning that into something different and selling albums, and that was not the area that Mike Pedan came from. Clive countered that Mike would have an assistant who would work in that area and so Max Bloom came to the Company. Max, like Mike, is a pleasant man, and he would in due course go on to have a career in the record business after leaving Jive, but to my mind he was inexperienced in the field we needed for progress.

To say I was gutted was an understatement. I felt I had rebuilt Zomba over the past few years and now it was time to move forward and go for it, yet once again the A & R department was looked at separately from the record company and, I felt, controlled with an elitist attitude. The circle of that control was headed by Clive and discussed with Steven, and the business affairs area was handled still by Mark Furman. None of them really liked my style. After the meetings and the decisions, John Fruin had to do long sessions of therapy with me. I could not believe that after all that we had achieved in the past three years I would again have A & R people forced upon me and, to make matters worse, they were musically nowhere near the reality of what was happening in our world.

That decision messed me up badly. Throughout my life I have only ever really done what I have wanted to do, regardless of the consequences, and this sometimes makes me hard to handle. I have never been frightened of being fired or removed from my position, I have always believed I would just do something else if that were to happen. I had been offered so many jobs by so many labels I thought I could just move on now, but Impulse was the sticking point. It was now twelve years old and I owed loyalty to the staff, some of who had started that company with me. Furthermore, I felt that my new team at Jive, which had taken six years to build up, was now ready to move into the top league. Despite feeling pessimistic about the future, I decided to continue, be professional and manage the situation as the owner wanted.

Legends of football – On record!:

Sally Mattis joined the company as my assistant while Tina gained control of the US product for Jive Records. Andy hired Hans Griffiths as his sales assistant and the company started to move forward whilst still being at No 1 with the Rednex. Some pleasure, success and an opening for my creative juices came via Phil Cokell. Phil and I had been friends for nearly twenty years and during his long career at Chrysalis Records, where he had risen to Marketing Director, he at Chrysalis and I at Impulse had achieved many hits together. Chrysalis and Phil had now agreed that he would become Managing Director of Dover Records, a label that gave him the opportunity to do the projects he wanted to and become his own boss. Dover Records had success with compilation albums and albums built around TV stars and icon artists such as Tom Jones. Over lunch one day Phil and I were talking about the rise of the new football Premier League that was now entering its third year and we were commenting how the players were becoming more and more successful. We exchanged views about our heroes in the game and slowly the idea of talking books came to fruition. We thought that if Denis Law and Paddy Crerand talked about the glory years of Sir Matt Busby's reign at Manchester we would buy that tape and, similarly, if Alan Hanson or Kenny Dalglish spoke about the glory years of Liverpool F. C. under Bill Shankly we would buy that tape too. And so we set about making this a reality.

I had met and played a round of golf with Alan Hansen, former Liverpool centre-back and winner of nine league titles and several cups with Liverpool. He is also a presenter and analyst with BBC's *Match Of The Day*. I managed to obtain his phone number and arranged a meeting with him on his next visit to London for *Match Of The Day*. We threw around our ideas and Alan had a few of his own, and in one meeting we agreed that this seemed a good idea and possibly profitable. Our first two projects would be *Liverpool F.C., The Shankly Years* with Ian St John, and *The Success Continues* with Alan Hansen. The Executive Producer would be Phil Cokell and co-ordination of the projects would be handled by Alan Hansen and Steve Jenkins. This project brought me immense joy. It enabled Phil and me to meet all our heroes in the game and make a product that we were all proud of. We went on to produce *Arsenal, My Arsenal* with David O'Leary, *The Making Of Champions* with Steve Bruce, *Manchester United, The Busby Years* with Denis Law and Paddy Crerand, *The Blues On Parade* with Peter Osgood, *My West Ham* with Trevor Brooking, *Life At Goodison* with Andy Gray, *Onwards And Upwards* with Gordon Strachan, *An Insight To The Villa* with Andy Gray and *The Highs And Lows* with Ray Clemence. We made eleven volumes in all and sold them directly into Woolworths. More than the profit or the success, just to spend time with the best footballers in the English league was a tremendous experience. If my Dad had been alive he would have been at all the recordings, as his loves of football, cricket and music were all as strong as mine.

Aaliyah – and Robert:

The first six months of 1995 with the new moves at Zomba, Jive and Silvertone just rolled along. R. Kelly was our top seller, Aaliyah's album continued to grow, and there were a few new artists who were making an impression on the chart and starting to take off. Aaliyah scored again in March with 'Age Ain't Nothin' But A Number', peaking at No 32, and again in May with 'Down With The Clique', a No 33 single. Aaliyah had now scored four hit singles and came to England in May to do her first gigs at Wolverhampton Civic and Hammersmith Apollo, where we had decided to do exactly the same plan that had worked so well for R. Kelly. It was wonderful to watch a fifteen year-old Aaliyah be so confident and command the stage on what were her first live gigs. We all loved Aaliyah, who was accompanied this time by her father Michael Haughton, a charming man. As she came off stage at the Apollo it was my pleasure to present them with silver discs for the album, which had now passed sixty thousand sales and was well on its way to being a debut gold album. We would have one more hit with Aaliyah that year before circumstances determined that she would leave Jive Records. 'That Thing I Like' was a hit in September and it brought to an end our contact with Aaliyah and her family.

Aaliyah's friendship with R. Kelly had grown during the making of the album *Age Ain't Nothin' But A Number* and it continued as the singles from the album became worldwide hits. They began performing on TV shows together and became inseparable whenever their schedules allowed. Robert was Aaliyah's favourite artist, friend, mentor, songwriter and producer. Robert adored her and said 'I can just look at her and write a hit song.' They played basketball together in their spare time and Aaliyah could play, occasionally beating Robert and rejoicing in the fact.

I knew them both well and they were compatible, both were down-to-earth, reserved, talented and unpretentious.

Immediately, Aaliyah returned to the US following her first enormously successful concert dates in the UK, first the press and then radio and TV began to question the relationship between her and Robert. Liyah was still a minor and Robert was ten years her senior. Finally, it exploded when it was reported that a marriage license had been issued to Robert Kelly and Aaliyah Haughton and that they were in fact now husband and wife. Jive Records defended the accusation several times and Aaliyah claimed that Robert and her were great friends and that the friendship would last. A few years later Liyah would admit that it had been a difficult time in her life, but her parents had sat her down and explained what she must do and put everything into perspective for her.

These problems had caused a situation where it was thought best that Robert and Aaliyah did not record for the same label and that their lives should not be so interlinked. The result was that Aaliyah would no longer record for Jive Records and would sign to Barry Hankerson's, Blackground Records, which in turn was signed to Virgin. Jive Records had lost a truly talented world star and we all were left with a feeling of disappointment, not only for the sales of her future records but more, that in knowing Aaliyah she had become a friend. I, like everyone else would watch her continued rise to fame through her next album *One In A Million*, and onto Hollywood to star in movies.

On 25th August 2001 I was at an airport in America waiting for a connecting flight to the UK. Across the airport lounge I saw photos of Aaliyah paraded on a television screen in a news broadcast. I moved closer to hear the reporter. My heart sank and I felt sick as I heard the tragic news of her death in a plane crash. After completing her latest video, Aaliyah and six crew members from the shoot had boarded the plane and taken off from Marsh Harbour International Airport at 6.50 pm. The small plane was later claimed to be overloaded with equipment and out of balance. It took off, rose to about forty feet and then crashed into the marsh leaving no survivors. Aaliyah was gone.

I believe if Aaliyah had lived she would have become one of the world's major stars with hit records, concerts and movies. She most certainly had it all as an incredibly talented performer. It will always be tragic that she lost her life so young at the age of just 22. I still have the photos and the notes she wrote me all those years ago. God bless Aaliyah Haughton.

A sign of the future:

Back to 1995. The The Rednex followed up their No 1, with a No 12 single, 'Old Pop In An Oak.' We tried another single later in the year, but it didn't hit. The Rednex were really a pop explosion that was over. Their album sold a reasonable amount of copies, but never threatened to be a huge seller. Times were changing. Meanwhile, Andy and I put together *The Complete Stone Roses*, an album of all the band's tracks and mixes that we owned, and it peaked at No 4 as Silvertone's bestseller of the year. We also issued a remix of 'Fools Gold' that became a No 25 hit single.

The Backstreet Boys – An uphill battle to the summit:

Breaking the Backstreet Boys was to prove one of the longest and most taxing challenges, but a salutary lesson in perseverance. In early 1995, not long after we had signed them up, they were high priority on our list of possible breakthrough artists and Tina and I went to Zurich to see a gig, meet with the band and begin to plan an assault on the UK. Lou Pearlman, their manager, would years later be found out as one of the most substantial Ponzi scheme felons in US history and thus spend his days behind bars. When Tina and I met him he was the Backstreet Boys' greatest supporter and remarkable manager. He had put the band together via auditions in Orlando and he had also contacted Johnnie and Donna Wright, the driving force behind New Kids On The Block, and enlisted them as part of the team behind The Backstreet Boys. Lou had financed everything and after we had completed our recording sessions of the band in Stockholm he had taken them to Germany, where he had many business contacts and started to build their career there. The Backstreet Boys were already polished performers. They practiced and worked every day on their performance, very quickly they managed to be on national TV and, soon after, they and we scored a hit with 'We've Got It Going On.'

All hell broke loose in Germany. The boys were a hit act almost immediately and soon followed up 'We've Got It Going On' with 'I'll Never Break Your Heart', which made them national stars and heroes in Germany. The swell of support began to spread to surrounding countries and BMG began to gear up for a European wide release. The ingredients were very unusual: an American band with Swedish songwriters and producers becoming German superstars. However, although it was fantastic that the boys had scored hits in Germany and their fame was spreading, England was becoming the focus of the whole worldwide Jive record label. This was not the usual way we released records and coordinated promotion campaigns. Most projects come out of America or England and gain some early success, and then the other countries' promotion campaigns are planned and timed around definite release dates. The German success made us all look at the campaign for The Backstreet Boys in a different way.

England had to come to the party quickly and break The Backstreet Boys, and we felt if that could happen then it would coordinate Europe in a better way, after which we could take the band back to the US as an international hit group and give them an enormous chance in their homeland.

Our main problem was that the UK has always had what had become known as Boy Bands. For a lot of the world markets this was a new concept, but in England it was not and we had lived through the biggest of them all, Take That. Robbie Williams had already left Take That and their runs of hits were coming to an end, although they were still tremendously popular. Nick Fleming and Matt Connolly as our main promotion people were called in and, with Tina and I, we set about forming a plan to release the first record in the UK. The first responses from radio and TV were as I had imagined they would be: 'Boy Bands are over. Take That finished that style of music, it will not happen again. Steve, you can't be serious, who would come with a boy band now?'

This appalling reaction caused Nick and Matt to suffer a lack of confidence, and I spoke with both Clive and Barry and honestly told them what we were up against. We would have to spend a lot more money than we had been used to doing on promotion, appearances and gigs, which would be tough and may take a little time. I asked Clive if he was sure he could go along with that. 'Do whatever you have to do', was his answer, 'but be sure you break the band.'

We decided to make October the month for our issue of 'We've Got It Going On', with a launch party planned two weeks before release. The band would come in, do any interviews we could get them and set the record up as best we could. I talked this over with Donna Wright and told her how difficult this was going to be given the UK's history of Boy Bands and the Take That effect. We had booked a club in Carnaby Street to stage our launch party and we had worked hard to get as many people as possible to the event from the media, including all the secretaries. I believed if the secretaries loved the band they would help us in the course of the next few months. When the night arrived not as many people showed up as we had hoped. The backlash to boy bands was beginning to tell, and even free food, drinks and a show had not caused the stampede we had hoped for. I got Andy, Tina, Nick, Matt and myself out in the street, stopping passers-by, and asking them to come to the party. Slowly, the place began to look a little more promising: I had even said to Andy 'pay passers by a fiver – just get them in.'

The band performed professionally and well. The evening was just about a success. The few people from radio we had managed to get there were impressed how The Backstreet Boys' routines were much more polished than their English counterparts – they were different and had at least put a question mark in the minds of radio. The TV reaction was much better, they could see that the boys would make good television, and the press reaction was even stronger than TV. The teen magazines had seen a group of good-looking lads that would photograph well, were fun and had a great stage show.

Our hard work brought a couple of breaks. Smash Hits liked the band and were operating their yearly tour in early December, which finished with a TV show broadcast live on a Sunday, a 'must see' for the UK pop fans. If you wanted your band on The Smash Hits Tour, the record company paid all the costs and more to Smash Hits – it was expensive, but it was the only way to put the band in front of the target audience. I spoke with Clive and Donna and said this is a 'must do', it may not deliver the hit, but it will start the ball rolling. Clive agreed, Donna set everything in motion, and thanks to our relationship with Will Smith he flew in to compere the show and was fantastic. We were also very fortunate to have Tim Byrne filming and he helped convince the people at Smash Hits that The Backstreets were worth a shot. Radio One were a tough nut to crack on this one, but they finally agreed to 'C' list 'We've Got It Going On.' The 'C' list on Radio One at the time was the third tier of the playlist and was used for artists or records that might hit, but which they were unsure about. It was by no means a guarantee of radio play, but being on the 'C' list meant that at least you had a chance.

Smash Hits started warming up their tour a few weeks in advance with photographs and stories about the Backstreet Boys. Radio One played the 'We've Got It Going On' single five times over a couple of weeks and TV started to show the video. It all came a little too late for the single to connect with the audience but we had made a dent. 'We've Got It Going On' came out in October and peaked at No 54.

The reaction from Europe was that we had failed miserably. America said it was early days, exactly as I had told them. I knew we had something going and with the tour to come the fan base could only increase. It is at times like these that Managing Directors earn their money, keeping the staff on the right track and pushing away the doubters from within their company, while maintaining the confidence of the band. We set the release date of 'I'll Never Break Your Heart' for December, just after the Smash Hits tour. I had no choice in this decision: we had to gamble that the tour would work, increase the fan base and propel the single into the chart. In realistic terms, December is totally the wrong time to launch a new band, it is when most records are sold in the year and established artists always prepare their albums and big hit singles for this period. But, the pressure was on and if we could just make the Top 40 it would give us a powerful chance for 1996.

The Backstreets came in and ripped the tour. Of the new acts they were by far the best and the teenagers, especially girls, loved them and claimed them for their own. The first signs of real support were seen on that tour and we had big hopes for the single. 'I'll Never Break Your Heart' then came out and under enormous pressure reached No 42 and then it dropped down the chart. We were gutted –

our big shot from the tour had failed. I studied the sales figures and totals over Christmas and New Year, and I soon began to realise that if we were to repeat the exercise in any other month of the year, the amount of records we had sold during that Christmas would firmly put this single in the Top 20. All was not lost.

The first six months of 1996 would be tough on the Backstreet issue. Our US company now thought we were failing and our European arm thought we already had failed. I maintained throughout the constant pressure that we were now close to a breakthrough, but everyone thought I was just talking a good game. Time, in due course, would tell who was right.

Out in Jamaica..:

Away from the pressures of Zomba, I started working with Yazz on her new project. We discussed the possibility of a 'lovers rock' album, a beautiful form of reggae music and always a passion for Yazz. I suggested we should try for UB40 to produce the record and I set about contacting their managers Mick Cator and David Harper. We travelled to Birmingham one Monday night and Yazz sang for the band. It was almost an audition, but Yazz sang her socks off and from that moment on the band were committed to recording the album. Dave Robinson joined our team and we set about getting a deal for the UB40 produced new Yazz album. The main companies were East West, a division of Warner Brothers, where the Managing Director was Max Hole, and Virgin Records where Ken Berry was Chairman. Dave and I had long conversations and meetings with both before deciding to go with Max Hole at East West. The deal was completed and we left the following day to record vocals in Jamaica, using Bob Marley's old studio in Ochos Rios. The basic tracks had been recorded in Birmingham, but we used Jamaican musicians to add to the vibe of the album. We managed to record ninety percent of the album and return to London to mix the tracks three weeks later. It had been a fabulous experience and the result would become an album to be proud of.

Adieu John Fruin – Bienvenue Lesley Rees:

Back at Zomba, through the summer, changes were happening again. The long and celebrated career of John Fruin was coming to a close. John had started working a four day week, then a three day week, and by now he just came into the office on a Monday. It was coming up to his sixty fifth-birthday and time for him to retire, although he would be retained as a consultant for the next few years. John and I always joked that I was so uncontrollable that his consultancy was based on being my minder and there may have been some truth in that statement. He alone was the one person who could get me to do things I did not want to. In the future, if Clive disliked something I was doing, there would be a lunch with John Fruin and he alone would, if need be, put me on the right track and keep the peace. John in my mind was on the same level as my father in my life: not to be questioned and I would do as I was asked. I would miss John's day-to-day influence and the meetings where I could bounce my ideas and refine the plans with his knowledge.

Lesley Rees, who had been assistant to Clive during his days in London and then to John Fruin, became my assistant and would continue to be so for the next nine years. I moved upstairs into John's old office, which was situated next to Lesley's, and a new era began. Lesley Rees was magnificent for me during the next nine years. She ran my office, made me look truly professional and was not slow to disagree with my ideas if she thought they were wrong. It was a partnership that would take Jive Records to unbelievable heights.

Impulse – Still continuing:

Meanwhile, Clive had insisted that I now report on the projects that the A & R team was working on, and the old questions about Impulse began to rise again. Despite reducing in size, the Impulse Promotion Company was still at the forefront of independent sales marketing and promotion. With the subsuming of Prime Time into the sales force and the closure of the club promotion company and the radio department, Impulse was purely an 'on the road' independent store operation, but as such, in its original format before expansion, it was still central to the record business, still making money and still obtaining hit records. I still liked the feedback from the team on all records going through the operation, and I believed it kept me fresh and on top of things at the important store level. Impulse achieved the No 1 slot on the singles chart three times during 1995, with 'Cotton Eyed Joe' by The Rednex on our own Internal affairs label in January, with 'Bombastic' by Shaggy on Virgin Records in September and with 'Gangsta's Paradise' by Coolio for Tommy Boy Records in October. Clive reluctantly accepted that it, and I as Chairman, could continue for now.

PWL – The end of the era:

The year of change had arrived at PWL. David Howells resigned and Warner Brothers employed Peter Price to become Managing Director of the label. Did Pete Waterman have much say in the decision? I don't think so. Peter Price was asked to create his own A & R policies and staff, which is quite unbelievable when you think about it, since Waterman was probably the most successful A & R man of the previous twenty years. Warners' decision to put him aside meant that Pete found himself with no control over his own company. Pete retreated into his office and his other companies. It is a well-known fact that he is a train buff, knows everything about trains and owns several train companies. If you were to ask, does Pete prefer trains or music, I would say trains would just edge it.

This slowdown in output from PWL hit Impulse. Pete was nowhere around, the records were not as good and were slowing in quantity and then Warners started to remove Impulse from the equation. Pete for the only time since I have known him disappeared and we rarely spoke during the year. I called a few times but all I got was, 'I'm playing trains. Warners have put me out to grass, I don't even belong in my own company.'

Jive still talkin':

Jive Records' year concluded with the launch of the new R. Kelly album, simply titled *R. Kelly*. The launch was held at George Martin's Air Studios in Hampstead. Rob spent the evening in a private room and rarely came out to meet the people from the press, radio and TV. I spent some time with him and encouraged him to meet a few people, but his shyness and disinterest was apparent. Nevertheless, Tina had organised a superb event and it worked like a dream as the album shot into the Top 20 at Christmas time and the sales helped to save our year and keep us in the game for the coming one.

Jive Records had also had some success through the year with new artists Smooth, Nuttin' Nyce and Zhane, compilation albums *Low Down Dirty Shame* from the movie, and our rap series titled *West 25th*. West 25 Street in New York was home to Jive US. Roddy also put together compilations from our Chicago studios, entitled *Chicago Club Classics*, and these albums sold reasonable amounts. Silvertone had its most successful album with *The Complete Stone Roses*, but the A & R for the label had come up short. Whiteout and Solar Race from the UK were failing after promising starts, Martin Dodd's Metal Molly from Europe failed and the US signings of Tupelo Honey and Jars of Clay were not fairing any better. My own personal A & R approaches had also failed in the short term but would bear fruit a little later. I had met and had lunch with Scott MacLachlan, who was A & R for Multiply Records, and I was direct with him right from the start that I wanted him to join me at Jive Records. Scott was having good success at Multiply, by licensing 12-inch singles and delivering hit records, and I knew that in Clive's school that was not the right way to approach the record business, however, I was sick of the A & R signings we had made without my approval and I just wanted to get on and get some hits. Scott at this time was happy where he was, but I told him at some time in the future he could always come and work for me.

1995 had its ups and downs, but I was happy with the rise of R. Kelly, the job we had done on Aaliyah, the No 1 single with The Rednex and *The Complete Stone Roses* album. The artists that we had signed to Jive, notably, R. Kelly and Will Smith, were reaching out beyond our record label. Robert was writing and producing for many artists including Janet Jackson and her brother Michael and, during 1995, Michael Jackson would hit No 1 in most countries with the R. Kelly written and produced 'You Are Not Alone.' The entire music community was recognising Robert's talent as a songwriter and producer. Will Smith was now making movies and his big breakthrough came in 1995 with *Bad Boys*. The last time I spoke with him was when he phoned to ask Tina and I to go and see *Six*

Degrees of Separation. By now, Jazzy Jeff & The Fresh Prince's contract had come to an end. Will signed as a solo artist to Sony, going on to rack up many hits with them, before some years later concentrating on movies. To this day, I am proud of Will, he was an incredibly hard worker and was not frightened of taking a chance. I see most of his new movies and he always makes me laugh. It was a great pleasure to know him for all those years and to play some part in what has become a wonderful career. And, without knowing it, it was Will who had saved my bacon with 'Boom! Shake The Room', enabling me to stay in charge of Jive Records. Thanks Will, and good luck.

The Impulse Roll Call of Hits for 1995

January			
Bump n Grind	R. Kelly	Jive	No 8
Cotton Eye Joe	Rednex	Internal Affairs	No 1
I Need Somebody	Loveland	Eastern Bloc	No 21
Glory Box	Portishead	Go Discs	No 13
This Time Of The Year	Runrig	Chrysalis	No 38
February			
Don't Give Me Your Life	Alex Party	Systematic	No 2
I've Got A Little Something For You	MN8	Columbia	No 2
Jackie's Racing	Whiteout	Silvertone	No 72
Shame	Zhane	Jive	No 66
March			
Age Ain't Nothin But A Number	Aaliyah	Jive	No 32
Old Pop In An Oak	Rednex	Internal Affairs	No 12
Here I Go	2 Unlimited	PWL Continental	No 22
Selling Jesus	Skunk Anansie	One Little Indian	No 46
April			
Fools Gold	Stone Roses	Silvertone	No 25
Chains	Tina Arena	Columbia	No 6
If You Love Me	Brownstone	MJJ	No 8
For All We Know	Nikki French	Bags Of Fun	No 42
Not Over Yet	Grace	Perfecto	No 6
Love City Groove	Love City Groove	Planet 3	No 7
May			
Down With The Clique	Aaliyah	Jive	No 33

The 4 Play EP	R. Kelly	Jive	No 23
The Complete Stone Roses LP	Stone Roses	Silvertone	No 4
Army Of Me	Bjork	One Little Indian	No 10
Living Next Door To Alice	Roy Chubby Brown	NOW	No 3
Move Your Body	Eurogroove	Avex	No 29
This Is How We Do It	Montel Jordan	Def Jam	No 11
Yes	McAlmont & Butler	Hut	No 8
Surrender Your Love	Nightcrawlers	Final Vinyl	No 7
June			
Reverend Black Grape	Black Grape	Radio Active	No 9
Marta's Song	Deep Forest	Columbia	No 26
Right In The Night	Jam & Spoon	Epic	No 10
Don't Make Me Wait	Loveland	Eastern Bloc	No 22
Down For Whatever	Nuttin Nyce	Jive	No 62
Secret Love	Daniel O'Donnell	Ritz	No 28
Love Love Love	Rollo	Cheeky	No 32
I Can Dream	Skunk Anansie	One Little Indian	No 41
July			
Mind Blowin'	Smooth	Jive	No 36
Humpin' Around	Bobby Brown	MCA	No 8
Did You Ever Really Love Me	Nikki French	Bags Of Fun	No 55
In The Summertime	Shaggy	Virgin	No 5
Bite It LP	Whiteout	Silvertone	No 71
August			
Isobel	Bjork	One Little Indian	No 23
Salva Mea	Faithless	Cheeky	No 30
Hope Street	The Levellers	China	No 12
Froggy Style	Nuttin Nyce	Jive	No 68
Waterfalls	TLC	LaFace	No 4
September			
The Thing I Like	Aaliyah	Jive	No 33
Can I touch You There	Michael Bolton	Columbia	No 6
Stayin' Alive	N'Trance	All Around The World	No 2
The Wonder Of Love	Loveland	Eastern Bloc	No 53
Bombastic	Shaggy	Virgin	No 1

Charity	Skunk Anansie	One Little Indian	No 40
October			
Wild And Free	Rednex	Internal Affairs	No 55
We've Got It Going On	The Backstreet Boys	Jive	No 54
It's Summertime, Let It Get Into You	Smooth	Jive	No 46
Do Whats Good For Me	2 Unlimited	PWL Continental	No 16
Gangsta's Paradise	Coolio	Tommy Boy	No 1
Brown Sugar	D'Angelo	Cooltempo	No 24
Missing	Everything But The Girl	Blanco Y Negro	No 3
Flavour Of The Old School	Beverley Knight	Dome	No 33
Where The Wild Roses Grow	Nick Cave & Kylie Minogue	Mute	No 11
November			
You Remind Me Of Something	R. Kelly	Jive	No 24
R. Kelly LP	R. Kelly	Jive	No 18
Hits Unlimited	2 Unlimited	PWL Continental	No 27
It's Oh So Quiet	Bjork	One Little Indian	No 4
Sentimental	Deborah Cox	Arista	No 34
I Believe	Happy Clappers	Shindig	No 7
I Need Somebody remix	Loveland	Eastern Bloc	No 38
Hungry Heart	Bruce Springsteen	Columbia	No 28
December			
I'll Never Break Your Heart	The Backstreet Boys	Jive	No 42
Boom! Shake The Room remix	Jazzy Jeff and The Fresh Prince	Jive	No 40
Insomnia	Faithless	Cheeky	No 27

Michael Haughton (Manager) Me, Aaliyah and Tina Wisby

The Backstreet Boys

CHAPTER 22
1996 AND 1997

Final jigsaw piece:

Jive Records started 1996 focusing on the R. Kelly project. Robert once again made a trip to England to stage four massive concerts at Manchester, Birmingham and Wembley Arena. We followed up the shows by releasing the single 'You Remind Me Of Something', which peaked at No 23 and continued the massive sales of the album R. Kelly. These sales provided the company with much needed turnover, but other hit singles from other projects were hard to find.

The Backstreet Boys were continuing to grow around Europe and the news of that growth and continued support from *Smash Hits* magazine and other teen publications was constantly improving the support for the band. We completely believed that we had collected enough fans to launch an attack on the UK chart and finally break the band.

The sales of Silvertone albums from Buddy Guy, John Lee Hooker, John Mayall and the Stone Roses catalogue also kept Silvertone's head just above water, but the new signings were selling very few records or not selling at all.

Mike Pedan and Max Bloom had now settled into their UK A & R positions and were making their first signings, which became a pleasant surprise for me. I thought that both bands were in the right area for the time and capable of making good albums that would give us a real shot. Crustation started work on their album *Bloom*, and Smoke City began on *Flying Away*. Both albums would not be ready until 1997, but work was under way.

Clive arrived in the UK that year for a prolonged summer stay. His main objective was to buy seventy-five percent of the independent distributor Pinnacle Records. This move would enable Jive Records to compete on a level playing field with the major companies in Europe. Clive also gave his first interview in twenty years to *Music Business International*. It was the most in depth interview he has ever given. He disliked interviews and photographs immensely and I believe he only did this one to publicise the growth of Zomba and attract artists, managers and labels to our group as a real alternative. *Music Business International* saw this interview as a real coup and publicised the magazine extensively. Most people in the industry wanted to read about the reclusive Clive Calder and the quiet growth of Zomba.

The Calder effect:

Clive Calder grew up in South Africa and learned to play bass guitar after hearing Jack Bruce in Cream with Eric Clapton and Ginger Baker. During the late Sixties, in his teens, he played in local Johannesburg Motown covers bands six nights a week, often performing for five hours a night. During the day he would play bass at recording sessions and, after gaining some studio experience, he gradually moved into record production. Cover versions of US and UK records were recorded and manufactured by Clive and Ralph Simon and sold into the local black areas. A big hit in the US would be re-recorded in a rougher style with a local black vocalist and an acetate would then be produced (a one off record) and played in a local store or local club where Clive and Ralph would judge the reaction and enquiries on the record. They would then decide whether or not to produce copies. This was a dangerous occupation in those days in South Africa, I have heard many stories about Clive and Ralph running through the bush clutching their earnings whilst being chased after a concert had gone wrong. Some of those stories were myth, but some are probably true.

Clive himself says he knew the black areas of South Africa better than he knew the white areas. The production of the cover versions were sometimes tested in Soweto, in the store at the railway station, and Clive being white was not allowed in Soweto after 7 pm but would enter in the back of a van with blankets over him until the test single arrived at the store. The acetate of the latest production was then played to the people as they arrived home from work. Clive would judge the response and enquiries before then proceeding to manufacture the record the following day – or not. A good response meant manufacture, a bad response meant the production was scrapped. Clive and Ralph's productions and business style was considered highly unusual, sometimes illegal and poorly regarded by the local music industry establishment. However, they obviously made enough money and made their first attempt at moving to the UK in 1969, which would fail.

This started the next phase of Clive's career. He joined EMI South Africa as an A & R man. EMI had noticed this 'street trader' and for eighteen months Clive worked and learnt about life and records within the corporate structure of EMI. When he left EMI he started his own CCP Records label, which specialised in local black music, and he used the knowledge gained from his early productions and from working with EMI. One of his major problems was getting airplay on his black productions and this led both Clive and Ralph into concert promotions to publicise their artists.

In all the time I have known Clive I have always seen him work all hours during the day and into the night – probably a slow starter in the mornings, but once he gets into his stride around midday, the work goes on until late into the evening. The same was true back in the early seventies. Always busy and always on the move with several projects on the go, this led to him being unable to attend a recording session and calling another local musician to step in. The other local musician was Robert John 'Mutt' Lange, who completed the production that day and would from that day on be Clive's main producer and songwriter.

CCP Records made a lot of money, no-one really knows how much, but the story goes that Clive was a millionaire by the time he was twenty-one years old. I have no idea if that is totally true or not or if Clive was a rand, dollar or pound millionaire, but certainly the proceeds of CCP Records were enough to enable another attempt at England. Mutt Lange travelled first and then a few weeks later in 1974 both Clive and Ralph arrived in the UK

The first few years were tough in the UK as they both began to get to know the industry. They managed the Birmingham band City Boy, a group I was very aware of coming from that neck of the woods myself. City Boy's biggest hit was '5705', a record Birmingham music fans, including me, were very proud of. I remember playing the single on my radio show and at warm-ups before my gigs in Birmingham. City Boy did manage to tour the US as the record did well in America and Clive, as their manager, was on tour with them. I remember him telling me years later that he was on that tour of the states and the thought came to him, 'what the hell am I doing here?' Clive was right, as he would be most of the time in the coming years, his time should be spent in an office, wheeling, dealing and building companies based around music.

Not long after returning to England from the tour Clive started a publishing company called Zomba, taking the name of a small town in South Africa. Zomba Music slowly began to grow, and Clive and Ralph hustled records and publishing to build up the company. The Village People were a sub-published act by Zomba on the condition they found a record deal in the UK, and the story goes that twelve companies turned them down before a deal was achieved. Zomba Music, after several years, had made enough money for Clive to invest in a studio with offices above in Willesden. In all the years I have known Clive all our offices around the world have been built around studios. He once told me 'When you're in trouble in the record business the only place to go to get out of trouble is back in the studio.' Just one of the lessons I learnt from a master of the game.

It would be 1981 before Zomba Music created its own label, Jive Records. The label's first release 'The Lion Sleeps Tonight' by Tightfit, was to go to No 1 in the UK, I was working at and owned a share of the company Promopeople at the time and we were contracted to work the single.

As I have said in an earlier chapter of this book, during my initial contact with Jive Records I was undoubtedly impressed with the way the company operated.

They seemed a straight up, unpretentious organisation and I enjoyed working on their records, which began to increase in number. After leaving Promopeople and looking to set up a new independent promotion company that would eventually become Impulse, I was looking for a partner and Jive Records was my chosen label for their direct and upfront style. I remember the first meeting I had with Clive, it was in the office that many years later would become mine as Managing Director of Jive. I went through my thoughts on the new company, and Clive asked piercing and direct questions before setting up a follow-up meeting with John Fruin, with the added note that if John said 'yes' to the idea, we would proceed.

When we began work on the setting up of Impulse, Samantha Fox was having her first hit and Billy Ocean had been signed, but Clive told me many years later that around that time he felt the label and the business could have gone either way – it was tough going, but Jive Records and Zomba Music managed to stay afloat and this enabled me to set up Impulse. It seems that after 1983 Jive's output became a constant stream of albums and singles that sold well – however, if you had been in there at the sharp end it was always a pressure cooker to get those records that sold time and time again. Jive Records had no catalogue to tide it over months without a hit single or album.

Clive always commanded great respect from the people that worked at Zomba and Jive. He was a musician, record producer and tremendous businessman. This is a rare package in the music business. Richard Branson, I would say, was a business man, but not a great record man. Chris Wright and Terry Ellis, who built Chrysalis Records combined their talents – Chris in business, Terry in music. The same can be said of Herb Albert and Jerry Moss in the building of A & M Records, Herb with music and Jerry with business. There are few people in the history of the record business who have had both disciplines. If you were searching for people with both disciplines then you would mention Berry Gordy in the building of Motown and possibly, Ahmet Ertegan building Atlantic Records – they have been few and far between.

'Mutt' Lange and I used to joke about Clive, believing that if he cut his leg, brain not blood would gush out. It seemed to us that his body was completely full of brain. In the early days, it was Clive alone who made the signings of Billy Ocean, Kool Mo Dee, Teddy Riley, KRS-One, Too Short, and A Tribe Called Quest. Later, a team of A & R people were hired, but, in reality, they were finders of talent for Clive to judge, and only he would decide if the act was signed and invested in. Jive Records was built on Clive's musical ability and business acumen and its success has been assisted by a stable management around the world that he has personally overseen. In the MBI interview it was stated that Steven Howard had been with the company 16 years, Barry Weiss 14 years, Bert Meyer 10 years, Neil Portnow, in Los Angeles 9 years and me 13 years. We all knew each other well and this gave us an advantage to see the company as a worldwide drive to success. I knew more about the record business in the US and Europe than any UK Managing Directors, and I had constant information from both Barry and Bert, who I would think were more knowledgeable than most about the UK record business. We all travelled the world together and in planning meetings about the direction of the company, the players were Clive, Barry, Bert and myself.

When new people joined the company, we would always say if they last a year then they may stay forever. Zomba was a stressful place to work in. There were few political games and it was all about getting the hits, increasing the turnover and, most importantly, making profit. In working at Zomba you simply could not busk it or pull the wool over Clive. If you managed to flannel him and he took it, only a matter of days later he would think about what you had said, realise he had been flannelled, and then the penalty was a colossal dressing down. Clive insisted on the truth even if the truth was bad news. He told me 'no matter how bad the news, you at least know where you are and have a chance to fix it. With flannel you are fighting your way through clouds and there is no chance of finding the problem.'

Deal of the Year:

Music Week reported the buying of Pinnacle Records as the deal of the year. Zomba bought seventy-five percent of Pinnacle and Steve Mason retained twenty-five percent. He remained Chairman, managing Pinnacle separately from the rest of the Zomba Group, under a five year service agreement. Zomba stated the deal sealed its position as the world's biggest independent music group. There was much speculation over how much Zomba had paid for Pinnacle and *Music Week's* best guess was that Pinnacle's value was about 12 million pounds and Zomba had paid around 15 million for seventy-five percent of the company. I actually do not know the final figures but what I do know is that getting two extremely tough negotiators together to make the deal could not have been easy. The upside, however, was magnificent. Pinnacle controlled distribution for Germany and Holland, as well as the UK, and this gave our record labels a foothold in Europe with our own distribution. The rise of The Backstreet Boys in Europe for the first time gave us a real opportunity to become a worldwide operation and take on the major record companies around the world.

The industry names all spoke about the deal. Derek Green at China Records said 'Zomba is now well placed to become the seventh major and will give strength to the independent sector.'

Roadrunner Records' Managing Director, Jimmy Devlin, said 'Zomba's business interests are so diverse and I think this is a good business philosophy.' Cliff Dane of Media Research Publishing stated 'The move makes Zomba a significant force and could be the springboard to acquire more repertoire.' John Craig of First Night Records said 'Calder and Mason together could make a dynamic team and there could be a germ of a pan European distribution network there, because they already own Rough Trade Germany and Rough Trade Holland.'

Whatever anyone said, it was without doubt the biggest deal of the year and would strike fear into all our competitors. It was even more frightening as we had never courted the press and had seemed to sneak up on the blind side and overnight become an awesome power. For me, the real trick had been the timing. Clive spent so much time strategising and thinking and his timing had always been immaculate. He knew exactly when our licensing deals around the world were coming up for renegotiation and he saw that The Backstreet Boys' European sales were about to explode and could help finance and put real record sales through the new joint company. The timing, most of all, was pure genius.

On a personal note, and for Jive UK it was manna from heaven, as Steve Mason and I had been having hits together since 1983, Pinnacle and Impulse had grown to industry leaders in their own fields, and our friendship had blossomed with that success. During the Eighties, we had teamed up with Pete Waterman and together had enjoyed the success of PWL Records and the Stock Aitken Waterman explosion with Kylie Minogue, Jason Donovan and the rest. Zomba and Jive were now in the big time, the pressure, always great, would now increase, we needed more hits and album sales, and England was once again the focal point of the group.

Pete comes back:

When you look back over a career you can see certain moments or happenings change the course of what is to come. One of those moments or happenings was about to occur. In March 1996, Warner Brothers politely told Pete Waterman that he should resign. His five-year deal was coming to a close and there was no will from Warner Brothers to continue. Pete had, by now, been playing with his trains for eighteen months, but on release from his contract he was fired up to succeed in the record business again. He rounded up the staff that had remained at PWL studios and were loyal to him, and he began to start his assault on the record charts again. He was cold in the UK record marketplace and there was not a queue of record labels wanting his skills, but through an old contact he was put in touch with VCI Recordings and was asked to record a single for Manchester United to celebrate getting to the FA Cup Final.

Early in May Pete called me and said 'Steve, I've got a record coming out on VCI, it's Manchester United's FA Cup Final single and they really don't know how to promote it, can you get down there and sort it out, it's a hit and I can't let them screw it up.' I knew Peter Stack at VCI and arranged a meeting. Peter is a charming man and we sorted out how we should go about working the Man U single with Impulse. 'Move Move Move (The Red Tribe)' by Manchester United Football Club would become a No 6 UK hit single and sell 400,000 copies. Pete had started on the long road back and scored a hit with his very first attempt.

We went to dinner to celebrate and catch up. Pete brought me up to date with what he had been doing. To compound his problems, his new bank manager hated Stock Aitken Waterman records and thought Pete was finished as a hit maker and, on top of that VCI were not paying him for the production or royalties for 'Move, Move, Move.' I knew Pete so well after all those years, if the world was against him and he was fired up I would put my money on him, however if he was just doing a few records and was then going to go back to his trains I would say he could be a bad bet. In his autobiography *I Wish I Was Me*, Pete remembers I asked him 'Why don't you retire and just enjoy the money you have made?' Pete found this question incomprehensible – why and how could he stop doing what he loved?

It probably took Pete years to get over my asking that question and it still stays with him to this day. I just wanted to be sure that my old pal still had that fire burning in his stomach, because if I was to go out on a limb for Pete I wanted to know he would give it everything he had. If he didn't, then he would bring the two of us down. At that dinner I suggested we work together and do a joint label deal with Zomba and Pete was instantly excited and wanted in. However, there was one condition. Pete said, 'We should have done this years ago. Here's my condition: if I tell you black is green or water flows up stream, you have to trust me.'

In Pete's world he had delivered hits when people thought he was mad. He wanted total trust in his ideas and one hundred percent backing, even when other people at the label would doubt him. I agreed without a problem. I knew that Pete is hard to handle and he can go off at what seems a tangent, but ultimately he or his idea will come back to the right path. He just works things out differently to others and you have to accept that or don't do a deal with him. I too had a condition, though. 'I do the business, the sales, the marketing, and the promotion, unquestioned.' Pete agreed.

I returned to Zomba to lobby for the deal with Waterman, certain issues were with me on this deal. I had moaned for nearly four years about the A & R people I had been forced to manage and Clive had once asked me:

'Why do you beat up the A & R people so badly?' I responded:

'I don't pick them, they are not real hit makers, most talk a good game without ever getting their hands dirty and they rest on their contracts. They only try when they are in their last year of contract, purely to get another one. I don't decide if they get another one or not, and for the most part their employment and operations seem to have little to do with me or my wishes.'

That little speech was about to pay dividends.

After the retirement of John Fruin, Nick Howe had taken over the running of most parts of the company without interfering with the labels, except on an accountancy level. Nick, without doubt, is the best financial brain I have ever met. Even Clive admitted Nick was better than him at finance. Nick had thankfully changed our business affairs department and to replace Mark Furman he had found Michael Smith from Shilling and Lom. I was given the courtesy of meeting and having lunch with Michael before any decisions were made. I liked Michael instantly and over the years he grew into one of the best record company lawyers in our business. He joined the company and played a major part in putting a deal together with Pete. Now, for the first time in my seven years at Zomba, I was connected to the business affairs department and no longer was I put down or not helped to make artist and record deals. Michael was there to help me succeed, the relief was immense, and our partnership would bear endless fruit.

Nick Howe, Michael Smith, Pete and I worked on the deal and agreed within weeks that the label umbrella was to be called EBUL/Jive. I never thought that was a pretty name, but it came about because the labels we would issue product on were established PWL brands. They were named after a couple of record stores Pete owned in the north of England, Eastern Bloc Records and Unity Records. Combining Eastern Bloc (EB) Unity (U) and Limited gave us EBUL/Jive Records. Pete liked it, perhaps because he has been called a bull in a china shop many times. Our first release was a remix of Atlantic Ocean's 'Waterfall', a dance record that made No 21 on the chart and got us moving some six weeks after the deal was signed.

The band Kaleef, who were just about to be dropped by London Records, had also approached Pete. They played Pete an idea they had about a rap over the Stranglers' hit 'Golden Brown.' The band knew it was a good idea, but couldn't get it to work. Pete went into the studio with it and the record achieved a No 22 position for Unity/Jive records in the busy December period. Two hits in the first three months of the deal – now that's an A & R man, right in there where it's hot and dirty, mining for gold and finding the first couple of pieces from a hunch.

Breaking The Backstreet Boys:

Apart from all the business dealings, the breaking of The Backstreet Boys in the UK was the biggest job of the year. The band had continued to grow in Europe and their album would be coming in August or September. England was lagging behind, though, and the timing was becoming enormously tight. We had to issue the album in Europe soon and if the UK were not up to speed, there was a chance that The Backstreets would then not break England and, even worse, have no platform from which to attack the US. I received one of those 'This just has to happen' phone calls from Clive. I have to say, I was confident, I believed and could see the fan base growing. All divisions of Jive around the world were doing their best to assist me, and in an attempt to get a more English sounding record to break the UK, Martin Dodd recorded 'Get Down (You're The One For Me)' with The Backstreets, with a producer who was not one of ours. To me, this track sounded like a European view of an English pop record and missed it by a mile. It was an attempt to help me out of a tough predicament, but I hated the record, and to this day it is The Backstreet Boys' worst ever single to me. Nevertheless, it would be the one we would issue as our third attempt at breaking the act.

'Get Down (You're The One For Me)', released in June '96, exploded into the Top 20. It peaked at No 14 and I believed this was because the fans were waiting after having been convinced of The Backstreet Boys on the previous year's Smash Hits Tour. The door was open; we were in and knew exactly what to do next.

There was some relief spreading from all parts of the US and Europe. Clive phoned to ask where we were. I told him we were in the door, and I now intended to make a quick re-issue of 'We've Got It Going On', which I believed was a Top 10 record, and then set up for the album and re-issue 'I'll Never Break Your Heart.' Clive asked if I was sure about the re-issue policy, I said I was completely sure and I had done it before with 'She's Got That Vibe' and R. Kelly.

'OK what do you need?'

'I need the boys for Smash Hits *TV show at Christmas, if and when I get it, and I need them to fly in for a day here and there to record* Top of the Pops *and do some magazine photo shoots and maybe a Saturday morning TV appearance.'*

Clive said he would let Barry know.

'I'm supporting you Steve, make sure you get it.'

Get it we did. The boys flew in and out throughout the next six months for radio, TV and press, and in August 'We've Got It Going On' finally peaked at No 3 on the UK Top 40. In November 'I'll Never Break Your Heart' was to peak at No 8 in the UK Top 10. In between those successes, the Backstreets' first album *The Backstreet Boys* would enter the album chart at No 12 and just keep on selling throughout the year. The timing was immaculate. Pinnacle Records was buzzing as we hit the big time with The Backstreet Boys, Jive Records staff knew they had accomplished something special and overnight the pressure of breaking The Backstreet Boys moved across the Atlantic to Barry in the US. We had come a long way from dropping fivers to people in Carnaby Street to come see this new band The Backstreet Boys.

Impulse – Sunset:

Through 1996 the Impulse Promotion Company had still maintained a high level of business, but the marketplace had changed. Independent record stores were now only nine percent of the chart. The growth of major chain record stores had started to kill the independent sector, with Woolworths, HMV, Virgin and Our Price now controlling ninety percent of the chart. These companies had taken the Impulse idea of charging for store space of single releases and they had developed it to a new level. Each week they would add around fifteen new releases to their own Top 75 singles and if you were not in their chart you could not get to the main market. This caused almost an auction for their store space. If a major chain changed fifteen records a week, so that fifteen older records slipped out of the Top 75, this allowed fifteen spaces for new releases. In any given week there are six or seven 'must stock' new releases, and these singles will be follow-ups to previous hit singles with a guaranteed sales base or they will be really established artists, again, with a guaranteed sales base. This left six, seven or eight places remaining for the industry's new records. At that time, maybe a hundred new releases were being issued each week and a hundred into six, seven or eight does not fit well, hence those spaces became incredibly valuable. Record companies went for the big game as they must and so investment went into major chain stores rather than the independent stores or companies like Impulse that serviced those stores.

Another problem for the Impulse client base was that over the past couple of years Virgin Records, Chrysalis Records, A & M Records and Island Records had been bought by the major companies and reduced the pool of records available to work. In the early stages, the majors had just too many records for their own promotion teams to handle and so Impulse had not felt the effect, but now, with the change in philosophy and the growth of major chain retailers, their teams could cope much more easily with the reduced volume of releases put through their teams.

We had been slowly reducing the staffing costs of the company to reach a level of profitability, but with the decline in releases coming through our doors even that could not stop the slide in income. Impulse had been a profit making company every year since its inception in 1983 and now 1996 was a breakeven year. It was the first year in which we had not made a profit. The deal Clive and I had made in 1991 to keep the company going for five years as long as it was profitable had concluded, and both the financial position, plus the timing of the end of our agreement, would put the focus back on Impulse in the following year. Furthermore, Zomba's purchase of Pinnacle meant that they already had a much larger sales force of representatives on the road and a much larger pre-selling operation on the phones.

Impulse would be looked at in 1997, of that I was sure. I was just hoping that we could start the year well and that the market would change in our favour, even though everything suggested that it would not. Meanwhile, during 1996, Impulse had still been involved in many hit records and had reached the No 1 position twice: in March with The Prodigy and the memorable 'Firestarter' for XL Recordings, and again in November with a re-issue of The Prodigy's 'Breathe.'

The full roll call of hits follows:

January			
Rollerblade	Nick Heyward	Epic	No 37
Single Girl	Lush	4AD	No 21
World Of Good	Saw Doctors	Shamtown	No 15
Anything	3T	MJJ	No 2
Change Your Mind	Upside Down	World	No 11
February			
Smoke Gets In Your Eyes	John Alford	Love This	No 13
Hyperballad	Bjork	One Little Indian	No 8
Lifted (re-issue)	Lighthouse Family	Wild Card	No 4
March			
Down Low Nobody Has To Know	R. Kelly	Jive	No 23
Love Groove	Smooth	Jive	No 46
Firestarter	Prodigy	XL Recordings	No 1
Soul Provider	Michael Bolton	Columbia	No 35
Stupid Girl	Garbage	Mushroom	No 4
Let's Whip It Up	Sleaze Sisters	Pulse 8	No 46
Always Music	Westbam	Low Spirit	No 51
April			
Goldfinger	Ash	Infectious	No 5
X Files	DJ Dado	ZYX	No 8
Baby Lee	John Lee Hooker	Silvertone	No 65
Love Is The Drug remix	Roxy Music	EG	No 33
Everytime I Fall In Love	Upside Down	World	No 18
May			
Blue Moon	John Alford	Love This	No 9
Peach	Gloria Esterfan	Epic	No 15
Rappaz R. N. Dainja	KRS One	Jive	No 47
Night To Remember	911	Ginga	No 38

Move Move Move	Manchester United Football Team	VCI	No 6
June			
Get Down, You're The One For Me	The Backstreet Boys	Jive	No 14
Thank God It's Friday	R. Kelly	Jive	No 14
Mysterious Girl	Peter Andre	Mushroom	No 2
Something For The Weekend	Divine Comedy	Setanta	No 14
That Girl	Maxi Priest	Virgin	No 15
Female Of The Species	Space	Gut	No 14
July			
Undercover Lover	Smooth	Jive	No 41
1nce Again	A Tribe Called Quest	Jive	No 34
Tattva	Kula Shaker	Columbia	No 4
Exodus Live	The Levellers	China	No 24
August			
We've Got It Going On (re-issue)	The Backstreet Boys	Jive	No 3
Beats Rhymes and Life LP	A Tribe Called Quest	Jive	No 28
Virtual Insanity	Jamiroquai	Sony S2	No 3
Love Sensation	911	Ginga	No 21
Everybody's Free	Rozalla	Pulse 8	No 30
September			
Backstreet Boys LP	The Backstreet Boys	Jive	No 12
Footsteps	Daniel O'Donnell	Ritz	No 25
Teenage Angst	Placebo	Elevator Music	No 30
October			
You're Gorgeous	Baby Bird	Echo	No 3
Trigger Hippie	Morcheeba	Indochina	No 40
Twisted	Skunk Anansie	One Little Indian	No 26
November			
I'll Never Break Your Heart (re-issue)	The Backstreet Boys	Jive	No 8
Stressed Out	A Tribe Called Quest	Jive	No 38
Waterfall (re-issue)	Atlantic Ocean	Eastern Bloc	No 21
Breathe (re-issue)	The Prodigy	XL Recordings	No 1

If	John Alford	Love This	No 21
Possibly Maybe	Bjork	One Little Indian	No 13
Don't Make Me Wait	911	Ginga	No 10
December			
Garage Flower LP	The Stone Roses	Silvertone	No 58
Golden Brown	Kaleef	Unity	No 22
Don't Cry For Me Argentina	Mike Flowers Pops	Love This	No 30
Cosmic Girl	Jamiroquai	Sony S2	No 6

A momentous time – of experimentation, triumph and personal loss:

1997 began with a hit for the Backstreet Boys. The song 'Quit Playing Games With My Heart' would eventually just miss out on the No 1 spot and peak at No 2. The Backstreet Boys were now a hit making band in the UK, with a huge following, and it had been a long and dedicated haul to achieve this position. 'Quit Playing Games With My Heart' had not been intended to be a single from the album, but as the track had begun to receive increased plays on radio throughout Europe an unforeseen demand had arisen for it. Brian Littrell had originally sung lead vocal on the album version from start to finish, but we had noticed on other tracks performed at gigs and on TV that when Nick Carter had a lead part on a song the audience of young girls went ballistic. Nick had become the darling of 12, 13, 14 and 15 year-old girls and, although they liked all the boys, Nick, being of the same age group, was their hero. During a trip to New York, Clive, Barry, Bert and I sat with the band and talked over 'Quit Playing Games.' We felt that if we went back in the studio and got Nick to sing the first verse of the song, this would create an enormous audience boost of noise whenever the track started and Nick stepped forward to sing. In many groups, such a request would have brought on ego trouble, but The Backstreet Boys were professional and thoughtful and Brian understood completely and agreed instantly to the change of vocal on the first verse. We immediately flew to Stockholm for the re-recording of the first verse with Nick and the result was as expected: the song would start and when Nick moved forward all hell broke loose. 'Quit Playing Games' rocketed up the charts around Europe dragging the album along with it and accumulating enormous sales and revenue.

Our operations were forever expanding in scope. There was a lot of travelling, with two visits in the first two months of 1997 to Cologne, where we had opened a new German office for Jive Records as a result of the success of the Backstreet Boys, and a trip to Singapore in January to present new product for our licensees in the Far East region, where a new office was opened by Paul Palliello. The company was growing at a rapid rate of knots and almost daily, Clive, Barry, Bert and I were in constant touch to plan the expansion around the world.

The EBUL deal with Pete Waterman, so successful in its birth at the end of the previous year, was slow to yield results during 1997. Kaleef were signed and we would issue singles in the second half of the year, and Tina Cousins had also been signed, but the right record had not appeared as yet. Pete was working hard with Mark Topham and Karl Twigg, the new PWL producers, and they showed real signs of being able to produce to the standards we required, but they had not gained enough experience or belief in Pete's system. It would take another year before they were to hit the gong.

February saw my mother return to hospital and, although we did not know it at the time, my dear old Mom would not return home. She spent some time in Walsall Manor Hospital, where she always said she was well looked after, and then onto the Walsall Hospice where all the staff were fantastic with her. Through March and April I went to Walsall Hospice to see Mom every Saturday, and when I could arrange a midweek visit I would go then too. The staff had looked after my Mom so well that she asked if I would bring copies of 'I Believe I Could Fly' by R. Kelly, so she could give them to the nurses.

R. Kelly had written 'I Believe I Can Fly' for the movie *Spacejam* starring Michael Jordan and The Looney Tunes Cast. Robert had not written for a movie before and it somehow freed him from writing R. Kelly designed songs or R&B songs of a similar style for other artists. I believe he was also inspired to work with his all time hero, Michael Jordan, and the combination produced one of those classic songs that go on forever. 'I Believe I Can Fly' is of all the songs and records I have been involved in by far the best known. Everyone knows that song, many artists have tried to cover it, and it is without doubt one of the most uplifting songs of all time, showing the depth of talent within R. Kelly. The record went to No 1 in the UK during March of 1997 and it was a favourite of my Mom's. It was the only record she ever asked me for and when the nurses at the Walsall Hospice got their copies my Mom was proud that her son was at No 1 with one of his records. Today whenever I hear that record on the radio, it brings back my Mom for just a few minutes. Thank you, Robert Kelly.

My mother's cancer spread quickly. As the weeks went by, she grew progressively weaker. One Saturday, as I arrived, the Matron called me into her office as I made my way to my Mom's bed. She told me that if I had anything I wanted to say to my Mom I should say it today as it would be doubtful that she would be here next Saturday. I was thankful for the information, but it knocked me sideways – I couldn't get my head around the realisation that this might be the last time I would see my Mom. She had been moved into a small private room, and as I reeled into the room from the information I tried to brighten my face, but she had deteriorated in the last seven days and although she recognised me and held out her hand, she was barely with me. I sat there for a couple of hours: Mom came around for seconds and then slept – by this time I think she was so full of morphine that she only had seconds of reality. Just the week before, although weak she had still been aware and talkative. She had told me she was proud of my achievements and that my Dad would have been too. She had also asked me not to play in Chris Marsh's Testimonial match at Walsall, she felt that professional footballers were too good for me now and I would get hurt. I told her I would be playing, but not to worry, I would come through just fine. She was disappointed, but said 'OK, but just be careful.' It was the final conversation I had with my Mom. I just sat with her.

I returned to work and fully expected Mom to be there the following weekend. I had planned to go to Walsall as usual. On Wednesday morning, Lesley came in my office and said 'Your sister's on the phone.' I knew before I spoke with Helen that Mom had gone. I went downstairs to the first floor where there was a fire escape; the smokers at Jive always went there for a cigarette as the offices were 'no smoking.' Fortunately, there was no one there and I lit up a cigarette to steady myself. Andy Richmond came bursting through the door and ripped into some problem that needed my instant reaction. I tried to listen, but could not focus. I said 'Andy, you've got to give me a few minutes, my Mom just died.' 'Sorry Mate', and Andy disappeared.

Since the death of my father at such a young age, my Mom had overcome so many difficulties and she had been the making of me. Without her I would not have been a success. Mom instilled into me that anything was possible, that I should never give in no matter what the odds were and that life's mantra would be work hard and play hard. All simple, direct philosophies and absolutely clear. I lived my life by those philosophies. Thanks, Mom.

Mom's funeral was on 14th May 1997; my sister Helen put the whole thing together as I was away in London and a bit of a mess with the whole thing. The day went well and I saw a lot of my mother's and father's friends from many years before come to pay their respects. I thank them all, I think Mom would have been pleased. We had a small reception after the funeral, where mainly family came to spend a few minutes, and then it all seemed over in an instant. My Mom and Dad have lived on through my sister and I, we remember them well and I can still recollect conversations with both of them through my life. I still miss them and I guess everybody has the same feelings towards their own parents.

Bread winner:

During the first few days of March, each year, a group of music business professionals would embark on a four day golf tournament at La Manga in Spain. I had been invited to the first tournament in 1996, but had been unable to attend and so made my debut in the event in 1997. It was won that year by the organiser and Chairman of Pinnacle Records, Steve Mason. On the third night Clive called me in the hotel and stayed on the phone so long that I missed the dinner that evening. Clive wanted to know if I knew the band Bread, as there was a possibility we could get their catalogue from Warner Brothers and issue their greatest hits album. Bread's current manager was Selwyn Miller, a personal friend of Clive's. I knew the Bread catalogue well and had bought their records in the seventies back in Walsall, so we hatched a plan that night to obtain the catalogue from Warner Brothers. I soon realised that although I would get support from Clive and Selwyn, obtaining the catalogue was all down to me.

I returned from La Manga and set about the task. Martin Craig had recently taken over control of all Warner back catalogue and so we arranged to meet and discuss the idea. Warners at the time were not in the business of reworking their back catalogue and the appointment of Martin Craig was their first step towards catalogue representation and exploitation. It seems strange now, but back then reissues of older artists were not seen as moneymakers, hence we were in a new and untested area as far as Warners were concerned. I believed that if you treated this catalogue as if it were a new release and focused on it as a series of frontline operations, then you had even more of a chance of success as the public already knew the songs. Fortunately, Martin and I got on well and Martin would eventually play golf in our music business events and become one of our band of players.

Martin went to the Board of Directors and tried to sell the idea of Jive Records issuing Warner Brothers' back catalogue. To start with he hit brick walls, but eventually through his persistence it went all the way to Ramon Lopez, the head of Warner Music International. His reaction, I was told, was 'Who is this kid from Jive that wants our product?' Eventually, the word came back from Martin that it was not impossible that this deal could happen. I spoke with Clive and said we had worked a crack in the system and I felt if we now made a financial offer we might get the catalogue. Clive and I agreed to offer 50,000 pounds and see what happened. I told Martin of the offer and again it went to Lopez. 'For 50,000 pounds, let's see what they can do' came back the message. We were in business.

The album was titled *Essentials, The Best Of Bread*. It was issued on Jive Records and debuted at No 9 on the national chart, eventually selling over 250,000 copies. David Gates, vocalist and main writer for the band, came to England for a short promotional trip and later in the year the band came to tour England for the first time in twenty years, playing packed houses on a twenty date tour. It was a phenomenal success.

Billy comes back:

I truly enjoyed putting together that album, promotion and tour, and I felt we could do the same operation with our own Billy Ocean. Billy had not recorded since 1991 and most of the public believed he lived in America when all the time he still lived in the same house in Virginia Water, Surrey. I had always maintained a very strong relationship with Bill and when we met up now I said, 'It's time Bill.' I had a plan that we could license Billy's earlier hits from Sony such as 'Love Really Hurts

Without You', 'Red Light Spells Danger', 'LOD', 'Love On Delivery', and 'Stop Me If You've Heard It All Before', along with a few others, and then include all the Jive hits from the eighties; it would become the ultimate Billy Ocean Greatest Hits. Billy liked the idea, but he did not want to come out of retirement and give artist support as Billy Ocean, which I told him we greatly needed in the circumstances, because he had been off the scene for so long. Finally, we made an agreement for just a one-off one hour radio special, pre-recorded, and Billy would perform only if I could get *The National Lottery* or *Noels' House Party,* the two biggest TV shows of the day. Billy commented to me that he only agreed to *The Lottery* and *House Party* because I had no chance of getting him on the shows. That decision would come back to bite him in the bum. For now, there was a lot of work to do.

John Aston at Sony helped me with the licensing of the hits I needed, which surprisingly was a simple task. Mark Goodier did a fine job of presenting a one hour radio special on Billy with Bill's own comments and thoughts. Billy told me after the interview how much he enjoyed it and it certainly gave him confidence. I was there at every appearance Billy made during the album's release, there were only three or four, but I was a condition. The only times I objected were shopping trips to get the suits for *The Lottery* and *The House Party* performances, and yes, we got the shows and Billy came back to perform magnificently. Tina went shopping with Billy and after trying on a few suits he commented, 'I'm starting to feel like Billy Ocean again.'

We released the album in August 1997. Billy came up with the title as he became more confident and interested: *L.I.F.E. The Best Of Billy Ocean.* L.I.F.E. also stood for 'Love Is Forever', one of Billy's big Jive hit records. The album became the highest entry of the week at No 7 and would go on to sell 250,000 copies in the UK alone. We followed up the success of the album with an appearance on the *Lottery*, and thankfully, Billy's longtime manager Laurie Jay was with us that day – Laurie is a master of difficult situations.

After that year's successful album I thought Billy might be interested in recording again, but that was not to be. He had enjoyed the experience, the performances and the success, but that was enough. It would be many years before he would record again.

Ups and Downs:

During April, Jive Records scored a debut-hit single with Smoke City. The driving force behind the record was its fortunate inclusion as the theme for the latest Levi TV advertisements. They brought 'Underwater Love' to an audience we would have struggled to reach without Levi's massive TV campaign, and this gave us an opportunity to invest in a groundbreaking video to accompany the single: in its use of bullet time motion, the video predated *The Matrix*. 'Underwater Love' peaked at No 4 on the UK singles chart and gave us a great start, or so we thought, with Smoke City. The blend of acid jazz and trip hop was a fashionable British sound and we worked hard with the band, which consisted of Nina Miranda, Mark Brown and Chris Franck. I thought they would become a good selling album band for the company, but as time went on the Levi advert became a double-edged sword. We would try with a further couple of singles and the album *Flying Away,* but we could not convince the public that this was a band to support. Personally, I really liked the members of the band and their music and would invest again in a second album and work in the studio with them. Sadly, the second album would be only marginally successful and the band would finally split in 2002.

Mike Pedan's second signing to Jive, Crustation, brought out their album *Bloom* in this year of 1997. It received good reviews and sold a small quantity of records to a dedicated few, but it never really got going with the public at large and it would be the band's one and only album for the label. The Smoke City and Crustation projects, especially the latter, had forced me to divide the promotion and marketing departments away from the A & R centre, a system that would remain in operation throughout the coming years.

After making the albums, Mike Pedan then thought he would decide on the promotion people that would work on the projects and have control over the marketing budgets to sell the albums. I completely disagreed with this philosophy. Once the singles and albums were made it was then the promotion, sales and marketing departments that had control over how we sold the product and how much we spent to achieve our goals, and all this was only approved by me.

Mike clearly was offended by this arrangement and tried many times to change the system that I had put in place, which caused some problems with the management of the acts as they had been misled on how we operated. This was the beginning of the end of Mike Pedan and Max Bloom at Jive Records; their contracts were up at the end of the year and would not be renewed.

During June, Jive Records changed again. Andy Richmond, one of my strongest allies and I still believe one of the best salesmen I ever met, left the company. Jive Records was not a political company as we were too busy getting the job done to be interested in politics, however, politics surrounded the departure of Andy. It seemed all year I had been defending Andy's position within the company, somehow Andy had upset the powers that be and I had been hauled over the coals on two occasions about his position. My response had been 'give me a good reason and if you cannot then he stays as I am the Managing Director and I personally do the hiring and firing.' I thought that the water had now passed under the bridge, but in early June I received a call from Clive insisting that Andy left the company. This was unusual as Clive never became involved in the hiring or firing of staff. I questioned him intently on the matter, but all I got was this had to happen and it was my job to do it.

I had known Andy Richmond since the early Eighties, he had taken a chance on me with the idea of Impulse and thrown his hat in the ring. Andy had become a senior operator at Impulse before leaving to return to Gainsboro to run the local public house in his village and then, missing the cut and thrust of the record business, returning to work for me as Sales Manager at Jive. In the early nineties when we were struggling for hits and sales, Andy was one of the main reasons we stayed afloat: he milked every available sale from our releases and he was without doubt a great player. Now, I was charged with telling him he was leaving the Company. Hard enough, but not knowing the crime was even worse. As a professional I had to do the job, but it damn near killed me. It remains one of the worst moments in my career. My relationship with Andy would never be the same again, but the biggest disappointment for me was that he would not be involved in the success that was to come; I felt he deserved to be after the hard years that had gone before.

I promoted Tina Wisby to General Manager, a position she would hold until Jive Records eventually closed, years later. Hans Griffiths, who Andy had hired, became Sales and Marketing Manager, again staying until the company closed. And now, an even worse blow was to come. My baby, the company that had given me a living, brought unbelievable success and built my reputation, was in trouble. The Impulse Promotion Company had been wobbling for almost a year. As I described in the previous chapter, the business had changed and the major chains, in the sales of both singles and albums, had overtaken the small independent retailers. Along with the demise of independent retailers, Impulse had lost its enormous power, and this coupled with the selling of A & M Records, Chrysalis Records, Island Records, Mute Records and more to major record companies had reduced the Impulse client base and its chance of profitability.

Impulse, for the first time in fourteen years, was now reliant on the product flow from Jive Records. The team at Impulse had shrunk to align itself to the decreasing numbers of record retailers and was now a much smaller operation than the Pinnacle Records team that we now owned. Something had to give.

Impulse – The end of an era:

Clive and Nick Howe were very gentle with me over the support of Impulse. They both knew it meant a lot to me and over a period of the first six months of 1997 they allowed Impulse every opportunity to reverse the position it found itself in. Unfortunately, the market dictates, and by June of 1997 the decision was made to close Impulse. I told Shaun King, Impulse's Managing Director, that the decision had been made and that in July we would inform the staff, some of who had worked for me for the whole duration of the company. It was a sad moment in my life.

We arranged a farewell lunch at The Man Chui Restaurant in Hendon, a restaurant we had used many times to entertain clients and secure deals during the Impulse years. We tried our best to be 'up' about the whole thing, but Impulse had been a way of life for us all for many, many years and sadly as we left that day, it would be no more.

The Impulse Group of Companies had at least one No 1 single in every year of its existence and the proud total of No 1 singles after fifteen years closed at 68. The last one was 'I Believe I Can Fly' by R. Kelly on Jive Records. Impulse did fly, it changed the record business and took promotion, sales and marketing to a new level. Impulse beat all its competitors and copy companies, and rightfully has its place in the history of the UK record business. I thank everyone who worked for the company over the years and I hope it remains in your memory as a great and successful achievement.

STEPS:

Shaun told the staff of Impulse about the company closing on 7th July 1997 and it is strange how in life one door closes and another opens. That day I was due to have lunch with Tim Byrne. Tina Wisby had arranged the lunch and knew Tim better than I from the days of the *Smash Hits* TV show. Tim had told Tina that he had formed a band and wanted to talk to me about them. Tina had put pressure on me to do the lunch and thankfully, I had gone along with her wishes. Tim wanted me to watch the band perform and we agreed he would bring them to our studios, on condition that I did watch them – he would not let me listen to any recordings. Afterwards, I suggested to Tina that as the project was in the pop area we should get Pete Waterman along to give us his reaction. If Pete didn't like it then it probably was not for us. Tina arranged the studio a week later and I phoned Pete to come and take a look.

At Battery Studios in Chaplin Road I met for the first time Faye Tozer, Claire Richards, Lisa Scott-Lee, Lee Latchford-Evans and Ian 'H' Watkins, the members of the band STEPS. They were young, rehearsed, and had a determined air about them, yet were down to earth and easy to get along with. Pete duly arrived a few minutes later and the band performed '5.6.7.8', a pop, country line dance sounding single. I knew of the boom in the north of England for line dancing in social clubs that had spawned a few dedicated magazines and I was aware there was some demand for that style of music. The version the band performed of '5.6.7.8' was not quite right and although it had the bones of an idea, at that moment, I did not believe it was a hit record at all. What did hit me though was the complete belief and dedication the band had to their performance, they absolutely went for it. I remember thinking '*if this group could have a great song they could really pull it off.*' Pete had said little and sat to watch the performance, while I stood at the side. About half way through the song we looked at each other and Pete nodded: I knew that meant we were going to sign the band and have a go. We chatted for a while and then the band performed the song again. When they finished I spoke to them all and said we would make a deal and give them a shot, but I would have to work with Pete on the details of what we did next. 'Do not worry, I will be in touch and make an offer.'

Pete and I went back to my office and discussed the project, we both agreed that the song had something, but it was a long way from a finished single, which Tim and the band thought it was.

I started work with Michael Smith on a deal for the band and Pete started to prepare to rework and add instruments to the record to bring it up to a reasonable standard for us to release.

Tina began to work on a video to enhance the release and the Jive machine slowly began to click into action on STEPS.

Everything moved very quickly. I wanted to get the record out in early September, as I knew that during October, November and December all the major record companies' priority acts would be in the marketplace and lessen the chance of exposure on radio and especially TV. Pete was in the studio within a week with Mark Topham and Karl Twigg working on the single, and Steve Crosby and Barry Upton, the original producers and writers, both who Pete and I knew from previous projects, were also involved. It was Steve, Barry and Tim that had conceived the line dancing idea and put the original advertisement in the *Stage* for a band to front the idea. The three of them had also sat through all the auditions to select Claire, Faye, Lisa, Lee and H.

Pete, Mark and Karl made the record sound like a techno country line dancing record complete with banjos and fiddles, and in doing so they made a huge improvement to the record. It did now sound like a hit. Mark and Karl, who were primarily jazz funk musicians, thought Pete and I had taken leave of our senses, and they thought the record was so appalling that they refused to have their names on the record as producers. They just couldn't see it all.

The new audience:

August, traditionally a slow time in the music business, was busy at Jive Records. The Backstreet Boys were touring the UK and we took advantage by launching the new album *Backstreets Back* at a party on the 12th. The band appeared and the press, radio and TV turned out in their droves. The Backstreet Boys were the biggest pop band in the land, and everybody had gone Backstreet crazy. We launched the first single, 'Everybody (Backstreet's Back)', and it was accompanied by an amazing huge production video. The single narrowly missed out on the No 1 spot and peaked at No 2, selling 400,000 copies. It was closely followed by the album which debuted at No 2 and stayed on the chart for months, achieving double platinum status and pushing on, eventually, to 800,000 sales. The tour was crazy, sell out shows everywhere, and we constantly moved the band from hotel to hotel as they became besieged and isolated within their rooms.

The ingenuity of 13, 14 and 15 year-old girls was quite remarkable. When the Backstreets flew into the UK, the girls would somehow find out what flight the boys were arriving on and be at Heathrow to welcome them. At the same time, they would dispatch two girls and station them at each hotel in London. We would whisk the boys straight from the airport to the designated hotel and within two hours the hotel would be besieged with girls looking for their heroes. It was a constant battle to keep the fans away and choose the most unlikely of hotels; all we managed to do in reality was to gain forty-eight hours before they were found. The staff of Jive Records became accustomed to fans in the street outside the offices, they would stand there all day, no matter what the weather, and talk to anyone who came in and out of our doors, searching for any information before using their mobile phones to ignite the army and move across London to wherever they thought the band were. It took some getting used to, but slowly we became proficient at moving a successful band around the country in the most secretive of manners.

As soon as The Backstreet Boys launch was over we went straight into preparing for the launch of STEPS and '5.6.7.8.' We had chosen The Atlantic Bar and Grill in central London as we wanted to make it a simple task for the media to attend. We used the Pete Waterman name and the current Jive success with The Backstreet Boys to get a very large turnout from the press, radio and TV.

The record '5.6.7.8' was about to become one of the strangest singles that we ever promoted and one to which I had never seen such a kind of response before, nor have I since. It all started at The Atlantic Bar and Grill. It was a fantastic launch and all the media, for once, let their hair down and had a carefree lunch break. STEPS performed and were well prepared, the record sounded good and even the 'cool' media copied the dance routine and generally had a great time. Many of them talked to Pete and I during and after the launch and said what a great time they had. However, they would not support the single as it was clearly a one-off novelty record and even if it became a hit, it was a flash in the pan and just a fun moment in time. We began trying to get any radio, TV and press exposure we could and put the band out in a transit van playing three or four clubs a night performing '5.6.7.8' – just that one song and then onto the next club. Some venues were full and others were empty, with the band playing to one man and a dog. I remember an early performance in a club in central London where we had expected a crowd and the band performed to Tim, Tina and I, with another three paying customers. Radio had proved to be an absolute no go area – no one was interested in '5.6.7.8.'

I felt the dance moves and the general 'up' feeling of the record gave us a chance on TV, and the pop magazines just came forward with news items and the odd photograph, which was achieved mainly by Jive Records using our power with the successful Backstreets campaign. Tony Wilson of Granada Reports and ex-boss of Factory Records was doing a piece on Line Dancing and its success in the north of England, and as Tony knew Pete and me well he asked Pete to do an interview 'live' on the show and 'bring up that band you've got, STEPS.' Although we didn't know it at the time, that show on Granada TV was the start point of the STEPS phenomenon. The band performed the song twice on the show and during the second time everyone in the studio started trying to mimic the dance routine. Pete did his interview in the middle and sold the idea brilliantly, as he always does, and the record started to sell the following day in the north of England.

I had given a cassette of the song to my sister Helen for the kids, Sally and David, to gauge a reaction. '5.6.7.8' would become the song that drove Helen crazy, as the kids would insist on it being played every morning in the car on the way to school, while they sat in the back attempting some of the dance moves in a seated position. They thought it was great fun. We were learning that the relatively simple dance moves were a real plus to the whole project and that the band's easy presentation style, looking like they were genuinely having real fun, added to the whole momentum.

'5.6.7.8' was still a difficult record to get going, though. It seemed every week we had to get something to propel the record upwards on the chart. Most weeks we only achieved a TV spot at the last minute and that would hold the single's position or move it up a couple of places. The weekly chart position of '5.6.7.8' responded like no other record I have ever seen: after a few weeks we were inside the Top 30 and more TV shows began to take a chance on the band and the record, but it still had a slow consistent growth as more and more people became aware of the record. The chart positions read like a lottery ticket: No 27 then 24, then 25, then 21, then 19, then 22. We got an appearance on the *Blue Peter* TV show and '5.6.7.8' went Top 20 at No 17, only to fall back to No 18 the following week. Then in came *Top of The Pops* which catapulted the record to its highest ever position of No 14. Back it went again after that to No 18, then back up to 15. I had never seen anything like it. Eventually, the record stayed on the chart for months but would never beat its highest position of No 14.

'5.6.7.8' was eventually swamped by the number of major releases hitting the chart for the Christmas sales rush, but the record remained a favourite throughout the Christmas party period and we knew we had something with STEPS. We were not quite sure what, but we knew it was truly something.

STEPS continued doing club gigs and building their fan base. They performed in clubs for months, gaining experience and becoming a splendid band. '5.6.7.8' would become a British record holder for the most sales of a single never to make the UK Top 10: it sold well over 200,000 copies and became a debut silver disc. Our licensees around the world, without understanding what the record was about, launched the single in their relative countries all with some success. It was perceived as a Christmas novelty record and would be all over by 1st January 1998.

New blood – New acts:

I was still chasing my first pick of A & R men Scott Maclachlan and, finally after several lunches over the months, there was a sense that maybe he would be interested in joining us. Our current success had obviously helped and on 4th September at 'il Barbino Restaurant' in central London we agreed to talk about what the offer would look like. Five days later we met again and within six weeks Michael Smith and I had agreed with Scott that he would join Jive Records in the coming year. I was elated: I now had Pete, who was beginning to get into his stride, and I felt that Scott would provide hit records in the dance area and then move into the album selling market with current new bands that we could build a future with.

EBUL Records fuelled by the success of STEPS clicked up a few gears and started to work on Tina Cousins' tracks which sounded good. Pete also found Will Mellor, an actor on Hollyoaks, and the storyline suggested there was an opportunity for him to have a hit single in the coming year, so we duly signed him to EBUL.

The hits were becoming constant through Jive Records. R. Kelly, fuelled with his success from the *SpaceJam* movie, was now accepted in Hollywood and was commissioned to write a track for the new *Batman* movie 'Gotham City', which would put him back in the UK Top 10 in July. Another real success story of 1997 was the Joe project. Joe Lewis Thomas had been signed in the US but we in England had helped with the signing, as Joe particularly wanted to have hits in England and had seen the progress we had made with R. Kelly. 1997 was a huge success year for Joe, as not only did his album *All That I Am* become a Top 20 record in the US, he also became a star and able record seller in the UK. The singles 'Don't Wanna Be A Player' and 'The Love Scene' became hits and the album *All That I Am* became a huge chart success resulting in a tour of big venues in Manchester, Birmingham and Wembley, London. Another success story for Jive Records.

Billy – and Nelson Mandela:

Billy Ocean's Greatest Hits had caused a worldwide stir and everyone thought that he was back and working. That was not exactly true as Billy and I had made a low key deal and a restricted performance agenda – however, when you start something, it sometimes has a life of its own and you just have to go along with it. The highest position entry in the UK chart had spread around the world and our companies began to sell the album in their territories, so soon, Billy, Laurie, Tina and I were off to Germany to record on *Wetten, dass...?* (Wanna bet that...?), the long running Saturday night TV show, to support our German label in their bid to sell records.

An unexpected trip arose at the end of the year and it was one that I will not forget. The Prince's Trust, operated by Prince Charles, was supporting a huge event in Johannesburg for Nelson Mandela. The finale was at the Johannesburg stadium, where The Spice Girls were top of the bill. The Trust along with Nelson Mandela wanted Billy to appear just before the girls and perform three songs including 'When The Going Gets Tough', which was their adopted anthem. I advised the Trust that I would speak with Billy and come back to them. Billy had not performed in front of a huge audience for nearly ten years. I believed he would go to South Africa purely because Mr. Mandela had asked him, although Bill is his own man and you can never be quite sure. The concert was planned for 1st November and it was organised by the Nations Trust with the title The Two Nations Concert. It was to be held at the Johannesburg Stadium and attending would be Prince Charles, Prince Harry and Nelson Mandela. The funds from the concert would go to create new jobs for the unemployed youth of South Africa.

I called Laurie Jay and told him about the request and he too thought Bill would be interested in going and performing. When I phoned Billy at home and told him about the concert and Mr. Mandela's request, as I expected, he did not turn down Nelson Mandela, especially as I had also been informed that we would meet him at some point during the trip. I phoned the Prince's Trust and we were soon making arrangements to fly to South Africa. Billy was to perform 'Caribbean Queen', 'Suddenly' and 'When The Going Gets Tough.'

Billy, Laurie and I took the direct flight into Johannesburg and were met at the airport by our two bodyguards for the trip. They were both big South African lads – one look was enough to suggest they were not to be messed with. The boys were with us throughout the five-day trip and whenever we left the hotel, it was only with them. The two of them had guns in ankle belts, normally not noticeable, but when they sat down and their trousers rose a little because of the knee bend, you could occasionally catch sight of the weaponry. The first couple of days were spent doing a little promotion for the concert, with a breakfast radio show, a TV interview and some press interviews, it was all very relaxed. We were just transported to whichever radio or TV studio around Johannesburg, but as usual we only saw parts of the city through car windows. I have seen so many cities through car windows around the world that it becomes easier to remember the airport or the hotel, and even those memories blur into one. The South African people we met were fantastic, I believe all were appreciative that we had made the trip and were there for the concert.

On the Friday, before the concert, at about six o'clock in the evening we were ushered up to a private entrance to the Hotel, and Prince Charles and Harry were introduced to us all individually. Laurie as ever was off with his camera and filming the whole event and Billy and I were standing in line awaiting the Princes. Slowly, Charles and Harry came towards us as Billy and I were having a great time chatting to everyone. Charles came up to us and said 'I've seen you two while I've been meeting people. Out of everyone, you seem to be having the best time.' We both spoke with Charles for a minute and then he moved on. A young Harry tagging on behind said 'Hello', shook our hands, and followed his dad. Laurie would later send me a copy of the moment Billy and I met Charles.

The Saturday of the concert we went to stage rehearsals in the afternoon. Billy sounded great and I got to walk around the stadium for half an hour, which also felt great after hours and hours in the hotel. We returned to the Johannesburg Stadium around 6.30, before the crowds came and awaited our call. It was around 9.30 that we first saw the enormous crowd, as we were driven from what I would imagine were sporting dressing rooms, which had been our place for the past three hours, to the back of the stage. As we got out of the people carrier, the noise was enormous. Jonathan Butler, a former Jive recording artist, was on stage and Billy was to follow.

When Billy gets nervous he just goes very quiet and within himself, and at this point it is best to leave him to it – he gathers himself in his own way. When the introduction of 'Ladies and Gentlemen, Billy Ocean' came, he was ready. Laurie was off with his camera recording Billy's performance from side and front of stage, I stayed side of stage at the monitor-mixing desk and watched. Billy performed 'Caribbean Queen' and the whole place was rocking. He spoke with the crowd after the song and then performed 'Suddenly.' The whole place was a picture as the crowd lit up cigarette lighters and held them aloft, a magical moment. Billy was by now really enjoying himself, thanking the crowd for inviting him, and he turned to cue the band, who ripped into the opening bars of 'When The Going Gets Tough.' The audience was ready, and expectant, and a wave of noise hit the stage. I think the whole stadium sang 'When The Going Gets Tough' so loud that Billy could not hear himself.

I was aware of a real commotion behind me. The Spice Girls had arrived and were jumping and leaping about to 'When The Going Gets Tough', providing their own dance routines and having a great time screaming and shouting. Billy finished the song, took his bow and started to exit the stage. The Spice Girls flew past me and surrounded him, all talking at once in amongst the noise of the audience. I saw Billy's hand push up from the middle of them and point at me, at which point five wild girls headed my way all talking to me at the same time. I tried to calm them down, but they were excited. Finally, Scary Spice and Posh calmed down enough to tell me they had their own TV special coming up in the New Year and definitely wanted Billy as their special guest. I told them I knew their manager and if they called Jive Records I would arrange it for them. The girls hung around for a few minutes all ready to perform and it was not long before the stage was set. Billy, Laurie and I watched them do their three numbers and then all the artists went back on stage for one last bow. The show was over and we were out of the stadium in minutes and back to the hotel.

The following day about thirty of us went to meet Nelson Mandela just outside Johannesburg. Jonathan Butler, Trevor Rabin, Billy and The Spices were all there.

Mr Mandela did the same as Prince Charles – he walked slowly around the group and thanked us for coming. The Spice Girls made a big fuss of him and he seemed to enjoy every moment of their attention.

Our South African Adventure was over, our bodyguards returned us to the airport and we caught the night flight home arriving in England early in the morning. A fantastic trip and one that Billy, Laurie and I will remember.

1997 had been an exceptional year in the history of Jive Records. We had built a roster of acts that were all selling records to various degrees, and we were the jewel in the crown of our distributor Pinnacle Records – and yet, still, we seemed to be under the radar as far as the rest of the record industry were concerned. Impulse was now over and committed to history, my staff had moved on and I missed having both Shaun King and Andy Richmond around on a daily basis.

My Mom had passed on and so had my great friend Tom Edmunds, just before the end of the year. I cannot deny I had a feeling of loneliness as the year began to come to a close. I was exhausted and needed some time to review all that had happened during this momentous year. I headed for some peace, quiet and golf on the islands of the Caribbean. Pete headed for India, a fishing trip and sleeping in tents in the middle of the jungle. Each to his own, eh?

1997 Impulse Hits until the end of June, including Jive Records and Jive hits from July to December:

1997 Hits

January			
Quit Playing Games With My Heart	The Backstreet Boys	Jive	No 2
February			
Ain't Talkin' 'Bout Dub	Apollo 440	Stealth Sonic	No 7
Candy Girl	Babybird	Echo	No 14
Da Funk	Daft Punk	Virgin	No 7
Word Perfect	KRS One	Jive	No 70
Children Of The Night	Nakatomi	Peach	No 47
Hedonism	Skunk Anansie	One Little Indian	No 13
March			
Anywhere For You	Backstreet Boys	Jive	No 4
I Believe I Can Fly	R. Kelly	Jive	No 1
Feels So Good	Lorna B	Avex	No 69
I Miss You	Bjork	One Little Indian	No 36
The World Is Mine	Ice Cube	Jive	No 60

Oxygene 8	Jean Michel Jarre	Epic	No 17
Show Me Love	Robin S	Champion	No 9
April			
Underwater Love	Smoke City	Jive	No 4
Step Into A World	KRS One	Jive	No 24
Can We	SWV	Jive	No 18
May			
Make The World Go Round	Sandy B	Champion	No 35
Dog On Wheels	Belle & Sebastion	Jeepster	No 59
Fireworks EP	Embrace	Hut	No 34
Going Out Of My Head	Fatboy Slim	Skint	No 57
I Got Next LP	KRS One	Jive	No 58
June			
Trials Of Life	Kaleef	Unity/Jive	No 75
Don't Wanna Be A Player	Joe	Jive	No 16
July			
Gotham City	R. Kelly	Jive	No 9
Essential The Best Of Bread	Bread	Jive	No 9
All That I Am	Joe	Jive	No 26
August			
Everybody Backstreets Back	Backstreet Boys	Jive	No 3
Backstreets Back LP	Backstreet Boys	Jive	No 2
The Jam EP	A Tribe Called Quest	Jive	No 61
L.I.F.E. The Best Of Billy Ocean	Billy Ocean	Jive	No 7
September			
Heartbeat/A Friend	KRS One	Jive	No 66
The Love Scene	Joe	Jive	No 22
October			
As Long As You Love Me	Backstreet Boys	Jive	No 3
I Like The Way	Kaleef	Unity/Jive	No 58
November			
5.6.7.8.	STEPS	Ebul/Jive	No 14

CHAPTER 23

THE HIGHEST PEAKS – 1998 AND 1999

Jive Records – The Hit Machine:

I returned to work on 5th January 1998 and chaired a riotous planning meeting at midday. It seemed all we had set up in the last couple of weeks of 1997 had come home to roost. STEPS had retained their No 14 chart position and would make their debut on *Top Of The Pops* on Friday; '5.6.7.8' had officially sold over 200,000 copies. Joe's single 'Good Girls' was a new entry at No 29, and 2 Pac's, 'I Wonder If Heaven's Got A Ghetto' was a new entry at No 21. The Backstreet Boys' single 'As Long As You Love Me' was sliding down the chart from last year, at No 24, but their album *Backstreets Back* had passed double platinum status, selling over 600,000 copies, while our new project Solid Harmonie had secured a performance on *The Lottery*. What a start, the company was buzzing.

Solid Harmonie had supported The Backstreet Boys on their tour and built up a following. The girls – three Brits: Melissa Graham, Rebecca Onslow, and Mariama Goodman, plus Elisa Cariera (born Orlando Florida) – were one of our big hopes for 1998. Their first single 'I'll Be There For You' performed on *The Lottery* that week, hit the Top 20 in the UK, finally peaking at No 18 during January – a splendid start to the campaign.

We had also tried three singles with Pete's signing Kaleef and were beginning to believe we had missed the boat when their fourth single 'Sands Of Time' also became a hit in January peaking at No 26. This breathed life into the project for a short while.

We had increased the turnover of Jive Records from 9 million to 25 million in just one year. I renegotiated my contract through the first three weeks of January, and although I was not particularly happy with the new contract, as I felt a little underappreciated, we were on the cusp of greater things and I wanted to stay and drive home the opportunity. It had taken eight years to obtain a team I felt that could deliver both artists and hit records and I wanted to stay and lead that team forward.

George Benson:

With last year's success of Billy Ocean and Bread's *Greatest Hits*, there was no doubt that our idea of treating the Best Of's as front line product was well in advance of other record companies. I had returned to Martin Craig at Warner Brothers and asked for the back catalogue of George Benson, one of my all time heroes. The reaction he and I received from the top of Warners was that George was difficult to deal with and would never agree to being involved with a Best Of. Warners felt it was a waste of time although Martin, still believing in me after the solid success of Bread, was as supportive as possible. After three weeks of talks and Martin working internally we agreed that I would call George Benson, tell him of our idea and see what the response would be. I agreed with Warners that if George said yes, then they would license the product on the same 50,000 pounds advance as per the Bread deal and just let me get on with it.

I called George's manager, Denis Turner, in Los Angeles and started by explaining my position and our achievements with Billy Ocean and the licensed *Bread Essentials* album. I wanted to continue the theme and call the album *Essentials, The Very Best Of George Benson*, and I spoke about treating the album as frontline product where artist involvement was an absolute must. The response was fantastic. Within a couple of days I had spoken with George who had asked many questions and had agreed to promote the album and come to the UK initially for five days, after which he would later return for concerts should we be successful. I believed there was no doubt that we would be successful! Warners were amazed that George had agreed and were left with no choice but to license the product. Jive Records would now have on its label such classic songs as 'The Greatest Love Of All', 'Give Me The Night', 'Love X Love', 'Turn Your Love Around', 'Never Give Up On A Good Thing', and 'In Your Eyes.' Two personal favourites of mine from my DJ days were 'Breezin' and 'This Masquerade', which I insisted on featuring on the record. George too was pleased at their inclusion.

We released the album in April and took a big gamble. I felt we had enough momentum to chart the record on Sunday the 19th and so we arranged for George to arrive in the UK on the 20th. Yes, it could have gone wrong but our commitment and total belief was not to be beaten. *Essentials, The Very Best Of George Benson* became a new entry at No 8. The following evening George arrived from Los Angeles with Denis and we celebrated with his favourite, a Japanese dinner. Although it certainly is not my preferred dish, I had over the years found a way to pick around the menu. I really had to pinch myself, here I was with one of my all time heroes. I had played his records in clubs all over the Midlands and now I was responsible for a Top 10 album and was having dinner with the man himself. George was extremely jet lagged and if you know that feeling it sometimes can be awful, sometimes you have to just close your eyes thinking it will only be for two or three seconds and suddenly you are gone, completely out. George's manager,

Denis, had to keep prodding him to stay awake – if you do that the lag disappears for a while and you feel fine again for a time. To be fair, George struggled that night, but was in a great frame of mind. Tina and I got to know him well during that week of promotion and the media treated him with great love and respect. George would return in July to play a few nights at the Royal Albert Hall and I remember watching the show and thinking how we had made possible the joy the audience was feeling. *Essentials, The Very Best Of George Benson* would become a gold album and sell 250,000 copies.

The Levellers:

News of our success with these types of albums was reaching widely across the artist community and slowly other labels began to call to see if we would become involved in joint ventures with them. We were offered Leo Sayer, Gladys Knight, Randy Crawford and The Levellers almost immediately, but I felt that we had to be selective and artistically discriminating about the whole matter. I did not want us to look like a 'cash in' company. It was vital we maintain a high standard and keep the selective tag that the company was now developing.

The Levellers were the most interesting to me. They had been nurtured by Derek Green at China Records and had been having Top 20 records since 1991. The band was self-contained, writing and recording its own material, and seriously looking after its fan base. It operated in the record business almost purely on its own terms. Although I had not been a personal fan, I loved The Levellers' independence, and when Derek Green contacted me and suggested we meet to discuss the project I readily agreed. We had a good discussion, but I decided I would not move forward without first seeing the band and looking at their audience, and then discussing the album personally with the members. I went to see The Levellers at Shepherds Bush Empire and spent most of the evening watching the audience rather than the band, noting their reaction to certain songs, and cross-checking with previous singles and chart positions. I was most certainly doing my homework.

The band came to Jive in July with Derek. We talked about Jive's previous successes, how different this album would be and what we would need to do to obtain the volume sales. I felt we could and must reach a larger audience than the traditional one they already had. I also explained to the band that I was not personally a fan, I appreciated their sound and truly loved their independence, but if they wanted a dedicated fan to be in charge of their album, then it was not me. I countered that I still felt I might just be the best man for the job, but I had to be honest. Derek's face was a picture as I launched into the speech, I think he felt I had blown it, but as time passed on I believe that brutal honesty was what brought the Levellers to Jive Records. We took a long time to set the record up and finally the band recorded three new songs for the record as I had requested. We took the chance of issuing the album in November in the middle of the Christmas rush of releases, and it made its debut at No 15, stayed on the chart for fifteen weeks and sold 200,000 copies.

The theory of Essentials – and others:

After the success of the George Benson album, Warners had wanted us to tackle the Everly Brothers under the tag Essentials. I wanted to continue with _Essentials, The Very Best of Otis Redding_, and when a few weeks later Martin called me into Warners for a meeting, I thought we would agree it. Not so. The Board had asked 'how come Jive Records are taking our catalogue, have sold almost half a million records and we are not doing this ourselves?' Martin had countered that the UK Company was not prepared to commit budgets to back catalogue and I believe from there that the order was given for no more licensing of product to Jive Records. Instead, Warners set up their own project taking our Essentials name and indiscriminately abused and plundered their catalogue everywhere they could. I admit they were not on their own, other major companies did exactly the same thing, with the result that over the years those great recordings and the history of our business have been devalued.

I believe we had a unique view of Essentials, Best Of's and Greatest Hits albums. We never made any albums without either talking to the artists or the artists' estates and we always tried to work together, attending to their wishes and thoughts. It was a class way of representing the history of our industry and unfortunately, what was to follow in our wake with most companies was simply a catalogue opportunity seen as a 'cash cow.' Their Best Of's and Greatest Hits albums were made purely to cover the mistakes of frontline A & R departments that had signed and spent too much money on the wrong artists. As our parents always told us, two wrongs don't make a right.

The other album I really pursued with great gusto for an Essentials release was owned by Ace Records, but I just could not obtain a satisfactory agreement and so _Essentials, The Creedence Clearwater Collection_ never did appear. However, Jive did issue two further greatest hits albums during 1998. The first appeared in May when _DJ Jazzy Jeff & The Fresh Prince Greatest Hits Collection_ charted at No 20. It stayed on the chart for eight weeks and sold 100,000 copies. The next one came out in December: _2 Pac, The Greatest Hits_ was an album I was particularly proud of. It made its debut at No 17 and then stayed on the UK chart for an unbelievable 35 weeks. It just kept on selling and selling, eventually reaching over 300,000 units.

I was constantly asked to provide finance for compilation albums that would be issued on Jive Records. This was not an area I was interested in, as I have never really been a fan of compilations, which, for the most part, have left me with a feeling of disappointment. There are a few good tracks accompanied by a large ratio of tracks that were not hits, or simply do not fit in to the album. I preferred to license our records to other companies for their compilations, although only on a restricted basis – I always felt that if you wanted a Jive Record, you should buy it from Jive Records. At Jive I can only really remember issuing one compilation album, which was an R&B release that had been compiled by Mario Warner, who would go on to operate Warners catalogue and compilation department. I liked Mario, who has been a friend for many years, and we made a deal for the album as at the time Mario was in between companies. If I had liked the experience I think we would have done more, but it never quite felt right for Jive Records, and so apart from this compilation we stayed away from that part of the business.

New singles, fresh hits:

On the singles front we were back on the hit trail during February as The Backstreet Boys took the No 2 spot again with 'All I Have To Give.' Pete's Unity/ Jive label scored again with Will Mellor's 'When I Need You' peaking at No 5. We had a good relationship with both Will Mellor and Raz Gold, Will's manager, until 'When I Need You' became a huge hit and then the problems started. This happens with a lot of artists, somehow, after only one hit, they can believe they know it all, what should happen next and what they should record. Will was on *Top Of The Pops* and the troubles began only days after. Pete wanted to record one way and Will wanted another way, Raz then got in the middle, but sided with Will, as he had too, and it was not long before I was called to the party. Pete always knew if there was trouble at the stage when we should be celebrating a hit single, then the project would not go much further. We managed to get another single together, which was like pulling teeth, and in June we released 'No Matter What I Do.' The record peaked at No 23 and Will Mellor's hit making career was over. I am pleased to see that in the years that have passed Will has gone on to have a successful acting career which I am sure has many years to run with many great parts to play. Personally, I was pleased to be involved in 'When I Need You', not only because it was a hit for Will but also because it had been the first No 1 record I had ever been involved with, when Leo Sayer took the same song to the top, twenty-one years earlier in 1977.

I had now rearranged the A & R department, so that Jane Austin was operating the department on a day to day basis and we now had Pete Waterman, Scott MacLaghlan, who had joined Jive in January, and Roddy McKenna on Silvertone. This made up a much happier group of people all focused on their own area of music and all trying to join in on the hit machine at Jive that was developing. We were in our best shape for over ten years and certainly the best since my arrival in 1989.

We were still making progress with Solid Harmonie and, in April, their single 'I Want You To Want Me' was to peak at No 16 in the UK. It looked like the band were making headway and they were selling records in Holland, Finland, Norway, Sweden, Switzerland and France as well as the UK. April also saw the first hit single for Jive from Scott and what a way to start! Scott had played me a record he really wanted to sign entitled 'Feel It' from a band named Tamperer, featuring

Maya, and on a first listen there was no doubt that this was a hit record. We called in Michael Smith and started to negotiate to buy the single from an Italian company. The negotiations were tough, but Michael duly did the job and the record was ours. We started club promotion and instantly the record began to create a demand. We quickly picked up the 'B' list on Radio One and that caused even more interest and demand. This was shaping up to be a big one, and that it certainly became. The pre-sales grew to almost 100,000 and the Tamperer would become the No 1 record in the UK by the end of April. The record gave Scott superb credibility at Jive Records.

The sorcerer and his apprentices:

The Tamperer and the second STEPS single were pivotal records in my career and they typified Jive's explosive successes in turnover and hits in the last twelve months, so you would think that I would be in a highly respected position by Clive Calder. Well, life at Jive Records was never that easy. Clive had arrived in the UK in March and from the start I had a feeling that all was not well. The following six weeks were hell.

It all started with a board meeting in Willesden. Clive, Nick Howe, Michael Smith, John Fruin and I attended, and almost from the off Clive proceeded to slaughter me in front of everyone. The issues were Pete Waterman's EBUL deal, the changes in A & R including Scott, the separation of Zomba Publishing from the record division, the staff costs, in fact, anything he could think of to erode my confidence and, I suppose, knock me down a peg or two. Personally, I think Clive's information sources, Steven Howard and Co, had been moved slowly out of the record company and now had no accurate information to give, so I believe they had started misleading him to prove their position and worth. It was a vicious attack and for six weeks I received faxes every Friday night and early on a Monday morning. In them, Clive said the new signings we were looking at were not good enough, the singles were not good enough and even though we were hitting the chart more regularly than ever before, nothing was right. My assistant Lesley even took to keeping the faxes from me for a day or so if I was not in the right mood to be able to deal with them, such was their intensity and venom.

I had lunch with John Fruin three weeks into the war and he told me I was showing an unbelievable streak of toughness to withstand such abuse. I really had to take it all on the chin and I did not want Pete, Scott or the staff to know that we were under such an attack from the owner as, in their eyes, we were on top of the world. The attacks were not confined to the UK either: in international meetings with Bert, Kurt Thielan from Germany and Martin Dodd, my proposed signings of Rick Astley and Kylie Minogue were completely demolished. The European boys also could not believe the pressure and insane attacks when we were doing so well and I was without doubt gaining support from them all for my refusal to buckle.

After four or five weeks of faxes, phone calls, written reports and God knows what else, for me it all came to a head when Pete called me one night in a panic. 'I hear you have resigned and are going to become MD at East West for Warner Brothers and Nick Howe is the new MD at Jive.' Pete thought I had let him down and not told him what I was doing and was leaving him at Jive. It took a good couple of hours to dispel the rumours from his mind by reminding him how long we had known each other and that I had not even spoken to East West. I had been in and out of the Warners building, but that was to do with George Benson not East West. I called a meeting in Nick Howe's office and let rip: 'If all this is all a set up to get me to resign, you've no chance. Either fire me or get lost.' Nick probably did not deserve the blast he was facing, but I did not deserve the abuse I was receiving. A couple of days later I was instructed to write a report on the deals I had commissioned and suddenly it all stopped. I never knew if it was the report or the blast at Nick that finally ended it, but end it did.

A week later Clive called me at home with a sort of apology and, sort of, was the best you would ever have from Clive. Unfortunately that was not to be the end of the war. At our yearly summer meetings in New York, again, I was called into the master's office and questioned on the record deals I had made and Clive stated he did not want to continue with the EBUL deal. I decided I would ride it out, keep all the unrest from the Jive and PWL staff and just keep charting records and making money. It was mentally exhausting. John Fruin, as ever, was supportive in our lunches together and once commented 'you have come the closest to getting the sack that I've ever seen without getting it.' I responded with, 'I know, and I would have been sacked if I hadn't made so much money.' We did laugh about the situation, but it was a painful period to go through.

In late August, Clive arrived in the UK to review our 'run in' to Christmas. The UK Company was in spectacular shape and we knew it was going to be a tremendous year-end, however, after all that had been happening with Clive in recent months I was apprehensive about the Board meeting. I got all the information together and was ready to do battle, but Clive backed right down, in fact, the meeting only went on for a couple of hours, which was a record in short time terms. The release schedule was too good and I was in too good a position for the situation to continue at that point. It would come back again, but not for a while. Our staff changes, bringing in Peter Berry and reorganising the press department and Paul Bultitude into International, with Kieron Fanning, were singled out for approval, and the waters would be calm for a while.

STEPS – to the summit:

A particularly special part of the release schedule that had strengthened my position at that meeting was the indication of a forthcoming bonanza with STEPS. During April, STEPS had debuted on the UK singles chart at No 6 with their second single, 'Last Thing On My Mind.' Pete and I felt we had a band that might just be able to perform the songs well and they were becoming more and more supported by the public around the world, especially as kids and teenagers were copying the dance routines from the dance plans of the steps to the song, which we added to the CD single.

STEPS' first album that would be titled *Step One* was nearing its completion and we felt we had an outstanding issue, but we were still looking for a third single. It was, in fact, to turn out that the most important record in STEPS' history was the last track to be recorded for the *Step One* album.

The backing track and song structure were almost finished and some of the lyrics were already written, but the key to the lyric and therefore the power behind the song had not arrived. It was one morning when it was pouring with rain that Mark Topham drove from home to the studios and started thinking about the song. Stuck in a traffic jam in London it came to him: 'One For Sorrow, Two Too Bad About Love.' At first, Mark thought it was too crass, but on arriving at the studios he tried it on the track and everyone agreed 'That's it.' Pete and I believed we had a smash hit single, the album was complete and we set about the pre promotion. The band recorded the video and the theme was based around the Enid Blyton book series *Five Go To*.... 'One For Sorrow' debuted in the UK Top 10 at No 2, sold 139,000 copies in its first week and would go on to sell over 400,000 in the UK alone. In Australia, it reached No 15, in New Zealand No 13, in Holland No 24, in Sweden No 34, in Ireland No 3 and it scored No 1's in Belgium and the Philippines.

We released the album *Step One* on 14th September 1998, the chart debut was No 2 and it would stay on the chart for an extraordinary 62 weeks. Eventually, the album would achieve eight times platinum status, selling over 2.4 million in the UK alone. Sales across the rest of the world would increase the album total to over 4 million copies. STEPS were here to stay.

Pete and I immediately started working on what would become the fourth single from the album and we planned to issue the record in November to stimulate the sales of the album going into Christmas. We had decided on a track from the album titled 'Heartbeat', written by Jackie James, and Tim Byrne had once again come up with the theme for the video, this time based on *The Ice Queen*. We then received a call from PolyGram to ask if STEPS would appear on a charity album with a variety of artists covering Bee Gee songs. Pete went along to the meeting and it was decided that 'Tragedy' would be the song that STEPS would cover. We agreed to the request only if Jive retained the single rights, with a license that the track could and would only appear on this one charity album. The current sales of the group made them important to the publicity of the charity album and so PolyGram agreed. At the time, we knew nothing about what was to come, and we decided to couple 'Heartbeat' with 'Tragedy' as a double 'A' side release. I believed that 'Heartbeat' was the band's Christmas single and their first ballad release, and then just after Christmas we could flip the 'A' side to 'Tragedy' and further stimulate the sales of the single.

We had already spent 80,000 pounds on the 'Heartbeat' video and we had used up the entire budget for videos on that track, so we now had the problem of making another video for 'Tragedy' or going without. We all felt that 'Tragedy' sounded like a smash hit and so Tim, Hermoine and I worked out how we could get a cheap video to go with the 'Tragedy' track. We promised the producer the next video, called in favours with everyone we knew and finally made the video that STEPS are probably most remembered for at a price of 40,000 pounds. Again, Tim came up with the story line: all the girls were to be married, the boys would sabbotage every wedding, then everyone would go off to a disco where the DJ was Pete Waterman. The video was filmed at All Saints Church in Harrow Weald, the fathers giving away their daughters were the girls' real fathers, the wedding guests were all from the bands' families and it was all a very special day. The video would feature what was to become the trademark of STEPS: putting both hands parallel to the side of the head in time with the word 'Tragedy.'

'Tragedy' exploded across the TV screens and the hand movement in time to 'Tragedy' could be seen everywhere you went. Sales took off like a rocket through the Christmas period and the first No 1 of 1999 on 3rd January was 'Heartbeat/ Tragedy' by STEPS. We had achieved more than we had hoped for and the band was set for the coming year. 'Heartbeat/Tragedy' is still the 48th best selling single in UK chart history with a total of 1,200,000 sales. That single outsold the previous combined sales of STEPS' first three singles. By January 1999, everyone in the UK knew Claire, Faye, Lisa, Lee and 'H.'

Jive Records was embarking on a chart dominance that would last for five years. By 15th November 1998 we had five singles inside the UK Top 30: STEPS at No 2, Tamperer at No 4, Shamrock at No 17, Tina Cousins at No 20 and R. Kelly at No 26. We all thought it was fantastic, but it was only the tip of the iceberg. R. Kelly hit a sequence of hit records with 'Half On A Baby', 'Home Alone', and the duet with Celine Dion 'I'm Your Angel', and we issued the album *R.*, which debuted at No 27 on the chart, but just sold and sold, achieving platinum status quickly and pushing on from 300,000 sales. The Tamperer followed up their No 1 single 'Feel It' with a No 3 single, the strangely titled, 'If You Buy This Record, Your Life Will Be Better.' Meanwhile, back in August, Tina Cousins, who had been signed to the EBUL deal for some time, had finally got her break as the featured vocalist for Sash. Sash was on a big run of hits at the time and Tina featured on his No 2 record 'Mysterious Times', appearing on *Top Of The Pops* a couple of times. We issued 'Pray' as Tina's follow up single, achieving a Top 20 record, and we released her album with two hits on it.

Baby One More Time – A phenomenon called Britney:

And now, after all that came, yet another Jive phenomenon. In 1994, a thirteen year-old girl called Britney Spears had featured on the American teenage television show the *All New Mickey Mouse Club*, which had also included Christina Aguilera and Justin Timberlake. The Spears family, in due course, sought advice about her future from Larry Rudolph, a New York lawyer, and this was the beginning of a journey that would eventually bring Britney to Jive Records. In 1996, Larry arranged for her to sing over a backing track of a Toni Braxton song. This demo, not in a suitable key for Britney, was sent to Jeff Fenster, our head of A & R in New York. Jeff liked the voice and although he knew she was singing in an inappropriate key, he was intrigued. In the meantime, Larry had set up appointments at six labels including Jive, and Britney over a few days was to sing three songs at each label as an audition. The response to Britney and family from Larry was that two labels said no, one was a maybe, Jive were slow to respond and the other two just disappeared.

The inside track at Jive was a little different; we had all been impressed by Britney's audition, not solely by her voice, but also by her movement and by the determined look in her eyes that suggested she would do whatever was needed to succeed in show business. Clive, Barry, Jeff, Bert and I had discussed for what seemed like eighteen months the idea of finding a new Madonna or Pop Princess, and although we had no working title for the project we knew we had the song. That song was 'Hit Me Baby One More Time', which had been written by Dennis Pop and Max Martin in early 1997, specifically for TLC and their album *Fan mail*, but by the time the band had received and listened to the song the album had been completed and 'Hit Me Baby One More Time' was rejected. At Jive we were all amazed about that, as we believed the song was a smash hit, and had TLC been on Jive I know we would have delayed the album and recorded the song: hits are more valuable than time.

We decided to put the song on hold and wait for the right artist to come along for it, one with guts, determination and an iron will to succeed. Hence, yes, in the eyes of the Spears family we were slow to respond, but we were checking all along the line to make sure of our choice. If it was to be Britney, she had to have the right credentials to become a world star. We finally believed she could and we offered her a contract with a ninety-day clause, in which we could get out if the project did not shape up. This kind of arrangement is known in the industry as a development deal. We sent Britney to Eric Foster White in New York to record a few songs, so we could see how she handled the process. We also arranged for her to dance with some professional dancers and she blossomed. Britney out danced the professionals.

I was part of the Jive meeting in New York when we discussed the possibility of combining Britney Spears and 'Hit Me Baby One More Time.' Clive, by this time, was sold on Britney and went on and on about her dancing ability. There is a boxing phrase used to describe a real champion in the making: 'He has the eye of the tiger.' I asked Clive that day 'Does Britney have the eye of the tiger?' He responded 'You know what Steve, I believe that's exactly what she's got.' 'Good enough for me Clive.'

Britney's contract was duly extended into a full deal and off she went to Sweden to record our coveted 'Hit Me Baby One More Time.' In that meeting with Clive I had also raised the point about the title of the song and advised for a number of reasons that it should be renamed 'Baby, One More Time', which in any case I felt was a sexier sounding title. That was how it was known from then on.

The next time I would see Britney was in early 1998, when we had travelled to Singapore to present our new product to our far eastern companies. The trip involved a couple of days of speeches and performances from Britney, STEPS, Jessica, an artist from our Holland company, and Julian Lennon who had made a new album for a label through Pinnacle. I met Lynne Spears, Britney's mother, on that trip for the first time and spent more time with Britney than I had before. It would still be another ten months before we launched 'Baby One More Time', and during those months Britney recorded in Stockholm and New York as we slowly put the album together.

When the album was almost complete we set about putting the video and promotion together.

The 'Baby One More Time' video was a landmark in the history of pop music. I had never before seen a video cause such a stir and become such compulsive viewing. The original idea and one that we were going with was a comic strip blend of Power Rangers and the Warrior Princess, but Britney hated the idea and after consulting her mother came back with an idea of her own. She wanted a video that represented girls of her age just leaving school, with love interest and dancing. Nigel Dick the producer agreed and we went along with it. The script was rewritten and the video that we all know today was shot. Filmed at Venice High School in Los Angeles, the same location as the film Grease many years before, all the clothes worn by the cast and Britney were bought at Wal-Mart and not one piece cost more than 17 dollars. Just that alone shows how well that video was tuned to Britney's age group. It was Britney herself who came up with the idea of wearing a school uniform, as the video told the story of leaving school and going out into the world. The reason the shirt was tied in a knot above her waist was because she felt it looked more cool than having the shirt tucked into the skirt. I was not responsible, as quite a number of people have thought, for devising some kind of a voyeuristic scenario. Case over, not guilty your honour.

In the months leading up to the release of the single, Britney toured shopping malls in the USA learning her trade. Performing day after day to a live audience is the only way to become confident in your vocals and general performance. We had operated a similar idea before with The Backstreet Boys; they completed a six-month tour of schools in America even though they were performing to 10,000 people a night in Europe. STEPS had performed night after night in clubs all over the UK and sometimes to just two or three people in the build up to their first single release. It is what you have to do, you have to learn your trade.

The US went with the Britney single first, starting work in October 1998, and slowly building, with 'Baby One More Time' cracking the Top 20 at No 17 in December and then in mid-January reaching No 1. The UK started promotion in December 1998 and everyone who saw the video or heard the record knew it was a hit, so we became instantly supported by radio and TV. Now the press really wanted to know about Britney Spears.

'Baby One More Time' was just one of those records that comes along every now and again and captures everyone, it is just perfect. I believe Britney was perfect, the song was perfect, the video perfect, Jive Records confident and in its best shape since its inception, and our knowledge of the mainstream pop market perfect from the experience we had gained with The Backstreet Boys and STEPS. In the UK record industry at the time, a well-used sales ploy was to reduce the price of the CD single for a period of time, usually the first week of release, from £3.99 or £2.99 to the price of £1.99. This educated the public that if they bought the single in the first week they could obtain it at the cheaper price of £1.99, also it made them very aware of the release date of their favourite single and caused them to purchase the record very quickly within the first seven days. Jive Records was sitting on a huge pre-sell for 'Baby One More Time' and, theoretically, there was no need to reduce the price of the single in the first week, but I was very keen to reduce the price to £1.99 to try and cause a real explosion. I believe almost every other record company would have not reduced the price and just taken the money. I have to admit, I agonised over that decision and there was some internal concern about the idea, particularly as Clive was always very miffed at any suggestion of giving away product. I had about forty-eight hours to make up my mind and went this way and that before finally deciding that I would reduce the price of 'Baby One More Time' to £1.99 for the first week, after which it would be a £3.99 item in all stores. I felt I had 10 days to wait for the result and I held my breath.

What happened next was that the record sold 250,000 copies in three days, after six days the working week's total was 464,000 and 'Baby One More Time' by Britney Spears was No 1 in the UK by a country mile. *Music Week* sprung into action writing how ridiculous the pricing of the Britney Spears CD was. Why, when you have a sure fire hit, would you reduce the price of the record? I was almost accused of mismanaging the system. The national press, however, sprung into action for information, the statisticians went into overdrive and, soon, information and demand for Britney Spears was at an all time high for any artist, probably the highest since 'Please Please Me' hit the charts for The Beatles in 1963. We very soon knew that Britney Spears was the highest selling first week sales by a female artist in the history of popular music. She was top of the tree in the history of the record business at her first attempt. The press poured on for weeks.

A week or so after the *Music Week* comment appeared, Clive read it and called. He asked me to explain in great detail every nuance of my thoughts on the issue of a £1.99 Britney single. After the debate he said he would think about it and watch what happened to find his conclusion.

Six weeks later, *Music Week* revisited the £1.99 Britney issue and corrected their stance as Britney Spears was now all over every newspaper, TV show and radio programme. They felt they had misjudged the sales explosion and could see the reasons why it had been a good, but unorthodox idea. Clive phoned again a week later and said 'so who's wrong now, eh Steve?' I knew it had been a risk, but I felt I had the right song, the right artist and the right company to take the chance and deliver it.

And a little bonus to end the year:

At the end of most years, with the party season in full swing, there is the chance for unorthodox records to become hits. I heard a record that I thought would become a hit and we signed the single 'Tell Me Ma' by Sham Rock, a band from Northern Ireland. It proved to be their one and only hit in the UK, spending 11 weeks on the chart, peaking at No 13 and selling 200,000 copies.

My contract at Jive was quickly renegotiated and after all the problems that had occurred between Clive and me, we finished the year on a high. There would be more battles to come, but Jive Records was firmly on the map, a power in the record business and a hit making machine.

1998 Jive Hits

January			
Good Girls	Joe	Jive	No 29
I Wonder If Heaven Got A Ghetto	2 Pac	Jive	No 21
I'll Be There For You	Solid Harmonie	Jive	No 18
February			
All I Have To Give	The Backstreet Boys	Jive	No 2
When I Need You	Will Mellor	Jive	No 5
April			
Essentials The Best Of George Benson	George Benson	Jive	No 8

I Want You To Want Me	Solid Harmonie	Jive	No 16
Feel It	The Tamperer	Jive	No 1
May			
Jazzy Jeff & The Fresh Prince Greatest Hits	Jazzy Jeff & The Fresh Prince	Jive	No 20
London Town	JDS	Jive	No 49
Last Thing On My Mind	STEPS	Jive	No 6
June			
No Matter What I Do	Will Mellor	Jive	No 23
Do For Love	2 Pac	Jive	No 12
July			
Lovely Daze	Jazzy Jeff & The Fresh Prince	Jive	No 37
Be Careful	Sparkle featuring R. Kelly	Jive	No 7
August			
Find A Way	A Tribe Called Quest	Jive	No 41
I Wanna Love You	Solid Harmonie	Jive	No 20
Sparkle	Sparkle	Jive	No 57
September			
Half On A Baby	R. Kelly	Jive	No 16
One For Sorrow	STEPS	Jive	No 2
Step One	STEPS	Jive	No 2
October			
The Love Movement	A Tribe Called Quest	Jive	No 38
November			
Pray	Tina Cousins	Jive	No 20
Home Alone	R. Kelly	Jive	No 17
I'm Your Angel	Celine Dion & R. Kelly	Jive	No 3
Time To Move On	Sparkle	Jive	No 40
R.	R. Kelly	Jive	No 27
Best Of The Levellers	The Levellers	Jive	No 15
To Love Once Again	Solid Harmonie	Jive	No 55
Heartbeat/ Tragedy	STEPS	Jive	No 1 (Jan'99)
If You Buy This Record Your Life Will Be Better	Tamperer	Jive	No 3

Tell Me Ma	Sham Rock	Jive	No 13
December			
Greatest Hits	2 Pac	Jive	No 17
Baby One More Time	Britney Spears	Jive	No 1

One more time:

Jive Records started January 1999 no longer under the radar of the rest of the music Industry. We were now the undisputed largest independent record company in the world. During 1999, we would benefit from yet more confidence and yet better records, and that would bring a second wind that blew us way out in front of all the others.

The TV channel The Box was the most important indicator of the late nineties. It recorded the public's votes and plays on videos and was watched by all music enthusiasts – adults, kids and teenagers. Their January Top 10 featured 'Baby One More Time' by Britney Spears at No 1, 'Changes' by 2 Pac at No 2, 'Tragedy' by STEPS at No 3, the new STEPS single 'Better Best Forgotten' at No 5 and the six month old 'One For Sorrow' by STEPS at No 7. Jive Records had 5 of the Top 7 most popular records in the UK and STEPS were recognised as a phenomenon.

The Pete Waterman deal that the industry had mocked and, which even within the walls of Jive had not been wanted and seen as a burden, posted a 2.8 million pounds profit in its first eighteen months. Jive was so busy that we did not issue any records during January – the sales of the singles and albums we had issued in the fourth quarter of 1998 were still selling enormous amounts and I wanted the company to make sure no sales were lost on those artists and to prepare properly for the next wave. For the first time in our careers, Tina and I had a long meeting about 'thinning out' the release schedule rather than trying to fill it.

The month of February was about to be manic and in just four short weeks the whole world was about to know the name Britney Spears. Britney arrived in the UK while 'Baby One More Time' was still at No 1. The list of TV and radio shows, newspapers and magazines that wanted her was enormous, and we chose just those that would make the most impact. Britney was in great form, she had exploded in the USA. and the UK, and the rest of the world was about to fall the same way. She was just seventeen and could hardly really believe what was happening, but the interviews were very upbeat and the performances, with added confidence, were fantastic.

'Baby One More Time' would be the best selling single in the UK for 1999, and it became the bestseller in every country that released it, topping sixty charts around the world. The album, with the same title, came quickly on the back of the single, shot to No 2 on release in March and would stay on the UK chart for an astonishing eighty-two weeks.

Awards season:

Whilst Britney was selling bundles of records, February brought the award ceremonies of the year. *The Brits* and *The Music Week Award* shows were on the agenda. One was filled with disappointment and a feeling of being let down, the other was filled with elation. Pete and I were involved in the Brits for 1999 and the committee had come to us with a request to produce the finale to the show. Pete came up with the idea of 'Thank Abba for The Music', which eventually featured the pop stars of the day, including our own STEPS and Tina Cousins along with B*Witched, Cleopatra and Billie. The track was finally finished on the day and the routine was completed about an hour before the show. It became a real success and a superb finish to the Brits. The record was released on Sony and would peak at No 4.

The huge disappointment was the gong for Best British Newcomer, supposedly voted for by the Radio One listeners. There was no doubt that STEPS had broken all records in their debut year and Pete and I were even told earlier that day that STEPS had won. There was indeed no real competition, however, on the night the award went to Belle and Sebastian – right, who? I have no bad feelings for Belle and Sebastian, but awarding them the gong caused a deep intake of breath at The Brits and was obviously humorous to the powers that be. STEPS management, STEPS themselves, Jive Records and Pete Waterman were absolutely gutted. It started a volume of paperwork and within days was front-page news in *The Sun* and many more of the dailies, STEPS had been swindled out of their award.

Pete and I attacked the BPI, the major record companies and BBC Radio One for their disgraceful behaviour, as it was obvious that the result had not come from Radio One listeners as it was meant to. It must be said now that the complete disbelief of the public and the outcry from the press did change the Brits forever. As each year went by, the public's contribution to the result became increasingly more safely protected and such a travesty has not occurred again.

The Music Week Awards, on the other hand, were the complete opposite to *The Brits*. The major award for services to the record industry is known as The Strat Award, after Tony Stratton Smith, and it is awarded to a high profile or successful individual in the industry. It is a highly secretive affair as on arrival at the ceremony the recipient doesn't know he or she has been selected. *Music Week* had contacted me and asked me to get Pete there on the night and although Pete, like me, is not really an awards show person, I thought that it was right and proper that Pete receive his Strat Award. He deserved it and was at last being recognised for his achievements, so I agreed to get him there – without him knowing that he would receive the award, of course. The presentation starts with video clips of prominent industry figures talking about the winner and I filmed my piece to camera for the intro. Pete joined the staff of Jive Records on our tables and the evening went along with a swing. Towards the end of the presentations of the gongs, Label of

The Year was next on the agenda. 'Ladies and Gentlemen, Label Of The Year is Jive Records, and to collect the award, here is Managing Director, Steve Jenkins.' I accepted the award on stage and thanked my staff, who had really stuck in there through thick and thin and were now reaping the rewards of dedication. I held the award aloft as I went back to our tables and everyone in turn held the trophy.

The Strat Award was the final gong of the night and as the video clips rolled on Pete became aware it was him. There is no doubt it took him by surprise and, finally, being officially recognised by the industry was a moment for him. To be fair, Pete struggled with his acceptance speech, which is most unusual, as normally nothing outwardly fazes him. After the ceremony was over, the two of us retired to the bar. Pete obviously knew that I had seen to it that he would be there that night.

'I know you did that for all the right reasons', he said,
'but you are my mate, don't ever do that again.'

'Ok mate, I never will, no matter what.'

And I never have done, our friendship is valued at a much higher level than any award.

Chart domination:

A week later on 21st February, Jive records would have three of the UK's Top 10 records: at No 1 Britney Spears, at No 8 2 Pac and at No 10 STEPS. We were beginning to dominate the chart and the people's choice.

I was still in search of more Greatest Hits projects and I had been dealing with Mushroom Records over a Kylie package. Negotiations continued, with me being invited to Shepherd's Bush Empire to watch her show, and a few days later we had dinner at Julies in Holland Park. Kylie really was the master at not being recognised out in public – she wore very little make up and had all her hair pinned in an old fashioned style. Occasionally, someone would take a second look but dismiss the thought it was Kylie Minogue, it was just someone who looked a little like her. I hadn't seen Kylie for some time, we had a great evening together, and I was up for doing the package, but the complication of Mushroom and PWL ownership of rights could not be worked out at that time. Years later it would eventually happen.

Our chart domination continued in March as STEPS' 'Better Best Forgotten', a Waterman title, would become their best-selling single of the year passing 400,000 sales and peaking at No 2 with 17 weeks on the chart. Tina Cousins continued her hit run with 'Killing Time', peaking at No 15, and as a build up to the tenth anniversary album of The Stone Roses at the end of the year, we re-issued a remix of 'Fools Gold', which peaked at No 25. Silvertone Records, for all its woes and unable to find new big selling artists, had made a profit of 500,000 pounds in 1998, primarily due to working the catalogue and Buddy Guy's continuing releases. We were to be notified in March of the following year, 2000, that Jive Records had been the biggest UK label in terms of single sales for 1999, beating all the major companies.

We were about to issue *Millennium*, the third album of The Backstreet Boys, who now had not only conquered their homeland America, but were also world stars. The first single from the album, 'I Want It That Way', shot straight to No 1, their first No 1 single in the UK. The band arrived for a three-day promotional trip including a *Top Of The Pops* performance and the album hit the No 2 spot on the charts a couple of weeks later. We continued the promotion throughout the year with an arena tour to 12,000 people a night and the release in October of 'Larger Than Life', which became a No 5 single. By the end of the year, we had sold over 500,000 copies of *Millennium*.

New signings – more hits:

May also delivered our fourth No 1 single of the year with 'Sweet Like Chocolate' by Shanks and Bigfoot. Scott had first brought me the record, which had been made by a small label. A batch of 1000 copies had been issued to nightclubs. I immediately chased up negotiations – I was certain this would be a big hit. The discussions were difficult and went on for weeks as the artists Steven Meade and Danny Longsman had since fallen out with the label Chocolate Boy Recordings and this brought with it a dispute over ownership. Michael Smith, in business affairs, slowly picked his way through the problems and we agreed to release it with the Chocolate Boy logo on the label, which finally healed all the problems. By this time, the demand was enormous and we knew we had another huge record. 'Sweet Like Chocolate' debuted on the UK chart at No 1 and it would become the eighth biggest selling record of the year. It turned out to be the biggest ever single from the UK Garage scene and the first single in the history of the record business that simultaneously topped The National Chart, The Dance Chart, The Independent Chart, and the R&B Chart. The record completely swept across the nation.

We also enjoyed our first success with Groove Armada during May 1999. Once again, it was Scott who had found something for us in the form of a single titled 'At The River.' When he played it to me I truly thought that it was an amazing record and we set off to investigate its origin, which was from Andy Cato and Tom Findlay's Tummy Touch Records. I went to meet both Andy and Tom at their lawyer's office and told them I believed in the record so much that I would sit there all day to conclude a deal. We did, in fact, sit there for a long time, but the deal was not to be done that day, however during that time the boys could see that I was deadly serious. I listened to some of their ideas and instantly offered to record an album. The trombone on 'At The River 'gave me the feeling that these boys could produce something different, yet still commercial, and they could become major album sellers.

Over the next few weeks, Michael Smith concluded the deal and we were all set to record.

Andy and Tom thought my enthusiasm for 'At The River' had meant that would be the first single, but I was a much more experienced record man than that. I explained that 'At The River' was most definitely an album selling song, but we needed a record that would introduce the band to a wider audience. It had to be up-tempo and the earliest I would release At The River would be as their second or third single, preferably the third. Although I didn't know it at the time, this had disappointed the boys; I think they thought they would control the single releases and call the shots. Nevertheless they went into the studio and after a few weeks came up with a fantastic first single: the moment I heard 'If Everybody Looked The Same', I knew we were on our way. For Groove Armada's first proper single release it did well in reaching No 25 on the chart and that opened the door for them to become an album selling act.

The band finished their album, titled *Vertigo*, and we decided to release it and work the record live, with 'At The River' following in August and some live dates to establish the band. *Vertigo* charted at No 23 and stayed on the charts for 19 weeks. Over the coming year it would pass 100,000 sales. 'At The River' peaked at No 19. We ended the year for Groove Armada by releasing 'I See You Baby, Shakin' That Ass', another truly superb record that peaked at No 17.

A STEPS Spectacular:

Meanwhile, back in the summer we had issued Britney's second single 'Sometimes', which went to No 3, selling 250,000 copies, and we had put out STEPS' 'Love's Got A Hold Of My Heart' as the first release from their next album, *Steptacular*. It was an instant sounding smash hit record and peaked at No 2, Ricky Martin this time just edging us out by a few sales. Ricky dancing down Oxford Street I think made the difference, a great stunt by Sony Records. When I listened to the playback of the completed *Steptacular*, which was Lee's idea and word, I believed the album had five hit singles on it. Pete, Helen, Tina and I celebrated over dinner and we decided that the second single from the album would be 'After The Love Has Gone.' We would hold back releasing it until October and then issue the album right on the back of the single at the start of November, giving it two months of the best selling weeks of the year. Finally, we would issue a double A sided single right in the last couple of weeks of the year, a track from the album and a new recording not on the album, to go for the No 1 spot right at the turn of the year and the new Millennium.

'After The Love Has Gone' peaked at No 5, which was a something of a disappointment, yet it still sold over 250,000 copies by staying on the chart for 11 weeks. We launched the album at Fabric, a new venue in London at the time, on 25th October, and it became a fun party. I gave the speech to launch the record and presented the group with five time platinum discs for the previous album *Step One*. *Steptacular* released in early November, shot straight to No 1 and stayed there for three weeks, when it dropped to No 2. We then started the promotion of 'Say You'll Be Mine', which featured one our best videos. The band re-enacted well-known moments from hit movies: *Titanic*, *There's Something About Mary*, *Romeo and Juliet*, *Batman Returns*, *Armageddon*, and *Austin Powers*. Tim Byrne had pulled it off again.

A couple of weeks later we issued the video to 'Better The Devil You Know.' As we were running out of time, we used the recording from Wembley of the live arena show. I was there that night to see the recording and the audience just went wild when the band broke into 'Better The Devil.'

The great thing about STEPS concerts was the audience. They were full of small kids with their Moms and Grandmas. The kids just loved STEPS, the Moms got off on the kids enjoyment and the Grans could cope with the music as it sounded like Abba. STEPS also had a huge teenage and gay following and the feeling at every concert was of people having a good time singing and dancing without inhibitions. You didn't have to be cool or posture at a STEPS concert; you just got on with having a good time. STEPS were more than just a pop band. Their music, their dances and their videos were loved by a huge amount of people who would have supported them no matter what, and their style of having fun and not taking themselves too seriously brought them a dedicated audience.

As planned, we released 'Say You'll Be Mine/ Better The Devil You Know' on 13th December, to go for the new Millennium No 1 and follow up last year's success of 'Tragedy.' This time we would fail. The double A side stalled at No 4 and Westlife claimed the No 1. We were not to be beaten on the albums front however, selling 1.3 million copies of *Steptacular* in ten weeks.

Encore R. Kelly:

Our main selling artists at Jive were STEPS, Britney Spears and The Backstreet Boys, but R. Kelly was still an international world seller. We kept up the pressure through the year by releasing 'Did You Ever Think' from the album *R.*, which was still selling, and the single peaked at No 20, bringing more sales to the album total. Robert's next single will always remain in my memory for the absolute fight I had to make it a hit record. 'If I Could Turn Back The Hands Of Time', for me, was a classic song and hit single on first listen. I originally thought that the record would be a 'walk on', in other words I had to just send it to radio, they would play it and the demand would be created. I started by having lunch with Jeff Mullen, the head of BBC Radio 2. Afterwards, I thought I would soon get a call to say, 'you're on the playlist.' Quite the reverse occurred. Jeff said he didn't quite hear the record and it was not one of R. Kelly's best. I was flabbergasted.

We sent the video out and started to pick up radio from commercial stations across the country. It was slow progress, but a constant trickle of support. I went back to Radio 2 and told Jeff I was going to have a hit, come what may, I simply would not give up, please listen again. Still, Jeff held out. I knew I had to get Radio 2, as I had no chance with Radio One on this one. Back we went again to commercial radio, and I traded STEPS tickets, Britney photos, anything I could to get play for 'Turn Back The Hands Of Time', as I completely believed that if the public heard the record then they would buy it in their droves.

Back yet again to Jeff, who by now had heard the record a few times and was beginning to think I might be right, but still no playlist. I knew that radio people listen to other radio stations to hear what is being played, so I decided to advertise the single with thirty second shots all over Capital Radio. One more time I went to see Jeff, who was by now getting fed up with it all, but, and I don't know if it was my persistence, the radio adverts or the increasing play around commercial radio, he agreed to a 'C' list with about six plays a week to gauge a reaction. The British public did not let me down now. Jeff phoned a week later to say the reaction was excellent and we would be 'B' list for a week and then 'A' list.

We set the release date further away than Jeff wanted, but he had committed now and it would be difficult to get out. 'Turn Back The Hands Of Time' was released in October to huge demand and again we just missed the No 1 slot, peaking at No 2. It sent the album *R.* into a massive sales boost and catapulted the single Top 10 across Europe. It would become R. Kelly's biggest single since 'I Believe I Can Fly' two years previously.

Jive at its peak:

October also brought the third hit single from Britney Spears. 'You Drive Me Crazy' would have the same effect on Britney's album as 'Turn Back The Hands Of Time' had on R. Kelly's R. album: the sales catapulted again and drove the albums back up the chart. 'You Drive Me Crazy' would peak at No 5 because everyone wanted the album for Christmas, and we still sold over 250,000 copies.

STEPS presented the Smash Hits Awards in 1999, two years after they had been a reserve act for the show, and that year it seemed like the Jive Show: The Backstreet Boys won five awards and Britney Spears won three Awards. Live on TV Jive artists presented awards to Jive artists – I could never have afforded to buy that kind of TV advertising.

The albums in 1999 racked up enormous sales: STEPS 1.3 million, Britney Spears 750,000, The Backstreet Boys 500,000, R. Kelly 300,000, and 2 Pac 300,000. All this plus millions of singles sales. The staff headed for the *Record Of The Year* TV Show at LWT Studios on 11th December. We expected to win Record of The Year for Britney's 'Baby One More Time' and probably should have done so, however, Westlife had been doing well and Britney's single was way back in February, so we were beaten into second place by Westlife. The Industry Awards were also presented that night and I would go up twice to receive our awards. I expected Jive to win the Label Of The Year Award, but I did not expect or even consider thinking that Managing Director Of The Year for 1999, finally, and after all those years, was to go to one Steve Jenkins.

1999 ended with *Music Week* announcing that the Britney Spears single that had caused so much controversy with the £1.99 pricing was now a sales changing single, whatever that meant. Staff changes occurred, Roddy McKenna left Silvertone Records to return to Scotland, he was replaced by Dave Wibberley. Russell Heir joined the company to work with me on licensing tracks to advertising companies and for compilations. Stuart Watson joined the company as Managing Director of Zomba International, a move that upset a lot of our Managing Directors, especially Bert Meyer, as they all had to report to him. I was called into Nick Howe's office and told before I could even speak that I would not be reporting to Watson. I simply asked 'Is that because I'm an awkward bastard?' 'Yes', was the answer.

The year before, Pete had believed the untrue rumour that I was leaving to be Managing Director of East West Records. In September of 1999, they did actually make an approach and I had thought about it, but I rejected it as I had just built a company that was dominating the industry and I believed would do so for some years to come. It had taken me ten years to arrive where we now were and I was not about to leave Tina, Pete and a whole host of people that had stood by me and fought with and for me.

In October, in response to an invitation from LWT, Pete had made a prime time TV show, *Abbamania*, and we worked together on pulling in all the artists. STEPS, Martine McCutcheon, Culture Club, Westlife, Madness and Stephen Gately all performed an Abba song on the show. The record industry suggested it was old hat; the public just loved it, watched the show in their millions and bought half a million of the album. We had a great time.

When you look back in detail on your career, the statistics I suppose show all the peaks and troughs. Although there were great years to come, I believe 1999 was the peak of my career, we could do no wrong. Jive had four No 1 singles, four No 2 singles, two No 3 singles, two No 4 singles and two No 5 singles, in total, sixteen singles that hit the Top 5. Early in 2000, it was announced that Jive Records in 1999 had the best year for an independent record company in the history of the music business.

Jive Records Hits 1999

January			
Heartbeat/Tragedy	STEPS	Jive	No 1
February			
Baby One More Time	Britney Spears	Jive	No 1
Changes	2 Pac	Jive	No 3
Tonight	Supercar	Jive	No 15
March			
Killing Time	Tina Cousins	Jive	No 15
Better Best Forgotten	STEPS	Jive	No 2
Baby One More Time LP	Britney Spears	Jive	No 2
Fools Gold remix	Stone Roses	Jive	No 25
April			
Thank Abba For The Music	Tina Cousins, Billie Piper, STEPS, Cleopatra, B*Witched	Jive	No 4
Sweet Lies	Ellie Campbell	Jive	No 42
May			
I Want It That Way	Backstreet Boys	Jive	No 1
Millennium LP	Backstreet Boys	Jive	No 2
Sweet Like Chocolate	Shanks & Bigfoot	Jive	No 1
If Everybody Looked The Same	Groove Armada	Jive	No 25
June			
Sometimes	Britney Spears	Jive	No 3
Vertigo LP	Groove Armada	Jive	No 23
July			
Did You Ever Think?	R. Kelly	Jive	No 20
Love's Got A Hold On My Heart	STEPS	Jive	No 2
Dear Mama	2 Pac	Jive	No 27
August			
At The River	Groove Armada	Jive	No 19
So Many Ways	Ellie Campbell	Jive	No 26
October			
Stone Roses Tenth Anniversary LP	Stone Roses	Jive	No 26
Larger Than Life	Backstreet Boys	Jive	No 5

If I Could Turn Back The Hands Of Time	R. Kelly	Jive	No 2
You Drive Me Crazy	Britney Spears	Jive	No 5
After The Love Has Gone	STEPS	Jive	No 5
November			
Steptacular LP	STEPS	Jive	No 1
I See You Baby	Groove Armada	Jive	No 17
December			
Say You'll Be Mine/ Better The Devil You Know	STEPS	Jive	No 4

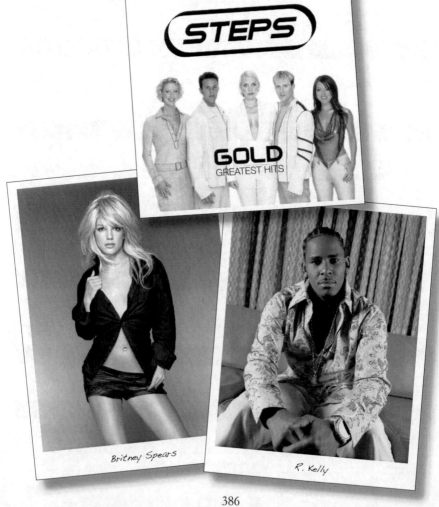

Britney Spears

R. Kelly

CHAPTER 24

2000 AND 2001 – OOPS... JIVE
DID IT AGAIN

The hits just keep on coming:

We opened a new decade and a new millennium with four huge selling acts in Britney Spears, STEPS, The Backstreet Boys and R. Kelly and, what is more they were all current and making records every year. Jive Records was becoming the new Tamla Motown. We discovered our own artists, they were recorded in our own studios by our own producers and using our own song writers. Not since the days of Tamla Motown in the 1960's had any label been so independent and so world dominating and we were about to open offices all around the world in different countries.

We had issued Britney's video for 'Born To Make You Happy' to TV stations in the week before Christmas 1999, believing that new footage of Britney would add to our sales of the album before the end of the year. Once again, I was looking for my January hit, to kick start the company and chase away the New Year blues and 'Born To Make You Happy' was issued as a single in Europe to keep up momentum for Britney's career and album sales. I had originally thought that it was probably a Top 5 single, after all, we had already sold 700,000 copies of the album and a large quantity of the fans already had the track. I would have been happy with a Top 5 single to get the wheels turning for 2000 and so it was a great surprise when the midweek chart indicators came through that the record looked like it could be No 1. By Sunday night it was the UK's No 1 record and we achieved the previous year's success of a No 1 in January.

During the previous year I had found Russell Hier to operate our licensing department, which I had previously been running myself. I had very strict rules about how we would license our records to major record companies for compilations. Firstly, if you wanted to license a Jive hit record you had to take one of our lesser hits, which helped us recoup money on those lesser hits that had probably not made money, and this slowly helped us balance the books. I had seen major record companies begin to start operating this system of lesser hits on the album and I saw no reason why Jive should not participate. The majors hated the rule and they whined and moaned at Russell about it, but I had told him that for as long as we are having hits, this was the rule and there were no exceptions.

Now That's What I Call Music!

Now That's What I Call Music! is the most successful compilation the record business has ever known. It was originally initiated in 1983, as a joint venture between EMI Music and Virgin (now part of EMI Music), and later there was also collaboration with PolyGram (now part of Universal Music Group). A rival brand titled *Hits* was initiated the following year by CBS (now part of Sony Music Entertainment) and WEA (now Warners Music Group), and soon BMG joined in too. Given that Jive Records was delivering more hits than Warners and BMG and probably rivaling Sony, I believed that if we became a partner in *Hits* it would take the compilation to another level and even closer to rivaling *Now That's What I Call Music!* Also, given that our artists were 'of the moment' and to a huge degree we had cornered the Pop and R&B markets, I saw Jive as a driving factor, should we be able to make a deal. This we attempted to do through our connections at Sony, but it was rejected by Warners, who, I only learned nine years later, had said they felt *Hits* did not need Jive per se.

I decided that now everyone would have to take two of our lesser hits to get one of our big ones. At this time, I also would not license 'Tragedy' by STEPS or 'Baby One More Time' by Britney Spears, as I believed these were iconic singles that come along once or twice in a lifetime. If you wanted to buy either, then you had to buy it from Jive Records, they were part of our crown jewels. This caused big problems with all the major companies, as to have one of these two tracks on a compilation would guarantee a lot more sales. Holding out on these two records increased their sales: STEPS' Tragedy reached 1.25 million copies and Britney's 'Baby One More Time' achieved 1.45 million. I was delighted, but the majors began to become more and more angry.

A couple of months later, Ashley Abraham, creator of *Now That's What I Call Music!* came to see me. I had known Ashley for some years and he knew how to handle me. He spoke about Jive Records and our rise in the industry and slowly got round to Britney's 'Baby One More Time' and STEPS' 'Tragedy.' The series *Now That's What I Call Music!* could ill afford not to have the biggest records of 1999 appear. I saw the opportunity and thought I would just take the shot, though I didn't think it would come off.

'Ashley you can have these two and all the rest of my hits, but I want to be a partner and I want ten percent of Now That's What I Call Music!*'*

A smile came across Ashley's face. He knew it was a cheeky stance, but I explained my reasoning and how we had a grip on the youth market. I said I thought it was right and proper and we certainly should be partners in the *Now That's What I Call Music!* series because of our achievements. Ashley left with a simple 'I'll get back to you.' Ashley did come back to me quickly: 'ten percent, put the lawyers on it and welcome to the partnership.' We would have a four year relationship with *Now That's What I Call Music!* In the meantime the *Hits* compilation sold less and less and within a few years it disappeared.

Brave new world:

In February 2000, I started to learn the new world. Jan Haley would come in every Monday afternoon and teach me the complexities of the computer. The start of the new world had arrived for me four weeks into the 2000's and over the next ten years computers, the internet and all that came with it would change the way every business worked and how everyone lived. Computers were the new Rock 'n' Roll.

February also brought a one day trip to Portugal to hail one of my best friends on a milestone achievement in his life: the sixtieth birthday of Brian Bennett MBE. Years before I had been invited to play golf at Elstree Golf Club on a Sunday morning by Brian Berg of PolyGram TV. It was Brian who had begun to teach me about compilations and TV advertising all those years ago and, in return, I had licensed my tracks to him for his compilations. We set off that Sunday morning with Adrian, Brian's brother-in-law, another Brian and Bergie in a four ball. The game was going well and the banter increased as we made our way around. Bergie and Adrian had made a couple of Cliff and The Shadows jokes around the course but not excessively, and I was concentrating so much on not making a fool of myself with the clubs that it had passed me by. Only did it strike my consciousness at about the fifteenth hole – I walked down the fairway with the other Brian and plucked up the courage to say 'Are you Brian Bennett from The Shadows?' 'Yes I am', he said. This was a big moment for me. Cliff Richard and The Shadows were the first group that had really opened my mind to records and music: I had seen their movies, bought their records, well, my Dad had bought them for me, to be truthful. Cliff Richard, Hank Marvin, Bruce Welch and Brian Bennett were heroes that stay with you for a lifetime and here I was knocking a ball around Elstree with Brian Bennett. I am pleased to say that twenty years on we all still spend our Sunday mornings together. The golf may not be much better, but the banter is at an unbelievable high.

N'Sync:

Shortly after my trip to Portugal I met Justin Timberlake, JC Chasez, Lance Bass, Joey Fatone and Chris Kirkpatrick for the first time. N'Sync had finally signed to Jive Records and we were about to increase our huge selling artists total to five. The band had originally been formed years before in Orlando when Lou Pearlman was losing his grip on the Backstreet Boys and was very early on thinking he could build another band in a similar fashion. Slowly, the group members came together and Pearlman called in Backstreets manager, Johnny Wright to manage them. Eventually, N'Sync were signed to BMG/Ariola in Munich and obviously Lou's connections and the path the Backstreets had already taken was being copied. N'Sync recorded with Jive producers in Stockholm and first of all they scored a hit in Germany that set them on their way. The band's reputation spread across Europe and back into America quicker than the Backstreet Boys and N'Sync would end up with four hit singles and a diamond album in America. Meanwhile, by 1998 they were in the middle of a legal battle. The premise was that Lou Pearlman had taken fifty percent of N'Sync's income instead of the agreed one sixth. At the same time, at Jive, we knew there were problems with the band's recording contract, as BMG and RCA, who had subsequently signed them for the US, had not taken the correct steps when signing artists under sixteen years of age. We had in-depth knowledge of the legal situation when, what are termed minors, are signed and we meticulously adhered to the law correctly. The powers that be in Munich had not done their job properly and were about to pay the price. When N'Sync threatened to leave both Pearlman and RCA and sign to Jive Records, we assured the band that we would support them through all their problems. The case eventually went to court and the injunction put on N'Sync by Pearlman and RCA was thrown out. That left Pearlman and RCA with no choice but to release the band and try for an out of court settlement. Jive remained the guiding hand in the background and we contributed to the settlement, N'Sync were then free to sign to Jive Records, which they duly did. Although I was not involved in the signing of N'Sync, Clive and I had many conversations about the band during the legal battle and we were both convinced that at some stage N'Sync would become a Jive artist.

We had already been recording the album and it was finished before the legal battle ended. The recordings took place in Stockholm and the US but, unlike The Backstreet Boys, N'Sync recorded seventy percent of their material in the US as opposed to The Backstreets who had recorded seventy percent of their material in Europe. This gave N'Sync a tougher, more R&B sound. It was still Pop, but the tracks were more shaped by R&B. Justin always referred to their sound as 'Dirty Pop' and I guess he summed it up well.

Clive had spoken to me often as we prepared for N'Sync's release in the UK, I had researched their history and chart positions, their fan-base and what had happened up to that date. It seemed to me that N'Sync had been treated by BMG as a band that came out of Germany and the records were just issued without serious intent. 'Tearing Up My Heart' and 'I Want You Back' had been released in the UK following European success and achieved chart positions of No 40 and No 62 respectively. BMG had then just moved on. After N'Sync cracked the US almost two years later, BMG reissued 'I Want You Back', scoring a Top 5 single, and they followed it with 'Tearing Up My Heart' which made No 9 in June 1999. The album,

N'Sync, which had been such a huge success in America, was released in July '99 achieving a chart position of No 30, but only staying on the chart for two weeks. The promotion of N'Sync in the UK looked bitty, unfocused and not driven with any passion or belief.

Tina and I went to meet the boys as soon as they arrived in the UK. We spoke all afternoon about their and my views of what had happened to their career in the UK, and after three or four hours the band knew that they were a priority in my mind and that their singles and albums would be treated with the greatest care and respect while we tried to sell as many copies as possible during our first year together.

By the end of March, 'Bye Bye Bye', Jive's first single from N'Sync, was proudly standing at No 3 and hot on its heels in April we issued the album *No Strings Attached*, a title born out of the band's escape from Lou Pearlman and BMG. *No Strings Attached* charted at No 14 and in America the story became a massive sensation. The album sold 1.4 million copies there on the day of release, an astonishing figure, and sales stood at 2.4 million by the end of the first week. America quickly became the focus for the band out of necessity. The promotion time needed in the UK to make them as big as The Backstreets Boys was not available. Europe also suffered from lack of live access. This was nobody's fault, there was just no time in the band's schedule, and when you are selling that amount of records in the US, that territory must become the priority.

We would release further N'Sync records later in 2000. 'I'll Never Stop' peaked at No 13 in July and 'It's Gonna Be Me' reached No 9 in September. We followed that in December with 'This I Promise You', which peaked at No 21. Even so, in the UK, the lack of live access to the band meant the public could not get attached in the way they had to The Backstreets. The UK also had its own Boy Bands like Westlife, 5ive, Ronan Keating from Boyzone, and Robbie Williams from Take That, so there was plenty of competition, especially if you then include The Backstreet Boys and STEPS. In the UK *No Strings Attached* would sell 120,000 copies during 2000, achieving Gold status, which was an excellent and much better start than N'Sync had achieved before, but a drop in the ocean compared to sales in the US.

Rolling on:

The Backstreet Boys were still churning out the hits and touring the UK and the world. It is fair to say that their visits to the UK were becoming less as the demands around the world grew. Also, they were being overtaken by the new British Boy Bands on the block, but, had created their own loyal fan base that would serve them well for their dedication to the UK 'Show Me The Meaning Of Being Lonely' became a No 3 single, just ahead of N'Sync's release in March. 'The One' became a Top 10 single peaking at No 8 in June and, by November, we were releasing 'Shape

Of My Heart', the new single from the new album *Black and Blue*. 'Shape Of My Heart' peaked at No 4 and the *Black And Blue* album debuted at No 13 in December and then sped through 400,000 copies by the end of the year.

The Awards season was upon us again in March and The Brits committee did not want any more bad publicity over rigged awards, in fact, they went out of their way to make sure Jive, Jenkins and Waterman were happy. The Jive tables were the best we ever had, positioned at the front of a low balcony with a superb view of the stage. STEPS made a performance and were presented with a new Brit Award for Best Touring Act. STEPS had sold more tickets to concerts in 1999 than any other artist. The band were delighted to have won their Brit, and Pete and I felt that at least they had been recognised for their extraordinary rise to fame, hit records and now live shows. The big disappointment was that the biggest star of 1999, Britney Spears, did not win a Brit Award – another in the long list of major record companies dividing the spoils between themselves. A few days later came the *Music Week Awards* once again and, I was on stage accepting for the second year running, our Label Of The Year gong. Again, I gave it to the staff who, once more, all had their moment with the trophy.

Oops – She Did It Again:

During April, we started to prepare for the launch of the second Britney album and single 'Oops I Did It Again.' Britney had been recording in short spells in Sweden and Switzerland with Mutt Lange and in the US. The album was ready to go, the video had been shot and had once again the theme had come from Britney: 'I want to dance on Mars with a cute guy' was where it all started. 'Oops I Did It Again' sounded like a huge hit from the moment you heard it and coupled with Britney's now manic following in the press and a huge fan base it had to go to No 1 around the world. We began the promotion with a video which quickly became a No 1 TV video, the single came out in May and debuted at No 1, and the album followed closely and debuted at No 2. Britney came to the UK for two days of intense promotion just as the record went to No 1. Further singles followed through the year with 'Lucky', in August, peaking at No 5, and 'Stronger', in December, peaking at No 7, and these singles kept the *Oops I Did It Again* album selling throughout the year. It eventually stayed on the chart for 45 weeks. In between releases during October Britney brought The 'Oops Tour' to England, playing sold out arenas. Britney's Mom, Lynne, made the trip and so did a young Jamie Lynn, they were great to have around and I nicknamed Lynne The Queen Mother.

STEPS – In a new direction:

STEPS were now on my agenda and had been for some months. During May they were out on another arena tour and selling tickets by the bucket load. Their singing and dancing shows were fantastic fun and their reputation as a live act was growing at a pace. The build up to what was to become STEPS' third album *Buzz* was difficult from the start. The band, the management, Clive and Pete were all pulling in different directions. It became a most frustrating situation that almost cost us the popularity of the band and it would eventually affect our sales. From the first meeting with the band there was trouble. Claire, Faye, Lisa, Lee and 'H' had made a decision that they wanted to write all the songs for the new album, regardless of the fact they were not songwriters and had not ever written any songs to play to me. Naturally, Pete was offended. From being the master designer of both *Step One* and *Steptacular* and delivering a constant stream of hits, the band wanted to abandon the successful formula and proceed in their own way.

Behind the whole affair was the issue of publishing income. The writers of the songs generate income that goes on for years, especially if the songs become hit records and are played frequently. Tim and the band wanted to be included in this income stream and therefore, wanted to write the songs. My point of view was that we simply could not go from world class songwriters and producers to first time writers. On top of that, who would produce? Pete most definitely would not. The other problem that compounded what was already a difficult situation was that Clive had decided that his publishing company, Zomba Music, was also not benefitting from publishing income from STEPS albums. I finally decided there was only one way to go. We had to make a fifteen track album, with Pete completing five tracks, Jive completing five tracks and each member of the band delivering one track and thereby making up a further five tracks. It was a total compromise, however, it would widen the net in search for material and who knew what might appear. Finally. an agreement was made with all parties, and I insisted that each band member wrote a song with the assistance of experienced songwriters. The album already had a hit on it from 1999's double 'A' side single 'Better The Devil You Know', and the single that was not on *Steptacular,* would appear on *Buzz*, the third album. We continued to work *Steptacular* through 2000 and 'Deeper Shade Of Blue' would peak at No 4 in April, stimulating the album with a spurt of sales.

We needed another single to promote the tour, keep the album selling and prepare the new album *Buzz*. STEPS, up until that point, had only put out double 'A' side singles at Christmas and I now decided I would use that system during the summer by coupling 'When I Said Goodbye', from *Steptacular*, with 'Summer Of Love', from the forthcoming album *Buzz*. I had spoken with Pete and told him the idea, knowing he was the only one that would understand the plan and be able to deliver a record not only on time, but also one of great quality. Pete delivered 'Summer Of Love', and we were off to the races. 'When I Said Goodbye' kept *Steptacular* selling, and 'Summer Of Love' registered hit No 2 for the up-and-coming unfinished *Buzz* album. A bonus, a piece of luck, call it what you will then arrived. When Pete is working on a project he goes quite inward and deep thinking for periods of time. I was pressuring him to come up with a new direction for STEPS, something that would be unexpected. During July, I got an excited Waterman on the phone 'Get down here pal. I've got something.' I was off to PWL and there heard what was to become another No 1 record for STEPS: 'Stomp' was just a magnificent pop record in a new direction, just what I had asked for.

There was no dispute from the management or the band or anyone else regarding 'Stomp.' The reaction was 'just get it out.' 'Stomp' debuted at No 1 in October of 2000 and added hit No 3 to the forthcoming *Buzz* album. *Buzz* was released on 3rd November and debuted at No 4 on the UK album chart. The album stayed on the chart throughout the Christmas period and would eventually sell 1 million copies. We had just about got away with it: the first album, *Step One*, had sold 1.5 million copies in the UK, album two *Steptacular* had also sold 1.5 million in the UK, and the third album *Buzz* would sell just over 1 million copies. We had lost half a million sales by messing with the formula and issuing, rather than a cohesive album, a mixed bunch of songs pulling in different directions. I felt deflated that we had messed around with a winning team and formula, but elated that we had got away with selling one million copies of what I thought was a poor album. The videos were again all themed: Futuristic STEPS on 'Deeper Shade Of Blue', romantic STEPS in Rome with 'When I Said Goodbye', Good STEPS versus Bad STEPS in 'The Summer Of Love', and Party STEPS in 'Stomp.' These videos kept STEPS on TV throughout the year.

Another great year:

Our end of year sales were boosted by our other worldwide act R. Kelly. Work on his career continued throughout the year and during April Robert's '4 Play EP' made the UK Top 30, peaking at No 24. The first single from the new album, 'I Wish', debuted at No 12 in October and we issued the new album *TP-2.com* on 18th November. It entered the chart at No 21 and stayed in the Top 40 through Christmas.

The gross turnover of Jive Records improved in 2000 and the profit margin increased accordingly.

As Managing Director of the most profitable record label in the UK, having five top selling artists on the books that command huge radio and TV airtime, plus being constantly in the press spotlight, all this attracts a lot of attention and invites from the most unusual places. Lesley used to come in most mornings with the post and we would sit and review enquiries, problems, invites and requests. I have to admit that I refused ninety-nine percent of everything that was sent in. I was not the party animal MD, not least because I was vastly too busy. Five international artists, their singles, videos, albums and tours are hard to handle. One act selling the kind of volume of records we were achieving is tough and five takes somewhere between ten to fifteen hours a day. Added to that, much of my work took place in the US. A lot of my evenings were spent on the phone to New York and the

New York office sometimes forgot the time difference and called in the middle of the night. Therefore, my free time became more and more valuable the busier we were. My interests outside music were confined to sport. I loved and still love my hometown football club, it has always been a place where both Pete and I have unfailingly been made welcome. The games and the involvement with the players and team stopped my brain thinking about records for a period of time. The club was my mental release.

In 2000, Pete and I worked on another LWT Saturday Night television Special called *Motownmania*. The principle was the same as *Abbamania*, a group of artists performing well known Motown Songs.

Universal Records would issue the *Motownmania* album, which would sell 150,000 copies. The *Abbamaninia* album, also released on Universal, sold three times that many. John Kennedy, then Chairman of Universal, helped Pete and I with all the LWT projects and also issued Pete Waterman's *Greatest Hits* in 2000, an idea I had that would develop into a book on Pete's life, published by Virgin Books. John also oversaw the album, which would debut at No 3.

The BBC also approached me to do a 'fly on the wall' documentary. Their idea was that a TV camera would follow me round for months and this would eventually make up a ten part series for BBC2. I went along to the first meeting but I felt that they just wanted to hear my private conversations with STEPS, The Backstreet Boys, N'Sync, R. Kelly and, obviously, Britney. This I could not do. Those conversations were my private domain and the faith these artists had in my integrity would have gone for good. I called the Beeb and said 'No Thanks.' They just could not believe I would give up a golden opportunity for what they called 'national stardom.' Whether you think I was right or wrong, I have absolutely no regrets. I felt the artists were the stars and I was definitely behind the scenes. If you wanted an interview then speak to Pete Waterman, that was his game and part of our partnership, not mine.

When Britney came in on one of her promo trips to the UK we went to the lunch and afternoon presentations for The Capitol London Awards. Britney won and accepted her London's Favourite International Female Award. Tina and I spent the lunch and afternoon with Britney, but the moment for me was later, towards the end of the function. I have always been a Rod Stewart fan, ever since all those club gigs and the breakthrough record 'Maggie May.' Ever since then I have always bought Faces and Rod's solo records, all through the years. Rod is without doubt a musical hero of mine. He played a couple of songs that day and picked up an award and afterwards he cruised the room with Penny Lancaster greeting the guests. Then he retired backstage to the dressing rooms. I had access via Britney to the dressing rooms and spent an amazing 20 minutes just chatting with Rod and Penny. Many times, when you meet a hero after many years of worship, it is a disappointment, however Roderick was most definitely not.

I travelled to New York in September for company meetings with Bert Meyer and Kurt Thielan. Both were big football fans and from the landing at JFK we were searching for a bar that would be showing the England versus Germany match. We eventually found a bar showing the game and headed there early one morning to eat breakfast and watch the game. It was to be an unhappy breakfast for me: Germany won the game 1-0 and after the match Kevin Keegan resigned. Kurt really let me have it through the next couple of days with his constant reminders of our defeat. It would be a while before I could return the abuse, but when it came it was unbelievable. On 1st September 2001, England went to play in Germany in the match all England fans remember: Germany went 1-0 to the good before Michael Owen and the rest of the team destroyed them 5-1. The video of that match became a big seller in England and we at Jive Records, for some promotion, received a bundle of them. I arranged with our International department to send a copy of the video to Kurt every three days, so that he would keep opening packages that always said the same thing: England 5 Germany 1. I don't believe Kurt ever watched the video, I just can't think of a reason why.

Also in 2000 we signed an act named Kinobe. Scott had found and signed them and they would produce two albums for us over the next three years. Julius Waters and Dave Pemberton produced their first album *Soundphiles*, which I liked, and it featured a really great track 'Slip Into Something.' The album sold a fair quantity of records, however, they needed to up their game for the second album. The recording of this second album was slow going and we were missing out on the awareness we had built on the first album. I had spoken with Scott many times as he brought track after track up to my office when they were completed. I was concerned that the boys were moving musically further and further away from taking a step forward on their second album. In sheer frustration, after months of slow recording and without any really great track, I spoke with them about the structure of a song, explaining what I had learned from great songwriters and passing on to them the rules that would bring better material and tracks to the project. They listened and didn't comment very much but must have left with the idea of 'Old Fart' in their minds. They continued with their snail pace, over-thinking method of recording and finally delivered their album. Their come back at me was to title the album *Versebridgechorus?* Whenever I see that album on the net or in someone's collection all these years later, it always reminds me of those boys: they did provide me with the only album titled after ideals.

Jive Hits 2000

January			
Born To make You Happy	Britney Spears	Jive	No 1
February			
Hammer To The Heart	Tamperer	Jive	No 6
March			
Show Me The Meaning Of Being Lonely	The Backstreet Boys	Jive	No 4
Bye Bye Bye	N'Sync	Jive	No 3
April			
A Deeper Shade Of Blue	STEPS	Jive	No 4
4 Play EP	R Kelly	Jive	No 24
No Strings Attached LP	N'Sync	Jive	No 14
My Name Is Joe LP	Joe	Jive	No 46
May			
Oops I Did It Again	Britney Spears	Jive	No 1
Oops I Did It Again LP	Britney Spears	Jive	No 2
The Remixes LP	Groove Armada	Jive	No 68
June			
The One	The Backstreet Boys	Jive	No 8
July			
When I Said Goodbye/ Summer Of Love	STEPS	Jive	No 5
Sing-A-Long	Shanks & Bigfoot	Jive	No 12
I'll Never Stop	N'Sync	Jive	No 13
Treat Her Like A Lady	Joe	Jive	No 60
August			
Lucky	Britney Spears	Jive	No 5
September			
It's Gonna Be Me	N'Sync	Jive	No 9
October			
Stomp	STEPS	Jive	No 1
I Wish	R. Kelly	Jive	No 12
November			
The Remixes LP	The Stone Roses	Jive	No 41
Buzz LP	STEPS	Jive	No 4

Shape Of My Heart	The Backstreet Boys	Jive	No 4
TP-2.com LP	R. Kelly	Jive	No 21
December			
Stronger	Britney Spears	Jive	No 7
Black and Blue LP	The Backstreet Boys	Jive	No 13
This I Promise You	N'Sync	Jive	No 21

STEPS – forwards – and then…

On New Year's Day 2001, we issued STEPS' 'It's The Way You Make Me Feel/ Too Busy Thinking About My Baby.' It was another record for our 'kill the New Year blues and get a hit early' philosophy. We were not to be disappointed. The single debuted at No 2 and we were once again off and running. 'The Way You Make Me Feel' was STEPS' twelfth single and the video theme, Dangerous Liaisons, that accompanied became one of the band's favourite releases. 'Too Busy Thinking About My Baby' was a cover of Marvin Gaye's classic Motown track, which the band had performed on our Motown Mania TV show towards the end of the previous year.

Our double 'A' side singles were now being copied by new pop groups, but without the reasoning that had brought us to operate the system. Other companies just issued double 'A's without using them in the correct fashion that had been so successful for us and for STEPS. We would first work one side of the single and then as the first track began to falter we would work the other side and therefore slow the decline in sales, attracting a few more sales and maintaining a slow decline on the chart. We were about to operate this structure and flip to 'Too Busy Thinking About My Baby' when Faye decided she hated the version and was not prepared to perform the song on TV. This was unusual. Faye was normally the most easy-going of the group and usually just got on with the job, and in meetings with the band Faye asked questions, but was normally thoughtful in her responses and I always got along with her very well. Lee was always protective of the band and in general looked after everyone. Lisa, always strong and direct, would push for more success and although sometimes her passion was misdirected, she was a driving force and contributed a lot to STEPS. Claire and 'H' never really rocked the boat; they just got on with everything and let everyone around them make most of the decisions. So it was quite a surprise when Faye completely refused to perform 'Too Busy Thinking About My Baby.' When I spoke with her about this she said she was completely convinced that our version had ruined the original. I could not change her mind and 'Too Busy Thinking About My Baby' did not realise its potential. We had, however, achieved a No 2 single and we just moved on.

Tim and I met several times during January and February to decide upon the next move with the band. *Buzz* we already knew, had lost almost a third of our record buying public – the album was simply too 'bitty', not cohesive and with songs that were not good enough to keep our selling momentum. I could not face another album being pulled this way and that over who wrote the songs, who published the songs, who sang lead on the songs and all the problems that had occurred in the build up to *Buzz*. I thought we should issue the *Greatest Hits* album, with two or three new songs, which would be easier to achieve, therefore giving us a slightly more convenient recording schedule for 2001. I also saw the *Greatest Hits* as the end of phase one, surely increasing the sales base back to 1.5 million in the UK and probably beyond. This coupled with the touring would put STEPS right at the top of the pile in terms of Pop acts, after which we should take three months off with the individual band members doing whatever they wanted until April 2002, when we should meet up and plan the start of phase two.

I truly believed that with 'Stomp' we had found a way forward. This record and 'It's The Way You make Me Feel' had started to move the band forwards musically and I felt we had a splendid opportunity to develop, beginning to carry our fans with us as they got older. The next STEPS sound, I believed, would be somewhere between Chic and Barry White on one side and Carol King's *Tapestry* and New Seekers on the other. It would still be pop, but the songs would begin to be more adult as our audience started to grow up.

Tim and I agreed without any argument that the Hits album should be 2001's event and we began to plan accordingly. By the time recording came around, though, it was clear that STEPS no longer wanted to record at PWL. No matter how hard I had tried to mend the differences, *Buzz* had put a rift between PWL and STEPS. For now, we continued the promotion of *Buzz* with another double 'A' side single that came out in June. It was titled 'Here And Now/ You'll Be Sorry.' I guess all the management and Pete have their favourite and least favourite STEPS singles, and I have to say that of all the singles we issued, this pair of 'A' sides are my least favourite. I didn't like the songs or the titles and I didn't much care for the videos, but the record again proved STEPS' popularity and it peaked at No 4 to keep their hit ratio in perfect condition.

We began work on the new tracks for the *Greatest Hits* album that would be titled *Gold*. It was Tim who came up with the idea for 'Chain Reaction', always one of his favourite songs, coupled with a hospital video, which set the girls dressed as nurses and the boys as patient and doctor. The package seemed like a winner from its inception and we worked towards finishing what would become the lead single from the album. We had also decided upon a huge arena winter tour, our biggest, and the word of a *Gold* tour began to sell tickets immediately. After a summer of recording and shooting videos, the band started rehearsals for the *Gold* tour and we exploded back into the public's consciousness. We opened with Chain Reaction and the hospital video in early October and, again, it was a double 'A' sided single, this time with a remix of one of our biggest sellers, 'One For Sorrow.' The single debuted at No 2 and would become our biggest selling single for over two years.

The launch party for the *Gold* album was held on its release date 15th October, the pre-orders were enormous and STEPS were back on track. The album debuted at No 1 and would go back to No 1 on a further two occasions. *Gold* was November 2001's biggest selling album and as we approached the huge selling month of December we were in great shape.

The *Gold* tour commenced and we issued 'Words Are Not Enough' coupled with 'I Know Him So Well', a track not available on *Gold*. During the pressurised weeks of December the single peaked at No 5 and the *Alice Through The Looking Glass* video was all over the TV. The concerts were huge and a riot, just hit after hit. Gold continued its huge sales through December and stood at 1.25 million by the close of the year, eventually going on to sell 1.6 million copies and becoming STEPS' biggest album in the UK. During December, I went to see them play their concerts in Wembley and Birmingham. After the Birmingham concert on 11th December they were all tired, but we discussed taking off the three months as planned and I left for holiday, tired myself, on 16th December. It was the last time I saw them all.

The first I learned of the band splitting up was halfway round the world on 27th December. I was staying in a hotel and they put the local national paper under the door each day. I was just skimming through the paper when I saw a picture of STEPS and the 'Band Split' headline. Initially, I thought it was one of the usual stories that had been doing the rounds for the past months, but something in the way it was written suggested that, at the very least, someone from within the group or management had said something. I phoned Pete who told me the news that the group had told the press on Boxing Day of the split. Pete was fending off press calls every few minutes as he had no knowledge himself of what had occurred. The fans, and probably rightly so, thought they had been misled and were vicious in their disappointment.

After all these years it is clear that the whole affair was handled badly, and there was no need to announce a split at that time. There are factors to take into account about the demise of STEPS, but I offer them not as an excuse – the way the split was announced and concluded was poor and not befitting of a group that had brought so much pleasure to so many people. The factors were that within the wheels of the group their management company was going through its own problems of conflicts and disagreements and, at the same time there were divides and rivalries in the band, with individual members feeling they were the most important. The cohesive unity of the band had been one of its greatest attractions, and whereas the attempts at solo careers over the following years had some successes these were never anywhere near the kind of success they all had together. STEPS' power was as a unit, not as individuals, and it is sad that they chose not to respect that any more.

STEPS' career finished with some phenomenal statistics. At the time, they had more Wembley performances under their belt than any other pop group and they kept that record for many years, only eventually being overtaken by a reformed Take That. In the list of consecutive Top 5 records they are fourth highest in the history of popular music: The Beatles have twenty consecutive Top 5 singles, Westlife twenty also, Oasis are third with eighteen, then STEPS with fourteen, a remarkable achievement. STEPS' total sales have still continued to increase as the years have been going by and at the time I write this, the figure stands at 19 million. They deserve their place in the history of pop, they worked extremely hard and were dedicated for five years, I only wish the end could have been handled with the class it deserved.

From the Backstreet Boys to Shirley Bassey:

The first four months of 2001 were a breeze. The Backstreet Boys scored another Top 10 record in February with 'The Call', peaking at No 8, the month was made even better with Joe scoring his biggest UK hit, 'Stutter', which reached No 7 and brought Joe in for promotion on *Top Of The Pops*, resulting in a sales boost for the album *My Name Is Joe*. During March R. Kelly came back with 'The Storm Is Over Now', peaking at No 18, and April was the return of Britney with 'Don't Let Me Be The Last To Know', reaching No 12. As a company we were back out there looking for hot new artists: Pete signed Luke Galliana, Scott had signed Jason Downs and I was talking with Shirley Bassey.

Shirley had not been recording for some time and I believed if we could sign her and produce the right album on a label that was having back to back hits, it would provide us with a great story and a lot of album sales. I believed her audience was just waiting for a new record. Shirley did not have a manager, just an agent and it was with them that we opened negotiations. I had the great fortune to meet Shirley and spend a couple of hours in her company as we discussed her feelings about a new record and how we should approach it. Everything was going according to plan and we opened negotiations with her agent, however, the demands of the agent, rather than Shirley, were what brought the whole deal to fail. I am sure that Shirley never knew why the deal had failed, as she was very excited about the possibility and I reckon the agent cooked up some story. I was pleased to see that over a year later another label signed Miss Bassey and achieved success, my gut feeling had been correct. I had felt it an honour to spend just a little time with such an iconic performer.

On and On:

March, again, would bring The *Music Week Awards* and once again and for a third year in a row, a feat never matched before or since, Jive Records was

Label Of The Year. Soon we were on the verge of an English summer and May brought a hit for Jason Downs', 'White Boy With A Feather.' It peaked at just No 19, but it was all over the radio and at the time it looked as though we had found an artist who could go on to sell a lot of records. Luke Galliana also scored a No 41 single with 'To Die For.' I have always felt that had that record cracked the Top 40, it would have gone on to be a Top 20 record and the future may just have been different for Luke.

June brought the 'Here and Now/ You'll Be Sorry' No 4 hit for STEPS and R. Kelly continued his long list of hits with 'Fiesta' at No 23. Their albums just kept on selling. In July, 'More Than That' scored a No 12 single for The Backstreet Boys, their final single for 2001 in the build up to their *Greatest Hits* album for Christmas. And as the Backstreets wound down, N'Sync delivered their new album *Celebrity*. The first single from the album, 'Pop', became a No 9 record in July and was quickly followed by the album, which entered the chart at No 12 in August. *Celebrity,* in the UK would double the sales of the previous album *No Strings Attached* and conclude at 200,000 sales.

The problem for N'Sync in the UK was their lack of visits into the country. Many have said that N'Sync believed the huge success they were having in America – upwards of 7 million sales – would automatically spread across the world without them having to travel. I do not agree with that statement. Had they promoted in the UK and Europe, the sales achieved would not have matched the incredible figures in the much larger conglomerate area of the US, furthermore, the UK has a history of Boy Bands and the ones that were here all the time were the ones that became successful – Take That, Boyzone and Westlife. Their priority was the United States and rightly so – but if they had appeared with a presence in the UK it would probably have helped their popularity here quite a lot.

Jive Records' run in to Christmas began in September. Groove Armada led the charge, with the single 'Superstylin'' scoring a No 12 hit and setting up the album *Goodbye Country, Hello Nightclub*. Andy and Tom delivered a first single immediately to stop my involvement in searching for one and, as they saw it, interfering. I was happy that 'Superstylin'' sounded like a hit and also a great record, and I just rolled the project. Following this, the months of October, November and December brought enormous sales to the company. STEPS' singles 'Chain Reaction' and 'Words Are Not Enough' drove the album *Gold* to No 1. Britney Spears came back with 'I'm A Slave For You', being the first single from her third album *Britney*, which peaked at No 4; the album also debuted at No 4. The Backstreet Boys released *The Greatest Hits, Chapter One* and that too debuted in the Top 5 of the UK album charts.

After all the No 1 singles and the huge amount of other hits we had achieved over the past three years, Christmas 2001, for me, delivered our biggest and best achievement. We scored three albums in the UK Top 10 at the same time, and thus our sales and therefore our income went through the roof, making this our most profitable year. The chart read No 1 STEPS, No 4 Britney and No 9 The Backstreet Boys. From the backwaters of Willesden we were outselling Universal, EMI, Sony, Warner Brothers and BMG – the five major companies, who were left trailing in our wake.

The tours were also rolling. This year, R. Kelly returned to the UK with huge shows in Birmingham, Manchester and London. I remember watching the huge London Arena Show with Robert in total command of the audience. He had come a long way from 'She's Got That Vibe', and the struggle we originally had to get his live performance career going was now a distant past. He was a complete professional and a worldwide star. I remember thinking that Jive UK had a lot to do with what we were now watching. STEPS were also on the last tour, although we didn't know it at the time. With two shows a day in some cities, over 250,000 people were making their way to see STEPS.

The live shows I always loved. The hits were what I was all about, but to go and see the enjoyment created by the artist and the hits was the best part, to see the reaction to big hits and the singing and dancing by the audience that accompanied the bands was fantastic. Generally, the first time I watched one of our artists shows I was there from start to finish, then on a second or third occasion, by then knowing the set, I watched the audience and their reaction to the hits.

A Star Is Born:

My old pal Pete was busy and embarking on a new opportunity. He took a call from Simon Cowell, whom he and I had known for years, going back to the mid-Eighties when Pete made Sinitta's records for Simon and Impulse promoted them. Pete's development of Simon's idea would become a long running project that changed television broadcasting and made Pete a household name. For years he and I had spoken every evening at some time regarding our businesses and how the day had gone and one evening he told me about Simon's idea and that he had been asked to be a judge. Simon had been away on holiday in Barbados the previous Christmas, something he did every year and continues to do today. Simon was bored; he had been having a successful run of hit records with both 5ive and Westlife and had established himself at BMG Records after years of trying. Everyone in the UK had been watching a show titled *Popstars*, the first of the talent search shows, and it intrigued Simon, who came to the conclusion there was a better show to make. On his return to England he set about putting together what would become known as *Pop Idol*.

Having obtained commitment from LWT and ITV, Simon started to search for the judges. Pete was on top of the list, as he would bring a credibility to the show on account of his track record for hits and artists. The group set off to audition in Manchester and Pete called me every night to let me know how things were going, while I told him of our sales and the way STEPS were shaping up for the tour and *Gold* album. After a couple of days filming the auditions Simon called a judge meeting. The show was not working. Simon came to the conclusion that being honest was the only way to go: if the audition was awful, they should be told. That changed the whole show and would become the successful 'hook' the show needed and, on that basis, the auditions went on around the country, finally returning to London.

The press launch was scheduled and just after it Pete called, 'We've got a winner of a show, the press are all over it, this is big.' He was right. That first show lit up Saturday night TV, I watched every week and then discussed it with Pete the following week. I went to quite a few of the shows and sat just behind the judges, and I was amazed at the amount of people who called the week after and said, 'Hey I saw you at *Pop Idol*.' It had gripped the nation. Ant and Dec made the show, with their adlibs and compere technique, and ITV had got it right. *Pop Idol* was huge.

That first show was definitely about finding a real pop star, someone who could sell records and last at doing so. The climax was a duel between Gareth Gates and Will Young. Simon believed that Gareth should be the winner, Pete thought it should be Will, the public would, however, decide. It was a big night, the final, and I think we all believed that the public would go for Gareth. It was a surprise that Will eventually won. I believe the right man won; Will definitely had something special and more than Gareth. Eventually they both became pop stars, but Will had the longevity and was the first *Pop Idol*. I think that has stood him in good stead through the years. Meanwhile, Pete had become a national TV star, and by the time the next UK *Pop Idol* came around Simon was a household name in America. *Pop Idol* did in the US exactly what it had done in the UK – become a huge TV success.

I would say 2001 was one of the most enjoyable years, I was just left to get on with it at Jive and the sales were enormous. Walsall FC were promoted at The Millennium Stadium, a huge memory for any Walsall fan, and the record business tournament that meant the most, the La Manga Golf Classic, had seen me become Champion for the second time. Always a music lover, I even got to see two of my favourite bands that year: The Eagles, who for me give the best live shows in that they play the hits note perfect, and Hall and Oates, writers of great songs and a privilege to have worked with them.

Could I have foreseen what was to come?

Jive Hits 2001

January			
It's The Way You Make Me Feel/Too Busy Thinking About My Baby	STEPS	Jive	No 2
February			
The Call	The Backstreet Boys	Jive	No 8
Stutter	Joe	Jive	No 7
March			
The Storm Is Over Now	R. Kelly	Jive	No 18
April			
Don't Let Me Be The Last To Know	Britney Spears	Jive	No 12
May			
I Wanna Know	Joe	Jive	No 37
White Boy With A Feather	Jason Downs	Jive	No 19
Too Die For	Luke Galliana	Jive	No 41
June			
Here And Now/ You'll Be Sorry	STEPS	Jive	No 4
Fiesta	R. Kelly	Jive	No 23
July			
More Than That	The Backstreet Boys	Jive	No 12
POP	N'Sync	Jive	No 9
White Boy With A Feather	Jason Downs	Jive	No 64
August			
Celebrity	N'Sync	Jive	No 12
Superstylin'	Groove Armada	Jive	No 12
September			
Goodbye Country, Hello Nightclub	Groove Armada	Jive	No 5
October			
Chain Reaction/ One For Sorrow remix	STEPS	Jive	No 2
Gold, The Greatest Hits	STEPS	Jive	No 1
I'm A Slave For You	Britney Spears	Jive	No 4
Songbook, A Lifetime In Music	David Gates	Jive	No 11

November			
Britney	Britney Spears	Jive	No 4
The Hits: Chapter One Greatest Hits	The Backstreet Boys	Jive	No 5
My Friend	Groove Armada	Jive	No 36
December			
Words Are Not Enough/ I Know Him So Well	STEPS	Jive	No 5
Gone	N'Sync	Jive	No 24

Paris launch of Oops with Britney and Tina

London – N'Sync, Tina and Me

With Brian Bennett MBE, Shadows Drummer, composer and great friend

CHAPTER 25

2002 AND 2003 – ALL THINGS MUST PASS

Life in the fast lane:

January 2002 opened and we once again got the year off quickly with 'Drowning' by The Backstreet Boys peaking at No 4 on the chart. Britney arrived in the UK for just two days of promotion for her next single 'Overprotected', which would also become a No 4 single in February. These two singles kept The Backstreets' Greatest hits, *The Hits - Chapter One* album and Britney's *Britney* album selling through January and February into March.

'Drowning' was to be The Backstreet Boys' last single for a long while. The boys had done almost seven years of constant touring and needed a break. Wisely they did not announce any split, but said they were taking a hiatus. Even though in the next year or so they would involve themselves in a host of solo projects, they always denied the rumours of a split and would eventually return to both recording and touring.

In April, 'Girlfriend' by N'Sync became their biggest UK hit, peaking at No 2 and selling bundles of the *Celebrity* album. This was the first time after nearly three years of hard work by Jive that N'Sync were at their closest to cracking the UK market. And then, almost immediately, the band announced that they too were taking a hiatus from recording and touring. Although they did regroup for a huge TV show now and again, we did not know at the time that this was the end of N'Sync.

The awards season arrived with *The Brits* in February and the *Music Week Awards* in March.

Jive Records won Label Of The Year for the fourth year running and as I had now been on stage for the past three years accepting the award I felt that this year it should be another member of the team who did the honours. Tina did not want to accept it and neither did Hans, so I decided that the recipient should be John Fruin, for his loyal support of my career and his influence over Jive Records. It would be John Fruin's last public appearance and he accepted immaculately, as I knew he would. The audience stood for his acceptance, a tribute to one of the UK's finest music executives. John handed the award to me as he was applauded off the stage and I again handed it to all the Jive staff to have their moment with their fourth consecutive label of the year award. I don't believe any company has won that award four times on the trot, before or since.

A film – and a drama – for Britney:

The 25th of March brought a new area for Jive Records with our first movie, *Crossroads*, starring Britney Spears. This was a Jive investment achieved on a shoestring budget of 12 million dollars and Pepsi also had an involvement of 2 million dollars, which is why you see plenty of Pepsi drinking during the movie. I have been asked many times if *Crossroads* was meant to be the start of Britney going into the movies and becoming a film star. Well, I believe that Britney and Jive were testing the water on that question. She had left her teens and was no longer the Teen Princess, so the huge worldwide brand of Britney Spears had to move on: we could not keep repeating 'Baby One More Time' or 'Oops I Did It Again.' The third album, *Britney,* had been a move away from the first two albums and recorded mainly in the States with US producers, rather than mainly in Europe with European producers and, as I have said earlier, the album had a more grown up sound. Although not as easily accessible as the first two albums, certainly, it was a move forward for Britney. Many people suggested during this time that Britney's star was waning in that the *Baby One More Time* album had sold 14 million, whereas *Oops I Did It Again* achieved 10 million and *Britney* eventually only 7 million. It may look like that from the figures, but 7 million is enormous in anyone's book. No, *Crossroads* just added to the Britney mix: the records, the touring, the merchandise, and the books. Clive decided the time was right for a Britney movie and that Jive would finance it, probably to protect our prize asset. The deal was struck and Britney would make far more money with Jive than with any film studio in Hollywood as she was a partner in the movie.

A lot of people have also said to me that the movie failed. Well, I'm not so sure. Financially, definitely it did not. The first week's gross in the US was 17 million dollars and, eventually, it would make back 35 million dollars, almost three times its cost. Failed in the fact that Britney did not go on to be a major movie star? Well, possibly, but since then Britney has not tried or wanted to make movies, although I would not rule it out of her life forever. *Crossroads* did well in the UK and achieved better press here than in America. It might be said that the public was starved of regular Britney Spears in the UK, and so to get the Britney fix the movie did the job for the fans and that is what it was all about. I thought Britney did well in the movie portraying an eighteen year-old, it was fun, it was up, and it had a chic flick story. What's wrong with all that?

Singles from the movie filled our year. 'I'm Not A Girl, Not Yet A Woman' peaked at No 4 in April. 'Boys' peaked at No 7 in August, and 'I Love Rock 'n' Roll' peaked at No 13 in November. The *Britney* album sold over 500,000 copies in the

UK and the movie was a success making 5 million pounds, so altogether, Britney Spears had another great year and came in and out of the UK on flying visits.

In the lives of most people there are years that go unbelievably well and others that just collapse around you. Britney's collapsing year in personal terms started in 2002. The first big story of the year was the possible split of the long running relationship between Britney and Justin Timberlake. They had known each other since they were teen presenters on the Mickey Mouse Club, they had both grown into music stars in their own right and then both become world stars. The history and the success could only have put a special bond between them and a relationship would seem the only way to go for two individuals who had a similar experience of life. At Jive Records, we always tried to protect their relationship and a strict 'No comment' was in place on anything that was not to do with the promotion and sales of their albums.

After several denials of a split, which were true at the time, finally, the inevitable happened, and Britney and Justin were no longer together. For any of us, the trauma of the breakup of our first true love is horrifically painful, but to have it played out on every TV show, the news, the papers, the magazines, in fact, everywhere you look, is beyond comprehension.

Britney and Justin both had to do interviews, it was part of their job, and all those interviews wanted the 'dirt' on what had happened to the Prince and Princess of Pop. No matter how careful you are in your responses, something always comes out and is propelled across the press and TV. It was an awful position.

Britney and Justin both handled their pain differently. Britney started to go off the rails and finally and gladly decided to take six months off at the end of 2002. In England, the bad press came to roost on the opening night of *Crossroads* in Leicester Square. The week before, Tom Cruise had been at the premier of his new movie *Vanilla Sky* and had treated the fans to over an hour of walkabout, signing and photo taking, a huge Cruise success that made all the news shows. Hence, everyone expected the Pop Princess to do the same. The crowds were enormous in that expectation. I was already inside the theatre awaiting Britney's arrival, the mobiles were hot and time was passing. Britney eventually arrived an hour late. Probably because she knew she was late, she got out of the car, waved to the fans and disappeared inside. The groundswell of disappointment blew straight out of Leicester Square into the theatre. Everyone inside knew a problem had just occurred and within seconds three or four of us were around Britney saying 'you have to go back out there for ten minutes, it will make it all OK.' Britney, however, was not in a good state, she was clearly upset and had made an enormous effort to get there and hold herself together through the premiere. She could not face going out to the fans and so we decided that we would go onto the balcony for a few minutes and wave so that people could take photos. We expected to do that for maybe four or five minutes.

The theatre quickly lit up the balcony and then Britney, Tina, Felicia, me and a couple of bodyguards headed for the balcony. As we got closer to the public, we held back a step or two to be supportive of Britney and give her the limelight with the fans. After an initial cheer, it started to go badly with a few people shouting unsavoury comments that then built like a plague. We decided to abandon quickly and go back inside the theatre. Much has been written about that night, but I do feel, had the reception been warmer, Britney would have stayed on the balcony longer and who knows may have found a little comfort and eventually returned outside. As it was, we will never know, it was a P.R. disaster and the papers went for it.

In contrast, Justin reacted differently and would commence recording the album *Justified* in a whirlwind of day and night work, finishing the album in six weeks. Justin probably said a couple of things he would have reversed in hindsight, but in general, because of the album, he stayed out of sight and away. He poured all his feelings into *Justified* and only really shocked with the video to the second single from the album 'Cry Me A River.'

Both Britney and Justin are from the show business world and operate to the mantra 'the show must go on.' No matter how much they didn't want to, they got up there and did the job. Notwithstanding Britney's stress, she recorded her videos and then went on tour, while Justin made his album and then set about making it a success.

Justifiably Justin:

When Justin delivered the album *Justified* I was in New York for discussions on the UK promotion. Justin and his manager, Johnny Wright, had decided to commit to the UK in a way that N'Sync had never done. Justin felt that being really successful in the UK would spread back to the US and into Europe, and once again we were to be pivotal in the solo career of a star performer. The first single from the album, 'Like I Love You', was received well by radio and the video caused an instant reaction. We knew quickly that we were going to have a hit. Justin flew into England to a whirlwind press radio and TV campaign, recording *Top Of The Pops*, doing interviews on Radio 1 and Capitol, plus a couple of 'A' grade press interviews, then out of the country again as quickly as he came in. The campaign worked and grew quickly and 'Like I Love You' would debut on the chart at No 2 in the UK. This happened before the US started their release pattern, and this news spread across the Atlantic as we had hoped.

Two weeks later the US released *Justified* on the same day as the UK. It flew onto the UK album chart and debuted at No 1. Meanwhile, 'Like I Love You' spent sixteen weeks on the chart and drove *Justified* right through the Christmas period as one of the year's best-selling albums. Our next single release after that would not be until February 2003 and it would come with a blaze of publicity establishing Justin Timberlake as the new King of Pop.

The World's Greatest:

R. Kelly kept the company ticking over in the first few months of the year, with the first hit coming in March and peaking at No 4. 'The World's Greatest' was a track written by Robert for the movie *Ali*, the part of Mohammed Ali played brilliantly by our own Will Smith. Robert had been invited to LA to discuss writing a song for the movie and was sitting in the meeting as the producers of the movie explained how they pictured the film and what the music might sound like. Inspiration is something that just appears for an artist, especially when the artist is as talented as Robert. In the middle of the meeting, Robert felt it coming and got uncomfortable knowing he had to do something about it or it might be lost. He excused himself by requesting a toilet break and left the meeting, locking himself in the toilet, where he wrote the song 'The World's Greatest.' The meeting continued and thirty minutes later the executives were wondering where R. Kelly was. Eventually, Robert returned to the meeting and apologised for leaving, explaining that the idea for the song had come to him and proceeding to sing the verse and chorus to what would become the record 'The World's Greatest.' The producers were flabbergasted, and Robert went back to Chicago to record the song from the notes he had made in the L.A. toilet. 'The World's Greatest' easily became a theme in the movie and then a worldwide hit record.

Jive issued the album *Best Of Both Worlds* during the same month. It peaked at No 37, and then during May we released 'Honey' to keep the momentum going on it. 'Honey' peaked at No 35 on the UK chart. Robert then disappeared into the studio for the rest of the year and the following year, 2003, we would issue two R. Kelly albums as he was on the verge of a huge selling bonanza.

Lauren Waterworth:

In June Pete and I had a hit with Lauren Waterworth. To me, she was the best female vocalist we ever worked with. Pete had heard a track that Lauren had recorded and fell in love with her voice. He had been told that the voice he was hearing was of a 12 year-old girl, which he dismissed as untrue, but with the rider that 'if it is, then send me some film footage of her singing.' A few weeks later film appeared of this little girl with an unbelievable voice. Pete brought it over to my office and we sat in wonder at what we were watching. We decided we had to sign her even though we had no plan of action at that moment and also the signing of a minor was a difficult objective. We overcame that problem and Lauren Waterworth became an EBUL/Jive artist.

We were looking for some kind of a route for success with Lauren when I remembered a single I had heard a few years before that I thought should have been a hit in the UK but wasn't. The single by Alison Krauss was a cover of the Foundations 60's hit 'Baby Now That I've Found You', although it was played and recorded in a gentle country blue grass style. I took the record to Pete who loved it and we recorded Lauren singing 'Baby Now That I've Found You' in Manchester, close to Wigan where Lauren was at school. The record became a No 24 hit single in June, and we had started the career of the 13 year-old Lauren Waterworth.

Best of's...and Greatest Hits:

Most of my summer was spent in negotiation for three Best Of albums for the winter campaigns. Firstly, I wanted to issue a _Best Of The Stone Roses,_ but I wanted the band to support the project. Simon Moran was the only route to the boys and, although he was defensive in our first meeting, I believe he realised that I wanted real approval from the band, also, I needed John Squires to produce the artwork. I wanted the boys to be proud of the project and not simply to 'cash in.' Simon and I began to get on well and it was mainly Simon who worked with the band to obtain their approval, prepare artwork and help with the selection of tracks that would become _The Best Of The Stone Roses._

I was also working on a _Best Of Kylie_ album. The first nineteen hit singles that Pete and I had made with Kylie were owned by PWL, but under strict conditions of consent by Kylie. It would take a few months to reach an agreement both with Terry Blamey, Kylie's long-standing manager, and Kylie herself. In the end the record would be released and become a hit album, although I think all parties were not totally happy with the resulting album. Nevertheless, it went on to be a great success and still stands as a splendid record of Kylie's early career. I also put together _Songbook, A Lifetime In Music_ by David Gates, a complete collection of songs David had written over thirty years, and this would become another big seller for Jive.

Bang:

And then came 11th June 2002. On that day the Jive Records world changed forever. Clive had been in town for a few days, but we had not seen him. The rumours were around that Jive Records was to be sold. They had been circulating before, indeed quite a number of times, but this time they seemed to be sticking. My view was, 'I am busy, and when Clive tells me he is selling, then I'll believe it.'

I was called to Clive's house, where we had held many meetings over the years. Clive and I had known each other at this time for twenty years and I was beginning my fourteenth year as Managing Director of the UK Company. Our conversation was pretty short. Clive said he had decided to sell the company to BMG and by the end of the year he would be gone. He insisted he would look after his major executives in the sale of the company and I would be one of those. He elaborated that it would not be a Richard Branson operation, where when Richard sold Virgin he basically looked after no-one and poured all the money into Virgin Airlines, nor would it be an Island situation, where when Chris Blackwell sold Island he looked after everyone. Jive would be somewhere in the middle. I thanked Clive and we spoke about all we had achieved and then I left. My belief was that the company was Clive's and the decision to sell or not sell was also Clive's. As for being 'looked after', I believed that might happen and it might not, but I would not rely on anything. After the death of my father all those years ago, I became unable to completely believe or trust anyone and that saved me from many disappointments that life could and does bring. I relied only on myself.

Evidently, my meeting with Clive, I was told, was his easiest. Most other key executives were prone to 'What about me?' syndrome. To be honest, I would never lower myself to that. I knew from that meeting on, that at some point I would be working for BMG Records, if only for a short while. The thought did not fill me with joy and I already knew what would happen when they finally got hold of Jive. Normally, companies like that in buy-outs issue a press release saying nothing will change and they are going to embrace the successful culture of the bought label. Then, within months, they slaughter it. I had watched it happen to A & M Records, Island Records, Chrysalis Records and Virgin Records. Even though at Jive we were the most successful and still at the top of our game, I knew it would be no different. At some point in the future, one way or another, it would end.

I quickly decided that to fight the beast that would come we needed to be in the best shape possible and I set about a flawless release schedule for the final quarter of 2002. The Jive staff were initially disappointed, but as nothing changed in the coming months, they began to just get on with the job. None of us knew what would happen by the end of the year, so whatever was to come, we might as well enjoy the moment, get the hits and then face the future.

The press were soon onto the sale of Jive Records and Zomba as a group to Bertelsmann (BMG) and the phrase that was apparent was 'put option' until 2002, I had never really heard of a put option and did not know what it meant. To understand a put option in the Jive Records sense we have to go back to 1991, when the first of the deals between Jive and BMG were completed. Jive/Zomba sold twenty-five percent of our publishing company to BMG, making BMG a junior partner in that business. In 1996, we sold twenty percent of our record company to BMG with an agreement that Zomba received an option that forced Bertelsmann to buy the rest of the entire Zomba group – Records, Publishing, Studios, Equipment Hire etc – by the end of 2002. Clive alone could only call this option. Hence, the phrase put option. The sale price of the company was agreed in 1996, based on the average profits in the years 1999, 2000 and 2001. As history would show that our most profitable years were 1999, 2000 and 2001, in short, it meant that BMG would have to overpay for Zomba to the tune of 1 billion dollars. The total sale price was estimated at 2.8 billion dollars and some people thought that at even 1.8 billion Zomba was overpriced.

BMG at the time were trying to merge with EMI, which had been an on/off affair. Thomas Middlehoff, CEO of Bertelsmann, had done all he could to renegotiate the put option clause, one that had been conceded by Michael

Dornemann and Thomas Zelneck years before. At first, BMG tried a three way deal between EMI, BMG and Zomba with Clive and Ken Berry operating the new company, but Clive declined. Middlehoff then tried the idea of handing back BMG stakes in Zomba and subsequently selling us Virgin Records to enable the deal to go ahead between BMG and EMI, and Clive again declined. Finally, Middlehoff considered combining Zomba and BMG, offering Clive fifty percent of the new company and the CEO position. Clive declined. BMG were facing paying a bill for Zomba Records that would nearly bankrupt the company and the sale price would be the biggest ever figure for an independent record company. I doubt it will ever be beaten. The sales of A & M, Chrysalis, Island and Virgin Records pale into insignificance at the price for Zomba/Jive. Bertelsmann would have to sell off some of their assets to pay the bill.

When BMG realised there was no way out, some people had to pay with their jobs. Dorneman and Zelnick were fired and Middlehoff resigned. Early in 2003, I would be greeted by a new management at Bertelsmann who opened talks with 'the Bertelsmann company wants to be out of the record business by 2005.' Obviously, seriously hurt, Bertelsmann had fallen out with the record business completely and wanted to cash out.

My first meeting with any BMG executive was in August when I was called to have lunch with the newly appointed, if unfortunately named, Michael Smellie. As he was an Australian cricket fan there was room for good banter and I would say we got on well for a first meeting. Jive UK were then pretty much left alone for the year. Although there were lots of talks going on behind closed doors, we were not called to any meetings or informed of anything.

The deal between Zomba and Bertelsmann was completed on 27th November and on 28th November I was working for BMG, although still in the same building, operating the same staff and the same artists. A week later some of Zomba's European Managing Directors and I were called to the Metropolitan Hotel in London for our first meeting. It was a tense and false affair. It was clear that the BMG heads did not like the Jive people, as we had changed their company on account of Clive running off with all their money. A few arguments broke out, especially between the Dutch and the Germans. I pretty much kept out of it all and just watched. The German Managing Director of Bertelsmann obviously was looking for a fight and pretty much got one from Bert Meyer. Evidently, they had not liked each other for years. He also approached me and sneered 'It's going to be different now you're here.' I responded 'Really, who are you?' He turned and walked away.

Michael Smellie did his best to welcome us to the company, but it was very uncomfortable. We then sat through a talk on how BMG worked. That was shown to us by a series of charts and graphs, something I had never experienced in all my time at Jive. Boring, you bet it was, it was an accountancy meeting and one of those that disguises the truth from the owners and shareholders. I left disappointed at what I had seen.

Clive phoned me that night to ask what it was like and what I thought. 'Clive, it was just endless charts and graphs for two hours and you know what, no-one asked me if I'd got any hit records. In fact, it bore no resemblance to a record company at all. I think if a hit record jumped up and smashed them in the face, they wouldn't know what it was.' Clive and I laughed about it all and he found great fun in my Midland pronunciation of the word 'graph' said with a flat 'a' rather than sounding 'grahhph.' Clive for some time described BMG as a 'graph' company, many a true word said in jest. My final meeting of the year with BMG was on 13th December when I met the incoming Chairman Tim Bowen. I would suggest our first meeting went OK. I wouldn't say 'we hit it off', but we didn't injure each other and the New Year would start with a clean slate.

Hit records in corporate mayhem:

The summer with all this going on was relatively poor in sales terms for Jive. Our biggest hit was Britney's No 7 single 'Boys', but apart from that it was slow. We had, however, a good schedule for the final quarter and I set about gearing up for that. I had called the staff together and explained that we either wait to get shot by BMG or we get as many hits as we can, make it difficult for them, and fight the beast that will surely come. Thankfully, the troops rallied and we attacked every project with determination and passion. The records and the hits still kept coming and we would make another huge profit for the year, more profit, in fact, than our owners, the label BMG Records. The Best Of's all fared well: Kylie sold 400,000 copies, The Stone Roses 300,000 and David Gates 120,000. Our artists continued to sell high quantities: Britney 400,000 singles, Groove Armada 60,000 and the big winner, Justin Timberlake, with 800,000. The Justin Timberlake album going to No 1 and the huge profit it made saved Jive Records in the UK. Instead of being merged into the BMG black hole we were considered too important to close and by January, we had secured our operation for 2003.

We then completed the year with a 400,000 unit sale of the single from One True Voice, titled 'Sacred Trust', and it was a Waterman story. Pete's TV job for 2002 was the ITV show *Popstars, The Rivals*. It pitted him against Louis Walsh to form a band. Pete had mainly worked with girl bands and Louis with boy bands, so they switched it around and Pete got the boys and Louis the girls. The public voted off contenders as the weeks went by and eventually One True Voice became Pete's band and Girls Aloud, Louis.' The race was then on for No 1, which was eventually won, and only just, by Girls Aloud. I thought 'Sound Of The Underground' was a great record and they deserved their victory. It was disappointing that we did not win, but we sold a very large number of records and had a group that might just go on to sell records in the coming year.

2002 ended dramatically for Jive Records. Clive was gone and, although he would still be visible for another few months in 2003, we had to face the unknown quantity of BMG. I found in my mind that there was no use wishing it was different, it was what it was. BMG owned us and the great ride we had been on for the past fourteen years was over. Especially for Tina and me it was a brand new world with new kinds of people and I intended to do what I had always done: attack the situation with thought, take calculated risks and see where it took us. Right now, I needed a couple of weeks off.

2002 Jive Hits

January			
Drowning	The Backstreet Boys	Jive	No 4
February			
Overprotected	Britney Spears	Jive	No 4
Let's Stay Home Tonight	Joe	Jive	No 29
March			
The World's Greatest	R. Kelly	Jive	No 4
Best Of Both Worlds LP	R. Kelly	Jive	No 37
April			
I'm Not A Girl, Not Yet A Woman	Britney Spears	Jive	No 4
Girlfriend	N'Sync	Jive	No 2
Leave It Up To Me	Aaron Carter	Jive	No 22
May			
Honey	R. Kelly	Jive	No 35
Only A Woman Like You LP	Michael Bolton	Jive	No 19
June			
Baby Now That I Found You	Lauren Waterworth	Jive	No 24
August			
Boys	Britney Spears	Jive	No 7
September			
What If A Woman?	Joe	Jive	No 53
You & Me	Easyworld	Jive	No 57
October			
Help Me	Nick Carter	Jive	No 17
November			
Like I Love You	Justin Timberlake	Jive	No 2

I Love Rock & Roll	Britney Spears	Jive	No 13
Purple Haze	Groove Armada	Jive	No 36
The Best Of Kylie Minogue	Kylie Minogue	Jive	No 20
The Best of The Stone Roses	The Stone Roses	Jive	No 19
Songbook, A Lifetime In Music	David Gates	Jive	No 11
Lovebox	Groove Armada	Jive	No 41
Justified	Justin Timberlake	Jive	No 1
December			
Sacred Trust	One True Voice	Jive	No 2

Survival of the fittest:

I returned from holiday on Sunday 5th January on an overnight flight and twenty four hours later I was making my way to BMG Records in Putney to have the first meeting of the year with new Chairman, Tim Bowen. The main outcome of that meeting was Tim's decision on Jive Records UK: 'If I have my way, I'll close you down!' I thought at the very least that was honest, probably not the way to welcome your best and most profitable label to the company, but nevertheless truthful. I obviously told him I thought that would be a huge mistake and that I would endeavour to keep our doors open. I have to admit, it was not the situation I had hoped for: first day back at work and the decision was shut it down. I knew, however, there was a long way to go, but if it was Tim's decision then I would already be starting the car.

I was at BMG for various meetings on the 14th, 15th, and 16th January. These were all about finance and staff. There was no sign of a record or artist meeting. Barry Weiss flew into the UK the week after to lend his support to the Jive UK cause, we met on the 22nd and then Barry travelled into Europe to assess what was about to occur there. The 23rd brought the accountant, set to change our way of doing things and instruct us to account in a BMG way. Dennis Kooker would be a regular visitor to Jive and was a decent man just doing his job. We had many discussions over the change in accounts, it seemed almost stupid to me the way they went about it all: reams and reams of paperwork and at the end of it all you had no idea how much you had spent and how much you had earned. The simple mathematics of profit and loss had disappeared. I guess the way the accounts were done at BMG was to keep the owners mystified, to be able to shape them this way or that, depending on how well or badly you were doing. I must have said a hundred times 'Dennis, why would you do that? It's much simpler this way, and then we know where we are.' Dennis got used to me and in the end I think agreed with me, but he had to toe the company line.

BMG had put Nick Howe immediately on 'gardening leave' to see out his contract as he was not wanted by them. Another mistake. Nick could have put

BMG in the best shape possible, but his involvement in Clive's 'sting' had put him in a position where they wanted nothing to do with him. No offence to Dennis, but I was now dealing with people who were not of the same calibre as Nick, who I had learnt from for the past eight or nine years. Almost my whole month was taken up with the fight against closure with BMG. Then, on the 26th January, came my first break: *Justified* by Justin Timberlake did what few records ever do, it survived the Christmas rush of the previous year and came into a New Year rising stronger in sales, returning to No 1 on the album chart.

We were preparing Justin's second single 'Cry Me A River,' and the pre-release video was all over the TV, as was the controversy surrounding its portrayal of Justin's girlfriend having an affair and Justin finding out. To make matters worse, the girlfriend was played by a Britney look-a-like actress. The storm started within the walls of Jive: our best-selling female artist was the subject of a video made by our best-selling male artist supposedly depicting their break-up. The Spears family did not want it released, but Justin had delivered it and wanted it out. It was a torrid time and we were in the middle. We felt that the Spears family could not stop Justin releasing his video, just as Justin or the Timberlake family could not stop Britney releasing her videos or records. The personal issue was between them and we would remain in our position of 'no comment.' Meanwhile, the 'Cry Me A River' video became a 'must see', and Jive benefitted from the exposure as *Justified* went back to No 1 and 'Cry Me A River' debuted at No 2 in February, finally bringing the crown of 'King of Pop' to Justin's door.

As Justin stood at No 1 with *Justified* and No 2 with 'Cry Me A River', I was summoned again to a visit with Michael Smellie on 6th February. I had gathered by now that it would rest on Michael's shoulders whether Jive Records UK stayed open or not. I took him on a tour of the offices and showed him the studios that surrounded us, both our own and other peoples.' That was all I could do – and I believe he left impressed.

The Brits came around again and the new King of Pop appeared with Kylie Minogue singing a duet of the Blondie single 'Rapture.' We all attended the *Music Week Awards*, and this year there was to be no Label Of The Year award for us. If we had still been the independent Jive Records company we would have won it, and by a country mile, but the sale to BMG had put us in with their corporate group and *Music Week* took the opportunity to award the prize elsewhere. It had been a great run, four consecutive Label of the Year wins is probably enough, but I would have enjoyed the moment had we been given a fifth.

After silence from BMG for many weeks, suddenly at the end of March the phones and e-mails began lighting up. I was back with Tim Bowen on 21st March and told 24th March was D. Day. Then we would know what was to happen next. Come that day, Bowen pretty much just read the press release that was to be issued the following day. 350 Zomba music group staff were to be let go during the coming months and Zomba's 18 international offices would be integrated into BMG (that meant they would close). A statement from Rolf Schmidt-Holtz said that Zomba's key assets were its people, BMG was therefore retaining key executives including President Barry Weiss, who would now add the UK operation to his responsibilities and Steve Jenkins would remain as Managing Director of Zomba UK, Tim Bowen became Chairman of the Board of Zomba UK

We had survived the first phase of the demolition of Zomba/Jive. I was encouraged, as this gave us a chance to compete again, and, notwithstanding, my awareness that in a corporation things can change quickly, I thought we had secured a year and for now that was as good as could be expected. The appointment of Tim as Chairman meant the next time we were in danger of being closed, it probably would happen.

Corporate Life:

On 25th and 28th April I was informed of the buildings we were to put up for sale, which included our studios. To me again this was all alien. A good record company revolves around its studios, it is where we make the records. The plans were poorly thought out and just an instant reaction: cut the costs, sell everything, try and get some money back.

The main thing I noticed quickly was how isolated you are operating a major company label. BMG did not want me dealing with anything that was not UK based, whereas at Jive I had been used to working on a worldwide basis. I felt as though I had been plucked from the sea and put in a goldfish bowl, everything seemed so small.

Our next battle was days away. Tim, now as Chairman, had direct control over how many staff we retained in the record company at Jive UK. In the first few days of May I worked with Michael Smith, William Rowe and Stephen Richards to find a minimum number that we could operate with and still achieve our results. It was a horrible job that went on for many days. I was being forced to play with the lives of people who had been loyal and hardworking for the company. It kept me awake at night and I hated it all. I thought many times during this period, maybe I should quit, let BMG do its own dirty work, I think no one would have blamed me. However, Barry and Michael kept me on the tracks and suggested it was better to save some than none at all and if I left it would be over for everyone. We came up with what we thought was the best possible solution of 60 people. It would mean a lot of redundancies, but the company could survive on that number, given that all our support structures, accounts, purchasing, distribution and manufacturing were eventually going to be handled by BMG.

As Michael and I went to present the numbers and the figures to BMG, *Justified* went back to No 1 on the chart for a third time. The Chairman had no words of well done or congratulations, it seemed a disappointment. Achieving a

No 1 in the business is always a moment for appreciation, they are unbelievably hard to get. I was now in a position where a No 1 was a disappointment.

On 7th May came meetings titled Jive Consultations, in which we outlined our staffing plans to BMG accountants and lawyers. On 8th May we did the same thing to Tim Bowen and heard the responses from BMG's accountants, the people we had seen the day before. The upshot of it all was they wanted the staff cut to 25. I saw that as impossible and it would definitely make the company fail. By the 13th May Barry Weiss was back in the UK fighting with us to achieve more staff and a shot of making it work. And now, another piece of good fortune and hard work solved the situation to the dismay of Lord Tim of BMG: on 18th May, *Justified* returned to No 1 for the fourth time, which was probably bad enough for BMG, and on the same day R. Kelly debuted at No 1 on the singles chart with 'Ignition.'

Well, I was forced in to doing interviews with the press about Jive Records' achievements, wasn't I? The radio and television stations were full of how it was the first time the hugely successful Jive Records had topped both the singles and albums chart in the same week, with the sales figures that accompanied this. Justin's album had now passed a million sales and R. Kelly's album *Chocolate Factory* was exploding. I simply stated 'I'm delighted for Justin and Robert and the company. All have worked incredibly hard to achieve these chart positions.' R. Kelly's 'Ignition', a truly magnificent record, would stay at No 1 for three weeks.

The following week we issued 'Rock Your Body', Justin's third single from *Justified*. It was the most played record on UK radio at the time, and it entered the chart at No 2. It was only held off the top spot by our own R. Kelly, so we were now No 1 and 2 on the chart.

I was called again to BMG. The compromise was 43 people and that's all. We had another small victory under our belts, but I still knew that we could not keep up these chart positions forever. There would come a time when we would have a cold patch, then I would have no defence.

King of R & B:

'Ignition' was a belter of a record – Robert hit the gong right on the nose with that one. *The Chocolate Factory* album, which was his highest charting album up to that point at No 10, was equally an outstanding issue. The work Robert had put in at the studio through 2002 paid off enormously and this year Robert, in the studio, was to give Tina, Barry and I a unique and unforgettable experience. With Tina, I had travelled to Chicago, the windy city, where Robert had his own studio, and we met up with him and Barry to listen to a playback of *Chocolate Factory* ahead of release. There were three other people in the studio and Robert said a few words to us all about the album. Then he started playing the first track. Before it had ended, he switched off the track and said 'You know, I just cannot sit here and listen to the album and watch your faces, so I'm going to perform the album for you.' The album started again and Robert sang along with it all the way through to seven people in the room. You cannot buy a moment in time like that: probably the most talented artist I ever worked with singing his new album to his loyal supporters and record company. There were no photos that day, but Robert called over Tina and me and we had a photo taken to remind us of the moment in Chicago.

Meanwhile, back at the ranch:

June was more BMG, this time a presentation to the UK Company. I had to deal with a rehearsal and a day of preparation – 'what are you going to say?' As a speaker I have worked out mentally where I am going and I have points to hit, but most of the time I am spontaneously improvising. BMG could not get to grips with that style. They had me there all afternoon.

'You must know what you're going to say, surely?'

'Well, sort of.'

'Do it now then.'

'OK, but it won't be the same on Wednesday.'

In the end I said:

'Just have the videos ready and I'll cue you, it'll be obvious anyway. I'll stick to the order of videos, you just be ready.'

Panic had set in. I presented our entire product, which looked incredibly promising. I knew we would deliver big sales, I even told a few stories and got a few laughs, and I think it was the first time BMG staff had laughed in years, so much so, that they seemed unsure whether it was allowed or not. The other presenters then either tried to copy the presentation style and add a little humour or delivered absolutely straight.

London to New York and back – for Robert and Britney:

In July, August and September I spent a week each month in New York. July's visit was to work with Barry and R. Kelly on his *Greatest Hits* album scheduled for December that year. Barry and I knew we would be in another battle at the end of the year for Jive's survival and Robert's *Greatest Hits* could be a huge seller for both him and the company. We wanted to get a worldwide view on the record and hence I was there to add tracks that might not have been included by American ears. In August, I was there to view up-and-coming Jive US signings and to meet Britney who had almost finished her next album *In The Zone*, which she had begun recording in June. September's visit was for the marketing and preparation for the final quarter, including a presentation to just BMG executives about our profitability.

Back in England, Barry flew in to discuss with Tim and me the finance meetings for 2004 and a week later BMG and Sony announced their proposal for a joint company to be called Sony/BMG. It would take a long time to come to fruition, but it was a definite statement of intent. BMG could not exit the record business yet, but they were lessening their involvement and trying to become a stronger company by joining forces with Sony.

Meanwhile, as R. Kelly's huge success with the 'Ignition' single and the *Chocolate Factory* album had put him right back at the top in terms of popularity and sales, Barry and I were sure that this was now the time for a *Best Of R. Kelly* release. To fly to New York and work with Robert and Barry on that album was fantastic. It was a celebration of thirteen years of working together and of all the records that had made a once unknown Robert Kelly the world superstar R. Kelly. We launched *The R in R&B, Greatest Hits* album in October 2003 and it rocketed to No 4, sticking on the chart throughout Christmas and the New Year and selling 600,000 copies. It was a 'must have' release for a huge amount of people.

The R. Kelly singles we released in 2003 also gave Robert his most consistent year of single chart positions: following 'Ignition' came 'Snake', which debuted at No 10, and then another great record in November, 'Step In The Name Of Love', which peaked at No 14, at any other time of the year it would easily have been Top 10.

Come back Britney:

In October, Tina and I were in Paris with Britney Spears in advance of her forthcoming flying visit to the UK to set up the promotion for the single 'Me Against The Music' and the album *In The Zone*. Madonna had come to Britney's aid by starting to wear a Britney T-Shirt to events, and Britney had responded by wearing a Madonna T-Shirt. Britney's heroine had always been Madonna and that she was coming to her aid and lending support added to her confidence after all the personal unhappiness she had suffered and all the exploitive abuse she had received from the press. Many Hollywood stars, including George Clooney, had come to Britney's defence at this time. Madonna, who is remarkable at changing her image and direction and coming up with a record to go along with the change, was, I am sure, protecting Britney, but she also saw the value of the enormous publicity her involvement would bring. The end game came at that year's MTV Awards when Britney and Madonna performed and Madonna kissed Britney. Britney had not been too sure about it all at the rehearsals and was a little stiff about it, but when the moment came 'live' the 'show must go on' attitude kicked in, and the papers all over the world printed the photo.

Madonna had also made a couple of changes to our recording of 'Me Against The Music', and we launched the record in November. With such public and press interest in a new Britney single aided by Madonna, the record went straight to

No 2. We had overcome the first hurdle of a big hit single, but the mood of the nation was still unsure. We issued the album quickly and it disappointingly charted at No 14, although we stayed on it through to Christmas and managed to extract 300,000 sales. That was not bad and we had got through the initial comeback stage – but there was still plenty to do. The disappointment obviously hit Britney hard, as the record was not selling as she and we had hoped, but even so we still had a long way to go. We all stopped for Christmas, all tired and worn out from our efforts. By New Year's Day Britney Spears would be a married woman.

And once more with feeling:

The year ended on a screaming conclusion. In December I was back with Justin, this time at Earls Court, where the demand for tickets to the *Justified* tour were massive and increasing. Tina and I presented Justin with a five time platinum disc for 1.5 million sales and we were still not finished: the tour would return again to England and Earls Court in 2004 and the *Justified* album would eventually sell 1.9 million copies making it Jive's biggest selling UK album in the history of the company.

That was the year that was:

So much of 2003 had been taken up with constant BMG meetings. It seemed I had no time to work on projects, records and artists, they almost became secondary with the constant rounds of staff and finance meetings. I needed a break. All of the Jive offices around the world had been closed, Jive UK's support departments had all gone, that is distribution, manufacturing and accounts, and the studios were being rented off one by one in long term deals until buyers could be found. Our offices all over Willesden were empty and up for sale. The worst part for me, however, was in making our staff redundant. I had spent fifteen years building up that company and now was pulling it apart bit by bit and it was heartbreaking making people redundant week after week after week. Some would accept it well and thank me for sticking in there and trying, others would just lose it completely and the worst part was that as you started the conversation you never knew which way it would go.

So, that was the first year of our ownership by BMG Records, it was a completely different world to the one we had known. Jive Records had grown up and become the market leader being cocooned in its own world with its own way of doing things. Most of our staff had worked at Jive for years and really knew only one way of operating, one that was straightforward and built on strong contracts and strict profit and loss accounts. I knew when we were in trouble, knew when we had to find a hit or pressurise sales from an album to balance the books, knew which acts we had to recoup losses on. Clear knowledge is half the battle. In contrast, BMG accounts were confusing and in a constant state of flux as they adjusted them month after month. They seemed to want the record business to react like Heinz Baked Beans – how many tins did we sell last year, we are down twenty percent, correct the projections. In the record business, no matter how hard you try, you cannot react like beans. The industry is built on emotion, inspiration, character and good fortune, and the more you try to make it into beans the more it will react badly.

I always remember going to see Tim Bowen when I had some ideas for a couple of artists on the BMG label. I asked if I could play him a couple of songs, but even as they were playing his face revealed that there was no point, he could not tell if they were good or bad ideas. I realised that most of the upper echelon of BMG had never been near a studio, never been up until three in the morning trying to get something right, it was not their job and they had no clue. I had spent twenty years with Clive who, like me, had started booking studios and making records in his early years. Clive could also pick up a bass guitar and play it if he had to. Barry Weiss also knew about records, you could not fool him, he knew the market and so all of our discussions were both musical and business. Within BMG I was still in the record business, but like a fish out of water.

Pete Waterman's deal was still intact throughout the BMG/Jive trauma, but looking back it was a poor year for hit records at EBUL. One True Voice followed up their No 2 record 'Sacred Heart' with 'Shakespeare's Way With Words', a record that would peak at No 10. We thought One True Voice would be our major seller of 2003, but it was not to be. This band that was put together by the public were mismatched as people: they did not have common aims and had big differences in age and experience. Pete and I could tell after the first record that this was not really going to work. I had several meetings with the boys and tried to explain their position as I recommended to them that they should grab this chance as opportunities on this scale do not come along that often. The boys saw things differently. They said that because of their fame from the TV show, each one of them was always stopped in the street. Well, they were not aware how fickle that is. They all wanted to be solo acts and cash in on the fame they had made with just one hit single. Pete and I fought to hold them together and we got the second record out, but the whole affair became a disaster. They were nice enough lads, but they all wanted something different, and One True Voice came to a shuddering halt. In contrast, Girls Aloud handled themselves properly and time has shown how successful they have become. They obviously saw that they had a chance and boy did they take it. Well done you girls.

Jive Records 2003 year was made by Justin Timberlake, R. Kelly and Britney Spears. We had not achieved as many hits as the previous years, but with now only carrying a staff of 43 we were hugely profitable. We had done all we could to preserve Jive Records.

2003 Jive Hits

February			
Cry Me A River	Justin Timberlake	Jive	No 2
Junkies	Easyworld	Jive	No 42
March			
Chocolate Factory	R. Kelly	Jive	No 10
May			
Ignition	R. Kelly	Jive	No 1
Rock Your Body	Justin Timberlake	Jive	No 2
Easy	Groove Armada	Jive	No 31
August			
Snake	R. Kelly	Jive	No 10
September			
Senorita	Justin Timberlake	Jive	No 13
But I Feel Good	Groove Armada	Jive	No 50
October			
2nd Amendment	Easyworld	Jive	No 42
R In R&B Greatest Hits	R. Kelly	Jive	No 4
November			
Me Against The Music	Britney Spears	Jive	No 2
In The Zone	Britney Spears	Jive	No 14
Step In The Name Of Love	R. Kelly	Jive	No 14

Earls Court - Tina, Justin and Me

NewYork - Britney and Me

Chicago - Tina, R. Kelly and Me

CHAPTER 26

2004 – REQUIEM AETERNAM DONA EIS (GRANT THEM ETERNAL REST)

Tragedy:

I didn't return to work until the 11th January 2004. I had taken three weeks off as I knew that instantly, on my return, the battle with BMG would commence again. It started immediately with the issue of paperwork under the heading 'head count.' In all my years at Jive that phrase had never been used, but here it was, a head count was issued for all labels within BMG and not just Jive. The falling yearly revenue from sales meant there were staff reductions everywhere. Jive's reductions were to be over fifty percent and that meant we had to go from a staff of 43 to just 23. I presumed there was some logic to the No 23 but the paperwork gave no clue. As all BMG labels' staff were being cut, there really was no argument, however, other labels were certainly not being cut by fifty percent.

In management meetings over the next two weeks, Michael Smith, Stephen Richards and our human resources manager, Emma Harvey, discussed how we could carry out the cuts and still remain operational. In these changes Emma would soon switch to a BMG employee.

We worked on who, where and how we could make the changes, and the final document came out at 23 people with four part-time staff for the next few months. It was the best we could do. BMG finally agreed the package and at the start of a New Year I was again making staff redundant, although this time assisted by Emma, who was a real help. The meetings were the same as last time: some reacted well and others with pain and aggression. I could understand it all: the sleepless nights and the distaste of breaking down Jive Records was awful. I nevertheless believed that if we did as BMG wished, then we would eventually become a satellite label of BMG and could return to making and selling records within the group instead of spending nearly all our time on cuts and politics. When Jive stood at 23 people, there was little more to cut.

No support but still winning:

Some respite from all this came with Justin Timberlake's return tour to England, where he was at the Earls Court arena for ten nights. The sum of this and his previous four nights there made Justin's fourteen performances at Earls Court a record number for an artist at Earls Court at that time. I went to see Justin with Tina and we posed for photographs with a 5 x Platinum disc representing 1.5 million sales of *Justified*. The concerts were superb and Justin introduced me to his girlfriend of ten months, Cameron Diaz. She was a pleasure: pretty, quiet and always in the background giving Justin his time at work. Nothing was about Cameron, it was all about Justin. I came away with enormous respect for Cameron, she is a proper woman.

Justin came once again to the Brits and another great night was had by all, not performing this time, but scooping two big awards: Justin Timberlake – Best International Male Artist and *Justified* – Best International Album. *Justified* was still on the UK album charts where it had remained for an extraordinary sixteen months, going to No 1 on four separate occasions.

Jive had Pete Waterman back and focusing on making records in the studio after the TV experiences with *Pop Idol* 1 & 2 and *Popstars The Rivals*. We showcased Lauren Waterworth and her new album *Beyond Her Years*, and we started to work again with Tim Byrne, ex STEPS manager, as we prepared to sign a band simply called Pop. There would be no hiding place for the band, they were exactly what their name suggested: Pop.

Because of all the other duties I now had with BMG, we did not open the year with a hit straight out of the box, which we had done in each of the past five years. Even so, this had not affected our profitability as *Justified*, *The R in R&B*, and *In The Zone* were still big selling albums.

Britney – Just One More Time:

The news of Britney's marriage had burst into the press on New Year's Day. I was away on holiday and was pretty much away from it all, including the marriage's annulment after fifty-five hours. I never mentioned it to Britney when I next saw her: it was another situation that had occurred mainly because of the traumatic eighteen months that had gone before.

The record from the album *In The Zone* that changed Britney's career again had been on the list of potential singles, but was not definite until the feedback from the album started to filter through. The buildup of demand showed us that 'Toxic' was looking like it might be something special. The record would become as important to Britney's career as 'Baby One More Time' and the public bought 'Toxic' because it was an outstanding record and not just because it was Britney Spears. 'Toxic' topped both airplay and the dance charts before we released it and we thought we had a great shot at No 1 with the single. We issued the record on 1st March and on the 7th it was the UK's No 1 record and Britney's first No 1 since 'Oops I Did It Again' in May 2000.

'Toxic' was Britney's fourth No 1 single and her Onyx Hotel Tour on the back of it hit the UK during April 2004. I met up with her at the Wembley Arena shows on the 26th and 27th and again when she performed in Birmingham: she was back and on top of her game. 'Toxic' in March and the tour during April and May set up the follow-up single, which looked a huge hit way before release: we issued 'Every Time' on 14th June and by the 27th Britney was again No 1 on the UK chart. And once again the video caused a storm in the press. In the story of the video Britney commits suicide by drowning in her bath. The press seized on the footage and said it promoted suicide with young girls, but all that did was make it a 'must see' video and keep it played on all the TV video channels. 'Every Time' racked up Britney's fifth UK No 1 single, and her second in a row in 2004.

Watching paint dry:

Meanwhile, the BMG front had been quiet. I had not been called to the Putney offices through January or February and even the reduction in staff at Jive had not caused me to go there. Then news came through that I had to go to Toronto for a BMG conference. I arrived and went straight to the closing Jive office, where I met with Laura Bartlett, our Managing Director, and Barry Weiss. Neither of us had been to the office before and it was sad to be going as it was about to close. The conference was like any other I had been to – two days of up-and-coming product sold to the other countries in the group. Clive Davis had a reputation for staying on stage for hours presenting everything he had signed and everything he might sign and once again, he must have been on stage for three hours, which was like watching paint dry. I felt pretty detached at that conference, I always had the feeling there were better things to do in the UK and I could not influence the company from Toronto. BMG announced that they were in talks with Sony and the merger was coming along – these deals can always go wrong, but this one had not faltered yet.

The final shot:

Back in England we were launching a second Jason Downs album and JC Chasez from N'Sync was in town to promote his new single and album. JC was enjoyable to be with and we promoted his single and album with great determination. It was neither a pop record nor an N'Sync commercial record: JC had wanted to try other styles and although we achieved a No 13 position with the single 'Some Girls' (Dance With Women), it was only a reasonable seller. The album *Schizophrenic* also sold moderately achieving a position of No 46.

Joe was also in England on a short tour taking in Manchester, Birmingham and winding up at Hammersmith Apollo. I saw the London show and we had lunch together the next day before he flew back to the States. His single 'Ride Wit You/ More And More' peaked at No 12 and kept up his now consistent run of hit singles.

Only ten days after the Toronto conference, came the UK BMG conference where I presented our records for the year: Eamon, JC Chavez, POP, Groove Armada Greatest Hits, R. Kelly and The Best Of Britney – we were again looking good for a successful year.

The surprise hit during April rocked the UK to the core: one of the greatest anti establishment records of all time would soon be No 1. Barry and I had been sitting on a record from Eamon for about eighteen months. We both knew this could be a huge hit, but how to promote it and get it started had been the problem. Eventually in 2003, Barry decided to leak it out to clubs and just see how it responded. It almost immediately started to get support and action, and we agreed that we would release it in the UK in 2004. Tina started the promotion with a simply marvellous idea: for Valentine's Day you could buy a clip of the song and send it with a Valentine card to your girlfriend or most probably a girl that had rebuffed you. The card looked loving and for real, and as it was opened the lyric of the song kicked in. The idea and therefore the track exploded across the internet and the demand for the record grew, bringing press and lots of it. And then BBC Radio One called and wanted an edit with the word 'Fuck' taken out. Well this single holds the world record for expletives in a three-minute pop song. It was a tricky edit, to say the least, there was not much left of the song, but Radio One still played it. The pre sales just grew and we shipped over 150,000 – we knew it had the greatest chance to be No 1. Fuck It (I Don't Want You Back) entered the chart at No 1 and would be Jive's second No 1 of the year.

At that time we had four singles in the Top 20: Eamon, Joe, JC Chavez, and a falling Britney Spears. Once again we were right on top of our game as the leading popular music record company by a mile, and for us Britney was in the UK on tour again with dates in Manchester, two nights at Wembley and a final gig in Birmingham. I went to the London gigs and then waved her goodbye in Birmingham as she left for Europe.

Assassination:

On 10th May 2004, the announcement came that Sony and BMG had merged and would now become one company Sony/BMG. BMG itself would now be under the pressure that we had felt at Jive: staff cuts, redundancies and who is getting what job in the new company. Twenty-one days later Michael Smith and I were called to BMG. It was a Friday morning and we had been called to BMG many times. Michael and I always met early in a café around the corner from their Putney offices and tried to work out what the meetings would be about before we went in. Many times we had said 'this might be it' as we had expected that one day they would close us down.

Michael and I walked into an empty boardroom. Strangely, this time it was the big boardroom not the smaller one. Coffee and biscuits were ready, and so we helped ourselves and sat at the end of the room facing the door. After five or so minutes, the door opened and an army of BMG people came through the door: they must have gathered outside or down the corridor to march in all together. There were lawyers, accountants, analysts, promotion people, sales people, managing directors, general managers and finally, Tim Bowen. Michael and I looked at each other: we knew already what was coming. A huge audience was seated, so there could be no arguments, and they had all come to watch the hanging, desperate to get their hands on *Britney Spears' Greatest Hits* and what they imagined would be a new Justin Timberlake album for December. Bowen opened to the point.

'We are closing Jive Records. Today, we will decide on the objectives and the company will close on 30th September.'

There was no discussion, no defence. Michael and I then had to work with the puppets, go through the staff and the buildings, and do what had to be done, all of which took over three hours. We both went back to what remained of the Willesden offices, but I was in no mood for working. I knew first thing Monday I would have to tell the staff that the company was closing. I spoke with Lesley and told her it was all over. We would arrange an 11.00 am meeting in the canteen for all the remaining staff, the studio people, accounts, Dreamhire and record company staff. I then left for home and a weekend of reflection to steady myself for the meeting to come.

The decision to close Jive was most definitely a wrong one. Three weeks earlier we had four records in the Top 20 of the UK chart, we had just come off our second No 1 of the year with Eamon and were about to have our third and last ever No 1 with 'Every Time' by Britney Spears. The staff of Jive was now 26 people and would be 23 by the start of September, yet the big selling Justin Timberlake, R. Kelly and Britney Spears albums had put us in great profit. The end of the year would bring a new R. Kelly album, *Britney Spears' Greatest Hits,* and *Groove Armada Best Of.* These and some other projects would all add up to another seriously profitable year for Jive. It was not exactly a poorly functioning, over-staffed, debt ridden company on the verge of collapse! Jive was one of the most profitable record companies in the country and held up as a label that was correctly operated.

The knee jerk closure of Jive by the senior management of BMG went back two years to the sale of Jive to BMG. Jive Records had never been well received within the walls of BMG and the massive sale price Clive had forced out of them, added to their legal costs of trying to wriggle out of their deal, had changed Bertelsmann's desire to remain in the record business. They had set new management in place at Bertelsmann with the brief of 'get BMG out of the record business by 2005.' Although this was almost an impossible task, the management had pulled off a merger with Sony that had healed some pain and eventually provided BMG with its escape route.

From the start the management had not been interested in building labels or seeking the new idea that may turn the ailing BMG Company around: they were in 'sell or merger' mode. Hence close all the Jive offices as fast as possible, keep Jive US and Jive UK for now, they will probably fail in the next couple of years and then close them. In Jive UK's case, closing Label Of The Year in 2002 would look poor in anyone's eyes, so we have to hang on for now. Tim Bowen, the newly elected Chairman of BMG in the UK, had in fact wanted to close Jive UK immediately in 2002, but was restrained by the New York board. His other problem was that BMG were over staffed, had poor and unfocused staff, were losing money, and lacked direction. Hence, that question arose 'How come Jive is doing so well and BMG isn't?' Imagine the embarrassment for the BMG Chairman. It would be better to take Jive's profit-making artists, put them on BMG and close the embarrassment down.

The advent of the Sony merger finally gave Tim Bowen his great chance to close Jive and obtain a B*ritney Greatest Hits album*, an R. Kelly album and a *Groove Armada Best of*, amounting to probably a million sales from nowhere for BMG's Christmas push in 2004. All that had to be done was to convince the Board of Directors. The line Tim used was a winner: 'I must merge Jive now, you cannot expect me to merge both Jive and Sony at the same time.' The Board approved the closure.

Tim Bowen's personal reason for closing Jive was that in the very near future a new Sony/BMG UK Chairman would be appointed, and there were two candidates, one of which would no longer be a Chairman of the respective company he ran. Rob Stringer, Chairman of Sony, and Tim Bowen, Chairman of BMG, were the competitors. Naturally the staff of Sony wanted to protect their jobs and wished for Stringer, while at BMG the staff wanted Tim. The way to put yourself in the best position is to have a good year-end and make a profit and 1 million Jive albums were crucial to the chairman's position for Tim. I felt from the very beginning that Tim was fighting a losing battle and I believed Rob would become Chairman, simply because after the merger the company had to be built again and could only be done so by making records and signing artists. Rob is a record man, Tim is a lawyer, game over.

Death by indifference:

On Monday 4th June 2004 as the Britney Spears single 'Every Time' was the best selling single of the day and would be No 1 by the end of the week, the Jive staff assembled in the canteen. On a makeshift stage I explained what had happened and what would be happening over the next three months. Was I upset? Yes. I cracked at one point and Michael took over before I returned to finish. Jive Records died that day, there was no more motivating the staff and no more hustling

Jive Records with the passion and commitment we had given for years. BMG had won the war.

'Every Time' by Britney went to No 1 the following Sunday, but to be honest it passed me by. The next three months of Jive Records was just a case of turning up and sorting out the offices that were due to close. The passion had gone overnight, now it was just a job of conclusion. Lesley Rees took charge of sending relevant paperwork to BMG, Michael Smith packaged and forwarded the contracts, Jane Austin organised the tapes of all our records to go to the BMG libraries and Graham Stewart began to empty the buildings and make them ready for sale. I worked with the remaining staff on their contracts, bringing lawyers to prepare their redundancies and payoffs. It had nothing to do with records, I was closing the company I had spent fifteen years of my life building. Every day was heartbreak.

The staff began to leave as their contracts were concluded and it seemed every Friday was a 'goodbye day' as they moved on to other jobs or took a break before planning their next move in life. Three members of the Jive staff accepted jobs at BMG and the few others that were offered employment declined. As we approached the final days, the offices that had been hustling and bustling for years were empty and in various stages of being packed up.

30th September came and seven remaining staff turned up for the final day. The work was all done, our offices had been emptied and I walked the corridors and offices one last time. At twelve thirty, seven people watched Lesley lock the door for the final time and we headed for a restaurant for our very last lunch. We consumed a few bottles of wine and all said our goodbyes before heading off home. The greatest ride in the record business was finished, there was no more Jive Records.

I was at home when the phone went at six thirty that evening. It was Michael. He told me that BMG had already cut the phones off to the building. I phoned the number I had been calling for twenty years through Impulse and Jive and got that dull tone. It hit me that life would never be the same again, it was over.

I have no animosity towards Tim Bowen or even the BMG Board of Directors. They were working on a different plan and Jive Records was not really on their radar. They only wanted our artists to prop up their ailing company, it's just life and one of those things. I am pleased that Jive finished at the top with three No 1 records in its final year, still making profit and still on top of its game. Slowly falling into debt and being wound up was not the way that Jive should conclude what had been an unbelievable rise to prominence. Jive had been the Motown of the 1990s and the first part of the 2000's and I was delighted to have been its Managing Director through those years.

The industry was shocked that Jive Records was closing, it was questioning how a company could shut down with three No 1 records and the huge sales of Justin, Britney and R. Kelly. My phone never stopped. The incoming Chairman of

Sony/BMG, Rob Stringer, called me to his office and told me straight that Sony would not have closed Jive. They were kind words, but too late.

I doubt that any independent record company will ever achieve the success of Jive Records again and certainly no independent music company will ever be sold for 2.8 billion dollars.

2000 with Steve Mason, Chairman of Pinnacle Records celebrating 25 million sales in 3 years

Susan and I on a rare night out, whilst recovering from my operation

CHAPTER 27

2004, 2005 AND 2006 – THE WORLD
MOVES ON

EBUL Records:

Although they were closing Jive on 30th September, BMG were still left with the joint venture Jive/EBUL, and Pete and I were offered a deal for two and a quarter years to continue with the label under the banner of Sony/BMG/EBUL. I believe that somewhere in Tim Bowen's mind he knew that he had made a poor decision over Jive Records and as some compensation had decided to invest in EBUL Records. The deal was signed on 28th September and meant that after Jive shut down on the 30th I would take off three days and commence work at PWL Studios on 4th October.

That move gave me no time to think. I was straight into a new operation and, although at least it was with my longstanding pal, we pretty much had no artists to work with and had to start all over again in building the company. Pete and I both have a 'go for it' mentality and so we started to reshape the company along with Pete's assistant Helen Dann. Helen had been a trusted member of the team for a long time, all through the Kylie, Jason and STEPS years, and she had always been the main contact between Jive and EBUL. There is no doubt that PWL studios was a calm haven for me after the previous two years of fighting BMG, with no personality clashes and no politics. It was simply a matter of what were we going to do with this company.

October, November and December 2004 were a learning curve as to how we should reshape PWL Studios and the EBUL label. At the time we had one band that was showing signs of selling records and that band was POP. We had signed POP in March of 2004, with Tim Byrne as manager, and their very first release 'Heaven And Earth' had become a No 14 single in June. Glenn Ball, Hannah Lewis, Jamie Tinkler and Jade McGuire were all good people and enjoyable to work with and their second single 'Can't Say Goodbye', released in September, had peaked at No 26, but we felt that was probably the song not quite being good enough rather than a lack of support from the public. Their fan base was growing. EBUL issued their third single 'Serious' on 17th December and, intentionally, I was back on the trail of an early hit in January to set up the company for the New Year.

'Serious' peaked at No 16 and showed that POP could become a viable act for EBUL Records. Pete then had the idea to cover 'Xanadu.' When we had produced the record we all felt it would be a Top 10 single and the breakthrough record, so we started working on the album that would follow. All seemed to be going well.

So often in the record business, just when you think it's safe to go back in the water, life deals a blow. Jade McGuire came from Glasgow and was travelling back and forwards to London: obviously she was staying away from home more and more and this lead to a decision she had to make. She either had to stay in Glasgow in a relationship or pursue her career in London. I believe she made her mind up quickly, but the situation dragged on for weeks. Eventually, she left the band, and as she was POP's lead singer, just as we were about to launch the breakthrough single and album, there was no band. At the very same time Pete's son Paul Waterman, who had been ill for over six months, tragically died. Paul was a valued member of our production team and had made many hits in our Manchester studios, and it was also Paul who played Pete and I lots of new records and new ideas. He was family and special to us all. This was a huge enough shock to the company and everyone within it, but for Pete it was devastating. It broke his heart and, day after day Helen and I were propping him up just to get through it all. We all attended Paul's funeral in February, it was a sad day and one that would take some time to recover from, if we ever did.

PWL Studios was changing. The producers we had worked with for years were moving on and we set about the search for new producers. We took the decision after Paul's death to close the Manchester Studios: Pete could no longer go there and so we started to sell off the equipment and sell the building. We also felt that a new beginning was needed, so we began to build new studios in County Hall and prepare to move from the existing studios and offices. Eventually we moved from The Borough, home of PWL for twenty-one years, to County Hall at the end of December 2005. Pete and I were still to make a few singles during the coming months, but it was not the same anymore. We did not have our own staff to promote the records and were using marketing people that Sony/BMG hired. We were just one in a list of many with no real passion and support.

I believed we needed a big selling album for Christmas and we had little on the horizon, so I suggested to Pete that we should put together the *Best of Stock Aitken Waterman*. This would be the definitive hits package and it would straighten out our year financially with a big selling album. Pete said he was up for it, but he had not spoken to Mike and Matt in years because of the court cases between them that had concluded in 1999. It became my job to pull the whole thing together and I started with Mike Stock. The meeting went well as I told him of the idea and that it would require the three of them getting together for promotion and putting the past to bed. Mike was very up for the idea and said he would contact Matt and come back to me. Over the early summer I managed to get everyone to agree the deal and the track listing. They also agreed that the organisation of promotion and marketing would be left to me and Sony/BMG. We would all do P.R. as a team. Matt's only request was no early morning interviews and no *GMTV* for him, so Mike and Pete would do the *GMTV* interview.

Finally, after all those years, the four of us convened at Sheppard's restaurant on 28th September. We had a superb dinner and shared a lot of laughs about all those years ago. *S.A.W Gold* was issued in mid-November and went into the Top 10, eventually selling 150,000 copies. EBUL had its big selling record for 2005 and a friendship had been rekindled between us all. The promotion went well and we all spent three days in a people carrier travelling around London doing interviews for radio, TV and press.

Dicing with death:

Five days later, the beginning of a trauma appeared in my life. I had decided to have a Saturday afternoon out at the home of Milton Keynes Dons, as Walsall Football Club were the visitors that day. I knew Pete Winkleman, MK Dons Chairman well, after his years in the record business, and I also could have asked Roy Whalley, Chief Executive of Walsall FC, for a ticket and sat in the warmth of the Directors' box, but as I do most times I opted for sitting behind the goal with the travelling Walsall fans, in the company of my pal Joe Savage. I think being in the crowd reminds me of my youth and I love the banter and passion that swells up during a game with 'the faithful.' MK Dons' old stadium had very little cover and the wind whips across the pitch. It was bloody freezing. At the time I knew I was not feeling great, but there had been nothing that inhibited me or really bothered me that much. I could still run and keep fit. The only thing I really had been noticing was that I had been losing weight – not in large amounts, but constantly losing. In early November I had got on the scales, something I rarely do, and saw with shock that I was in danger of dropping below ten stone. I still didn't think too much about it and thought 'well I'm sure it will sort itself out, maybe I'll eat a little more and see how we go.'

MK Dons were victorious that day 2–1, and straight after the game I said to Joe 'I'm off.' I was freezing and just couldn't get warm. I got through Milton Keynes and headed south on the M1 and suddenly had the feeling all was not well. I made it back to the flat and for the next day or so just lay around until Monday morning came, when I phoned my friend and doctor, Adrian Whiteson OBE. On Tuesday I was in his surgery.

Adrian referred me to Dr Charles Akle BSc MS FRCS in Harley Street. Charles is a very funny man with an enormous amount of skill and talent in his chosen profession. Within ten days I was in the London Clinic for exploratory surgery. My sister Helen came down from Walsall for a day to help me through. I would be in hospital for at least a week and by the end of that week, I would know where I was. And I did. I would be back on 9th January 2006 for an operation. I pretty much stayed around home over the Christmas period and just got on with life: January would come soon enough.

The night before the operation, I was allocated my room, and Susan, who you will find out about further along in this chapter, was with me all of the time. Then came the big day – Monday 9th January 2006. The moment comes when they wheel the transport bed into the room to take you down to the theatre. Now, I had always been tough, but I have to admit I was only calm above the water: the legs were going like mad below the surface. I asked if I could walk to the theatre because I was sure as hell I wouldn't be walking back, but I was declined and was wheeled in. Charles was a comforting face all dressed up and ready to go, and I pretty much knew nothing about anything for a couple of days after: the morphine and the valium kicked in and I was just floating through life. The TV was on all hours and I drifted in and out, starting to come around by Wednesday. The nurses and everyone who looked after me in the London Clinic were first class and, looking back, I am so thankful to Charles and his staff.

Dr Akle came to visit and then the moment came. I had escaped colon cancer by a whisker: he said the speed of Dr Adrian Whiteson's work had saved the day and I should be ever thankful to him. I am.

Colon cancer is a tough subject to talk about, no one really wants to discuss the inner workings of the backside and couple that with the word cancer, it's not a dinner conversation. I decided that I would keep everything confined to the doctors, Susan and I, and that way I didn't have to deal with anything anyone might say or anything I might have to respond to. I would go it alone apart from Susan and see where life would take me.

I guess you could say I got away with it: close, but not quite. An experience like that does change your view on life, and it would change mine completely.

Susan and I still had a sense of humour, and I think that is imperative when these moments occur in life. A sense of humour can enable you to get through a lot and for me it was a must.

Dr Charles Akle became privately known to Susan and I, as Dr Arse, obvious but funny, sorry Charles. My huge knowledge of records came up with James Brown's 'Papa's Got A Brand New Bag' the word Bag being replaced with Arse, it helped.

Dr Akle did not want me to leave the hospital on the Saturday and wanted me to stay in for a few more days, but when you are in hospital all you want to do is get back home. Dr Akle conceded and Susan arrived with the car. As we headed for home, after only a mile I knew Charles Akle was right and I should have stayed: I felt every small bump in the road from central London to home.

Reflecting in recovery:

The next two months were a write off, but I slowly started to grow in strength and put some weight on. Susan and I went out to a few gatherings of friends and appointments, but they were spread apart, as the following day I would be too exhausted to do much. Susan was slowly nursing me back to health: the process was slow but steady, even though I always wanted to run before I could walk.

I believe the whole situation had come around after living life at speed for all those years. At the time, as I have said previously, the national average service for a Managing Director of a record company was two and a quarter years. I had done six years at Impulse and fifteen in charge of Jive Records. A part of the national average is based on failing Managing Directors on three-year contracts. I had not failed and had built a huge winner of a company, but although that feels great, it is a stressful arena. I was dealing with millions of pounds on a monthly basis, gambling, if you like, on artists, songs and producers. It obviously took its toll. The flying around the world and the poor sleep with time differences all contributed to my problem. And then the final straw had not been the closing of Jive as a company but making people redundant every month for nearly two years and pulling apart something I had spent fifteen years building. The body has a mind of its own and when you are going at full speed for years it keeps going, but when you start to slow down, I believe it thinks 'OK it's alright now to sort out the mechanics that are going wrong.' You relax a little and the body notices the change and responds. I learnt quickly that no matter how many hit records you have had it makes no difference to your body. I had spent nearly forty years of my life 'Chasin' the Hits' and they were all worthless in the London Clinic.

I managed to gain enough strength to return to work at the end of April. We had signed Darren Sampson to EBUL Records: better known as Daz, he had recorded a song 'Teenage Life', which had been entered for *The Eurovision Song Contest*. Pete and I never really had any interest in Eurovision, but as we were trying to get our company going we thought we would give it a go and see how we went. On 4th March Daz had won the BBC TV Show *Making Your Mind Up*, and so he was representing Britain in Athens. *The Eurovision Song Contest* took place on 20th May and Daz fell victim to the political voting that has foiled Britain's recent attempts, and which I believe will continue to happen consistently. He and Britain eventually came 19th out of 24 countries. In contrast, back in the UK the record had huge public support and became a Top 10 single peaking at No 8. It was the biggest British Eurovision song in eight years and at least suggested that Pete and I could still get a hit whenever we wanted.

Goodbye to all that:

In my absence, our relationship with a disinterested Sony/BMG had grown even more distant. Sony/BMG were only interested in the 'quick buck.' A Daz record with national TV support was no problem for them, a *S.A.W Gold Greatest Hits* was no problem, but a new record from an unknown artist meant hard work and investment and that proved all too much. Our recording budgets began to get tighter and our marketing and promotion budgets were at the bare minimum. Pete and I are too experienced and know that simply does not work. The Jive/EBUL arrangement was built on full support for records, but the Sony/BMG/EBUL arrangement was built on a defensive, spend as little as possible ideal, which we really were unaccustomed too. Rather than constantly fight the system, Pete and I began to become less interested in making records for a company that, to be fair, was in merger turmoil.

The merging of Sony and BMG was a tough job and was taking a long time to settle. The staff were in constant fear of losing their jobs and the way to keep them was not to rock the boat. So, don't make any decisions, don't champion ideas or records, stay quiet and hope the axe does not fall on you. That ideal is not the way Pete or I are made. We champion ideas and records, force the issue and rock the boat, and that is why we had been so successful over all those years. In hindsight, I also believe that the BMG/EBUL deal was based on Tim Bowen's poor decision about Jive Records. When he had forced the closure, he then had some guilt about it all and made a deal with EBUL to calm the waters rather than build a new source for hit records.

I remember how one day, only weeks after the EBUL deal had been concluded I had walked into the Sony/BMG offices in Putney, just as I had been doing for over two years. Everyone knew me and I would talk to the receptionist and the security men that controlled the entrance. That was something I always did, I always tried to speak with staff on every level within the business and gave them some of my time, then I would just go to whichever area in the company I wished. This day, one of the security guards I knew said 'Steve, come with me.' I went outside and he apologised profusely in telling me I now had to sign in as a visitor and whoever I was going to see or their secretary had to collect me from reception. I was no longer allowed to walk the departments. I told him not to worry, I knew it was nothing to do with him and I would sort it out. I went to see Tim and said 'Tim, I'm now not allowed in the company without an escort, what is this?' Tim responded with 'Yes, I know, I cannot allow you in the company unannounced and not escorted.'I simply said 'Why?' Tim explained that the staff of BMG had great respect for the achievements of Jive Records, and had gained an even greater respect for me personally, through my company speeches. They believed in my honesty and systems for obtaining success and hit records. Tim claimed when the BMG staff asked me questions, I gave them honest answers, regardless of the company line, which in turn made them very vocal about how BMG were operating. I can only presume my presence was causing a minor mutiny. Tim concluded he didn't need that from his staff, and so, I would be escorted in and out of the building from now on.

I accepted Tim's reasoning and just let it go. Looking back, it is obvious that from the start Pete and I were being paid to stay away. If we came up with hits OK, but we were never really given a shot. EBUL Records was an expensive 'gardening leave label.'

As 2006 progressed Pete and I became more disillusioned with Sony/BMG. Pete, who owned a few railway companies, trains being his greatest passion, began spending more and more time on those companies and hardly any time in the studio or with records. I cannot blame him. As I have always said, to get the best out of the raw talent that is Pete Waterman he has to be one hundred percent supported and his motivation comes from not ever letting anyone down. Without support he wanders off into his own world of hobbies, trains, reading, war films and smoking a big cigar. Who the hell can blame him. As for me, I was still not fit, my body had taken a colossal battering and I could not muster the power to change the situation and do my usual thing of 'fighting all comers.' And so, as 2006 came to a close, Pete and I decided not to contact Sony/BMG regarding the deal or negotiations. Sony/BMG on their part must have decided not to contact us, so the deal just expired and Pete and I were free. By this time I had spent four and a quarter years working with BMG and then Sony/BMG. Although we had delivered many hits and made an enormous amount of money I believe I was seen as a maverick in their eyes. I had their respect, but never their support, and four and a quarter years of no support is long enough for anyone.

So – what has happened to the record industry, and why?

In the years that have passed since then, all the Sony/BMG Board of Directors, including Tim Bowen, have been removed from the company. Bertelsmann finally got out of the record business in 2008. It had happened three years later than they had wanted, but eventually they made it out. Sony/BMG has been rechristened Sony Music Entertainment and I believe the inclusion of the word 'Music' is a statement of going forward and trying to find artists and hit records and finally a move away from the corporate politics surrounding Bertelsmann's BMG Records. Sony were always a more classy and music based company than BMG and the CBS history and heritage they have inherited gives them a basis to work from. The great years of the sixties, seventies and eighties are well behind them, but a form of that success is carried forward into today's company in that they have a fine historical background to operate from. In August 2006, Sony UK Chairman, Rob Stringer, made his move to New York to be Chairman of the Epic label within Sony and good luck to him: I liked Rob a lot and at the end of it all he had spent his life dedicated to records.

Sony was a moving piece as people came and went, but it has steadied itself over the past couple of years and got back to records. Its problem is now the same as EMI's, Warners' and the biggest of them all, Universal's: the record business had been shrinking in sales each year for the past ten years. The world now knows that the record business completely missed the internet and has spent nearly ten years trying to catch up in the most catastrophic and foolish way. It became King Canute trying to push back the sea and eventually it got completely soaked.

The decline in major record companies is mainly blamed on the internet, downloading and piracy, etc, etc. To me, yes they are titles you put a tag on, but I think the problem is deeper. The record companies needed to make deals with the internet companies quickly, but instead they waged a fruitless war and, in doing so, the industry alienated the worldwide youth. All its problems, certainly in the popular music field, were brought about by its attacks on downloading and its general hostility to the young peoples' new Rock 'n' Roll: the internet. If you alienate the world's youth you poison the very lifeblood of the popular record business. The industry just kept digging a bigger hole, so deep it could not get out of it, and once the record companies and the young people were in different corners, respect was gone and the game was over. It is not only the record business that performed badly in this arena, but it had the highest of profiles and so commanded the most press in its decline.

Today, record companies are still standing their corner and they suggest to us that CD album sales still account for seventy-five percent of their business. That statement is probably true on the surface, but they are quoting seventy-five percent of their business today. Compared with their business of eight or ten years ago, the figure is probably thirty-five percent. As a 'for instance', Britney albums were selling 15 million copies around the world, and The Backstreet Boys, N'Sync and R. Kelly were averaging about 8 million copies, whereas today, an album commanding 6 million is considered huge selling. Thus, from the year 2000 to 2009 the top selling album is down roughly from 15 million to 6 million sales. Now, 6 million units is still a figure not to be sniffed at, but the glory years have gone and if you couple this with the prices of the sales you can also see a significant difference. CD album sales were once £13.99. As the independent record stores failed and supermarkets took over the bulk of our sales, the price steadily reduced to £6.99 and in some cases £5.99 or £5.79. That, in only a few years, is £8 difference. Hence, even when you get a 6 million seller today it has not anything like the value of the past.

Singles have simply collapsed. A decade ago I was selling Britney Spears' 'Baby One More Time' at mainly £3.99, following a week on promotion of £1.99, and we sold over a million copies. Although, admittedly, this was the top end of the market, look at the contrast with today when a single or track is bought or downloaded for 0.79 pence and a top seller is probably 150,000 in the UK – another huge loss of value.

Compilations or Greatest Hits albums for years were the 'Cash Cow' departments within record companies. If you had not broken any new acts or had a poor year with new artists' sales you could balance the books by exploiting your back catalogue and issuing Greatest Hits albums or compilations. Now, this area too is over, and the main reason is that it has been done to death. Six different volumes of *Stevie Wonder's Greatest Hits* no longer has any interest: after the first couple of volumes the people that want it have already got it, therefore it's a small market play. Compilations apart from the *Now That's What I Call Music!* series are all poor copies: occasionally one comes along, but in general 'Who really cares?'

The CD itself I don't think was ever a sexy item. Technology made it a seller and replacing your collection of vinyl records with CDs became a passion for a part of the music buying public, but the CD was never sexy or warm like vinyl. Vinyl, in fact, has made a comeback in recent years as a small collectors' market and has now progressed into 'Vinyl Parties' where people bring along their pride and joy vinyl records and play them at parties. I have never been to a vinyl party but it sounds like a good night. CD I believe will eventually become like vinyl – a small collectors' market. It will take a few years, but nevertheless it will happen.

Here is an interesting fact. At the time of writing this, my two daughters Josie and Hanna are seventeen and fifteen. They know I spent my life in the record business and have seen some of my artists like Britney Spears, who they are fans of. Neither of them has ever asked for a CD. If they copy music onto a CD, you will find it a few days or a week later in a pile somewhere. Recorded music is not a treasured item with the youth of today as it has been for previous generations. Neither Josie nor Hanna has ever asked to go to a record store – film stores, yes, but record stores have never crossed their mind. They program YouTube on their computers and get their music and video fix that way. They don't watch MTV or other music channels very often and if they do it is on the computer. The new generation is here, computer and internet savvy, and the old way of selling records has only a few years to go – by 2015 it could be all over.

Personally, I think the iPod and the iPhone are incredible inventions. If your music library is on the iTunes facility as mine is, it means you can travel anywhere with your 'life soundtrack' in your top pocket. No more boxes or racks of CDs. The shuffle item is magical, it throws up your own songs at random and brings surprise after surprise. No more loading a CD and knowing what's coming – the element of surprise is a beautiful thing.

I believe the future of today's record company is in its history. The great thing about the youth of today is that they only see tracks rather than albums or singles and this means they are open to a track from the sixties as much as they are to a track from today. My girls already have a vast knowledge of music, they are fans of Elvis, The Beatles, Abba and on. They watch Elvis when he appears in concert on TV, it really doesn't matter that it was forty years ago, they know he was great and appreciate his performance. Is that not truly wonderful?

In 2010, the complete world record company catalogue is already fifty percent sold on the internet by downloading. This is a major move. In recent years the older generation has supported Greatest Hits CDs releases in their thousands, buying the music of their youth, but this is also coming to a close. Their children, computer savvy, are buying them iPods: they are copying their parents' favourite records onto an iPod, and then giving them the loaded iPod as a gift. That is probably one of the best gifts they will ever receive, bestowed with knowledge and crafted with care.

Having said all this, I do not believe we are experiencing the death of the music business. More and more people are listening to music as it is more accessible. Every day I listen to music on the radio, the TV or the iPhone, and so do millions more. The musicians of today have a real chance to record and sell the music they want to without business interference. They know the internet, PayPal principals, YouTube, Facebook, Twitter and Myspace. They can build their own following and then sell their own product. They will soon learn to make more commercial records rather than music for themselves, the area will grow and recorded music could well return to the open market it was in the 50's, 60's and 70's when all sorts of different sounding records appeared on the Top 40 chart.

I am enthused by the future of music but not enthused by the current defensive, contract protecting players in the record business. That said, at the time that I am writing this I do still think there are good people in the industry – however, they are few and far between, and as the years go on the good ones become increasingly scarce.

My design for a major record label at present would be to have a small and focused team that deals with the catalogue and the licensing for TV adverts and special products for hotels, car manufacturers and other companies that need music and I would be aggressive in pursuit of that licensing. If I was Warners, EMI, Universal or Sony, I would cut as many label idents as possible: no-one cares any more about label ID. Cut them to one or two labels, build a dynamic promotion, marketing and sales operation around the label and tend to the artists that command sales. In terms of signing, I would go back to bringing on three acts a year and have a focused, small, but top drawer A & R team. When those acts are signed, back them with proper budgets that are designed to succeed. Do not sign ten acts and then work with reduced budgets, that is poor and shallow thinking, the stakes are high and like it or not you have to be a high roller. The target is 5 million albums not 100,000 with a 'Oh, didn't we do well attitude.'

The record business today has lost the respect of the public. In football, when the manager loses the confidence of the dressing room or the player's belief, he is gone. Precisely this has happened with the management of a lot of record companies.

The final kick:

2005 and 2006 bring back some memories. I played my final football match on 21st May 2005 and it all ended at the Banks's Stadium in Walsall. Chris Marsh had organised an end of season game in aid of The Walsall Hospice, the place that had looked after my Mom so well in the final weeks of her life, and Chris phoned and asked if I would play in the event.

I told Chris that in all honesty, although I still ran most days and was fit, I hadn't kicked a ball in over a couple of years. I agreed on the condition that I could warm the bench and come on for the last fifteen minutes when everyone would be tired and I would just about get through it. The problem is, running is good, but football is all about stop, start, and turn, and that was something I had not done in a long while. I turned up on the day for The Walsall Old Dogs versus The Walsall Mad Dogs. I believe I qualified for both teams, but played for The Mad Dogs. Chris Marsh, Andy Rammall, Dean Keates, Martin O'Connor, Colin Harrison, Mark Rees and many more of my lifetime heroes and pals turned up to play, all ex-professionals. We pulled a near two thousand crowd, and I went out to warm up prior to kick-off. I was chipping in crosses to Ron Green, former Walsall goal-keeper when Marshy jogged over.

'Don Goodman just phoned, can't make it until half time, can you do the first half?'

'Come on Chris, I was up for ten minutes.'

'Yeh, but I'm stuck, play in front of me on the right flank it will be OK.'

So I started the game on the right of four across the middle. Cutting a long story short, I made twenty-seven minutes and was forced to leave the field having ripped both Achilles heels. It would be my final football match at the age of 53 and it would take twelve weeks and much therapy for me to walk properly again, but I had finished at the home of Walsall Football Club and that in itself was right and proper for me.

The greatest hit of all:

If my life has been built around hit records, the greatest worldwide hit of my life walked into my office on 10th November 2004. Her name: Susan Gregory. Susan was producing the animated TV show *Friends and Heroes* and PWL Studios were providing the music. I had inherited the project after arriving at PWL Studios from Jive Records and was not that interested, but professionalism had brought about the meeting and I would judge the project from there. Helen Dann organised Susan coming over and she sat in on the meeting as Helen knew all the background from a PWL point of view. It is true that from the moment we met electricity was bouncing through the air. The one-hour meeting attended to all the business of the project, but was filled with humour and mental jousting. Helen always reminds us both of that meeting, claiming that in the whole of her life she has never seen an interaction like that between two people.

I consider our lives together to be very private, so we have spent nearly every day together since the end of 2004 and today we spend most of every day together. Susan is the woman I waited for my entire life. She has made me well and changed my life completely and we will be together until our last breath. Susan is the most important part of my life bar none, nothing is above her in my mind.

Once more with Kylie:

On 4th May 2005, Pete, Mike, Matt and I were invited to Kylie's last Earls Court Show in the UK before she headed for Australia. It was a nice gesture from both Kylie and Terry her longtime manager. We watched the show and then went backstage to spend a few minutes with Kylie, who as ever was charming and funny about the past, it was a great few minutes.

After we left the arena Pete and I remarked that Kylie looked weak and a little too thin, but we thought that was the effort put into a huge tour, with many costume changes and being the centre of the whole event. It was a shock that only six or seven days later she was diagnosed with cancer and the whole world worried about the Pop Princess. Thankfully, and as is well documented, Kylie faced the fight as she always does and has returned fit and well. These days I know that just like Robbie Williams and Justin Timberlake, Kylie has learnt the game of golf. Although I have not played a round of golf with her, knowing her character as I do, I am sure she has become a competent and able golfer. See you on the course one day Kyles!

A hole in one? no, but the next best thing:

Golf was always important in my life and over the years I began to become a better player and be invited to many events and charity events in the UK and abroad. Through golf I have met many celebrities that we all see on TV and have spent between four and five hours in their company during a round. Some have become friends and the beautiful game of golf has been the catalyst to those friendships. I have met a wider group of people through the game of golf than I have through music. One of the great events is The Footballers Golf Classic organised by the great Terry Mancini. Susan has come along to four of these events over the past few years, they are held mainly in Spain at La Manga and in Dubai. Through those events I have become friends and golf partners with a lot of football heroes. If you know football you will know these names: Alan Ball, Andy Gray, Mike England, Eddie Gray, Glen Hoddle, Francis Lee, Alan McInally, Frank McLintock, Russell Osman, Graeme Sharpe, Pat Jennings, Lee Sharpe, Mick Bates, Dave Beasant,

Steve Bull, Gary Gillespie, Mark Lawrenson, Matt Le Tissier, Mick McCarthy, Derek Mountfield, Gary Owen, Danny Wilson, Sir Ray Graydon, Chris Nichol and Kenny Hibbitt.

In other events around the UK, I have had the pleasure of playing with my great friend Rick Wakeman, also with Jimmy Hill, Bernard Cribbins, Ray Clemence and many more people who have become national heroes at some time or another. The game of golf has been good to me and continues to be so.

Our daughter Josephina has only been playing golf for two years, but she has already represented Middlesex and is the Middlesex Junior Champion. Josie has been the subject of many professional golfers wanting to nurture what seems to be an unbelievably gifted golfer. I adore that Josie is addicted to a sport I am passionate about. She is fortunate to have inherited her mother's athleticism (Susan is a former professional ballet dancer, trained by the Royal Ballet) and innate power that cannot be coached: you either have it or you don't. Josie believes that one day she will win the US Open. I have told her I will believe it for as long as she does and so we train together as much as possible around her school times. I am positive I shall play golf until I can no longer swing a club, although it won't be long before both Josie and Susan will be beating me regularly. I am fortunate that I have a golfing family and as long as I can get out there, I'll take the defeats.

Dr Peter Alan Waterman OBE:

Pete and I are now into our thirty-eighth year of friendship. We are still on the phone to each other many weeks of the year discussing all aspects of music, the industry, trains, football, golf and the passing years. Susan and I, Pete and Helen Dann get together for dinner two or three times a year and much fun is had by all as we remember past glories, past mistakes and the incredible quirks of fate that affected our lives. It seems that Pete and I only have to be together for a matter of moments before the banter and stories start, shortly followed by raucous laughter. As our partnership has lasted all these years without failing, I can say with certainty it will last in our lives forever.

Final flame extinguished:

Sony Music in the US has gone through many changes in the past three years. Jive Records in America, the last of Jive's offices, had managed to retain a small identity within the Sony empire until the summer of 2011. Then there was further change at Sony and the final flame was extinguished. The handful of remaining staff that had experienced the glory years and the rise of Jive Records were 'let go' and the story finally concluded. A label that had started in Willesden, North-West London, in 1981, ended in Manhattan, New York City, in 2011. Its lifespan had been 30 years.

Clinging to the wreckage:

The remaining corporate record companies are in decline. As I write this, everyone knows that the final UK major company E.M.I. Records, will soon be no more, broken up and sold off. That will leave only Universal Music, Sony Music and Warner Music. How long will it be before the industry is left with two?

The staff at all these companies are in complete defensive mode, protecting contracts that have a time to run and just sticking in there until the axe finally falls. Not the environment to move forward, create passion and build for the future. It is indeed a sad ending to an industry that brought so much joy.

We are now in the final chapter of all we have known in the past sixty years. I feel I must add that it is not entirely the fault of the record companies. To suggest they have been operated poorly is probably true; however, what surrounds the companies is also in disarray. Radio is now spread thinly in audience terms with the existence of so many stations and the systematic playlists and 'no character' presenters make the sound of them boring and repetitious. No surprise, then, that the youth market has left the building. The most popular radio stations with the highest listening figures play music from the Sixties, Seventies and Eighties. Television no longer supports the old ways of bringing new artists to the public: gone are the Saturday morning kids shows and gone is the focal point of *Top Of The Pops*. Sure, I see guest artists on *X-Factor* and *Strictly Come Dancing,* but they are just guests adding to the overall package of the transmissions – those programmes are not specifically about those artists or music. Retail has also collapsed, and gone are almost all the record shops. HMV remains, but it has diversified into games and anything else they can sell – they too as a company are teetering on the brink. Therefore, it is wrong to place all the blame onto to the record company: the world is changing and with it so is all that went before.

For those of us that enjoyed the Glory Years, weren't we lucky and wasn't it just fantastic?

It's only Rock 'n' Roll, but I like it:

I've given my all to the Music Industry for most of my life and no matter how much I try to distance myself from the business, I can never distance myself from the music. Today I hear new records from new artists and bands I like. Sometimes they come to me via the internet, sometimes on radio, sometimes my daughters and friends in the industry send me CD's, and sometimes artists get in touch with me directly. I still love music and always will do, it has been my life.

I have had many offers to return to the Music Industry, but so far I have declined them all. People still ask me 'Will you go back?' also 'You know too much not to be involved.' In answer to this I believe you have to know yourself well. The first statement to make is 'Never say Never': life normally bites you if you make that kind of statement. In my own character, I know I am a one hundred percent passion player, in all I do I give everything I have, which sometimes is detrimental to what is around me and that normally includes my personal life. But I am now at an age where I will not allow that to happen. Susan is the most important person in my world and my time with her is all important. I will not risk that for any amount of No 1 records or money, it just will not happen. Also, The Impulse Group of Companies and then Jive Records were market leaders in their field, and I would never be able to repeat that high level of success. It happened to me twice and a third time would be too much to ask. I don't intend to have failure after all that success. I am treated well by the people that still work in the Music Industry, even the young ones that I believe should not know my name or the history of Jive Records. I am forever surprised when a 25 year-old comes up to me and says 'Are you Steve Jenkins from Jive Records? You know I bought all those records.' That is a pleasant moment and it makes me feel I added a little something to life's great tapestry of music. There is just something about finishing at the top, just like a footballer concluding his career in the Champions League Final. I just believe that is my place and time.

Tomorrow never knows:

I returned from holiday to England in October 2011 to the news that STEPS had reformed, and Sony had issued the *Gold Greatest Hits album* we had put out ten years previously under the title *Ultimate STEPS*. The album debuted at No 1 on 16th October. It was a perfect birthday present. To be back at No 1 on that day with the records we had made all those years ago was special. The tour during April 2012 will be fantastic I am sure, it should be just wall to wall hits and will bring joy to all those that attend.

In the very same week The Stone Roses announced they too were reforming and will play concerts in June 2012. Again, I believe the concerts will be sold out and a good time will be had by all.

The Backstreet Boys will also return to England as part of their world tour in April 2012 and play five arena dates, another night of hit after hit record.

November 2011 saw a woman in her thirties with two children return to the O2 Stadium to play concerts as part of her Worldwide Femme Fatale Tour. Britney Spears was back on the road and in England.

Justin Timberlake has successfully followed in the footsteps of Will Smith and made a smooth transition from Jive recording artist to international movie star.

During 2011, R. Kelly was voted The Most Important R&B Star of the Last Twenty Five Years.

So even though Jive Records has long gone, all those hit records and artists live on.

And finally:

I guess I lived my dream and I was lucky. I gave it everything I had and somehow I got there. My message to you is whatever your particular dream may be, chase it with passion and commitment. It will have moments of being incredibly difficult, but you should never give in: take a moment, regroup and go again, regardless of what faces you. Consistency is what wins the game. Put in a great day's work and then do it again tomorrow and keep doing it. One day the wall will fall and you will be on your way.

Good Luck.

Walsall – Up on the Roof

EPILOGUE
WALSALL TO THE WORLD AND
BACK AGAIN

Homecoming – An exhibition of my life:

I have always been a great supporter of Walsall, my home town, and not just the Football Club. Those same streets today are flashback moments and memories of my youth. I started doing DJ gigs at fourteen and that love of playing music to people took me around the world, but I still welcome any return to the old home town. I suppose all through my life I have promoted my birthplace to anybody who would listen and also to the ones who did not want to listen. That area in the middle of The Black Country will always be my home no matter where in the world I am.

Some dedicated people at Walsall Museum and Walsall Council organised my return to Walsall. They had grown to know of my achievements and instigated a homecoming.

I was first in touch with Walsall Council during August of 2004, when they asked me to a short meeting to discuss my career and what awards I had received and still had in my possession. A year was then to go by before I was subsequently contacted by the Museum, in August 2005, this time to attend a meeting with Stuart Warbiton and Dominic Bubb.

Stuart had recently become head of Walsall Museum and was looking at a list of possible ideas for exhibitions for the coming year. On that list was Steve Jenkins – Walsall Music Producer.

Stuart decided that my life was the subject of the exhibition he wanted to display. I agreed, but with a condition that the exhibition illustrated that anything is possible and that you should always chase your dreams: I was living proof for the kids in Walsall that whatever was their life plan and whatever was their dream they should 'Go for it.'

For the next ten months I would visit Stuart, relay my story, and inform him and Dominic of the awards, including the platinum, gold and silver records I had in my possession. Each month I would find photos and press clippings and list the awards and gold discs. Stuart then organised an interview to be recorded in which I told the story of my life from Walsall to Impulse and Jive Records, relating the scenario of the artists I had worked with through the years. This enabled Stuart and Dominic to design the exhibition in some kind of order and with the inclusion of photographs of my mother, my father and my sister Helen and their lives in the town. I just did whatever they asked of me as I knew nothing about museum exhibitions or had any inkling of what the exhibition would eventually look like.

The title of the exhibition was to be called *Kylie, Britney, Justin and Me – Steve Jenkins Adventures in the Pop Industry*, and the opening party would be on 6th July. Work was due to commence in early 2006, but my operation left Stuart and Dominic working on their own and communicating with me via e-mail and phone for the first three months. As soon as I was fit enough I made visit after visit up and down the M1 and M6. Time and again it reminded me of the days I had been doing the journey the opposite way round: working in London for two or three days and living in Walsall. It was enjoyable and Susan always came with me. Walsall aided my recovery and helped rebuild my life, just when I needed it most.

Stuart introduced me to Emma Marshall who was in charge of the local schools for the Council and Dan Slee, the Museum's press officer. Dan was destined to be my greatest ally and would put an enormous amount of work into the exhibition and be one of the main reasons it became such a huge success.

I contacted Sue Buckler, née Parsons, who is still promoting records to radio, now with her own company. She has made a great success of it after all those years working with me. I wanted Sue to be involved as she was the one who first set me on the course of working for a record company. I believed she had a great deal to do with the success I achieved and lived it with me through the years – the exhibition was hers as much as mine. Sue agreed to collaborate and help with the radio and TV promotion, and come along and generally take the mickey out of me. Now I wasn't the boss, Sue had a free reign and used it well. My Susan enjoyed the banter on our radio tours as well.

I did a photo shoot around the town with Paul Pickard and those photos were used in the press throughout the next year and beyond. I began to do press interviews in June and was supported wonderfully by *the Express* and *Star*, *The Birmingham Mail, Walsall Advertiser, Walsall Chronicle, Walsall Observer, Walsall Pride*, and the Football Club's programme *Saddlers TV*. In that month the press began to break the news of the up-and-coming event and from that press came radio. BBC WM were amazingly supportive and I did my first interview with them on the popular Janice Long Saturday morning show. I had known Janice from her years in London on Radio One, but some years had passed since we had spoken. We had a great time, it was just like a normal conversation you have with someone you haven't seen for a long time. These interviews are normally only a few minutes, three or four, but Janice and I spoke for over fifteen minutes live to the West Midlands before she called a halt to play a record. We had both got into chatting so much that Janice hit the wrong button and nothing came over the air. Her microphone was still on and you heard her saying 'What have I done, nothing's working?' I was already off and gone by this, time but I could hear the mayhem I had left behind. Janice quickly found the right button and normal service was resumed.

Over the months I would return to WM a few times to do an hour with Jimmy Franks and another hour with Paul Franks (no relation) along with the phone interviews that came along. The radio stations in the area all gave me superb support: Beacon, BRMB, Heart, Saga, Galaxy and many more. This would also bring in the TV stations and I did news pieces for *Midlands Today, Central News,* and *Black Country News*. The reaction to the exhibition before the opening was fantastic and they all managed to spread my words of encouragement to the youth of the Midlands: 'chase your dreams.'

The build up during the week of the exhibition was great fun for me. I had delivered the 270 Platinum Gold and Silver disc awards, photographs through the years, The Backstreet Boys Smash Hits Award and Justin Timberlake's two Smash Hits Awards. Meanwhile, Pete Waterman had sent his Ivor Novello Award, Brian Bennett had sent his The Shadows disc awards and Billy Ocean had provided his Grammy Award. I topped those up with all my personal awards. That some old friends of the status of Pete, Brian and Billy had sent some awards to the exhibition generated more and more press along with more and more interviews.

It had also been arranged that I would do an interview on Hospital Radio Stafford where I had been the Sunday afternoon DJ all those years before. In those days I used to follow Anton Emery who finished at 4.00pm and many times he sat with me through my show so he could get a ride home with me afterwards. I returned to the same radio building I had not seen in almost thirty years and was interviewed by the Station Head, Anton Emery. Brilliant, just brilliant. I was also pleased that Susan and the kids were there to watch my return home. They all came with me to do the interviews that week at the football club, the press offices and the radio and TV Stations.

We went to look at the completed exhibition before the opening and it was the first time I had seen it. When you see your life displayed like that it is difficult to take in and I found it hard to look at all. It would not be until a few months later that I could appreciate the whole show and the effort that people had put in and only then could I come to terms with all I had done. I had never thought about my career too much before, I was too busy just getting the next hit or selling as many albums as possible. To see it all there, finished and all behind me was not easy. The great part for me was the people of Walsall. So many people stopped me and asked me questions and I got the feeling they were proud of me. That I came from their town made it all so special.

The opening night for me was just a pleasure. My girls – Susan, Josie and Hanna – all went to the hair salon and dressed for the occasion, they were a picture. My sis Helen, her partner Dave, her children Sally and David, Walsall Football Club ex-manager Chris Nichol, Walsall Football Club players, Sue Buckler, Big Joe Savage and the great and the good of Walsall all came along and made the evening special for me. I could walk around the show and talk to everyone knowing that my girls were safe under the watchful eye of Big Joe. Josie and Hanna helped me to present flowers to the people who had contributed to the show. I did live interviews for the press, radio and TV, and the exhibition was off to the best possible start. John Aston also turned up and proceeded to take the mickey unmercifully, in his usual style. It topped off a great night.

During August, I was invited to have tea with the Lady Mayoress of Walsall in her private chambers. In the room sits the desk on which, in Walsall, Jerome K Jerome wrote the book *Three Men In A Boat*. Susan, Sue and I had a marvellous time with the Mayoress, she was charming and appreciated my promotion for Walsall.

Me with Billy Ocean at my Exhibition

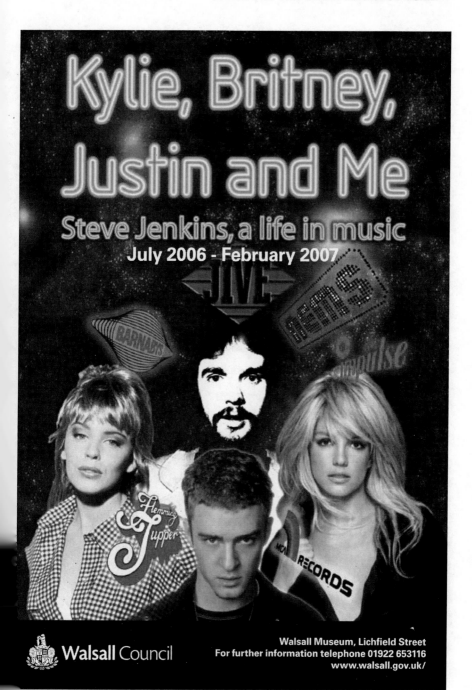

Bob Hope and Bing Crosby on the road to Walsall

Helen still supporting her wayward brother

I had organised some of my pals to make a visit to the exhibition and every one that came posed for photographs and did press interviews for Dan Slee and radio and TV for Sue Buckler. They all gave up a day in their life for me and Walsall. Pete Waterman had to be the first because of our work together. He came along on 1st September and did a great job: as long as you get a good bacon sarnie in Pete early on in the day he's good to go and he did all the interviews and photographs that were asked of him. In October, Brian Bennett came along on a day he was not feeling too well, refusing to let anyone down. Emma had invited 50 school kids to a talk we both gave and then Brian did the photographs, press and radio interviews he was asked to give. On a cold December day along came Billy Ocean. Billy did me a great favour in coming along as he rarely does interviews and has led a much quieter life since the world No 1's and tours. He remembered playing Walsall as an unknown singer years before.

The exhibition was due to close at the end of December, but because of the volume of people making visits, its term was extended until March. In January 2007, Jeff Bonser, Chairman of Walsall Football Club, came to the exhibition and had some interesting music stories of his own. Jeff, who also is not keen on interviews, did all that was asked of him and I was thankful he had made the effort. In between all the big events at the Museum I could also repay Jeff by appearing at his Business Breakfast Club at Walsall Football Club, where I gave a forty-five minute presentation about stories behind the hits.

I was also invited to speak at some of the local schools and the press always supported these events. At the end of the presentations there were lively question and answer sessions. Teenagers pull no punches and want to know is Kylie's bum great up close, did R. Kelly sleep with an under-age Aaliyah, etc: they get right to the point and want the answer. Hopefully, through it all I managed to get across the theme of 'chase your dreams, give it a go – and don't give up.' I explained how many times in my career, especially at the beginning, it was easier to give up than to keep going, but fortune favours the brave.

The exhibition finally closed at the end of March. It had been the most successful ever at Walsall's Museum and over 8,000 Walsall people had made a trip to the see my life story. I am forever honoured. I was informed that in the Museum's history I was the first living Walsall person to have an exhibition there: now that is an honour, at least I got to see it and be involved in it.

The best thought for me about the whole exhibition was that my Mom and Dad would have been proud. I had returned a hero to the town where they spent their lives. From what had been a poor start I had recovered, to rise in the record business to the very top. Those months of the exhibition made me feel close to them. It really felt as though they were with me through it all and were hopefully taking great pride and pleasure from all the events.

And the Saddlers are champs:

During the exhibition, Walsall Football Club, who had been relegated in May 2006 to Division Two, were having a superb season under the management of Richard Money. It had been even more special for me as two mates from years before, Martyn Butler and Dean Keates, had returned to the Club. Walsall had only ever won one championship, which was the Fourth Division Championship in the 1959/60 season (what was then the Fourth Division is now the renamed Division Two). My Dad had spoken many times of the team that had won that title and then been runners-up the following year in Division Three, getting promoted again to Division Two. I will have seen that team play with my Dad, but was very young and I have no recollection of the enormity of their achievement. I still have the Walsall Footballers half pint mug that my Dad bought to commemorate the achievement. In all my supporting days of Walsall FC I had seen them promoted many times, but never actually win a Championship.

As we went into late April we had a real chance. As usual in football it goes to the last game and we were away at Swindon Town needing at least a point to secure the title. It was a perfect sunny day and the Walsall faithful packed one end of the ground. Susan and I were in with the Directors that day as guests. Nothing is ever easy with Walsall Football Club, and with one minute to go we were 1-0 down and our hopes beginning to fade when Dean Keates hit a screamer from outside the box into the top corner and the 'faithful' went ballistic. Walsall FC had achieved the Championship of Division Two and only the second championship of their history. Susan and I danced, sang and laughed, a great day in the life of a Walsall boy.

The icing on the cake came on 5th May. Susan and I were invited to ride the open top bus around the town waving to the Walsall FC fans before we ended up at the Town Hall, where all the players were presented with their medals in front of a huge joyous crowd. We went to the gathering afterwards for sandwiches, tea and cake and there I had my photo taken with the Championship Trophy and Dean Keates, Player Of The Season, Leading Goalscorer and scorer of the goal that brought the trophy home. My return to Walsall had been all I could have hoped for and more: the Exhibition and the Second Division Championship Trophy had completed the circle for me.

The Forest Arts Centre, Walsall:

I would perform one more major duty some months later in Walsall when I was asked to open The Forest Arts Centre in Leamore, Walsall. The Forest Arts Centre is a great asset to the community and has been carefully built by Mike Parrott. Over 2,000 people of all ages pass through its doors each week. It majors on music, film, dance and art, and I feel I have more work to do for them in the years to come. The great moment for me with Forest Arts is its position in the world. It is only two hundred yards from where my Dad's parents lived and where he grew up as a child. Before I gave the opening speech I had to go and walk along May Street and look at No 25. That is where I jumped off the wall as a 6 year-old and when I could jump off the wall and over the hedge I truly believed I had achieved something. I stood and just stared at that house for a few moments. I am proud of the Forest Arts Centre and all they achieve and I am proud that the plaque standing in their reception states the day of opening by one Steve Jenkins.

Chase that dream!

The people of Walsall, the radio, press and TV, and all others who supported the exhibition event requested, demanded and insisted I write this book. People I have known in the record business have always said 'you should write a book about all those hits' and even Susan became insistent that I should do it. I was not so sure. Could I sit down and write all that? Would I give up halfway through? What if I managed to do it and I thought it was terrible? Would it just be a waste of time? All these questions were in my head, but the constant gentle pressurising of everyone around me began to change my mind and I believe at the very least I owe it to them to have given it a try.

For two seasons I wrote for Walsall FC's programme. To me it was a test – could I produce five hundred to six hundred words on demand once every two weeks or sometimes twice in a week? I believed if I could master that discipline I would find out if I liked writing, if I could sit and do it week after week and then see if the reaction was good or not. I found out I did like writing, I could give it time, I was passionate about the resulting piece and, fortunately, the feedback from the supporters was good. I put a lot of effort into it and used a variety of stories and photographs of the people I had met in music, golf and football. It became a success and then I contributed articles to a few journals and books, trying to learn the trade.

This book has taken me three years work to produce and I have written it at home in London, in a three month stay in Naples Florida and during a six week stay in Marbella. I can only hope that you have enjoyed the story and know a little more about some of the hits you listened to on the radio and how everything works in the record business. I hope you are also now Walsall FC supporters!

My life is great, I now only do the things I want to or am passionate about. Since the death of my father I have always had a general life plan. After watching him pay off his mortgage and tell me now he was going to enjoy his life more as his family were now safe, it was only three weeks later that he had his heart attacks and stroke. That left an impression on me that I carried throughout my life and at 16 years old I had decided if I could make enough money and made it to the age of 55, I would then quit and try and enjoy the following ten years while I still had full movement and flexibility. When you have a life plan like that, you never really think you will get there, but there I have arrived.

After giving my whole life to the music industry, I have been fortunate to meet Susan and gain an entire family. My life now is based around my family. The kids are doing well: Elaine has her own computer company and is a qualified fitness instructor, and she manages all that with her husband Ian and our two grandchildren. The kids Alexia and Zeusie give both Susan and I enormous fun when we see them: we can't work out if we are bigger kids than they are.

Jack is doing well and is making his way in the tough world of advertising: he seems calm and aware of what it takes to succeed and he operates himself well in that arena. I enjoy our games of golf whenever he has time or joins us on holiday. The girls are just terrific: Josie has her life before her and it seems she will have a career in golf. If that happens, what a wonderful outdoor life for a sportswoman that will be – and if you see her on TV, look for the old fella carrying her bag, he once had a few hits you know. Hanna is just reaching the age where her ideas will crystallize: for the moment I have no idea what shape her life will take, but I am keen to observe and help when needed. Susan and I intend to travel more: in a year or so we will spend winters away from the English cold weather and go where life leads us. However, you know what, you never can tell: life takes you where it will – but it will only take us both together.

It's been a great life. I have been able to work within my passion for music all these years. Songs have been my food, drink and sustenance for as long as I can remember. Paul Anka wrote for Frank Sinatra to sing 'Regrets I've had a few, but then again too few to mention' and John Lennon wrote 'Life is what happens to you, while you're busy making other plans.' My mother and father always taught me to 'Work hard and play hard.' I believe I did both, and I am now looking forward to the coming years.

Tomorrow the sun will rise and later set. The bit in the middle is all yours. Just remember, hope survives.

Happiness with Susan

ing: It's too late, **James Taylor:** You've got a friend, **T.Rex: Carole king:** It's too late, **James Taylor:** You've got a f

The Beatles: She loves you, **Paul McCartney and Wings:** Hot Love, **The Beatles:** She loves you, **Paul McCartney**

the Run, **Bread:** Make it with you, Astrud Gilberto: The Band on the Run, **Bread:** Make it with you, Astrud G

Ipanema, **Janis Ian:** At seventeen, **Eagles:** Hotel California, girl from Ipanema, **Janis Ian:** At seventeen, **Eagles:** Hot

natra: I've got you under my skin, **Dean Martin:** Everybody **Frank Sinatra:** I've got you under my skin, Dean Martin

ebody, **Steely Dan:** do it again, **David Bowie:** The Jean loves somebody, **Steely Dan:** do it again, **David Bowi**

reedence Clearwater Revival: Bad moon rising, Dusty Genie, **Creedence Clearwater Revival:** Bad moon ris

The Look of love, **Cliff Richard:** The next time, George Springfield: The Look of love, **Cliff Richard:** The next ti

On Broadway, **Aretha Franklin:** Until you come back to me, Benson: On Broadway, **Aretha Franklin:** Until you come

wart: Maggie May, **Glenn Miller:** Moonlight Serenade, Sam **Rod Stewart:** Maggie May, **Glenn Miller:** Moonlight Ser

ou send me, **Slade:** Gudbuy T'Jane, **Michael Jackson: Cooke:** You send me, **Slade:** Gudbuy T'Jane, **Michae**

you, **Tom Jones:** It's not unusual, **Elvis Presley:** Jailhouse Rock with you, **Tom Jones:** It's not unusual, **Elvis Presle**

a Fitzgerald: Everytime we say goodbye, Beach Boys: Rock, **Ella Fitzgerald:** Everytime we say goodbye, B

sed her, **Barry White:** Can't get enough of you babe, **Andy** Then I kissed her, **Barry White:** Can't get enough of

Can't take me eyes off you, **Marvin Gaye:** Come get to **Williams:** Can't take me eyes off you, **Marvin Gaye:** C

Day: Move over darling, **Ricky lee Jones:** Chuck E's in this, **Doris Day:** Move over darling, **Ricky lee Jones:** C

c Camera: Hoe men are, **Sugar Minnott:** Good thing love, **Aztec Camera:** Hoe men are, **Sugar Minnott:**

by Goldsboro: Summer the first time, **Four Tops:** I'm in a going, **Bobby Goldsboro:** Summer the first time, **Four T**

world, **Shanice:** I love your smile, **Todd Rungren:** I saw the different world, **Shanice:** I love your smile, **Todd Rungre**

Hayes: Joy, **Johnny Cash:** Ring of Fire, **Junior Walker:** light, **Isaac Hayes:** Joy, **Johnny Cash:** Ring of Fire, **Jun**

it take, **Chic:** I want your love, **Al Green:** Tired of being What does it take, **Chic:** I want your love, **Al Green:** Ti

y Como: And I love you so, **Major Harris:** Love wont let alone, **Perry Como:** And I love you so, **Major Harris:** Le

oobie Brothers: What a fool believes, Frank and Nancy me wait, **Doobie Brothers:** What a fool believes, Frank

omething Stupid, **Andrew Gold:** Never let her slip away, Sinatra: Something Stupid, **Andrew Gold:** Never let he

it: Nick of time, **Bee Gees:** Night Fever, **Hall and Oates: Bonnie Rait:** Nick of time, **Bee Gees:** Night Fever, **Hall**

for that, **Prince:** Purple Rain, **B.J. Thomas:** Raindrops I can't go for that, **Prince:** Purple Rain, **B.J. Thomas**

on my head, **Fontella bass:** Rescue Me, **Ray Charles:** keep falling on my head, **Fontella bass:** Rescue Me, R

loving you, **Otis Redding:** Sitting on the dock of the bay, I can't stop loving you, **Otis Redding:** Sitting on the doc

s: Close to you, **Diana Ross:** I'm still waiting, **Supremes: Carpenters:** Close to you, **Diana Ross:** I'm still waiting,

Temptations: Ain't to proud to beg, **Barbara Streisand:** Reflections, **Temptations:** Ain't to proud to beg, Barba

Squeeze: Up the junction, **Spinners:** Could it be I'm Evergreen, **Squeeze:** Up the junction, **Spinners:** Cou

e, **Patsy Cline:** Crazy, **Crystal Gayle:** Don't it make my falling in love, **Patsy Cline:** Crazy, **Crystal Gayle:** Don't

blue, **Thin Lizzy:** Boys are back in town, **Kinks:** Waterloo brown eyes blue, **Thin Lizzy:** Boys are back in town, Kin

nne Warwick: Do you know the way to San Jose, Isley Sunset, **Dionne Warwick:** Do you know the way to Sa

This old heart of mine, **Fleetwood Mac:** Dreams, Sly and Brothers: This old heart of mine, **Fleetwood Mac:**

Stone: Family Affair, **Petula Clark:** Downtown, Norah **the Family Stone:** Family Affair, **Petula Clark:** Down

't know why, **Chris Rea:** Fool if you thinks it's over, Stevie Jones: Don't know why, **Chris Rea:** Fool if you thinks it's

ately, **Boz Scaggs:** It's over, **Georgie Fame:** Sitting in the Wonder: Lately, **Boz Scaggs:** It's over, **Georgie Fame:**

Who: I can't explain, **Curtis Mayfield:** Move on up, **Sam** park, **The Who:** I can't explain, **Curtis Mayfield:** Move

Soul Man, **Ben E King:** Stand by me, **5th Dimension:** and Dave: Soul Man, **Ben E King:** Stand by me, 5th

ll Blues, **Bing Crosby:** White Christmas, **Jackie Wilson:** Wedding Bell Blues, **Bing Crosby:** White Christmas, **Jac**

weetest feeling, **Style Council:** You're the best thing, **The** I get the sweetest feeling, **Style Council:** You're the

t Back, **Percy Sledge:** When a man loves a woman, Beatles: Get Back, **Percy Sledge:** When a man love

mer; Every Kinda people, **Arthur Conley:** Sweet soul **Robert palmer;** Every Kinda people, **Arthur Conley:**

key Robinson: Tracks of my tears, **Chicago:** Saturday in music, **Smokey Robinson:** Tracks of my tears, **Chicago**

adows: Foot tapper, **Bob Marley:** Waiting in vain, **Mark** the Park, **Shadows:** Foot tapper, **Bob Marley:** Waiting i

: It's too late, **James Taylor:** You've got a friend, **T.Rex: Carole king:** It's too late, **James Taylor:** You've got a fr

e Beatles: She loves you, **Paul McCartney and Wings:** Hot Love, **The Beatles:** She loves you, **Paul McCartney**

Run, **Bread:** Make it with you, Astrud Gilberto: The Band on the Run, **Bread:** Make it with you, Astrud G

ema, **Janis Ian:** At seventeen, **Eagles:** Hotel California, girl from Ipanema, **Janis Ian:** At seventeen, **Eagles:** Hot

ra: I've got you under my skin, **Dean Martin:** Everybody **Frank Sinatra:** I've got you under my skin, Dean Martin

ody, **Steely Dan:** do it again, **David Bowie:** The Jean loves somebody, **Steely Dan:** do it again, **David Bowi**

lence Clearwater Revival: Bad moon rising, Dusty Genie, **Creedence Clearwater Revival:** Bad moon ri

The Look of love, **Cliff Richard:** The next time, George Springfield: The Look of love, **Cliff Richard:** The next ti

Broadway, **Aretha Franklin:** Until you come back to me, Benson: On Broadway, **Aretha Franklin:** Until you come

t: Maggie May, **Glenn Miller:** Moonlight Serenade, Sam **Rod Stewart:** Maggie May, **Glenn Miller:** Moonlight Sere

send me, **Slade:** Gudbuy T'Jane, **Michael Jackson: Cooke:** You send me, **Slade:** Gudbuy T'Jane, **Michae**

u, **Tom Jones:** It's not unusual, **Elvis Presley:** Jailhouse Rock with you, **Tom Jones:** It's not unusual, **Elvis Presle**

tzgerald: Everytime we say goodbye, Beach Boys: Rock, **Ella Fitzgerald:** Everytime we say goodbye, B

ner, **Barry White:** Can't get enough of you babe, **Andy** Then I kissed her, **Barry White:** Can't get enough of you

n't take me eyes off you, **Marvin Gaye:** Come get to **Williams:** Can't take me eyes off you, **Marvin Gaye:** C

ay: Move over darling, **Ricky lee Jones:** Chuck E's in this, **Doris Day:** Move over darling, **Ricky lee Jones:** C

Camera: Hoe men are, **Sugar Minnott:** Good thing love, **Aztec Camera:** Hoe men are, **Sugar Minnott:**

Goldsboro: Summer the first time, **Four Tops:** I'm in a going, **Bobby Goldsboro:** Summer the first time, **Four To**

d, **Shanice:** I love your smile, **Todd Rungren:** I saw the different world, **Shanice:** I love your smile, **Todd Rungre**

yes: Joy, **Johnny Cash:** Ring of Fire, **Junior Walker:** light, **Isaac Hayes:** Joy, **Johnny Cash:** Ring of Fire, **Jun**

take, **Chic:** I want your love, **Al Green:** Tired of being What does it take, **Chic:** I want your love, **Al Green:** Ti

Como: And I love you so, **Major Harris:** Love wont let alone, **Perry Como:** And I love you so, **Major Harris:**

bie Brothers: What a fool believes, Frank and Nancy me wait, **Doobie Brothers:** What a fool believes, Frank

ething Stupid, **Andrew Gold:** Never let her slip away, Sinatra: Something Stupid, **Andrew Gold:** Never let he

Nick of time, **Bee Gees:** Night Fever, **Hall and Oates: Bonnie Rait:** Nick of time, **Bee Gees:** Night Fever, **Hall**

that, **Prince:** Purple Rain, **B.J. Thomas:** Raindrops I can't go for that, **Prince:** Purple Rain, **B.J. Thomas**

my head, **Fontella bass:** Rescue Me, **Ray Charles:** keep falling on my head, **Fontella bass:** Rescue Me, R

ng you, **Otis Redding:** Sitting on the dock of the bay, I can't stop loving you, **Otis Redding:** Sitting on the dock

lose to you, **Diana Ross:** I'm still waiting, **Supremes: Carpenters:** Close to you, **Diana Ross:** I'm still waiting, S

mptations: Ain't to proud to beg, **Barbara Streisand:** Reflections, **Temptations:** Ain't to proud to beg, Barbara

ueeze: Up the junction, **Spinners:** Could it be I'm Evergreen, **Squeeze:** Up the junction, **Spinners:**

Patsy Cline: Crazy, **Crystal Gayle:** Don't it make my falling in love, **Patsy Cline:** Crazy, **Crystal Gayle:** Don't

e, **Thin Lizzy:** Boys are back in town, **Kinks:** Waterloo brown eyes blue, **Thin Lizzy:** Boys are back in town, Kink

e Warwick: Do you know the way to San Jose, Isley Sunset, **Dionne Warwick:** Do you know the way to

old heart of mine, **Fleetwood Mac:** Dreams, Sly and Brothers: This old heart of mine, **Fleetwood Mac:** Dream

one: Family Affair, **Petula Clark:** Downtown, Norah **the Family Stone:** Family Affair, **Petula Clark:** Downto